Principle Advancements in Database Management Technologies:
New Applications and Frameworks

Keng Siau
University of Nebraska–Lincoln, USA

John Erickson
University of Nebraska–Omaha, USA

INFORMATION SCIENCE REFERENCE

Hershey · New York

Director of Editorial Content: Kristin Klinger
Senior Managing Editor: Jamie Snavely
Assistant Managing Editor: Michael Brehm
Publishing Assistant: Sean Woznicki
Typesetter: Mike Killian, Sean Woznicki
Cover Design: Lisa Tosheff
Printed at: Yurchak Printing Inc.

Published in the United States of America by
      Information Science Reference (an imprint of IGI Global)
      701 E. Chocolate Avenue
      Hershey PA 17033
      Tel: 717-533-8845
      Fax: 717-533-8661
      E-mail: cust@igi-global.com
      Web site: http://www.igi-global.com/reference

Library of Congress Cataloging-in-Publication Data

Principle advancements in database management technologies : new applications and frameworks / Keng Siau and John Erickson, editors.
      p. cm.

  Summary: "This book presents exemplary research in a variety of areas related to database development, technology, and use"--Provided by publisher.

  Includes bibliographical references and index.
  ISBN 978-1-60566-904-5 (hardcover) -- ISBN 978-1-60566-905-2 (ebook) 1.
005.74/5. I. Siau, Keng, 1964- II. Erickson, John, 1956-
  QA76.9.D3P72995 2010
  005.74--dc22
                          2009046476

British Cataloguing in Publication Data
A Cataloguing in Publication record for this book is available from the British Library.

Advances in Database Research (ADR) Series

ISBN: 1537-9299

Editor-in-Chief: Keng Siau, University of Nebraska–Lincoln, USA

&

John Erickson, University of Nebraska–Omaha, USA

Advanced Principles for Improving Database Design, Systems Modeling, and Software Development

Information Science Reference • copyright 2008 • 305pp • H/C (ISBN: 978-1-60566-172-8) • $195.00 (our price)

Recent years have witnessed giant leaps in the strength of database technologies, creating a new level of capability to develop advanced applications that add value at unprecedented levels in all areas of information management and utilization. Parallel to this evolution is a need in the academia and industry for authoritative references to the research in this area, to establish a comprehensive knowledge base that will enable the information technology and managerial communities to realize maximum benefits from these innovations. Advanced Principles for Improving Database Design, Systems Modeling, and Software Development presents cutting-edge research and analysis of the most recent advancements in the fields of database systems and software development. This book provides academicians, researchers, and database practitioners with an exhaustive collection of studies that, together, represent the state of knowledge in the field.

This series also includes:

Contemporary Issues in Database Design and Information Systems Development

IGI Publishing • copyright 2007 • 331pp • H/C (ISBN: 978-1-59904-289-3) • $89.96 (our price)

Database management, design and information systems development are becoming an integral part of many business applications. Contemporary Issues in Database Design and Information gathers the latest development in the area to make this the most up-to-date reference source for educators and practioners alike. Information systems development activities enable many organizations to effectively compete and innovate, as new database and information systems applications are constantly being developed. Contemporary Issues in Database Design and Information Systems Development presents the latest research ideas and topics on databases and software development. The chapters in this innovative publication provide a representation of top notch research in all areas of the database and information systems development.

Research Issues in System Analysis and Design, Databases and Software Development

IGI Publishing • copyright 2007 • 286pp • H/C (ISBN: 978-1-59904-927-4) • $89.96 (our price)

New Concepts such as agile modeling, extreme programming, knowledge management, and organizational memory are stimulating new research ideas among researchers, and prompting new applications and software. Revolution and evolution are common in the areas of information systemsdevelopment and database. Research Issues in Systems Analysis is a collection of the most up-to-date research-oriented chapters on information systems development and database. Research Issues in Systems Analysis and Design, Databases and Software Development is designed to provide the understanding of the capabilities and features of new ideas and concepts in the information systems development, database, and forthcoming technologies. The chapters in this innovative publication provide a representation of top notch research in all areas of systems analysis and design and database.

Hershey • New York

Order online at www.igi-global.com or call 717-533-8845 x100 – Mon-Fri 8:30 am - 5:00 pm (est) or fax 24 hours a day 717-533-8661

Table of Contents

Detailed Table of Contents

Yingjiu Li, Singapore Management University, Singapore
Huiping Guo, California State University at Los Angeles, USA
Shuhong Wang, University of Wollongong, Australia

At the heart of the information economy, commercially and publicly useful databases must be sufficiently protected from pirated copying. Complementary to the Database Protection Act, database watermarking techniques are designed to thwart pirated copying by embedding owner-specific information into databases so that the ownership of pirated copies of protected databases can be claimed if the embedded information is detected. This chapter presents a robust watermarking scheme for embedding a multiple-bits watermark to numerical attributes in database relations. The scheme is robust in the sense that it provides an upper bound for the probability that a valid watermark is detected from unmarked data, or a fictitious secret key is discovered from pirated data. This upper bound is independent of the size of the data. The scheme is extended to database relations without primary-key attributes to thwart attribute-related attacks. The scheme is also extended to multiple watermarks for defending additive attacks and for proving joint ownership.

Pericles Loucopoulos, Loughborough University, UK
Wan M.N. Wan Kadir, Universiti Teknologi Malaysia, Malaysia

A critical success factor for information systems is their ability to evolve as their environment changes. There is compelling evidence that the management of change in business policy can have a profound effect on an information system's ability to evolve effectively and efficiently. For this to be successful, there is a need to represent business rules from the early requirements stage, expressed in user-understandable terms, to downstream system design components and maintain these throughout the lifecycle of the system. Any user-oriented changes could then be traced and if necessary propagated from requirements to design specifications and evaluated by both end-users and developers about their impact on the system. The BROOD approach, discussed in this chapter, aims to provide seamless traceability between requirements and system designs through the modelling of business rules and the successive transformations, using UML as the modelling framework.

Chapter 3

Kevin Crowston, Syracuse University, USA
Barbara Scozzi, Politecnico di Bari, Italy

Free/Libre open source software (FLOSS, e.g., Linux or Apache) is primarily developed by distributed teams. Developers contribute from around the world and coordinate their activity almost exclusively by means of email and bulletin boards, yet somehow profit from the advantages and evade the challenges of distributed software development. This chapter investigates the structure and the coordination practices adopted by development teams during the bug-fixing process, which is considered one of main areas of FLOSS project success. In particular, based on a codification of the messages recorded in the bug tracking system of four projects, this chapter identifies the accomplished tasks, the adopted coordination mechanisms, and the role undertaken by both the FLOSS development team and the FLOSS community. The chapter concludes with suggestions for further research.

Chapter 4

Kari Smolander, Lappeenranta University of Technology, Finland
Matti Rossi, Helsinki School of Economics, Finland

This chapter describes the architecture development process in an international ICT company, which is building a comprehensive e-business system for its customers. The implementation includes the integration of data and legacy systems from independent business units and the construction of a uniform Web-based customer interface. The authors followed the early process of architecture analysis and definition over a year. The research focuses on the creation of e-business architecture and observes that instead of guided by a prescribed method, the architecture emerges through somewhat non-deliberate actions obliged by the situation and its constraints, conflicts, compromises, and political decisions. The interview-based qualitative data is analyzed using grounded theory and a coherent story explaining the situation and its forces is extracted. Conclusions are drawn from the observations and possibilities and weaknesses of the support that UML and RUP provide for the process are pointed out.

Chapter 5

João de Sousa Saraiva, INESC-ID/Instituto Superior T´ecnico, Portugal
Alberto Rodrigues da Silva, INESC-ID/Instituto Superior T´ecnico, Portugal

Ever since the introduction of computers into society, researchers have been trying to raise the abstraction level at which software programs are built. Currently an abstraction level based on graphical models instead of source code is being adopted: MDE. MDE is the driving force for some recent modeling languages and approaches, such as OMG's UML or Domain-Specific Modeling. All these approaches are founded on metamodeling: defining languages that represent a problem-domain. A key factor for the success of any approach is appropriate tool support. However, only recently have tool creators started considering metamodeling as an important issue in their list of concerns. This chapter evaluates a small set of MDE tools from the perspective of the metamodeling activity, focusing on both architectural and practical aspects. Then, using the results of this evaluation, the authors discuss open research issues for MDE-based software development tools.

Chapter 6

Stefan Koch, Vienna University of Economics and Business Administration, Austria
Christian Neumann, Vienna University of Economics and Business Administration, Austria

There has been considerable discussion on the possible impacts of open source software development practices, especially in regard to the quality of the resulting software product. Recent studies have shown that analyzing data from source code repositories is an efficient way to gather information about project characteristics and programmers, showing that OSS projects are very heterogeneous in their team structures and software processes. However, one problem is that the resulting process metrics measuring attributes of the development process and of the development environment do not give any hints about the quality, complexity, or structure of the resulting software. Therefore, this chapter expands the analysis by calculating several product metrics, most of them specifically tailored to object-oriented software. The authors then analyzed the relationship between these product metrics and process metrics derived from a CVS repository. The aim was to establish whether different variants of open source development processes have a significant impact on the resulting software products. In particular, the authors analyzed the impact on quality and design associated with the numbers of contributors and the amount of their work, using the GINI coefficient as a measure of inequality within the developer group.

Chapter 7

Kris Ven, University of Antwerp, Belgium
Jan Verelst, University of Antwerp, Belgium

Previous research has shown that the open source movement shares a common ideology. Employees belonging to the open source movement often advocate the use of open source software within their organization. Hence, their belief in the underlying open source software ideology may influence the decision making on the adoption of open source software. This may result in an ideological—rather than pragmatic—decision. A recent study has shown that American organizations are quite pragmatic in their adoption decision. This chapter argues that there may be circumstances in which there is more opportunity for ideological behavior. The authors therefore investigated the organizational adoption decision in Belgian organizations. Results indicate that most organizations are pragmatic in their decision making. However, the authors have found evidence that suggests that the influence of ideology should not be completely disregarded in small organizations.

Chapter 8

Web Services, Service-Oriented Computing, and Service-Oriented Architecture:

John Erickson, University of Nebraska - Omaha, USA
Keng Siau, University of Nebraska - Lincoln, USA

Service-oriented architecture (SOA), Web services, and service-oriented computing (SOC) have become the buzz words of the day for many in the business world. It seems that virtually every company has implemented, is in the midst of implementing, or is seriously considering SOA projects, Web services projects, or service-oriented computing. A problem many organizations face when entering the SOA world is that there are nearly as many definitions of SOA as there are organizations adopting it. Further complicating the issue is an unclear picture of the value added from adopting the SOA or Web services paradigm. This chapter attempts to shed some light on the definition of SOA and the difficulties of assessing the value of SOA or Web services via return on investment (ROI) or nontraditional approaches, examines the scant body of evidence empirical that exists on the topic of SOA, and highlights potential research directions in the area.

Chapter 9

Wookey Lee, Inha University, Korea
Myung-Keun Shin, Telecom Business Division, SK C&C, Korea
Soon Young Huh, Korea Advanced Institute of Science and Technology, South Korea
Donghyun Park, Inha University, South Korea
Jumi Kim, Small Business Institute, Korea

Approximate Query Answering is important for incorporating knowledge abstraction and query relaxation in terms of the categorical and the numerical data. By exploiting the knowledge hierarchy, a novel method is addressed to quantify the semantic distances between the categorical information as well as the numerical data. Regarding that, an efficient query relaxation algorithm is devised to modify the approximate queries to ordinary queries based on the knowledge hierarchy. Then the ranking measures work very efficiently to cope with various combinations of complex queries with respect to the number of nodes in the hierarchy as well as the corresponding cost model.

Chapter 10

Joseph Fong, City University of Hong Kong, China
Herbert Shiu, City University of Hong Kong, China

Extensible Markup Language (XML) has become a standard for persistent storage and data interchange via the Internet due to its openness, self-descriptiveness and flexibility. This chapter proposes a systematic approach to reverse engineer arbitrary XML documents to their conceptual schema – Extended DTD Graphs — which is a DTD Graph with data semantics. The proposed approach not only determines the structure of the XML document, but also derives candidate data semantics from the XML element instances by treating each XML element instance as a record in a table of a relational database. One application of the determined data semantics is to verify the linkages among elements. Implicit and explicit referential linkages are among XML elements modeled by the parent-children structure and ID/IDREF(S) respectively. As a result, an arbitrary XML document can be reverse engineered into its conceptual schema in an Extended DTD Graph format.

Chapter 11

This chapter develops a model of open source disruption in enterprise software markets. It addresses the question: Is free and open source software (FOSS) likely to disrupt markets for enterprise business applications? The conventional wisdom is that open source provision works best for low-level system-oriented technologies while large, complex enterprise business applications are best provided by commercial software vendors. The authors challenge the conventional wisdom by developing a two-stage model of open source disruption in business application markets that emphasizes a virtuous cycle of adoption and lead-user improvement of the software. The two stages are an initial incubation stage (the I-Stage) and a subsequent snowball stage (the S-Stage). Case studies of several FOSS projects demonstrate the model's ex post predictive value. The authors then apply the model to SugarCRM, an emerging open source CRM application, to make ex ante predictions regarding its potential to disrupt commercial CRM incumbents.

Chapter 12

Active applications are characterized by the need for expressing, evaluating, and maintaining a set of rules that implement the application's active behavior. Typically, rules follow the Event-Condition-Action (ECA) paradigm, yet oftentimes their actual implementation is buried in the application code, as their enactment requires a tight integration with the concepts and modules of the application. This chapter proposes a rule management system that allows developers to easily expand its rule processing logic with such concepts and modules and, hence, to decouple the management of their active rules from the application code. This system derives from an exception manager that has previously been developed in the context of an industry-scale workflow management system and effectively allows developers to separate active and non-active design concerns.

Chapter 13

The UML is an industry standard for object-oriented software engineering. However, there is little empirical evidence on how UML is used. This chapter reports results of a survey of UML practitioners.

The authors found differences in several dimensions of UML diagram usage on software development projects, including frequency, the purposes for which they were used, and the roles of clients/users in their creation and approval. System developers are often ignoring the "Use Case-driven" prescription that permeates much of the UML literature, making limited or no use of either Use Case Diagrams or textual Use Case descriptions. Implications and areas requiring further investigation are discussed.

Chapter 14

Brenda Eschenbrenner, University of Nebraska-Lincoln, USA
Fiona Fui-Hoon Nah, University of Nebraska-Lincoln, USA
Keng Siau, University of Nebraska-Lincoln, USA

Three-dimensional virtual world environments are providing new opportunities to develop engaging, immersive experiences in education. These virtual worlds are unique in that they allow individuals to interact with others through their avatars and with objects in the environment, and can create experiences that are not necessarily possible in the real world. Hence, virtual worlds are presenting opportunities for students to engage in both constructivist and collaborative learning. To assess the impact of the use of virtual worlds on education, a literature review is conducted to identify current applications, benefits being realized, as well as issues faced. Based on the review, educational opportunities in virtual worlds and gaps in meeting pedagogical objectives are discussed. Practical and research implications are also addressed. Virtual worlds are proving to provide unique educational experiences, with its potential only at the cusp of being explored.

Chapter 15

Kamal Masri, Simon Fraser University, Canada
Drew Parker, Simon Fraser University, Canada
Andrew Gemino, Simon Fraser University, Canada

Making Entity-Relationship diagrams easier to understand for novices has been a topic of previous research. This study provides experimental evidence that suggests using small representative graphics (iconic graphics) to replace standard entity boxes in an ER diagram can have a positive effect on domain understanding for novice users. Cognitive Load Theory and the Cognitive Theory of Multimedia Learning are used to hypothesize that iconic graphics reduce extraneous cognitive load of model viewers leading to more complete mental models and consequently improved understanding. Domain understanding was measured using comprehension and transfer (problem solving) tasks. Results confirm the main hypothesis. In addition, iconic graphics were found to be less effective in improving domain understanding with English as second language (ESL) participants. ESL results are shown to be consistent with predictions based on the Cognitive Load Theory. The importance of this work for systems analysts and designers comes from two considerations. First, the use of iconic graphics seems to reduce the extraneous cognitive load associated with these complex systems. Secondly, the reduction in extraneous load enables users to apply more germane load which relates directly with levels of domain understanding. Thus iconic graphics may provide a simple tool that facilitates better understanding of ER diagrams and the data structure for proposed information systems.

Chapter 16

Researchers have argued that competitive necessities will require open source software companies to participate in cooperative business networks in order to offer the complete product / service (whole product) demanded by customers. It is envisaged that these business networks will enhance the business models of participant firms by supplementing their value adding activities and increasing responsiveness to customers. However, while such propositions have intuitive appeal, there is a paucity of empirical research on such networks. This study examines Zea Partners, a network of small open source companies cooperating to deliver the 'whole product' in the area of Content Management Systems (CMS). It investigates how network participation augments the business models of the participant companies, and identifies the agility challenges faced by the business network. The chapter concludes that reconciling the coordination needs of OSS networks with the operational practices of participant firms is of crucial importance if such networks are to achieve adaptive efficiency to deliver whole products in a 'bazaar-friendly' manner.

Chapter 17

Domain analysis provides guidelines and validation aids for specifying families of applications and capturing their terminology. Thus, domain analysis can be considered as an important type of reuse, validation, and knowledge representation. Metamodeling techniques, feature-oriented approaches, and architectural-based methods are used for analyzing domains and creating application artifacts in these domains. These works mainly focus on representing the domain knowledge and creating applications. However, they provide insufficient guidelines (if any) for creating complete application artifacts that satisfy the application requirements on one hand and the domain rules and constraints on the other hand. This chapter claims that domain artifacts may assist in creating complete and valid application artifacts and present a general approach, called Application-based DOmain Modeling (ADOM), for this purpose. ADOM enables specifying domains and applications similarly, (re)using domain knowledge in applications, and validating applications against the relevant domain models and artifacts. The authors demonstrate the approach, which is supported by a CASE tool, on the standard modeling language, UML, and report experimental results which advocate that the availability of domain models may help achieve more complete application models without reducing the comprehension of these models.

Chapter 18

Ontology has recently received considerable attention. Based on a domain analysis of knowledge representations in data mining, this chapter presents a structure of ontology for data mining as well as the unique resources for data mining with incomplete data. This chapter demonstrates the effectiveness of ontology for data mining with incomplete data through an experiment.

Preface

Databases and database systems continually assume a more critical place at the center of the information systems architecture for many companies and organizations. Coupled with data warehouses and advanced data mining techniques, an increasing number of organizations now have powerful analytic and predictive tools available to help them gain and maintain competitive advantage. In addition, connecting back office databases and data warehouses with the Web is becoming vital for a growing number of organizations. The preceding developments and events in the practical business world provide the backdrop for research into the creation of ever more sophisticated means to the ends regarding information systems.

In the current environment, research investigating the entire discipline of database should be at the core of teaching as well as extending research in all related areas of database. Database lines of research include business intelligence, query languages, query optimization, data warehouse design, data mining algorithms, XML tool development, and tools for the modeling, design, and development of information systems. Some of the more recent techniques involve design and deployment of object-relational databases that include support for object-oriented systems. Other research and development streams involve Web Services, Service Oriented Architectures, and Open Source Systems. As the complexity of database systems increases, modeling databases and database systems has assumed increased importance in database research. Future databases or data warehouses are likely to include real-time analysis using advanced statistical methods, with increasing immediacy and connection to the Web, Supply Chain Management, Customer Relationship Management, and Knowledge Management systems.

Over the past forty years, IS and database researchers have conducted empirical investigations that have resulted in a better understanding of the impacts and values of advanced database principles in business on a global basis. Past database research has focused primarily on technical and organizational issues, and less on social issues. Issues such as text mining and opinion mining that depend on state of the art database systems and can be used to infer meaning and emotional content are also likely to garner more attention in future research.

In accordance with the high standard of previous volumes in the Advances in Database Research Series, we edited this volume by including only the best research in the field. A majority of the chapters included in this volume are conducted by internationally renowned scholars. We believe this volume will provide a convenient store of valuable knowledge on the topic of database, systems analysis and design, design science, and software engineering. This volume can serve as a starting point for references and citation pieces for researchers, graduate students and practitioners in the field. This volume consists of eighteen chapters; three are focused on database, three on systems analysis and design, four on modeling, two on architecture, five on open systems development, and one on educational efforts. A brief description of each chapter is presented below.

Chapter 1, "A Multiple-Bits Watermark for Relational Data," by Yingjiu Li, Huiping Guo, and Shuhong Wang, presents a technique to mark data in databases protected by copyright. The technique is robust enough that it can estimate the probability regarding whether the watermark itself can be detected. The technique can also work on databases that do not use primary key attributes and it can prevent attribute related attacks. Finally, the technique supports multiple watermarks so that joint owners can each place their own security measure, or to detect multiple (additive) attacks.

Chapter 2, "BROOD: Business Rules-Driven Object Oriented Design," by Pericles Loucopoulos and Wan Kadir, identifies a critical success factor for information systems as their ability to change with environmental changes. The authors go on to explicate their approach to deriving business rules that include means to evolve or change information systems from an object-oriented perspective. They propose the use of modelling techniques, in particular UML as the basis for modelling business rules that allow or encourage changes in the depicted information systems.

Chapter 3, "Bug Fixing Practices within Free/Libre Open Source Software Development Teams," by Kevin Crowston and Barbara Scozzi, examine the processes and practices of distributed development teams working on open source projects. They approach the issues involved by analyzing messages recorded in the error tracking system of fours projects. By doing this the authors were able to identify common tasks, coordination efforts, and roles of the development teams. The results can be compared with those of non open source teams and other open source teams as well to provide insight into improving development efforts.

Chapter 4, "Conflicts, Compromises and Political Decisions: Methodological Challenges of Enterprise-Wide E-Business Architecture Creation," by Kari Smolander and Matti Rossi, examines how an international ICT company developed its architecture. The authors monitored the early architectural phases of the development effort as part of the research project. Results indicate that the final architecture often derives from the conditions and environment present at the time of its creation. According to the authors, other elements affecting the architecture can include political compromises and constraints.

Chapter 5, "Evaluation of MDE Tools from a Metamodeling Perspective," by João de Sousa Saraiva and Alberto Rodrigues, explores and enhances the ideas of Model Driven Architecture (MDA) by creating an additional abstraction layer that they call the graphical model layer. The paper goes on to describe the evaluation of tools supporting metamodels from the MDA perspective. Based on the evaluation, the chapter closes with a possible research agenda for MDA development tools.

Chapter 6, "Exploring the Effects of Process Characteristics on Products Quality in Open Source Software Development," by Stefan Koch and Christian Neumann, proposes metrics that purport to measure open system development processes. In particular, the metrics are aimed at object-oriented processes. A problem the authors note is that the existing metrics do not measure quality, complexity or structure. The goal of the research is to determine whether metrics can be used to assess the aforementioned issues.

Chapter 7, "The Impact of Ideology on the Organizational Adoption of Open Source Software," by Kris Ven and Jan Verelst, examines the ideology underlying the open source community of developers. Other studies have indicated that US organizations are more interested in the practical uses of open source. The authors propose that other opportunities might exist that allow more of the underlying ideologies to emerge. The findings indicate that most organizations favor the practical over the ideological, but that, in small organizations, ideological influences might yet play a role in the adoption of open source.

Chapter 8, "Web Services, Service-Oriented Computing, and Service-Oriented Architecture: Separating Hype from Reality," by John Erickson and Keng Siau, provides an overview of the Service Oriented Architecture (SOA), Web services, and Service Oriented Computing (SOC) areas of software and systems development. The authors note that the definitions of the system types are not agreed upon by business or researchers, and provide a framework for understanding the components of SOA. The authors provide some evidence suggesting that the areas are understudied in terms of research, and suggest future directions or gaps in the current research for investigators.

Chapter 9, "Approximate Query Answering with Knowledge Hierarchy," by Wookey Lee, Myung-Keun Shin, Soon Young Huh, Donghyun Park, and Jumi Kim, creates an efficiency relaxation algorithm to change approximation queries into ordinary queries. The approach uses the knowledge hierarchy as a means to enable this transformation. Then the authors apply ranking measures to help deal with the many complex nodes generated by using the knowledge hierarchy to simplify the approximation query.

Chapter 10, "Abstract DTD Graph from an XML Document: A Reverse Engineering Approach," by Joseph Fong and Herbert Shiu, proposes a means to reverse engineer XML documents back into their "conceptual schema," which they call Extended DTD graphs. The authors argue that their approach can do two tasks; first to determine the structure of XML documents, and second to extract the data schemas from the XML elements. They accomplish these tasks by considering the XML element instances as records in a relational database.

Chapter 11, "A Dynamic Model of Adoption and Improvement for Open Source Business Applications," by Michael Brydon and Aidan R. Vining, proposes a way to model open source disruption in software markets. Their two stage model includes an incubation stage, where the initial adoption and development are nurtured, followed by a snowball stage, where momentum is gathered. The authors then apply their model to a Customer Relationship Management application named SugarCRM as a test case.

Chapter 12, "Aiding the Development of Active Applications: A Decoupled Rule Management Solution," by Florian Daniel and Giuseppe Pozzi, examines the set of rules that commonly describe what they call active applications. They use the Event-Condition-Action paradigm as the starting point for their explanatory vehicle, and the rules management system they derive allows developers to separate active and non-active design issues.

Chapter 13, "Dimensions of UML Diagram Use: Practitioner Survey and Research Agenda," by Brian Dobing and Jeffrey Parsons, examines field use of UML. The research was executed by means of a survey to UML practitioners. Results indicate that practitioners generally tend not to use UML Use Case diagrams. They either do not utilize Use Cases at all or instead make use of textual based Use Case descriptions. This finding is directly at odds with much of the literature on UML, and is also counter to how the OMG (Object Management Group) prescribes best practices for UML.

Chapter 14, "A 360-Degree Perspective of Education in 3-D Virtual Worlds," by Brenda Eschenbrenner, Fiona Fui-Hoon Nah, and Keng Siau, examines education from the perspective of 3D virtual worlds, such as Second Life. The research assesses the impact of such virtual worlds on education via a review of current literature on the subject. Based on the literature, pedagogical, practice, and research objectives are discussed. The literature suggests that research into the impacts of virtual worlds on education is at a very early stage, and many opportunities for education and research remain unexplored.

Chapter 15, "Using Graphics to Improve Understanding of Conceptual Models," by Kamal Masri, Drew Parker, and Andrew Gemino, provides the results of an experiment involving the replacement of standard identity boxes in ERDs (Entity Relationship Diagrams) with iconic graphics (small representative graphics). The primary problem under investigation was how to enhance novice understanding of ERDs. Findings indicate that a reduction in "extraneous" cognitive load for those using the iconic graphics was possible, further allowing an increase in "germane" cognitive load. This implies better understanding of the diagrams.

Chapter 16, "Beyond Open Source: The Business of 'Whole' Software Solutions," by Joseph Feller, Patrick Finnegan, and Jeremy Hayes, examines a common research notion that open source developers will be forced (by competitive pressures) to join cooperative type networks so that a complete product can be provided to customers. The chapter uses a case study at Zea Partners, an open source content management application developer, to conclude that if such networks are to succeed, then the participant organizations must reconcile the coordination concerns with the operational concerns.

Chapter 17, "The Application-Based Domain Modeling Approach: Principles and Evaluation," by Iris Reinhartz-Berger and Arnon Sturm, investigates the area of domain analysis with the goal of developing an approach that can overcome some of the shortcomings of modeling the domain using metamodeling techniques. The authors propose that domain artifacts can be used to assemble relatively complete and valid artifacts in their approach called Application based Domain Modeling. They demonstrate the viability of their approach using a CASE tool created for UML.

Chapter 18, "The Use of Ontology for Data Mining with Incomplete Data," by Hai Wang and Shouhong Wang, demonstrates how a domain analysis of knowledge representations in a data warehouse or other data set, can be used in combination with a formal ontology, developed specifically for data mining, to extract relatively complete results with incomplete data. They provide experimental evidence supporting their claim.

Keng Siau & John Erickson
Editors, Advances in Database Research

Chapter 1
A Multiple-Bits Watermark for Relational Data

Yingjiu Li
Singapore Management University, Singapore

Huiping Guo
California State University at Los Angeles, USA

Shuhong Wang
University of Wollongong, Australia

ABSTRACT

At the heart of the information economy, commercially and publicly useful databases must be sufficiently protected from pirated copying. Complementary to the Database Protection Act, database watermarking techniques are designed to thwart pirated copying by embedding owner-specific information into databases so that the ownership of pirated copies of protected databases can be claimed if the embedded information is detected. This article presents a robust watermarking scheme for embedding a multiple-bits watermark to numerical attributes in database relations. The scheme is robust in the sense that it provides an upper bound for the probability that a valid watermark is detected from unmarked data, or a fictitious secret key is discovered from pirated data. This upper bound is independent of the size of the data. The scheme is extended to database relations without primary-key attributes to thwart attribute-related attacks. The scheme is also extended to multiple watermarks for defending additive attacks and for proving joint ownership.

INTRODUCTION

With the development of information technology, databases are becoming increasingly important in a wide variety of applications such as parametric specifications, surveys, and life sciences. While demand for the use of databases is growing, pirated copying has become a severe threat to such databases due to the low cost of copying and the high values of the target databases. To fight against pirated copying, database watermarking techniques are designed to embed owner-specific information into database relations; when a pirated copy is found, the owner can extract the embedded information and use the detection process to assert the ownership of data. This complements the effort of the Database Protection Act (Vaas, 2003) as people realize that the law does not provide sufficient protection to valuable databases (Gray & Gorelick, 2004).

While watermarking multimedia data has long been rigorously studied (Cox, Miller, & Bloom, 2001; Johnson, Duric, & Jajodia, 2000; Katzenbeisser & Petitcolas, 2000), the approaches developed for multimedia watermarking cannot be directly applied to databases because of the difference in data properties. In general, database relations differ from multimedia data in significant ways and hence require a different class of information-hiding mechanisms. Unlike multimedia data whose components are highly correlated, database relations consist of independent objects or tuples. The tuples can be added, deleted, or modified frequently in either benign updates or malicious attacks. No existing watermarking techniques for multimedia data are designed to accommodate such tuple operations.

Perhaps the most well-known scheme for watermarking relational data is the one proposed by Agrawal and Kiernan (2002). For convenience, we call it the AK scheme. The main idea of the AK scheme is to change a small portion of numerical data according to a secret key such that the change can be detected for ownership proof. Without access to the secret key, a pirate cannot localize exactly where the change is made. It is difficult for a pirate to confuse the ownership detection unless he or she introduces an intolerable error to the underlying data. The AK scheme can be used in many real-world applications such as watermarking parametric specifications, surveys, and life-science data (Agrawal, Haas, & Kiernan, 2003; Agrawal & Kiernan).

Consider a database relation R that has a primary key P and v numerical attributes $A_0,..., A_{v-1}$. Let there be η tuples. A portion of tuples is selected for embedding watermark information according to a control parameter γ ($\gamma < \eta$). The selection is also determined by a secret key K, known only to the owner of the data, as well as the primary key. Any tuple r is selected if $S_1(K, r.P) \bmod \gamma = 0$, where $S_1(K, r.P)$ is the first number generated by $S(K, r.P)$, and $S(K, r.P)$ is a cryptographic pseudorandom sequence generator seeded with a secret key K and the primary key $r.P$ of tuple r. Given a sequence of numbers $S_1, S_2,...$ generated by S, it is computationally infeasible to derive the secret key or to predict the next number in the sequence. Due to the uniqueness of the primary key, roughly one out of every γ tuples is selected for embedding watermark information.

For each selected tuple r, the AK scheme selects exactly one least significant bit j from attribute A_i and replaces it with a mark bit x, where $i = S_2(K, r.P) \bmod v, j = S_3(K, r.P) \bmod \xi$, and $x=0$ if $S_4(K, r.P)$ is even and $x=1$, otherwise. Here, ξ is another control parameter determining the range of least-significant bits of each value that may be modified.

For ownership detection, the mark bits are located using the same process provided that the secret key is known and the primary key remains unchanged. Let ω be the number of mark bits being localized ($\omega \approx \eta/\varphi$). To increase the robustness of the detection process, the ownership is claimed if more than $\tau\omega$ of the localized bits are as expected, where $\tau \in [0.5, 1)$ is a control parameter that is related to the assurance of the detection process.

The AK scheme has the following advantages: It is (a) key based, meaning all aspects of the scheme are determined by a secret key and a primary key, (b) blind, that is, the detection process does not require the knowledge of the original database or the embedded information, (c) incrementally updatable, where each tuple is marked independently of all other tuples, (d) error tolerable, meaning the error introduced by embedding mark bits can be controlled such that its impact on the mean and variance of marked attributes is minuscule, and (e) robust, where the detection process is robust to a variety of attacks including bit-flipping attacks, mix-and-match attacks, additive attacks, and invertibility attacks. In particular, the scheme is robust against tuple-related attacks such as tuple modification, deletion, and insertion.

To motivate our research, we examine the following assumptions that are used in the AK scheme:

- *Error tolerance:* A database relation being watermarked consists of a number of numeric attributes. It is acceptable to change a small number of ξ least-significant bits in some numeric values; however, the value of data will be degraded significantly if all or a large number of such bits change.
- *Primary-key criticality:* A database relation being watermarked has a primary-key attribute that either does not change or can be recovered. The primary-key attribute contains essential information such that modification or deletion of this information will substantially reduce the value of data.
- *Attribute order dependence:* A database relation being watermarked has a fixed order of attributes that either does not change or can be recovered. This assumption is implicit in Agrawal and Kiernan (2002).

The scheme depends critically on a primary key and the original order of database attributes. The scheme does not apply if the data have no primary-key attribute or if either the primary key or the order of attributes is modified. The scheme is therefore not robust against attribute-related attacks such as attribute deletion and insertion.

In this article, we present the view that the AK scheme actually embeds a 1-bit watermark, and we extend it to a multiple-bit watermark. The extended scheme provides an upper bound for the probability that a valid watermark is detected from unmarked data, or a fictitious secret key is discovered from pirated data. This upper bound is independent of the size of the data. Then we drop the assumptions for primary-key criticality and attribute order dependence by constructing a virtual primary key from some most-significant bits of some selected attributes. The attributes used for constructing the virtual primary key may vary from tuple to tuple, and the scheme does not depend on a priori ordering over the attributes. Our extended scheme is robust against not only tuple-related attacks, but also attribute-related ones. We also extend our scheme for embedding and detecting multiple watermarks so as to thwart additive attacks or prove joint ownership. As a result of our study, ownership detection can be fully automated for detecting any database relations with a guarantee of low false-detection rates.

The remainder of this article is organized as follows. We first present a multiple-bits watermarking scheme for relational data. We then extend it by removing the assumptions on the primary key and attribute order. We also extend our scheme to multiple watermarks. In the related-work section, we compare our work with many other solutions including newly published ones. The final section presents our conclusion. For ease of reference, Table 1 gives the notation that is used in this article.

RELATED WORK

In this section, we summarize the related work in three categories: robust watermarking, fragile watermarking, and public watermarking.

Robust Watermarking

Recent development of watermarking techniques has been targeted on relational databases to accommodate typical database operations such

Table 1. Notation in watermarking

η	Number of tuples that can be used in watermarking
ν	Number of numerical attributes that can be used in watermarking
ξ	Number of least-significant bits available in each value for watermarking
$1/\gamma$	Fraction of tuples that are used for watermarking
K	Secret key
S	Cryptographic pseudorandom sequence generator
τ	Threshold in watermark detection

as tuple insertion, deletion, and modification. The AK scheme (Agrawal & Kiernan, 2002) is a typical robust watermarking scheme that embeds a single-bit watermark to relational data. The scheme alters some least-significant bits in numerical attributes such that the alteration does not degrade the data beyond their usability and that the pattern of alteration can be detected even if the data have been modified. In this article, we extend the AK scheme to (a) allow multiple-bit information to be embedded and detected, (b) provide an upper bound for the probability that a valid watermark is detected from unmarked data, or a fictitious secret key is discovered from pirated data, regardless of the size of data, (c) deal with database relations without primary-key attributes, and (d) embed and detect multiple watermarks for thwarting additive attacks and for proving joint ownership.

Parallel to our work, a multibit watermark scheme was proposed by Sion, Atallah, and Prabhakar (2003). The scheme is designed primarily for watermarking a set of real numbers $\{x_1,..., x_n\}$ by manipulating its distributions. The first step of watermark insertion is to sort the values according to a cryptographically keyed hash of the set of most-significant bits of the normalized values. Then, a maximum number of nonintersecting subsets of values are formed, where each subset consists of a certain number of adjacent items after sorting. Embedding a watermark bit into a subset is achieved by making minor changes

to some of the data values in this subset such that the number of values that are outliers in the distribution is less than a smaller threshold (for watermark bit 0) or greater than a larger threshold (for watermark bit 1). Note that some of the groups may not be able to be watermarked given user-specified change tolerance. Also note that some redundant bits must be embedded such that the original multibit watermark can be recovered in watermark detection even if some of the encoded bits are destroyed in data attacks. Compared with our multibit watermarking scheme, this scheme is robust against linear transformation and does not depend on the existence of a primary key. On the other hand, since it requires sorting, grouping, and distribution manipulating, it incurs more watermarking overhead, especially expensive for watermarking large data sets or frequently updated databases.

Robust watermarking schemes have also been developed for protecting copyrights for categorical data, XML (extensible markup language) data, and data cubes. In Sion (2004), the author proposed to watermark a categorical attribute by changing some of its values to other values of the attribute (e.g., *red* is changed to *green*) if such change is tolerable in certain applications. Sion's scheme is equivalent to the AK scheme in selecting a number of tuples for watermarking a categorical attribute A based on a secret key K and the primary-key attribute P. For each selected tuple r, exactly one bit is chosen from watermark information *wm_data* and is embedded to *r.A*, where the watermark information *wm_data* is generated from a shorter watermark *wm* using the error-correcting code (ECC). The bit position is determined by a pseudorandom value generated from the secret key and the primary key *r.P*. To embed the chosen bit *b*, the current categorical value *r.A* is changed to another valid value of *A*, which is chosen from a list L_A of all valid values of *A*. In this process, any value *a* can be chosen from L_A (to replace *r.A*) as long as *a*'s index in L_A has the least-significant bit *b*. For watermark detection, a number of tuples are selected the same way as in watermark insertion. Then, for each selected tuple *r*, a bit position in *wm_data* is located and the corresponding bit value in *wm_data* is extracted from the least-significant bit of the index of *r.A* in the list L_A. After all of the tuples are processed, the ECC takes as input *wm_data* and produces the corresponding *wm*. The ECC can tolerate certain errors in detecting *wm_data* and still produce the same *wm* in watermark detection. This scheme has been extended to protect the ownership and privacy of outsourced medical data (Bertino, Ooi, Yang, & Deng, 2005) that are subject to generalization (Kim, Sengupta, Fox, & Dalkilic, 2007) and aggregation (Woo, Lee, Lee, Loh, & Whang, 2007) attacks.

The AK scheme has also been extended by Ng and Lau (2005) to watermarking XML data. In this scheme, the owner of XML data is required to choose locators, which are XML elements having unique values that can serve as primary keys as in the AK scheme. While a textual value of an element is selected to embed a mark bit, one of its words is replaced by a synonym function based on a well-known synonym database WordNet.

Gross-Amblard (2003) considered relational or XML data that are only partially accessible through a set of parametric queries in his query-preserving watermarking scheme. The scheme modifies some numerical values in watermark insertion in a way that the distortions introduced to the results of those parametric queries are small

and that the watermark can be detected from the results of those queries. Another work on watermarking XML data was conducted by Zhou, Pang, and Tan (2007). They proposed creating queries to identify the data elements in XML data that can be used for embedding watermarks. The identifying queries are resilient against data reorganization and redundancy removal through query rewriting. If an identified element is a leaf node, watermark insertion is performed by modifying its value; otherwise, it is performed by adding to or deleting its child nodes. The usability of XML data is measured by query templates. The results of certain basic queries on the data remain useful after watermarking or attacks.

J. Guo, Li, Deng, and Chen (2006) proposed a robust watermarking scheme to protect the owner's rights in data-cube applications. The basic assumption is that all values able to be watermarked in a data cube are numeric, and those small changes in a small portion of these values are acceptable. For each cell in a data cube, the owner of the data seeds a cryptographically secure pseudorandom sequence generator *S* with a secret key *K* in concatenation with the cell's feature attributes. A small portion of cells are selected and for each selected cell, a bit position among ξ least-significant bits is selected to embed a mark bit in the same way as in the AK scheme. Since the most prevalent data-cube operations are aggregation queries (Pears & Houliston, 2007), a minicube is constructed for each cell that is modified in watermark insertion so as to eliminate the errors introduced by watermarking to aggregation queries. J. Guo et al. have shown that this can be done effectively and efficiently in real-world applications even for very large data cubes.

The AK scheme has also been extended to fingerprinting relational databases (Li, Swarup, & Jajodia, 2005). Fingerprinting is used to insert digital marks for the purpose of identifying the recipients who have been provided data, which is different from watermarking in which digital marks are inserted for the purpose of identifying the source of data. The challenge is to address the collusion attack in which a group of legitimate users work collaboratively to create a pirated copy of protected data (Boneh & Shaw, 1995, 1998; Safavi-Naini & Wang, 2001).

Fragile Watermarking

Different from robust watermarking, the purpose of fragile watermarking is not to protect copyright, but to detect and localize possible attacks that modify a distributed or published database. Li, Guo, and Jajodia's scheme (2004) is an example of fragile watermarking. This scheme embeds a watermark to relational data by partitioning the tuples into groups and manipulating the order of the tuples in each group, where the grouping and ordering of the tuples are determined by a secret key and the primary key of the tuples. A watermark can be computed by hashing or signing all tuple values in a group. Note that even though the watermark can be derived from a digital signature, it is embedded into the data, which is different from integrating digital signatures with relational databases (Reid & Dhillon, 2003). Any change to the underlying data can be detected at a group level with a high probability in watermark detection. This solution introduces no error to the underlying data and can be easily extended to watermarking multidimensional data cubes.

To improve the precision in tamper localization, H. Guo, Li, Liu, and Jajodia (2006) proposed another fragile watermarking scheme under the assumptions that the database relation to be watermarked has numerical attributes and that the errors introduced in two least-significant bits of each value can be tolerated. In this solution, the tuples are first divided into groups, as in the previous scheme. Within each group, a tuple hash (keyed) is computed for each tuple (with attributes organized in a fixed order), and an attribute hash (keyed) is computed for each attribute (with tuples organized in a fixed order). When these hash values are computed, the two least-significant

bits of all attribute values are ignored. Each tuple hash is embedded into the corresponding tuple and each attribute hash into the corresponding attribute. The embedded hash values actually form a watermark grid, which helps to detect, localize, and characterize database attacks.

Recently, H. Guo, Li, and Jajodia (2007) proposed a fragile watermarking scheme for detecting malicious modifications to streaming data. The scheme partitions a numerical data stream into groups based on synchronization points. A data element x_i is defined to be a synchronization point if its keyed hash $HMAC(K, x_i)$ mod $m=0$, where K is a secret key, and m is a secret parameter. For each group of data that falls between two synchronization points, the scheme computes and embeds a fragile watermark so that any modification to the data can be detected and localized at a group level in watermark detection.

Public Watermarking

One common feature of most robust watermarking techniques is that they are secret-key based, where ownership is proven through the knowledge of a secret key that is used for both watermark insertion and detection. The secret-key-based approach is not suitable for proving ownership to the public (e.g., in a court). To prove ownership of suspicious data, the owner has to reveal his or her secret key to the public for watermark detection. After being used one time, the key is no longer secret. With access to the key, a pirate can invalidate watermark detection by either removing watermarks from protected data or adding a false watermark to nonwatermarked data.

Li and Deng (2006) proposed a unique database watermarking scheme that can be used for publicly verifiable ownership protection. Given a database relation to be published or distributed, the owner of the data uses a public watermark key to generate a public watermark, which is a relation with binary attributes that are derived from the original database. Anyone can use the watermark key and the watermark to check whether a suspicious copy of the data is watermarked, and, if so, prove the ownership of the data by checking a watermark certificate officially signed by a trusted certificate authority, DB-CA. The watermark certificate contains the owner's ID, the watermark key, the hashes of the watermark and database relation, the first time the relation was certified, the validity period of the current certificate, and the DB-CA's signature. The watermark certificate may be revoked and recertified in the case of identity change, ownership change, DB-CA compromise, or data update. Therefore, the revocation status also needs to be checked in proving the ownership.

EMBEDDING AND DETECTING MULTIPLE-BITS WATERMARK

In this section, we extend the AK scheme under the same set of assumptions: error tolerance, primary-key criticality, and attribute order dependence. The extended scheme is used for embedding a multiple-bits watermark rather than a 1-bit watermark as in the AK scheme. Multiple-bits watermarks are useful for embedding owner information such as name, logo, signature, or description about the underlying data. We prove that certain false-detection rates are bounded in our extended scheme.

Embedding Multiple Bits

The AK scheme embeds a 1-bit watermark only. This can be seen clearly by extending it to embedding a multiple-bits watermark $W = (w_0,..., w_{L-1})$. To embed W, the same scheme is used to (a) select some tuples, (b) select one attribute for each selected tuple r, (c) select one least significant bit for each selected attribute, and (d) compute a mark bit x for each selected bit. Now the difference is that the mark bit is not used to replace the selected bit in data directly; instead, one watermark bit w_l is selected from W where $l = S_5(K, r.P) \bmod L$, and

x XOR w_l is used to replace the selected bit in the data. In watermark detection, the watermark bit w_l is recovered by computing XOR on a located bit in the data with the computed mark bit x. The ownership is claimed as long as the original watermark string W can be recovered from the data. The AK scheme can be considered to be a special case of this extended scheme where W is 1-bit 0.

Compared to the AK scheme, the same number $\omega \approx \eta/\varphi$ of least-significant bits is selected in our extended scheme for embedding watermark information; thus, the error introduced by the embedding process is the same as the AK scheme. The reader is referred to Agrawal et al. (2003) for more details on the analysis of watermarking error. The difference is that each watermark bit w_l is embedded $\varpi \approx \omega/L$ times as compared to ω times in the original scheme; thus, the robustness analysis on the watermarking scheme must be adapted to take this into consideration. A preliminary analysis of our extended scheme was first reported in Li, Swarup, and Jajodia (2003a).

Robustness Analysis for Multiple-Bits Scheme

The robustness of a watermarking scheme can be measured by the following probabilities: (a) false hit rate, in which a valid watermark is detected from unmarked data, (b) invertibility rate, where a fictitious secret key is derived from marked data, and (c) false miss rate, in which no valid watermark is detected from marked data in the presence of various types of attacks. The smaller these probabilities, the more robust the watermarking scheme.

In the robustness analysis, we use the following notation: (a) the probability function of binomial distribution $b(k; n, p) = C_n^k p^k q^{n-k}$ (i.e., probability of obtaining exactly k successes out of n Bernoulli trials with probability p of success in any trial), and (b) the survival function of binomial distribution $B(k; n, p) = \sum_{i=k+1}^{n} b(i; n, p)$ (i.e., probability of having more than k successes in n independent Bernoulli trials).

False Hit

Being aware of the existence of a watermarking technique, a pirate may modify marked data so as to confuse ownership proof. Therefore, watermark detection may be applied to not only the original marked data, but also unmarked data, both of different sizes.

Claim 1. If the detection algorithm is applied to unmarked data, then the false-hit rate is $\prod_{i=0}^{L-1} B(\tau\omega_i; \omega_i, 0.5) \leq \frac{1}{2^L}$, where $\omega_i > 0$ is the number of times that the watermark bit i is extracted from data.

Proof. If the detection algorithm is applied to unmarked data, it may possibly return some binary string $(w_0,..., w_{L-1})$ as a potential watermark. Let w_i be extracted from data ω_i times and $\omega_i > 0$. Due to the use of pseudorandom generator S in detection, w_i is extracted each time from unmarked data as 0 or 1 with the same probability 0.5. Due to the use of threshold τ in detection, w_i is detected as 0 or 1 with the same probability $B(\tau\omega_i; \omega_i, 0.5)$. The probability that a binary string $(w_0,..., w_{L-1})$ is obtained in detection is $\prod_{i=0}^{L-1} 2B(\tau\omega_i; \omega_i, 0.5)$. Now, there is only one watermark in the space of 2^L possible binary strings. Thus, the probability that the binary string obtained matches the original watermark is $1/2^L$. The false-hit rate is $\frac{1}{2^L}\prod_{i=0}^{L-1} 2B(\tau\omega_i; \omega_i, 0.5) = B(\tau\omega_i; \omega_i, 0.5)$. The false-hit rate has an upper bound $1/2^L$ due to $B(\tau\omega_i; \omega_i, 0.5) \leq 0.5$ for $\tau \in [0.5, 1)$.

The upper bound is independent of ω_i and τ. Therefore, no matter what the size of the data and the detection threshold are, the false-hit rate can be reduced exponentially by increasing L.

The AK scheme corresponds to a special case of our scheme where $L=1$. In the AK scheme, the false-hit rate is $B(\tau\omega; \omega, 0.5)$, where ω is the total number of mark bits extracted from targeted data. The false-hit rate in the AK scheme may be con-

trolled by the detection threshold τ. For example, for $\omega = 1,000$, it is required that $\tau = 0.6$ so that the false-hit rate is less than 10^{-10}. To reduce the false-hit rate, one needs to increase the detection threshold τ.

The side effect of increasing threshold τ in detection is that the scheme is more vulnerable to some attacks. For example, the scheme will return no valid watermark from marked data if an attacker flips at least $100(1-\tau)\%$ of the ξ least-significant bits of all values. The smaller the parameter τ, the more robust the scheme is against such attacks at the price of a larger false-hit rate.

In our extended scheme, we can choose $\tau=0.5$ to maximize the robustness without degrading the false-hit rate significantly as it is bounded by $1/2^L$; therefore, a simple majority vote can be used in our watermark detection as long as the length of the watermark is long enough (e.g., $L=40$). In comparison, the false-hit rate is close to 50% for $\tau=0.5$ in the AK scheme, which is intolerable in most cases.

Note that in the AK scheme, the false-hit rate depends not only on τ, but also on the size of data (in terms of ω). Since the size of data may change due to various attacks, one has to determine an appropriate τ by solving a false-hit equation for different sizes of data. The smaller the size of the data, the more a larger τ is required (thus the weaker the scheme is against attacks). For example, if ω decreases from 1,000 to 100, then τ must increase from 0.6 to above 0.7 so as to keep the false-hit rate below 10^{-10}. In our extended scheme, a simple majority vote (i.e., $\tau=0.5$) can be used uniformly for any size of data, which significantly simplifies the detection process.

Invertibility

Now consider when a pirate discovers a secret key from marked data that yields a satisfactory watermark. A pirate can use the discovered key to claim legitimate ownership of the data. Alternately, a pirate can claim innocence by claiming that data owner used this type of invertibility attack to obtain the evidence of piracy.

Claim 2. If a pirate randomly selects a secret key, then the probability that this key causes a valid watermark to be detected from pirated data is

$$\max(\frac{1}{2^{|K|}}, \prod_{i=0}^{L-1} B(\tau \omega_i; \omega_i, 0.5)) \leq \frac{1}{2^{|K|}}, \frac{1}{2^L}),$$

where $\omega_i > 0$ is the number of times that watermark bit i is extracted from data.

Proof. The first term $\frac{1}{2^{|K|}}$ is the probability that the tried key is the real secret key K (assume that the length of the secret key is fixed and public). The second term is the probability of detecting a valid watermark from pirated data using a different secret key, which is the same as the probability of detecting a valid watermark from unmarked data. An attacker may choose his or her own parameters γ, L, and τ to increase this probability. In particular, if τ=0.5 is selected, this term reduces to its upper bound $1/2^L$.

Thwarting this invertibility attack requires choosing a long-enough watermark and secret key (e.g., $L \geq 40$ and AES $|K| \geq 128$). This requirement can be enforced by a standard process or public announcement. Note that an alternate convention might be to require τ to be greater than 0.5; however, an attacker may get around that convention by first reducing ω_i (e.g., via a subset attack) before launching an invertibility attack.

Consider the AK scheme, which corresponds to a special case of our scheme where L=1. No matter how long a secret key is, the invertibility attack could succeed with high probability because the second term $B(\tau\omega; \omega, 0.5)$ in the invertibility rate may approach 50% when an attacker manipulates the size of the data and the detection threshold. In comparison, this term in our scheme has the upper bound $1/2^L$, which is independent of the size of the data and the detection threshold τ.

Since the false-hit rate and invertibility rate in our scheme are controlled by the length of the watermark, we choose τ=0.5 in the following so as to maximize the robustness of our scheme against various attacks.

False Miss

Watermarking schemes should be robust against malicious attacks or benign update operations that may destroy the embedded watermark. Since the embedded watermark can always be destroyed by making substantial modifications to marked data, we assume that when attacks modify data, they also degrade the value of the data. We consider the robustness of our watermarking scheme relative to typical database attacks. In this section, we focus on typical tuple-related attacks that have been considered in Agrawal and Kiernan (2002).

Value Modification

Consider value modification in which an attacker randomly selects some data values and flips their least-significant bits. Assume that the attacker toggles each least-significant bit with probability p_f, where $p_f > 0.5$ (if $p_f > 0.5$, then watermark detection can be applied to transformed data in which each bit is flipped back) is called the flipping probability (subscript f stands for *flipping*).

Claim 3. If a value modification attack is applied to a watermarked relation with flipping probability p_f, then the false-miss rate is

$$1 - \prod_{i=0}^{L-1} (1 - B(\frac{\omega_i}{2}; \omega_i, p_f)),$$

where $\omega_i > 0$ is the number of times that watermark bit w_i is embedded in the data.

Proof. Due to the majority vote, watermark detection fails to detect watermark bit w_i only if at least $\omega_i/2$ embedded bits that correspond to w_i are toggled. Thus, the probability that the watermark bit is not recovered is $B(\frac{\omega_i}{2}; \omega_i, p_f)$. The probability that the entire watermark is not recovered (i.e., the false-miss rate) is

$1 - \prod_{i=0}^{L-1} (1 - B(\frac{\omega_i}{2}; \omega_i, p_f))$.

In an average case, we have $\omega_i = \varpi = \omega/L$ and the false miss rate $1 - (1 - B(\frac{\varpi}{2}; \varpi, p_f))^L$. Figure 1 plots the false-miss rate in the average case. The two parameter values that are varied are ϖ and p_f. The figure uses the default value 100 for L. The figure shows that with a proper choice of parameters, a successful attack requires p_f being large, causing a perceptible change to the data relation.

Tuple Deletion and Insertion

Consider tuple deletion, in which an attacker deletes a subset of tuples from a watermarked relation. Suppose that the attacker examines each tuple independently and selects it with probability p_d for inclusion in the pirated relation.

Claim 4. If a tuple deletion attack is applied to a watermarked relation, then the false-miss rate is

$1 - \prod_{i=0}^{L-1} (1 - p_d^{\omega_i})$,

where $\omega_i > 0$ is the number of times that watermark bit w_i is embedded in the data, and p_d is the probability that a tuple is deleted in the attack.

Proof. For the attack to be successful, it must delete all embedded bits for at least one watermark bit. Now, each watermark bit w_i is embedded ω_i times, so the probability that all the embedded bits for w_i are deleted is $B(\omega_i - 1; \omega_i, p_d) = p_d^{\omega_i}$. Therefore, the false miss rate is

$1 - \prod_{i=0}^{L-1} (1 - p_d^{\omega_i})$.

In an average case where $\omega_i = \varpi = \omega/L$, we have the false-miss rate $1 - (1 - p_d^{\varpi})^L$.

Figure 2 shows that a tuple deletion attack is unlikely to succeed unless a large number of tuples are deleted.

A tuple deletion attack is a less effective attack than a value modification attack. However, it is more potent when used in combination with a value modification attack. A tuple deletion attack reduces the average times a watermark bit is embedded and hence makes the pirated relation more susceptible to value modification attacks. Figure 3 plots the false-miss rate as a function of the ratio of tuples deleted and the flipping probability in a combination attack.

Another type of attack is tuple insertion attack, in which an attacker takes a marked relation and mixes it with $\eta \cdot p_i$ tuples from other sources, where η is the number of tuples in the

Figure 1. False-miss rate under value modification attack

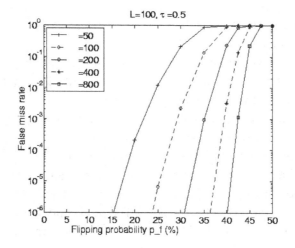

original relation and $p_i \geq 0$ is the insertion rate. In watermark detection, each watermark bit w_l is extracted from those additional tuples roughly $\omega_l \cdot p_i$ times, where ω_l is the number of times the watermark is extracted from the original data. Then the probability that this watermark bit is not recovered due to the attack is

$$B(\frac{\omega_l(1+p_i)}{2}; \omega_l p_i, 0.5).$$

It is then fairly straightforward to derive the false-miss rate for the tuple insertion attack. It is more difficult for an attacker to confuse ownership proof by launching a tuple insertion attack

than manipulating the same number of tuples in a tuple deletion attack.

WATERMARKING WITHOUT PRIMARY KEY

Both the AK scheme and our extended scheme depend critically on a primary key and the original order of database attributes. These schemes do not apply if the data have no primary key attribute or in the case that either the primary key or the order of attributes is modified. These schemes are therefore not robust against attribute-related

Figure 2. False-miss rate under tuple deletion attack

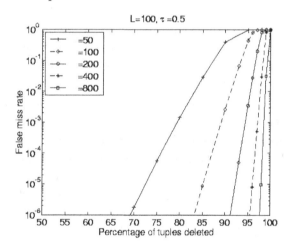

Figure 3. False-miss rate under combination attack

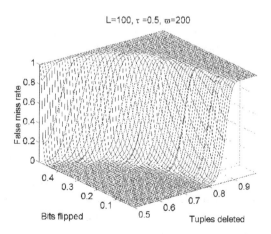

attacks such as attribute deletion and insertion. In this section, we propose alternative schemes that do not depend on primary-key attributes or the attribute order. A preliminary analysis of these schemes was first reported in Li, Swarup, and Jajodia (2003b).

Element-Based Scheme

The multiple-bits scheme discussed in the above section can be called tuple based as it processes data tuple by tuple in watermark insertion and detection. An alternative approach is to process each numerical value independently. A virtual primary key vpk is constructed from each attribute value or data element. We call such scheme element based.

For each element $r.A_i$ of tuple r, the bits of $r.A_i$ are partitioned into two parts: $lsb(r.A_i)$ and $vpk(r.A_i)$, where $lsb(r.A_i)$ may be used to embed a watermark bit and $vpk(r.A_i)$ is used as its virtual primary key. The least-significant bit portion lsb consists of ξ bits in which a watermark bit may be embedded. The virtual primary key vpk consists of the (most significant) bits except the bits in lsb. Changing vpk would introduce intolerable error to the underlying data.

Recall that tuple-based schemes embed one bit per γ tuples. To maintain the same ratio, the element-based scheme embeds one bit per γv elements: An element $r.A_i$ is selected for embedding a watermark bit if $S_1(K, vpk(r.A_i))$ mod γv equals 0. If element $r.A_i$ is selected, its least-significant bit j in the $lsb(r.A_i)$ portion is selected, where $j = S_3(K, vpk(r.A_i))$ mod ξ. Then the element-based scheme embeds (or extracts) a watermark bit to (or from) the selected bit exactly as the tuple-based scheme does.

Combination-Based Scheme

Another solution is to combine some significant bits from multiple attributes for constructing the virtual primary key and process the data tuple by tuple, based on each tuple's virtual primary key. We call such scheme combination based. The construction of the virtual primary key does not depend on the order of the attributes.

For each tuple r, the combination-based scheme computes its virtual primary key r.V by concatenating k ($1 \leq k \leq v$) keyed hash message authentication codes (in the case that the concatenation results in too-long binaries, the virtual primary key can be constructed from hashing the concatenation result) in {$HMAC$ $(K, vpk(r.A_i))$: $i=0,...,v-1$} that are closest to 0 (hash values are interpreted as natural numbers when comparing with 0). The attributes used for constructing the virtual primary key are not fixed but may change from tuple to tuple. Without knowing the secret key, an attacker is unable to determine which attributes are selected for constructing the virtual primary key in each tuple.

The combination-based scheme then uses the tuple-based technique to process each tuple, but with two modifications. First, the combination-based scheme uses the virtual primary key in place of the real primary key. Second, for each tuple r that has been selected, attribute A_i is chosen if its hash value $HMAC$ $(K, vpk(r.A_i))$ is closest to 0 among all attributes' $HMAC$ hash values. Multiple attributes may be selected if they have the same lowest $HMAC$ hash value. In comparison, the tuple-based scheme selects a single attribute A_i if $i = S_2(K, vpk(r.A_i))$ mod v.

Note that in the combination-based scheme, the attribute(s) selected for embedding a watermark bit is (are) among those that are used for constructing the virtual primary key (i.e., the lowest hash value is among the k lowest hash values). The construction of the virtual primary key depends on the hash values rather than the order of the attributes.

Robust Analysis for Virtual-Primary-Key-Based Schemes

Recall that the analysis on the tuple-based scheme is independent of the composition of the primary key; thus, it holds for the combination-based scheme as long as the virtual primary key has the same uniqueness property as the real primary key. In this section, we first extend the robustness analysis to attribute-related attacks and then study the impact of using the virtual primary key instead of the real primary key in robust analysis. Unless otherwise stated, our analysis is applied to the combination-based scheme. A comparison of the combination-based scheme with the element-based scheme is given at the end.

Attribute Deletion and Addition

Assume that k out of v attributes are selected for constructing the virtual primary key and that the k attributes are randomly distributed among v attributes from tuple to tuple. We analyze the false-miss rate of watermark detection when applied to marked data in which some attributes may be deleted or added. Our analysis is similar to that for a value modification attack, where the false-miss rate is measured in terms of flipping probability p_f. The flipping probability is the probability that each extracted watermark bit is not as expected. In the context of attribute deletion and addition, this probability is renamed equivalent flipping probability $\hat{p}_f$. We study how to calculate $\hat{p}_f$ in attribute deletion and addition attacks. As long as $\hat{p}_f$ is obtained, the false-miss rate can be computed the same way as in a value modification attack (by replacing p_f with $\hat{p}_f$).

Claim 5. If d out of v attributes are deleted in a watermarked relation where the virtual primary key is constructed from k attributes, then the false-miss rate is

$$1-\prod_{i=0}^{L-1}(1-B(\frac{\omega_i}{2};\omega_i,\frac{1}{2}-\frac{C_{v-d}^k}{2C_v^k})),$$

where $\omega_i > 0$ is the number of times that watermark bit w_i is extracted from the data.

Proof. An extracted bit is not as expected only if the virtual primary key is altered; that is, some of the k attributes that are involved in the construction of the virtual primary key are deleted. Since the k attributes are randomly distributed from tuple to tuple, the probability that the virtual primary key is altered is

$$1-\frac{C_{v-d}^k}{C_v^k}.$$

It is equally likely that the altered virtual primary key leads to a correct or incorrect bit being detected. Therefore,

$$\hat{p}_f = \frac{1}{2} - \frac{C_{v-d}^k}{2C_v^k}.$$

Note that the false-miss rate is computed based on the extracted times rather than the embedded times of each watermark bit. If the extracted times are unknown, it can be estimated as d/v of the embedded times.

The false-miss rate in an attribute deletion attack is computed exactly as in a value modification attack, except that p_f is replaced with $\hat{p}_f$. Figures 4 and 5 plot $\hat{p}_f$ as functions of d and k, respectively. Figure 4 shows that the more the attributes are deleted, the larger the equivalent flipping probability and the larger the false-miss rate. Figure 5 indicates that the less attributes are involved in the construction of the virtual primary key, the less the impact of attribute deletion. However, as it shall be shown in the next subsection, using less attributes in the construction of the virtual primary key will degrade the uniqueness property of the virtual primary key, which increases the false-miss rates against tuple-related attacks. Therefore, there is a trade-off between tuple-related attacks and attribute deletion in terms of the number of attributes in the virtual-primary-key construction. The optimal number can be decided by minimizing the overall false-miss rates in the evaluation of these attacks.

Figure 4. Equivalent flipping probability for attribute deletion with respect to d

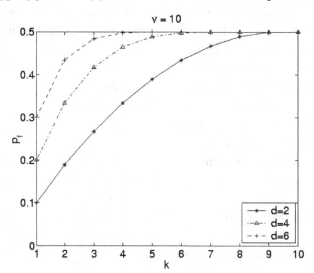

Now consider attribute addition. We assume that all hash values *HMAC(K,vpk(r.A))* are uniformly distributed from 0 to *U*, where *U* is the largest possible hash value.

Claim 6. If *d>0* attributes are added to a watermarked relation where the virtual primary key is constructed from *k* out of *v* attributes, then the false-miss rate is

$$1-\prod_{i=0}^{L-1}(1-B(\frac{\omega_i}{2};\omega_i,\frac{1}{2}-\frac{1}{2}(1-\frac{k}{v+1})^d)),$$

where $\omega_i>0$ is the number of times that watermark bit w_i is extracted from the data.

Proof. For each tuple *r* where a watermark bit is embedded, *k HMAC* hash values $h_0,...,h_{k-1}$ are used for constructing the virtual primary key, where the *k* hash values are selected from {*HMAC(K,vpk(r. A_i)): i=0,...v-1*} that are closest to 0. The watermark bit is embedded into the attribute whose hash value is the closest to 0. Now consider that one attribute A_x is added. The virtual primary key of tuple *r* is unaffected by the adding of A_x only if the hash value *HMAC (K,vpk(r.A_x))* is greater than $\max_{i<k}h_i$. With the assumption that all *HMAC* hash

values are uniformly distributed from 0 to *U* (the largest possible hash value), the probability that the virtual primary key is altered is

$$\frac{\max_{i<k}h_i}{U}\approx\frac{k}{v+1}.$$

If *d* attributes are added, the probability that the virtual primary key is altered is

$$1-(1-\frac{k}{v+1})^d.$$

It is equally likely that the altered virtual primary key leads to a correct or incorrect watermark bit being detected. Therefore, the equivalent flipping probability is

$$\hat{p}_f=\frac{1}{2}-\frac{1}{2}(1-\frac{k}{v+1})^d.$$

Note that the false-miss rate is computed based on the extracted times rather than the embedded times of each watermark bit. If the extracted times are unknown, it can be estimated as 1+*d*/*v* of the embedded times.

Figure 6 plots the equivalent flipping probability as functions of *d* and *k*, indicating that the more attributes are added, the larger the

Figure 5. Equivalent flipping probability for attribute deletion with respect to k

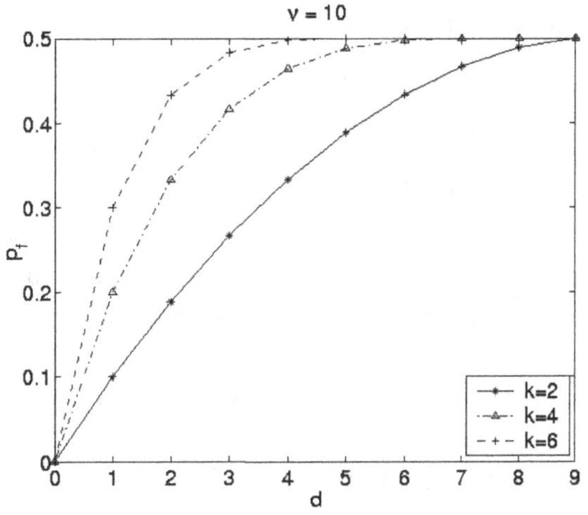

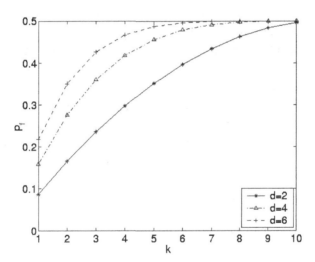

Figure 6. Equivalent flipping probability for attribute addition

equivalent flipping probability and the larger the false-miss rate.

Duplicate Problem

Because the virtual primary key may not be unique to each tuple, the average number of marked bits may not be $\omega = \eta/\gamma$, and each watermark bit may not be embedded in the data roughly the same number of times $\varpi = \eta/(\phi L)$. Due to the possible duplicates of virtual-primary-key values, some watermark

bits may be embedded fewer times than the others, rendering the scheme less robust to various attacks. We call this the duplicate problem.

Due to the duplication of virtual-primary-key values, different watermark bits are not embedded (or extracted) evenly. Let ω_i be the actual times that watermark bit w_i is embedded (or extracted), where $i = 0,\ldots,L-1$. Let $\omega_{max} = \max_i \omega_i$ and $\omega_{min} = \min_i \omega_i$. We use the following duplicate index δ to measure the severeness of the duplicate problem.

- Duplicate index $\delta = (\omega_{max} - \omega_{min})/\omega_{min}$

There will be no duplicate problem if the duplicate index is 0 (i.e., $\omega_i = \varpi$). If some watermark bit is not embedded into the data (i.e., $\min_i \omega_i = 0$), then the duplicate index is infinity ($\delta = \infty$). The smaller the duplicate index, the more evenly the watermark is embedded (or extracted).

We now investigate the influence of the duplicate index on false-miss rates. The duplicate problem affects both tuple-related attacks and attribute-related attacks. In this article, only the impact on tuple-related attacks (value modification and tuple deletion) is illustrated. The impact on attributed-related attacks can be easily derived from the impact on value modification attacks as discussed in the previous subsection.

In the case of $\delta = 0$, Figures 1 and 2 illustrate the false-miss rates under the value modification attack and the tuple deletion attack. In the case that $\delta \neq 0$, we compute the false-miss rate based on the assumption that the embedded times of different watermark bits are uniformly distributed in the interval $[\omega_{min}, \omega_{max}]$ with mean ϖ, where $\varpi = \sum_i \omega_i / L$. Given ϖ and δ, ω_{min} and ω_{max} can be computed as

$$\omega_{min} = \frac{2\varpi}{2+\delta}$$

and

$$\omega_{max} = \frac{2(1+\delta)\varpi}{2+\delta}.$$

Figures 7 and 8 plot the false-miss rates under the value modification attack and the tuple deletion attack for different duplicate indices, where $L=100$ and $\varpi=200$. The figures show that a larger duplicate index renders the scheme more vulnerable to the attacks.

Numerical Results

The duplicate index is content based and thus should be evaluated case by case. We used a real-life data set, forest cover-type data, as an example for the evaluation of the duplicate index. The data set is available from the University of California-Irvine KDD Archive (http://kdd.ics. uci.edu/databases/covertype/covertype.html). The data set consists of 581,012 tuples, each with 61 attributes and no primary key. The first 10 integer-valued attributes are chosen for embedding

Figure 7. False-miss rate under value modification attack

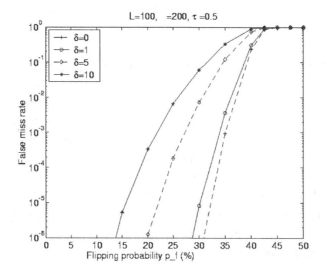

the watermark (i.e., $v=10$). Let the default length of the watermark be $L=58$, and the default ξ be one fourth of the bits (least-significant part) in the binary representation of each attribute value. For the combination-based scheme, two attributes are used in the construction of the virtual primary key (i.e., $k=2$) unless otherwise stated.

Table 2 compares the combination-based scheme with the tuple-based scheme and element-based scheme in terms of duplicate index. For the tuple-based scheme, we added an extra attribute called *id* to serve as the primary key. Due to the uniqueness of such primary key, the duplicate index of the tuple-based scheme is closest to 0 compared to the other schemes. On the other hand, the duplicate index of the element-based scheme is always infinity, indicating that the element-based scheme cannot be used for watermarking this relation.

Figure 9 shows the duplicate index as a function of the number of attributes used in the construction of the virtual primary key (i.e., k). In the figure, the duplicate index is illustrated for different γ values and for the combination-based scheme only. The trend is that the more the attributes used in the construction of the virtual primary key, the less the duplicate index. The duplicate index may not be a strict monotonic function of k because it depends also on the set of tuples that is chosen for embedding the watermark. Combining this figure with Figure 5, one may conclude that using three attributes ($k=3$) for constructing the virtual primary key is a good choice for watermarking the forest cover-type data.

Figure 8. False-miss rate under tuple deletion attack

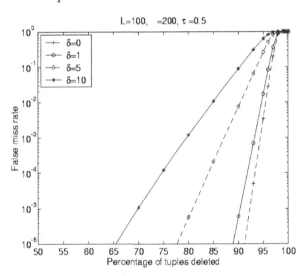

Table 2. Duplicate index for different watermarking schemes

γ	Duplicate index δ		
	Tuple-based scheme	Combination-based scheme	Element-based scheme
100	0.58	5.46	∞
50	0.61	2.73	∞
25	0.14	0.85	∞
12	0.07	1.03	∞

Figure 9. Change of duplicate index (the duplicate indices for all γ values at k=1 are infinity)

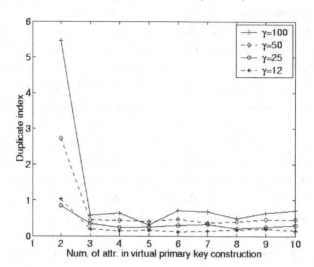

EXTENSION TO MULTIPLE WATERMARKS

Our multiple bits scheme can be easily extended to allow for multiple watermarks. Assume that n watermarks $W_1,..., W_n$ of length L are embedded into database relation R sequentially with different secret keys $K_1,..., K_n$ but with the same watermarking parameters γ, v, and ξ. Interference exists among multiple watermarks, as an embedded bit of one watermark could be flipped back and forth by some later embedded watermarks. The interference among multiple watermarks can be quantified as follows. Let $p_c = 1/(\gamma v \xi)$ be the probability that a least-significant bit is used in embedding a single watermark. For any mark bit of watermark W_{n_1}, the probability that this mark bit is modified by other watermarks is

$$p_{n_1,n} = \frac{1}{2}[1 - (1 - p_c)^{n-n_1}] < 0.5.$$

For any least-significant bit of the original data, the probability that this bit is modified by all watermarks is

$$p_{0,n} = \frac{1}{2}[1 - (1 - p_c)^{n}] < 0.5.$$

If watermark detection is applied to unmarked data using each of n different valid secret keys $K_1,..., K_n$, then the probability that at least one valid watermark is detected, or the false-hit rate, is $1 - (1 - 1/2^L)^n$, which has a lower bound $1/2^L$ and an upper bound $n/2^L$. Given the number n of watermarks, the false-hit rate can be made low enough by increasing the length L of the watermark.

The false-miss rate can be analyzed under a typical modification attack in which an attacker randomly toggles each least-significant bit with a probability $p_f < 0.5$. Under this attack, the probability that the n_1^{th} watermark cannot be detected from the modified data, or the false-miss rate, is

$$1 - \prod_{i=0}^{L-1}(1 - B(\omega_{n_1,i}/2; p_{n_1,n}(1 - p_f) + (1 - p_{n_1,n})p_f)) \approx$$
$$1 - (1 - B(\omega/2; p_{n_1,n}(1 - p_f) + (1 - p_{n_1,n})p_f))^L,$$

where $\omega_{n_1,i}$ is the number of times that the watermark bit w_i in W_{n_1} is embedded in the data, and ϖ is the average times each watermark bit is embedded. The reason is that after modification, each mark bit of the n_1^{th} watermark could be modified either due to watermark interference or by data modification. The probability of it being modified due to watermark interference is $p_{n_1,n}$, and the probability of it being modified by a data modification attack is p_f. Therefore, the probability of it being modified in any way is $p_{n_1,n}(1 - p_f) + (1 - p_{n_1,n})p_f$. The false-miss rate in this case is the probability of at least $W_{n_1,i}/2$ embedded bits out of $\omega_{n_1,i}$ bits of the n_1^{th} watermark being modified. It is clear that the false-miss rate of the first embedded watermark is the largest while that of the last embedded watermark is the smallest among n watermarks.

It can be verified that as $n \rightarrow \infty$, the false-hit rate approaches 100% and the false-miss rate approaches 50%. The more watermarks embedded into a data copy, the larger the false-detection rates in watermark detection, and the more errors introduced to the underlying data in watermark insertion.

The watermarking errors should be carefully evaluated so as to preserve data quality. The errors can be controlled at two different levels. At the item level, the errors introduced to individual values are bounded because no alteration is allowed beyond ξ least-significant bits. At the aggregation level, the errors introduced to descriptive statistics of attribute values can be quantified. In particular, one can study the watermarking error introduced to the mean of an integer-valued attribute with values $x_1,..., x_\eta$. After embedding n watermarks, value x_i becomes $x_i + e_i(n)$, where $e_i(n)$ is a random variable. For x_i, if its least-significant bit j is modified in watermark insertion, the modification will cause change $+ 2^j$ or $- 2^j$ to x_i with the same probability 1:2.

Knowing that the least-significant bit j will be modified in watermark insertion with a probability $p_{0,n}$ (due to watermark interference), one can derive that the mean of $e_i(n)$ is 0 and the variance of $e_i(n)$ is

$$\frac{p_{0,n}(2^{2\xi} - 1)}{3}.$$

Let

$$\mu = \frac{\sum_{i=1}^{\eta} x_i}{\eta}$$

be the mean of original attribute values and let

$$\mu_e(n) = \frac{\sum_{i=1}^{\eta} e_i(n)}{\eta}$$

be the error in computing μ after watermarking. The expected error in computing μ after watermarking is $E[\mu_e(n)] = 0$ and the variance of the error is

$$V[\mu_e(n)] = \frac{p_{0,n}(2^{2\xi} - 1)}{3}.$$

It can be verified that the variance of watermarking error is monotonic, increasing with n to approach its upper limit

$$\frac{2^{2\xi} - 1}{6\eta}.$$

An application of multiple watermarks is to defend against additive attacks. In an additive attack, a pirate inserts additional watermarks to watermarked data so as to confuse ownership proof. A pirate can insert watermarks to claim ownership of the data or claim that the data were provided to a buyer legitimately. An additive attack can be thwarted by raising the watermarking error to a predetermined threshold such that any additive attack would introduce more errors than the limit (Li, Swarup, & Jajodia, 2004). In the case of an additive attack, the ownership dispute can be resolved by determining whose watermarks can be detected more. To gain advantage in an ownership dispute, a pirate is forced to embed a large-enough number of watermarks. Consequently, the pirated data are less useful or less competitive compared to the originally watermarked data and it is not necessary for the owner to claim ownership over such data.

Multiple watermarks can also be used for proving joint ownership in a scenario where a database relation is jointly created by n participants. Each participant can embed a watermark with his or her own key so that he or she can prove the ownership independently. The question is whether the underlying data can be watermarked. Given a certain robustness requirement and error constraint, a maximum number of watermarks can be determined based on our analysis on false-detection rates and watermarking errors.

CONCLUSION

In the area of database watermarking, the research on the AK scheme is innovative. Nonetheless, the AK scheme can be strengthened from both theoretical and practical perspectives. In this article, we pointed out the weaknesses of the AK scheme and proposed our solutions to address these weaknesses.

The theoretical contributions of this research can be summarized as follows. First, we exposed a unique view that the AK scheme actually embeds 1-bit watermark information, which cannot be conveniently used to encode multibit information about database owners or users. Based on such a view, we extended the AK scheme to embed a multiple-bit watermark. Our extension not only inherits the same set of properties as the AK scheme, but also provides an upper bound for the probability that a valid watermark is detected from unmarked data, and that a fictitious secret key is discovered from pirated data. Second, we realized that the AK scheme depends critically on the existence of a primary key and the order of the attributes. Due to this weakness, an attacker can easily create a pirated copy by changing the primary key or attribute order without being detected by the AK scheme. To solve this problem, we proposed to construct a virtual primary key from some selected attributes. With a high probability, our solution ensures that a pirated data copy can still be detected even if its primary key or attribute order has been manipulated by an attacker. Finally, our scheme is extended to allow for multiple watermarks to be embedded and detected for the purpose of thwarting additive attacks or proving joint ownership. Rigorous analysis has shown that our scheme is robust against a variety of

attacks including tuple-related attacks, attribute-related attacks, invertibility attacks, primary-key attacks, and additive attacks.

The practical contributions of this research include the following. First, as a result of our study, copyright detection can be fully automated for detecting any database relations with a guarantee of low false-detection rates. Our scheme can be directly applied to protecting database relations of any size since the false-detection rates are bounded as a function of the length of the watermark regardless of the size of the data. Second, our scheme can be used to protect database relations without primary keys, and protect databases that are subject to a variety of attacks including attribute-related attacks and additive attacks. In the AK scheme, however, one may need to adjust the watermark detection threshold appropriately for detecting data of different sizes so as to keep the false-detection rates low. One may also need to manually check the primary key as well as the order of attributes before launching the watermark detection in the AK scheme.

One future research direction is to model common database queries and minimize the watermarking impact on those queries. It is possible that different watermarking schemes should be designed to accommodate different types of queries. Another future research direction is to study the impact of watermarking to database usability in various application contexts such as in e-business (Pons & Aljifri, 2003).

REFERENCES

Agrawal, R., Haas, P. J., & Kiernan, J. (2003). Watermarking relational data: Framework, algorithms and analysis. *The VLDB Journal, 12*(2), 157-169.

Agrawal, R., & Kiernan, J. (2002). Watermarking relational databases. *Proceedings of VLDB* (pp. 155-166).

Bertino, E., Ooi, B. C., Yang, Y., & Deng, R. (2005). Privacy and ownership preserving of outsourced medical data. *Proceedings of IEEE International Conference on Data Engineering* (pp. 521-532).

Boneh, D., & Shaw, J. (1995). Collusion secure fingerprinting for digital data (extended abstract). *Crypto*, 452-465.

Boneh, D., & Shaw, J. (1998). Collusion secure fingerprinting for digital data. *IEEE Transactions on Information Theory, 44*(5), 1897-1905.

Cox, I. J., Miller, M. L., & Bloom, J. A. (2001). *Digital watermarking: Principles and practice.* Morgan Kaufmann.

Gray, B., & Gorelick, J. (2004, March 1). Database piracy plague. *The Washington Times.* Retrieved from http://www.washingtontimes.com

Gross-Amblard, D. (2003). Query-preserving watermarking of relational databases and XML documents. *Proceedings of ACM Symposium on Principles of Database Systems (PODS)* (pp. 191-201).

Guo, H., Li, Y., & Jajodia, S. (2007). Chaining watermarks for detecting malicious modifications to streaming data. *Information Sciences, 177*(1), 281-298.

Guo, H., Li, Y., Liu, A., & Jajodia, S. (2006). A fragile watermarking scheme for detecting malicious modifications of relational databases. *Information Sciences, 176*(10), 1350-1378.

Guo, J., Li, Y., Deng, R. H., & Chen, K. (2006). Rights protection for data cubes. *Proceedings of Information Security Conference (ISC)* (pp. 359-372).

Johnson, N. F., Duric, Z., & Jajodia, S. (2000). *Information hiding: Steganography and watermarking. Attacks and countermeasures.* Kluwer.

Katzenbeisser, S., & Petitcolas, F. A. (2000). *Information hiding techniques for steganography and digital watermarking.* Artech House.

Kim, H. M., Sengupta, A., Fox, M. S., & Dalkilic, M. (2007). A measurement ontology generalizable for emerging domain applications on the Semantic Web. *Journal of Database Management, 18*(1), 20-42.

Li, Y., & Deng, R. (2006). Publicly verifiable ownership protection for relational databases. *Proceedings of ACM Symposium on Information, Computer and Communication Security (ASIACCS)* (pp. 78-89).

Li, Y., Guo, H., & Jajodia, S. (2004). Tamper detection and localization for categorical data using fragile watermarks. *Proceedings of ACM Digital Rights Management Workshop (DRM)* (pp. 73-82).

Li, Y., Swarup, V., & Jajodia, S. (2003a). Constructing a virtual primary key for fingerprinting relational data. *Proceedings of ACM Digital Rights Management Workshop (DRM)* (pp. 133-141).

Li, Y., Swarup, V., & Jajodia, S. (2003b). A robust watermarking scheme for relational data. *Proceedings of 13th Workshop on Information Technology and Systems (WITS)* (pp. 195-200).

Li, Y., Swarup, V., & Jajodia, S. (2004). Defending against additive attacks with maximal errors in watermarking relational data. *Proceedings of 18th Annual IFIP WG11.3 Working Conference on Data and Applications Security (DBSEC)* (pp. 81-94).

Li, Y., Swarup, V., & Jajodia, S. (2005). Fingerprinting relational databases: Schemes and specialties. *IEEE Transactions on Dependable and Secure Computing, 2*, 34-45.

Ng, W., & Lau, H. L. (2005). Effective approaches for watermarking XML data. *International Conference on Database Systems for Advanced Applications* (pp. 68-80).

Pears, R., & Houliston, B. (2007). Optimization of multidimensional aggregates in data warehouses. *Journal of Database Management, 18*(1), 69-93.

Pons, A. P., & Aljifri, H. (2003). Data protection using watermarking in e-business. *Journal of Database Management, 14*(4), 1-13.

Reid, R., & Dhillon, G. (2003). Integrating digital signatures with relational databases: Issues and organizational implications. *Journal of Database Management, 14*(2), 42-51.

Safavi-Naini, R., & Wang, Y. (2001). Collusion secure q-ary fingerprinting for perceptual content. *Digital Rights Management Workshop* (pp. 57-75).

Sion, R. (2004). Proving ownership over categorical data. *Proceedings of IEEE International Conference on Data Engineering (ICDE)* (pp. 584-596).

Sion, R., Atallah, M., & Prabhakar, S. (2003). Rights protection for relational data. *Proceedings of ACM SIGMOD International Conference on Management of Data* (pp. 98-108).

Vaas, L. (2003, September 24). Putting a stop to database piracy. *eWeek: Enterprise News and Reviews*. Retrieved from http://www.eweek.com/print_article/0,3084,a=107965,00.asp

Woo, J. H., Lee, B. S., Lee, M. J., Loh, W. K., & Whang, K. Y. (2007). Temporal aggregation using a multidimensional index. *Journal of Database Management, 18*(2), 62-79.

Zhou, X., Pang, H. H., & Tan, K. L. (2007). Query-based watermarking for XML data. *Proceedings of ACM Symposium on Information, Computer and Communication Security (ASIACCS)* (pp. 253-264).

This work was previously published in the Journal of Database Management, Vol. 19, Issue 3, edited by K. Siau, pp. 1-21, copyright 2008 by IGI Publishing (an imprint of IGI Global).

Chapter 2
BROOD:
Business Rules–Driven Object Oriented Design

Pericles Loucopoulos
Loughborough University, UK

Wan M.N. Wan Kadir
Universiti Teknologi Malaysia, Malaysia

ABSTRACT

A critical success factor for information systems is their ability to evolve as their environment changes. There is compelling evidence that the management of change in business policy can have a profound effect on an information system's ability to evolve effectively and efficiently. For this to be successful, there is a need to represent business rules from the early requirements stage, expressed in user-understandable terms, to downstream system design components and maintain these throughout the lifecycle of the system. Any user-oriented changes could then be traced and if necessary propagated from requirements to design specifications and evaluated by both end-users and developers about their impact on the system. The BROOD approach, discussed in this article, aims to provide seamless traceability between requirements and system designs through the modelling of business rules and the successive transformations, using UML as the modelling framework.

INTRODUCTION

The ubiquitous nature of information systems and the increasing dependency of organizations, government and society on such systems highlight the importance of ensuring robustness in their operation. At the same time rapid changes in the environment of information systems places an increasing emphasis on the ability of these systems to evolve according to emerging requirements. A large proportion of a total systems' lifecycle cost is devoted to introducing new requirements, and removing or changing existing system functionality (Grubb & Takang, 2003). Software evolution therefore is considered as a key challenge in the development and maintenance of information systems (Erlikh, 2000).

In recent years there has been an increasing interest of the IS community in business rules, which has resulted in dedicated rule-centric modeling frameworks and methodologies (Ross & Lam, 1999; Zaniolo et al., 1997), international initiatives for the investigation of business rules' role in the context of knowledge management (Hay & Healy, 1997), conferences, workshops and tutorials (Mens, Wuyts, Bontridder, & Grijseels, 1998), and rule-centric rule management tools and application development support environments (e.g., Blaze Advisor Builder, BRS RuleTrack, Business Rule Studio, Haley Technologies, ILOG Rules, Platinum Aion, Usoft Developer and Visual Rule Studio). Whilst these efforts make significant contributions in their own right, a key challenge remains unanswered namely the *linking of business rules specifications to software designs*.

The aim of the BROOD (business rules-driven object oriented design) approach is to address the issue of software evolution from both *requirements* and *design* perspectives. This confluence should provide a seamless and traceable facility that arguably should bring about a more effective way of dealing with software evolution, by aligning changes of the information system to changes in its environment. BROOD adopts as its methodological paradigm that of object orientation with UML as its underlying graphical language. It augments UML by explicitly considering business rules as an integral part of an object-oriented development effort. To this end BROOD aims:

i.   To explicitly model business rules in a manner understandable to end-user stakeholders.
ii.   To map these to formal descriptions amenable to automation and analysis.
iii. To provide guidelines on the deployment of business rules in the development process.
iv.   To provide guidelines on the evolution of requirements and related design specifications.

The article is organized as follows. Section 2 discusses the background to business rules modeling. Section 3 introduces the motivation for BROOD. Section 4 introduces the BROOD metamodel as the foundation for modeling business rules. Section 5 discusses the manner in which business rules are linked to design components via the concept of 'rule phrase.' The BROOD process is detailed in section 6. The BROOD approach is supported by an automated tool and this is briefly discussed in Section 7. The article concludes with an overview of BROOD, observations on its use on a large application and comparisons with traditional approaches.

The language details for business rules definition are given in appendix A. The BROOD approach is demonstrated through an industrial application which is described in appendix B. This application had originally been developed using a traditional approach. Therefore, it proved useful not only as a means of providing a practical grounding on BROOD but also on comparing and contrasting the use of BROOD with a traditional development effort.

BUSINESS RULES MODELLING

The motivation of BROOD is to provide a development environment whereby the business analysis and system design domains are supported by business rules modeling with the specific aim to facilitating more effective software evolution.

The term "business rule" has been used by different authors in different ways. For example, in (Rosca, Greenspan, Feblowitz, & Wild, 1997), business rules are:

statements of goals, policies, or constraints on an enterprise's way of doing business.

In (Herbst, 1996a), they are defined as:

statements about how the business is done, i.e. about guidelines and restrictions with respect to states and processes in an organization.

Krammer considers them as "programmatic implementations of the policies and practices of a business organization" (Krammer, 1997) whilst Halle states that:

depending on whom you ask, business rules may encompass some or all relationship verbs, mathematical calculations, inference rules, step-by-step instructions, database constraints, business goals and policies, and business definitions. (Halle, 1994).

In general, business rules in the information systems field may be viewed in terms of two perspectives: (a) business rules as applied to conceptual modeling and (b) business rules as applied to evolvable software systems development.

Business Rules in Conceptual Modeling

1. Business rules as part of requirements gathering and systems analysis have not been ignored by structured analysis, information engineering or object-oriented analysis approaches (Moriarty, 1993) which, to varying degrees, subsume or represent business rules as part of notation schemes used to specify application requirements (Gottesdiener, 1997) Ross (1997) comments that traditional IS methodologies have addressed rules poorly, and only relatively late in the system development lifecycle. (Hay & Healy, 1997) mention that rules dealing with information structure may be represented by any of several flavors of entity—relationship or object class diagrams, and responses to events may be shown via essential data flow

diagrams (McMenamin & Palmer, 1984) or as entity life history diagrams (Robinson & Berrisford, 1994).

From a conceptual perspective there are approaches that consider business rules as an integral part of the modeling and analysis of systems' requirements. An early effort in this direction was the *RUBRIC* project (Loucopoulos & Layzell, 1986; van Assche, Layzell, Loucopoulos, & Speltinex, 1988) parts of which were integrated into the information engineering (Martin, 1989) method.

In *BROCOM* (Herbst, 1996b, 1997), the rule language is a type of structured English, and therefore it is highly expressive. Moreover, rules are organized according to a rich meta-model, and can be retrieved based on a number of different criteria. As far as methodological guidance is concerned, Herbst proposes the development of various models which are helpful during the analysis phase, but the process of creating and using them is not clearly defined. The transition from analysis to design and implementation has not been addressed by this approach.

The *DSS* approach (Rosca, Greenspan, & Wild, 2002; Rosca et al., 1995) focuses on the analysis phase of IS development by supporting the rationale behind the establishment of rules. DSS adopts the ECA (event-condition-action) paradigm for structuring rule expressions and also links these expressions to the entities of an underlying enterprise model. The absence of a formal rule language confines the use of DSS on modeling tasks.

The Business Rules Group (*BRG*), formerly known as the GUIDE Business Rule Project (Hay & Healy, 1997), investigated an appropriate formalization for the analysis and expression of business rules (Hay & Healy, 2000). This approach identifies terms and facts in natural language rule statements, and consequently, it offers a high level of expressiveness. The meta-model it provides for describing the relations between these terms and facts is very detailed. Therefore, rule models are (a) highly manageable and (b) formal and fully consistent with the information models of a specific organization.

The *IDEA* method (Zaniolo et al., 1997) focuses on the maintenance of formality and consistency with underlying business models. The method offers guidance for every activity being involved in the development of a rule-centric information system. The IDEA method is directed towards the use of specific active and deductive databases, and of the corresponding rule languages. As a result of this, (a) IDEA rules are rather difficult to be expressed or even understood by business people; and (b) the choice of technologies to be employed for the development of an information system is rather limited.

The *BRS* approach (Ross, 1997) is formal, in accordance with the underlying data models of an organization, offers sufficient methodological guidance, and allows management of rule expressions based on a very detailed meta-model. It is also one of the few methods that adopts a graphical notation for expressing rules. Regarding the development process, BRS introduces a business rule methodology called BRS Proteus™ methodology that defines a number of steps for both business and system modeling (Ross, & Lam, 2003). BRS also provides the BRS RuleTrack™, an automated tool for recording and organizing business rules.

The object constraint language (*OCL*) of UML (Eriksson & Penker, 2000) is tightly bound with the widely accepted UML but lacks methodological guidance for the collection of rules. Rule structures are implied by the allocation of rules to classes, attributes, associations and operations.

A comparative evaluation of the treatment of business rules for conceptual modeling by three widely used approaches is shown in Table 1.

Business Rules in Evolvable Software Evolution

The majority of approaches in this category aim to improve the understanding and evolution of a software system by logically and physically separating business rule components from other software components.

The adaptive object model (*AOM*), which is also known as the dynamic object model (Riehle, Tilman, & Johnson, 2000), is *"a system that represents classes, attributes, and relationships as metadata"* (Yoder, Balaguer, & Johnson, 2001). Unlike traditional object-oriented design, AOM is based on objects rather than classes. It provides descriptions (metadata) of objects that exist in the system. In other words, AOM provides a meta-architecture that allows users to manipulate the concrete architectural components of the model such as business objects and business rules. These components are stored as an object model in a database instead of in code. The code is only used to interpret the stored objects. Thus, a user only needs to change the metadata instead of changing the code to reflect domain changes.

The *coordination contract* method aims to separate coordination from computation aspects (or core components) of a software system (Andrade, Fiadeiro, Gouveia, & Koutsoukos, 2002). It is motivated by the fact that there should be two different kinds of entities in a rapidly changing business environment—core business entities which are relatively stable and volatile business products which keep changing for the business to remain competitive (Andrade & Fiadeiro, 2000). Volatile business products are implemented as contracts. A contract aims to externalize the interactions between objects (core entities) by explicitly define them in the conceptual model. It extends the concept of association class by adding a coordination role similar to other components in architecture-based software evolution such as architectural connectors (Oreizy, Medvidovic, & Taylor, 1998), glue (Schneider, 1999), actor (Astley

Table 1. Comparative evaluation of business rule in conceptual modeling

BR Approach / Criteria	BRG	BROCOM	BRS
Concepts			
Business Rule Definition	IS	IS	Business
Business Rule Taxonomy			
- **Structural Rules**	High (10)	Low (0)	Medium (1)
- **Behavioural Rules**	Medium (8)	High (>30)	Medium (8)
- **Derivation**	Medium (2)	Low (0)	Medium (2)
Bus. Rule Management Elements	Medium (5)	Medium (9)	High (>30)
Modelling Language			
Understandability	Medium	Medium	High
Expressiveness (business rules)	Medium	High	High
Unambiguity	Medium	High	Medium
Formality	Medium	Medium	High
Evolvability	Medium	Medium	High
Process			
Lifecycle coverage	A	A	A + D
Process description	N/A	High	High
Coherence	N/A	High	High
Support for evolution	No	Yes	Yes
Pragmatics			
Communicability	Medium	High	High
Usability	Medium	High	High
Resources availability	Low	Medium	High
Openness	High	Medium	High

Lifecycle coverage: A-Analysis, D-Design, I-Implementation, M-Maintenance

& Agha, 1998) or change absorbers (Evans & Dickman, 1999).

Business Rule Beans (*BRBeans*), formerly known as accessible business rules (Rouvellou, Degenaro, Rasmus et al., 1999; Rouvellou, Degenaro, Rasmus et al., 2000), is a framework that provides guidelines and infrastructures for the externalization of business rules in a distributed business application (IBM, 2003). Business rules are externally developed, implemented and managed to minimize the impact of their changes on other components such as core business, application, and user interface objects. They are implemented as server objects, which are fired by embedded trigger points in application objects. A rule management facility is provided to help users to understand the existing rules and to locate the rules when changes are required. BRBeans is implemented as a part of WebSphere Application Server by IBM *"to support business applications that externalize their business rules"* (Kovari, Diaz, Fernandes et al., 2003).

A comparative evaluation of the treatment of business rules evolvable software systems development by the three approaches is shown in Table 2.

Table 2. Comparative evaluation of business rules in evolvable software systems

Criteria BR Approach	Adaptive Object Model (AOM)	Coordination Contract	Business Rule Beans (BR-Beans)
Concepts			
Business Rule Definition	Implicit	Implicit	Explicit
Business Rule Taxonomy	primitive, composite, workflow	ECA	derivation, constraint, invariant, script, classifier
Business Rule Management Elements	Nil	Nil	Yes
Modelling Language			
Understandability	High	Medium	Medium
Expressiveness (business rules)	Low	Medium	Medium
Formality	Low	High	Medium
Evolvability	High	High	High
Process			
Lifecycle coverage	(Evolutionary)	D + I + T + M	A + D + I + T + M
Process description	Low	Medium	High
Coherence	Medium	Medium	Medium
Support for evolution	Low	Medium	High
Pragmatics			
Communicability	High	Medium	Medium
Usability	Low	Medium	Medium
Resources availability	Medium	Medium	High
Openness	Medium	Medium	Low

MOTIVATION FOR THE BROOD APPROACH

According to Lehman's laws (Lehman & Belady, 1985), a software system that is used in a real-world environment inevitably must change or become progressively less useful in that environment. Lehman's laws also state that the software structure tends to become more complex due to the implemented changes and its size must continue to grow to accommodate new user requirements. Therefore, there is a need to introduce a method that facilitates the management of the increasingly complex and larger size software system due to its evolution.

The position put forward in this article is that developers need to identify the sources of changes for software evolution in the system's environment and that some of the most volatile of these components tend to be business rules. In section 0 many contemporary approaches were reviewed all of which aim to externalize business rules from software components.

At the conceptual modeling level, there are approaches that separate syntax and semantics for modeling business rules. This effort localizes the changes to business rule components, and also increases the understanding and maintainability of business rules specification. This category of approaches provides a great deal of help in dealing with the concepts related to business rules, but they provide relatively little description on the design and implementation aspect of business rules.

At the implementation level, approaches create separate software components that implement business rules. As a result, the business rule changes will only localize to such components, and reduce the impact of changes to the overall software structure. This group of approaches provides very good facilities for developing evolvable software components but is less helpful in representing business rules at the conceptual business level.

The BROOD approach addresses both business modeling and the linking of business model components to software architecture components. By focusing on the conceptual level, BROOD attempts to externalizing changes from software components. This user-oriented view enhances understandability and maintainability since it encourages the direct involvement of business stakeholders in the maintenance of their business rules.

By introducing a linking component between the conceptual model of business rules and software design, BROOD attempts to increase business rule traceability. Traceability is highly desirable since one can keep 'forward' and 'backward' tracks of changes between business and software.

BROOD considers both *product* and *process* perspectives of the development and evolution of a software system. The *product* is defined using the BROOD metamodel, which specifies the structure for business rule specification, software design, and their linking elements. The *process* refers to a set of systematic and well-defined steps that should be followed during software development and evolution. The BROOD process emphasizes several important activities in a software lifecycle that contribute to a more resilient software system.

THE BROOD METAMODEL

The initial concept of the metamodel was introduced in (Wan Kadir & Loucopoulos, 2003; Wan Kadir & Loucopoulos, 2004). The metamodel is complemented by a language definition based on the context-free grammar EBNF, which is included in appendix A. The language definition defines the allowable sentence patterns for business rule statements and describes the linking elements between business rules and the related software design elements.

At the outset, three main desirable characteristics were set for developing an appropriate business rule metamodel, which would be consistent with the aims of BROOD:

- It should have an exhaustive and mutually exclusive typology to capture different types of business rules.
- It should have the structured forms of expressions for linking the business rules to software design.
- It should include rule management elements to improve business rule traceability in a business domain.

These three characteristics form the basis for the development of the business rule metamodel, which is shown in Figure 1. This figure shows the business rules metamodel together with parts of the UML metamodel that deal with static (classes) and dynamic (actions and events) aspects. The key requirement of BROOD for tracing changes from business to software through the use of business rules is achieved by integrating these three metamodels.

Business Rules Typology

The metamodel classifies business rules into three main types, which are constraint, action assertion, and derivation.

Figure 1. The BROOD business rule metamodel

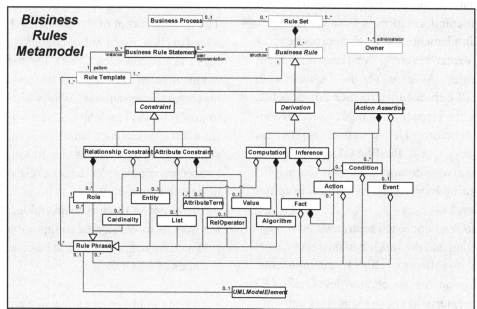

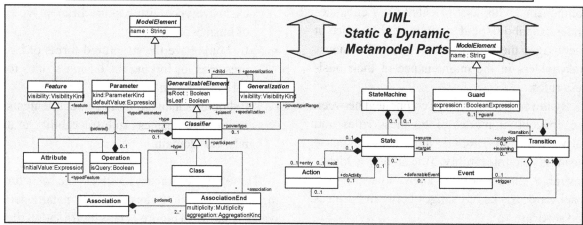

Constraints

Constraint rules specify the static characteristics of business entities, their attributes, and their relationships. They can be further divided into attribute and relationship constraints. The former specifies the uniqueness, optionality (null), and value check of an entity attribute. The latter asserts the relationship types as well as the cardinality and roles of each entity participating in a particular relationship.

Examples of attribute constraints from the MediNet application expressed according to the BROOD syntax (see `attribute constraint` definition in appendix A) are the following:

- Patient must have a unique patient registration number.
- Patient may have a passport number.
- Bill must have a unique bill number.
- The amount of Bill must be less than the maximum bill amount set by the paymaster.

- An employee level of a Panel Patient must be in {employer, executive, production operator}.

Examples of relationship constraints for MediNET (see `relationship constraint` definition in appendix A) are:

- Clinic item is a/an item type of bill item.
- Bill must have zero or more bill item.
- HCP Service Invoice is a/an Invoice.

Actions

Action assertion concerns a behavioral aspect of the business. Action assertion specifies the *action* that should be activated on the occurrence of a certain *event* and possibly on the satisfaction of certain *conditions*. An event can be either a simple or a complex event where the latter is constructed by one or more simple events using the logical connectives AND/OR. A condition may be a simple or complex condition. A simple condition is a Boolean expression which compares a value of an entity attribute with any literal value or the value of another entity attribute using a relational operator. It can also be an inspection of the existence of a value of an entity attribute in a list of values.

An action is performed by a system in response to the occurrence of an event and the satisfaction of the relevant condition. The execution of action may change the state of the system. An action may be a simple action or a sequence of simple actions. Simple actions can be further categorized into three different types, trigger actions, object manipulation actions, and user actions. Trigger action invokes an operation, a process, a procedure, or another rule under certain circumstances. Object manipulation action sets the value of the attribute or create/delete an instance of an entity. User action is a manual task that is done by system users. During implementation, user action is often implemented as a message displayed to the user.

Examples of action assertion for MediNET (see `action assertion` definition in appendix A) are:

- When new invoice created then calculate invoice end date.
- When patient consultation completed then removed the patient from consultation queue and create bill for the patient.
- When invoice entry updated if stock of drug smaller than re-order threshold then reorder the drug.

Derivation

A derivation rule derives a new fact based on existing facts. It can be of one of two types, *computation*, which uses a mathematical calculation or algorithm to derive a new arithmetic value, or *inference*, which uses logical deduction or induction to derive a new fact. Typically, an inference rule may be used to represent permission such as user policy for data security. An example of a computation derivation rule such as "*The amount HCP MediNET usage invoice is computed as the amount of transaction fees, which are calculated as the transaction fee multiply by the total number of transactions, plus the monthly fee*" would be expressed as:

- let a = transaction_fee;
- let b = number_of_treated_patient;
- transaction_fees = a * b;
- invoice_amount = transaction_fees + monthly_fee;

Examples of inference rules are given below:

- If the paymaster's last quarter transaction is more than RM12,000.00 and the paymaster has no past due invoices then the paymaster is a preferred customer.

- If the user type is equal to HR Officer and the user company is equal to patient paymaster then the user may view the patient's medical certificate.

The Rule Template

Rule templates are the formal sentence patterns by which business rules can be expressed. They are provided as a guideline to capture and specify business rules as well as a way to structure the business rule statements. Each rule template consists of one or more well-defined rule phrases, which are discussed in section 0.

By using the available templates, an inexperienced user may easily produce a consistent business rule statement. Rule templates help users to avoid tedious and repeated editing when creating many similar rules; and ensure uniformity by restricting the type of rules that can be written by business users. The use of templates also allows the precise linking of business rules to software design elements. The templates can be directly derived from the rules definition in Appendix A. Business rules templates are shown in Table 3.

The Rule Management Elements

Management elements are also included in the BROOD metamodel for facilitating the organization and management of business rules. These elements include the *rule set, business process*, and *owner*.

Rule set is used to group business rules into a set of closely interrelated rules. Each business rule model must have a single rule set, which is considered as the root rule set. This rule set must have at least one rule statement or another rule set.

One of the popular ways to identify a rule set is through its related business process. For example, the rules *'The bill amount is calculated as the sum of amounts of all bill items'* and *'If a patient is a panel patient and his paymaster pays the bill in* *full, the balance is set to 0 and the bill status is set to paid'* can be grouped in a rule set which is related to *'bill preparation'* process. By properly organizing rules, the complexity of managing a large set of rules can be reduced.

Each business rule model must have an owner. An owner may also be defined for a rule set. The owner of a parent rule set is assumed to be the owner of its child rule set if the child does not define its owner. It is important to define the owner information in a business rule model to determine the access rights and responsibility to a business rules repository, especially for software systems with multiple user groups that possess different business rules. An owner may be an organizational unit, an individual user, a user group or role that is responsible for the management of the respective business rules. During business rule implementation, each rule set, business process, and owner is given a unique identifier.

THE RULE PHRASE

A rule phrase in BROOD links a user-oriented business rule definition to a software design component. There are alternative ways in which this may be achieved. For example, using a rule object or rule engine, or making use of OCL. The use of rule object or rule engine increases the semantic distance between analysis and design and imposes implementation considerations. The use of constraints expressed using OCL may provide a link between business rule specifications and software design but OCL is still hard to understand by business users although OMG claims that no mathematical background is required in using OCL.

Rule phrases are considered as the building blocks for rule statements. They can be maintained independently during implementation, in other words, they are not deleted when a business rule is deleted. However, the modification and deleting of a rule phrase is not recommended since a care-

Table 3. Business rule templates

Types	Templates
Attribute Constraint	<entity> must have | may have [a unique] <attributeTerm>. <attributeTerm1> must be | may be <relationalOperator> <value> | <attributeTerm2>. <attributeTerm> must be in <list>.
Relationship Constraint	[<cardinality>] <entity1> is a/an <role> of [<cardinality>]<entity2>. [<cardinality>] <entity1> is associated with [<cardinality>]<entity2>. <entity1> must have | may have [<cardinality>] <entity2>. <entity1> is a/an <entity2>.

Action Assertion	When <event> [if <condition>] then <action>.
	The templates of <event> :
	    <attributeTerm> is updated
	    <entity> is deleted | is created
	    <operation>|<rule> is triggered
	    the current date/time is <dateTime>
	    <number> <timeUnit> time interval from <dateTime> is reached
	    <number> <timeUnit> after <dateTime>
	    <userEvent>
	The templates of <condition> :
	    <attributeTerm1> <relationalOperator> <value | attributeTerm2>
	    <attributeTerm> [not] in <list>
	The templates of <action> :
	    trigger <process> | <operation> | <rule>
	    set <attributeTerm> to <value>
	    create | delete <entity>
	    <userAction>

Computation	<attributeTerm> is computed as <algorithm>

Derivation	if <condition> then <fact>.
	The templates of <fact> :
	    <entity> | <attributeTerm> is [not] a <value>
	    <entity> may [not] <action>

ful effort is needed in reviewing its aggregated business rules. In addition to playing a role as the building blocks for business rule statements, rule phrases are also important in linking business rules to software design elements.

The mappings between rule phrase types and UML model elements are summarized in Table 4. Most of the rule phrases are directly linked to class diagram model elements. Entity and attribute term are directly connected to the respective class and attribute in the class diagram. Cardinality and role are correspondingly linked to multiplicity and role of an association end of a relationship. Algorithm is linked to operation specification.

Rule phrases for event, condition, and action, which are the building blocks for action assertion rules, are naturally linked to statechart diagram. Event, condition, and action are respectively linked to event, guard, and action of a state transition in a statechart diagram. Consequently, event and action may be linked to a class operation, and guard may be linked to an operation specification, in a class diagram. List and relational operator contain enumerated values whilst value contains a literal value. However, value and list can be linked to an operation that return a single and multiple values respectively.

Table 4. Association between rule phrases and design elements

Rule Phrase Type	Software Design Elements
Entity	Class
Attribute Term	Attribute
Operation Term	Operation
Attribute Constraints	Attribute.isUnique, Attribute.notNull
Cardinality	AssociationEnd.multiplicity
Role	AssociationEnd.role
Event	Transition.event → Class.operation
Condition	Transition.guard, Operation.specification
Action	Transition.action → Class.operation
Algorithm	Operation.specification
Value	- (literal value), Operation.
List	- (enumeration), Operation
Relational Operator	- (enumeration)

THE BROOD PROCESS

The BROOD process is described using the process model based on the syntax and semantics of the OMG software process engineering metamodel (SPEM). SPEM was developed by the Object Management Group to provide a metamodel and notations for specifying software processes and their components (OMG, 2002). SPEM extends the unified modeling language (UML) (OMG, 2001) metamodel with process specific stereotypes. A part of SPEM that shows most of the important components of a process structure is shown in Figure 2.

In SPEM, a *work product* is an artifact produced, consumed, or modified by a process. It may be a piece of information, a document, model, or source code. It is either used as an input by workers to perform an activity, or a result or an output of such activities. A work product is called a deliverable if it is needed to be formally delivered by a process. The examples of work products in BROOD are class diagram, statechart diagram, and business rule specification. Each work product

is associated with a process role that is formally responsible for its production.

A *process role* defines the responsibilities of an individual, or a group of individuals working together as a team. Each process role performs or assists with specific activities.

The core activities of the BROOD process are situated in the analysis, design, and evolution phases. Analysis phase produces analysis model that contains two main work products: the initial business rule specification and preliminary software design models. Both work products are refined and linked during the design phase to produce a more traceable and consequently evolvable software system. The flow of activities in each BROOD phase is shown in Figure 3.

The Analysis Phase

As shown in Figure 4, the analysis phase starts with an architectural analysis activity that considers the work products from requirements phase such as use-case model, business model, initial architecture descriptions, and supplementary

Figure 2. An excerpt from OMG software process engineering metamodel (OMG, 2002)

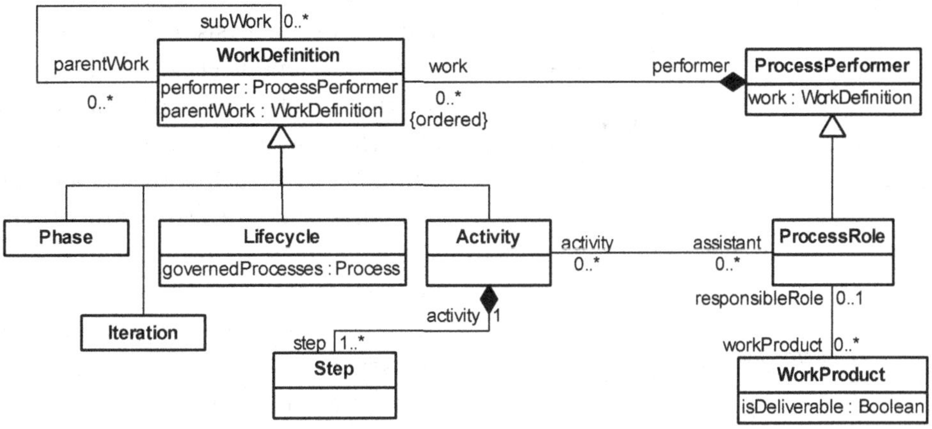

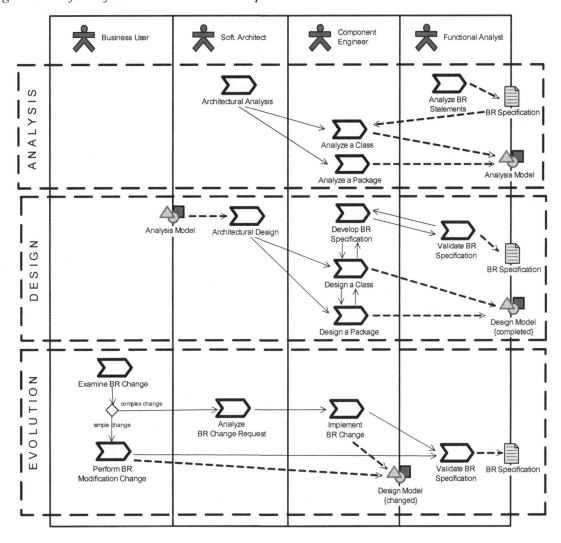

Figure 3. The flow of activities in the BROOD process

Figure 4. Packages for the MediNet application

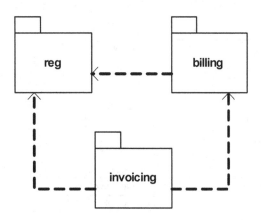

requirements. A software architect performs architectural analysis by identifying the analysis packages based on the functional requirements and knowledge of the application domain. Each package realizes a set of closely related use cases and business processes to minimize the coupling between packages, which in turn localizes business changes. This activity identifies analysis classes and outlines their name, responsibilities, attributes, and relationships. In order to extract more information about the behavior of the classes, collaboration or interaction diagrams can be developed based on the process flows (scenario) in the use case models. The main work products produced by this activity are analysis class diagrams and packages in their outline version.

Considering the MediNet application, architectural analysis resulted in three packages *business processes* i.e. *registration*, *billing*, and *invoicing*. The registration package groups all classes related to patient registration such as Patient, Paymaster, HCProvider, Clinic, User, and RegLocation. Billing package contains classes related to billing and drugs inventory such as Bill, BillPayment, Bill_Item, TransType, TransItem, and ExpenseItem. Invoicing package includes classes related to invoicing and invoice payment for example Invoice, InvoiceItem, Payment, and PaymentAllocation.

The outline of analysis class diagrams and packages are further refined by class analysis and package analysis activities, respectively. A component engineer identifies more detailed information about responsibilities and attributes of each class. Different types of relationships between classes such as association, aggregation, and inheritance are also identified. The possible states and their transitions can be identified to understand the behavior of objects from certain classes. These steps are repeated until a complete analysis class diagram, statechart diagram and package are achieved.

The activity of business rule modeling considers the informal statements captured during initial requirements and identifies the types for each business rule statement based on the BROOD typology. Business rule statements are transformed into more structured business rule specifications according to the templates' definition.

Table 5 shows a set of structured rules for the MediNet application. This template provides the means of managing rules as they get discovered and analyzed and acts as a 'repository' of rules for their entire lifecycle.

The Design Phase

The design phase involves the identification of application-specific and application-general subsystems. The application-specific subsystems are related to packages that group a set of closely related services in an application domain. The application-general subsystems are related to implementation technology decisions such as the introduction of user interface and database connectivity layers. The MediNet subsystems definition is shown in Figure 5.

The class design activity elaborates further the static and dynamic information of classes that were defined during the analysis phase. Additional information on the operations, attributes, and relationships can be added to each class. The specification of operations and attributes is made

Table 5. Business rule statements for the MediNET application

Business Process	Business Rule Example	Rule Type
Registration	A patient must have a unique registration number.	Att. Constraint
	A patient may have more than one paymaster.	Rel. Constraint
	If a patient has an outstanding balance, then the patient should be banned from consultation registration	Action Assertion
	When consultation registration is successfully completed, then put the patient into the consultation queue.	Action Assertion
	If a patient's condition is critical then the patient is an emergency patient.	Inference
Billing	The amount of a panel patient's bill must not exceed the maximum bill amount set by the paymaster.	Att. Constraint
	Each bill item is associated with an item from the clinic transaction items	Rel. Constraint
	When consultation is completed then create bill.	Action Assertion
	If the bill is a panel patient's bill then create panel transaction item.	Action Assertion
	The amount of a bill is computed as the sum of all amounts of bill items.	Computation
	The amount of bill item is computed as the unit amount multiply by the quantity.	Computation
	A bill can be modified only if the user role is Chief Clinic Assistant.	Inference
Invoicing	One invoice must have zero or more payments.	Rel. Constraint
	When a payment is not received within 30 days from the invoice date, then the first reminder will be sent.	Action Assertion
	The amount of HCP MediNET usage invoice is computed as the sum of monthly subscription fee plus transaction fees.	Computation
	A paymaster (panel company) is under probation if the paymaster has an invoice with category 1 past due and the current balance is more than RM 5,000.00.	Inference

using the syntax of the chosen programming language. If necessary, the methods that specify the algorithm for the implementation of operations are specified.

The class design activity for the MediNet application resulted in detailed specification of for the three packages of registration, billing and invoicing. The class association diagram of Figure 6 shows the class details for invoicing. In order to reduce diagrammatic complexity all parameters and return values are hidden in the class operations.

The calculation of invoice amount is different for different types of invoice. The amount for healthcare service invoice is calculated as the total of its item amounts after applying additional computation rules such as bill limit, invoice limit and discount. MediNET uses the open item invoicing method that allows an invoice issuer to track each unpaid invoice as an individual item for aging purposes. Panel patient bills are considered as the items for HCP MediNET usage and HCP service usage invoices. For HCP MediNET usage invoice, the number of bills issued by a particular HCP is counted as the number of transactions, which is later used in the invoice amount calculation. In terms of payment, MediNET allows balance

Figure 5. Software architecture for the MediNet application

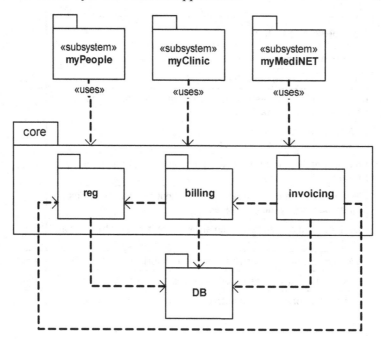

forward invoicing method in addition to open item method.

Within the design process classes are further elaborated in terms of the events and conditions that trigger their transition from one state to another. These are shown as statechart diagrams. For example, a statechart diagram for the HCServiceInvoice object is shown in Figure 7.

Within the BROOD design phase, rule phrase specifications are developed. Each rule phrase definition is stored in the repository called rule phrase entries. The possible values for rule phrase may be a set of enumerated values or the values of the linked software design element. A component engineer may define certain attributes for each business rule specification such as rule priority, owner, and business process. Each business rule statement can also be arranged in an appropriate rule set to assist the future management of the business rules.

For the MediNet application, the rules shown in Table 5 are specified according to rule phrases syntax as shown in Table 6.

The first rule in Table 6 shows the rule phrase derived from the attribute constraint rule, informally defined in the analysis phase as *"A patient must have a unique registration number."* The rule phrases 'a patient' and 'registration number' are respectively linked to Patient class and patRegNo attribute. The keywords 'must have' and 'a unique' are not statically linked to any design element. Instead, they are used to dynamically toggle the optionality and uniqueness values of patRegNo attribute during the creation or modification of the business rule statement. In other words, they are used to enable the automated change propagation to software design.

The second rule in Table 6 shows a relationship constraint., The rule phrases 'clinic item' and 'bill item' are respectively linked to TransItem class and Bill_Item class. The rule phrases 'one and only one' and 'clinic item' play a similar role to keywords as in the attribute constraint rule, that is their purpose is to propagate business changes to design elements. The former specifies the multiplicity of an asso-

Figure 6. Class association diagram for invoicing for the MediNet application

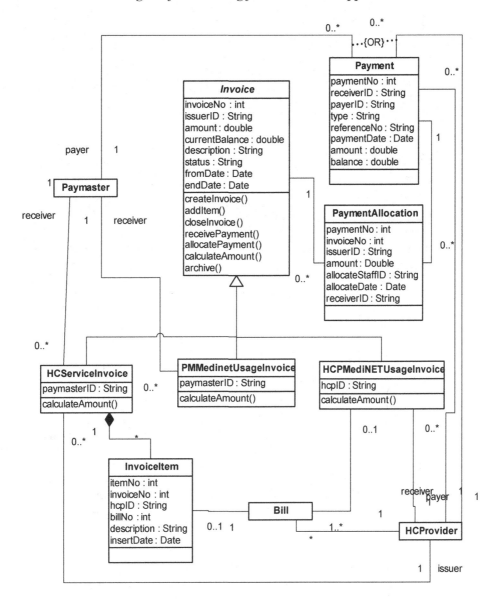

ciation end whilst the latter specifies the role of an association end.

In the *action assertion* rule *"When a payment is not received within 30 days from the invoice date, then the first reminder will be sent,"* the rule phrases that represent the event, condition, and action are not directly linked to any design element but they are respectively used to generate the specifications of the transition's event, guard,

and action in the HCP service usage invoice STD. Since event, condition, and action rule phrases are themselves composed by other rule phrases, they may be indirectly linked to the related design components via these rule phrases.

The *computation* and *inference* rules are linked to the operation specification —the computation rule is linked to the specification of calculateAmount() operation in HCPMediNETUsageInvoice

Figure 7. The STD `HCServiceInvoice` *object for the MediNet application*

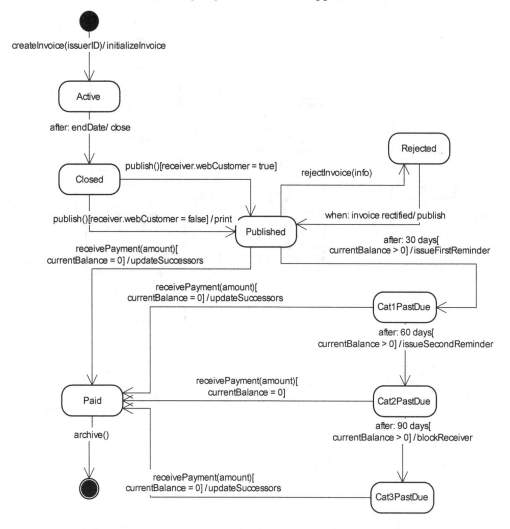

class and the inference rule is linked to getStatus() operation from Paymaster class. During the development of an inference rule, a new operation is often needed to be added in its associated class to perform the derivation and return the inferred value.

The Evolution Phase

In general, business rule changes may be classified into simple and complex changes. A simple change is concerned with the modification, addition, or deletion of business rules that do not need to in-

troduce new rule phrases or design elements. A complex change involves the addition or deletion of rule phrases or design elements.

Ordinarily, *simple business rules changes* could be performed by business users. The examples of five change scenarios that require simple business changes in MediNET system are shown in Table 7.

The implementation of a *complex* business rule change requires more effort than that of simple change. It involves the introduction of new rule phrases or design elements, which is needed to be performed by an individual with the knowl-

Table 6. Rule phrases and linked software design elements for the MediNet application

B Rule Category	Business Rule Phrases	Software Design Elements
Attribute Constraint	\<entity\> = 'a patient'	Patient (class)
	'must have'	- (patRegNo.optionality)
	'a unique'	- (patRegNo.uniqueness)
	\<attributeTerm\> = 'registration number'	Patient.patRegNo (attribute)
Relationship Con-straint	\<cardinality\> = 'one and only one'	- (AssociationEnd.multiplicity)
	\<entity\> = 'transaction item'	TransItem (class)
	\<role\> = 'item type'	- (AssociationEnd.name)
	\<entity\> = 'bill item'	Bill_Item (class)
Action Assertion	\<event\> = '30 day after the creation date of the invoice'	- (Trans1.event.spec)
	\<condition\> = 'current balance of the invoice is greater than 0'	- (Trans1.guard.body)
	\<action\> = 'trigger issue the first reminder'	- (Trans1.action.initialiseIn-voice().spec)
Computation	\<attributeTerm\> = 'the amount of HCP MediNET Usage invoice'	HCPMediNETUsageInvoice. amount
	\<algorithm\> = 'the sum of monthly subscription fee plus transaction fee'	HCPMediNETUsageInvoice. calculateAmount().specification
Inference	\<attributeTerm\> = 'a paymaster status'	Paymaster.status
	\<value\> = 'under probation'	- (literal value)
	\<condition\> = 'the paymaster has an invoice with category 1 past due' AND 'the current balance is greater than RM 5,000.00'	Paymaster.getStatus().speci-fication

edge of software design. In addition to technical skills, it often requires creative skills in making a design decision. Three examples of complex rules changes are shown in Table 8.

The first scenario initiates the modification of two existing business rule statements, the calculation of bill and the calculation of invoice amount. These business rule changes consequently lead to a minor change in software design, that is the introduction of hasMaxBill attribute in the Paymaster class.

In the second scenario, the paymaster decided to introduce different healthcare benefit coverage to different levels of their payees. For example, executive staff is entitled to any medical treatment and medical procedures whilst production staff is only paid for outpatient treatments. It is obvious that simply implementing this new requirement into the existing Paymaster or PanelPatient class may increase the complexity of these classes. Therefore, additional classes that are responsible to manage the healthcare benefit coverage are required to be added to the existing software design. The possible candidates for these classes include BenefitCoverage, SelectedClinic, MedicalProcedure, and Entitlement.

Table 7. Simple change scenarios for the MediNet application

Change Scenarios	Changed Business Rules
1. HCP allows patients to make 'more than one payment for their bills' instead of the previously set 'single payment for each bill'.	One patient bill is associated with zero or more payments.
2. HCP makes small changes on the conditions to issue the reminder and block paymaster.	WHEN *15 days* from the invoice date IF a payment is not received THEN issue the first reminder. WHEN *30 days* from the invoice date IF the payment is not received THEN issue the second reminder. WHEN *45 days* from the invoice date IF the payment is not received THEN block the paymaster.
3. The MediNET supplier offers a more attractive usage charge to HCPs. They are charged based on the number of treated patients regardless the number of patient visits.	The amount of HCP usage invoice IS CALCULATED AS if (opt new package) then the transaction fee multiply by the number of registered patients, else, the transaction fee multiply by the number of treated patients, plus the monthly fee.
4. HCP introduces 5% discount to its internet customer.	If the paymaster is an internet customer, then give 5% discount to their invoices.
5. The HCP decides that each expense item must belong to one of the pre-defined types.	Zero or more expense item is associated with one and only one transaction item.

Table 8. Complex change scenarios for the MediNet application

Change Scenarios	Changed Business Rules

1. HCP introduces new package for paymaster. In this package, the paymaster may limit the maximum amount of each patient bill to RM 20.00, and the excessive cost is absorbed by HCP. However, the paymaster must pay a monthly fee of RM5.00 for each patient.	The amount of a bill is computed as
	    let amount = the sum of all amounts of bill items
	    if (patient is a panel patient) AND (paymaster has maximum bill amount) AND (amount > RM 20.00)
	        amount = 20
	
	The amount of HCP service invoice is computed as
	    let amount = the total of the invoice items
	    if (paymaster has maximum bill amount)
	        amount = amount + 5 * the number of paymaster's patients

2. Paymaster wishes to provide different healthcare benefit coverage for different groups of its payees.	If (the patient is a panel patient) AND (the patient is an executive staff) then the patient is entitled to any type of treatments and medical procedures. If (the patient is a panel patient) AND (the patient is a production staff) then the patient is entitled for an outpatient treatment.

3. HCP would like to introduce a 5% discount on the invoices to preferred paymasters as a way to express gratitude to the loyal, potential, and good paying paymasters.	If (a paymaster has been a paymaster panel for more than 5 years) then (the customer is a 'loyal' customer).
	If (a paymaster has an average of at least RM24000.00 for the invoices over the last five years) then (the paymaster is considered as a 'potential' customer).
	If (a paymaster never has a past due invoice for the last two years) then (the paymaster is considered as a good paying paymaster).
	When (the invoice in created) if (the paymaster is a loyal, potential and good paying customer) then (set the discount of the invoice to 5%)

The third scenario requires the intervention of a software developer. This scenario requires a number of new inference rules to be added to define a loyal, potential, and good paying customer. In addition to these business rules, an action assertion rule that initializes the value of the invoice discount during invoice creation should also be added. The introduction of the new inference rules consequently requires isLoyal(), isPotential(), and isGoodPaying() operations to be added to the Paymaster class. Similarly, the newly introduced action assertion rule requires component engineers to modify the action component of the transition from the initial state to 'Active' state in the STD for HCServiceInvoice object.

THE BROOD SUPPORT TOOL

The BROOD process introduces several additional activities to the traditional object-oriented software design process. These additional activities include the documentation of business rules and their linking to software design components. To assist a developer with these BROOD-specific activities, a tool has been developed that supports the activities of business rule specification and management, software design editing, and business rule change propagation.

The BROOD tool was developed on top of the generic modeling environment (GME) (Ledeczi et al., 2001; VU, 2003), which is a configurable modeling environment.

The metamodel and templates, which are discussed in section 0, were used to implement the BROOD tool environment.

GME was used to visually edit the software design models, business rule specification, and rule phrase entries. Three main modules (known as interpreters in GME) were developed to simplify the rule phrase management, business rule composition, and business rule modification. These modules also perform the *automated propagation* of business rule changes to the respective software design elements, since a manual undertaking of such propagation would be impractical for most applications.

The BROOD tool has been designed to be used by both software developers and business users. A user-friendly interface is provided to ease the management and traceability of business rules by non-IT users. An overview of the BROOD support tool is shown in Figure 8.

The metamodel, the graphical model editor, the rule phrase management, the business rules composition and the business rules modification functions are part of the core component and user application layer in the BROOD tool architecture. The rule phrase entries, business rule specification, and software design models are stored in the storage layer.

The BROOD tool maintains the consistencies between business rule and the linked software design each time a business rule is created or modified. It provides full automated support in performing simple changes and partial support for complex changes since these require creative skills of software engineers in making a design decision.

There are four main types of model that can be managed using the BROOD tool: rule phrase entries, business rule, class diagram, and statechart diagram. Users may select the type of model to be created from a set of choices. An example of the BROOD model editor is shown in Figure 9. The model editor provides a convenient way to create a model and also to connect it or parts of it to other models.

While graphical model editing is convenient for visual models such as those of class and statechart diagrams, it is less helpful for business rules specification.

The graphical model editor can be used for some simple business rules definition such as cardinality, relational operator, list, and optionality but for more complex rules the BROOD tool offers a dedicated rule editor, the add business rule (ABR) module. This module performs two main tasks:

Figure 8. Overview of the BROOD tool

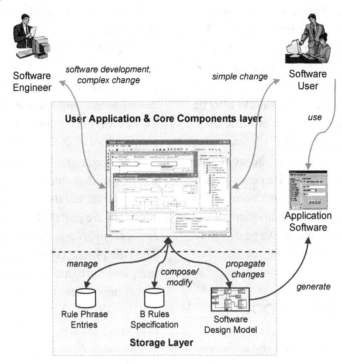

Figure 9. Example of the BROOD model editor

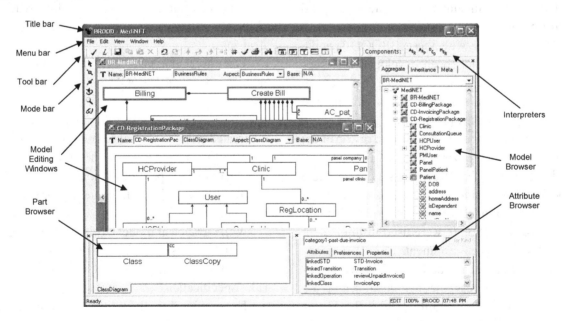

business rule composition and software design updating. In business rule composition mode, rule phrases are used to construct a business rule statement. In software design updating mode the module updates the software design model that corresponds to the composed rule.

Figure 10. Example of the BROOD business rules modifier

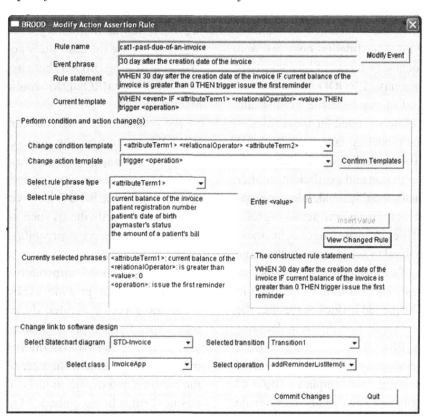

The BROOD tool also helps with the implementation of business rule changes. The modify business rule (MBR) module was developed to assist tool users in performing this task, an example of which is shown in Figure 10.

A full description of the tool is beyond the scope of this article. It should be stressed however, that the tool plays an important part in the effective application of the BROOD approach by simplifying a sometimes tedious, error-prone, and time-consuming task of linking and propagating business rule changes to software design components.

DISCUSSION

The main aim of BROOD has been to facilitate the process of software evolution through: (a)

externalization of business rules and their explicit modeling and (b) the linking of each modeled business rule with a corresponding software component. This approach provides full traceability between end-user concepts and software designs. By combining BROOD to design traceability in source code (Alves-Foss, Conte de Leon, & Oman, 2002), it is possible to achieve effective traceability in a software system.

The BROOD metamodel offers a complete foundation and infrastructure for the development of a software system that is resilient to business rule changes.

With regard to business rule typology, BROOD introduces three main business rule types: constraints, action assertion, and derivations. These types are further divided into an adequate number of sub-types and templates. In contrast to BRG, BROCOM, and BRS approaches, BROOD attempts to remove the redundancy by reducing the unnecessary business rule types. At the same time, it improves the incompleteness of business rule types in AOM, coordination contract, and BRBeans approaches. In terms of business rule management elements, BROOD provides the concept of *ruleset* to organize the groups and hierarchy of the closely related business rules.

In terms of its modeling language, BROOD offers a high level of expressiveness. The keywords in the language definition and a sufficient number of sentence templates should provide adequate representation constructs. In general, achieving total expressiveness of the modeling language business rules is relatively hard to achieve due to the large number of ways of expressing business rules in a natural language. The usability of BROOD in this context will be proved in due course once the approach has been applied on different domains and applications. BROOD was found to have a high level of un-ambiguity by the introduction of the appropriate typology and templates. BROOD provides a mutually exclusive set of business rule types and removes the superfluous templates in order to avoid conflict and redundancy in representing the meaning of business rules.

In practical terms, BROOD can be applied using the UML-based SPEM metamodel, which provides a set of concepts and notations to describe various software process components such as lifecycle phases, activities, process roles, and work products. The use of business rule templates and UML improves the usability of the BROOD approach. The templates allow users to create a business rule statement by simply composing the existing rule phrases whilst UML provides abstractions for users to naturally design a software system. Moreover, the detailed process description is provided to guide users especially in performing complex tasks such linking business rules to software design and handling different types of changes.

The utility of BROOD was demonstrated in this paper through the use of the MediNet indus-trial application. This application had originally been developed using a standard object-oriented approach. It was therefore possible (and indeed desirable) to use the case study not only as a way of demonstrating BROOD but also for comparing and contrasting BROOD to a traditional development approach.

By considering UML for software design, BROOD maintains the well-known object-oriented design quality attributes such as modularity, high cohesion, low coupling, efficiency, and portability. BROOD however provides additional quality attributes such as *requirements traceability*, *software evolvability*, and *approach usability.*

The traditional approach deployed for MediNet did not provide explicit traceability of business policy defined during the requirements specification phase. Instead, it provides a so-called 'seamless transition' from the use case models that document the user requirements to the analysis and design models. This resulted in business rules being embedded in both requirements specification and software design models. In contrast, with BROOD there was a natural transformation of the MediNET requirements into the structured business rules specification and in turn this specification was directly related to software design components.

Concerning software evolution, the implementation of changes using the traditional approach required the use of expertise with specific knowledge of the MediNET software design. Since software engineers do not normally initiate business changes, they had to repeat all phases in MediNET development lifecycle especially requirements and analysis phases. Locating the related software design components was hard since there was no explicit link between the MediNET design models and its user requirements.

In relation to approach usability, the traditional approach was easier to apply during development since it did not have to deal with additional steps that were added to explicitly specify, document, and link business rules specification to software design. These steps were found to increase the complexity and duration of software development process. However, the availability of the business rule typology and templates, which provide the guidelines for the analysis of business rule statements and the identification of rule phrases, were found useful in minimizing these problems. The business rule templates have improved the MediNET system understandability and increased the involvement of business users in the Medi-NET development. During evolution, BROOD was found easier to be used than the traditional approach. Using BROOD, business users could perform the simple business rule changes as demonstrated in the MediNET application. Rapid change implementation is important especially in business critical applications with intolerable downtime. The detailed process description facilitated the implementation of complex changes in MediNET.

In summary, BROOD contributes to three critical areas namely business rules specification, object-oriented design, and software evolution process. The proposed business rule specification extends the state-of-the-art approaches to business rule representation by reducing redundancy and avoiding conflict among business rule types in its typology. The structures of rule templates have been defined so as to make them suitable for linking to software designs in support of future software evolution. A specification is aligned to changing user requirements via the linking of business rules to software designs through a detailed transformation of business rule into the specification of related software design components. Thus, the externalization of frequently changing aspects of a system into detailed business rules and the maintenance of associations between these and corresponding software components should provide a strong framework for effective software evolution.

ACKNOWLEDGMENT

The authors would like to thank the human resource department of Universiti Teknologi Malaysia (UTM) for partially sponsoring this research, and Penawar Medical Group, Malaysia for the permission to use its MediNET healthcare information system requirements specification as the case study. The authors wish to also express their gratitude to the three anonymous reviewers and to the editor of the special issue, Professor Dinesh Batra, whose insightful and detailed comments have contributed to the production of a much improved version of this article.

REFERENCES

Alves-Foss, J., Conte de Leon, D., & Oman, P. (2002). *Experiments in the use of xml to enhance traceability between object-oriented design specifications and source code.* Paper presented at the 35th Annual Hawaii International Conference on System Sciences.

Andrade, L., & Fiadeiro, J. (2000, October 15-19). *Evolution by contract.* Paper presented at the ACM Conference on Object-Oriented Programming, Systems, Languages, and Applications 2000, Workshop on Best-practice in Business Rules Design and Implementation, Minneapolis, Minnesota USA.

Andrade, L., Fiadeiro, J., Gouveia, J., & Koutsoukos, G. (2002). Separating computation, coordination and configuration. *Journal of Software Maintenance and Evolution: Research and Practice, 14*(5), 353-359.

Astley, M., & Agha, G. A. (1998, 20-21 April). *Modular construction and composition of distributed software architectures.* Paper presented at the Int. Symposium on Software Engineering, for Parallel and Distributed Systems, Kyoto, Japan.

Eriksson, H.-E., & Penker, M. (2000). *Business modelling with uml*: OMG Group, Wiley Computer Publishing, John Wiley & Sons, Inc.

Erlikh, L. (2000). Leveraging legacy system dollars for e-business. *IEEE IT Professional, 2*(3), 17 - 23.

Evans, H., & Dickman, P. (1999, October). *Zones, contracts and absorbing change: An approach to software evolution.* Paper presented at the Conference on Object-Oriented Programming, Systems, Languages and Applications (OOPSLA '99), Denver, Colorado, USA.

Gottesdiener, E. (1997). Business rules show power, promise. *Application Development Trends, 4*(3, March 1997).

Grubb, P., & Takang, A. A. (2003). *Software maintenance: Concepts and practice.* Singapore: World Scientific Publishing.

Halle, B. V. (1994). Back to business rule basics. *Database Programming and Design*(October 1994), 15-18.

Hay, D., & Healy, K. A. (1997). *Business rules: What are they really?* GUIDE (The IBM User Group). Retrieved from http://www.Business-RulesGroup.org/):.

Hay, D., & Healy, K. A. (2000). *Defining business rules ~ what are they really?* (No. Rev 1.3): the Business Rules Group.

Herbst, H. (1996a). *Business rule oriented conceptual modelling.* Verlag: Physica .

Herbst, H. (1996b). Business rules in system analysis: A meta-model and repository system. *Information Systems, 21*(2), 147-166.

Herbst, H. (1997). *Business rule-oriented conceptual modeling.* Germany: Physica-Verlag.

IBM (Cartographer). (2003). *Ibm websphere application server enterprise*

Kovari, P., Diaz, D. C., Fernandes, F. C. H., Hassan, D., Kawamura, K., Leigh, D., et al. (2003). *Websphere application server enterprise v5 and programming model extensions: Websphere handbook series* (First Edition ed.): International Business Machines Corporation.

Krammer, M. I. (1997). Business rules: Automating business policies and practicies. *Distributed Computing Monitor*(May 1997).

Ledeczi, A., Maroti, M., Bakay, A., Karsai, G., Garrett, J., Thomason, C., et al. (2001, 17 May). *The generic modeling environment.* Paper presented at the Workshop on Intelligent Signal Processing, Budapest, Hungary.

Lehman, M. M., & Belady, L. A. (1985). *Program evolution: Processes of software change.* London: Academic Press, Inc.

Loucopoulos, P., & Layzell, P. J. (1986, 1987). *Rubric: A rule based approach for the development of information systems.* Paper presented at the 1st European workshop on fault diagnosis, reliability and related knowledge based approaches, Rhodes.

Martin, J. (1989). *Information engineering*: Prentice-Hall.

McMenamin, S. M., & Palmer, J. F. (1984). *Essential systems analysis.* Englewood Cliffs, NJ: Yourdon Press.

Mens, K., Wuyts, R., Bontridder, D., & Grijseels, A. (1998). *Tools and environments for business rules.* Paper presented at the ECOOP'98, Brussels, Belgium.

Moriaty, T. (1993). The next paradigm. *Database Programming and Design.*

OMG (Cartographer). (2001). *Omg unified modeling language specification*

OMG (Cartographer). (2002). *Software process engineering metamodel specification*

Oreizy, P., Medvidovic, N., & Taylor, R. N. (1998, April 19-25). *Architecture-based runtime software evolution.* Paper presented at the International Conference on Software Engineering 1998 (ICSE'98), Kyoto, Japan.

Riehle, D., Tilman, M., & Johnson, R. (2000). *Dynamic object model* (No. WUCS-00-29): Dept. of Computer Science, Washington University.

Robinson, K., & Berrisford, G. (1994). *Object-oriented ssadm.* Englewood Cliffs, NJ: Prentice Hall.

Rosca, D., Greenspan, S., Feblowitz, M., & Wild, C. (1997, January 1997). *A decision support methodology in support of the business rules lifecycle.* Paper presented at the International Symposium on Requirements Engineering (ISRE'97), Annapolis, MD.

Rosca, D., Greenspan, S., & Wild, C. (2002). Enterprise modeling and decision-support for automating the business rules lifecycle. *Automated Software Engineering, 9*(4), 361 - 404.

Rosca, D., Greenspan, S., Wild, C., Reubenstein, H., Maly, K., & Feblowitz, M. (1995, November 1995). *Application of a decision support mechanism to the business rules lifecycle.* Paper presented at the 10th Knowledge-Based Software Engineering Conference (KBSE95), Boston, MA.

Ross, R. G. (1997). *The business rule book: Classifying, defining and modelling rules*: Data Base Newsletter.

Ross, R. G., & Lam, G. S. W. (1999). *Ruletrack: The brs meta-model for rule management*: Business Rule Solutions, Inc.

Ross, R. G., & Lam, G. S. W. (2003). *The brs proteus^{tm} methodology* (Fourth ed.): Business Rule Solutions.

Rouvellou, I., Degenaro, I., Rasmus, K., Ehnebuske, D., & McKee, B. (1999, November 1-5). *Externalizing business rules from enterprise applications: An experience report.* Paper presented at the Conference on Object-Oriented Programming, Systems, Languages, and Applications, Denver, Colorado.

Rouvellou, I., Degenaro, L., Rasmus, K., Ehnebuske, D., & McKee, B. (2000, June). *Extending business objects with business rules.* Paper presented at the 33rd International Conference on Technology of Object-Oriented Languages and Systems (TOOLS Europe 2000), Mont Saint-Michel/ St-Malo, France.

Schneider, J. (1999). *Components, scripts, and glue : A conceptual framework for software composition.* Bern:University of Bern.

van Assche, F., Layzell, P. J., Loucopoulos, P., & Speltinex, G. (1988). *Rubric: A rule-based representation of information system constructs.* Paper presented at the ESPRIT Conference, Brussels, Belgium.

VU (Cartographer). (2003). *Gme 3 user's manual*

Wan Kadir, W. M. N., & Loucopoulos, P. (2003, 23-26 June). *Relating evolving business rules to software design.* Paper presented at the International Conference on Software Engineering Research and Practice (SERP), Las Vegas, Nevada, USA.

Wan Kadir, W. M. N., & Loucopoulos, P. (2004). Relating evolving business rules to software design. *Journal of Systems Architecture, 50*(7), 367-382.

Yoder, J. W., Balaguer, F., & Johnson, R. (2001, October 14-18). *Adaptive object models for implementing business rules.* Paper presented at the Third Workshop on Best-Practices for Business

Rules Design and Implementation, Conference on Object-Oriented Programming, Systems, Languages, and Applications (OOPSLA 2001), Tampa Bay, Florida, USA.

Zaniolo, C., Ceri, S., Faloutsos, C., Snodgrass, R., Subrahmanian, V. S., & Zicari, R. (1997). *Advanced database systems*: Morgan Kaufmann.

Chapter 3
Bug Fixing Practices within Free/Libre Open Source Software Development Teams

Kevin Crowston
Syracuse University, USA

Barbara Scozzi
Politecnico di Bari, Italy

ABSTRACT

Free/Libre open source software (FLOSS, e.g., Linux or Apache) is primarily developed by distributed teams. Developers contribute from around the world and coordinate their activity almost exclusively by means of email and bulletin boards, yet some how profit from the advantages and evade the challenges of distributed software development. In this article we investigate the structure and the coordination practices adopted by development teams during the bug-fixing process, which is considered one of main areas of FLOSS project success. In particular, based on a codification of the messages recorded in the bug tracking system of four projects, we identify the accomplished tasks, the adopted coordination mechanisms, and the role undertaken by both the FLOSS development team and the FLOSS community. We conclude with suggestions for further research.

INTRODUCTION

In this article, we investigate the coordination practices for software bug fixing in Free/Libre open source software (FLOSS) development teams. Key to our interest is that most FLOSS software is developed by distributed teams, that is, geographically dispersed groups of individuals working together over time towards a common goal (Ahuja et al., 1997, p. 165; Weisband, 2002). FLOSS developers contribute from around the world, meet face to face infrequently, if at all, and coordinate their activity primarily by means of computer mediated communications (Raymond, 1998; Wayner, 2000). As a result, distributed teams employ processes that span traditional boundaries of place and ownership. Since such teams are increasingly commonly used in a diversity of settings, it is important to understand how team members can effectively coordinate their work.

The research literature on distributed work and on software development specifically emphasizes the difficulties of distributed software development, but the case of FLOSS development presents an intriguing counter-example, at least in part: a number of projects have been outstandingly successful. What is perhaps most surprising is that FLOSS development teams seem not to use many traditional coordination mechanisms such as formal planning, system level design, schedules and defined development processes (Mockus et al., 2002, p. 310). As well, many (though by no means all) programmers contribute to projects as volunteers, without working for a common organization and/or being paid.

The contribution of this article is to document the process of coordination in effective FLOSS teams for a particularly important process, namely bug fixing. These practices are analyzed by adopting a process theory, that is, we investigate which tasks are accomplished, how and by whom they are assigned, coordinated, and performed. In particular, we selected four FLOSS projects, inductively coded the steps involved in fixing various bugs as recorded in the projects' bug tracking systems and applied coordination theory to identify tasks and coordination mechanisms carried out within the bug-fixing process.

Studying coordination of FLOSS processes is important for several reasons. First, FLOSS development is an important phenomenon deserving of study for itself. FLOSS is an increasingly important commercial issue involving all kind of software firms. Million of users depend on systems such as Linux and the Internet (heavily dependent on FLOSS software tools) but as Scacchi notes "little is known about how people in these communities coordinate software development across different settings, or about what software

processes, work practices, and organizational contexts are necessary to their success" (Scacchi, 2002, p. 1; Scacchi, 2005). Understanding the reasons that some projects are effective while others are not is a further motivation for studying the FLOSS development processes. Second, studying how distributed software developers coordinate their efforts to ensure, at least in some cases, high-performance outcomes has both theoretical and managerial implications. It can help understanding coordination practices adopted in social collectives that are not governed, at least apparently, by a formal organizational structure and are characterized by many other discontinuities that is, lack of coherence in some aspects of the work setting: organization, function, membership, language, culture, etc. (Watson-Manheim et al., 2002). As to the managerial implications, distributed teams of all sorts are increasingly used in many organizations. The study could be useful to managers that are considering the adoption of this organizational form not only in the field of software development.

The remainder of the article is organized as follows. In Section 2 we discuss the theoretical background of the study. In Section 3 we stress the relevance of process theory so explaining why we adopted such a theoretical approach. We then describe coordination theory and use it to describe the bug-fixing process as carried out in traditional organizations. The research methodology adopted to study the bug-fixing process is described in Section 4. In Section 5 and 6 we describe and discuss the study's results. Finally, in Section 7 we draw some conclusions and propose future research directions.

BACKGROUND

In this section we provide an overview of the literature on software development in distributed environment and the FLOSS phenomenon.

Distributed Software Development

Distributed teams offer numerous potential benefits, such as the possibility to perform different projects all over the world without paying the costs associated with travel or relocation, or ease of reconfiguring teams to quickly respond to changing business needs (DeSanctis & Jackson, 1994; Drucker, 1988) or to exploit available competences and distributed expertise (Grinter et al., 1999; Orlikowski, 2002). Distributed teams seem particularly attractive for software development, because software, as an information product, can be easily transferred via the same systems used to support the teams (Nejmeh, 1994; Scacchi, 1991). Furthermore, while many developed countries face a shortage of talented software developers, some developing countries have a pool of skilled professionals available, at lower cost (Metiu & Kogut, 2001, p. 4; Taylor, 1998). As well, the need to have local developers in each country for marketing and localization have made distributed teams a business need for many global software corporations (Herbsleb & Grinter, 1999b, p. 85).

While distributed teams have many potential benefits, distributed workers face many real challenges. The specific challenges vary from team to team, as there is a great diversity in their composition and in the setting of distributed work. As mentioned, distributed work is characterized by numerous discontinuities that generate difficulties for members in making sense of the task and of communications from others, or produce unintended information filtering (de Souza, 1993). These interpretative difficulties make it hard for team members to develop a shared mental model of the developing project (Curtis et al., 1990, p. 52). A lack of common knowledge about the status, authority and competencies of participants brought together for the first time can be an obstacle to the creation of a social structure and the develop-

ment of team norms (Bandow, 1997, p. 88) and conventions (Weisband, 2002), thus frustrating the potential benefits of increased flexibility.

Numerous studies have investigated social aspects of software development teams (e.g., Curtis et al., 1988; Humphrey, 2000; Sawyer & Guinan, 1998; Walz et al., 1993). These studies conclude that large system development requires knowledge from many domains, which is thinly spread among different developers (Curtis et al., 1988). As a result, large projects require a high degree of knowledge integration and the coordinated efforts of multiple developers (Brooks, 1975). However, coordination is difficult to achieve as software projects are non-routine, hard to decompose perfectly and face requirements that are often changing and conflicting, making development activities uncertain.

Unfortunately, the problems of software development seem to be exacerbated when development teams work in a distributed environment with a reduced possibility for informal communication (Bélanger, 1998; Carmel & Agarwal, 2001; Herbsleb & Grinter, 1999a). In response to the problems created by discontinuities, studies of distributed teams stress the need for a significant amount of time spent in "community building" (Butler et al., 2002). In particular, members of distributed teams need to learn how to communicate, interact and socialize using CMC. Successful distributed cross-functional teams share knowledge and information and create new practices to meet the task-oriented and social needs of the members (Robey et al., 2000). Research has shown the importance of formal and informal adopted coordination mechanisms, information sharing for coordination and communications, and conflict management for project's performance and quality (Walz et al., 1993). However, the processes of coordination suitable for distributed teams are still open topics for research (e.g., Orlikowski, 2002).

The FLOSS Phenomenon: A Literature Overview

The growing literature on FLOSS has addressed a variety of questions. Some researchers have examined the implications of free software from economic and policy perspectives (e.g., Di Bona et al., 1999; Kogut & Metiu, 2001; Lerner & Tirole, 2001) as well as social perspective (e.g., Bessen, 2002; Franck & Jungwirth, 2002; Hann et al., 2002; Hertel et al., 2003; Markus et al., 2000). Other studies examine factors for the success of FLOSS projects (Hallen et al., 1999; Leibovitch, 1999; Pfaff, 1998; Prasad, n.d.; Valloppillil, 1998; Valloppillil & Cohen, 1998, Crowston and Scozzi, 2003). Among them, an open research question deals with the analysis of how the contributions of multiple developers can be brought into a single working product (Herbsleb & Grinter, 1999b). To answer such a question, a few authors have investigated the processes of FLOSS development (e.g., Jensen & Scacchi, 2005; Stewart & Ammeter, 2002). The most well-known model developed to describe FLOSS organization structure is the bazaar metaphor proposed by Raymond (1998). As in a bazaar, FLOSS developers autonomously decide the schedule and contribution modes for software development, making a central coordination action superfluous. While still popular, the bazaar metaphor has been broadly criticized (e.g., Cubranic, 1999). According to its detractors, the bazaar metaphor disregards some aspects of the FLOSS development process, such as the importance of the project leader control, the existence of de-facto hierarchies, the danger of information overloads and burnout, the possibility of conflicts that cause a loss of interest in a project or forking, and the only apparent openness of these communities (Bezroukov, 1999a, 1999b).

Nevertheless, many features of the bazaar model do seem to apply. First, many teams are largely self-organizing, often without formally appointed leaders or formal indications of rank or role. Individual developers may play different roles in different projects or move from role to role as their involvement with a project changes. For example, a common route is for an active user to become a co-developer by contributing a bug fix or code for a new feature, and for active and able co-developers to be invited to become members of the core. Second, coordination of project development happens largely (though not exclusively) in a distributed mode. Members of a few of the largest and most well-established projects do have the opportunity to meet face-to-face at conferences (e.g., Apache developers at *ApacheCon*), but such an opportunity is rare for most project members. Third, non-member involvement plays an important role in the success of the teams. Non-core developers contribute bug fixes, new features or documentation, provide support for new users and fill a variety of other roles in the teams. Furthermore, even though the core group provides a form of leadership for a project, they do not exercise hierarchical control. A recent study documented that self-assignment is a typical coordination mechanism in FLOSS projects and direct assignment are nearly non-existent (Crowston et al., 2005). In comparison to traditional organizations then, more people can share power and be involved in FLOSS project activities. However, how these diverse contributions can be harnessed to create a coherent product is still an important question for research. Our article addresses this question by examining in detail a particular case, namely, coordination of bug-fixing processes.

CONCEPTUAL DEVELOPMENT

In this section, we describe the theoretical perspectives we adopted to examine the coordination of bug fixing, namely, a process-oriented perspective and the coordination theory. We also introduce the topic of coordination and discuss the literature on coordination in software development and the (small) literature on coordination in FLOSS teams.

Processes as Theories

Most theories in organizational and information system research are variance theories, comprising constructs or variables and propositions or hypotheses linking them. By adopting a statistical approach, such theories predict the levels of dependent or outcome variables from the levels of independent or predictor variables, where the predictors are seen as necessary and sufficient for the outcomes. In other words, the logical structure of such theories is that if concept *a* implies concept *b*, then more of *a* means more (or less) of *b*. For example, the hypothesis that the adoption of ICT makes organization more centralized, examined as a variance theory, is that the level of organization centralization increases with the number of new ICTs adopted.

An alternative to a variance theory is a process theory (Markus & Robey, 1988). Rather than relating levels of variables, process theories explain how outcomes of interest develop through a sequence of events. In that case, antecedents are considered as necessary but not sufficient for the outcomes (Mohr, 1982). For example, a process model of ICT and centralization might posit several steps each of which must occur for the organization to become centralized, such as development and implementation of an ICT system and use of the system to control decision premises and program jobs, resulting in centralization of decision making as an outcome (Pfeffer, 1978). However, if any of the intervening steps does not happen, a different outcome may occur. For example, if the system is used to provide information directly to lower-level workers, decision making may become decentralized rather centralized (Zuboff, 1988). Of course, theories may contain some aspects of both variance and process theories (e.g., a variance theory with a set of contingencies), but for this discussion, we describe the pure case. Typically, process theories are of some transient process leading to exceptional outcomes, for example, events leading up to an organizational change or to acceptance of a system. However, we will focus instead on what might be called "everyday" processes: those performed regularly to create an organization's products or services. For example, Sabherwal and Robey (1995) described and compared the processes of information systems development for 50 projects to develop five clusters of similar processes.

Kaplan (1991, p. 593) states that process theories can be "valuable aids in understanding issues pertaining to designing and implementing information systems, assessing their impacts, and anticipating and managing the processes of change associated with them". The main advantage of process theories is that they can deal with more complex causal relationships than variance theories. Also they embody a fuller description of the steps by which inputs and outputs are related, rather than noting the relationship between the levels of input and output variables. Specifically, representing a process as a sequence of activities provides insight into the linkage between individual work and processes, since individuals perform the various activities that comprise the process. As individuals change what they do, they change how they perform these activities and thus their participation in the process. Conversely, process changes demand different performances from individuals. ICT use might simply make individuals more efficient or effective at the activities they have always performed. However, an interesting class of impacts involves changing which individuals perform which activities and how activities are coordinated. Such an analysis is the aim of this article.

Coordination of Processes

In this subsection, we introduce the topic of coordination and present the fundamentals of coordination theory. Studying coordination means analyzing how dependences that emerge among the components of a system are managed. That stands for any kind of system, for example, social, economics, organic, or information system. Hence, the coordination of the components of a system is a phenomenon with a universal relevance (Boulding, 1956). The above definition of coordination is consistent with the large body of literature developed in the field of organization theory (e.g., Galbraith, 1973; Lawrence & Lorsch, 1967; Mintzberg, 1979; Pfeffer & Salancik, 1978; Thompson, 1967) that emphasizes the importance of interdependence.

For example, according to Thompson (1967), organizational action consists of the coordination of the interdependences and the reduction of the costs associated to their management. Two components/systems are said to be interdependent if the action carried out by one of them affect the other one's output or performance (McCann & Ferry, 1979; Mohr, 1971; Victor & Blackburn, 1987). For space reason, it is not possible to present all the contributions on coordination in the literature, but because of its relevance, we here briefly report on Thompson's seminal work. Thompson (1967) identified three main kinds of interdependence, namely *pooled, sequential* and *reciprocal interdependence.* Pooled interdependence occurs among organization units that have the same goal but do not directly collaborate to achieve it. Sequential dependence emerges among serial systems. A reciprocal dependence occurs when the output of a system is the input for a second system and vice versa. The three kinds of interdependence require coordination mechanisms whose cost increases going from the first to the last one. The coordination by standardization, that is, routine and rules, is sufficient to manage pooled-dependant systems. Coordination by plan implies the definition of operational schemes and plans. It can be used to manage pooled and sequential dependences. Finally, coordination by mutual adjustment is suitable for the management of reciprocal dependences.

The interest devoted by scholars and practitioners to the study of coordination problems has recently increased due to the augmented complexity of products, production processes and to the rapid advancement in science and technology. To address these issues scholars have developed coordination theory, a systemic approach to the study of coordination (Malone & Crowston, 1994). Coordination theory synthesizes the contributions proposed in different disciplines to develop a systemic approach to the study of coordination. Studies on coordination have been developed based on two level of analysis, a micro and a macro level. In particular, most organization studies adopt a macro perspective, so considering dependencies emerging among organizational units. Other studies adopt a micro perspective, so considering dependencies emerging among single activities/actors. Coordination theory adopts the latter perspective and, in particular, focuses on the analysis of dependencies among activities (rather that actors). Hence, it is particularly useful to the description and analysis of organizational processes, which can be defined as a set of interdependent activities aimed to the achievement of a goal (Crowston, 1997; Crowston & Osborn, 2003). In particular, this approach has the advantage of making it easier to model the effects of reassignments of activities to different actors, which is common in process redesign efforts. We adopted this perspective because the study focuses on analyzing coordination mechanisms within processes.

Consistent with the definition proposed above, Malone and Crowston (1994) analyzed group action in terms of *actors* performing *interdependent tasks.* These tasks might require or create *resources* of various types. For example, in the case of software development, actors include the customers and various employees of the software company. Tasks include translating aspects of a customer's problem into system requirements and code, or bug reports into bug fixes. Finally, resources include information about the customer's problem and analysts' time and effort. In this view, actors in organizations face *coordination problems* arising from dependencies that constrain how tasks can be performed.

It should be noted that in developing this framework, Malone and Crowston (1994) describe coordination mechanisms as relying on other necessary group functions, such as decision making, communications, and development of shared understandings and collective sensemaking (Britton et al., 2000; Crowston & Kammerer, 1998). To develop a complete model of a process would involve modeling all of these aspects: coordination, decision making, and communications. In this article though, we will focus on the coordination aspects, bracketing the other phenomenon.

Coordination theory classifies dependencies as occurring between a task and a resource, among multiple tasks and a resource, and among a task and multiple resources. Dependencies between a task and a resource are due to the fact that a task uses or creates a resource. Shared use of resources can in turn lead to dependencies between the tasks that use or create the resource. These dependencies come in three kinds. First, the flow dependence resembles the Thompson's sequential dependency. Second, the fit dependence occurs when two activities collaborate in the creation of an output (though in the case where the output is identical, this might better be called synergy, since the benefit is that duplicate work can be avoided). Finally, the share dependency emerges among activities that share the use of a resource. Dependencies between a task and multiple resources are due to the fact that a task uses, creates or produces multiple resources or a task uses a resource and create another resource. For example, in the case of software development, a design document might be created by a design task and used by programming tasks, creating a fit dependency, while two development tasks might both require a programmer (a share dependency) and create outputs that must work together (a fit dependency).

The key point in this analysis is that dependencies can create problems that require additional work to manage (or provide the opportunity to avoid duplicate work). To overcome the coordination problems created by dependences, actors must perform additional work, which Malone and Crowston (1994) called *coordination mechanisms*. For example, if particular expertise is necessary to perform a particular task (a task-actor dependency), then an actor with that expertise must be identified and the task assigned to him or her. There are often several coordination mechanisms that can be used to manage a dependency. For example, mechanisms to manage the dependency between an activity and an actor include (among others): (1) having a manager pick a subordinate to perform the task; (2) assigning the task to the first available actor; and (3) having a labour market in which actors bid on jobs. To manage a usability subdependency, the resource might be tailored to the needs of the consumer (meaning that the consumer has to provide that information to the producer) or a producer might follow a standard so the consumer knows what to expect. Mechanisms may be useful in a wide variety of organizational settings. Conversely, organizations with similar goals achieved using more or less the same set of activities will have to manage the same dependencies, but may choose different coordination mechanisms, thus resulting in different processes. Of course, the mechanisms are themselves activities that must be performed by some actors, and so adding coordination mechanisms to a process may create additional dependences that must themselves be managed.

Coordination in Software Development

Coordination has long been a key issue in software development (e.g., Brooks, 1975; Conway, 1968; Curtis et al., 1988; Faraj & Sproull, 2000; Kraut & Streeter, 1995; Parnas, 1972). For example, Conway (1968) observed that the structure of a software system mirrors the structure of the organization that develops it. Both Conway (1968) and Parnas (1972) studied coordination as a crucial part of software development. Curtis et al. (1988) found that in large-scale software project, coordination and communication are among the most crucial and hard-to-manage problems. To address such problems, software development researchers have proposed different coordination mechanisms such a planning, defining and following a process, managing requirements and design specifications, measuring process characteristics, organizing regular meetings to track progress, implementing workflow systems, among the others.

Herbsleb and Grinter (1999b), in a study of geographically-distributed software development within a large firm, showed that some of the previously mentioned coordination mechanisms—namely integration plans, component-interface specifications, software processes and documentation—failed to support coordination if not properly managed. The mechanisms needed to be modified or augmented (allowing for the filling in of details, handling exceptions, coping with unforeseen events and recovering from errors) to allow the work to proceed. They also showed that the primary barriers to coordination breakdowns were the lack of unplanned contact, knowing whom to contact about what, cost of initiating a contact, ability to communicate effectively and lack of trust or willingness to communicate openly.

Kraut and Streeter (1995), in studying the coordination practices that influence the sharing of information and success of software development, identified the following coordination techniques: formal-impersonal procedures (projects documents and memos, project milestones and delivery schedules, modification request and error-tracking procedures, data dictionaries), formal-interpersonal procedures (status-review meetings, design-review meetings, code inspections), informal-interpersonal (group meetings and co-location of requirements and development staff, electronic communication such as e-mail

and electronics bulletin boards, and interpersonal network). Their results showed the value of both informal and formal interpersonal communication for sharing information and achieving coordination in software development. Note though that this analysis focuses more the media for exchanging information rather than particular dependencies or coordination mechanisms that might be executed via these media. That is, once you have called a group meeting, what should you talk about?

Coordination in FLOSS Development

A few studies have examined the work practices and coordination modes adopted by FLOSS teams in more detail, which is the focus of this article (Iannacci, 2005; Scacchi, 2002; Weber, 2004). Cubranic (1999) observed that the main media used for coordination in FLOSS development teams were mailing lists. Such a low-tech approach is adopted to facilitate the participation of would-be contributors, who may not have access to or experience with more sophisticated technology. The geographical distribution of contributors and the variability in time of contributors precluded the use of other systems (e.g., systems that support synchronous communication or prescriptive coordination technology, such as workflow systems). Mailing lists supported low-level coordination needs. Also, Cubranic (1999) found no evidence of the use of higher-level coordination, such as group decision making, knowledge management, task scheduling and progress tracking. As they are the main coordination mechanisms, the volume of information within mailing lists can be huge. Mailing lists are therefore often unique repositories of source information on design choices and evolution of the system. However, dealing with this volume of information in large open source software projects can require a large amount of manual and mental effort from developers, who have to rely on their memory to compensate for the lack of adequate tools and automation.

In a well-known case study of two important FLOSS projects, namely Apache and Mozilla, Mockus et al. (2002) distinguished explicit (e.g., interface specification processes, plans, etc.) and implicit coordination mechanisms adopted for software development. They argued that, because of its software structure, the Apache development team had primarily adopted implicit coordination mechanisms. The basic server was kept small. Core developers worked on what interested them and their opinion was fundamental when adding new functionality. The functionality beyond the basic server was added by means of various ancillary projects, developed by a larger community that interacted with Apache only through defined interfaces. Such interfaces coordinate the effort of the Apache developers: as they had to be designed based on what Apache provided, the effort of the Apache core group was limited. As a result, coordination relied on the knowledge of who had expertise in a given area and general communication on who is doing what and when. On the other hand, in the Mozilla project, because of the interdependence among modules, considerable effort is spent in coordination. In this case, more formal and explicit coordination mechanisms were adopted (e.g., module owners were appointed who had to approve all changes in their module).

Jensen & Scacchi (2005) modelled the software-release process in three projects, namely Mozilla, Apache and NetBeans. They identified tasks, their dependencies and the actors performing them. However, they did not analyze the coordination issues in depth and did not focus specifically on the bug-fixing process, which is the aim of this article. Rather, their final goal was to study the relationships among the three communities that form a Web Information Infrastructure.

Iannacci (2005) adopted an organizational perspective to study coordination processes within a single large-scale and well-known FLOSS development project, Linux. He identified three main

(traditional) coordination mechanisms, namely standardization, loose coupling and partisan mutual adjustment. Standardization is a coordination mechanism to manage pooled dependencies emerging among different contributors. It implies the definition of well-defined procedures, such as in the case of patch submission or bug-fixing procedures. Loose coupling is used to manage sequential dependencies among the different subgroups of contributors. It is the coordination mechanisms used to, for example, incorporating new patches. Finally, partisan mutual adjustment is a mechanism used to manage what Iannacci (2005) called networked interdependencies, an extension of the reciprocal dependencies as proposed by Thompson (1967). Networked interdependencies are those emerging among contributors to specific part of the software. Partisan mutual adjustment produces a sort of structuring process so creating an informal (sub-)organization. However, these findings are based on a single exceptional case, the Linux project, making it unclear how much can be generalized to smaller projects. Indeed, most of the existing studies are of large and well-known projects and focused on the development process. To our knowledge, no studies have analyzed the bug-fixing process in depth within small FLOSS development teams.

A Coordination Theory Application: The Bug-Fixing Process

To ground our discussion of coordination theory, we will briefly introduce the bug-fixing process, which consists of the tasks needed to correct software bugs. We decided to focus on the bug-fixing process for three reasons. First, bug fixing provides "a microcosm of coordination problems" (Crowston, 1997). Second, a quick response to bugs has been mentioned as a particular strength of the FLOSS process: as Raymond (1998) puts it, "given enough eyeballs, all bugs are shallow". Finally, it is a process that involves the entire developer community and thus poses particular coordination problems. While there have been several studies of FLOSS bug fixing, few have analyzed coordination issues within bug-fixing process by adopting a process view. For example, Sandusky et al. (2004) analyzed the bug-fixing process. They focus their attention on the identification of the relationships existing among bug reports, but they do not examine in details the process itself. In contrast to the prior work, our article provides empirical evidence about coordination practices within FLOSS teams. Specifically, we describe the way the work of bug fixing is coordinated in these teams, how these practices differ from those of conventional software development and thus suggest what might be learned from FLOSS and applied in other settings.

We base our description on the work of Crowston (1997), who described the bug-fixing process observed at a commercial software company. Such a process is below defined as traditional because 1) it is carried out within a traditional kind of organization (i.e., the boundary are well defined, the environment is not distributed, the organization structure is defined) and 2) refers to the production of commercial rather than FLOSS software. The process is started by a customer who finds a problem when using a software system. The problem is reported (sometimes automatically or by the customer) to the company's response center. In the attempt to solve the problem, personnel in the center look in a database of known bugs. If a match is found, the fix is returned to the customer; otherwise, after identifying the affected product, the bug report is forwarded to an engineer in the marketing center. The assigned engineer tries to reproduce the problem and identify the cause (possibly requesting additional information from the reporter to do so). If the bug is real, the bug report is forwarded to the manager responsible for the module affected by the bug. The manager then assigns the bug to the software engineer responsible for that module. The software engineering diagnoses the problem (if she finds that the problem is in a different module, the report is

forwarded to the right engineer) and designs a fix. The proposed fix is shared with other engineers responsible for modules that might be affected. When the feedback from those engineers is positive, the proposed design is transformed into lines of code. If changes in other module are needed, the software engineer also asks the responsible engineers for changes. The proposed fix is then tested, the eventual changed modules are sent to the integration manager. After approving, the integration manager recompiles the system, tests the entire system and releases the new software in the form of a patch. To summarize then, in the traditional bug-fixing process, the following tasks have been identified (Crowston, 1997):

Report, Try to solve the problem, Search database for solution, Forward to the marketing manager, Try to solve the problem/Diagnose the problem, Forward to the Software Engineering Group, Assign the bug, Diagnose the problem, Design the fix, Verify affected modules and ask for approval, Write the code for the fix, Test it, Integrate changes, Recompile the module and link it to the system.

After describing the above process, Crowston (1997) went on to analyze the coordination mechanisms employed. A number of the tasks listed can be seen as coordination mechanisms. For example, the search for duplicate bugs as well as the numerous forward and verify tasks manage some dependency. Searching for duplicate outputs is the coordination mechanism to manage a dependency between two tasks that might have the same output. In this case, the tasks are to respond to bug reports from customers. These tasks can be performed by diagnosing and repairing the bug, but if the solution to the bug report can be found in the database, then the effort taken to solve it a second time can be avoided. Thus, searching the database for a solution is a way to manage a potential dependency between the two bug-fixing tasks. Forwarding and verifying tasks are coordination mechanisms used to manage dependency between a task and the actor appropriate to perform that task. These steps are needed because many actors are involved in the process and each of them carry out a very specialized task, requiring additional work to find an appropriate person to perform each task.

RESEARCH METHODOLOGY

To address our research question, how are bug fixes coordinated in FLOSS projects, we carried out a multiple case study of different FLOSS projects, using the theoretical approach developed in the previous section. In this section, we discuss sample selection and data sources, data collection and data analysis, deferring a discussion of our findings to the following section.

Sample Section

In this sub-section we describe the basis for selecting projects for analysis. Projects to be studied were selected from those hosted on SourceForge, (http://sourceforge.net/), a Web-based system that currently supports the development of more than 100,000 FLOSS projects (although only a small proportion of these are actually active). We chose to examine projects from a single source to control for differences in available tools and project visibility. Because the process of manually reading, rereading, coding and recoding messages is extremely labor-intensive, we had to focus our attention on a small number of projects. We selected projects to study in-depth by employing a theoretical sampling strategy based on several practical and theoretical dimensions.

First, we chose projects for which data we need for our analysis are publicly available, meaning a large number of bug reports. (Not all projects use or allow public access to the bug-tracking system.) Second, we chose teams with more than 8 developers (i.e., those with write access to the source code control system), since smaller proj-

ects seemed less likely to experience significant coordination problems. The threshold of eight members was chosen based on our expectation that coordinating tasks within a team would become more complicated as the number of members increases. We assumed that each member of the team could manage 4 or 5 relationship, but with eight members, we expected some difficulty in coordination to arise. Only 140 projects of Source-Forge met the first two requirements in 2002 when we drew our sample. Third, projects were chosen so as to provide some comparison in the target audience and addressed topic, as discussed below. Finally, because we wanted to link coordination practices to project effectiveness, we tried to select more and less effective development teams. To this aim we used the definitions of effectiveness proposed by Crowston et al. (2006a), who suggest that a project is effective if it is active, the resulting software is downloaded and used and the team continues in operation. We selected 4 FLOSS projects to satisfy the mentioned criteria. Specifically, from the 140 large active projects, we selected two desktop chat clients that are aimed at end users (KICQ and Gaim) and two projects aimed primarily at developers (DynAPI, an HTML library and phpMyAdmin, a web-based database administration tool). A brief description of the projects is reported in Table 1, including the project goal, age at the time of the study, volume of communication and team membership. A consequence of the requirement of a significant number of bug reports is that all four projects are relatively advanced, making them representative of mature FLOSS projects. Based on the definition proposed by Crowston et al. (2006a), Kicq, Gaim and phpMyAdmin were chosen as examples of effective projects because they were active, the resulting software was being downloaded and the group had been active for a while. DynAPI was chosen as an example of a less effective project because the number of downloads and programming activity had rapidly decreased in the months leading up to the study.

Table 1. Four examined projects

	KICQ	DynAPI	Gaim	phpMyAdmin
Goal	ICQ client for the KDE project (a chat client)	Dynamic HTML library	Multi-platform AIM client (a chat client)	Web-based database administration
Registration date	1999-11-19	2000-05-15	1999-11-13	2001-03-18
Development Status	4 Beta, 5 Production Stable	5 Production Stable	5 Production Stable	5 Production Stable
License	GPL	LGPL, GPL	GPL	GPL
Intended Audience	Developers, End Users/ Desktop	Developers	Advanced End Users, Developers, End Users/ Desktop	Developers, End Users/ Desktop, System Administrators
Topic	ICQ, K Desktop Environment (KDE)	Dynamic Content	AOL Instant Messenger, ICQ, Internet Relay Chat, MSN Messenger	Front-Ends, Dynamic Content, Systems Administration
Open bugs/ Total # of bugs	26 /88	45/220	269 /1499	29 /639
Open Support Requests/ Total # of requests	12/18		20/107	3/125
Open Patches/ Total # of Patches	1/8	14/144	75/556	7/131
Open Features requests/ Total # of requests	9/9	5/12	214/447	214/447
Mailing lists	813 messages in 3 mailing lists	9595 in 5 mailing lists	304 in 1 mailing list (developers)	5456 in 5 mailing lists
# of team members	9	11	9	9
Team member roles (# in role)	Admin/project manager (2); packager (1); developers (3); advisor/ mentor/ consultant(1); not specified (2)	Admin/project manager (1); developers (4); admin (3); not specified (3)	Project manager (1); admin/ developer (1); support manager (1); web designer (1); developers (3) not specified (2)	Project manager/ admin (1); admin/ developer (2); developers (6)

Data Collection

In this sub-section we describe how data were selected and collected. As mentioned above, all of these projects are hosted on SourceForge, making certain kinds of data about them easily accessible for analysis. However, analysis of these data poses some ethical concerns that we had to address in gaining human subjects approval for our study. On the one hand, the interactions recorded are all public and developers have no expectations of privacy for their statements (indeed, the expectation is the opposite, that their comments will be widely broadcast). Consent is generally not required for studies of public behaviour. On the other hand, the data were not made available for research purposes but rather to support the work of the teams. We have gone ahead with our research after concluding that our analysis does not pose any likelihood of additional harm to the poster above the availability of the post to the group and in the archive available on the Internet.

We collected several kinds of data about each of the cases. First, we obtained data indicative of the effectiveness of each project, such as its level of activity, number of downloads and development status. Unfortunately, no documentation on the organization structure, task assignment procedures and coordination practices adopted was available on the projects' web sites (further supporting the position that these teams do not employ formal coordination methods). To get at the bug-fixing process, we considered alternative sources of data. Interviewing the developers might have provided information about their perceptions of the process, but would have required finding their identities, which was considered problematic given privacy concerns. Furthermore, reliance on self-reported data raises concerns about reliability of the data, the response rate and the likelihood that different developers would have different perceptions. While these issues are quite interesting to study (e.g., to understand how a team develops shared mental models of a project, for example, Crowston & Kammerer, 1998), they seemed like distractions from our main research question. Because of these concerns, we elected to use objective data about the bug-fixing process. Hence, the main source of data about the bug-fixing process was obtained from the archives of the bug tracking system, which is the tool used to support the bug-fixing process (Herbsleb et al., 2001, p. 13). These data are particularly useful because they are unobtrusive measures of the team's behaviors (Webb & Weick, 1979) and thus provide an objective description of the work that is actually undertaken, rather than perceptions of the work.

In the bug tracking system, each bug has a request ID, a summary (what the bug is about), a category (the kind of bug, e.g., system, interface), the name of the team member (or user) who submitted it, and the name of the team member it was assigned to. An example bug report in shown in Figure 1 (the example is fictitious). As well, individuals can post messages regarding the bug, such as further symptoms, requests for more information, etc. From this system, we extracted data about who submitted the bugs, who fixed them and the sequence of messages involved in the fix. By examining the name of the message senders, we can identify the project and community members who are involved in the bug-fixing process. Demographic information for the projects and developers and data from the bug tracking system were collected in the period 17–24 November 2002. We examined 31 closed bugs for Kicq, 95 closed bugs for DynAPI, 51 bugs for Gaim and 51 for PhPMyAdmin. The detailed text of the bug reports is not reported because of space restriction but is available on request.

Data Analysis

In this section we present our data analysis approach. For each of the bug reports, we carefully examined the text of the exchanged messages to identify the task carried out by each sender. We first applied the framework developed by Checkland & Scholes (1990), who suggested identifying the owners, customers and environment of the process, the actors who perform it, the transformation of inputs into outputs, the environment and the worldview that makes the process meaningful. We then followed the method described by Crowston & Osborn (2003), who suggested expanding the analysis of the transformation by identifying in more detail the activities carried out in the transformation. We identified the activities by inductively coding the text of the messages in

Figure 1. Example bug report and followup messages

[bug# 0000000] crash with *alfa* chat

Date: Priority:
2024-05-28 12:56   5
Submitted by: Assigned to:
kub (kkhub)   Gill Coudan (gills)
Category: Status:
system   closed
Summary:
Crash with *alfa* chat
Each time I try an *alfa* chat session the whole program closes itself immediately

Followsups

Message
Date: 2024-07-29 08:56
Sender: cenis
Ok, since kkhub reported it works for me, I am closing this bug.
To cobvnl I repeat:
"please try latest sources from CVS
_____
Date: 2024-06-29 13:02
Sender: cobvnl
Module name: cicq
Latest release is xxxxx1
Is written here did I probably install a beta version xxxxxx?
It would be great to can chat again
_____
Date: 2024-06-18 01:10
Sender: kkhub
I've trieds the lastes version, it seems to work perfectly
That's marvellous...
_____
Date: 2024-06-17 06:50
Sender: cenis
Ok, lets try it one more time – WHAT VERSION OF CICQ do you use?
There was dramatic improvements in chat code since xxxxxx beta, so please try latest s
CVS and report your comments back.
_____
Date: 2024-06-08 12:32
Sender: cobvnl
Hi, I have the exact same problem. It doesn't make difference whether I initiate or the c
initiates the chat. I use CIC 6.2 and compiled CICQ with the export bbbbbb/bbb/lib
previous lib) because it needed it. Also it doesn't make difference to run with the old o
Sometimes the chat request results in a user ABORTed at the other side and ....
_____
Date: 2024-05-29 05:03
Sender: cenis
What version do you try?

the bug tracking systems of the four projects. We started by developing a coding scheme based on prior work on bug fixing (Crowston, 1997), which provided a template of expected activities needed for task assignment (those listed above). The coding system was then evolved through examination of the applicability of codes to particular examples. For example the message:

I've been getting this same error every FIRST time I load the dynapi in NS (win32). After reloading, it will work... loading/init problem?

represents a report submitted by another user (someone other than the person who initially identified and submitted the bug). This message was coded as "report similar problems". Table 2 shows the list of task types that were developed for the coding. The lowest level elementary task types were successively grouped into 6 main types of tasks, namely *Submit, Assign, Analyze, Fix, Test & Post,* and *Close*. A complete example of the coded version of a bug report (the one from Figure 1) is shown in Figure 2.

Once we had identified the process tasks, we studied in depth the bug-fixing process as carried out in the four cases. Specifically, we compared the sequence of tasks across different bugs to assess which sequences were most common and the role of coordination mechanisms in these sequences. We also examined which actors performed which tasks as well as looked for ways to

Table 2. Coded tasks in the bug-fixing process

1.0.0 **Submit (S)**
1.1.0 Submit bug (code errors)
1.1.1 Submit symptoms
1.1.2 Provide code back trace (BT)
1.2.0 Submit problems
1.2.1 Submit incompatibility problems (NC)
2.0.0. **Assign (As)**
2.1.0 Bug self-assignment (A*)
2.2.0 Bug assignment (A)
3.0.0 **Analyze (An)**
3.1.0 Contribute to bug identification
3.1.1Report similar problems (R)
3.1.2 Share opinions about the bug (T)
3.2.0 Verify impossibility to fix the bug
3.2.1 Verify bug already fixed (AF)
3.2.2.Verify bug irreproducibility (NR)
3.2.3 Verify need for a not yet supported function (NS)
3.2.4 Verify identified bug as intentionally introduced (NCP)
3.3.0 Ask for more details
3.3.1 Ask for Code version/command line (V)
3.3.2 Ask for code back trace/examples (RBT/E)
3.4.0 Identify bug causes (G)
3.4.1 Identify and explain error (EE)
3.4.2 Identify and explain bug causes different from code (PNC)
4.0.0 Fix (F)
4.1.0 Propose temporary solutions (AC)
4.2.0 Provide problem solution (SP)
4.3.0 Provide debugging code (F)
5.0.0 **Test & Post (TP)**
5.1.0 Test/approve bug solution
5.1.1 Verify application correctness (W)
5.2.0 Post patches (PP)
5.3.0 Identify further problems with proposed patch (FNW)
6.0.0 **Close**
6.1.0 Close fixed bug/problem
6.2.0 Closed not fixed bug/problems
6.2.1 Close irreproducible bug (CNR) and close it
6.2.2 Close bug that asks for not yet supported function (CNS)
6.2.3 Close bug identified as intentionally introduced (CNCP)

Figure 2. Coded version of bug report in Figure 1

Bug ID	Summary	Assigned to	Submitter
0000000	crash with *alfa* chat	gills	kkhub

Task	Person	Comments
(S)	kkhub	
(V)	cenis	asks what version kkhub is running
(R)	cobvnl	reports the same problem as kkhub. submits information about the operating systems and the libraries
(V)	cenis	asks again what version both users are running
(W)	kkhub	reports the most recent version of cicq works
(TP&C)	cobvnl	reports version information and close the bug
(C)		bug closed

Table 3. The bug-fixing process: Main results

	Kicq	DynAPI	Gaim	phpMyAdmin
Bugs submitted by team members	9.7%	21%	0%	21.6%
Bugs submitted by members external to the team	90.3%	78.9%	100%	78.4%
Bug assigned/self-assigned of which:	9.7%	0%	2%	1%
Assigned to team members	0%	-	100%	100%
Self assigned	66%			0%
Assigned to members external to the team	33%	-	-	0%
Bug fixed	51,6%	42,1%	51%	80%
Fixed by team members	81,3%	50%	84%	90,2%
Bug fixed by members external to the team	18,7%	50%	16%	9.8%

more succinctly present the pattern of tasks, for example, by presenting them as Markov processes. Because of the shortness and relative simplicity of our task sequences, we could exactly match task sequences, rather than having to statistically assess the closeness of matches to be able to form clusters (Sabherwal & Robey, 1995). Therefore, we were able to analyze the sequences by simple tabulation and counting, though more sophisticated techniques would be useful for larger scale data analysis. In the next Section we present the results of our analysis.

FINDINGS

In this section we present the findings from our analysis of the bug-fixing process in the four projects and the coordination mechanisms employed. Data about the percentage of submitted, assigned and fixed bugs both by team members and individuals external to the team for each project are reported in Table 3. Table 4 summarizes our findings regarding the nature of the bugs fixing process in the four projects.

We now present our overall analysis of the bug-fixing process. Each instance of a bug-fixing

Table 4. Observed characteristics of the bug-fixing processes in the four projects

	Kicq	**DynAPI**	**Gaim**	**phpMyAdmin**
Min task sequence	3	2	2	2
Max task sequence	8	12	9	13
Uncommon tasks (count)	Bug assignment (3)	Bug assignment (0)	Bug assignment (0)	Bug assignment (1)
Community members	18	53	23	20
Team members' participation	2 of 9	6 of 11	3 of 9	4 of 10
Most active team members Role/ name	Project mgr: denis; Developer: davidvh	Admin: rainwater; Ext member: dcpascal	Admin-developer: warmenhoven; Developer: rob-flynn	Admin-developer: loic1; Admin-developer lem9.
Max posting by single community member	2	6	4	3
Not fixable bug closed	8	5	5	-

process starts (by definition) with a bug submission (S) and finishes with bug closing (C). Submitters may submit problems/symptoms associated with bugs (Ss), incompatibility problems (NC) or/and also provide information about code back trace (BT). After submission, the team's project managers or administrators may assign the bug to someone to be fixed ((A); (A*) if they self-assign the bug). Other members of the community may report similar problems they encountered (R), discuss bug causes (T), identify bug causes (G) and/or verify the impossibility of fixing the bug. Participants often ask for more information to better understand the bug's causes (An). In most cases, but not always, after some discussion, a team member spontaneously decides to fix (F) the bug. Bug fixing may be followed by a test and the submission of a patch (TP). Testing is a coordination mechanism that manages usability between producing and using a patch, by ensuring that the patch is usable. However, as later explained, in the examined projects this type of activity is not often found. The bug is then closed (C). Bugs may also be closed because they cannot be fixed, for example, if they are not reproducible (CNR), involve functions not supported yet

(CNS) and/or are intentionally introduced to add new functionality in the future (CNCP). Notice that the closing activity is usually attributed to a particular user.

For our analysis, we consider *Submission, Analysis, Fix* and *Close* to be operative activities, while *Assignment, Test* and *Posting* are coordination mechanisms. As already discussed, *Assignment* is the coordination mechanisms used to manage the dependency between a task and the actor appropriate to perform it. *Posting* is the mechanisms used to manage the dependency between a task and its customers (it makes the fix available to the persons that need it).

The tasks identified above are linked by sequential dependencies as shown in Figure 3. These dependencies were identified by considering the logical connection between tasks based on the flow of resources. For example, a patch can not be tested before it is created. Because the dependencies can be satisfied in different orders, different sequences of the activities are possible. The tasks and their sequence change from bug to bug. Figure 3 shows the most frequent sequences observed, as identified by tabulating and counting the sequences.

Figure 3. Task dependencies in the bug-fixing process

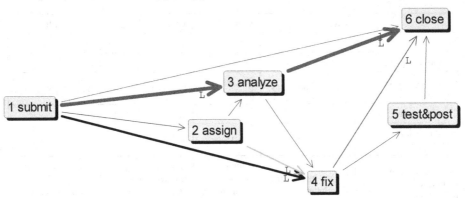

Table 5 shows the portion of processes that follow each possible paths, based on the collected ways the bug-fixing process is observed to be performed within the FLOSS teams. For example, row 1 of Table 5 is read as follows. In the Dynapi project, submission always occurs as the first task (as it does for all of the groups, by definition), while the second task is S in 26% of cases, An in 39% of cases, F in 19% of cases, TP in 1% of cases and C in 15% of cases, and so on.

In Table 6, we describe the occurrences per task for the four projects and the average number of tasks to fix bugs. A χ^2 test shows a significant difference in the distribution of task types across projects (p<0.001). On all projects, *submit* is the task that always appears first, while *analyze* is the most common second task and *fix*, third. The first three most frequent task sequences are reported in Table 7. As noted above, given the limited number of examined sequences, the sequences were manually identified. Finally, in Table 8 we show which tasks are carried out by which roles. Please notice that differences in percentage shown in Table 3 and Table 8 are due to the fact that results reported in Table 8 are calculated based on the total number of tasks carried out per bug. For example, in Table 3 the considered submissions are those carried out only as first task. In Table 8 all submissions tasks (i.e., also those carried out as second, third etc. task) are considered. As

reported in Table 2, submissions tasks can be more than one per bug because submissions can occur also in the form of a *submit* sub-task. The same stands for the fixing tasks. In Table 3 only the final fixing tasks are considered.

A detailed description of the process as performed in the four cases is provided below considering both the sequence of tasks and the participation in the bug-fixing process.

Kicq

The minimal sequence is composed of three tasks, the longest by eight. Bug fixing is usually the second task in the sequence, meaning that it is most common for bugs to be fixed immediately after they are submitted, which is different from the overall picture in which analysis was most common. *Bug assignment* is a quite rare task, as only three bugs are formally assigned. Eight bugs were closed because they were considered to be not fixable.

There are 18 identified users, but many (anonymous) users submitted bugs and contributed to analysis and fixing. Team members are not very active in bug fixing, except for one of the two project managers (denis), who is involved in all the tasks and, in particular, in bug analysis and fixing. Out of 23 fixed bugs, 16 are fixed by

Table 5. Portion of processes for each possible path

i	task i-1	task i	Kicq	Dynapi	Gaim	PhPmyadmin
2	S	S	42%	26%	4%	2%
		As	6%	-	2%	2%
		An	39%	39%	61%	41%
		F	13%	19%	24%	45%
		TP	-	1%	2%	8%
		C	-	15%	8%	2%
3	S	An	38%	36%	50%	100%
		F	62%	40%	50%	-
		TP	-	8%	-	-
		C	-	16%	-	-
	As	An	-	-		100%
		F	50%	-	100%	-
		TP	50%	-	-	-
	An	S	8%	-	-	5%
		An	25%	41%	58%	52%
		F	8%	11%	3%	29%
		TP	-	-	3%	-
		C	58%	49%	35%	14%
	F	An	-	11%	-	13%
		F	50%	22%	8%	4%
		TP	-	6%	-	4%
		C	50%	61%	92%	78%
	TP	An	-	-	-	50%
		F	-	100%	100%	-%
		TP	-	-	-	-50%
		C	-	-	-	-
	C	An	-	7%	-	-
		C	-	93%	-	-
4	S	S	-	-	-	-
		An	100%	-	-	-
		F	-	-	-	100%
		TP	-	-	-	-
		C	-	-	-	-
	An	S	-	4%	5%	-
		An	13%	48%	53%	50%
		F	25%	11%	21%	11%
		TP	-	4%	-	6%
		C	63%	33%	21%	33%

continued on following page

Table 5. continued

i	task i-1	task i	Kicq	Dynapi	Gaim	PhPmyadmin
	F	S	-	-	-	-
		As	8%	-	-	-
		An		11%	20%	
		F	33%	16%	-	14%
		TP	-	5%	-	29%
		C	58%	68%	80%	57%
	TP	S	-	-	-	-
		An	-	-	-	-
		F	-	33%	-	33%
		TP	-	-	-	33%
		C	-	67%	100%	33%
	C	C	-	-	100%	-
5	S	AN	-	-	100%	-
		F	-	-	-	-
		TP	-	100%	-	-
	As	F	100%	-	-	-
	An	S	-	-	-	-
		An	50%	27%	73%	67%
		F	-	13%	18%	11%
		TP	-	-	-	11%
		C	50%	60%	9%	11%
	F	An	17%	14%	-	20%
		F	--	-	25%	-
		TP	-	-	25%	-
		C	83%	86%	50%	80%
	TP	An	-	-	-	-
		F	-	-	-	50%
		TP	-	100%	-	-
		C	-	-	-	50%
6	An	S	-		11%	-
		As	50%	-	-	14%
		An	-	20%	22%	43%
		F	-	-	11%	29%
		TP	-	20%	-	-
		C	50%	60%	56%	14%
	F	S	-	-	-	-
		An	-	-	-	-
		F	-	-	-	-

continued on following page

Table 5. continued

i	task i-1	task i	Kicq	Dynapi	Gaim	PhPmyadmin
		TP	-	-	-	33%
		C	100%	100%	-	67%
	TP	An	-	-	-	-
		F	-	100%	-	-
		TP	-	-	-	-
		C	-	-	-	100%
7	S	AN	-	-	50%	-
		©	-	-	50%	-
	As	F	100%	-	-	100%
	An	S	-	-	-	33%
		An	-			33%
		F	-	100%	100%	-
		TP	-	-	-	-
		C	-	-	-	33%
	F	An	-	100%	-	-
		F	-	-	-	-
		TP	-	-	-	-
		C	-	-	100%	100%
	TP	F	-	100%	-	100%
8	S	An	-	-	-	100%
		F	-	-	-	-
	An	An	-	100%	-	-
		F	-		100%	100%
	F	An	-	50%	-	-
		TP	-	-	-	50%
		C	100%	50%	100%	50%
9	An	An	-	50%	-	100%
		C	-	50%	-	-
	F	AN	-	-	-	100%
		C	-	-	100%	-
	TP	TP	-	-	-	100%
10	An	An	-	100%	-	50%
		F	-	-	-	50%
	TP		-	-	-	100%
11	An	An	-	100%		50%
		F	-	-	-	50%
	F	C	-	-	-	100%
12	An	An	-	-	-	100%

continued on following page

Table 5. continued

i	task i-1	task i	Kicq	Dynapi	Gaim	PhPmyadmin
		C	-	100%	-	-
	F	C	-	-	-	100%
13	An	C	-	100%	-	100%

Table 6. Task occurrences and average number of tasks per projects

Task / Project (bugs)	(S)	(Ag)	(An)	(F)	(TP)	(C)	Avr. tasks per bug
KICQ (31)	44	4	24	23	0	31	4.4
Dynapi (95)	121	0	94	54	9	95	3.8
Gaim (51)	71	1	77	28	4	51	4.2
Phpmyadmin (51)	54	2	66	45	15	51	4.6

Table 7. Most frequent task sequences

	First task	Second task	Third task	Fourth Task	Occurrences
Kicq	S	An	C	-	13
	S	F	C	-	11
	S	An	F	C	2
DynAPI	S	An	C	-	34
	S	F	C	-	24
	S	C	-	-	17
Gaim	S	An	C	-	21
	S	F	C	-	13
	S	An	F	C	6
phpMyAdmin	S	F	C	-	19
	S	An	C	-	8
	S	An	F	C	7
All projects	S	An	C	-	76
	S	F	C	-	67
	S	C	-	-	22

denis. Apart from a developer (davidvh), the other project members seem not take part in the bug-fixing process at all. However, it is noteworthy that the bug tracking system register three bugs as submitted and assigned to the administrator (bill), although he does not otherwise take part in the process. Most of the community members have posted just one bug, and only two of them posted 2 bugs each.

Dynapi

The minimal sequence is composed of two tasks, the longest by 12. Again, *bug assignment* is not explicitly carried out; apparently community or team members decide autonomously to take part to the bug-fixing process. However, the system reports that six bugs (out of 95) are assigned to an administrator and the rest to a member external

Table 8. Tasks carried out by different roles

task	ROLES/PROJECT Kick				
	devel	pm			% of total tasks
S		4			9%
As		4			100%
An		18			75%
F	1	15			70%
TP					
	Dynapi				
	devel	admin	admin/develop	no role	% of total tasks
S	9	6	1	10	21%
As					
An		27		3	32%
F		18	1	2	35%
TP		2	1		33%
	Gaim				
	admin/develop	develop	supp. mang.		% of total tasks
S					0%
As		1			100%
An	33	11	1		58%
F	17	6			82%
TP					100%
	Phpmyadmin				
	admin/develop	pm			% of total tasks
S	11	1			22%
As	2				100%
An	49				74%
F	40				89%
TP	10				93%

to the team. Five bugs are closed because they are said to be not fixable. Bug fixing is usually the second or the third task in the sequence.

Team members are not very active except for an administrator (rainwater), who is involved in all the tasks and, in particular, in bug *analysis* and *fixing*. The other five team members (two without a specific role, one administrator/developer, one developer and one administrator) are mostly involved in bug *fixing*. The community members involved in the process are 47 persons plus some anonymous posts. Most of them submitted just one bug, but some submitted more (e.g., one submitted six bugs). Community members are mostly involved in bug *submission* but some also carry out other tasks. In particular, one of them (dcpascal) is very active in all the process tasks. Out of 57 fixed bugs, 20 are fixed by a team member (the project manager).

Gaim

The minimal sequence is composed of two tasks, the longest by nine. *Bug assignment* is not explicitly carried out, as community or team members decide autonomously to take part to the bug-fixing process. However, the system reports that 24 bugs (out of 51) are assigned to an administrator (and the rest to member external to the team). Five bugs are directly closed because they are said to be not fixable.

Team members are not very active in bug fixing except for the administer/developer (warmenhoven) and a developer (robflynn), who are involved in many tasks and, in particular, in bug analysis and fixing. Apart from them, just another member of the project team, a developer (lschiere), is also involved in the bug fixing. The community members involved in the process are 21 persons plus some anonymous users. Most of them posted just one bug (2 of them posted five bugs, one 4 bugs). Some of them are also involved in bug analysis and fixing. Out of 29 fixed bugs, 23 are fixed by a team member (the project manager).

Phpmyadmin

The minimal sequence is composed of two tasks, the longest by thirteen. *Bug assignment* is a quite rare task, as only one bug is formally assigned. The assignment is carried out by an administrator/developer (lem9) and directed to a team member (loic1). However, the system reports that all 51 are assigned, of which 40 to team members. Bug fixing is usually the second or the third task.

Team members are not very active in the process, except for two administer/developers (loic1 and lem9), who are involved in all the tasks and, in particular, in bug analysis and fixing (but also submission). Apart from them, two team members take part to the process, a project manager/adminster (swix) and a developer (robbat2), that are involved (not heavily) in bug submission and analysis. The community is composed of 16 members plus some anonymous users. Most of them

have just posted one bug (two of them posted 3 bugs), but some are also involved in bug analysis and fixing. Out of 49 fixed bugs, 44 are fixed by team member (administrator/developers).

DISCUSSION

In this section, we discuss the implications of our findings for understanding the coordination of bug fixing in FLOSS teams. Our findings provide some interesting insights on the bug-fixing process for FLOSS development in these teams. First, process sequences are on average quite short (four tasks) and they seem to be quite similar: submit, (analyze), fix and close. As shown in Table 3, formal task assignments are quite uncommon: only few bugs are formally assigned. Coordination seems rather to spontaneously emerge. From bug description and initial analysis, those who have the competencies autonomously decide to fix the bug and simply go ahead and do so. That activity is facilitated by the supplied bug report and analysis, which is often undertaken by several contributors. Apart from the procedure to submit bugs (we analyzed only bugs submitted through the bug tracking system), we do not observe any other formal process: roles are not predefined, delivery dates are not assigned nor are formal-interpersonal, formal-impersonal or informal-interpersonal procedures adopted. The lack of assignment is one of main aspects differentiating the process as it occurs in FLOSS development team from the traditional commercial bug-fixing process described above.

Testing is also quite an uncommon task in the data. Most of the proposed fixes are directly posted, though presumably after personal testing that is not documented. If no one describes the emergence of new problems with these fixes, they are automatically posted and the relevant bug closed without a formal test process. It is important also to note that many of the posted problems do not represent real bugs (i.e., they have been already fixed, are not reproducible, have been intentionally produced, are associated to functions not yet supported or are associated to related programs), so they are directly closed with that explanation.

Another striking finding is that the bug-fixing process is apparently carried out without any explicit discussion about where knowledge is located in the team, contrary to the findings of Faraj and Sproull (2000), who stress the importance of expertise coordination for team effectiveness (they distinguish expertise coordination from what they call administrative coordination, which is the focus of this article). They define expertise coordination as the management of knowledge and skill dependencies. To manage knowledge it is necessary to know where it is located within development team, where it is needed and how to access it. However, in our observations, the knowledge needs seem to emerge by "(informal and asynchronous) electronic meetings".

The bug tracking system represents a sort of organizational memory, storing bug reports and solutions found to submitted problems (which not always are real bugs). However, as discussed in Cubranic (1999), the large number of emails stored makes it difficult for contributors to easily identify the solutions to their own problems, so making different users repeat the same (already fixed or addressed) submission more times. In those cases (i.e., for bugs closed without being fixed or the attended patches posted), it is usually the team members that act as "memory".

A further difference is that in these projects, the process is performed by few team members (usually not more that two or three) working with a member of the larger community. Team members (usually project managers, administrators or developers) are most involved in bug fixing, testing and posting. Surprisingly, only a few members of the team are involved in the process. The other participants are active users who submit bugs or contribute to their analysis. We also noted striking differences in the level of contribution to the process. The most active users

in the projects carried out most of the tasks while most others contributed only once or twice. Most community members submit only one bug; only two or three members of the involved community are involved in fixing tasks and can be referred to as co-developers. As expected, the most widely dispersed type of action was submitting a bug, while diagnosis and bug-fixing activities were concentrated among a few individuals.

As we have few members of the team and few members of the community (co-developers) mostly involved in bug fixing and many users/members of the community (active users) mostly involved in bug submission, the organizational models proposed in the literature (Cox, 1998) seem to be valid for the bug-fixing process. It would be interesting to further investigate if those, among the active users also involved in bug fixing also contribute to software coding, for example, by analysis of contributions of source code independent of bug fixes.

As an apparently less effective project, we expected to find that DynAPI had a smaller active user base than the other projects. However, as noted above, our data shows the opposite. However, our estimation of the effectiveness of the projects is based on activity levels. It appears that DynAPI somehow does not benefit from its larger community in increased activity. One striking difference is the proportion of bugs fixed by the team members, shown in Table 3, which is much lower in DynAPI than in the other projects. This finding suggests that the contribution of core members may be particularly important in the effectiveness of the team. The case studies presented here are not sufficient to test this hypothesis, so it is one that should be followed up in future studies.

CONCLUSION

In this article, we investigated the coordination practices adopted within four FLOSS development teams. In particular, we analyzed the bug-fixing process, which is considered central to the effectiveness of the FLOSS process. The article provided some interesting results. The task sequences we observed were mostly sequential and composed of few steps, namely *submit, fix and close*. Second, our data supports the observation that FLOSS processes seem to lack traditional coordination mechanisms such as task assignment. Third, effort is not equally distributed among process actors. A few contribute heavily to all tasks, while the majority just submit one or two bugs. As a result, the organization structure reflected in the process resembles the one proposed in the literature for the FLOSS development process. Few actors (core developers), usually team project managers or administrators, are mostly involved in bug fixing. Most of the involved actors are active users instead of developers, who just submit bug reports. In between are few actors, external to the team, who submit bugs and contribute to fixing them. Finally, while we did not find obvious associations between coordination practices and project effectiveness, we did notice a link to participation: our least effective team also had the lowest level of participation from core developers, suggesting their importance, even given the more widely distributed participation possible.

The article contributes to fill a gap in the literature by providing a picture of the coordination practices adopted within FLOSS development team. Besides, the article proposes an innovative research methodology (for the analysis of coordination practices of FLOSS development teams) based on the collection of process data by electronic archives, the codification of message texts, and the analysis of codified information supported by the coordination theory.

Based on the analysis of the tasks carried out and the attendant coordination mechanisms, we argue that the bazaar metaphor proposed by (Raymond, 1998) to describe the FLOSS organization structure is still valid for the bug-fixing process. As in a bazaar, the actors involved in

the process autonomously decide the schedule and contribution modes for bug fixing, making a central coordination actor superfluous.

As with all research, the current article has some limitations that limit the scope of our current conclusions and suggests directions for further research. First, although the selected projects are quite different in terms of target audience and topic, other characteristics (not examined because they are not explicitly present on the project web sites) could be shared among projects so affecting the obtained results. In the future, we would like to deepen our knowledge about the coordination practices adopted by the four projects by directly interviewing some of the involved actors. Second, due to the limited number of examined bugs, the process sequences have been manually examined. In the future, we intend to enlarge the number of examined bugs and adopt automatic techniques (e.g., the optimal matching technique) to analyze and classify the task sequences. In particular, we plan to further explore the hypothesis about the importance of core group members by examining a larger number of projects (e.g., to examine the change in the population over time). Finally, in the article we only examined administrative coordination. In the future, we intend to examine also expertise coordination in more detail. A particular interesting consideration here is the development of shared mental models that might support the coordination of the teams' processes.

REFERENCES

Ahuja, M. K., Carley, K., & Galletta, D. F. (1997). *Individual performance in distributed design groups: An empirical study.* Paper presented at the SIGCPR Conference, San Francisco.

Alho, K., & Sulonen, R. (1998). *Supporting virtual software projects on the Web.* Paper presented at the Workshop on Coordinating Distributed Software Development Projects, 7th

International Workshop on Enabling Technologies: Infrastructure for Collaborative Enterprises (WETICE '98).

Anthes, G. H. (2000, June 26). Software Development goes Global. *Computerworld Magazine.*

Bandow, D. (1997). Geographically distributed work groups and IT: A case study of working relationships and IS professionals. In *Proceedings of the SIGCPR Conference* (pp. 87–92).

Bélanger, F. (1998). Telecommuters and Work Groups: A Communication Network Analysis. In *Proceedings of the International Conference on Information Systems (ICIS)* (pp. 365–369). Helsinki, Finland.

Bessen, J. (2002). *Open Source Software: Free Provision of Complex Public Goods*: Research on Innovation.

Bezroukov, N. (1999a). A second look at the Cathedral and the Bazaar. *First Monday, 4*(12).

Bezroukov, N. (1999b). Open source software development as a special type of academic research (critique of vulgar raymondism). *First Monday, 4*(10).

Boulding, K. E. (1956). General systems theory— The skeleton of a science. *Management Science, 2*(April), 197–208.

Britton, L. C., Wright, M., & Ball, D. F. (2000). The use of co-ordination theory to improve service quality in executive search. *Service Industries Journal, 20*(4), 85–102.

Brooks, F. P., Jr. (1975). *The Mythical Man-month: Essays on Software Engineering.* Reading, MA: Addison-Wesley.

Butler, B., Sproull, L., Kiesler, S., & Kraut, R. (2002). Community effort in online groups: Who does the work and why? In S. Weisband & L. Atwater (Eds.), *Leadership at a Distance.* Mahwah, NJ: Lawrence Erlbaum.

Carmel, E. (1999). *Global Software Teams.* Upper Saddle River, NJ: Prentice-Hall.

Carmel, E., & Agarwal, R. (2001). Tactical approaches for alleviating distance in global software development. *IEEE Software* (March/April), 22–29.

Checkland, P. B., & Scholes, J. (1990). *Soft Systems Methodology in Action.* Chichester: Wiley.

Conway, M. E. (1968). How do committees invent. *Datamation, 14*(4), 28–31.

Cox, A. (1998). Cathedrals, Bazaars and the Town Council. Retrieved 22 March, 2004, from http://slashdot.org/features/98/10/13/1423253.shtml

Crowston, K. (1997). A coordination theory approach to organizational process design. *Organization Science, 8*(2), 157–175.

Crowston, K., & Howison, J. (2006). Hierarchy and centralization in free and open source software team communications. *Knowledge, Technology & Policy, 18*(4), 65–85.

Crowston, K., Howison, J., & Annabi, H. (2006a). Information systems success in Free and Open Source Software development: Theory and measures. *Software Process—Improvement and Practice, 11*(2), 123–148.

Crowston, K., & Kammerer, E. (1998). Coordination and collective mind in software requirements development. *IBM Systems Journal, 37*(2), 227–245.

Crowston, K., & Osborn, C. S. (2003). A coordination theory approach to process description and redesign. In T. W. Malone, K. Crowston & G. Herman (Eds.), *Organizing Business Knowledge: The MIT Process Handbook.* Cambridge, MA: MIT Press.

Crowston K., Scozzi B., (2003). Open Source Software projects as virtual organizations: competency rallying for software development. *IEE Proceedings Software, 149*(1), 3-17.

Crowston, K., Wei, K., Li, Q., Eseryel, U. Y., & Howison, J. (2005). *Coordination of Free/ Libre Open Source Software development.* Paper presented at the International Conference on Information Systems (ICIS 2005), Las Vegas, NV, USA.

Crowston, K., Wei, K., Li, Q., & Howison, J. (2006b). *Core and periphery in Free/Libre and Open Source software team communications.* Paper presented at the Hawai'i International Conference on System System (HICSS-39), Kaua'i, Hawai'i.

Cubranic, D. (1999). *Open-source software development.* Paper presented at the 2nd Workshop on Software Engineering over the Internet, Los Angeles.

Curtis, B., Krasner, H., & Iscoe, N. (1988). A field study of the software design process for large systems. *Communications of the ACM, 31*(11), 1268–1287.

Curtis, B., Walz, D., & Elam, J. J. (1990). Studying the process of software design teams. In *Proceedings of the 5th International Software Process Workshop On Experience With Software Process Models* (pp. 52–53). Kennebunkport, Maine, United States.

Cutosksy, M. R., Tenenbaum, J. M., & Glicksman, J. (1996). Madefast: Collaborative engineering over the Internet. *Communications of the ACM, 39*(9), 78–87.

de Souza, P. S. (1993). *Asynchronous Organizations for Multi-Algorithm Problems.* Unpublished Doctoral Thesis, Carnegie-Mellon University.

DeSanctis, G., & Jackson, B. M. (1994). Coordination of information technology management: Team-based structures and computer-based communication systems. *Journal of Management Information Systems, 10*(4), 85.

Di Bona, C., Ockman, S., & Stone, M. (Eds.). (1999). *Open Sources: Voices from the Open Source Revolution.* Sebastopol, CA: O'Reilly & Associates.

Drucker, P. (1988). The coming of the new organization. *Harvard Business Review,* 3-15.

Faraj, S., & Sproull, L. (2000). Coordinating Expertise in Software Development Teams. *Management Science, 46*(12), 1554–1568.

Finholt, T., Sproull, L., & Kiesler, S. (1990). Communication and Performance in Ad Hoc Task Groups. In J. Galegher, R. F. Kraut & C. Egido (Eds.), *Intellectual Teamwork.* Hillsdale, NJ: Lawrence Erlbaum and Associates.

Franck, E., & Jungwirth, C. (2002). *Reconciling investors and donators: The governance structure of open source* (Working Paper No. No. 8): Lehrstuhl für Unternehmensführung und -politik, Universität Zürich.

Gacek, C., & Arief, B. (2004). The many meanings of Open Source. *IEEE Software, 21*(1), 34–40.

Galbraith, J. R. (1973). *Designing Complex Organizations.* Reading, MA: Addison-Wesley.

Grabowski, M., & Roberts, K. H. (1999). Risk mitigation in virtual organizations. *Organization Science, 10*(6), 704–721.

Grinter, R. E., Herbsleb, J. D., & Perry, D. E. (1999). The Geography of Coordination: Dealing with Distance in R&D Work. In *Proceedings of the GROUP '99 Conference* (pp. 306–315). Phoenix, Arizona, US.

Hallen, J., Hammarqvist, A., Juhlin, F., & Chrigstrom, A. (1999). Linux in the workplace. *IEEE Software, 16*(1), 52–57.

Hann, I.-H., Roberts, J., Slaughter, S., & Fielding, R. (2002). Economic incentives for participating in open source software projects. In *Proceedings of the Twenty-Third International Conference on Information Systems* (pp. 365–372).

Herbsleb, J. D., & Grinter, R. E. (1999a). Architectures, coordination, and distance: Conway's law and beyond. *IEEE Software*(September/October), 63–70.

Herbsleb, J. D., & Grinter, R. E. (1999b). *Splitting the organization and integrating the code: Conway's law revisited*. Paper presented at the Proceedings of the International Conference on Software Engineering (ICSE '99), Los Angeles, CA.

Herbsleb, J. D., Mockus, A., Finholt, T. A., & Grinter, R. E. (2001). *An empirical study of global software development: Distance and speed*. Paper presented at the Proceedings of the International Conference on Software Engineering (ICSE 2001), Toronto, Canada.

Hertel, G., Niedner, S., & Herrmann, S. (2003). Motivation of Software Developers in Open Source Projects: An Internet-based Survey of Contributors to the Linux Kernel. *Research Policy, 32*(7), 1159–1177.

Humphrey, W. S. (2000). *Introduction to Team Software Process*: Addison-Wesley.

Iannacci, F. (2005). Coordination processes in OSS development: The Linux case study. Retrieved 21 September, 2006, from http://opensource.mit.edu/papers/iannacci3.pdf

Jarvenpaa, S. L., & Leidner, D. E. (1999). Communication and trust in global virtual teams. *Organization Science, 10*(6), 791–815.

Jensen, C., & Scacchi, W. (2005). Collaboration, Leadership, Control, and Conflict Negotiation in the Netbeans.org Open Source Software Development Community. In *Proceedings of the Hawai'i International Conference on System Science (HICSS 2005)*. Big Island, Hawai'i.

Kaplan, B. (1991). Models of change and information systems research. In H.-E. Nissen, H. K. Klein & R. Hirschheim (Eds.), *Information Systems Research: Contemporary Approaches and Emergent Traditions* (pp. 593–611). Amsterdam: Elsevier Science Publishers.

Kogut, B., & Metiu, A. (2001). Open-source software development and distributed innovation. *Oxford Review of Economic Policy, 17*(2), 248–264.

Kraut, R. E., Steinfield, C., Chan, A. P., Butler, B., & Hoag, A. (1999). Coordination and virtualization: The role of electronic networks and personal relationships. *Organization Science, 10*(6), 722–740.

Kraut, R. E., & Streeter, L. A. (1995). Coordination in software development. *Communications of the ACM, 38*(3), 69–81.

Krishnamurthy, S. (2002). Cave or Community? An Empirical Examination of 100 Mature Open Source Projects. *First Monday, 7*(6).

Lawrence, P., & Lorsch, J. (1967). *Organization and Environment*. Boston, MA: Division of Research, Harvard Business School.

Leibovitch, E. (1999). The business case for Linux. *IEEE Software, 16*(1), 40–44.

Lerner, J., & Tirole, J. (2001). The open source movement: Key research questions. *European Economic Review, 45*, 819–826.

Madanmohan, T. R., & Navelkar, S. (2002). *Roles and Knowledge Management in Online Technology Communities: An Ethnography Study* (Working paper No. 192): IIMB.

Malone, T. W., & Crowston, K. (1994). The interdisciplinary study of coordination. *Computing Surveys, 26*(1), 87–119.

Markus, M. L., Manville, B., & Agres, E. C. (2000). What makes a virtual organization work? *Sloan Management Review, 42*(1), 13–26.

Markus, M. L., & Robey, D. (1988). Information technology and organizational change: Causal structure in theory and research. *Management Science, 34*(5), 583–598.

Massey, A. P., Hung, Y.-T. C., Montoya-Weiss, M., & Ramesh, V. (2001). When culture and style aren't about clothes: Perceptions of task-technology "fit" in global virtual teams. In *Proceedings of GROUP '01*. Boulder, CO, USA.

McCann, J. E., & Ferry, D. L. (1979). An approach for assessing and managing inter-unit interdependence. *Academy of Management Review, 4*(1), 113–119.

Metiu, A., & Kogut, B. (2001). *Distributed Knowledge and the Global Organization of Software Development* (Working paper). Philadelphia, PA: The Wharton School, University of Pennsylvania.

Mintzberg, H. (1979). *The Structuring of Organizations*. Englewood Cliffs, NJ: Prentice-Hall.

Mockus, A., Fielding, R. T., & Herbsleb, J. D. (2002). Two case studies Of Open Source Software development: Apache And Mozilla. *ACM Transactions on Software Engineering and Methodology, 11*(3), 309–346.

Mohr, L. B. (1971). Organizational technology and organizational structure. *16*, 444–459.

Mohr, L. B. (1982). *Explaining Organizational Behavior: The Limits and Possibilities of Theory and Research*. San Francisco: Jossey-Bass.

Moon, J. Y., & Sproull, L. (2000). Essence of distributed work: The case of Linux kernel. *First Monday, 5*(11).

Nejmeh, B. A. (1994). Internet: A strategic tool for the software enterprise. *Communications of the ACM, 37*(11), 23–27.

O'Leary, M., Orlikowski, W. J., & Yates, J. (2002). Distributed work over the centuries: Trust and control in the Hudson's Bay Company, 1670–1826. In P. Hinds & S. Kiesler (Eds.), *Distributed Work* (pp. 27–54). Cambridge, MA: MIT Press.

Orlikowski, W. J. (2002). Knowing in practice: Enacting a collective capability in distributed organizing. *Organization Science, 13*(3), 249–273.

Parnas, D. L. (1972). On the criteria to be used in decomposing systems into modules. *Communications of the ACM, 15*(2), 1053–1058.

Pfaff, B. (1998). Society and open source: Why open source software is better for society than proprietary closed source software. from http://www.msu.edu/user/pfaffben/writings/anp/oss-is-better.html

Pfeffer, J. (1978). *Organizational Design*. Arlington Heights, IL: Harlan Davidson.

Pfeffer, J., & Salancik, G. R. (1978). *The External Control of Organizations: A Resource Dependency Perspective*. New York: Harper & Row.

Prasad, G. C. (n.d.). A hard look at Linux's claimed strengths…. from http://www.osopinion.com/Opinions/GaneshCPrasad/GaneshCPrasad2-2.html

Raymond, E. S. (1998). The cathedral and the bazaar. *First Monday, 3*(3).

Robey, D., Khoo, H. M., & Powers, C. (2000). Situated-learning in cross-functional virtual teams. *IEEE Transactions on Professional Communication*(Feb/Mar), 51–66.

Sabherwal, R., & Robey, D. (1995). Reconciling variance and process strategies for studying information system development. *Information Systems Research, 6*(4), 303–327.

Sandusky, R. J., Gasser, L., & Ripoche, G. (2004). *Bug Report Networks: Varieties, Strategies, and Impacts in an OSS Development Community*. Paper presented at the Proceedings of the ICSE Workshop on Mining Software Repositories, Edinburgh, Scotland, UK.

Sawyer, S., & Guinan, P. J. (1998). Software development: Processes and performance. *IBM Systems Journal, 37*(4), 552–568.

Scacchi, W. (1991). The software infrastructure for a distributed software factory. *Software Engineering Journal, 6*(5), 355–369.

Scacchi, W. (2002). Understanding the requirements for developing Open Source Software systems. *IEE Proceedings Software, 149*(1), 24–39.

Scacchi, W. (2005). Socio-technical interaction networks in Free/Open Source Software development processes. In S. T. Acuña & N. Juristo (Eds.), *Software Process Modeling* (pp. 1–27). New York: Springer.

Stewart, K. J., & Ammeter, T. (2002). An exploratory study of factors influencing the level of vitality and popularity of open source projects. In *Proceedings of the Twenty-Third International Conference on Information Systems* (pp. 853–857).

Taylor, P. (1998, December 2). New IT mantra attracts a host of devotees. *Financial Times, Survey—Indian Information Technology,* p. 1.

Thompson, J. D. (1967). *Organizations in Action: Social Science Bases of Administrative Theory.* New York: McGraw-Hill.

Torvalds, L. (1999). The Linux edge. *Communications of the ACM, 42*(4), 38–39.

Valloppillil, V. (1998). Halloween I: Open Source Software. from http://www.opensource.org/halloween/halloween1.html

Valloppillil, V., & Cohen, J. (1998). Halloween II: Linux OS Competitive Analysis. from http://www.opensource.org/halloween/halloween2.html

Victor, B., & Blackburn, R. S. (1987). Interdependence: An alternative conceptualization. *Academy of Management Review, 12*(3), 486–498.

Walz, D. B., Elam, J. J., & Curtis, B. (1993). Inside a software design team: knowledge acquisition, sharing, and integration. *Communications of the ACM, 36*(10), 63–77.

Watson-Manheim, M. B., Chudoba, K. M., & Crowston, K. (2002). Discontinuities and continuities: A new way to understand virtual work. *Information, Technology and People, 15*(3), 191–209.

Wayner, P. (2000). *Free For All.* New York: HarperCollins.

Webb, E., & Weick, K. E. (1979). Unobtrusive measures in organizational theory: A reminder. *Administrative Science Quarterly, 24*(4), 650–659.

Weber, S. (2004). *The Success of Open Source.* Cambridge, MA: Harvard.

Weisband, S. (2002). Maintaining awareness in distributed team collaboration: Implications for leadership and performance. In P. Hinds & S. Kiesler (Eds.), *Distributed Work* (pp. 311–333). Cambridge, MA: MIT Press.

Zuboff, S. (1988). *In the Age of the Smart Machine.* New York: Basic Books.

ENDNOTE

[1] This research was partially supported by US NSF Grants 03-41475, 04–14468 and 05-27457. An earlier version of this article was presented at the *First International Workshop on Computer Supported Activity Coordination (CSAC 2004)*. The authors thank previous anonymous reviewers of the article for their comments that have helped to improve the article.

Chapter 4
Conflicts, Compromises, and Political Decisions:
Methodological Challenges of Enterprise-Wide E-Business Architecture Creation

Kari Smolander
Lappeenranta University of Technology, Finland

Matti Rossi
Helsinki School of Economics, Finland

ABSTRACT

This article describes the architecture development process in an international ICT company, which is building a comprehensive e-business system for its customers. The implementation includes the integration of data and legacy systems from independent business units and the construction of a uniform Web-based customer interface. We followed the early process of architecture analysis and definition over a year. The research focuses on the creation of e-business architecture and observes that instead of guided by a prescribed method, the architecture emerges through somewhat non-deliberate actions obliged by the situation and its constraints, conflicts, compromises, and political decisions. The interview-based qualitative data is analyzed using grounded theory and a coherent story explaining the situation and its forces is extracted. Conclusions are drawn from the observations and possibilities and weaknesses of the support that UML and RUP provide for the process are pointed out.

INTRODUCTION

Robust technical architecture is considered one of the key issues when building successful e-business systems. The design of technical architecture is usually seen as a set of trade-offs between available resources (such as available personnel and money) and operational requirements related to technical architecture, such as scalability, capacity, response times, security, and availability. The software architecture research provides design tools for technical architecture design, including, for instance, architecture description languages (Dashofy, Van der Hoek, & Taylor, 2005; Medvidovic & Taylor, 2000), common architectural patterns and styles (Monroe, Kompanek, Melton, & Garlan, 1997), architectural trade-off methods (Kazman, Klein, & Clements, 2000), architectural frameworks (Leist & Zellner, 2006), and technologies for e-business implementation (Bichler, Segev, & Zhao, 1998). In an ideal world, the work of an architect would be to find the explicit requirements for architecture, and select the best possible design tools and technologies to implement the architecture. Furthermore, the architecture development team would make rational trade-offs concerning the requirements, and produce the best realistic solution for the architecture with the selected design tools and implementation technologies.

However, the literature contains many examples of cases where technical rationality has not been sufficient for the success in IS projects (e.g. Sauer, Southon, & Dampney, 1997). Architecture researchers have found that the work of an architect and the usage of architecture are bound by more diverse organizational issues and limitations that the classical technical software architecture research ignores. These include for example the diverse role of an architect in an organization observed by Grinter (1999) and varying uses and meanings of architecture in practice (Smolander & Päivärinta, 2002a). The main message of these studies is that an architect has a social, and even political, role in an organization and that different stakeholders relate different meanings to architecture to fulfill their informational requirements in the development process. This phenomenon has remarkable similarities to information systems development in general. As pointed out by Klein & Hirscheim, the implicit assumption of rationality of the development processes hides the legitimating of the goals and differing political

agendas of various stakeholders (Hirschheim & Klein, 1989).

To understand the issues involved in architecture development, we observed a project that was developing e-business architecture in an international ICT company. We interviewed various stakeholders to gain a deep insight into the process. The company already had several e-commerce systems in individual business units, but it needed a more uniform customer interface for its various systems. The e-business project included the integration of data and legacy systems from these units and the construction of a uniform Web-based customer interface hiding the differences of the business units. Our goal was to find ways for supporting architecture development by means of methods and description languages, such as UML. We were aware of efforts of supporting architecture design with UML (e.g., Conallen, 1999; Garlan & Kompanek, 2000; Hofmeister, Nord, & Soni, 1999b; Object Management Group, 1999, 2006), but these efforts were mostly targeted to technical software design and we did not know how well these would support a large socio-technical or organizational project, such as enterprise or e-business architecture development. Therefore we decided to observe a real world project and concentrate on the requirements that e-business architecture development in its complex organizational context state on description languages and development methods. Next, we decided to compare the observed requirements to the support that UML and RUP offer, because they, together, form the current methodological basis for many systems development organizations. UML is the de-facto standard language in software and systems development and RUP (Jacobson, Booch, & Rumbaugh, 1999) is a widely known process model that claims to improve development process maturity (Kuntzmann & Kruchten, 2003). We believed that this kind of knowledge would benefit both practitioners in process improvement and developers of UML extensions.

Another interest was to find out what factors influenced the creation of e-business architecture: was it designed purposefully by software architects through rational decisions and trade-offs, or did it emerge through somewhat non-deliberate actions obliged by the situation and its constraints, conflicts, compromises, and political decisions? This is a very important issue, as unlike software architecture, e-business architecture is very tightly coupled with the business models of the company and thus the architecture has a far more direct impact on business than for example low-level system architecture. Furthermore, if the business models are not supported by the e-business architecture, then the business strategy will not work (Ross, Weill, & Robertson, 2006).

We used open interviews of various actors in the projects to gather the necessary information about the project. We analyzed the qualitative data from the interviews using grounded theory (Glaser & Strauss, 1967) as the research method and concluded the analysis by categorizing the issues that had emerged using the taxonomy of Lyytinen (1987). Thus, we classified the issues as belonging into technical, language and organizational context. From this classification of issues, we extracted requirements for development methods when developing integrated e-business solutions and compared these requirements to the support that the combination of UML and RUP provides.

We observed that most of the problems encountered had very little to do with descriptions of the architecture per se. Rather what was problematic were the issues that architecture development exposed about the underlying organization. This is an important finding, as most of the research into architecture has been about effective description languages and design processes and there is a void of research about the organizational consequences of architecture development.

The article is organized as follows: we start by explaining in more detail what is meant by architecture in this article (section 2). In section 3, we describe the research process and method used. section 4 describes the situation the company is facing and the motives for the change and implementation of the e-business system. In section 5, we describe the situation and the context of the development project aiming at e-business implementation and the consequences of the situation for the progress of the development project. From the observed issues faced by the development project we draw conclusions and extract the requirements for development methods in e-business architecture development and compare the requirements to support that the combination of UML and RUP provides (section 6). We point out areas where current research is not supporting the needs of the practice of general and particularly e-business architecture development.

ARCHITECTURE IN SYSTEMS DEVELOPMENT

In this study, we describe a process where comprehensive e-business architecture is being created. In addition to e-commerce systems serving external customer transactions, e-business includes both the integration of and streamlining of internal information systems to serve the new digitally enabled business processes (Kalakota & Robinson, 2001) and the unified customer interface (Ross et al., 2006). For the sake of simplicity, we understand e-business here to cover both the transactions and processes within a firm and the integrated external e-commerce systems as in (Kalakota & Robinson, 2001). This enables us to interpret the process in the studied organization as the process of building an integrated e-business architecture. Ross et al. (2006) stress the architecture as the necessary foundation for execution of comprehensive, across the functions operating, e-business.

Conventionally, architecture is understood as a high-level logical abstraction of the system defining the main components of the system and their relationships. The term architecture is also used both in the context of an individual system and in the context of systems integration. The software architecture typically concentrates on the architecture of a single software system, whereas the terms information systems (IS) architecture and enterprise architecture (Kim & Everest, 1994; Ross et al., 2006; Sowa & Zachman, 1992) refer to the overall architecture of all information systems in an organization.

In practice, however, the borderline between a single system and a set of systems is difficult to determine. Practically no system today is isolated from other systems, and the relationship of a system to its environment may be architecturally more important than the inner structure of the system, especially when developing e-business systems. Usually, systems rely on a common technical infrastructure, (including networks, processing services, operation services, etc.) which is common for all the systems in an organization. Organizationally, architecture design is a co-operative effort involving many roles in the development environment. These roles include the role of an architect who is specifically associated with the task of architecture design. An architect needs contribution and commitment from many individuals, teams, and parts of organization to succeed in the effort (Grinter, 1999).

By architecture development, we mean a process where early design decisions are realized into an architecture defining that defines system's composition from various viewpoints. Architecture also contains the blueprints for system's implementation from conceptual and physical components. This process forms a set of documents which different stakeholders can use to relate their concerns to the issues made concrete by the architecture and discuss their needs in the terms defined by the common architecture. They can also make decisions concerning system development strategies and policies using architecture as a common reference. This conception sees architecture not only as a technical artifact but also as a boundary object (Star & Griesemer, 1989) having strong organizational connotations.

The conventional role of architecture is to serve as an enabler for further design and implementation (Hofmeister, Nord, & Soni, 1999a; Shaw & Garlan, 1996). Obviously, sound and well-designed technical architecture makes the detailed design and implementation of a system easier and less risky than it would be without such architecture. Architecture defines, for example, the modules or components which the system is composed of, and therefore it focuses and constrains the solution space of individual designers that develop individual components. This technical view of architecture has produced also studies related to UML. In the end of last decade, possibilities and weaknesses of UML as an architecture description language, and its complexity (Siau & Cao, 2001; Siau, Erickson, & Lee, 2005) were widely evaluated and enhancements were proposed (Conallen, 1999; D'Souza & Wills, 1998; Egyed & Medvidovic, 1999; Garlan & Kompanek, 2000; Hofmeister et al., 1999b; Medvidovic, Egyed, & Rosenblum, 1999; Rumpe, Schoenmakers, Radermacher, & Schürr, 1999). The recent developments in this area include the SysML extension of UML (Object Management Group, 2006). Different profiles and enhancements to UML have been proposed to tackle its limitations in electronic commerce (Dori, 2001).

RESEARCH PROCESS

The studied organization is a globally operating ICT company having thousands of employees worldwide. Its customers include both consumers and businesses for which the organization provides various products and services. Software is one of the key assets in the organization's service production and product development. Historically, the organization has had several independent business units targeted at diverging business sectors. In addition, the information management of the organization has been distributed to these business units and the functions of enterprise level information management have included mainly the provision of network infrastructure, enterprise level accounting, and basic office tools. Most of the information systems in use have been implemented and operated by the business units that have been quite independent in their decisions concerning strategies for information management. However, recent developments in markets and technology have led the organization to set its strategies to a more integrative direction. For this reason, the organization has set an objective to provide an integrated e-business solution to both its consumer and business customers. This will include both implementation of a uniform Web-based customer interface and sufficient integration between the distributed operative back-end information systems, such as customer management and billing systems.

The research process followed the grounded theory method (Glaser & Strauss, 1967), which is a research method developed originally for social sciences by Glaser and Strauss in the 1960s and later developed and re-interpreted by the original authors (e.g., Glaser, 1978; Strauss & Corbin, 1990) and others (e.g., Locke, 2001; Martin & Turner, 1986). Grounded theory promotes inductive theory creation from the data. The objective is not to validate or test theories but to create one. The analysis process of the grounded theory is explicitly defined and consists of several coding phases. The coding starts from *open coding* in which any incident, slice, or element of the data may be given a conceptual label for the identification of commonalities. These commonalities are called *categories* and they are described in terms of their properties (Fernández, Lehmann, & Underwood, 2002). The coding continues with *axial coding* (Strauss & Corbin, 1990) or theoretical coding (Glaser, 1978), where relationships between the categories are resolved. The coding ends at *selective coding* (Strauss & Corbin, 1990) where the resulting theory is "densified" (Glaser,

1978) or a core category selected (Strauss & Corbin, 1990) and theory about that is described. The data collection is based on the notion of *theoretical sampling*, which means adjusting the data collection process according to the requirements of the emerging theory. The sources of data may be adjusted during the process and the data collection can be stopped whenever a state of *theoretical saturation* is achieved, meaning a situation where no additional data would further develop the categories and their properties.

In the study, we interviewed 19 participants of the ongoing e-business system architecture design project during 2002, first in January and February and then later in November and December. The interviewees included six system architects, five enterprise system managers, three project managers, two software development managers, one project leader, one system analyst, and one marketing manager. Table 1 describes their relationship to the e-business development project. The interviews lasted from 45 to 120 minutes and they were completely transcribed as text.

The interview themes of this study were adjusted during the data collection to reflect better the developing theoretical understanding of the researchers and the specific knowledge of the interviewees. The emphasis of the interviews changed according to the interviewee and the special knowledge in his or her possession. Because the data collection proceeded partly in parallel with the analysis, the emerging theory also caused changes in the emphasis of the interview themes. In grounded theory this kind of adaptation is called *theoretical sensitivity*, and for theory-building research this is considered legitimate because "investigators are trying to understand each case individually and in as much depth as feasible" (Eisenhardt, 1989, p. 539). Eisenhardt calls the process where the emergence of a new line of thinking causes the altering of data collection *controlled opportunism* "in which researchers take advantage of the uniqueness of a specific case and

Table 1. Interviewed persons and their roles

Role	Tasks	Interviews
System architect	Deals with technological solutions and architectural structures in the e-business development project	6
Enterprise system manager	Is responsible for a portfolio of systems and technologies that are used in a particular organization. Acts as a customer in the internal e-business development project or participates it as an expert.	5
Project manager	Manages resources and is responsible for the execution of a sub-project of the e-business development project	3
Software development manager	Is responsible for a permanent software development organization	2
Project leader	Manages the e-business development super-project and supervises its set of sub-projects.	1
System analyst	Participates the requirements gathering and analysis phases as an intermediate between customers and technical experts.	1
Marketing manager	Is responsible for the public image and services of the electronic channel. Requirements setter and a customer to the development project.	1

the emergence of new themes to improve resultant theory" (Eisenhardt, 1989, p. 539).

The analysis in this study started with the open coding phase. In the beginning, we did not have any explicit *a priori* constructs for the analysis. Our task was to search mentions from the interviews that could be interpreted as meaningful related to the research question, "What are the conditions and constraints for creating and designing architecture in a large information systems development project?" The identified mentions related to this question were categorized using the software tool ATLAS.ti. During the open coding phase, altogether 187 emergent categories were found, and the categories were assigned to emerging scheme of super categories or category families, including for instance changes, conflicts, consequences, experiences, problems, purposes, and solutions occurring during the e-business architecture design and implementation process.

The axial coding started in parallel with the open coding and causal relationships between categories were recorded with Atlas.ti's semantic network capability. Figure 1 shows an example of such a network diagram. In the figure, the boxes

represent categories, the arrows between them interpreted causalities, and the lines associations between categories. The number of categories and the number of identified relationships between the categories added up to 187 categories and 200 relationships, which created a problem of how to report such a multitude of categories and relationships. The solution was sought through abstracting out those categories that were rarely occurring in the data and interpreted as not so relevant regarding the research question. In addition, more attention was paid to those categories that occurred frequently in the data.

Inductively, we produced an explaining story to the events and forces under which the e-business development project had to work. The organization is facing market changes and changing the organization according to the changing markets. The objectives for the e-business development emerge from these changes and because the change is continuous and it brings all the time new requirements for the e-business system, the objectives are quite fluctuating. In addition, the history and legacy structures of the organization cause conflicts and problems in the development

Figure 1. An example of a semantic network from axial coding

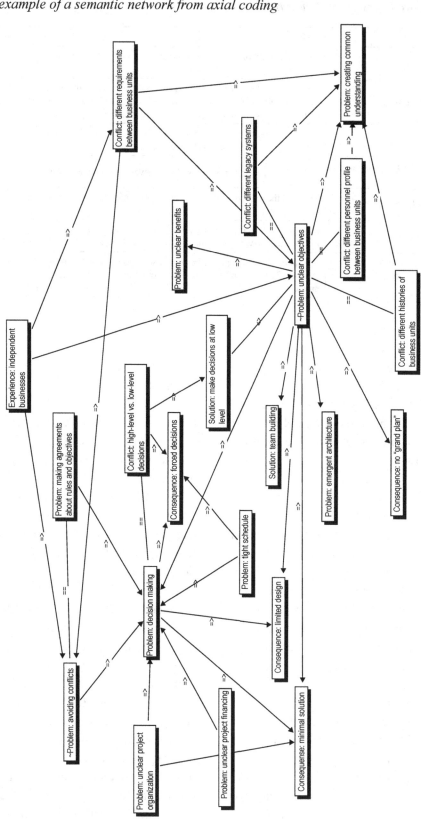

when combined with the need for change. These fluctuating objectives and emerging conflicts and problems brought certain consequences to the e-business architecture development in the organization. The formation and description of this explaining story can be considered as selective coding (Strauss & Corbin, 1990) and its details in the studied organization are explained in the next three sections.

The study has required extensive interpretation and exploration in the studied organization and therefore the main instruments of the research has been the researchers and their ability to interpret events and people's actions correctly. Robson (2002) lists three threats to validity in this kind of research, reactivity (the interference of the researcher's presence), researcher bias, and respondent bias, and strategies that reduce these threats. We have used these strategies in the following way:

- **Prolonged involvement:** Although this study lasted for one year, the research project altogether lasted for more than two years in the same organization and consisted of several phases and data collection rounds.
- **Triangulation:** The study has used data and observer triangulation as presented by Denzin (1978). To reduce the bias caused by researchers, we used *observer triangulation*, because the data collection was done by two researchers. The bias caused by data was minimized using *data triangulation*, where different sources of data were used. Interviews were the primary data collection method, but we also received many kinds of project and company documents and architecture descriptions.
- **Peer debriefing and support:** The research has included regular meetings and discussions with involved research participants from several research institutions. In addition, preliminary results of research phases have been presented and discussed in con-

ferences and workshops (Smolander, 2003; Smolander, Hoikka, Isokallio et al., 2002; Smolander & Päivärinta, 2002a, 2002b; Smolander, Rossi, & Purao, 2002, 2005).
- **Member checking:** The interpretation of the data has been confirmed by presenting the results to company participants in the research project.
- **Audit trail:** All interviews have been recorded and transcribed. The notes and memos of the study have been preserved and data coding and analysis results are available through the analysis tool used, ATLAS.ti.

CHANGES AND THEIR EFFECTS IN THE DEVELOPMENT CONTEXT

Starting Point: Changing Markets, Changing Organization

During the time of the data collection, there was a considerable change going on in the ICT market and the organization under study had undergone a deep change. A few years ago, the strategies emphasized growth and utilization of the possibilities in the stock market. This enforced independent business units inside the organization since the growth was easier to handle through independency. Each of the business units built independent e-commerce solutions and customer extranets, which resulted to a fragmentary set of e-commerce solutions to customers with own Internet sites, sales and billing systems, and Web-based customer support.

When the beliefs in the possibilities of ICT sector's continuing growth diminished, the organization had to change its strategies from growth to profitability and from stock market to customer orientation. With independent business units, there was no authority in the organization, which would see a customer as a whole. Instead, each business unit kept track of the customers only in the context of its independent business. To produce a unified customer interface a profound change to the way of building information systems and an integrated e-business solution was needed. This change would also require changes in business practices and organization. The organization should operate in a more integrated fashion and the barriers between independent units should be lowered.

The organization began to see technical e-business architecture as an enabler of change. The IS organizations in independent business units were obliged to cooperate and enforce commitment to the integration of information systems. This also emphasized the role of central information management, which had been in a minor role this far. Now, its roles would include the enforcement of information systems integration and enabling the unification of the sales channels and customer management for the planned e-business solution. At this point, the organization decided to establish a working group of systems architects from various parts of the organization. In the following section, we shall describe the context and the forces under which this group of architects were developing and designing the unified e-business architecture.

Conflicts, Problems and Varying Purposes

The context for e-business architecture development included many issues, which the working group for technical architecture development had to face and be aware of. These included the market changes as described above, historical organizational inertia, fluctuating requirements and objectives, and conflicts and problems emerging from the market changes, inertia, and unclear objectives.

Historical Inertia

The organization's history with independent businesses and their diverging functions and objectives had both psychological and technical consequences causing slow progress and conflicts in the integrated e-business development. Each of the business units had legacy systems with incompatible information structures, technical architectures, and operating principles. It was not possible in practice to replace these systems with a uniform solution at once.

The historical inertia had effects also on the organization responsible for information management and information systems. Because of the independence, the organization had no clear central information management that could take responsibility of the e-business architecture development. Many of the conflicts and problems described later arose from this situation.

The Observed Objectives for the E-Business System

The fluctuating objectives, meanings, and requirements for the e-business architecture created another source of conflicts and problems. In a large organization with a high degree of independency, the conceptions among different business units and individuals about the purposes of an e-business solution vary considerably. Among the interviewees, we identified a large set of different purposes for the e-business system, which were then classified in five distinct classes:

- Creation of a unified electronic customer interface.
- Reduction of costs.
- Integration of information systems.
- Gaining business advantage.
- Implementing an organization change.

This list of observed purposes for the e-business system looks quite comprehensive and ambitious. Different interviewees emphasized the purposes differently and many saw that the only realistic objective was to implement a single sign-on procedure with a minimal level of customer information integration. The list anyhow shows the complicated and conflicting nature of objectives for the e-business system when it is developed for a large enterprise.

Emerging Conflicts and Problems

Changes in markets and organization, the history of the organization, and the complicated objectives for the e-business system put the architecture development group in a difficult situation. The group and its members were obliged to respond by some means and these responses shaped mitigated the role of deliberate design in the development process. In open coding, we identified in total 48 categories of conflicts and problems. This list was further combined to seven main categories, as follows:

- Varying requirements and unclear objectives
- Problems in the cooperation between technical and business people
- Conflict avoidance and problems in decision-making
- Problematic role of the central information management and its missing working practices
- Difficulties in creating common understanding about the architecture
- Difficulties in determining the level of integration
- Problems of implementing the integration

As described earlier, the purposes of the system were manifold and complicated and the requirements varied according to the business needs in the business units. The architects held this ambiguity of objectives and requirements as the biggest obstacle in the development. Those in the managerial level recognized the problem as well, but explained it as unavoidable in the situation and expected that the first prototypes of the system will bring more clarity to the objectives. This resembles

the chicken-egg problem: architects must know well the objectives to design the architecture, but the objectives are further clarified only after the first version of the architecture is built.

There were several mentions about the problems in the cooperation between technical and business people. Architects expected the business managers to explicate clear requirements and objectives for the system and its architecture. However, they considered the task impossible, because they thought that the business managers do not possess enough understanding about the possibilities of current technology. They felt that this leads to unrealistic objectives, which were manifested especially when considering the possibilities of legacy systems integration: people with business background had far more optimistic views than architects.

Conflict avoidance and problems in decision-making slowed the progress. Again, because of the history of independency, a central authority that could take care of the architectural decisions for the integrated e-business solution was missing. Because nobody took a full responsibility of the situation, this led to avoidance of conflicts and enforced the tendency towards compromises. A frequently occurring phrase among the architects included the term "lowest common denominator," which was usually noting to the compromised solution with a single sign-on procedure and a minimal level of customer information integration.

The role of the central information management was unclear and it was lacking the routine of large development efforts. The independency of businesses and the minor role of central information management had implications on the working practices. The architectural and development practices of the business units contained considerable differences implying that also common working practices needed to be established for the development process of the e-business system.

Even the understanding of the designed architecture and related technical solutions were difficult to communicate across the organization. Since the business units have had their own histories and produced their own legacy systems and information architectures, the interpretations on the situation and objectives diverged. This, combined with changing organization, unclear objectives, and missing common working practices, created difficulties in understanding and transferring architectural knowledge between the participants from different business units.

It was also difficult to determine the level of integration between the systems. The ownership of the information becomes an issue even in the most modest single sign-on e-business solution serving the whole organization. The question becomes, "who owns the customer information?" and relates to determining the integration level to the currently independent back-end legacy systems. The more ambitious integration, the more out-of-control the customer information (and possibly other information too) shifts from the business units.

In addition to determining the integration level, the actual implementation of integration proved to be problematic. Since the diverging legacy systems could not be replaced, they all had to be interfaced. Of the seven conflicts and problems occurring when creating e-business architecture, only the problem of implementing the integration was mainly a technical problem. The others were more related to the change in organization and practices that happen when developing an e-business system in a large organization with independent businesses. In the following, we shall look closer on what consequences these conflicts and problems cause for the architecture design and development process.

CONSEQUENCES: LIMITED DESIGNS AND MINIMAL SOLUTIONS

In the beginning of the project a unified architecture was seen as a panacea for solving the problems of systems integration, streamlining the organization and unifying the customer interface. However, during the project it became clear that the aforementioned conflicts and problems would have some unfavorable consequences. While it was of paramount importance for the company to be able to streamline its systems and develop a more coherent architecture enabling the creation of an e-business system, the realities of legacy systems and the organization led to situation where it was best to seek satisfying, even minimal, solutions instead of optimal ones.

In the early phases of the project architecture was seen as general blueprints or roadmaps, largely drawn from scratch. Soon, however, the technical experts realized that evolutionary prototyping was the only possibility for progress in the architecture development. Because the schedule was tight, the objectives and requirements unclear and changing, and because the business units were rather independent, it was hard to achieve common understanding and commitment. With prototyping, it would be possible to clarify objectives and commit stakeholders by showing them visible results and benefits. This could be seen as "extreme" architecture design (Merisalo-Rantanen, Tuunanen, & Rossi, 2005). This could however lead to new problems. The technically oriented architects were specially worried that, combined with the quarter-based reporting system in the organization, evolutionary prototyping can easily produce quick-and-dirty and ad hoc solutions. We could classify the interviewees to those with positive attitudes towards prototyping and to those with negative or doubtful attitudes. In general, the project management believed positively that "somehow" the prototypes would transform to the final e-business solution, whereas technical architects presented more doubts and wanted to have explicit requirements and objective statements before committing to certain architectural solutions.

Prototyping and minimal solutions formed a vicious circle that made the development of robust and clear architectures nearly impossible by severely limiting the options available for the architecture developers. Existing legacy systems, the evolutionary approach, varying requirements, unclear objectives, difficulties in creating common understanding, and problems in decision making created a complex situation where textbook methods, description languages, and rational architecture design, as it is conceived in the literature, had no possibilities for immediate success. The degrees of freedom of design became limited. The system and its architecture could not be designed rationally as a whole, but rather one needed to accept the conditions and limitations caused by the factors above and to keep the day to day operations running while the new systems are continuously created through evolution.

The situation had also organizational consequences. We found clear hints of low-level networking and formation of shadow organizations as the result of unclear project organization and problems of decision-making and objective setting. As the organization and responsibilities change, new and perhaps inexperienced persons come into crucial official positions related to the e-business development. At the same time, the experienced architects and other key persons continued to stay in contact with each other. This unofficial shadow organization balanced the mismatch in skills and experience that might otherwise seriously impede the development.

The final consequence from all the above is, that in fact the e-business architecture becomes emergent: it is created gradually through compromises, constraints, and conflicts (c.f., Ciborra, 2000; Hanseth, Monteiro, & Hatling, 1996). The exact objectives and responsibilities will be resolved as the architecture emerges through evolutionary prototyping. Compared to the conventional view on software architecture design (Hofmeister et al., 1999a), most of the claimed benefits of rigorous architecture development seem to be lost. There is no "grand plan" since the work is proceeding in a day-to-day basis and

the well defined responses and interfaces between systems do not necessarily emerge in a rationally planned way, but rather most duplicate functions are kept and there is agreement only on a few items that become the "architecture."

DERIVED REQUIREMENTS FOR E-BUSINESS SYSTEMS DEVELOPMENT METHODOLOGY

From the previous observations and explanations, we can derive a set of requirements that an e-business systems development methodology should meet. The grounded theory process resulted in an explanation model (Figure 2), from which a set of methodological requirements can be extracted. Changing markets and organization, historical inertia, and unclear objectives for the development produced a complex combination of conflicts and problems that brought various difficult consequences to the e-business development process. We analyzed the complex socio-technical situation and its consequences and reasoned the set of most pertinent methodological requirements. This was done by identifying and coding the methodological requirements in the interview transcripts and further combining them in 13 requirements as described below.

According to Lyytinen et al. a design methodology should conform to a set of key requirements (Lyytinen, Smolander, & Tahvanainen, 1989). It must embed several conceptual structures and description languages, and support several levels of abstraction at which the development process takes place. It should also cover the whole spectrum of activities in information systems development (ISD), include a prescribed model of activities to be carried out during the development process, include a model of the organizational form of the development (a set of human roles), and try to reuse existing descriptions and implementations. Tools for drawing, manipulating, and managing

Figure 2. Deriving the methodology requirements

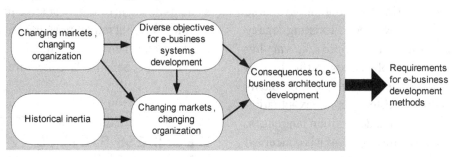

the descriptions should also support the methodology, in a balanced manner.

We can further elaborate this conception of ISD methodology by distinguishing between three separate contexts in ISD, namely the technical, language, and organization contexts (Lyytinen, 1987). The technical context is concerned with the technical components of the system (like hardware and software), language context forms the environment for linguistic communication, and the organization context provides the environment for systematic human interactions, including decision-making and operative control. An ISD methodology includes assumptions, models, languages, and tools related to these three contexts. In the following, we shall extract from the case the general requirements for e-business development methodology and classify them according to these contexts. The objective of this classification is to illustrate the nature and requirements of e-business architecture development in large organizations with several business areas and to highlight the areas with a weak methodical support.

Lyytinen commented already in 1987 that most development methodologies have too limited scope and they tend to concentrate on technological issues late in the development lifecycle (Lyytinen, 1987). This limited scope omits most of the institutional and governance issues which seemed to be central for most stakeholders according to this study on architectural practice.

One could argue that the organizational context is particularly relevant for e-business area, as most proponents of e-business emphasize the changes it brings about to work processes and organizations (Kalakota & Robinson, 2001).

The research into e-business architecture development is in a relatively immature stage. Previous literature has largely assumed that it solves technical issues for known problems (Taylor, McWilliam, Forsyth, & Wade, 2002). However, from the previous passages it has become obvious that methods for forming the problem statement and reaching a mutual agreement on what the architecture is in the end of the day are crucial. In this section, we take this as a starting point and observe the issues that rose in the described case starting from the inner, technical context and ending to the general organizational issues. This corresponds to Lyytinen's idea that the contexts are hierarchically ordered, because languages are presented by material carriers of technology context and language is needed for organized social action (Lyytinen, 1987). We identify e-architecture approaches in these areas and show how they propose solutions to the issues raised in our study.

In the following, we shall present the methodological requirements for each context. We also refer to the rows in Table 1 with the notation R1-R13.

Requirements from the Technology Context

Observed Requirements

The technical requirements of e-business development methods do not differ much from those of methods for traditional transaction-based information systems. E-business system development includes methodical requirements concerning e.g. distribution, error recovery, and networking, but those requirements can be met without a special "e-business support." A standard way to describe such technical solutions is of course required /R1/.

Integrated e-business architecture necessitates the integration of information systems in the organization and the rationalization of technology and development processes. Existing legacy systems will be integrated to the e-business functionality. This requires the selection of an integrative technology and the construction of development processes supporting the implementation of the integration. Because the integration is the basis and characteristic to e-business development, the development methodology should have specialized and usable techniques for describing information systems integration /R2/.

The key issue in the development of e-business systems is the keeping of the day-to-day operations running and at the same time implementing the integration between existing legacy systems and the new e-business functionality. This means that the nature of development is in many cases more analogous to a maintenance project than to a green-field development project. Current systems development methodologies and models of thought are mostly aimed at designing new systems instead of changing existing ones. This problem has been recognized before the advent of e-business, but it becomes more critical in the e-business development. From this we can derive a requirement that the development methodology for e-business

systems should support evolutionary approaches to architectures and systems /R3/.

Existing Solutions

Most research on e-business systems development in general, and e-business architecture in particular, concentrates on this view. Much of the support that UML and RUP or their derivatives provide seems to concentrate on this area. Component aware methodologies, such as the Catalysis extension to UML, seem suitable for e-business. In addition, there are UML 2.0 extensions, such as SysML (Object Management Group, 2006), that provide better support for technical architecture design. Bischler and Segev (Bichler et al., 1998) investigate the possibilities of component oriented approach for e-business. They take a technical viewpoint, and provide a useful listing of enabling technologies for e-business. An applicable standard in this area is the SysML extension to UML (Object Management Group, 2006). A work by Rossi & Schwabe (Rossi & Schwabe, 2000) uses patterns and frameworks as building blocks for e-business systems. This kind of approach could be particularly useful for a relatively well-specified domain, such as trade processes, which are assumed to be generic in nature. Baskerville & Pries-Heje see a relatively fixed architecture as a common ground, on top of which e-business systems can be built (Baskerville & Pries-Heje, 2001).

As mentioned earlier, in the e-business domain there are several layers of components available. The InterNCA architecture in (Lyytinen, Rose, & Welke, 1998) describes some of these and outlines needs for new breed of development methodologies, which would take into the account the particular problems of e-business systems development. Greunz & Stanoevska-Slabeva present an extension of UML, which can be used to realize systems on top of "media platform" architecture (Greunz & Stanoevska-Slabeva, 2002).

Requirements from the Language Context

The language context provides a means and an environment for linguistic communication which encompasses the use, nature, content, context and form of signs (Lyytinen, 1987). The methodology requirements coming from the language context deal with the ability of stakeholders to communicate successfully during the e-business architecture development process.

Observed Requirements

The chicken-egg problem between objectives and architecture becomes problematic in e-business development. To design a robust technical architecture, one must have clear objectives, and to select realistic objectives, one must understand the possibilities of the technical architecture. To overcome this problem, it is necessary to have a close cooperation between technical architects and those responsible of the business. This, however, induces a language problem. These groups often do not have a common language. To overcome the language problem, we need architecture description languages that business managers understand /R4/ and business descriptions that are explicit enough for technical people /R5/.

The problems of objectives and integration culminate on architecture design because the designs and prototypes related to technical architecture become the first concrete artifacts in the development showing implications of decisions to businesses and to the information management. Before architecture design, the plans and designs have been on the "PowerPoint presentation" level, showing ambiguous and general roadmaps and noble objectives. The more concrete the architecture becomes, the more various stakeholders become aware of the consequences, conflicts, and problems they will be facing. This leads to two distinct requirements for the development methodology: the methodology should take the development to a very concrete level (both politically and technically) very soon after the project initiation /R6/ and the architecture designs and descriptions (and their implications) should be approachable and intelligible by the various stakeholders participating the process /R7/.

Existing Solutions

As a description language, UML and its extensions offer a fairly strong support for engineering in the language context. Yet, there are very few articles describing these issues of having a common language in e-business area, but one could expect that methodologies used in other domains for participative processes and joint application development could be applied here (August, 1991). In this context, architecture serves as a language between the participants in the development process, enabling communication and making the consequences of the implementation concrete to the participants. Using architecture as an enabler of communication between a diverse set of participants (including various levels of management and technical experts) requires informal and expressive approaches, which are practically non-existent in the field of software architecture research. This kind of conception of "architecture as language" can be associated with approaches that include rich and informal description techniques, like "rich pictures" in (Wood-Harper, 1985), the wall-charting technique (Saaren-Seppälä, 1988), and genre-based approaches (Päivärinta, Halttunen, & Tyrväinen, 2001).

Requirements from the Organization Context

Observed Requirements

These problems formed the largest bulk in our study. They included issues such as organizational inertia as well as environmental limitations, characteristics of a given business environment, codes of conduct in business, and regulatory and societal factors. These factors form together the 'ballpark' for an organization to act in relationship with its providers and customers.

The first organizational requirement comes from the overall conclusion of the case. The transition from heterogeneous e-commerce to integrated e-business is not only technically challenging. It is more a profound change to the organization. In fact, the primary challenge is in the change of the organization, not in the implementation of the technology. Therefore, e-business systems development methodology should support also the description of organizational change /R8/.

In this change of organization and implementation of technology, the role of central information management or some kind of central authority in the organization is crucial. The central authority should take care of the multitude of conflicts occurring when aiming at integration and coordinate the creation of objectives for the system. An e-business development methodology should enable the creation of a common vision /R9/, which can then be enforced by the central authority.

Evolution with modest but growing objectives may be the only way to develop integrated e-business systems. To foster commitment, some immediate benefits should be shown with the prototypes for each stakeholder. However, at the same time, the path to robust architecture should also be secured and enough time and resources must be given to technical architects. This very difficult and complex trade-off must be made in every e-business project /R10/.

The implementation of e-business integration deals not only with technical issues but also with difficult political ones. An organization shifting to integrated e-business must resolve issues concerning the internal ownership of information related for instance to customers, sales, contracts, and products. The ownership and responsibilities related to information must be decided and described during the development process. The development methodology should include descriptions for organizational responsibilities and ownership of information /R11/.

Identifying and agreeing about objectives became the most difficult problem in this case. Thus, to become valuable in practice, e-business development methodology should support not only the formation and recording of objectives but also measuring of success related to objectives /R12/.

The requirements directed to an e-business development organization are quite conflicting. On the other hand, the development requires a strong authority that can control the process through conflicts, and on the other hand, the formation of unofficial and shadow organization (peer-level networking) should be fostered to allow creative solutions and frictionless cooperation between businesses /R13/. This requirement is, however, not a new one when developing organizations.

Existing Solutions

From a more managerial and decision oriented view one could look at business- and strategy development methods, which aim at creation of a common understanding and vision of business strategy. This view sees building of architecture as a common vision building effort rather than a system building effort. It could also be argued that e-business architecture building is quite similar to organizational change processes, especially the introduction of enterprise wide information systems, such as ERP. Koontz has argued for this by presenting e-business architecture development model, which is very generic (Koontz, 2000).

Organizational issues are largely neglected by the traditional systems development methodologies, but form important context and frame for the implementation of the e-business systems and architectures. The work on organizational change and observation of the power-play could be fruitful if applied to early stages of architecture development. However, they do merely observe the issues than provide solutions. Checkland's SSM methodology is one of the few general-purpose methodologies that identifies and models the "essence" of the organizational idea of the system and then proceeds to actual development of the system (Checkland & Scholes, 1990). It is clear from the observations in this case study that the explicit identification and framing of the problem to be solved, and then resolving the actual goals of the architecture forms the basis for architecture development.

Most studies thus far seem to assume that the development of e-architecture and infrastructure can be guided by the deliberate actions and decisions of management. However, as can be seen here the technological changes often evolve from designers' and users' experience with such technologies and are often unpredictable (Ciborra, 2000).The problem of loosing the original target while developing partial solutions and prototypes (e.g., see R10) could be helped by explicitly recognizing emergent and opportunistic possibilities created on the process.

Summary of Issues

The list above shows that most solutions and research this far, has concentrated on the technical level. Unfortunately, most of the problems seem to be non-technical in nature, they are rather more of the linguistic or organizational. E-business cuts across functional borders in organization and is built on a complex infrastructure of ERP and legacy systems and it shares many of the challenges and opportunities of these organizational technologies.

Table 2 summarizes these derived requirements for e-business development methodology.

Table 2. Summary of the requirements for e-business development methodology

	Requirement	Type	Rationale	Support in RUP employing UML
R1	Technical issues (like distribution, error recovery, and networking) must be described in a standard way.	T	These issues will occur as in all modern systems development	Good; this is what UML and RUP are for
R2	Specialized techniques for describing the information systems integration	T	IS integration is characteristic to e-business development	Poor; no specialized technique for the description of integration in standard UML. Some UML 2.0 extensions are however available.
R3	The development methodology should support evolutionary approaches to architectures and systems.	L/T	The change and maintenance of existing systems forms a major part of the e-business systems development	Moderate; UML and RUP are mainly targeted at the development of new systems
R4	Architectural description languages that business managers understand	L	To enable realistic objective selection, business managers must have some understanding on architecture	Poor; the descriptions necessitate too much technical skills and knowledge
R5	Business descriptions that are explicit enough for technical people	L	To understand the objectives, technical people must have understanding on business	Moderate; no description techniques showing overall aggregate view

continued on following page

Table 2.continued

	Requirement	Type	Rationale	Support in RUP employing UML
R6	The methodology should take the development to a very concrete level (both politically and technically) soon after the project initiation	T/L/O	The more architecture becomes concrete, the more stakeholders become aware of the consequences, conflicts, and problems	Good (technically), none (politically)
R7	The architecture designs and descriptions (and their implications) should be approachable and intelligible by the various stakeholders participating the process	L/O	To enable wide understanding to the consequences of architectural selections (cf. R4).	Moderate; no relevant description technique besides Use Case diagrams
R8	Support for the description of organizational change	O	e-business involves deep changes to organization	Poor; some thoughts of "organization engineering" in RUP's Business Architecture
R9	Support for the description of a common vision	O	Resolve conflicts, build objectives	Poor; no common language for all stakeholders
R10	Both prototyping and careful architecture design needed	T	Gain commitment and resolve objectives through prototyping, aim at robust architecture	Moderate; iterative basis in RUP, but its implementation is difficult in practice
R11	Methodology should contain descriptions for organizational responsibilities and ownership of information	L/O	The ownership of information becomes an issue when aiming at e-business integration	Poor; only general thoughts
R12	e-business development methodology should support the formation and recording of objectives and measuring of success related to objectives	L/O	Identifying and agreeing about objectives is one of the most difficult issues in e-business development	Poor; the objectives are mostly supposed to be given to the development project
R13	The development process should support organizationally both effective control structures and flexibility	O	Strong authority is needed to handle the conflicts and unofficial structures for creative solutions	Poor; development organization "design" in a general level

The requirements and their rationale are described in the text above. The 'Type' column places the requirement to the appropriate context or contexts (T: technology, L: language, O: organizational). The last column in the table ("Support in RUP employing UML") analyzes how unified modeling language (Object Management Group, 2005) and the Unified Process (Rational Software Corporation, 2001) support the e-business specific characteristics of the development process. This is important, because UML and RUP together form the current methodological basis for many software organizations. The column shows that the support is generally poor. The e-business specific requirements are not met by UML and RUP —only the standard technical issues are well covered. This conclusion calls for method development supporting better these e-business specific requirements.

Figure 3. Support and requirements

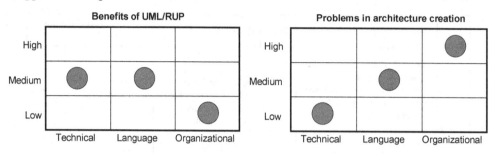

In the technical context we noted that e-business development would benefit from method enhancements in IS integration and evolutionary development. However, the language and especially the organization context appeared to have more importance in the development. In the language context, there was an urgent need for more understandable and concrete architecture descriptions that could be used among many groups involved in the process, including technical and non-technical people. The organization context appeared as the most important target for research and practical methodical improvements. In that context, we could identify a multitude of issues requiring improvements, including better understanding and usable methods for the design and implementation of organization change, organizational vision, organizational ownership of information, and organizational responsibilities.

Figure 3 shows concisely our findings. When creating e-business or enterprise architecture, the major problems to be solved are organizational. This does not align with the support that UML and RUP provides, because they mostly concentrate on solving the problems in the language and technical contexts. It is the task of future research to provide improvements to this, but, as can be seen from Table 2, it might need quite radical extensions or changes to UML and RUP to be able to support effectively the formation of e-business architecture.

CONCLUSION

We have described a process where a large ICT company is building architecture for a comprehensive e-business system. From the case, we extracted 13 requirements for methodology supporting integrated e-business systems development and classified the requirements to technology, language, and organization contexts. We also compared the requirements to the support that UML and RUP offers and concluded that the e-business specific requirements are not met in UML and RUP. Successful e-business development requires alternative approaches that support better organization change, communication between stakeholders, systems integration, objective formation, and evolutionary development.

In our study, architecture manifested itself as a catalyst that makes business and organizational conflicts and problems concrete. When making decisions about architecture, the systems architects had to take into account the organizational situation in the company. At the same time the architecture starts shaping and changing the organization, thus forming a double mangle (e.g., Jones, 1998). The architects also realized that technical rationality is not enough for success in this kind of a situation. To succeed in e-business architecture development, one has to be aware of the political and organizational forces that are driving the development and its objectives. E-business architecture development can therefore be characterized as a process of seeking boundaries, finding sufficient consensus, and identifying commonalities across organizational borders. Most previous literature on architectural methods has neglected this and sought to develop description languages for describing the actual architectures for systems with clear problem statements, whereas we claim that it would be more important to seek tools that aid in building common understanding about the system and its architecture and tools for processing the emerging conflicts. Thus, we maintain that the field of architecture for e-business would benefit from tools that help to identify and process the emerging conflicts than tools that aid in developing a technically "perfect" and optimized solution. These tools could be used in early phases of development to augment UML and RUP based tools. Examples of such tools are group support systems and different participation facilitation systems. Thus we do not call for replacing UML, but rather adding tools that can be used to communicate with nontechnical people about the architecture.

ACKNOWLEDGMENT

We would like to thank the anonymous reviewers of this paper for their valuable instructions and especially the reviewer that gave us the simple idea of Figure 3.

REFERENCES

August, J. H. (1991). *Joint application design: The group session approach to system design.* Englewood Cliffs, NJ: Yourdon Press.

Baskerville, R., & Pries-Heje, J. (2001, July 27-29). *Racing the e-bomb: How the internet is redefining information systems development methodology.* Proceedings of the IFIP TC8/WG8.2 Working Conference on Realigning Research and Practice in Information Systems Development: The So-cial and Organizational Perspectice (pp. 49-68). Boise, Idaho.

Bichler, M., Segev, A., & Zhao, J. L. (1998). Component-based e-commerce: Assesment of current practices and future directions. *SIGMOD Record, 27*(4), 7-14.

Checkland, P. B., & Scholes, J. (1990). *Soft system methodology in action.* Chichester: John Wiley and Sons.

Ciborra, C. (2000). Drifting: From control to drift. In K. Braa, C. Sorensen & B. Dahlbom (Eds.), *Planet internet.* Lund: Studentlitteratur.

Conallen, J. (1999). Modeling web application architectures with UML. *Communications of the ACM, 42*(10), 63-70.

D'Souza, D. F., & Wills, A. C. (1998). *Objects, components, and frameworks with UML: The catalysis approach:* Addison-Wesley.

Dashofy, E. M., Van der Hoek, A., & Taylor, R. N. (2005). A comprehensive approach for the development of modular software architecture description languages. *ACM Transactions on Software Engineering and Methodology, 14*(2), 199-245.

Denzin, N. K. (1978). *The research act: A theoretical introduction to sociological methods:* McGraw-Hill.

Dori, D. (2001). Object-process methodology applied to modeling credit card transactions. *Journal of Database Management, 12*(1), 4.

Egyed, A., & Medvidovic, N. (1999, Oct). *Extending Architectural Representation in UML with View Integration.* Proceedings of the 2nd International Conference on the Unified Modelling Language (UML), (pp. 2-16). Fort Collins, CO.

Eisenhardt, K. M. (1989). Building theories from case study research. *Academy of Management Review, 14*(4), 532-550.

Fernández, W. D., Lehmann, H., & Underwood, A. (2002, June 6-8). *Rigour and relevance in studies of IS innovation: A grounded theory methodology approach*. Proceedings of the European Conference on Information Systems (ECIS) 2002, (pp. 110-119).Gdansk, Poland.

Garlan, D., & Kompanek, A. J. (2000). *Reconciling the needs of architectural description with object-modeling notations*. Proceedings of the Third International Conference on the Unified Modeling Language - UML 2000, (pp. 498-512). York, UK.

Glaser, B. (1978). *Theoretical sensitivity: Advances in the methodology of grounded theory*. Mill Valley: Sociology Press.

Glaser, B., & Strauss, A. L. (1967). *The discovery of grounded theory: Strategies for qualitative research*. Chigago: Aldine.

Greunz, M., & Stanoevska-Slabeva, K. (2002). *Modeling business media platforms*. 35th Annual Hawaii International Conference on System Sciences, Maui, HI.

Grinter, R. E. (1999). Systems architecture: Product designing and social engineering. *ACM SIGSOFT Software Engineering Notes, 24*(2), 11-18.

Hanseth, O., Monteiro, E., & Hatling, M. (1996). Developing information infrastructure: The tension between standardization and flexibility. *Science, Technology & Human Values, 21*(4), 407-426.

Hirschheim, R., & Klein, H. K. (1989). Four paradigms of information systems development. *Communications of the ACM, 32*(10), 1199-1216.

Hofmeister, C., Nord, R., & Soni, D. (1999a). *Applied software architecture*. Reading, MA: Addison-Wesley.

Hofmeister, C., Nord, R., & Soni, D. (1999b). *Describing software architecture with UML*.

Proceedings of the First Working IFIP Conference on Software Architecture (WICSA1), (pp. 145-160). San Antonio, TX.

Jacobson, I., Booch, G., & Rumbaugh, J. (1999). *The unified software development process*. New York: Addison-Wesley.

Jones, M. (1998). *Information Systems and the Double Mangle: Steering a Course Between the Scylla of Embedded Structure and the Charybdis of Strong Symmetry*. IFIP WG8.2/8.6 Joint Working Conference, Helsinki, Finland.

Kalakota, R., & Robinson, M. (2001). *e-Business 2.0: Roadmap for Success*: Addison-Wesley.

Kazman, R., Klein, M., & Clements, P. (2000). *ATAM: Method for Architecture Evaluation* (Technical report No. CMU/SEI-2000-TR-004): Software Engineering Institute.

Kim, Y.-G., & Everest, G. C. (1994). Building an IS architecture: Collective wisdom from the field. *Information & Management, 26*(1), 1-11.

Koontz, C. (2000). Develop a solid e-commerce architecture. *e-Business Advisor*(January).

Kuntzmann, A., & Kruchten, P. (2003). The rational unified process—an enabler for higher process maturity. Retrieved April 19, 2007 from http://www-128.ibm.com/developerworks/rational/library/content/03July/0000/0579/Rational_CMM_WhitePaper.pdf.

Leist, S., & Zellner, G. (2006, April 23-27). *Evaluation of current architecture frameworks*. SAC'06, (pp. 1546-1553). Dijon, France.

Locke, K. (2001). *Grounded theory in management research*: SAGE Publications.

Lyytinen, K. (1987). A taxonomic perspective of information dystems fevelopment: Theoretical constructs and recommendations. In R. J. Boland, Jr. & R. A. Hirschheim (Eds.), *Critical issues in information systems research* (pp. 3-41): John Wiley & Sons.

Lyytinen, K., Rose, G., & Welke, R. (1998). The brave new world of development in the internetwork computing architecture (InterNCA): Or how distributed computing platforms will change systems development. *Information Systems Journal, 8*(3), 241-253.

Lyytinen, K., Smolander, K., & Tahvanainen, V.-P. (1989). *Modelling CASE environments in systems development.* Proceedings of CASE'89 the First Nordic Conference on Advanced Systems Engineering, Stockholm.

Martin, P. Y., & Turner, B. A. (1986). Grounded theory and organizational research. *The Journal of Applied Behavioral Science, 22*(2), 141-157.

Medvidovic, N., Egyed, A., & Rosenblum, D. S. (1999). *Round-trip software engineering using UML: From architecture to design and back.* Proceedings of the 2nd Workshop on Object-Oriented Reengineering (WOOR), Toulouse, France, Sept. 1999, 1-8.

Medvidovic, N., & Taylor, R. N. (2000). A classification and comparison framework for software architecture description languages. *IEEE Transactions on Software Engineering, 26*(1), 70-93.

Merisalo-Rantanen, H., Tuunanen, T., & Rossi, M. (2005). Is extreme programming just old wine in new bottles: A comparison of two cases. *Journal of Database Management, 16*(4), 41.

Monroe, R. T., Kompanek, A., Melton, R., & Garlan, D. (1997). Architectural styles, design patterns, and objects. *IEEE Software, 14*(1), 43-52.

Object Management Group. (1999). *UML Profile for Enterprise Distributed Object Computing: Request for Proposals (ad/99-03-10)*: OMG.

Object Management Group. (2005). *Unified modeling language: Superstructure version 2.0* (No. formal/05-07-04).

Object Management Group. (2006). *OMG SysML Specification (ptc/06-05-04).*

Päivärinta, T., Halttunen, V., & Tyrväinen, P. (2001). A genre-based method for information system planning. In M. Rossi & K. Siau (Eds.), *Information modeling in the new millennium* (pp. 70-93). Hershey, PA: Idea Group.

Rational Software Corporation. (2001). Rational Unified Process [Online documentation, Version 2001A.04.00].

Robson, C. (2002). *Real world research, (2ⁿᵈ ed.).* Blackwell Publishing.

Ross, J. W., Weill, P., & Robertson, D. C. (2006). *Enterprise architecture as strategy: Creating a foundation for business execution*: Harvard Business School Press.

Rossi, G., & Schwabe, D. (2000). Object-oriented web applications modeling. In M. Rossi & K. Siau (Eds.), *Information modelling in the next millennium.* Hershey: IDEA Group Publishing.

Rumpe, B., Schoenmakers, M., Radermacher, A., & Schürr, A. (1999). *UML + ROOM as a Standard ADL.* Fifth IEEE International Conference on Engineering of Complex Computer Systems, (pp. 43-53).

Saaren-Seppälä, K. (1988). *Wall chart technique: The use of wall charts for effective planning.* Helsinki: Kari Saaren-Seppälä Ky.

Sauer, C., Southon, G., & Dampney, C. N. G. (1997). *Fit, failure, and the house of horrors: Toward a configurational theory of IS project failure.* Proceedings of the eighteenth international conference on Information systems, (pp. 349-366). Atlanta, Georgia.

Shaw, M., & Garlan, D. (1996). *Software architecture: Perspectives on an emerging discipline*: Prentice Hall.

Siau, K. & Cao, Q. (2001). Unified modeling language (UML) — a complexity analysis. *Journal of Database Management, 12*(1), 26-34.

Siau, K., Erickson, J., & Lee, L. Y. (2005). Theoretical vs. practical complexity: The case of UML. *Journal of Database Management, 16*(3), 40-57.

Smolander, K. (2003, January 6-9,). *The birth of an e-business system architecture: Conflicts, compromises, and gaps in methods.* Hawaii International Conference on System Sciences (HICSS'36), Hilton Waikoloa Village, Big Island, Hawaii.

Smolander, K., Hoikka, K., Isokallio, J., Kataikko, M., & Mäkelä, T. (2002, April, 8-11). *What is included in software architecture? A case study in three software organizations.* Proceedings of 9th annual IEEE International Conference and Workshop on the Engineering of Computer-Based Systems (pp. 131-138). (ECBS) 2002, Lund, Sweden.

Smolander, K., & Päivärinta, T. (2002a, May 27 - 31). *Describing and communicating software architecture in practice: Observations on stakeholders and rationale.* Proceedings of CAiSE'02 - The Fourteenth International Conference on Advanced Information Systems Engineering, (pp. 117-133).Toronto, Canada.

Smolander, K., & Päivärinta, T. (2002b, Aug 25-30). *Practical rationale for describing software architecture: Beyond programming-in-the-large.* Software Architecture: System Design, Development and Maintenance - IFIP 17th World Computer Congress - TC2 Stream / 3rd Working IEEE/IFIP Conference on Software Architecture (WICSA3), (pp. 113-126). Montréal, Québec, Canada.

Smolander, K., Rossi, M., & Purao, S. (2002, December 18). *Software architecture: Metaphors across contexts.* AIS Theory Development Workshop, Barcelona.

Smolander, K., Rossi, M., & Purao, S. (2005, May 26-28). *Going beyond the blueprint: Unraveling the complex reality of software architectures.* 13th European Conference on Information Systems: Information Systems in a Rapidly Changing Economy, Regensburg, Germany.

Sowa, J. F., & Zachman, J. A. (1992). Extending and formalizing the framework for information systems architecture. *IBM Systems Journal, 31*(3), 590-616.

Star, S. L., & Griesemer, J. R. (1989). Institutional cology, "translations" and boundary objects: Amateurs and professionals in berkeley's museum of vertebrate zoology, 1907-39. *Social Studies of Science, 19*, 387-420.

Strauss, A. L., & Corbin, J. (1990). *Basics of qualitative research: Grounded theory procedures and applications.* Newbury Park, CA: Sage Publications.

Taylor, M. J., McWilliam, J., Forsyth, H., & Wade, S. (2002). Methodologies and website development: A survey of practice. *Information and Software Technology, 44*(6), 381-391.

Wood-Harper, T. (1985). Research methods in information systems: Using action research. In E. Mumford, R. A. Hirschheim, G. Fitzgerald & T. Wood-Harper (Eds.), *Research methods in information systems.* New York: North-Holland Publishers.

Chapter 5
Evaluation of MDE Tools from a Metamodeling Perspective

João de Sousa Saraiva
INESC-ID/Instituto Superior T'ecnico, Portugal

Alberto Rodrigues da Silva
INESC-ID/Instituto Superior T'ecnico, Portugal

ABSTRACT

Ever since the introduction of computers into society, researchers have been trying to raise the abstraction level at which we build software programs. We are currently adopting an abstraction level based on graphical models instead of source code: MDE. MDE is the driving force for some recent modeling languages and approaches, such as OMG's UML or Domain-Specific Modeling. All these approaches are founded on metamodeling: defining languages that represent a problem-domain. A key factor for the success of any approach is appropriate tool support. However, only recently have tool creators started considering metamodeling as an important issue in their list of concerns. In this paper, we evaluate a small set of MDE tools from the perspective of the metamodeling activity, focusing on both architectural and practical aspects. Then, using the results of this evaluation, we discuss open research issues for MDE-based software development tools.

INTRODUCTION

Ever since the appearance of computers, researchers have been trying to raise the abstraction level at which software developers write computer programs. Looking at the history of programming languages, we have witnessed this fact, with languages evolving from raw machine code to machine-level languages, afterward to procedural programming languages, and finally to object-oriented languages, which allow developers to write software by mapping real-world concepts into modular segments of code (called objects). Still, object-oriented languages are too "computing-oriented" (Schmidt, 2006), abstracting over the solution domain (computing technologies) instead of the problem domain.

Currently, the abstraction level is being raised into the model-driven engineering (MDE) paradigm (Schmidt, 2006). In this abstraction level, models are considered first-class entities and become the backbone of the entire MDE-oriented software development process; other important artifacts, such as code and documentation, can be produced automatically from these models, relieving developers from issues such as underlying platform complexity or the inability of third-generation languages to express domain concepts.

MDE is not a new idea. Already in the 1980s and 1990s, computer-aided software engineering (CASE) tools were focused on supplying developers with methods and tools to express software systems using graphical general-purpose language representations. The developer would then be able to perform different tasks over those representations, such as correction analysis or transformations to and from code. However, these CASE tools failed due to issues such as (a) poor mapping of general-purpose languages onto the underlying platforms, which made generated code much harder to understand and maintain, (b) the inability to scale because the tools did not support concurrent engineering, and (c) code was still the first-class entity in the development process while models were seen as only being suited for documentation (Schmidt, 2006). Currently, there are better conditions for such modeling tools to appear. Software systems today are reaching such a high degree of complexity that third-generation languages simply are not sufficient anymore; another abstraction level over those languages is needed. This need, combined with the choices of IT development platforms currently available (Java, .NET, etc.), to which models can be somewhat easily mapped, is the motivation for the adoption of MDE. There are already a few MDE-related case studies available, such as Zhu et al. (2004) and Fong (2007), but since most MDE work is still in the research phase, there is

still a lack of validation through a variety of real business case studies.

There are already multiple MDE initiatives, languages, and approaches, such as the unified modeling language (UML), the MetaObject Facility (MOF), the model-driven architecture (MDA), and domain-specific modeling (DSM) (Kelly & Tolvanen, 2008). There are also other derivative approaches, such as software factories (http://msdn2.microsoft.com/en-us/teamsystem/aa718951.aspx) that follow the MDE paradigm. Nevertheless, it is important to note that these initiatives are not a part of MDE; rather, MDE itself is a paradigm that is independent of language or technology, and is addressed by these initiatives.

All these approaches share the same basic concepts. A model is an interpretation of a certain problem domain, a fragment of the real world over which modeling and system development tasks are focused, according to a determined structure of concepts (Silva & Videira, 2005). This structure of concepts is provided by a metamodel, which is an attempt at describing the world around us for a particular purpose through the precise definition of the constructs and rules needed for creating models (*Metamodel.com*, n.d.). These basic concepts are the core of metamodeling, the activity of specifying a metamodel that will be used to create models, which is the foundation of MDE.

From the developer's point of view, a key issue for acceptance of any approach is good tool support so that software programs can be created in an easy and efficient manner. There is a wide variety of modeling tools available today, covering most modeling standards and approaches in existence. For example, Rational Rose and Enterprise Architect (EA)(SparxSystems, n.d.) are only two examples of a very long list of tools that support UML modeling. DSM has recently become popular with the developer community, with tools such as Microsoft's DSL Tools (MSD-SLTools) or MetaCase's MetaEdit+.

The aim of this article is to present our evaluation framework for tool support of the metamodeling activity, and to evaluate a small set of tools according to this framework; although these tools do not reflect everything that is currently available in MDE tools, they address the MDE-based approaches presented in this article by providing the features typically found in tools of their corresponding approach. The evaluation framework used in this article focuses on the following issues: (a) supported exchange formats, (b) support for model transformation and code generation, (c) tool extensibility techniques, (d) the logical levels that can be manipulated, (e) support for specifying metamodel syntax and semantics, and (f) complexity of the meta-metamodel hard-coded into the tool. The final purpose of this evaluation is to determine the strengths and weaknesses of the support that each of these MDE tools offer to the developer's tasks.

This article is divided as follows. The second section presents a brief overview of MDE and some related concepts, standards, and approaches. Then the article describes the evaluation framework, the selected modeling tools, and the results of their evaluation. Next it discusses the current status of MDE-based software tools and some open research issues for metamodeling. The final section presents the conclusions of this work.

MODEL-DRIVEN ENGINEERING

Software systems are reaching such a high degree of complexity that the current third-generation programming languages (like Java or C#) are not sufficiently adequate to create such systems in an easy and efficient manner. One of the problems with current programming languages is that they are still too oriented toward specifying how the solution should work instead of what the solution should be. This leads to a need for mechanisms and techniques that allow the developer to abstract over current programming languages and focus on creating a good solution to a certain problem.

Model-driven engineering (sometimes called model-driven development, or MDD) is an emerging paradigm based on the systematic use of models as first-class entities of the solution specification (Schmidt, 2006). Unlike previous software development paradigms based on source code as a first-class entity, models become first-class entities, and artifacts such as source code or documentation can then be obtained from those models.

It is very important to note that, although MDE is often mentioned alongside MDA (which is explained further later), MDE does not depend on MDA, nor is MDA a subset of MDE. In fact, MDA is one of several initiatives that intend to address the MDE paradigm.

The OMG's Approach to MDE

The Object Management Group (OMG) has created its own MDE initiative based on a set of OMG standards that make use of techniques for metamodeling and model transformation.

Unified Modeling Language

UML (http://www.omg.org/cgi-bin/apps/doc?formal/05-07-04.pdf), currently in Version 2.1.1, is a general-purpose modeling language originally designed to specify, visualize, construct, and document information systems. UML is traditionally used as a metamodel (i.e., developers create models using the language established by UML). However, the UML specification also defines the profile mechanism, which allows for new notations or terminologies, providing a way to extend metaclasses to adapt them for different purposes. Profiles are collections of stereotypes, tagged values, and constraints (Silva & Videira, 2005). A stereotype defines additional element properties, but these properties must not contradict the properties that are already associated with the model element; thus, a profile does not allow the user to edit the metamodel.

Although UML was definitely a step forward in setting a standard understood by the whole software engineering community and aligning it toward MDE, it is still criticized for reasons such as (a) being easy to use in software-specific domains (such as IT or telecom-style systems) but not for other substantially different domains, such as biology or finance (Thomas, 2004), (b) not being oriented to how it would be used in practice (Henderson-Sellers, 2005), and (c) being too complex (Siau & Cao, 2001). Nevertheless, UML is often the target of overzealous promotion, which raises user expectations to an unattainable level; the criticisms that follow afterward are usually influenced by this (France, Ghosh, Dinh-Trong, & Solberg, 2006). An example of such a criticism is the one regarding the difficulty in using UML to model non-software-related domains: Although UML is a general-purpose modeling language, it is oriented toward the modeling of software systems and is not intended to model each and every domain.

MetaObject Facility

MOF (http://www.omg.org/cgi-bin/apps/doc?formal/06-01-01.pdf), currently in Version 2.0, is the foundation of OMG's approach to MDE. UML and MOF were designed to be themselves instances of MOF. This was accomplished by defining the UML Infrastructure Library (http://www.omg.org/cgi-bin/apps/doc?formal/05-07-05.

pdf), which provides the modeling framework and notation for UML and MOF, and can also be used for other metamodels. Figure 1 illustrates the dependencies between UML and MOF; note that MOF can be described using itself, making it reflexive (Nóbrega, Nunes, & Coelho, 2006). Besides UML, the OMG has also defined some other MOF-based standards, such as the XML (extensible markup language) metadata interchange (XMI) and query-views-transformations (QVT).

XMI allows the exchange of metadata information by using XML, and it can be used for any metadata whose metamodel can be specified in MOF. This allows the mapping of any MOF-based metamodel to XML, providing a portable way to serialize and exchange models between tools. Nevertheless, users often regard XMI as a last resort for exchanging models between tools because tools frequently use their own vendor-specific XMI extensions; thus they lose information when exchanging models between different tools. The QVT specification defines a standard way of transforming source models into target models by allowing the definition of the following operations: (a) queries on models, (b) views on metamodels, and (c) transformations of models. One of the most interesting ideas about QVT is that the transformation should itself be considered an MOF-based model, which means that QVT's syntax should conform to MOF. Figure 2 presents OMG's typical four-layer architecture: (a) MOF is

Figure 1. The dependencies between UML and MOF

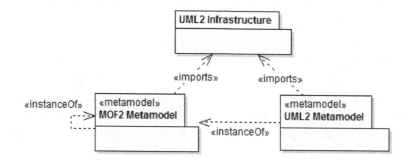

the meta-metamodel in the M3 layer, (b) UML, an instance of MOF, is the metamodel in the M2 layer, (c) the user model contains model elements and snapshots of instances of these model elements in the M1 layer, and (d) the M0 layer contains the runtime instances of the model elements defined in the M1 layer.

Model-Driven Architecture

MDA is OMG's framework for the software development life cycle driven by the activity of modeling the software system (Kleppe, Warmer, & Bast, 2003). It is based on other OMG standards such as UML, MOF, QVT, and XMI, and places a greater emphasis on UML model transformation techniques (through QVT) than on metamodeling itself; however, it should be noted that QVT model transformations are made possible only because

of the model-metamodel relationship between UML and MOF.

MDA defines two types of models (Kleppe et al., 2003): (a) the platform-independent model (PIM) and (b) the platform-specific model (PSM). A PIM is a model with a high level of abstraction that makes it independent of any implementation technology, making it suitable to describe a software system that supports a certain business without paying attention to implementation details (like specific relational databases or application servers). A PSM also specifies the system, but in terms of the implementation technology. A PIM can be transformed into one or more PSMs, each of those PSMs targeting a specific technology because it is very common for software systems today to make use of several technologies. Figure 3 presents an overview of MDA; the solid lines connecting the boxes are transformations, which are defined by transformation rules. MDA pre-

Figure 2. An example of OMG's four-layer metamodel architecture

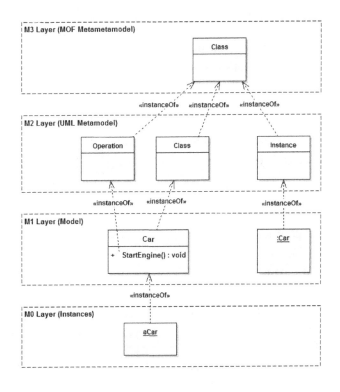

Figure 3. An overview of MDA

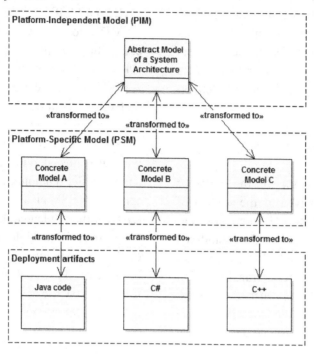

scribes the existence of transformation rules, but it does not define what those rules are; in some cases, the vendor may provide rules as part of a standard set of models and profiles.

MDA still faces some criticism in the software engineering community because of issues such as its usage of UML (Thomas, 2004) and the view that while current MDA generators are able to generate a significant portion of an application, they are not particularly good at building code that works within an existing code base.

Domain-Specific Modeling

DSM (Kelly & Tolvanen, 2008) uses problem-domain concepts as the basic building blocks of models unlike traditional CASE, which uses programming-language concepts. From a techno-logical perspective, DSM is supported by a DSM system, which can be considered as an application for making domain-specific CASE tools (or as a tool-building environment to create CASE tools

Figure 4. How CASE and DSM systems are related

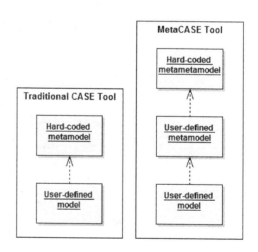

that can be used to produce applications). Thus, DSM adds an abstraction layer over traditional CASE, enabling the domain-specific configuration of the resulting modeling application as illustrated in Figure 4. Because of this, DSM systems are

Figure 5. Using the expertise of some developers to orient other developers toward the problem domain

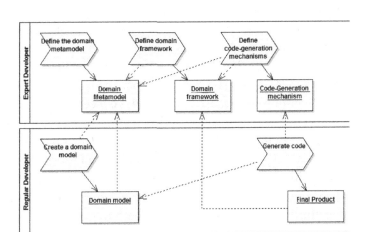

also called meta-CASE tools. DSM is closely related to the concept of domain-specific language (DSL). A DSL is a language designed to be useful for a specific task (or a specific set of tasks) in a certain problem domain unlike a general-purpose language (Kelly & Tolvanen). As Figure 5 illustrates, due to a DSL's highly specialized nature, DSLs and corresponding generators are usually specified by experts (i.e., experienced developers) in the problem domain; other developers, less experienced with the mapping between domain concepts and source code, will invoke the DSL in their own code. A well-known example of a DSL is the standard query language (SQL), which is a standard computer language for accessing and manipulating databases (so, SQL's problem domain is the domain of database querying and manipulation).

Developers usually prefer DSLs to UML because of the set of used concepts: The latter uses programming concepts directly, which places models at the same abstraction level as source code; a DSL uses concepts from the problem domain, which means developers do not need to worry about how those concepts will map to code.

UML itself can be seen as a set of DSLs (corresponding to use-case diagrams, class diagrams, activity diagrams, etc.); however, these would be dependent on each other in a "DSL spaghetti" manner. UML can also be used to define DSLs using the profile mechanism, although this does bring some limitations that DSLs do not, such as the ability to ignore the semantic constraints already defined in UML.

Metamodeling

The approaches presented lead us to the point where we can see that all concepts presented here are deeply related among themselves. We have a recurring pattern—the usage of metamodels and their instances of models—and the only real difference (in modeling terms) between all these approaches is in the number of layers each one uses. So, aside from a question of vocabulary, all these MDE-based variants have their foundation on the same topic: metamodeling.

But what is metamodeling? Metamodel.com (*Metamodel.com*, n.d.) provides the following definitions: "metamodeling is the activity that produces, among other things, metamodels" and "a metamodel is a precise definition of the constructs and rules needed for creating models." These definitions agree with other definitions that can be found in literature, such as the ones in Kleppe et al. (2003) and Söderstrom, Andersso, Johannesson, Perjons, & Wangler (2002). This means that a metamodel provides a language used to create a model, as Figure 6 illustrates; similarly, a metamodel that defines the language in which another metamodel is specified is called a meta-metamodel.

Similar in concept to DSM, metamodeling is about developing a language (a metamodel) adapted to the problem domain; for example, MOF is a language adapted to the domain of object-oriented approaches to modeling (Atkinson & Ku¨hne, 2005), while UML is a language adapted to the domain of object-oriented programming languages (OOPLs). A possible example, in the context of an organization, of what could be done with metamodeling can be the following: (a) the specification of a new language or metamodel (with an existing language as its metamodel, e.g., MOF or UML) that reflects the concepts, syntax, and semantics of the corresponding problem domain, which is the organization, (b) after creating a tool that supports the metamodel, the modeling of a solution using the organization's terms (e.g., the organization specifies a certain role R1 that can perform activities A1 and A2),

and (c) depending on the features provided by the tool, an application that implements the designed solution could be generated (either by model transformations, or by direct generation of source code). In fact, the PSMs for the MDA approach (oriented toward the implementation domain) can be obtained by using UML profiles tailored to an OOPL's concepts (such as C#'s class, struct, etc.). This would present an advantage over traditional development approaches as the solution would be created using the organization's terms instead of using implementation terms; we later present a more detailed view of how software development can be done combining metamodeling and model transformations. An example of the need of using metamodeling and metamodels can be found in Zhao and Siau (2007), which uses metamodels to handle the mediation of information sources.

The main difference (in modeling terms) between the presented modeling approaches is their number of modeling layers (i.e., model-metamodel relationships). Theoretically, the number of layers could be infinite, but any particular approach should have a specific number of layers; otherwise, its implementation would be impractical, if not impossible.

It is still rare to find a development tool that has explicit support for metamodel creation and/or configuration, which can be surprising if we consider that metamodeling is one of the found-

Figure 6. A metamodel defines a language used to create a model

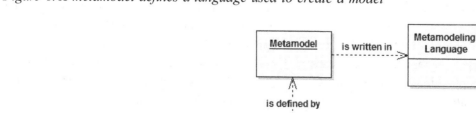

ing principles of MDE. This means that, until recently, a developer who wanted to use a certain metamodel would probably have to either (a) create a new modeling tool, which is not reasonable at all (Nobrega et al., 2006) or (b) settle on a CASE tool (with a hard-coded metamodel) that allows the developer to perform the desired task with the least possible hassle. However, adding metamodeling support to a tool does bring some practical issues that should be mentioned, such as (a) separating the OOPL class- instance relation from the metamodel-model relation, (b) deciding whether the number of logical levels should be limited or potentially unbounded, and (c) deciding whether the tool should support model transformation and/or code generation.

In addition to these issues, it is also necessary to consider how to change a metamodel, which should be considered a very high-risk activity because models, consistent in the context of a certain metamodel, can become inconsistent with only some changes to that metamodel. Obviously, this introduces a potential element of disruption that should be avoided at all costs. One possible way of ensuring the validity of existing models when changing their metamodels is through the specification and application of model transforma-

tions (e.g., UML transformations, such as those presented in Selonen, Koskimies, & Sakkinen, 2003): For any change to a metamodel, a corresponding transformation must be defined that receives the previously consistent models and produces new models consistent with the new metamodel.

However, in our research we have found no tool that addresses all of these metamodeling issues (although there are tools that address some of the presented issues).

Implementing a modeling tool with just one logical level (i.e., user model editing and a hard-coded metamodel) is easily done with current OOPLs using the class-instance relation: The logical level is implemented by the instance level. Metamodeling adds one (or more) logical level to the modeling tool, complicating the implementation as the instance level now has to hold two or more logical levels (Atkinson & Kühne, 2003). Level compaction (Atkinson & Kühne, 2005), an example of which is illustrated in Figure 7, is a technique that addresses this problem. Instead of the representation format for a level being defined by the level above, the format for a level is supplied by the modeling tool.

Figure 7. An example of using level compaction to compact three logical levels

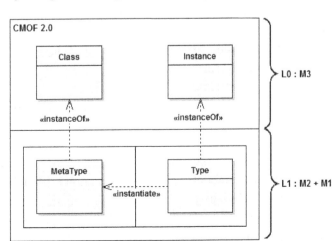

Although level compaction is essential for supporting multiple modeling levels, it is also important to determine whether the metamodel hard-coded into the tool allows such a number of levels. Atkinson and Kühne (2005) present the language and library metaphors, which allow tool creators to choose whether the number of layers in the tool's architecture should be restricted or potentially unbounded. When using the language metaphor, the basic elements of each layer (e.g., object, class, metaclass, etc.) are contained in the hard-coded metamodel itself; if the user wanted to add other basic elements, necessary for additional layers, it would be necessary to alter the hard-coded metamodel. This metaphor helps in supporting a standard (such as OMG's), but at the cost of not being able to edit the metamodel. On the other hand, in the library metaphor, the hard-coded metamodel consists only of a minimal core language, and the basic elements of each layer are available as predefined types in libraries to which the user can add elements (or remove them, if the tool allows it). With this metaphor, users can experiment with all metamodel layers because only the minimal core is hard-coded; the burden of syntax checking and language semantics is placed on the remaining metamodel layers. Note that if a tool does not use level compaction, then it obviously uses the language metaphor because the supported modeling levels are limited by the class-instance relation, which only allows one modeling level (in the instance level) besides the hard-coded metamodel (in the class level).

Another important aspect to consider in metamodeling tools are model-to-model transformations. It would be natural that, after some time using such a tool, a developer has created or adopted some languages adjusted to relevant problem domains. However, after modeling a solution using the problem-domain language, the developer would then need to re-create the model in the language of the target domain. Obviously this would render the first model useless. So, if the tool also provided some kind of framework or language for specifying transformations between model languages, this would certainly benefit the developer.

EVALUATION OF MDE TOOLS

One of the key issues for the success of MDE is appropriate tool support as developers will only use a certain approach if it is supported by available tools. This section first presents the evaluation framework used through the rest of this article. Afterward, we present the tools that are evaluated. Finally, the evaluation's results are presented.

Evaluation Framework

This subsection presents the proposed evaluation framework used in this article. This framework focuses on a tool's support for metamodeling and involves the following dimensions, as illustrated in Figure 8:

1. supported exchange formats,
2. model transformation support,
3. usage of the level-compaction technique (Atkinson & Kühne, 2005),
4. usage of the language and library metaphors (Atkinson & Kühne, 2005),
5. the logical levels that the user can manipulate,
6. support for specifying metamodel syntax and semantics, and
7. the size of the hard-coded meta-metamodel.

The third and fourth dimensions were directly based on the conceptual framework defined in Atkinson and Kühne (2005); the other dimensions are derived from the issues described in the previous section ("Model-Driven Engineering") since this evaluation also tries to focus on the practical usage of these tools instead of exclusively considering architectural details. Note

Figure 8. An overview of the proposed evaluation framework

Dimension		Measurement range	Observations
Supported standard exchange formats	Metamodels	Set of standards (possibly None)	Measure can only be either a combination of standards, or None
	Models		
Model transformation framework		Yes, No	Values are mutually exclusive
Level Compaction		Yes, No	Values are mutually exclusive
Language and Library metaphors		Language metaphor, Library metaphor	Values are mutually exclusive: If *Level Compaction* is *No*, value is *Language metaphor*
Number of levels the user can manipulate		Set of natural numbers	Values are mutually exclusive
Support for metamodel specification	Syntax / Supports specification	Yes, No	Values are mutually exclusive.
	Syntax / Languages used	Set of languages (possibly None)	Measure can only be either a combination of languages, or None: If "*Supports specification*" is *No*, this should be empty
	Semantics / Supports specification	Yes, No	Values are mutually exclusive
	Semantics / Languages used	Set of languages (possibly None)	Measure can only be either a combination of languages, or None: If "*Supports specification*" is *No*, this should be empty
Hard-coded metametamodel size		Small, Average, Large	Values are mutually exclusive

that we do not define a ranking system because the ultimate objective of this evaluation is not to determine the best tool but rather if (and how) the industry is currently addressing metamodeling. In addition, we believe it is up to each developer to determine what approach and tool characteristics are required for development. However, we do believe that this framework provides a practical contribution through its generic set of guidelines that help determine whether a tool can appropriately address metamodeling (both as an activity in itself and as an activity in the context of software development). Moreover, metamodeling is still an active research topic that is not addressed by many tools, and we believed that ranking these tools would ultimately yield unfair results (as some of the tools were not created to address this issue in the first place).

We also highlight the fact that, although this evaluation framework has been empirically validated (in the context of our experience with various MDE-based tools), some of these criteria and measurement metrics are still subjective and can be refined by performing an explicit validation of the existing criteria and their measurements metrics, according to approaches such as Moore and Benbasat (1991), and by adding further (and more objective) criteria that address other issues regarding metamodeling.

Supported Standard Exchange Formats

With all the modeling tools now available, the ability to exchange models between tools is becoming a very important requirement; the lack of this ability can easily lead to a situation in which a developer is stuck with a certain tool. This would require that tools be able to export and import models to and from a standard format, such as XMI. Although each tool creator is free to create or choose his or her own exchange format, it should be taken into account that developers usually choose tools that can import or export to standard formats, allowing models to be independent of the tools in which they are manipulated.

This dimension is divided into two subdimensions: (a) metamodels, which involves determining whether metamodels can be imported or exported, and (b) models, which involves determining whether user models can be imported or exported.

This division is useful because the formats used by a tool to import, or export metamodels and models may be different; also, a tool may only allow the import or export of models but not metamodels. The values for both dimensions are the set of standards used (possibly none).

Model Transformation Framework

This dimension measures whether the tool supports model transformations, and only allows a single value from its measurement range: *yes*, meaning that the tool additionally provides a framework or language based on the metamodel or the meta-metamodel for specifying transformations between user models (such as QVT), and *no*, meaning that the tool does not provide such a framework.

Level Compaction

This dimension measures whether the tool uses the level-compaction technique (Atkinson & Kühne, 2005) and only allows a single value from its measurement range: *yes*, meaning that the tool uses level compaction and can therefore easily be adjusted to support additional logical levels, and *no*, meaning that the tool does not employ level compaction.

Language and Library Metaphors

This dimension measures which of the two metaphors (language or library; Atkinson & Kühne, 2005) are used in the tool, and only allows a single value from its measurement range: language metaphor or library metaphor, according to the metaphor used. Note that if the dimension level compaction evaluates as *no*, then the value of this dimension will obviously be the language metaphor, as presented in the previous section ("Model-Driven Engineering").

Number of Logical Levels the User Can Manipulate

Despite what architectural options are present in a tool, one of the aspects that directly affects a tool's user is the number of logical levels that can actually be manipulated in the tool (by creating, editing, or deleting elements) as a limited number may force the user to compact two or more metamodel levels into a single layer (i.e., the user places elements from several logical levels in a single level).

This dimension measures how many metamodel-model relationships can be handled by the tool, and it only allows the usage of a single natural number (i.e., 1, 2, etc.). For example, a typical UML CASE tool only allows the manipulation of one logical level (M1) as the creation of instances is still performed in M1.

Support for Metamodel Specification

In the evaluation of the support that a tool provides for specifying metamodels, it is important to analyze what a tool supports.

This dimension is divided into two other dimensions, syntax and semantics, evaluating the support that the selected tools provide to the specification of the syntax and semantics of metamodels, respectively. The definitions of *metamodel syntax* and *metamodel semantics* are similar to the ones found at http://www.klasse.nl/research/uml-semantics.html and are described next.

- *Syntax.* A metamodel's syntax consists of the set of model elements (i.e., graphical representations of domain elements) and the relationships between those model elements; this is very similar to the definition of *syntax* in the context of linguistics, in which syntax is the study of the way words are combined together to form sentences.

The syntax dimension is divided into two subdimensions: specification support and languages used.

- *Specification support.* This dimension evaluates whether the tool supports the specification of the syntactic component of a metamodel (i.e., the graphical representation of its elements). It only allows a single value from its measurement range: *yes*, meaning that the tool allows the specification of the metamodel's syntax, and *no*, meaning that the tool does not support this.

- *Languages used.* This dimension determines the set of languages used by the tool to specify the metamodel's syntax (including proprietary or standard languages). Note that this dimension can only have a meaningful value when the specification-support dimension's value is *yes*.

- *Semantics.* A metamodel's semantics can be seen from two perspectives: the semantic domain and the semantics of each model element. The semantic domain consists of the whole set of domain elements that the metamodel is supposed to represent (i.e., the concepts that were captured during the analysis of the problem domain). On the other hand, the semantics of a certain model element is determined by the relation(s) between that model element and one or more domain elements.

This dimension is divided into two subdimensions, specification support and languages used, which evaluate some aspects of the mechanisms provided for defining metamodel semantics.

- *Specification support.* This dimension measures whether the tool supports the specification of the semantic component of a metamodel. It only allows a single value from its measurement range: *yes*, meaning that the tool allows specification of a metamodel's semantic constraints, and *no*, meaning that the tool does not support this.

- *Languages used.* This dimension, like the languages-used dimension of syntax, determines the set of languages used by the tool to define a metamodel's semantic constraints (such as OCL for MOF-based models, available at http://www.omg.org/cgi-bin/apps/doc?formal/06-05-01.pdf). Note that this dimension can only have a meaningful value if the specification-support value is *yes*.

Hard-Coded Meta-Metamodel Size

An important aspect to consider is the size of the meta-metamodel hard-coded into the tool (or metamodel if the tool only allows creating user models) because it reflects how wide the range of metamodel primitives is. In this evaluation, we consider the size of a model (or a meta-metamodel, in this case) to be defined by the quantity of information involved in the formal specification of the model (i.e., how many objects, relationships, and constraints are used to specify the model); the explanation for this lies in the amount of information that the user should be aware of when creating a metamodel in order to take full advantage of the language provided by the meta-metamodel.

This dimension only allows a single value from its measurement range: (a) *small*, meaning that the tool's hard-coded meta-metamodel consists of 15 elements or less (in this article, we consider an element to be either an object, a relationship between objects, or a constraint), (b) *average*, meaning that it consists of 16 to 30 elements, and (c) *large*, meaning that it consists of more than 30 elements. It is important to note that this measurement is highly subjective since we know of no framework to objectively classify a model's size or complexity; ultimately, it is up to the reader to make his or her own definition of how large a meta-metamodel must be before it can be considered large.

117

MDE Tools

Figure 9 presents an overview of the small set of MDE tools used in this evaluation: Enterprise Architect (SparxSystems, n.d.), MetaSketch (Nobrega et al., 2006), MetaEdit+ (MetaCase, n.d.), and Microsoft's DSL Tools (MSDSLTools, n.d.).

The initial criteria used for the selection of MDE tools to evaluate were the following: (a) The tool must be recent (or still be under development) to ensure it addresses current MDE approaches, (b) each tool must address one of the MDE initiatives presented in the previous section, and (c) the tool must have a relatively smooth learning curve as developers are usually more inclined to choose tools that they find to be user friendly and that facilitate their activities. We searched the Internet for candidate tools that fit these criteria; however, we found many candidate tools, so we limited this evaluation to popular tools in order to keep the evaluation (and this article) simple. We also included MetaSketch in this evaluation because, although it is not yet popular, it explicitly addresses the metamodeling activity, so we believed that including it in the evaluation could yield some interesting results. We did not consider

any of our own tools (i.e., developed in-house) as candidates for this evaluation in order to maintain an independent perspective over this tool evaluation and prevent us from inadvertently specifying dimensions that would favor any one of the tools being evaluated.

These tools were chosen because we consider that this set is a good representative of the current status of MDE-supporting tools currently available (e.g., Enterprise Architect can do most of what can be done with ArgoUML, http://argouml.tigris. org; Poseidon for UML, http://www.gentleware. com; Rational Rose 2003, http://www-306.ibm. com/software/awdtools/developer/datamodeler; or other UML modeling tools); they also presented enough differences amongst themselves to justify their inclusion in this evaluation. Although these tools do not reflect everything that is currently available in MDE tools, they address the MDE-based approaches defined earlier by providing the features that can often be found in typical tools of their corresponding approach.

The reason we evaluate only a small number of tools is article simplicity and size. However, it is important to reiterate that there are a great number of other tools available, such as the Generic Modeling Environment (GME; http://www.

Figure 9. The selected MDE tools

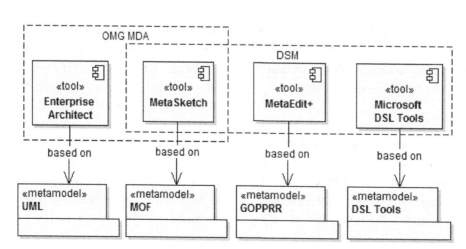

isis.vanderbilt.edu/projects/gme) or the Eclipse Graphical Modeling Framework (GMF; http://www.eclipse.org/gmf). Although in this article we only evaluate this small set of tools, we believe that an evaluation of a greater number of tools, including a wider range of areas such as ontology modeling or enterprise architecture modeling, would yield some very interesting results to complement those obtained here. An added advantage of such an evaluation would also be the diverse set of metamodels used by the evaluated tools (e.g., enterprise modeling tools tend to use enterprise-oriented metamodels, such as the TOGAF or Zachman framework).

Traditional CASE Tools

Although traditional CASE tools may be adequate for the development of small and simple software systems, they clearly do not support the development tasks that come with larger, complex systems. One of the main problems of such tools is that they only support a specific metamodel, usually UML, and do not offer support for altering that metamodel (although UML does provide the profile mechanism, supported by some UML modeling tools).

This type of tools is included in this evaluation to determine whether current typical CASE tools could easily be adapted to allow the creation of models based on a user-specified language. For the evaluation purposes of this work, we chose Enterprise Architect (SparxSystems, n.d.) to represent traditional CASE tools as it is quite easy to use, provides good support for UML and its profile mechanism (in fact, EA makes the definition of a UML profile a simple and easy task), and seems to be one of the best representatives of the current status of CASE tools.

(For this evaluation, we used Enterprise Architect 6.5, which was the latest version of this tool at the time this work was written.)

MetaSketch

MetaSketch (Nobrega et al., 2006) is a MOF-based editor, unlike most editors, which are usually based on UML. It is based on the following ideas: (a) A metamodel is a model that conforms to MOF 2.0, not to UML 2.0, (b) the UML profile mechanism is not powerful enough to support the definition of new modeling languages, (c) a metamodel should be the primary artifact of a modeling language definition and developers should not need to code metamodels, and (d) a metamodel is not the final goal but the means used to produce models, so it is not reasonable to create another modeling tool each time another metamodel is specified. These ideas lead to MetaSketch, an editor that is MOF compliant, allowing the definition of any language that can be specified using MOF (i.e., a MOF-based metamodel). Thus, MetaSketch is best defined as a metamodeling tool.

MetaSketch does not offer code generation capabilities by itself, but it can import or export defined models and metamodels to XMI; the tool adheres strictly (with no vendor-specific extensions) to XMI 2.1 (Nobrega et al., 2006), so code generation could easily be handled by any code generator that can understand XMI. The tool also supports the definition of models conforming to metamodels specified in XMI (e.g., MOF or UML). Three metalevels, M3, M2, and M1, are supported by using level compaction. Figure 10 illustrates two interesting scenarios that are made possible by MetaSketch: the definition of a MOF metamodel by using itself (top), and the definition of the UML and CWM metamodels (bottom). In the first scenario, the user takes advantage of MOF's reflexive property in order to define a metamodel consisting of MOF itself (note the hard-coded MOF and the user-defined MOF); UML and CWM can then be defined as user models from that metamodel. In the second scenario, the user defines the UML metamodel by using the hard-coded MOF meta-metamodel. UML user models can then be created based on

Figure 10. MOF is used as a meta-metamodel and as a metamodel

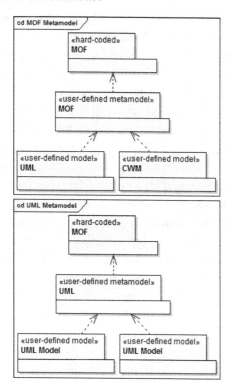

that metamodel (note that this second scenario is very similar to the typical OMG architecture, illustrated in Figure 2).

MetaEdit+

MetaEdit+, available at http://www.metacase.com, is a DSM-oriented environment (i.e., a meta-CASE tool) that allows the creation of modeling tools and generators fitting to application domains without having to write code (Tolvanen & Rossi, 2003). It uses a meta-metamodel called GOPPRR (graph, object, property, port, relationship, and role), named after the metatypes that are used when specifying the metamodel.

In MetaEdit+, an expert creates a modeling method by (a) defining a domain-specific language containing the problem domain's concepts and rules (in this article, we will treat a DSL in

MetaEdit+ as a metamodel since the tool does treat DSLs as metamodels), and (b) specifying the mapping from that language to source code in a domain-specific code generator. Once the expert creates the modeling method (or even a prototype), the development team can start using it in MetaEdit+ to define models, and the corresponding code will be automatically generated from those models. The code generator itself uses a DSL that allows the developer to specify how to navigate through models and output its contents along with additional text. The tool also provides a repository for all modeling method information, allowing the storage and modification of modeling method definitions; any modifications to definitions are also reflected in their corresponding tools, models, and generators.

(For this evaluation, we used MetaEdit+ 4.5, which was the latest version of this tool at the time this work was written.)

Microsoft DSL Tools

Microsoft's DSL Tools, available at http://msdn. microsoft.com/vstudio/dsltools, is a suite of tools for creating, editing, visualizing, and using domain-specific data for automating the enterprise software development process. DSL Tools allow developers to design graphical modeling languages and to generate artifacts (such as code or documentation) from those languages; the visual language tools are based on Microsoft Visual Studio.

The process of creating a new DSL begins with the DSL Designer Wizard, which provides some metamodel templates (such as class diagrams or use-case diagrams) and guides the developer through specifying the features of the desired DSL. As a result of executing the wizard, a Visual Studio solution is created, containing a DSL project with the language's domain model (classes and relationships), its visual representation (diagram elements), and the mappings between domain elements and visual elements. The source code that will support the DSL tool is generated by using text templates, which process the DSL's specification and output the corresponding code. Developers can provide additional code to refine aspects of the model designer, define constraints over the language, and/or even alter the text templates (which can have substantial effects on the generated source code). Testing is done within Visual Studio by launching another instance of the environment with the specified DSL tool. After ensuring that the tool is working correctly, the final step is creating a deployment package that allows its distribution.

(For this evaluation, we used the DSL Tools' Version 1 release, which was the latest version of this tool at the time this article was written.)

Applying the Framework

This subsection describes the small case study used to support this evaluation and the results obtained by applying the evaluation framework to each of the selected tools.

A Small Case Study: Social Network Metamodel

An essential part of the evaluation of a tool is determining how that tool actually supports the activities necessary toward the resolution of a certain problem. Thus, we use the facilities provided by each tool to specify and implement (when possible) a simple metamodel that supports the specification for simple social networks. This metamodel can be textually described by the following statements:

- A social network is composed of people and relationships between people.
- A person's participation in a relationship is defined by the role they play in it.
- A role must have a corresponding relationship.

- A role must have a corresponding person.
- A social relationship must involve at least two different people.

Figure 11 presents this metamodel (and two user models, for illustrative purposes) modeled in Enterprise Architect.

Note that this case study, because of its simplicity, could also be addressed with typical CASE tools (in fact, this is done in Enterprise Architect). However, the main objective of this article is to evaluate how the selected tools behave in specifying the Social Network metamodel and afterward producing and adapting a tool that can be used to create user models (i.e., with types and instances) using the language defined by that metamodel.

Evaluating the Tools

The evaluation framework's application to the presented tools was performed by us, so we did not need to resort to agreement measures, such as Cohen's Kappa coefficient. To compensate for the lack of a greater number of test participants, we tried not to define any dimensions that depended on the user's previous familiarity with one (or more) of the tools. Thus, the usage of each tool to define the Social Networks metamodel case study was accompanied by thorough reading of available tool documentation and previous tests of the tool in order to gain a reasonable amount of experience with each of the selected tools. Nevertheless, we acknowledge that such dimensions are important to measure usability and the tool's learning curve (and can be a good indicator of whether the tool will be accepted by the community).

- *Enterprise Architect.* Enterprise Architect is an easy-to-use tool with a minimal learning curve. However, its traditional CASE-tool roots make it extremely limited when it comes to metamodeling. Since EA is a UML modeling tool, the only mechanism that it provides for metamodeling support

Figure 11. The Social Network metamodel and two user models

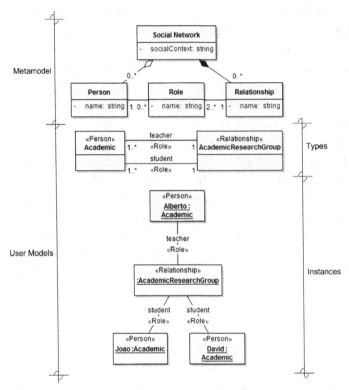

is the UML profile mechanism, which only allows adding elements and semantics to the metamodel, but not altering it (i.e., editing or removing elements and constraints).

The definition of a profile in EA is limited to specifying the generic syntax of the profile (i.e., defining stereotypes and what metaclasses they extend, enumerations, etc.). Other semantic and syntactic relationships and constraints entered in the profile definition (using a text-based notation such as OCL) are not enforced when the user creates a model using that profile; the only validation that EA does enforce is the application of a stereotype to an instance of a metaclass (e.g., a stereotype that extends the metaclass Association cannot be applied to an instance of the metaclass Class). EA does present the advantage of not requiring the creation of a new tool adapted to the problem domain as it supports both the definition

and application of a UML profile (as is typically the case with profile-supporting CASE tools).

Like other CASE tools, EA does not appear to use level compaction or any similar technique because modeling is limited to one logical level; in this case, adapting the tool to support more logical levels (by using level compaction) would require an extra effort in order to separate the metamodel-model and class-instance relationships. The tool offers code generation capabilities and some predefined basic model transformations to support MDA, such as PIM to PSM. However, they require that PIMs and PSMs be specified in UML as it is the tool's hard-coded metamodel.

Figure 12 shows the definition of a profile representing the Social Networks metamodel previously presented; additionally, Figure 11 presents two user models (obtained through the application of the profile) modeled in EA.

Figure 12. A screenshot of Enterprise Architect with a profile definition

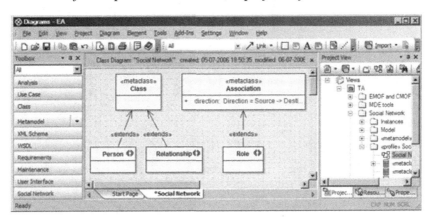

It is important to reiterate that the reason why EA is used in this evaluation is to show that typical CASE tools are not adequate for the metamodeling needs that are currently surfacing, even though EA (as other CASE tools) is not designed to support metamodeling; this evaluation is not meant in any way to diminish EA as a tool, and these results should not be interpreted as such.

- *MetaSketch.* From the set of evaluated tools, only MetaSketch supported metamodeling based on the MOF standard. The tool supports the XMI import and export of models and metamodels, so a user-defined model can become a metamodel simply by exporting it to XMI and then importing it from XMI as a metamodel. In fact, the tool can easily handle the XMI-based specifications of MOF and UML available on the OMG Web site.

MetaSketch uses the language metaphor (Nobrega et al., 2006), which in this case limits the user to manipulating two logical levels: the metamodel and the user model. However, MetaSketch uses level compaction, so it could be adapted to use the library metaphor with relatively little effort. Although MetaSketch does not support model transformations (to either source code or other models), this can be remedied because of

the tool's XMI import and export capabilities; the user could export the model to XMI, and then process it with a code generator (such as the Eclipse Modeling Framework, available at http://www.eclipse.org/emf) or a model transformation tool (likely based on QVT).

The syntax of the metamodel is specified in XML (outside the tool's environment) by composing simple shapes (rectangles, ellipses, etc.) and using the tool's geometry management mechanism (Nobrega et al., 2006), which dynamically adjusts the spatial arrangement of those shapes. The semantics of the metamodel is specified in the tool itself when modeling the user model that later becomes the metamodel; however, there is no support yet for constraint specification. Nevertheless, it is important to note that the tool is still a prototype under active development, so it can be expected that such issues will be corrected in the future. Thus, the results obtained in this evaluation do not reflect the full potential of this tool.

- *MetaEdit+.* MetaEdit+ is based on a very simple and flexible meta-metamodel, GOP-PRR; however, this meta-metamodel does not include behavioral features (only structural features), which can impact the possible set of metamodels that can be defined by the tool.

123

Figure 13. Social Network metamodel and user model in MetaSketch

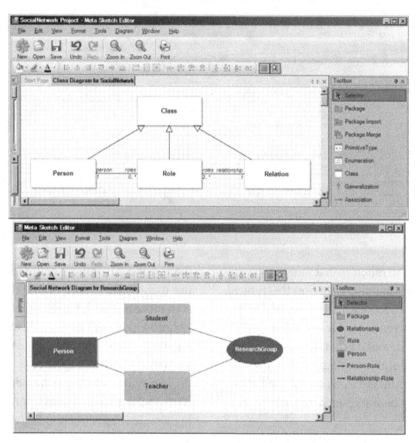

MetaEdit+ apparently uses the language metaphor, limiting the number of logical levels the user can edit to the metamodel and the user model. However, this metaphor is used not because of programming-language restrictions, but by choice of the tool creators, so the tool could be adapted to use the library metaphor with relatively little effort. Although the tool does not offer support for model transformations, it does provide a report mechanism that allows the generation of text-based artifacts (such as source code, HTML [hypertext markup language], or XML) based on the information available in the model's repository.

Syntax specification is done by creating instances of the meta-metamodel's elements and, eventually, creating vectorial images to represent those instances. Semantic specification is done when creating an instance of a graph (which corresponds to a type of model, like UML's class diagram or use-case diagram); constraints are then entered in the graph's corresponding form (e.g., "Objects of a certain type may be in, at most, a certain number of relationships"), which is designed to avoid as much manual text entering as possible (since it is prone to errors).

This tool did present a few important usability problems, such as the fact that it does not allow the altering of the superclass-subclass relationships between object types: Once the user chooses an object type's superclass (when creating the object type), it cannot be changed; the user should first draw the metamodel on a piece of paper or another modeling tool in order to obtain the definitive metamodel, and then re-create it within MetaEdit+.

Figure 14. Models of the Social Network metamodel in MetaEdit+

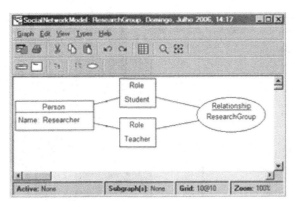

Figure 14 presents a model derived from the Social Network metamodel presented earlier.

- *Microsoft DSL Tools for Visual Studio.* This tool's meta-metamodel consists of the following elements: (a) class, (b) domain property, (c) embedding, (d) reference, and (d) inheritance. Like MetaEdit+, this meta-metamodel is highly object oriented but does not include behavioral features.

The tool's architecture is based on the language metaphor and limits the possible logical levels editable by the user to the metamodel and the user model. However, this limitation is because DSL Tools are based on the class-instance relation, so the adaptation of DSL Tools to use the library metaphor would likely require a great deal of effort.

The DSL designer itself is divided into two panes: Domain Model and Diagram Elements. In Domain Model, the developer identifies the relevant concepts of the problem domain and expresses them in the domain-model section of the designer along with model details like cardinality and source-code-specific details such as whether an association end should generate a property. Validations and constraints can also be specified by typing source code in additional validation classes. In Diagram Elements, aspects relating to the graphical layout of the model elements are specified, such as shapes used, association line styles, the shapes that can be on either end of an association, and how value properties are graphically displayed. Thus, the specification of the syntax and semantics of the metamodel is done entirely in the DSL designer (except for validations and constraints, which are expressed in source code) as the DSL Tools are highly focused on the graphical specification of user models and subsequent generation of text-based artifacts. Figure 15 presents the Social Network user model specified in DSL Tools.

Results

The results of this evaluation are shown in Figure 16. From these results, we can see that some tools already treat metamodel exchange as an important issue as only Enterprise Architect and MetaEdit+ do not export their metamodel definition. However, in Enterprise Architect's case, this is understandable since the metamodel (UML) is hard-coded into the tool and never changes. We find noteworthy the fact that MetaSketch is the only tool allowing metamodel import and export using a well-defined standard (XMI). User-model

Figure 15. Models of the Social Network metamodel in Microsoft's DSL Tools

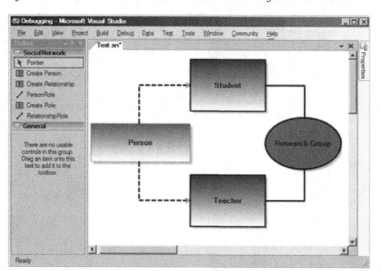

Figure 16. The evaluation results

Dimension \ Tool			Enterprise Architect	MetaSketch	MetaEdit+	Microsoft DSL Tools
Supported standard exchange formats		Metamodels	None	XMI	None	Other (DSL definition format)
		Models	XMI	XMI	XML	XML
Model transformation framework			Yes	No	No	No
Level Compaction			No	Yes	Yes	No
Language metaphor or Library metaphor			Language metaphor	Language metaphor	Language metaphor	Language metaphor
Number of logical levels the user can manipulate			1	2	2	2
Support for metamodel specification	Syntax	Supports specification	Yes	Yes	Yes	Yes
		Languages used	None (Association between stereotypes and icons)	XML	None (Graphical vectorial drawing within the tool)	XML
	Semantics	Supports specification	No	No	Yes	Yes
		Languages used	-	-	GOPPRR (uses metamodel concepts to establish constraints)	.NET source-code (e.g., C#)
Hard-coded metametamodel size			Large (MOF + UML metamodel)	Large (MOF metamodel)	Small (GOPPRR - 6 elements)	Small (5 elements)

exchange, however, is supported by all tools, using either XMI or XML.

Model transformation does not currently seem to be a major concern as most tools do not provide any kind of support for it (only Enterprise Architect provides a framework for model-to-model or model-to-code transformations in the context of the MDA initiative), likely because of the immature state of the area.

Another interesting conclusion is that each of the evaluated tools uses the language metaphor, although most of them support the specification of two logical levels. This is likely due to the fact that a tool that supports more than two logical levels is likely to reveal itself as confusing since it can usually be assumed that developers will not need more than two logical levels (one to specify a language that represents the problem domain—and perhaps another language that represents the solution domain—and another to specify a solution to the problem). However, both MetaSketch and MetaEdit+ use level compaction, and thus could be adapted to use the library metaphor (therefore supporting additional logical levels) with little effort; DSL Tools would require a much more extensive effort to support such additional logical levels.

Most tools support the specification of a metamodel's syntax to some degree (either by associating elements with external image sources or by providing internal facilities to create such graphical representations). However, the specification of a metamodel's semantic constraints seems to be sketchy at best, with only MetaEdit+ and DSL Tools supporting such constraint specifications. (MetaEdit+ uses its meta-metamodel concepts to establish constraints in the metamodel, while DSL Tools requires that developers use source code to specify constraints.)

Finally, the tools that do not follow a standard meta-metamodel (e.g., MetaEdit+ and MS DSL Tools) seem to prefer using a meta-metamodel that is as simple as possible: MetaEdit+'s consists of six elements, while DSL Tools' consists of five.

Discussion

Although CASE tools failed on their first appearance some years ago (Booch, Brown, Iyengar, Rumbaugh, & Selic, 2004), they brought the idea that development processes could be supported by such tools as long as those tools were adjusted to the development process. Early CASE tools were too inflexible, usually forcing the development process to be adjusted to the CASE tool instead of having the CASE tool support the development process. This led to the area of meta-CASE systems, which allow the automatic creation of development tools tailored to specific design processes, determined by organizational requirements.

The core problem with traditional CASE tools is that they only support specifying the solution; the identification of the problem-domain requirements is often done apart from these tools (usually in a word processor or similar). Hence, developers do not have a problem-domain-oriented language in which they can express the solution to the problem, forcing them to think of the solution in computational terms (toward which traditional CASE tool metamodels are especially oriented) rather than in problem-domain terms. The solution inevitably becomes misaligned with the problem domain and, therefore, with the problem itself. The consequences of this can be seen over the entire development process, but become especially critical during the product maintenance phase, when the product must be adapted to additional problem conditions and requirements, usually requiring extensive developer effort because of the difficulty of assuring that the product still solves the old problems while also solving additional problems.

However, when considering metamodeling and meta-CASE tools, we need to be careful because of possible meta-metamodel fragmentation: In this evaluation, we can see an example of this as Microsoft DSL Tools uses its own meta-metamodel and so does MetaEdit+. This could lead to a panorama much like the one from a few years ago, in which there was a myriad of modeling languages (i.e., metamodels) all doing the same and yet all different among themselves. Now that the community (and the industry) is beginning to focus on metamodeling and meta-metamodels (i.e., metamodel languages), we need to start considering meta-metamodel standards as they help eliminate gratuitous diversity (Booch et al., 2004). Otherwise, the diversity of languages that would be defined would very likely lead to the fragmentation that UML was designed to eliminate in the first place.

All this is theory that must be put into practice in tools that developers can use. For such tools to be of help to the developer, they must support the whole software development life cycle, from requirements specification to deployment and maintenance. This also requires that tools allow developers to specify solutions in problem-domain terms, which of course requires that tools support some form of metamodeling. However, as the results of this evaluation show, the current tool support is primarily directed toward DSM, and issues such as model-to-model transformations (upon which MDA is based) are being left out in all but a few tools (such as the Eclipse Modeling Project, available at http://www.eclipse.org/modeling).

We believe MDA and UML have the potential to adequately cover the development phases more directly related to software itself, like implementation design and coding. However, MDA does not address the requirements phase, leading to the known gap between what the client wants the system to do and what the system actually does; in part, this is because UML is not adequate for requirements modeling. On the other hand, DSM's strength over MDA comes from the fact that it is more than adequate for requirements specification. Using a DSM system, a developer experienced in the problem domain creates a metamodel reflecting that domain and specifies how domain concepts are mapped to code (or any other artifact type). Requirements are then specified as models (oriented toward not the implementation but what the client wants the system to do) using the defined metamodel. These models are then mapped into code using the mappings initially defined. However, DSM as it is used today has a weak point: the transformation between models and code (or even between models of different languages). If the DSM system user wishes to switch target platforms (for example, from Java to .NET), the mappings will have to be re-created by the expert developer, unlike what happens with MDA, as PIMs and PSMs provide the ability to exchange target platforms with minimal extra effort. This is not unlike what is said in Schmidt (2006), which states that MDE is evolving toward DSLs combined with transformation engines and generators;

in other words, MDE seems to be evolving toward MDA and DSM working together.

This is why we consider tools such as MetaSketch to be of utter importance to the industry, as MetaSketch reveals a genuine concern with adhering to OMG standards (which opens the door for its usage in MDA-oriented development scenarios) while also trying to address the metamodeling problem that we are facing today.

Another issue that we consider important to the success of metamodeling is complexity. The usage of standards is always conditioned by their complexity and how well adapted they are to the domain of interest. These points can be decisive factors over the difficulty of creating a model that correctly represents the problem (from the perspectives of syntax and semantics), which is where DSM differentiates itself. The fundamental issue is that developers and clients need to identify themselves with the metamodels they use; otherwise, they will look upon those metamodels as nuisances. An example can be seen in MOF, sometimes considered too complex for defining user metamodels, because it includes concepts that would only be useful in the context of OMG-defined metamodels. This is why tools such as MetaEdit+ (with simple meta-metamodels) are gaining popularity throughout the developer community, and MOF/UML CASE tools (with complex meta-metamodels) are typically considered as only good for documentation and a last resort for code generation.

Finally, we consider that the evaluation framework defined in this article is quite relevant because it provides a good insight into the main problems that metamodeling tools would face: Its dimensions include support for language specification (syntax and semantics) and model transformations, which are essential to the creation of metamodels and models, as well as to obtaining new models in an automatic, MDE-oriented fashion.

CONCLUSION

Just as development paradigms changed and evolved over the last decades from assembly code to subsequent generations of programming languages, the development paradigm is changing from our current third-generation programming languages to a higher abstraction level. This shift is gradually happening as MDE is gaining importance as an abstraction mechanism over traditional programming activity.

However, tools need to follow and support this paradigm change. The only way that a modeling tool can effectively support the software developer's complex tasks is by providing metamodeling support: Such a tool should allow a software developer or architect to specify a language or metamodel and be able to automatically create tools that enable the creation of models based on that metamodel.

This article presented a framework for evaluating a tool's adequacy in the metamodeling activity. This framework defines some criteria that address both theoretical and practical issues in metamodeling and in modeling tools; nevertheless, it is still subjective and open to further refinement by adding more important criteria and by defining measurement metrics that can establish a higher degree of consensus regarding metamodeling issues.

After presenting the framework, we applied it to a small set of current modeling tools that we believe to be representative of the status of the mainstream MDE area. Finally, this article discussed some open research issues for metamodeling-based software development tools.

ACKNOWLEDGMENT

We would like to thank Leonel Nobrega for his promptness in supplying the latest version of his MetaSketch tool as well as all the documentation that was available at the time. We would also like to thank the reviewers of this article for all their excellent constructive suggestions to improve its quality.

REFERENCES

Atkinson, C., & Kühne, T. (2003, September-October). Model-driven development: A metamodeling foundation. *IEEE Software, 20*(5), 36-41. Retrieved June 5, 2006, from http://doi.ieeecomputersociety.org/10.1109/MS.2003.1231149

Atkinson, C., & Kühne, T. (2005, October). Concepts for comparing modeling tool architectures. In L. Briand & C. Williams (Eds.), *Model Driven Engineering Languages and Systems: Eighth International Conference, MoDELS 2005* (pp. 398-413). Springer. Retrieved June 23, 2006, from http://dx.doi.org/10.1007/11557432 30

Booch, G., Brown, A., Iyengar, S., Rumbaugh, J., & Selic, B. (2004, May). An MDA manifesto. *Business Process Trends/MDA Journal.* Retrieved June 15, 2006, from http://www.bptrends.com/publicationfiles/05-04COLIBMManifesto-Frankel-3.pdf

Fong, C. K. (2007, June). *Successful implementation of model driven architecture: A case study of how Borland Together MDA technologies were successfully implemented in a large commercial bank.* Retrieved November 23, 2007, from http://www.borland.com/resources/en/pdf/products/together/together-successful-implementation-mda.pdf

France, R. B., Ghosh, S., Dinh-Trong, T., & Solberg, A. (2006, February). Model-driven development using UML 2.0: Promises and pitfalls. *Computer, 39*(2), 59-66. Retrieved June 5, 2006, from http://doi.ieeecomputersociety.org/10.1109/MC.2006.65

Henderson-Sellers, B. (2005, February). UML the good, the bad or the ugly? Perspectives from a panel of experts. *Software and Systems Modeling, 4*(1), 4-13. Retrieved June 5, 2006, from http://dx.doi.org/10.1007/s10270-004-0076-8

Kelly, S., & Tolvanen, J.-P. (2008). *Domain-specific modeling.* Hoboken, NJ: John Wiley & Sons.

Kleppe, A., Warmer, J., & Bast, W. (2003). *MDA explained: The model driven architecture. Practice and promise.* Reading, MA: Addison-Wesley.

MetaCase. (n.d.). *MetaCase: Domain-specific modeling with MetaEdit+.* Retrieved June 5, 2006, from http://www.metacase.com

Metamodel.com: Community site for meta-modeling and semantic modeling. (n.d.). Retrieved June 5, 2006, from http://www.metamodel.com

Moore, G. C., & Benbasat, I. (1991, September). Development of an instrument to measure the perceptions of adopting an information technology innovation. *Information Systems Research, 2*(3), 192-222.

Nobrega, L., Nunes, N. J., & Coelho, H. (2006, June). The meta sketch editor: A reflexive modeling editor. In G. Calvary, C. Pribeanu, G. Santucci, & J. Vanderdonckt (Eds.), *Computer-Aided Design of User Interfaces V: Proceedings of the Sixth International Conference on Computer-Aided Design of User Interfaces (CADUI 2006)* (pp. 199-212). Berlin, Germany: Springer-Verlag.

Schmidt, D. C. (2006, February). Guest editor's introduction: Model-driven engineering. *Computer, 39*(2), 25-31. Retrieved June 5, 2006, from http://doi.ieeecomputersociety.org/10.1109/MC.2006.58

Selonen, P., Koskimies, K., & Sakkinen, M. (2003). Transformations between UML diagrams. *Journal of Database Management, 14*(3), 37-55.

Siau, K., & Cao, Q. (2001). Unified modeling language: A complexity analysis. *Journal of Database Management, 12*(1), 26-34.

Silva, A., & Videira, C. (2005). *UML, metodologias e ferramentas CASE* (Vol. 2, 2nd ed.). Portugal: Centro Atlântico.

S̈oderstrom, E., Andersso, B., Johannesson, P., Perjons, E., & Wangler, B. (2002, May). Towards a framework for comparing process modelling languages. In *CAiSE '02: Proceedings of the 14th International Conference on Advanced Information Systems Engineering* (pp. 600-611). London: Springer-Verlag. Retrieved June 21, 2006, from http://portal.acm.org/citation.cfm?coll=GUIDE&dl=GUIDE&id=680389#

SparxSystems. (n.d.). *Enterprise architect: UML design tools and UML CASE tools for software development.* Retrieved June 5, 2006, from http://www.sparxsystems.com/ products/ea.html

Thomas, D. (2004, May-June). MDA: Revenge of the modelers or UML utopia? *IEEE Software, 21*(3), 15-17. Retrieved June 5, 2006, from http://doi.ieeecomputersociety.org/10.1109/MS.2004.1293067

Tolvanen, J.-P., & Rossi, M. (2003, October). MetaEdit+: Defining and using domain-specific modeling languages and code generators. In *OOPSLA '03: Companion of the 18th Annual ACM SIGPLAN Conference on Object-Oriented Programming, Systems, Languages, and Applications* (pp. 92-93). New York: ACM Press. Retrieved June 5, 2006, from http://doi.acm.org/10.1145/949344.949365

Visual Studio 2005: Domain-specific language tools. (n.d.). Retrieved June 5, 2006, from http://msdn.microsoft.com/vstudio/dsltools

Zhao, L., & Siau, K. (2007, November). Information mediation using metamodels: An approach using XML and common warehouse metamodel. *Journal of Database Management, 18*(3), 69-82.

Zhu, J., Tian, Z., Li, T., Sun, W., Ye, S., Ding, W., et al. (2004). Model-driven business process integration and management: A case study with the Bank SinoPac regional service platform. *IBM Journal of Research and Development, 48*(5/6), 649-669. Retrieved November 23, 2007, from http://www.research.ibm.com/journal/rd/485/zhu.pdf

Chapter 6
Exploring the Effects of Process Characteristics on Product Quality in Open Source Software Development

Stefan Koch

Vienna University of Economics and Business Administration, Austria

Christian Neumann

Vienna University of Economics and Business Administration, Austria

ABSTRACT

There has been considerable discussion on the possible impacts of open source software development practices, especially in regard to the quality of the resulting software product. Recent studies have shown that analyzing data from source code repositories is an efficient way to gather information about project characteristics and programmers, showing that OSS projects are very heterogeneous in their team structures and software processes. However, one problem is that the resulting process metrics measuring attributes of the development process and of the development environment do not give any hints about the quality, complexity, or structure of the resulting software. Therefore, we expanded the analysis by calculating several product metrics, most of them specifically tailored to object-oriented software. We then analyzed the relationship between these product metrics and process metrics derived from a CVS repository. The aim was to establish whether different variants of open source development processes have a significant impact on the resulting software products. In particular we analyzed the impact on quality and design associated with the numbers of contributors and the amount of their work, using the GINI coefficient as a measure of inequality within the developer group.

INTRODUCTION

In recent years, free and open source software (OSS) has drawn increasing interest, both from the business and academic worlds. Projects in different application domains, like most notably the operating system Linux, together with the suite of GNU utilities, the office suites GNOME and KDE, Apache, sendmail, bind, and several programming languages, have achieved huge successes in their respective markets. Undeniably, they constitute software systems of high quality. This has led to discussions and analyses of the underlying development process, as OSS is unique not only in its licenses and legal implications.

The main ideas of this development model are described in the seminal work of Raymond (1999), *The Cathedral and the Bazaar,* first published in 1997. Raymond contrasts the traditional model of software development, which he likens to a few people planning a cathedral in splendid isolation, with the new 'collaborative bazaar' form of open source software development. In the latter model, a large number of developer-turned-users come together without monetary compensation to cooperate under a model of rigorous peer review and take advantage of parallel debugging, which altogether leads to innovation and rapid advancement in developing and evolving software products. In order to enable this while minimizing duplicated work, the source code of the software needs to be accessible, which necessitates suitable licenses, and new versions need to be released often. Most often, the license a software is under is used to define whether it is open source software, applying for example the open source definition (Perens, 1999) or the approach of free software as embodied in the GNU GPL (Stallman, 2002). Nevertheless, usually a certain development style and culture are also implicitly assumed, although no formal definition or description of an open source development process exists, and there is considerable variance in the practices actually employed by open source projects. Also the re-

lationship to and insights regarding practices of agile software development (Erickson, Lyytinen, & Siau, 2005; Turk, France, & Rumpe, 2005; Merisalo-Rantanen, Tuunanen, & Rossi, 2005) have been discussed (Koch, 2004a).

Possible advantages and disadvantages to the development of software of this new development model have been hotly debated (Vixie, 1999; McConnell, 1999; Bollinger, Nelson, Self, & Turnbull, 1999; Cusumano, 2004; Feller, Fitzgerald, Hissam, & Lakhani, 2005). For example the question of whether open source development positively or negatively impacts quality and security has been a topic of several analyses (Witten, Landwehr, & Caloyannides, 2001; Hansen, Köhntopp, & Pfitzmann, 2002; Payne, 2002; Stamelos, Angelos, Oikonomou, & Bleris, 2002; Koru & Tian, 2004; Feller et al., 2005). Different viewpoints have also developed regarding whether or not the open source development approach increases efficiency of software production (Feller et al., 2005). Critics argue that the largely missing requirements engineering and design phases, together with the trend to search for bugs in the source code late in the lifecycle, lead to unnecessarily high effort hidden by the relative ease of spreading it throughout the world (McConnell, 1999; Vixie, 1999). Proponents of the OSS development model counter with arguments of very high modularity, fast release cycles, and efficient communication and coordination using the Internet (Bollinger et al., 1999; Raymond, 1999).

Currently, much empirical research is proceeding on OSS processes. Often, the research relies on data available through mining the communication and coordination tools and their repositories (Cook, Votta, & Wolf, 1998; Dutoit & Bruegge, 1998; Atkins, Ball, Graves, & Mockus, 1999; Kemerer & Slaughter, 1999) in place in OSS projects in order to describe and characterize the development team and processes. Most notably, the source code control systems used have been found to be a source of information, together with mailing lists and bug tracking systems. These analyses have been useful in providing an indication of how OSS development works in practice. Work performed has included both in-depth analyses of small numbers of successful projects (Gallivan, 2001) like Apache and Mozilla (Mockus, Fielding, & Herbsleb, 2002), GNOME (Koch & Schneider, 2002), or FreeBSD (Dinh-Tong & Bieman, 2005) and also large data samples, such as those derived from Sourceforge.net (Koch, 2004; Long & Siau, 2007). Primarily, information provided by version control systems has been used, but so have aggregated data provided by software repositories (Crowston & Scozzi, 2002; Hunt & Johnson, 2002; Krishnamurthy, 2002), meta-information included in Linux Software Map entries (Dempsey, Weiss, Jones, & Greenberg, 2002), or data retrieved directly from the source code itself (Ghosh & Prakash, 2000). Other approaches taken include ethnographic studies of development communities (Coleman & Hill, 2004; Elliott & Scacchi, 2004), sometimes coupled with repository mining (Basset, 2004). Indeed, it can be shown that important information about project characteristics and participating programmers can be retrieved in this fashion.

However, a key problem is that the resulting process metrics (Conte, Dunsmore, & Shen, 1986; Fenton, 1991; Henderson-Seller, 1996) measuring attributes of the development process and of the development environment, such as distinct programmers, number of commits, or inequality, do not address the quality, complexity, or structure of the resulting software product. Therefore, we expanded the analysis in this article by selecting and calculating several product metrics pertaining to these characteristics of the software product.

This allows us to analyze whether different development practices have an impact on product quality. We will use process metrics derived from the respective source code control systems as predictors for quality as portrayed by relevant product metrics. Uncovering these relationships will answer the question of which values for these variables—for example, low inequality in

participation—lead to a higher product quality. For this analysis, we use OSS Java frameworks as a data set. The most similar work available is by Koru and Tian (2005), who have used two large open source projects as a dataset to uncover a relationship between high-change modules and those modules rating highly on several structural measures. They used, among others, size measures such as lines-of-code or number of methods, coupling measures such as coupling between objects, cohesion measures such as lack of cohesion in methods, and inheritance measures such as depth in inheritance tree.

The research objective of this article therefore is as follows: We investigate whether there is an influence of different forms of open source software development processes characterized by process metrics on the resulting software. Most importantly, we check for impacts on different quality aspects as measured by appropriate product metrics. A comparison with proprietary products and processes is out of scope and will not be treated in this study.

In the following section the method employed for arriving at the necessary data is described, starting with the data set chosen and its importance, and proceeding to the data collection of both product and process metrics and their combination. Then we present the analysis regarding any relationship between process and product metrics, both on the level of classes and of projects, followed by a discussion. The article finishes with conclusions and future research directions.

METHOD

Data Set

For this empirical study, a certain fixed domain of OSS was chosen, in order to limit variance to the areas of interest by holding the application domain constant. All projects included therefore roughly implement the same requirements and with the same programming language, so differences in software design and quality can directly be attributed to different development practices in place.

We examine 12 OSS frameworks for the presentation layer of Web applications. A framework is a reference architecture for a concrete application which offers basic structures and well-defined mechanisms for communication. Only specific application functionality has to be implemented by the programmer, which is achieved by using abstract classes and interfaces that have to be overridden (Johnson, 1997; Fayad & Schmidt, 1997). All frameworks are based on J2EE components like JSP, Servlets, and XML, and can be used within every Servlet container that implements the J2EE standard. The frameworks are: ActionServlet, Barracuda, Cocoon, Expresso, Jetspeed, Struts, Tapestry, Turbine, Japple, Jpublish, Maverick, and Echo.

Besides having a fixed domain thus reducing any noise in the results, frameworks are an important part in modern software development. Frameworks are one possibility of reusing existing software, thus promising reduced costs, faster time to market, and improved quality (Morisio, Romano, & Stamelos, 2002). OSS especially lends itself to white box reuse (Prieto-Diaz, 1993), as it per definition contains the source code, offers a deeper view into the architecture, and may be modified or adapted. This reduces the disadvantages encountered with using components-off-the-shelf (COTS) offered by software companies. Another critical issue that can be solved by using OSS is the maintenance of frameworks, which is usually done by the contributors of project. On the other hand, although the source code is available and the program could be maintained by the community, some serious problems could accompany the development process, due to low-quality code, design, or documentation. Object-oriented metrics as used here provide a capability for assessing these qualities (Chidamber & Kemerer, 1991,

1994) and may help to estimate the development effort for adaptation and adjustment.

First, all classes are treated as a single data set; afterwards an analysis on project level is presented. An analysis on class level is performed for two reasons: As we analyze the development process and style, the differences between classes might be larger than those between projects, and indeed for some metrics the variation is higher within the projects than between them. For example an abstract class for database access might be developed similarly in all projects. We therefore might find paired classes among different projects. In addition, using a framework does not necessarily mean adopting all classes within this framework. Therefore an analysis on this detailed level is of interest out of a reuse perspective. Afterwards, we will try to consolidate both perspectives by using multilevel modeling which explicitly incorporates effects on both levels.

Data Collection

For the following analysis, several steps of data collection were conducted. As mentioned above, this study focuses on frameworks for Web applications written in an object-oriented language. Many of the available frameworks are not written in object-oriented languages but scripting languages like Perl or PHP. This would preclude using most of the product metrics designed for object-oriented languages. Therefore we focused on frameworks written in Java. We conducted preliminary research to identify potential candidates that fulfilled the criteria of both language and application area. This initial phase consisted of performing extended Web research (online developer forums, search engines) and perusing reports in professional publications for developers. This led to the identification of 12 frameworks. The functions and features of the resulting frameworks were compared in a prior study (Neumann, 2002) and are not part of this article.

After the data set as defined above had been identified, both product and process metrics had to be retrieved and merged for further analysis. In order to calculate the product metrics, the latest stable version of each framework was determined and downloaded as a packed distribution. We used the metric plug-in (*http://metrics.sourceforge. net/*) for the Eclipse SDK (*http://www.eclipse. org*) to calculate these product metrics. The necessary compilation of the downloaded source files required utilization of stable versions over the current snapshot from the source code repository, the latter of which might produce complications due to inconsistent code and the exclusion of additional libraries. The plug-in creates an XML representation of the calculated metrics which we used in our study. This is done for source code files only (i.e., .java-files in Java). A simple Java program was written to process this XML file and to store the metrics on class level into a database. The resulting product metrics will be described in the next section.

To retrieve the required process metrics, we used the methodology applied in other studies (Mockus et al., 2002; Koch & Schneider, 2002; Robles-Martinez, Gonzalez-Barahona, Centeno-Gonzalez, Matellan-Olivera, & Rodero-Merino, 2003; Dinh-Tong & Bieman, 2005; Hahsler & Koch, 2005), relying on mining the source code control repositories, for the data set in all cases of the concurrent version system (CVS). First, we looked up the CVS tag associated in the repository with the stable version already downloaded. Using this information, a local checkout of the files was performed, and a log file was generated from the initial check-in until the corresponding date of the stable release. This assures that the same source code is used to calculate both the product and process metrics. Data from the log files were extracted for every check-in for every available file in the local CVS repository. Once extracted, these were stored in a normal database as has been done in prior studies (Fischer, Pinzger, & Gall, 2003; Koch & Schneider, 2002; Koch, 2004;

Hahsler & Koch, 2005). Each database entry therefore consists of the filename, the name of the committer which was anonymized for privacy reasons (Thuraisingham, 2005), LOC added and deleted, and the date. The end result was a total of 45,164 records within a single table. We then used database queries to calculate process metrics, for example, overall commits, number of different committers, and so on, for each class (i.e., .java-file). Using another program, additional metrics like the standardized GINI coefficient were computed for every file and again stored in the database. The product and process metrics were merged using the file name as a unique key, resulting in one entry for every class containing both types of metrics. We therefore only consider source code files (i.e., .java-files) and exclude additional files possibly found in the CVS repository, like documentation files or the projects' Web sites. Figure 1 gives a graphical overview of the data-collection process.

Description of Process Metrics

In selecting the metrics used in this study, we both considered the goals of the analysis (i.e., to be able to both characterize the software process and quality aspects of the resulting product) and the availability of metrics within the data. We use several well-discussed process metrics to characterize the OSS development processes in the projects analyzed. The metric of commit refers to a single change of a file by a single programmer. Therefore the number of commits of a file is the sum of changes conducted over a certain period of time and is also an indicator for the activity of a file. In our study we cover the time from the initial commit of a file until the last commit before the stable version was released. The total lifetime of a file includes all the time elapsed, not only that time which was spent on developing and coding. Another important process metric is the total number of distinct programmers involved in writing and maintaining a file. A programmer is defined

Figure 1. Data-collection process

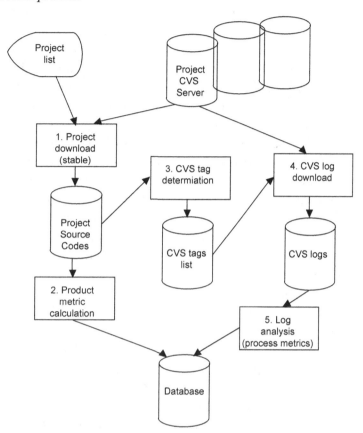

by counting those people committing source code changes through their CVS account, thus only people with such accounts are measured. In some projects, depending on the change and commit policy in place, people could be contributing code without CVS account, which sometimes is only granted to long-time participants, by sending it to one of those persons who then does the actual commit. For example, German (2006) found that 110 out of 364 modification records of a user were patches submitted by 46 different individuals. Therefore, the number of programmers might actually be higher than the number reported here. This fact is very problematic to check. In general, there are several possibilities of attributing authorship of source code to persons, which are to use the associated CVS account (as done here), to mine the versioning system comments for any

additional attributions, to infer from attributions in the source code itself, or by questionnaires or intimate knowledge of a project and its participants. Attributions in source code or commit comments are highly dependent on existence and form of a project's standards, and therefore are also difficult to implement for larger data sets. Ghosh and Prakash (2000) have implemented a solution based on source code attributions for a set of more than 3,000 projects, with about 8.4% of the code base remaining uncredited, and with the top authors containing organizations like the Free Software Foundation or Sun Microsystems. Nevertheless, they have found a similar distribution of participation as found in this study's data set, as have most other approaches like questionnaires (Hertel, Niedner, & Hermann, 2003) or case studies of larger projects (Mockus et al.,

2002, Koch & Schneider, 2002; Dinh-Trong & Bieman, 2005). In a case study of the OpenACS project under participation of project insiders and using the strict standards for CVS comments, Demetriou, Koch, and Neumann (2006) have found that only 1.6% of revisions pertained to code committed for someone without CVS privilege. In this study, we have used two approaches for checking the validity of this measure: Using simple heuristics, we have checked all commit comments for attributions. This shows that 11.7% of revisions seem to be contributed by other people. We have also manually inspected all revisions of the Maverick project: no revision seemed to have been committed for somebody else, which was identical to the heuristics result.

As the participation of programmers in open source projects is less continuous than in commercial development, the number of programmers alone does not adequately reflect the effort invested. Therefore we include the open source software person month (OSSPM) as a new process metric that characterizes the amount of work that is committed to the object considered. This is defined as the cumulated number of distinct active programmers per month over the lifetime of the object of analysis. As Koch and Schneider (2002) have shown, this number of active programmers can be used as an effort predictor. It should be noted that this measure assumes that the mean time spent is constant between objects of analysis.

As several prior studies (Koch, 2004; Mockus et al., 2002; Ghosh & Prakash, 2000; Dinh-Tong & Bieman, 2005) have shown the distribution of effort between participants to be highly skewed and differing from commercial software development, we add an additional process metric to characterize the development style. We used the normalized GINI coefficient (Robles-Martinez et al., 2003), a measure of concentration, for this. The GINI coefficient is a number between 0 and 1, where 0 is an indicator for perfect equality and 1 for total inequality or concentration. We cal-

culated the GINI coefficient both based on LOC added per person (which can be extracted from the CVS repository) and on the number of commits a person has done. As the further analyses did not show significant differences between both measures, we will only report the findings for the GINI coefficient based on LOC added. Therefore in the terms of OSS development, a GINI coefficient of 1 means that one person has written all the code. We performed a slight modification: As some files only have one author, calculating the normalized GINI coefficient results in 0 (equality). For these cases we changed the value from 0 to 1 because, for us, the fact that one person has written all the code is an indicator of inequality rather than equality.

Description of Product Metrics

The most popular product metric is the size of a program, which can be derived by counting the number of lines-of-code (LOCs). There are many different ways to count LOCs (Humphrey, 1995; Park, 1992; Jones, 1986). In this analysis we apply the definition used by the CVS repository, therefore including all types of LOCs: source code lines as well as commentaries (Fogel, 1999). The size of the largest method ($LOCm$) is another important descriptor in object-oriented classes which can also be measured by counting LOCs. These size metrics can be regarded as indicators for complexity as it is very difficult to read and understand classes with long methods and many fields (Henderson-Seller, 1996). Other indicators are the number of regular/static methods (NOM/NSM) and the number of regular/static fields (NOF/NSF). We propose that these size measures are affected by nearly all process metrics: If more people are working on a class, its size will increase. The same will tend to be true for the time the class exists and the number of commits performed. Especially the amount of effort invested in the class will increase the size. Most importantly, we propose that the inequality in contributions will affect different size measures: If the class is programmed and maintained by a small team, or a small core group within a team, these participants will tend not to see the need for promoting higher modularity. This would presumably lead to them not splitting up a class, thus affecting LOC, or a method, thus affecting LOCm.

The probably most well-known complexity metric is McCabe's definition of cyclomatic complexity (VG) (McCabe, 1976). *VG* counts the number of flows through a piece of code, (i.e., a method). Each time a branch occurs (if, for, while, do, case, catch, and logic operators), this metric is incremented by one. We determined the maximum (*VGmax*) and the average (*VGavg*) method complexity on class level. Weighted Methods per Class (WMC) are part of the Chidamber and Kemerer suite, but they leave the weighting scheme as an implementation decision (Chidamber & Kemerer, 1994). In our study WMC is defined as the sum of all method's complexities (*VG*) that occur within a class. VG and WMC are indicators of how much time and effort must be spent to understand, test, maintain, or extend this component (Chidamber & Kemerer, 1991; 1994), with McCabe giving *VG = 10* as a reasonable limit for proper testing (McCabe, 1976). But this measure should be treated with special care, as this metric is based on experiences in procedural languages including C or COBOL (Lorenz & Kidd, 1995). Subramanyam and Krishnan (2003) have shown that WMC is highly correlated to LOC, which supports the thesis that LOC can be used as a low-level complexity metric. The influence of WMC on software quality was examined in several studies (Basili, Briand, & Melo, 1996; Subramanyam & Krishnan, 2003). Regarding the relationship of complexity measures with process metrics, the most important effect is proposed to exist in connection with the inequality: Analogous to the reasoning for size, complexity reduction will not be a high priority when a small core group who would know the code in any case is present. Also, classes, and software overall, tend to accumulate more complexity as

time passes, if no counter-measures are taken. This will decrease maintainability, which again is less of an issue if the software is consistently maintained by a small group.

The object-oriented product metrics we investigated are mostly based on a subset of the Chidamber-Kemerer-Suite (Chidamber & Kemerer, 1991, 1994; Chidamber, Darcy, & Kemerer, 1998). The authors argued that the product metrics commonly used before were not suitable for object-oriented development (Chidamber & Kemerer, 1991). From their point of view, the modern object-oriented analysis, design, and programming processes, which encapsulate functionality and entities in objects, were too different from the traditional software engineering process. The prior product metrics were not designed to measure object-oriented characteristics like classes, inheritance, and the usage of methods and attributes. They proposed six metrics, derived from a theoretical analysis, which should be able to assist in making predictions about the complexity and quality of object-oriented programs. We used a subset of the CK-suite (NOC, DIT, WMC) for which concrete threshold values were suggested. The remaining metrics (LCOM, RFC, CBO) are not part of this study, as no threshold values are available. In addition, CBO and RFC have been found to be highly correlated with WMC (Chidamber et al., 1998), so they would not give additional information. These CK-metrics for our analysis are complemented by some of the metrics defined by Lorenz and Kidd (1995).

Number of Children (NOC) and Depth in Inheritance Tree (DIT) are metrics for the level of inheritance of a class. Chidamber and Kemerer (1994) state that the deeper a class in the hierarchy, the more complicated it is to predict its behavior and the greater its design complexity. Though this may lead to greater effort in maintenance and testing, it has greater potential for the reuse of inherited methods. In a Java environment, DIT is defined as the longest path from the class to the root in the inheritance hierarchy—that is, the class Object. Some studies have shown that DIT is related to fault-proneness (Basili et al., 1996; Briand, Wüst, Ikonomovski, & Lounis, 1998). NOC counts the number of classes inherited from a particular ancestor—that is, the number of children in the inheritance hierarchy beneath a class. A class implementing an interface counts as a direct child of that interface. Chidamber and Kemerer (1991) expose a similar relationship between design complexity and NOC. The greater the number of children of a class, the greater is the reuse. However, an excessive number of children may indicate the misuse of sub-classing. NOC also hints to the importance of that class within the application, as well as to the corresponding additional effort likely required for testing and maintaining. NOC was evaluated by Basili et al. (1996) and Briand et al. (1998), who differ in their findings related to fault-proneness. NORM, like NOC and DIT, is an inheritance metric for class design (Lorenz & Kidd, 1995). It measures the number of inherited methods overridden by a subclass. Lorenz and Kidd (1995) state that, especially in the context of frameworks, methods are often defined in a way that requires them to be overridden. However, very high values may indicate a design problem because a subclass should extend new abilities to its super-class that should result in new method names. Similar to the other product measures, we again propose a relationship of the process metrics with these object-oriented metrics. Especially the metrics giving an indication of the use of inheritance will be affected by different process attributes, most importantly on project level. The correct use of inheritance helps in achieving a modular design which in turn allows for parallel work by many participants. In addition, it significantly enhances maintainability. We therefore propose that analogous mechanisms will be found here as for complexity measures.

We suggest two additional metrics that can be used to describe the interior design of a class. The number of classes (NCL) counts the number of classes within a class and should be either 0 for interfaces or 1 for classes. Other values indicate the utilization of interior classes, which should be avoided in object-oriented design. The number of interfaces within a class (NOI) aims at the same direction. Interfaces are used to define entry points within or even across applications and therefore should not be defined within a class but in separate files.

Most of these product metrics presented are discrete variables, where increasing (or decreasing) values are not necessarily a sign of good or bad quality, or aspects thereof. For example, whether the cyclomatic complexity VG of an entity is 4 or 6 is mostly determined by its function, and does not signal any deviation from good practice or negatively influence maintainability. Only if a certain value is surpassed does this metric give an indication of possible problems. Therefore, most of these metrics can be assigned a threshold for this purpose. Currently, there is a paucity of threshold values for the defined metrics provided by literature based on empirical studies, especially using Java. This requires us for most metrics to use the values proposed by Lorenz and Kidd (1995) for C++ classes.

Based on the threshold values in Table 1, we created dummy variables that take on the value of one or zero, depending on whether the associated metric values exceed the threshold value for that class. These dichotomous variables try to categorize the given metrics based on different aspects to be explored like size or complexity (see Box 1).

MSIZE and *CSIZE* depend on metrics that measure size, *MCOMP* on complexity, *CINH* on inheritance, and *CDESIGN* on interior class design.

ANALYSIS ON CLASS LEVEL

In total, 6,235 Java classes (i.e., distinct files) have been analyzed, for which a total of 45,164

Table 1. Overview of metrics with corresponding threshold values

Metric	Name	Threshold	Definition
NOC	Number of Children		Total number of direct subclasses of a class
NOI	Number of Interfaces		Total number of interfaces of the file
DIT	Depth of Inheritance Tree	< 6	Distance from class Object in the inheritance hierarchy
NORM	Number of Overridden Methods	< 3	Total number of methods that are overridden from an ancestor class
NOM	Number of Methods	< 30-40	Total number of methods
NOF	Number of Fields	< 3-9	Total number of class variables
NSM	Number of Static Methods	< 4	Total number of static methods
NSF	Number of Static Fields	< 3	Total number of static variables
LOCm	Lines of Code	< 24	Total lines of code of the greatest method in the selected scope
VGmax	McCabe Cyclomatic Complexity Maximum	< 10	Maximum VG for all methods within a class
VGavg	McCabe Cyclomatic Complexity Average	< 10	Average VG for all methods within a class
WMC	Weighted Methods per Class	< 65	Sum of the McCabe Cyclomatic Complexity for all methods in a class
NCL	Number of Classes	= 1	Indicates possible interior classes

Box 1.

$$MSIZE \quad \begin{cases} 1 & if \quad LOC\,/\,NOM > 18 \vee LOCm > 24 \\ 0 & else \end{cases}$$

$$MCOMP \quad \begin{cases} 1 & if \quad VGmax > 10 \vee VGavg > 10 \\ 0 & else \end{cases}$$

$$CSIZE \quad \begin{cases} 1 & if \quad NOM > 30 \vee NSM > 4 \vee NOF > 9 \vee NSF > 4 \\ 0 & else \end{cases}$$

$$CINH \quad \begin{cases} 1 & if \quad DIT > 6 \vee (NOC * DIT) > 15 \\ 0 & else \end{cases}$$

$$CDESIGN \quad \begin{cases} 1 & if \quad NCL > 1 \vee NOI > 1 \\ 0 & else \end{cases}$$

commits were made, with 2,109,989 LOCs added and 913,455 LOCs deleted. A total of 133 distinct programmers have contributed with at least one commit. The number of classes investigated therefore is considerably higher than the datasets used in former studies on object-oriented metrics (634 by Chidamber & Kemerer, 1994; 97 by Chidamber et al., 1998; 180 by Basili et al., 1996; 698 by Subramanian & Corbin, 2001; 180 by Briand, Wüst, Daly, & Porter, 2000).

Table 2. Descriptive statistics for all classes

Process Metrics							
	N	Min	Max	Mean	s.d.	75% Percentile	Median
Authors	6,235	1.00	15.00	2.66	1.59	3.00	2.00
Commits	6,235	1.00	209.00	7.24	9.96	8.00	5.00
Days	6,235	0.00	1,628.91	357.44	298.90	459.81	350.78
GINI	6,235	0.00	1.00	0.78	0.24	0.98	0.85
OSSPM	6,235	1.00	58.00	4.80	4.02	6.00	4.00
Product Metrics							
	N	Min	Max	Mean	s.d.	75% Percentile	Median
LOC	6,235	0.00	7,546.00	207.99	279.44	237.00	124.00
DIT	5,339	1.00	10.00	2.60	1.58	3.00	2.00
NCL	5,339	1.00	51.00	1.16	1.24	1.00	1.00
NOF	5,339	0.00	119.00	2.50	4.67	3.00	1.00
NOI	915	1.00	28.00	1.07	1.19	1.00	0.00
NOM	5,339	0.00	252.00	8.37	12.32	10.00	4.00
NORM	5,339	0.00	65.00	0.61	1.89	1.00	0.00
NOC	5,339	0.00	185.00	1.18	7.05	0.00	0.00
NSF	5,339	0.00	69.00	1.54	4.30	1.00	0.00
NSM	5,339	0.00	69.00	0.71	3.03	0.00	0.00
VGavg	5,339	0.00	42.00	2.41	2.60	2.77	1.67
WMC	5,339	0.00	871.00	20.77	37.22	23.00	10.00
LOCm	5,339	0.00	601.00	22.96	35.85	30.00	24.00
VGmax	5,339	0.00	159.00	5.51	8.38	7.00	3.00

Descriptive Statistics

Descriptive statistics for all product and process metrics can be found in Table 2. The highest number of commits (209) can be found in the Barracuda project. This file is a change history in Java format containing only comments. The file with the second highest number of commits (188) is also the class with the highest value of LOCs added (19,252), LOCs deleted (11,706), and the largest file overall (7,546 LOCs). This file is one of the most important classes of the Expresso framework (DBObject.Java) and is responsible for DB communication. The class that is responsible for dispatching the requests of the Struts framework (ActionServlet.Java) is the file with the third highest number of commits (150). An abstract class of the Jetspeed framework that forms the behavior of a portlet has another high value of commits. It is obvious that components providing key functionalities need a special amount of interest because they are usually engaged with several other objects. In accordance with prior studies, all of the process metrics are not 'normal distributed' which can be ascertained using a Kolmogorov-Smirnov test.

In accordance with other studies (Koch, 2004), the number of distinct programmers is quite small with low standard deviation. The histogram of distinct programmers per file shows a heavily skewed distribution. Only 12.2% of the files have more than three distinct authors. Most of the files have one (24.0%) or two (56.1%) programmers, and only 3% have more than five distinct authors. The number of commits per file follows a similar distribution. Only 16.3% have more than 10 commits. Although our values depend on files' respective classes, there are similarities to other studies that have investigated the distribution of distinct authors and commits (Koch, 2004; Krishnamurthy, 2002; Mockus et al., 2002; Ghosh & Prakash, 2000) on the project level.

All of the product metrics are clearly not 'normal distributed' as well. The distribution of LOC is also heavily skewed, which is in accordance with other studies (Koch, 2004; Krishnamurthy, 2002).

Due to the fact that most of the metrics mentioned above measure attributes of classes, we regard real interfaces as missing values (*NOI = 1 and NCL = 0*). Classes that have interior interfaces are valid. Most of the median values are below the threshold suggested by Lorenz and Kidd (1995), as are most of the values for the 75% percentile. The only metric that exceeds this recommendation is the 75% percentile of the size of a method (30>24). The median of the average method complexity per class *VGavg* (1.67) and of the maximum method complexity (3) are below the threshold of 10 suggested by McCabe (1976), and only 11.5% of the classes have a maximum method's complexity greater than 10. Most of the studies which investigate object-oriented metrics

used C++ source files (Briand et al., 2000; Chidamber & Kemerer, 1994), so our results cannot directly be compared to them. We are aware of only one study that investigates Java classes (Subramanyam & Krishnan, 2003). Compared to that study we have higher WMC values and our classes are more deeply nested in the inheritance hierarchy. One possible reason for this may be the fact that we examined frameworks that provide abstract classes that are meant to be overridden. The percentage of classes that exceed our dichotomous variables are 5.3% (*CINH*), 6.0% (*MCOMP*), 6.1% (*CDESIGN*), 14.9% (*CSIZE*), and 34.9% (*MSIZE*). The fact that one-third of the classes investigated do not meet the requirements for small method size gives rise to the question whether these threshold values are suitable for object-oriented Java programs. Our data set consists of frameworks that provide functionality for a lot of different scopes. Therefore the average and maximum values may be greater than in normal applications. However we do not adjust the threshold value as it is an indicator for easy understanding and maintenance. The remaining values for the dichotomous variables seem to be reasonable.

RESULTS

In this analysis, we explore relationships between the metrics mentioned above. Results for correlations between the different process metrics can

Table 3. Correlation between process metrics (Spearman coefficient, all at a significance level of p<0.01)

	Authors	Commits	Days	GINI	OSSPM
Authors	1.000				
Commits	0.554	1.000			
Days	0.471	0.685	1.000		
GINI	-0.524	-0.370	-0.528	1.000	
OSSPM	0.639	0.925	0.689	-0.393	1.000

be found in Table 3, respectively Figure 2, using ellipses (Murdoch & Chow, 1996). Due to the fact that all metrics are not 'normal distributed', we used the nonparametric Spearman coefficient.

The correlation analysis shows expected relationships, like the older a file the more distinct programmers are involved (0.471), the more commits are conducted (0.685), and the more work is contributed (0.689). The amount of work (OSSPM) is highly correlated to authors, commits, and the active time, what is indeed reasonable. More interesting are the relations between the inequality as measured by the GINI coefficients and the remaining process metrics. The results show that the older a file, the more homogeneous is the distribution of the added input. The negative correlation between authors and GINI reveals the same tendencies. The more people are involved, the more the work is equally distributed among the participating authors. The number of commits only has slight influence on the GINI coefficient. The correlation between product metrics is not that important, but it should be mentioned that

metrics that measure size attributes of a class (NOM, NSM, NOF, and NSF) are positively correlated to the total size in LOC. Furthermore there is a very strong correlation of WMC to LOC (0.734), which is almost identical to the correlation coefficient of 0.741 found by Subramanyam and Krishnan (2003). More importantly, correlations between product and process metrics have been explored, and the results are shown in Table 4, respectively Figure 3, using ellipses (Murdoch & Chow, 1996).

The complexity metrics *WMC* and *VGavg* have a slight correlation to the number of authors and commits as well as to the effort indicator OSSPM. A similar slight relationship appears regarding the group of metrics that measure the size of a class like *LOC, LOCm*, or *NOM*. The influence of the active time on the product metrics can be disregarded. Metrics concerned with the use of inheritance (DIT and NOC) do not seem to be correlated to any of the process attributes. As DIT and NOC are important indicators of reuse and well-structured programming, a deeper look into source code is necessary to gather that kind of information. The GINI coefficient does not seem to be correlated to any product metric.

As described above we created dichotomous variables that indicate whether a class exceeds a certain quality threshold or not and compared these two samples with a non-parametric rank-sum test, the Mann-Whitney-U test, also known as Wilcoxon rank-sum test, for example also applied by Koru and Tian (2005). The test assesses whether the degree of overlap between the two observed distributions is less than would be expected by chance. The resulting hypotheses are:

H0: *There is no difference in process characteristics between the group S1 that exceeds the threshold values and the group S0 that does not.*

HA: *There is a difference between these groups.*

Figure 2. Correlation between process metrics (Spearman coefficient, black showing significance level of p<0.01)

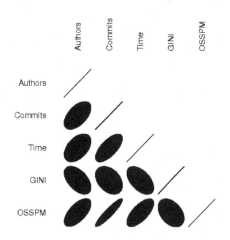

Table 4. Correlation between selected process and product metrics (Spearman coefficient, * p < 0.05, ** p < 0.01)

	Authors	Commits	Time	GINI	OSSPM
LOC	**0.157	**0.379	**0.179	**0.057	**0.370
DIT	0.015	0.019	0.025	*−0.027	0.021
LCOM	**0.109	**0.102	0.020	**0.044	**0.137
LOCm	**0.237	**0.432	**0.181	**−0.058	**0.408
NBD	**0.273	**0.290	**0.138	**−0.152	**0.292
NCL	**0.092	**0.139	**0.042	**0.048	**0.131
NOF	**0.149	**0.199	**0.071	**0.038	**0.199
NOI	**−0.080	**−0.097	0.001	**−0.034	**−0.119
NOM	**0.103	**0.253	**0.066	**0.037	**0.232
NORM	**0.095	**0.169	**0.108	**−0.078	**0.181
NOC	**0.085	**0.084	**0.091	*−0.029	**0.093
NSF	**0.129	**0.244	**0.155	−0.022	**0.235
NSM	−0.019	**0.044	*0.027	0.006	0.018
SIX	**0.076	**0.149	**0.108	**−0.086	**0.162
VGavg	**0.242	**0.332	**0.168	**−0.112	**0.337
WMC	**0.214	**0.389	**0.163	*−0.032	**0.366

Figure 3. Correlation between selected process and product metrics (Spearman coefficient, grey p < 0.05, black p < 0.01)

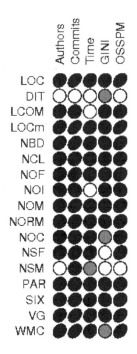

Table 5. Results of Mann-Whitney U-tests (↑ indicates that high values of the process metrics foster bad quality and ↓ indicates good quality)

	Authors	Commits	Time	GINI	OSSPM
MSIZE					
relationship (HA)	accepted (p<0.01)	accepted (p<0.01)	accepted (p<0.01)	accepted (p<0.01)	accepted (p<0.01)
direction	↑, *HA1* (p<0.01)	↑, *HA1* (p<0.01)	↑, *HA1* (p<0.01)	↓, *HA0* (p<0.01)	↑, *HA1* (p<0.01)
MCOMP					
relationship (HA)	accepted (p<0.01)	accepted (p<0.01)	accepted (p<0.01)	rejected	accepted (p<0.01)
direction	↑, *HA1* (p<0.01)	↑, *HA1* (p<0.01)	↑, *HA1* (p<0.01)		↑, *HA1* (p<0.01)
CSIZE					
relationship (HA)	accepted (p<0.01)	accepted (p<0.01)	accepted (p<0.01)	rejected	accepted (p<0.01)
direction	↑, *HA1* (p<0.01)	↑, *HA1* (p<0.01)	↑, *HA1* (p<0.01)		↑, *HA1* (p<0.01)
CINH					
relationship (HA)	accepted (p<0.01)	accepted (p<0.01)	accepted (p<0.01)	accepted (p<0.01)	accepted (p<0.01)
direction	↑, *HA1* (p<0.01)	↑, *HA1* (p<0.01)	↑, *HA1* (p<0.01)	↓, *HA0* (p<0.01)	↑, *HA1* (p<0.01)
DESIGN					
relationship (HA)	accepted (p<0.01)	accepted (p<0.01)	accepted (p<0.01)	accepted (p<0.01)	accepted (p<0.01)
direction	↑, *HA1* (p<0.01)	↑, *HA1* (p<0.01)	↑, *HA1* (p<0.01)	↑, *HA1* (p<0.01)	↑, *HA1* (p<0.01)

If H0 is rejected, an additional, one-sided Mann-Whitney U-test is used with the hypotheses:

HA1: *The rank-sum in S1 is greater than in S0, indicating that high values of process metrics foster bad quality.*

HA0: *The rank-sum in S1 is lesser than in S0, indicating that high values of process metrics foster good quality.*

The results of these tests are shown in Table 5. Except for the combinations *MCOMP/GINI* and *CSIZE/GINI*, the significance is smaller than 0.05, so in these cases we can accept the alternative hypothesis *HA* that the corresponding process metrics have an influence on the product metric. In this case we performed a one-sided Mann-Whitney U-test to determine the direction of relationship—that is, whether the process metrics have a positive (accept HA1) or negative (accept HA0) influence on the product metrics.

In case of a positive relationship (↑), the sum of the ranks in the group that exceeds the limit is higher than in the group that does not. In quality terms, these results indicate that the higher the process metric is, the lower the quality is. Therefore a higher number of distinct programmers, commits, time, and invested effort have a negative influence on the quality.

To validate our results we performed the same tests only with classes that have at least five different authors (n=668). The results are mainly the same, but we could not reject H0 for the combinations *MCOMP*/Time, *CSIZE*/Authors, and *CSIZE*/Time. The change in the number of authors had an influence on the relationship between GINI and the dichotome product metrics. All combinations had a positive influence (accept HA1 with p<0.01), which confirms our prior results that the more the work is concentrated, the worse is the quality of software. Or the other way around, an equal distribution of commits fosters good quality. We will discuss this important finding in more detail later on.

ANALYSIS ON PROJECT LEVEL

For an analysis on project level, we aggregated the product metrics from class level and calculated the process metrics for the whole project, based on those files that were examined in the former section. We stored these results in another table in the database.

Descriptive Statistics

Cocoon is the project with the highest number of distinct programmers, commits, and Java classes. The project ActionServlet, Jpublish, and Echo only have one author. Whether these should be included in further analysis can be discussed. Using a definition of OSS based on the respective license, these projects constitute open source projects, but they conflict with the development model normally associated. On the other hand, these projects might possibly have more participants but a very central control regarding the source code, such that any change must be reviewed and committed by the single maintainer, although other people actually write the code and submit it to this person. We have already discussed this problem with the

Table 6. Process metrics for all projects (ordered by number of authors)

	Authors	Commits	Days	GINI	Files	OSSPM
cocoon-2.1	40.00	10,131.00	439.49	0.85	2,298.00	244.00
jakarta-jetspeed	17.00	4,962.00	1,637.92	0.68	677.00	160.00
jakarta-turbine-2	17.00	2,621.00	748.17	0.81	388.00	83.00
jakarta-struts	16.00	3,092.00	1,122.33	0.60	496.00	146.00
expresso	10.00	6,389.00	761.08	0.84	649.00	94.00
jakarta-tapestry	9.00	3,001.00	409.62	0.85	535.00	53.00
Barracuda	9.00	3,543.00	1,279.08	0.75	453.00	71.00
japple	7.00	1,612.00	450.10	0.68	238.00	56.00
maverick	6.00	358.00	1,137.92	0.71	78.00	27.00
ActionServlet	1.00	199.00	223.15	1.00	106.00	4.00
echo	1.00	1,690.00	894.92	1.00	220.00	27.00
jpublish	1.00	886.00	1,172.03	1.00	97.00	34.00

respective metric description. In the following, we base the analysis on both the full set and a subset with these projects removed.

Struts is the framework with the lowest GINI coefficient, which is an indicator for equality of input. Cocoon, Jetspeed, Struts, Tapestry, and Turbine are projects that are hosted by the Apache Software Foundation. The great popularity of the Apache Web server may explain the encouragement of these frameworks. The very low number of commits for the ActionServlet is an indicator for inactivity of the project.

Table 7 shows the mean values of the most important product metrics. The Japple framework has the largest files and the highest WMC. As we have discussed in the previous chapter, there is a very strong linear relationship between LOC and WMC. Therefore this combination is not astonishing. Struts and Jetspeed are the projects with the highest DIT, which indicates extensive usage of subclassing, a form of reuse. The number of children differs across the projects. The frameworks with the lowest average number of children only have one author (ActionServlet, Jpublish).

To get an indication of quality and design, we again apply the dichotomous variables used for capturing different possible problem areas (*MSIZE, MCOMP, CSIZE, CINH,* and *DESIGN*). As the total number of classes that exceed our limits is not appropriate due to different numbers of classes between projects, we calculated the relative amount of faulty classes within a project (see Table 8). Metric *MSIZE* depicting problems with method size has rather high values for all projects, but more than 35% of the classes of Japple, Expresso, and Jetspeed exceed the limit. These three frameworks also have a large amount of methods that outrun the upper bound for complexity. The relative amount of misuse of inheritance *CINH* is small except for the Maverick framework (14.1%). The number of classes with interior classes or interfaces is small except for Barracuda, Maverick, and Echo.

Results

Due to the fact that only a small data set on project level is available, the usage of correlation analysis is not sufficient as the small number precludes any statistically significant findings. Therefore

Table 7. Product metrics for projects (mean values)

	DIT	NORM	NOC	SIX	VGavg	WMC
cocoon-2.1	2.54	0.50	1.13	0.24	2.30	18.02
jetspeed	2.97	0.81	0.81	0.45	2.63	22.41
turbine	2.53	0.42	1.40	0.26	1.82	16.33
struts	3.39	0.69	0.72	0.53	2.97	23.01
expresso	2.82	0.78	1.07	0.49	2.59	30.22
tapestry	2.28	0.29	0.92	0.18	1.65	13.49
Barracuda	2.44	1.29	2.88	0.27	2.83	26.74
japple	1.97	0.77	1.22	0.13	3.16	32.60
maverick	2.40	0.29	1.27	0.33	1.86	9.62
ActionServlet	1.87	0.23	0.33	0.12	2.73	17.01
echo	1.92	0.50	1.75	0.17	2.23	18.44
jpublish	1.97	0.24	0.46	0.10	1.73	13.70

Table 8. Percentage of classes that exceeds the limits of quality metrics

	MSIZE	MCOMP	CSIZE	CINH	CDESIGN
cocoon-2.1	24.06	4.05	11.27	4.35	7.57
jetspeed	37.08	6.06	15.36	8.71	2.81
turbine-2	26.55	1.55	12.37	4.12	2.32
jakarta-struts	34.68	8.67	17.34	3.63	1.61
expresso	45.30	8.01	15.25	4.47	2.77
tapestry	17.38	0.75	5.05	1.87	3.36
Barracuda	33.55	9.71	18.32	6.84	17.44
japple	53.78	7.98	13.03	1.26	3.36
maverick	17.95	0.00	10.26	14.10	11.54
ActionServlet	23.58	4.72	3.77	0.94	4.72
echo	28.18	5.45	22.27	3.18	15.00
jpublish	19.59	2.06	6.19	2.06	1.03

Table 9. Ranks and sum (ordered by decreasing ranksum)

	MSIZE	MCOMP	CSIZE	CINH	CDESIGN	Ranksum
jakarta-tapestry	12	11	11	10	6	50
jpublish	10	9	10	9	12	50
ActionServlet	9	7	12	12	5	45
jakarta-turbine-2	7	10	7	6	10	40
maverick	11	12	9	1	3	36
cocoon-2.1	8	8	8	5	4	33
japple	1	4	6	11	7	29
jakarta-struts	4	2	3	7	11	27
expresso	2	3	5	4	9	23
nextappecho	6	6	1	8	2	23
jakarta-jetspeed	3	5	4	2	8	22
Barracuda	5	1	2	3	1	12

we performed a simple ranking based on the relative amount of classes that exceed our threshold values. High relative amounts of 'faulty' classes result in high ranks (i.e., the project with the highest percentage of classes violating the threshold is ranked on the first place in this variable), and therefore the higher the sum of ranks the higher the overall quality. We do not weight the quality indicators. This ranking can be used to choose the best alternative among concurrent projects depending on their software quality. This ranking is on an ordinal scale and therefore should not be misused to perform any kind of quantitative comparisons, but we try to find some indicators for our findings on class level.

It is interesting that the two projects with only one author have the highest rank overall. Jpublish and ActionServlet also have very low numbers of Java-files and commits, and the OSS development effort is rather low as well. In contrast to these one-man-projects, Tapestry has nine distinct authors but the same Ranksum as Jpublish. But this project is not that old and the invested development effort is rather small. This can be seen as another proof for the hypothesis that over project lifetime, the quality decreases due to a missing necessary redesign of the software structure.

The largest project overall with 40 distinct authors, more than 10,000, commits and 244 OSSPM is Cocoon. Cocoon is ranked in sixth place—right in the middle—so that we cannot state the quality as extremely bad or good. The second largest project measured by OSSPM and .java-files is Jetspeed, which has the second worst quality ranking, which supports the findings on class level.

In order to statistically underline these results, we used the order produced by the ranksum to compare those projects ranking highly overall to those ranking very low. This was done by a set of Mann-Whitney U-tests as applied above. This time, membership in a project was used as a dividing factor for the classes, and the distribution of relevant process metrics was tested to uncover whether the top projects consistently have different distributions than the lower rated ones. We tested each of the top three projects against each of the bottom three projects, resulting in nine comparisons per process metric. For validation, we also eliminated the one-person projects within the top group, using the next lower ones with more participants. The results indicate that projects in the high-quality region have more authors and commits, but consistently lower GINI coefficient representing more equal distributions (in six, respectively seven, out of nine comparisons in the validation sample). While the first result seems in contradiction with the results on class level, the effects of a high concentration are valid on both levels. These results will be discussed in the following section.

MULTILEVEL ANALYSIS

Multilevel models (also sometimes termed nested or mixed-effect models) are statistical models with parameters arranged in a hierarchical structure (Goldstein, 1999; Snijders & Bosker, 2003; Kreft & de Leeuw, 2002). They are appropriate for data which involves multiple levels, for example on individual level and group level. A classical example is a study of students from different schools, attributes of which might have an impact on individual performance, or research in organizational science (Klein, Tosi, & Cannella, 1999). Multilevel models can account for direct effects of variables on each other within any one level, and also cross-level interaction effects between variables located at different levels.

In our study, we have data within two distinct levels: class and project, with classes being grouped into projects. Therefore, it is possible that aspects of a project like different processes or practices have an influence on the quality of a class. Using a multilevel model, these effects can be accounted for and tested. In the following, we use Akaike's information criterion (AIC) to compare the goodness of fit of the estimated models, which incorporates the number of parameters in selecting the best model, thus penalizing overfitting. For all analysis, we employed R, a freely available language and environment for statistical computing, using the nlme package for multilevel modeling.

First, we computed for comparison classical linear models without hierarchical effects for each dichotomous quality metric (*MSIZE, MCOMP*, etc.), using the independent factors Authors, Commits, Time, and GINI. The results are congruent with the class-level analysis and show the same general trend of negative effects on quality: In general, all of the parameters are significant, positive, and introducing them in a stepwise linear regression increases model quality significantly (all at *p< 0.01*). The following exceptions apply: Time has generally a positive effect on quality (except for *CINH* where the effect is negative, and for *CDESIGN* where it is not significant), and for *MSIZE* the GINI coefficient has a positive influence as well (again congruent with the prior analysis). The GINI coefficient also does

Figure 4. Ranking of projects based on the dichotomous variables (high relative amounts result in low ranks, the higher the sum of the ranks the better the quality)

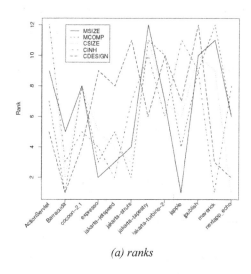

(a) ranks

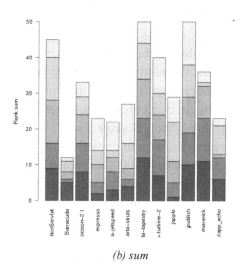

(b) sum

not have a significant effect on *CINH*. Overall, the resulting models only account for a relatively small part in overall variation, as the R-squared value ranges from about 0.05 to 0.10.

Following from this, we expand the analysis into multilevel models. We therefore both introduce additional fixed variables from the project level (i.e., the overall effort OSSPM of a project); the total number of programmers, files, and commits; total lifetime and GINI coefficient; and define an increasing range of first-level variables as random. This implies that for each unit, a different slope and intercept is estimated, so that the effect of these can differ between units. These different setups resulted in more than 10 different models being estimated for each quality indicator. Using statistical tests based on AIC, these models were compared with each other and also with the linear models without hierarchical effects computed before.

The first result is that the inclusion of project attributes like total number of programmers does not increase model quality. In all cases, these parameters are not significant in the regression. In the

model comparison, introducing these terms does therefore lead to a significant reduction in model fit measured by AIC (except for introducing the project's GINI coefficient, where the reduction is not significant) due to the penalty associated with a higher number of parameters. In comparison to the linear models without hierarchical effects, the results are generally slightly better if no or a small number of project attributes are included, due to the random slope introduced. This underlines that differences between the projects are significant. If the models which define more variables like authors as random (i.e., these are allowed to have a different intercept and slope depending on project) are inspected, the model quality does in all cases increase significantly. This is, with a few exceptions, true for an increasing number of variables becoming random, even though more parameters are penalized by AIC. The exceptions are: the GINI coefficient for both *MCOMP* and *CINH* does not exhibit significant random effects. This again shows that the differences between projects are manifold and encompass the effects of several attributes like concentration or number of developers. If the random effects estimated are evaluated further, we find that there are even differences in effect direction between projects: for example, the number of authors has a positive effect on method size in six projects, a negative effect in the others. For problems in inheritance structure on the other hand, the number of authors almost uniformly shows a negative effect throughout the projects. Also the concentration has negative effects almost throughout the project set.

From this analysis, we can draw the conclusion that the results achieved by other means hold mostly valid, but that the multilevel approach shows additional insights. We found that there are indeed differences between the projects in the way that the different process metrics have a relationship with product quality concepts, which can be accounted for with this analysis. We also found that the mechanisms and attributes of projects mitigating these effects do not currently seem to be captured by the measurements performed, as the metrics like total number of developers of projects did not show a significant impact. The reasons for the different effects might therefore lie in other attributes like process design which need to be incorporated in future analyses and models.

DISCUSSION

The analyses on class and project level showed several results which need to be discussed in their reasons and in their implications. As shown, a high number of programmers and commits, as well as a high concentration, is associated with problems in quality on class level, mostly to violations of size and design guidelines. This underlines the results of Koru and Tian (2005), who have found that modules with many changes rate quite high on structural measures like size or inheritance. On project level, there is a distinct difference: those projects with high overall quality ranking have more authors and commits, but a smaller

concentration than those ranking poorly. We will first address the effects associated with high concentration on few heads, which turn out on both levels, afterwards touching on the differences found.

A high concentration is often seen as a trademark of open source software development and has turned up in almost any study of open source projects (e.g., Koch, 2004; Ghosh & Prakash, 2000; Dinh-Tong & Bieman, 2005). Mockus et al. (2002) have shown this difference to commercial projects in a comparison. Reasons for this concentration are manifold: they reach from motivational aspects like status games which lead to different invested effort between participants, hugely different skills sets of participants in combination with self-selection for tasks, the founding process by one or a few people, to possible delays in achieving commiter status in some projects. On the other hand, we find that a high concentration is correlated with possible problems in the product quality and maintainability. It has to be noted that the direction of this relationship between design aspects and development organization is not determined: If the architecture is not modular enough, a high concentration might show up as a result of this, as it can preclude more diverse participation. The other explanation is that classes that are programmed and/or maintained by a small core team are more complex due to the fact that these programmers 'know' their own code and do not see the need for splitting large and complex methods. One possibility in this case is a refactoring (Fowler, 1999) for a more modular architecture with smaller classes and more pronounced use of inheritance. This would increase the possible participation, thus maybe in turn leading to lower concentration and maintainability, together with other quality aspects. At the beginning of the development process, a core developer team sets up the design which is not adjusted to cope with the increasing number of classes and complexity. In this case it might be better to split huge classes into several subclasses, which may also improve the quality of inheritance and abstraction.

Underlining these results, MacCormack, Rusnak, and Baldwin (2006) have in a similar study used design structure matrices to study the difference between open source and proprietary developed software, without further discrimination in development practices. They find significant differences between Linux, which is more modular, and the first version of Mozilla. The evolution of Mozilla then shows purposeful redesign aiming for a more modular architecture, which resulted in modularity even higher than Linux. They conclude that a product's design mirrors the organization developing it, in that a product developed by a distributed team such as Linux was more modular compared to Mozilla developed by a collocated team. Alternatively, the design also reflects purposeful choices made by the developers based on contextual challenges, in that Mozilla was successfully redesigned for higher modularity at a later stage.

Regarding the number of authors, the results need to be explored further and put into context of the findings on concentration: We found on class level a negative impact, while on project level a positive effect. This underlines a central statement of open source software development on a general level, that as many people as possible should be attracted to a project. On the other hand, these resources should, from the viewpoint of product quality, be organized in small teams. Ideally, on both levels, the effort is not concentrated on too few of the relevant participants. This is certainly not contrary to conventional software engineering knowledge, which can be found to hold in this context as well.

The implications of these findings need to be discussed in two different contexts, the first one being within open source projects, and also in general. These two settings differ significantly, most relevantly in the general aims, the possibilities for intervention by project management, and also the motivation of participants. In an open source project, a management in classical form does not exist, although often a maintainer, inner circle, or other authority (although with mostly minimal impact) could be interested in the organization of work within the project. Also the aims of a project, and interwoven with this, the motivations of participants are very much different from commercial settings, and they need to be considered. Therefore there are very limited possibilities for any central agency to manage and steer the participants, or they might lose motivation and leave the project. On the other hand, management responsibilities are often taken up by the founding group of a project. In case of early phases of a project, the design should therefore strive to allow for these teams to form by providing an appropriate number of classes within a modular architecture, termed by MacCormack et al. (2006) as "architecture of participation." Executing a refactoring within the context of a large and well-established open source project often might prove difficult, but a central agency should carefully monitor the respective metrics as described in this article to gain an understanding of possible future problems, both in quality and participation aspects. If those are identified, soft measures might be applied to encourage the participants to adjust, for example by using increased reputation and recognition for people participating in such efforts. In addition, the lack of formal design specification often associated with open source projects should be overcome. Again, taking up these tasks should be rewarded within the reputation structure, while other possible motivational factors like training are naturally offered in this context. MacCormack et al. (2006) have shown with the Mozilla case that such efforts can be successful. In our study, we have found evidence for a refactoring having taken place in the Maverick project based on log messages, which is now top ranking in method size and complexity measures.

In a commercial context, many of the problems as discussed above do not apply, so management has more possibilities to enforce a certain organization of work or a necessary refactoring. The organizational form of 'chief programmer team organization' (Mills, 1971; Baker, 1972), also termed 'surgical team' by Brooks (1995), has system development divided into tasks each handled by a chief programmer who is responsible for the most part of the actual design and coding, supported by a larger number of other specialists like a documentation writer or a tester. A similar form of development seems to be adopted by open source projects, although a too highly concentrated form does not perform well given the negative effects associated with high concentration. Possibly the single-author projects in our sample form an example of this organization. Only one person has access to the source code and is assisted by a larger number of other participants.

In arriving at the results of this study, we found that the creation of dichotomous variables helped in several ways, although the thresholds remain a problematic point. The huge number of available and sometimes highly correlated product metrics can be aggregated into a more manageable and interpretable set in this way, and effects on quality can more easily be analyzed. For the process metrics applied, we found that different calculation approaches for the GINI coefficient did not change the results in a significant way. The effort indicator OSSPM introduced did not give much additional information as well, although the high correlation to other metrics like commits need not be present in all data sets. We propose that the invested effort might still be considered as an important factor.

CONCLUSION

The analysis described in this article has tried to enhance prior studies on OSS by providing an empirical validation of relationships between process attributes and product quality. We presented and applied a method to calculate and merge both metrics, addressing both dimensions from online versioning repositories. In this article we have focused on the investigation of frameworks for the development of Web-based applications, which therefore offer similar functionalities and are suitable for a comparison. The results clearly show that it is possible to gather the necessary information to find relationships between process and product metrics. Using mostly object-oriented product metrics focusing on quality by employing a subset of the well-known Chidamber and Kemerer (1994) metrics, complemented with several metrics proposed by Lorenz and Kidd (1995) and several process metrics including total number of commits and the number of distinct programmers as well as the GINI coefficient as a measure of inequality within the developer group, we found that indeed significant relationships exist. This underlines the results of MacCormack et al. (2006). We identify the number of commits, the number of distinct programmers, and the active time as factors of influence which have a negative effect on quality. In particular, complexity and size are negatively influenced by these process metrics. Furthermore a high concentration of added work fosters bad quality. In discussing reasons for this finding, one explanation for this relationship might be found in a missing necessary refactoring of the design. We have also discussed the reasons for this and implications for practice.

Limitations of this work can certainly be found in the thresholds applied for defining methods as faulty based on experiences with C++ projects. Using preliminary sensitivity analysis, we have explored the impact of small changes of up to 20% on the threshold values and found that the main results presented here are still valid. Nevertheless, more work should be invested in this area to arrive at sensible thresholds, especially for Java and related programming languages. Another issue to be further explored in later studies are effects on different levels: we have tried to account for project-level influences on classes using a multi-level modeling approach, but the fact that some classes might be matched pairs across projects, while others are not, might still pose a problem. We have also found that differences between the projects in the effects of process metrics exist, but the attributes mitigating these still remain to be explored. Although we have tried to achieve a relatively homogeneous set of projects, differences in functionality and other aspects persist. Naturally, larger data samples would also be of high interest, especially a comparison of OSS projects with commercial software development, which might more prominently show differences in the development process. Furthermore, a longitudinal study of both product and process metrics over the lifetime and evolution of a project might provide more insights, as well as exploring the influence of process metrics on maintainability, which has been investigated in some studies (Deligiannis, Shepperd, Roumeliotis, & Stamelos, 2003; Fioravanti & Nesi, 2001; Samoladas, Stamelos, Angelis, & Oikonomou, 2004). Our study only gives qualitative evidence of maintainability.

Overall, we think that this study provides a first step despite these limitations. We have provided evidence regarding relationships between process and product measures in open source software development, and pointed out several characteristics tending to lead to lower product quality. This serves as a starting point for devising strategies to effectively manage projects for achieving higher quality and maintainability. Additional research can also benefit from observations regarding the method applied in this study, and might yield even more insights, leading to improvements in OSS and other software development processes.

REFERENCES

Atkins, D., Ball, T., Graves, T., & Mockus, A. (1999). Using version control data to evaluate the impact of software tools. *Proceedings of the 21st International Conference on Software Engineering* (pp. 324–333). Los Angeles: ACM Press.

Baker, F.T. (1972). Chief programmer team management of production programming. *IBM Systems Journal, 11*(1), 56–73.

Basili, V.R., Briand, L.C., & Melo, W.L. (1996). A validation of object-oriented design metrics as quality indicators. *IEEE Transactions on Software Engineering, 22*(10), 751–761.

Basset, T. (2004). Coordination and social structures in an open source project: Videolan. In S. Koch (Ed.), *Open source software development* (pp. 125-151). Hershey, PA: Idea Group.

Bollinger, T., Nelson, R., Self, K.M., & Turnbull, S.J. (1999). Open-source methods: Peering through the clutter. *IEEE Software, 16*(4), 8–11.

Briand, L., Wüst, J., Ikonomovski, S., & Lounis, H. (1998). *A comprehensive investigation of quality factors in object-oriented designs: An industrial case study.* Technical Report ISERN-98-29, International Software Engineering Network.

Briand, L.C., Wüst, J., Daly, J.W., & Porter, D.V. (2000). Exploring the relationship between design measures and software quality in object-oriented systems. *Journal of Systems and Software, 51*(3), 245–273.

Brooks, F.P. Jr. (1995). *The mythical man-month: Essays on Software engineering* (anniv. ed.). Reading, MA: Addison-Wesley.

Chidamber, S., & Kemerer, C.F. (1994). A metrics suite for object oriented design. *IEEE Transactions on Software Engineering, 20*(6), 476–493.

Chidamber, S.R., Darcy, D.P., & Kemerer, C.F. (1998). Managerial use of metrics for object-oriented software: An exploratory analysis. *IEEE Transactions on Software Engineering, 24*(8), 629–639.

Chidamber, S.R., & Kemerer, C.F. (1991). Towards a metric suite for object oriented design. *Proceedings of the 6th ACM Conference of Object Oriented Programming, Systems, Languages and Applications* (pp. 197–211). Phoenix, AZ: ACM Press.

Coleman, E.G., & Hill, B. (2004). The social production of ethics in debian and free software communities: Anthropological lessons for vocational ethics. In S. Koch (Ed.), *Open source software development* (pp. 273–295). Hershey, PA: Idea Group.

Conte, S.D., Dunsmore, H., & Shen, V. (1986). *Software engineering metrics and models.* Menlo Park, CA: Benjamin/Cummings.

Cook, J.E., Votta, L.G., & Wolf, A.L. (1998). Cost-effective analysis of in-place software processes. *IEEE Transactions on Software Engineering, 24*(8), 650–663.

Crowston, K., & Scozzi, B. (2002). Open source software projects as virtual organizations: Competency rallying for software development. *IEE Proceedings—Software Engineering, 149*(1), 3–17.

Cusumano, M.A. (2004). Reflections on free and open software. *Communications of the ACM, 47*(10), 25–27.

Deligiannis, I., Shepperd, M., Roumeliotis, M., & Stamelos, I. (2003). An empirical investigation of an object-oriented design heuristic for maintainability. *Journal of Systems and Software, 65*(2), 127–139.

Demetriou, N., Koch, S., & Neumann, G. (2006). The development of the OpenACS community. In M. Lytras & A. Naeve (Eds.), *Open source for knowledge and learning management: Strategies beyond tools* (pp. 298–318). Hershey, PA: Idea Group.

Dempsey, B.J., Weiss, D., Jones, P., & Greenberg, J. (2002). Who is an open source software developer? *Communications of the ACM, 45*(2), 67–72.

Dinh-Tong, T.T., & Bieman, J.M. (2005). The FreeBSD project: A replication case study of open source development. *IEEE Transactions on Software Engineering, 31*(6), 481–494.

Dutoit, A.H., & Bruegge, B. (1998). Communication metrics for software development. *IEEE Transactions on Software Engineering, 24*(8), 615–628.

Elliott, M.S., & Scacchi, W. (2004). Free software development: Cooperation and conflict in a virtual organizational culture. In S. Koch (Ed.), *Open source software development* (pp. 152–172). Hershey, PA: Idea Group.

Erickson, J., Lyytinen, K., & Siau, K. (2005). Agile modeling, agile software development, and extreme programming: The state of research. *Journal of Database Management, 16*(4), 88–99.

Fayad, M.E., & Schmidt, D.C. (1997). Object-oriented application frameworks. *Communications of the ACM, 40*(10), 32–39.

Feller, J., Fitzgerald, B., Hissam, S.A., & Lakhani, K.R. (Eds.). (2005). *Perspectives on free and open source software.* Cambridge, MA: MIT Press.

Fenton, N.E. (1991). *Software metrics—a rigorous approach.* London: Chapman & Hall.

Fioravanti, F., & Nesi, P. (2001). Estimation and prediction metrics for adaptive maintenance effort of object-oriented systems. *IEEE Transactions on Software Engineering, 27*(12), 1062–1084.

Fischer, M., Pinzger, M., & Gall, H. (2003). Populating a release history database from version control and bug tracking systems. *Proceedings of the 19th IEEE International Conference on Software Maintenance* (pp. 23–32), Amsterdam, The Netherlands.

Fogel, K. (1999). *Open source development with CVS.* Scottsdale: CoriolisOpen Press.

Fowler, M. (1999). *Refactoring: Improving the design of existing code.* Boston: Addison-Wesley.

Gallivan, M.J. (2001). Striking a balance between

trust and control in a virtual organization: A content analysis of open source software case studies. *Information Systems Journal, 11*(4), 277–304.

German, D. (2006). A study of contributors of PostgreSQL. *Proceedings of the International Workshop on Mining Software Repositories* (MSR'06), Shanghai.

Ghosh, R.A., & Prakash, V.V. (2000). The Orbiten free software survey. *First Monday, 5*(7).

Goldstein, H. (1999). *Multilevel statistical models.* London: Arnold.

Hahsler, M., & Koch, S. (2005). Discussion of a large-scale open source data collection methodology. *Proceedings of the Hawaii International Conference on System Sciences* (HICSS-38), Big Island, HI.

Hansen, M., Köhntopp, K., & Pfitzmann, A. (2002). The open source approach—opportunities and limitations with respect to security and privacy. *Computers & Security, 21*(5), 461–471.

Henderson-Seller, B. (1996). *Object-oriented metrics: Measures of complexity.* Upper Saddle River, NJ: Prentice Hall.

Hertel, G., Niedner, S., & Hermann, S. (2003). Motivation of software developers in open source projects: An Internet-based survey of contributors to the Linux kernel. *Research Policy, 32*(7), 1159–1177.

Humphrey, W. (1995). *A discipline for software engineering.* Reading, MA: Addison-Wesley.

Hunt, F., & Johnson, P. (2002). On the pareto distribution of sourceforge projects. *Proceedings of the Open Source Software Development Workshop* (pp. 122–129), Newcastle, UK.

Johnson, R. (1997). Frameworks=(components+patterns). *Communications of the ACM, 40*(10), 39–42.

Jones, C. (1986). *Programming productivity.* New York: McGraw-Hill.

Kemerer, C.F., & Slaughter, S. (1999). An empirical approach to studying software evolution. *IEEE Transactions on Software Engineering, 25*(4), 493–509.

Klein, K.J., Tosi, H., & Cannella, A.A. Jr. (1999). Multilevel theory building: Benefits, barriers, and new development. *Academy of Management Review, 24*(2), 243–248.

Koch, S. (2004). Profiling an open source project ecology and its programmers. *Electronic Markets, 14*(2), 77–88.

Koch, S. (2004a). Agile principles and open source software development: A theoretical and empirical discussion. *Extreme Programming and Agile Processes in Software Engineering: Proceedings of the 5th International Conference XP 2004* (pp. 85–93). Berlin: Springer-Verlag (LNCS 3092).

Koch, S., & Schneider, G. (2002). Effort, cooperation and coordination in an open source software project: GNOME. *Information Systems Journal, 12*(1), 27–42.

Koru, A.G., & Tian, J. (2004). Defect handling in medium and large open source projects. *IEEE Software, 21*(4), 54–61.

Koru, A.G., & Tian, J. (2005). Comparing high-change modules and modules with the highest measurement values in two large-scale open-source products. *IEEE Transactions on Software Engineering, 31*(8), 625–642.

Kreft, I., & de Leeuw, J. (2002). *Introducing multilevel modeling.* London: Sage.

Krishnamurthy, S. (2002). Cave or community? An empirical investigation of 100 mature open source projects. *First Monday, 7*(6).

Long, Y., & Siau, K. (2007). Social network structures in open source software development teams. *Journal of Database Management, 18*(2), 25–40.

Lorenz, M., & Kidd, J. (1995). *Object oriented metrics.* Upper Saddle River, NJ: Prentice Hall.

MacCormack, A., Rusnak, J., & Baldwin, C.Y. (2006). Exploring the structure of complex software designs: An empirical study of open source and proprietary code. *Management Science, 52*(7), 1015–1030.

McCabe, T. (1976). A complexity measure. *IEEE Transactions on Software Engineering, 2*(4), 308–320.

McConnell, S. (1999). Open-source methodology: Ready for prime time? *IEEE Software, 16*(4), 6–8.

Merisalo-Rantanen, H., Tuunanen, T., & Rossi, M. (2005). Is extreme programming just old wine in new bottles: A comparison of two cases. *Journal of Database Management, 16*(4), 41–61.

Mills, H.D. (1971). *Chief programmer teams: Principles and procedures.* Report FSC 71-5108, IBM Federal Systems Division, USA.

Mockus, A., Fielding, R.T., & Herbsleb, J.D. (2002). Two case studies of open source software development: Apache and Mozilla. *ACM Transactions on Software Engineering and Methodology, 11*(3), 309–346.

Morisio, M., Romano, D., & Stamelos, I. (2002). Quality, productivity and learning in framework-based development: An exploratory case study. *IEEE Transactions on Software Engineering, 28*(8), 340–357.

Murdoch, D.J., & Chow, E.D. (1996). A graphical display of large correlation matrices. *The American Statistician, 50*(2), 178–180.

Neumann, C. (2002). *Jsp- und Servlet-basierte frameworks für Web-applikationen.* Master's Thesis, Universität Karlsruhe, Germany.

Park, P. (1992). *Software size measurement: A framework for counting source statements.* Technical Report CMU/SEI-92-TR-20, Software Engineering Institute, Carnegie Mellon University, USA.

Payne, C. (2002). On the security of open source software. *Information Systems Journal, 12*(1), 61–78.

Perens, B. (1999). The open source definition. In C. DiBona, S. Ockman, & M. Stone (Eds.), *Open sources: Voices from the open source revolution* (pp. 171–188). Cambridge, MA: O'Reilly & Associates.

Prieto-Diaz, R. (1993). Status report: Software reusability. *IEEE Software, 10*(3), 61–66.

Raymond, E.S. (1999). *The cathedral and the bazaar: Musings on Linux and open source by an accidental revolutionary.* Sebastopol, CA: O'Reilly & Associates.

Robles-Martinez, G., Gonzalez-Barahona, J.M., Centeno-Gonzalez, J., Matellan-Olivera, V., & Rodero-Merino, L. (2003). Studying the evolution of libre software projects using publicly available data. *Proceedings of the 3rd Workshop on Open Source Software Engineering—25th International Conference on Software Engineering* (pp. 111–115), Portland, OR.

Samoladas, I., Stamelos, I., Angelis, L., & Oikonomou, A. (2004). Open source software development should strive for even greater code maintainability. *Communications of the ACM, 47*(10), 83–87.

Snijders, T.A.B., & Bosker, R.J. (2003). *Multilevel analysis: An introduction to basic and advanced multilevel modeling.* London: Sage.

Stallman, R.M. (2002). *Free software, free society: Selected essays of Richard M. Stallman.* Boston: GNU Press.

Stamelos, I., Angelis, L., Oikonomou, A., & Bleris, G.L. (2002). Code quality analysis in open source software development. *Information Systems Journal, 12*(1), 43–60.

Subramanian, G., & Corbin, W. (2001). An empirical study of certain object-oriented software metrics. *Journal of Systems and Software, 59*(1), 57–63.

Subramanyam, R., & Krishnan, M.S. (2003). Empirical analysis of ck metrics for object-oriented design complexity: Implications for software defects. *IEEE Transactions on Software Engineering, 29*(4), 297–309.

Thuraisingham, B. (2005). Privacy-preserving data mining: Development and directions. *Journal of Database Management, 16*(1), 75–87.

Turk, D., France. R., & Rumpe, B. (2005). Assumptions underlying agile software-development processes. *Journal of Database Management, 16*(4), 62–87.

Vixie, P. (1999). Software engineering. In C. DiBona, S. Ockman, & M. Stone (Eds.), *Open sources: Voices from the open source revolution* (pp. 91–100). Cambridge, MA: O'Reilly & Associates.

Witten, B., Landwehr, C., & Caloyannides, M. (2001). Does open source improve system security? *IEEE Software, 18*(5), 57–61.

This work was previously published in the Journal of Database Management, Vol. 19, Issue 2, edited by K. Siau, pp. 31-57, copyright 2008 by IGI Publishing (an imprint of IGI Global).

Chapter 7
The Impact of Ideology on the Organizational Adoption of Open Source Software

Kris Ven
University of Antwerp, Belgium

Jan Verelst
University of Antwerp, Belgium

ABSTRACT

Previous research has shown that the open source movement shares a common ideology. Employees belonging to the open source movement often advocate the use of open source software within their organization. Hence, their belief in the underlying open source software ideology may influence the decision making on the adoption of open source software. This may result in an ideological—rather than pragmatic—decision. A recent study has shown that American organizations are quite pragmatic in their adoption decision. We argue that there may be circumstances in which there is more opportunity for ideological behavior. We therefore investigated the organizational adoption decision in Belgian organizations. Our results indicate that most organizations are pragmatic in their decision making. However, we have found evidence that suggests that the influence of ideology should not be completely disregarded in small organizations.

INTRODUCTION

The free software movement—led by Richard M. Stallman—has always taken an ideological, political view on software. Adherents to the free software movement advocate that all software should be free, in the sense that it should be free to read, modify, and distribute. The open source movement on the other hand was created in order to facilitate the introduction of free software in organizations and takes a more pragmatic stance in its efforts to market open source software (OSS).

Previous research has shown that the open source movement is characterized by a shared, underlying ideology (e.g., Ljungberg, 2000; Bergquist & Ljungberg, 2001). Lately, an increasing number of developers are hired by commercial organizations to work on OSS projects. These developers may or may not share the OSS ideology. Nevertheless, many adherents to the open source movement still feel connected to the OSS ideology. Moreover, commercial organizations still need to find a balance between their commercial objectives and the traditional values of the open source movement (Fitzgerald, 2006).

Many organizations have already adopted OSS, especially mature server software such as Linux and Apache. Research on the organizational adoption of OSS has shown that its use was frequently a bottom-up initiative, suggested by technical employees within the organization who are an adherent to the open source movement (Dedrick & West, 2003; West & Dedrick, 2005; Lundell, Lings, & Lindqvist, 2006). In some cases, decision makers could also be considered an adherent to the open source movement. These employees will take on the role of *boundary spanners* in their organization, bringing the organization in contact with new innovations (Tushman & Scanlan, 1981). West and Dedrick (2005) have found in their study on American organizations that although such employees try to ensure that an open source alternative is considered in the decision making, the final decision is made on pragmatic grounds (i.e., based on characteristics of the software such as cost, reliability, and functionality), and not based on ideological feelings towards OSS. The organizations included in their study are rather large,[1] which may have had an impact on their results.

We argue that it is useful to perform a similar study in a context in which there is more opportunity for ideological behavior. We expect that this might be the case in smaller organizations. In order to investigate whether decision making in small organizations is ideological, we have conducted 10 case studies in Belgian organizations to investigate the organizational adoption of OSS. The article is structured as follows. We will start by discussing the theoretical background of this study. Next, we will discuss our research design. Subsequently, we will present the results of our study, focusing on three organizations that used fairly ideological decision making. This is followed by a discussion of our findings. Finally, we will offer our conclusions.

THEORETICAL BACKGROUND

OSS Ideology

Numerous definitions have been proposed in literature for the term "ideology." Usually, the term is used in a pejorative meaning. Such use implies that an ideology is based on false beliefs of reality. Several authors however recommend against using such a perspective (e.g., Hamilton, 1987). The definition of ideology that we will use in this article is proposed by Hamilton (1987, p. 38):

"An ideology is a system of collectively held normative and reputedly factual ideas and beliefs and attitudes advocating a particular pattern of social relationships and arrangements, and/or aimed at justifying a particular pattern of conduct, which its proponents seek to promote, realise, pursue or maintain."

This definition is non-judgmental, and as a result we do not make any pronouncements with respect to the correctness of the beliefs, values, and norms that characterize an ideology. Hence, acting according to an ideology will not necessarily have negative consequences for the organization.

Previous research has described several ideological principles of the open source movement (e.g., Markus, Manville, & Agres, 2000; Ljungberg, 2000; Stewart & Gosain, 2006). This ideology has been shown to enhance the effectiveness of the OSS community (Stewart & Gosain, 2006).

Stewart and Gosain (2006) identified a number of underlying norms, beliefs, and values of the open source movement (see Table 1). These norms, beliefs, and values are proposed as the tenets of the OSS ideology.

The tenets listed in Table 1 are used to describe the attitudes of developers within the OSS community. We argue however that some of the OSS beliefs and values (i.e., tenets 4–15 in Table 1) can also be shared by technical employees and decision makers in organizations. Hence, it is interesting to investigate whether decision makers who share these ideological ideas of the open source movement make an ideological—rather than pragmatic—decision. Although the study of West and Dedrick (2005) has shown that decision making on OSS is pragmatic, we believe that this may be different in small organizations. Some authors have pointed out that decision making with respect to IT in small organizations is often the responsibility of a single individual

(Harrison, Mykytyn, & Riemenschneider, 1997; Riemenschneider, Harrison, & Mykytyn, 2003). We argue that the impact of the OSS ideology will be greater if a single decision maker—who can be considered an OSS advocate—is present in the organization. In such situations, the adoption decision may be ideological since personal traits and beliefs of the decision maker are more likely to impact the final decision than in larger organizations.

Mindful Innovation

Nowadays, many things require the attention of managers, making their attention a scarce resource (Hansen & Haas, 2001; Swanson & Ramiller, 2004). One of the consequences is that much innovation in organizations is actually driven by bandwagon phenomena, in which organizations mimic the adoption behavior of other organizations and do not properly evaluate alternatives

Table 1. Tenets of open source ideology (Stewart & Gosain, 2006, pp. 294–295)

OSS Norms	OSS Beliefs	OSS Values
(1) *Forking*—There is a norm against forking a project, which refers to splitting the project into two or more projects developed separately. (2) *Distribution*—There is a norm against distributing code changes without going through the proper channels. (3) *Named Credit*—There is a norm against removing someone's name from a project without that person's consent.	(4) *Code Quality*—Open source development methods produce better code than closed source. (5) *Software Freedom*—Outcomes are better when code is freely available. (6) *Information Freedom*—Outcomes are better when information is freely available. (7) *Bug Fixing*—The more people working on the code, the more quickly bugs will be found and fixed. (8) *Practicality*—Practical work is more useful than theoretical discussion. (9) *Status Attainment*—Status is achieved through community recognition.	(10) *Sharing*—Sharing information is important. (11) *Helping*—Aiding others is important. (12) *Technical Knowledge*—Technical knowledge is highly valued. (13) *Learning*—There is a value on learning for its own sake. (14) *Cooperation*—Voluntary cooperation is important. (15) *Reputation*—Reputation gained by participating in open source projects is valuable.

(Abrahamson, 1991; Swanson & Ramiller, 2004). Recently, the bandwagon phenomenon has been framed into the broader context of *mindful innovation* (Swanson & Ramiller, 2004; Fiol & Connor, 2003). The concept of mindfulness originated in psychology and denotes a state of an individual involving: (1) openness to novelty; (2) alertness to distinction; (3) sensitivity to different contexts; (4) implicit, if not explicit, awareness of multiple perspectives; and (5) orientation in the present (Sternberg, 2000). Decision makers in organizations who are mindful have a "watchful and vigilant state of mind" (Fiol & Connor, 2003). An organization that innovates mindfully with IT will therefore not take generalized claims about advantages for granted, but will critically examine their relevance and validity in the organization-specific context (Fiol & Connor, 2003). Mindless innovation, on the other hand, is characterized by "…acting on automatic pilot, precluding attention to new information, and fixating on a single perspective" (Fiol & Connor, 2003; Weick, Sutcliffe, & Obstfeld, 1999).[2] Such innovation may result in making premature decisions based on beliefs that do not necessarily accurately reflect reality (Butler & Gray, 2006). Hence, a dogmatic belief in the OSS ideology may lead to mindless adoption, in which no proprietary alternatives are considered.

Swanson and Ramiller (2004) note that boundary-spanning activities are important for mindful organizational decision making, in order to obtain information on the innovation. We argue that in the case of OSS, this information may be ideologically colored. As a result, the presence of boundary spanners in the adoption of OSS may actually lead to ideological (mindless) behavior instead, especially if decision makers share the OSS ideology. There are at least two factors that can facilitate ideological behavior in such context. First, decision structures in small organizations tend to be less formal (bureaucratic) than in large organizations. Fiol and Connor (2003) argue that underspecified decision structures may encourage

further mindless behavior, if decision making was mindless to begin with. Second, Swanson and Ramiller (2004) point out that although personal mindfulness with respect to innovation does not necessarily equate to organizational mindfulness, it will definitely have an impact on it.

Ideology vs. Pragmatism

In order to investigate whether decision making in organizations exhibits ideological characteristics, we need to determine how ideological behavior can be identified. Based on the work of Stewart and Gosain (2006), we determine whether decision makers and other employees shared some of the beliefs and underlying principles (tenets) of the free and open source movements (see Table 1), *and* did not properly assess their relevancy for the organization. For example, proponents may argue that software should be free (similar to the views of the FSF), may have a negative attitude towards proprietary software, or may be convinced that OSS delivers software of a higher quality (Stewart & Gosain, 2006; Ljungberg, 2000). Consequently, decision makers may have a strong preference for using OSS, without (properly) considering proprietary alternatives. Such decision making may result in a less than optimal solution for the organization. In fact, decision makers are in that case rather mindless in their decision making. Mindless organizations will pay little attention to the organization's specifics or to studying new innovations. This will result in making decisions on "autopilot," using a single perspective (Swanson & Ramiller, 2004; Fiol & Connor, 2003). This means that the beliefs of the OSS ideology are taken for granted, without considering their suitability in the organization-specific context.

On the other hand, we consider an organization to be pragmatic in its decision making when the organization does not exhibit any of the tenets of the OSS ideology, or when decision makers do not take any claims of the OSS ideology for granted, but carefully examine their implications in the organization-specific context. Such organizations are mindful in their decision making. This means that decision makers base their decision on the characteristics of the innovation itself and consider how well the innovation fits within the organization. Pragmatic decision makers will probably consider both proprietary and OSS alternatives, outweigh the benefits of all alternatives, and choose the best solution based on factors such as cost and product features. In this case, no favoritism towards using OSS should be present.

It must be noted that ideological and pragmatic decision making is not a black and white phenomenon. In practice, we expect organizations to exhibit some ideological and some pragmatic characteristics. This is consistent with Geuss (1994), who remarks that an ideology is generally not only composed of the beliefs and values that are shared by *all* members of a group. Consequently, not all adherents to the open source movement will share *all* values proposed by the OSS ideology. This is similar to the statement of Ljungberg (2000) who suggests that developers vary in their adherence to the OSS ideology. Hence, there are many shades of gray in this classification. In this article, we will discuss decision making in three organizations in our sample which clearly exhibited ideological behavior.

RESEARCH DESIGN

To investigate whether decision making is ideological or pragmatic, we studied the organizational adoption of OSS in Belgian organizations. In this study, decision makers were questioned about the reasons for using OSS and their attitudes towards the open source movement. Based upon the information obtained from these organizations, we were able to determine whether their decision making was either pragmatic or rather ideological.

Scope

We decided to focus mainly on the adoption of open source *server* software. We use the term open source server software to refer to both open source operating systems (such as Linux and FreeBSD) and other OSS for server use (for example, the Apache Web server or the Bind name server). This choice is motivated by the fact that this type of OSS is generally considered to be stable and mature, and is already in use by a significant number of organizations. A similar research approach has been undertaken by other researchers (e.g., West & Dedrick, 2005). On the other hand, we also gathered information on other OSS that was being used in the organizations (such as desktop software, development, and networking tools).

Methodology

We used the exploratory case study approach to study the organizational adoption decision on open source server software. The case study approach is well suited to study a contemporary phenomenon in its natural setting, especially when the boundaries of the phenomenon are not clearly defined at the start of the study (Yin, 2003; Benbasat, Goldstein, & Mead, 1987). We conducted a series of in-depth face-to-face interviews with informants from 10 Belgian organizations to identify the factors that influence the decision to use open source server software as well as their attitudes towards the open source movement. Organizations were selected from the population of all Belgian organizations and were sampled on the basis of two criteria: the size of the organization measured by the number of employees and the sector in which the organization operated. Organizations were only included in our sample if they were using open source server software at the time of our study. Informants within each organization were selected using the *key informant method*. Since the use of a single informant has been shown to give inconsistent results (Phillips, 1981), we tried to speak to both a senior manager (e.g., the IT manager) and a technical person (e.g., the system administrator) whenever possible.

The interviews took place between July and November 2005. An overview of the cases in our study is shown in Table 2. As can be seen from this table, the organizations in our sample are considerably smaller than those in the study of West and Dedrick (2005).[3] In each organization, we have conducted a single interview during which all informants in the organization were present. The interviews were semi-structured, and the format was revised after each interview to incorporate new findings (Benbasat et al., 1987). In the first part of the interview, informants were asked to freely discuss their reasons for adopting OSS. In the second part of the interview, we probed for specific factors that were found relevant in previous studies, as well as the informants' perceptions of the free and open source movements. Each interview lasted 45-90 minutes, was recorded and transcribed verbatim. In order to increase the validity of our findings, informants were sent a summary of the interview and were requested to suggest any improvements if necessary. Follow-up questions were asked by telephone or via e-mail. The transcripts were coded and then further analyzed using procedures to generate theory from qualitative data, as described in the literature (e.g., Benbasat et al., 1987; Eisenhardt, 1989; Dubé & Paré, 2003). Various data displays were used to visualize and further analyze the qualitative data (Miles & Huberman, 1994; Eisenhardt, 1989).

EMPIRICAL FINDINGS

The dominant attitude towards OSS in seven organizations in our sample was pragmatism. These organizations did not exhibit any of the tenets of the OSS ideology, or their decision makers considered how the advantages of OSS could be realized in their organization. Consequently, these organizations could be considered pragmatic (and mindful) in their decision making with respect to the adoption of OSS. The most commonly cited advantages—and reasons for the adoption—of OSS were *cost* and *reliability*. In general, decision makers tended to consider both proprietary and OSS alternatives, and based their decision on the cost and functionality offered by the various alternatives. Some organizations even explicitly mentioned that they made a pragmatic adoption decision. These seven organizations did not have a preference for using OSS over proprietary

Table 2. Overview of the organizations in our study

Name	Sector	Employees	Informants	Extent of adoption
OrganizationA	Audio, video, and telecommunications	11	2	moderate
OrganizationB	Machinery and equipment	749	2	extensive
OrganizationC	Telecommunications	1346	1	limited
OrganizationD	Publishing and printing	31	1	extensive
OrganizationE	Food products and beverages	204	2	moderate
OrganizationF	Research and development	152	2	extensive
OrganizationG	Information technology	583	1	moderate
OrganizationH	Chemicals	4423	1	moderate
OrganizationI	Education	3303	3	limited
OrganizationJ	Publishing and printing	12	1	extensive

software, except OrganizationB where a slight preference for OSS was present. Although they would accept a minor workaround in order to be able to use OSS, this effort should be limited. Or, as expressed by an informant:

We are not going to program around something, because we really want to use that [open source] component. But if there is a little workaround, we will certainly take it.

The other six organizations were quite agnostic about using OSS. One informant in OrganizationF expressed this as:

[The fact that the software is open source] does not really matter for a company.

Some of the technical employees who served as informants in our study had a background in OSS. Although some indicated that they did suggest the use of OSS when appropriate, they did not try to force its use and remained pragmatic. Nevertheless, many OSS development and networking tools (e.g., Nagios, Eclipse, and Maven) were being used by the organizations in our sample.

The results obtained from these seven organizations are quite consistent with the results obtained by West and Dedrick (2005). On the other hand, we observed a different behavior in the three very small organizations in our sample (OrganizationA, OrganizationD, and OrganizationJ) consisting of less than 50 employees. In those organizations, we were able to detect several characteristics of ideological behavior. In the remainder of this section, we will discuss these three cases in more detail.

OrganizationA

OrganizationA specialized in telecommunication devices. It originally started as a research and development company. Initially, all projects within the organization aimed to gather knowledge and

experience in order to develop the initial product. Developers were free in their decision making on which products to incorporate into the final product. Consequently, decision making was significantly influenced by the personal experience of developers.

Our informants indicated that at the time of the organization's founding, many employees—including the organization's founders and the CIO—shared the same background, were very familiar with Linux, and shared the philosophical ideas of the open source movement. These employees had a "firm conviction" in OSS:

The firm conviction was coming from a number of people who said: 'It must be [OSS], we do not want anything else!'...The choice for using OSS was...just a conviction, rather than the result of a comparative assessment.

As a result, most software that was used in the organization was OSS. During package selection, no objective evaluation of (proprietary) alternatives was performed. Although some proprietary software was used, this was either on demand of a customer, or the software was eventually replaced by an OSS alternative.

The choice for OSS at that time was primarily motivated by the lower or non-existing license cost, the fact that there was more confidence in OSS, and the fact that OSS provides access to the source code. Our informants however admitted that these reasons were influenced by the philosophical view towards OSS and that this view on OSS dominated the adoption decision. They were for example aware that using OSS includes additional costs (e.g., packaging and updates), which makes it less clear whether OSS really offers a cost advantage. Such considerations were however not taken into account at that time.

Another factor that has influenced the decision is the avoidance of vendor lock-in. The open source movement generally depicts Microsoft as their common "enemy." This feeling was also present in the organization at that time. Vendor lock-in with Microsoft was feared, partly due to negative experiences in the past. The adoption decision appeared to be anti-Microsoft oriented. As expressed by one informant:

If you mentioned Microsoft, things exploded!

The organization also initiated its own OSS project. It consisted of a Java virtual machine for embedded devices. This project was started to try to benefit from the OSS community model (cf. tenets 4–15). This project was in fact quite successful, and the organization took the role of project maintainer. In the course of time, the project became less interesting for the community (as the product further matured) and participation of the community declined. The software is however still used in the organization's products.

As illustrated, the choice for using OSS was quite ideological in the early years of the organization. Interesting to note is that over the years, several employees of the organization who were adherents to the open source movement, and who advocated the use of OSS, left the organization. As a result, the choice for OSS became much more pragmatic. Another factor that may have influenced this evolution is that the organization finished its software products, gradually became less of an R&D organization, and other goals such as efficiency started to become more important.

At the time of our study, a slight preference for OSS still existed. One informant stated:

Our choice will in the first place go to open source or Linux, but less fanatical than in the past.

Furthermore, the organization seemed to be less willing to take risks in using OSS, or to invest additional effort to get OSS working. This was expressed by an informant as:

I think we are looking rather quickly towards open source products. But if it looks that it will deliver

us more worries than it yields advantages, we will not doubt to use a commercial product.

Hence, the organization will only consider using OSS if the product complies with the requirements. The "firm conviction" that was present in the organization has now faded away. The choice for OSS is now mainly based on the potential cost advantages.

Nevertheless, it appears that the organization still felt connected to the principles of the open source movement. When asked whether the organization contributed back any modifications they made to OSS, one informant appeared to feel guilty about not contributing:

...we did contribute quite little, rather naughty, isn't it?

He further noted that the organization tried to participate in OSS projects in other ways, for example by filling in bug reports or by participating in mailing lists (cf. tenets 10–15).

OrganizationD

OrganizationD was active in the publishing and printing sector. The organization had a single person responsible for decision making on IT, and had no internal IT staff. The organization used OSS on a variety of systems (i.e., one Internet gateway, two file servers, and one intranet server). The organization also had 3 LAMP (Linux–Apache–MySQL–PHP) servers, running custom-developed software for time registration. Finally, three desktops were equipped with the Linux operating system in the offices, and an additional 11 PCs function as terminals for the time registration system. The main reason for choosing OSS was to reduce vendor lock-in and maximize the freedom of the IT infrastructure. Consequently, the decision maker investigated OSS solutions without considering proprietary alternatives. Other reasons for using OSS were an increased control over the software, cost advantages, and an increased flexibility. These factors are consistent with the advantages proposed by the OSS community. We were able to detect a few additional ideological characteristics, although they were not that strong.

Our informant indicated that his extensive personal experience with Linux influenced his decision to start using OSS within the organization:

Following [new evolutions] is not enough: you try out software, and free software has the advantage that it is much easier to try out. And of course, since you have tried it yourself, it did influence the [organizational] decision.

His decision to start using OSS within the organization was also influenced by some negative experiences with proprietary software in the past (including vendor lock-in). For example, some proprietary application the organization was using contained a bug which the vendor refused to resolve. As a result, our informant tried to remain in full control over his IT infrastructure. He therefore wanted to maximize the degree of freedom in the IT infrastructure, not only by using open standards, but by using OSS as well: "I wanted to go a step further: not only by using open standards, but also by using open source applications to have full insurance" (cf. tenets 5–6). He felt that by having access to the source code of OSS, he had maximum control over his applications.

The organization was remarkably committed to its pursuit of freedom. This commitment has moved the organization to start its own OSS project, namely a time registration system for employees. Existing software either did not satisfy all requirements, or was too expensive and did not allow for customizing the software. Hence, the software needed to be custom developed. The decision maker did not want to become dependent on an external organization—not even on the external programmer who develops the software. Instead of performing in-house development or closing an escrow agreement, the organization has chosen a different path. The organization has hired a programmer from an external organization to develop the software, and our informant decided to release the software under an OSS license (the GPL) to ensure that the software would remain completely free (cf. tenet 5). This way, the organization aimed to remain in control over the application, avoid vendor lock-in, and be allowed to make modifications to the software at a later time. The software is being developed as a cooperation between our informant (who is mainly responsible for the analysis) and the paid external programmer. It was the intention of our informant to eventually share this application with other organizations in the same sector. He strongly valued the ability to cooperate with other organizations, and hoped that he would be able to leverage the OSS development model (cf. tenets 4–15) and to receive comments, bug fixes, and maybe even new code submissions.

Interestingly, he was the only informant in our sample who deliberately used the term *free software*.[4] He preferred this term since—in his experience—the term OSS is misused by some vendors to refer to software of which the source code is available, but whose license is still proprietary and does not offer the same freedom as OSS licenses. He felt that the Dutch term for *free software* did not suffer from the confusion in English, and that it better articulated the spirit of the open source movement (cf. tenet 5).

OrganizationJ

The most prominent form of ideological behavior was found in OrganizationJ. Our informant was the IT and business manager of the organization, who was the only one responsible for the IT infrastructure. No internal IT staff was present. The complete IT infrastructure of the organization was based on OSS. This included two important servers: an intranet server running ERP software and an Internet server running the e-commerce site of the organization. Recently, all desktops in the organization were migrated from MS Windows to Linux. The desktops consisted of lightweight terminals which booted from a server. All applications ran on the server, which placed very low demands on the desktop itself. All administration could be performed on the server. The desktops were running the XFCE desktop environment and OpenOffice.org was used as the office suite.

Our informant had a technical background and was an experienced programmer. In fact, he developed his own e-commerce application and was currently rewriting his own ERP software. His personal experience with Linux dates back from 1999. Based on this personal experience, he decided to migrate his Unix-based server to Linux when he was experiencing difficulties with that server.

Similar to our informant in OrganizationD, the IT manager wanted to remain in control of his IT infrastructure (cf. tenets 5–6). Consequently, he tried to make exclusive use of open standards. Moreover, he stated that he only considered using OSS (except for one PC running Microsoft Windows on which specific banking software was installed that is unavailable for Linux). He also did not want to pay for software, hence he did not use any of the commercial Linux distributions.

Similar to the other two organizations, our informant indicated that his organization had bad experiences with proprietary vendors in the past. In fact, when migrating the server that ran the ERP software, the organization faced huge switching costs when transferring the software from the Unix-based system (developed by a small company) to Linux. He was also suspicious of proprietary software, because it could contain hidden features. This prevented him from having total control over the software. OSS was believed to be more secure, thanks to the availability of the source code: "I think there are thousands, ten

thousands or millions of people who use and study it, so I don't have to worry" (cf. tenets 4 and 7).

As a result, he had a rule that proprietary software should not be used under Linux. Proprietary software was simply not considered as an alternative during decision making. This non-pragmatic decision making can be illustrated with two examples. First, the organization recently acquired a new printer/copier. Although the manufacturer provided drivers for Linux, they were proprietary; and the source code of the drivers was not provided. Consequently, the drivers were not installed on the Linux desktops. This means that default Postscript and PCL drivers were used. If specific features would be required, the IT manager stated that he would rewrite the drivers, based on the Postscript definition. He motivated his choice as follows:

Nothing is installed from which the source code is not available: I need control. ... [The manufacturer of the printer] will probably have no bad intentions, probably, but nowadays you never know.

Second, when the IT manager decided that the ERP software needed replacement, he reviewed some OSS alternatives. One of the reasons why Compiere was not properly examined as an alternative, was that it required the Oracle database server.[5]

The IT manager also started a small OSS project. It consisted of a Perl module to create OpenOffice.org documents. He also indicated that he valued the OSS development model. Two important advantages of this model were the peer review process (see supra) and that it offers more continuity. Although his ERP software was using a graphical library that was maintained by a single person, he was not afraid of becoming too dependent. If the maintainer would quit, our informant was convinced that other people would take over the project. Otherwise, he would still have access to the source code of the library and make any required changes himself (cf. tenets 5 and 14).

DISCUSSION

As can be gathered from our findings, ideological or pragmatic decision making is not a binary variable. Instead, decision making will exhibit both ideological as well as pragmatic characteristics, which places the organization's decision making on a continuum between both extremes. In practice, most organizations clearly use a pragmatic decision-making process with respect to the use of OSS. Nevertheless, we were able to detect rather ideological decision making in three small organizations in our sample. The degree of ideology varied between these three cases. A summary of the ideological characteristics in the decision-making process of these organizations is shown in Table 3.

Identifying Ideology

There were clear distinctions between the seven organizations that we labeled "pragmatic" and the three we identified as "ideological." First, within the three latter organizations, there was a clear push behind—or favoritism towards—using OSS. This was caused by the fact that decision makers were adherents to the open source movement and wanted to use OSS as much as possible, or even exclusively. Their personal experience and background was a major factor in this decision. The other seven organizations did consider OSS as one of the alternatives, but would not give preferential treatment to OSS.

Second, the tenets of the OSS ideology were only present in the three organizations. Among

Table 3. Ideological characteristics in the decision making of organizations in our sample

OrganizationA:
- Employees, including the organization's founders, shared the philosophical and cultural views of the OSS movement.
- A strong anti-Microsoft sentiment was present.
- Vendor lock-in was feared.
- The organization started its own OSS project to benefit from the OSS development model.
- All software that was used had to be OSS.
- The adoption decision was based on a "firm conviction" in OSS, not on an objective evaluation of alternatives.

OrganizationD:
- The IT manager strives to maximize the freedom in the IT infrastructure by using open standards and OSS.
- Extensive personal experience of the IT manager with Linux influenced the organizational adoption decision.
- The organization started its own OSS project to ensure that the software would remain totally free.
- Driven to OSS by negative experiences (including vendor lock-in) with proprietary software in the past.
- The IT manager uses the term "free software."

OrganizationJ:
- The IT manager does not want to pay for software, including application software.
- The switch to Linux was influenced by personal experience with Linux.
- All software that was used had to be OSS.
- Proprietary printer drivers were not used, even if this means that a work-around must be devised.
- Commercial software is not trusted because the source code is not available.
- Driven to OSS by negative experiences (including vendor lock-in) with commercial software in the past.
- The OSS development model is valued, because thousands of developers are reading the source code, correcting bugs, and ensuring the continuity of the project.
- The complete IT infrastructure was migrated to OSS.
- The IT manager started his own OSS project.

the tenets that were most prominently present were software freedom (tenet 5), information freedom (tenet 6), and cooperation (tenet 14).[6] These tenets are indeed central to the OSS ideology. The other seven organizations were rather agnostic about the values and beliefs of the open source movement and considered the OSS character irrelevant during decision making.

Third, several of the factors that influenced the adoption decision are consistent with the advantages put forward by the open source movement. Evidently, this is not sufficient to claim that these organizations shared the OSS ideology. However, there are indications (particularly in Organization A and Organization J) that the perceptions with respect to these adoption factors are influenced by the belief in the OSS ideology, and that their relevancy in the organization-specific environment were not or insufficiently evaluated. This indicates mindless decision making.

Finally, these three organizations were the only ones in our sample that initiated their own OSS projects. Organization A and Organization D clearly indicated that by starting their own OSS projects they wanted to try to leverage the OSS community model. This indicates a belief in the underlying principles of the open source movement (cf. tenets 10–15). If organizations would not be convinced of the advantages of the OSS development model, it seems likely that they would not initiate an OSS project and they would simply develop the software in-house. Nevertheless, principles such as sharing (tenet 10) and cooperation (tenet 14) were deemed quite important by the three organizations.

The previous four points demonstrate that the three organizations discussed in this article exhibited some form of ideological behavior. It is however not trivial to identify ideological tenets in organizations, since the ideas and beliefs of the OSS ideology are not explicitly formulated, as is often the case with ideologies (Hamilton, 1987). A second difficulty is that the presence of one of these characteristics by itself does not

automatically lead to ideological decision making. A good example is the avoidance of vendor lock-in. All three organizations indicated having had bad experiences with proprietary vendors in the past and wished to minimize vendor lock-in. The desire to avoid vendor lock-in can be a pragmatic reason for choosing OSS. It may however also lead to a situation in which the decision maker—based on negative experiences with some vendors in the past—only wants to use OSS without considering proprietary alternatives, leading to an ideological position towards OSS. Similarly, the list of characteristics in Table 3 is not exhaustive, and there may be other indicators of ideological behavior. A third issue is that there may be "instances where actors, genuinely or otherwise, do not interpret their behavior in terms of any commitment to a set of beliefs but as simply pragmatic, but where it is clear to the observer that it is, in fact, in conformity with such a set of beliefs" (Hamilton, 1987, p. 21). Nevertheless, the evidence presented in this article and the impression of the decision makers obtained during the interview allowed us to identify ideological characteristics in the decision making of these three organizations. These characteristics had a clear impact on the adoption decision on OSS, resulting in a strong favoritism towards OSS. The attitude in these three organizations was fundamentally different from the other seven organizations in our sample.

Limitations

This study has a number of limitations. First, we used a qualitative approach consisting of 10 case studies. Although we have found that small organizations may engage in ideological decision making, a large-scale quantitative study could provide more insight into the generalizability of this result.

Second, we only included organizations that have adopted OSS. Future research may provide more insight into the attitudes of non-adopters. We can make a meaningful distinction between two groups of non-adopters. On the one hand, there can be organizations that have considered using OSS, but decided not to adopt. The experiences of these organizations may provide more insight into the main drawbacks of using OSS. On the other hand, there are organizations that did not consider OSS as one of the alternatives. Such organizations may have negative perceptions towards OSS and did not further investigate them. For example, organizations may be convinced that OSS costs more in maintenance or is unreliable. Similarly, organizations may also have unverified ideas with respect to proprietary software. They may believe that using proprietary software is less expensive or may place more trust in a closed, proprietary software model. In the most extreme case, organizations may even only consider using software from one specific vendor. In either case, decision making will not be mindful, as not all alternatives are being considered.

Another interesting avenue for future research is to investigate whether decision making on OSS will become less ideological. Since the adoption of OSS is still a relatively recent phenomenon, less information is available on OSS than on proprietary software. It can be expected that as time passes, more information on an innovation becomes available, and decision makers will be able to make better informed choices. On the other hand, Swanson and Ramiller (2004) point out that later adoption can also be driven by diffusion itself, making later adoption not necessarily more mindful than early adoption.

A final topic for further investigation concerns situations in which the decision to start using OSS is triggered by the mere availability of OSS, rather than a concrete problem situation that gives rise to a search, evaluation, and decision-making process. This process resembles the *garbage can model* of decision making (Cohen, March, & Olsen, 1972). Hence, future research could investigate the applicability of this theory in situations in which decision makers share the OSS ideology.

CONCLUSION

The contribution of this article is that we were able to identify ideological characteristics in the decision making on OSS in very small organizations. This result further elaborates on the study of West and Dedrick (2005), who did not detect such behavior in their sample. We argue that while medium to large businesses are likely to be pragmatic in their decision making, the influence of ideological beliefs should not be completely disregarded in small organizations.

Although a minority of organizations in our sample has exhibited ideological behavior, it is remarkable that all three very small organizations in our sample—with a single decision maker—did to some degree. If that decision maker can be considered an open source advocate—which was definitely the case in Organization A and Organization J—it is more likely that personal beliefs and values of the decision maker have an impact on the final decision making. Hence, the adoption decision with respect to OSS is more likely to be ideological. This is consistent with the observation of Fiol and Connor (2003) who argue that mindlessness in combination with the absence of formal procedures will further enable mindlessness. In larger organizations, decision making is more likely to be pragmatic, since there are more decision makers and procedures involved in the OSS adoption decision.[7] Ideological decision making is however not necessarily a static phenomenon. Since it appears that ideological decision making is closely related to a single decision maker, the situation may change if that person leaves the organization, or if other decision makers join the organization. This could be observed in Organization A.

The definition of ideology we have used in this article is non-judgmental. Consequently, we do not want to make any claims with regard to whether the organizations have made a wrong decision in choosing for OSS. We have found no evidence to suggest that the decision has had a negative impact on the organizations. In fact, Organization A actually seemed to be able to innovate by using OSS and proved to be quite successful. On the other hand, it could be established that Organization A (at the time of founding) and Organization J were not sufficiently mindful in their decision. These organizations only considered using OSS and did not properly investigate alternatives. Such mindless behavior always entails the risk that the organization does not properly reflect on whether the innovation is suitable within the organization, resulting in a less-than-optimal solution for the organization (Swanson & Ramiller, 2004). A mindful organization that adopts OSS should not take the claims proposed by the OSS ideology for granted. Instead, it should investigate the implications of using OSS in the organization-specific environment. This is important since this situational context can be complex, rendering some claims irrelevant for the organization.

Swanson and Ramiller (2004) however point out that notwithstanding the risks, mindless decision making can have its merits for organizations. This can be the case when the rewards are likely to outweigh the risks, or when time limitations do not allow for a thorough decision-making process. Hence, mindless decision making can be a valid strategy for routine decisions and does not necessarily imply ideological decision making. However, we were able to exclude this possibility in the three small organizations in our sample by investigating the background of the decision-making process. In all three organizations, the adoption of OSS constituted an important change that concerned the replacement of existing proprietary software or the use of a new type of software. Therefore, no similar evaluation of OSS was previously undertaken, and decision making was indeed ideological.

REFERENCES

Abrahamson, E. (1991). Managerial fads and fashions: The diffusion and refection of innovations. *Academy of Management Review, 16*(3), 586–612.

Benbasat, I., Goldstein, D.K., & Mead, M. (1987). The case research strategy in studies of information systems. *MIS Quarterly, 11*(3), 368–386.

Bergquist, M., & Ljungberg, J. (2001). The power of gifts: Organizing social relationships in open source communities. *Information Systems Journal, 11*(4), 305–315.

Butler, B.S., & Gray, P.H. (2006). Reliability, mindfulness, and information systems. *MIS Quarterly, 30*(2), 211–224.

Cohen, M.D., March, J.G., & Olsen, J.P. (1972). A garbage can model of organizational choice. *Administrative Science Quarterly, 17*(1), 1–25.

Dedrick, J., & West, J. (2003). Why firms adopt open source platforms: A grounded theory of innovation and standards adoption. In J.L. King & K. Lyytinen (Eds.), *Proceedings of the Workshop on Standard Making: A Critical Research Frontier for Information Systems* (pp. 236–257), Seattle, WA.

Dubé, L., & Paré, G. (2003). Rigor in information systems positivist case research: Current practices, trends, and recommendations. *MIS Quarterly, 27*(4), 597–635.

Eisenhardt, K.M. (1989). Building theories from case study research. *Academy of Management Review, 14*(4), 532–550.

Fiol, C.M., & Connor, O.J. (2003). Waking up! Mindfulness in the face of bandwagons. *Academy of Management Review, 28*(1), 54–70.

Fitzgerald, B. (2006). The transformation of open source software. *MIS Quarterly, 30*(3), 587–598.

Geuss, R. (1994). Ideology. In T. Eagleton (Ed.), *Ideology* (pp. 260–278). Essex, UK: Longman Group.

Hamilton, M.B. (1987). The elements of the concept of ideology. *Political Studies, 35*(1), 18–38.

Hansen, M.T., & Haas, M.R. (2001). Competing for attention in knowledge markets: Electronic document dissemination in a management consulting company. *Administrative Science Quarterly, 46*(1), 1–28.

Harrison, D.A., Mykytyn, P.P. Jr., & Riemenschneider, C.K. (1997). Executive decisions about adoption of information technology in small business: Theory and empirical tests. *Information Systems Research, 8*(2), 171–195.

Ljungberg, J. (2000). Open source movements as a model for organizing. *European Journal of Information Systems, 9*(4), 208–216.

Lundell, B., Lings, B., & Lindqvist, E. (2006). Perceptions and uptake of open source in Swedish organizations. In E. Damiani, B. Fitzgerald, W. Scacchi, M. Scotto, & G. Succi (Eds.), *IFIP international federation for information processing: Volume 203—open source systems* (pp. 155–163). Boston: Springer.

Markus, M.L., Manville, B., & Agres, C.E. (2000). What makes a virtual organization work? *Sloan Management Review, 42*(1), 13–26.

Miles, M.B., & Huberman, A.M. (1994). *Qualitative data analysis: An expanded sourcebook* (2nd ed.). Thousand Oaks, CA: Sage.

Phillips, L.W. (1981). Assessing measurement error in key informant reports: A methodological note on organizational analysis in marketing. *Journal of Marketing Research, 18*(4), 395–415.

Riemenschneider, C.K., Harrison, D.A. & Mykytyn, P.P. Jr. (2003). Understanding IT adoption decisions in small business: Integrating current theories. *Information & Management, 40*(4),

269–285.

Sternberg, R.J. (2000). Images of mindfulness. *Journal of Social Issues, 56*(1), 11–26.

Stewart, K.J., & Gosain, S. (2006). The impact of ideology on effectiveness in open source software development teams. *MIS Quarterly, 30*(2), 291–314.

Swanson, E.B., & Ramiller, N.C. (2004). Innovating mindfully with information technology. *MIS Quarterly, 28*(4), 553–583.

Tushman, M.L., & Scanlan, T.J. (1981). Characteristics and external orientations of boundary spanning individuals. *Academy of Management Journal, 24*(1), 83–98.

Weick, K.E., Sutcliffe, K.M., & Obstfeld, D. (1999). Organizing for high reliability: Processes of collective mindfulness. In R.I. Sutton & B.M. Staw (Eds.), *Research in organizational behavior* (vol. 21, pp. 81–123). Greenwich, CT: JAI Press.

West, J., & Dedrick, J. (2005). The effect of computerization movements upon organizational adoption of open source. *Proceedings of the Social Informatics Workshop: Extending the Contributions of Professor Rob Kling to the Analysis of Computerization Movements,* Irvine, CA.

Yin, R.K. (2003). *Case study research: Design and methods* (3rd ed.). Newbury Park, CA: Sage.

ENDNOTES

[1]   These organizations had on average 41,885 employees (25,529 when only counting the unit studied in the organization).

[2]   The term "mindless" generally has a pejorative meaning, such as "unintelligent." In academic literature however, the term is used to refer to automatic or inattentive behavior (e.g., Swanson & Ramiller, 2004; Fiol & Connor, 2003; Butler & Gray, 2006;

Sternberg, 2000). We use the term "mindless" in the second sense. Hence, we do not wish to imply any negative connotations.

3   The organizations in our case studies have on average 1,081 employees.

4   Actually, the Dutch equivalent was used, namely "*vrije* software," which is similar in meaning as the French term *libre* software and refers to "freedom" rather than "free of charge."

5   Other reasons were that it used Java (which the IT manager did not like very much),

and the fact that he preferred using custom-developed software that fits his business.

6   This may indicate that these organizations preferred to cooperate with other organizations within the same industry in order to extend their own capabilities, rather than to outsource development to an external firm.

7   On the other hand, Fiol and Connor (2003) have noted that formal procedures may also lead to mindlessness (i.e., when decision makers follow procedures without critically considering them).

Chapter 8
Web Services, Service–Oriented Computing, and Service–Oriented Architecture:
Separating Hype from Reality

John Erickson
University of Nebraska - Omaha, USA

Keng Siau
University of Nebraska - Lincoln, USA

ABSTRACT

Service-oriented architecture (SOA), Web services, and service-oriented computing (SOC) have become the buzz words of the day for many in the business world. It seems that virtually every company has implemented, is in the midst of implementing, or is seriously considering SOA projects, Web services projects, or service-oriented computing. A problem many organizations face when entering the SOA world is that there are nearly as many definitions of SOA as there are organizations adopting it. Further complicating the issue is an unclear picture of the value added from adopting the SOA or Web services paradigm. This article attempts to shed some light on the definition of SOA and the difficulties of assessing the value of SOA or Web services via return on investment (ROI) or nontraditional approaches, examines the scant body of evidence empirical that exists on the topic of SOA, and highlights potential research directions in the area.

INTRODUCTION

Service-oriented architecture (SOA); Web services; mash-ups; Ajax; Web 2.0; some of their underlying middleware realization schemas such as SOAP (simple object access protocol), UDDI (universal description, discovery, and integration), XML (extensible markup language), and CORBA (common object request broker architecture); and many other ideas or approaches to cutting-edge information system architectures have become the buzzwords of the day for many in the business world and also in the IT and IS communities. It is quite difficult, perhaps nearly impossible, to pick up any relatively current practitioner publication without encountering an article focusing on at least one of the above topics. A recent library database search using keywords *service-oriented architecture*, *Web services*, and *SOA* resulted in 800-plus returns. Further investigation revealed that roughly 25 of those 800 articles were sourced in research journals while the other (still roughly 800) articles were all from more practitioner-oriented sources.

When it comes to adopting and implementing SOA, it appears that businesses are doing it at astounding rates. Of course, what they are actually doing, even though they may say that their efforts represent a move toward service-oriented architecture, may not match anyone else's definition of SOA but their own. Furthermore, how can SOA be defined, and how can we define the benefits of moving toward such architectures? It seems that there is little agreement among practitioners and researchers alike as to a standard definition of SOA.

Worse still, a growing number of practitioners are now beginning to question the business return of some of the approaches. For example, Dorman (2007), Havenstein (2006), Ricadela (2006), and Trembly (2007) indicate that there is doubt emerging as to the real value of SOA to adopting businesses and organizations. Perhaps the question of return on investment (ROI) should not be that surprising since it sometimes seems that each organization has its own definition of what SOA really is.

This article attempts to reach for a clearer understanding of what SOA really is, and proposes some possible areas of research into SOA that could help clear up some of the definitional confusion, which could in turn help lead to better understanding of ROI as it relates to SOA. First is the introduction. Second, the article provides existing definitions of SOA, Web services, and some of the related and underlying technologies and protocols. The next section combines the various definitions of SOA into a more coherent form, while the section after that proposes ideas about what SOA should be. The fifth section discusses research possibilities and provides recommendations for future research efforts. Next, we look at ways of measuring and justifying SOA and SOC (service-oriented computing) success. Finally, we conclude the article.

BACKGROUND AND HISTORY OF SERVICE-ORIENTED ARCHITECTURE

A minimum of nine formal definitions of SOA exist as of this writing, from sources such as the Organization for the Advancement of Structured Information Standards (OASIS), the Open Group, XML.com, Javaworld.com, Object Management Group (OMG), the World Wide Web Consortium (W3C), Webopedia, TechEncyclopedia, WhatIs.com, and Webopedia.org. In addition, many other definitions put forth by numerous industry experts, such as those from IBM, further cloud the issue, and worse yet, other formal definitions might also exist. In other words, the concept of service-oriented architecture appears in many ways to be a virtually content-free description of an IT-based architecture. It is not our intent here to add yet another definition to this already crowded arena of definitions, but to try to cull the common, base meanings from the various distinct definitions.

Prior to about 2003, the term service-oriented architecture was not in general use for the most part, according to Wikipedia ("SOA," 2007). However, since that time, SOA has exploded nearly everywhere in the business and technology world. SOA appears to derive or develop in many cases from more basic Web services. These services can include enabling technologies such as SOAP, CORBA, EJB (Enterprise Java Beans), DCOM (distributed component object model), and even SIP (session-initiated protocol) among many others; services may also include other middleware created with XML (Lee, Siau, & Hong, 2003; Siau & Tian, 2004; Sulkin, 2007; Walker, 2007).

Service-Oriented Architecture Definitions

The Open Group (2007) defines SOA as "an architectural style that supports service orientation." The definition goes on to also include descriptions of architectural style, service orientation, service, and salient features of SOA. OASIS defines SOA as "a paradigm for organizing and utilizing distributed capabilities that may be under the control of different ownership domains." The OASIS definition includes what they call a "reference model" in which the details of the definition are expanded and formalized. The Object Management Group (2007) defines SOA as "an architectural style for a community of providers and consumers of services to achieve mutual value." OMG adds that SOA allows technical independence among the community members, specifies the standards that the (community) members must agree to adhere to, provides business and process value to the (community) members, and "allows for a variety of technologies to facilitate (community) interactions" (OMG, 2007).

W3C (2007) defines SOA as "a form of distributed systems architecture that is typically characterized by…a logical view, a message orientation, a description orientation, granularity and platform neutrality." W3C adds details describing what it means by logical view, message and description orientations, granularity, and platform neutrality. XML.com (2007) defines SOA as follows:

SOA is an architectural style whose goal is to achieve loose coupling among interacting software agents. A service is a unit of work done by a service provider to achieve desired end results for a service consumer. Both provider and consumer are roles played by software agents on behalf of their owners.

The Javaworld.com SOA definition, composed by Raghu Kodali (2005), is as follows: "Service-oriented architecture (SOA) is an evolution of distributed computing based on the request/reply design paradigm for synchronous and asynchronous applications." Kodali also goes on to describe four characteristics of SOA. First, the interfaces composed in XML, using WSDL (Web services description language), are used for self-description. Second, XML schema called XSD should be used for messaging. Third, a UDDI-based registry maintains a list of the services provided. Finally, each service must maintain a level of quality defined for it via a QoS (quality of service) security requirement.

Finally, IBM proposes that SOA "describes a style of architecture that treats software components as a set of services" (UNL-IBM System in Global Innovation Hub, 2007). Furthermore, it insists that business needs should "drive definition" of the services, and that the value proposition be centered on the reusability and flexibility of the defined services.

SERVICE-ORIENTED ARCHITECTURE

We begin the SOA discussion with an overview of SOA provided by Krafzig, Banke, and Slama (2005). They proposed a three-level hierarchical perspective on SOA in which Level 1 includes the application front end, the service, the service repository, and the service bus (SB). Accordingly, only the service child has children, consisting of the contract, implementation, and interface. Finally, the last level of the proposed hierarchy is composed of business logic and data, children of implementation. The next subsections will discuss the general ideas of the elements included in the hierarchy proposed by Krafzig et al. described previously. This is not to recommend adoption of the hierarchy and description as the final description of SOA, but rather as a framework for discussing the meaning of SOA for the remainder of this article.

Application Front End

This part of SOA comprises a source-code interface, and in SOA terminology, it is referred to as the application programming interface (API). In accordance with most commonly accepted design principles, the underlying service requests, brokerage (negotiation), and provision should be transparent to the end user.

Service Repository

The service repository could be thought of as the library of services offered by a particular SOA. This would likely consist of an internal system that describes the services, and provides the means in the user interface to call a particular service. UDDI could be seen as a realization of the service repository idea. UDDI is a global registry that allows businesses to list themselves on the Internet. UDDI is platform independent and XML based. The point of UDDI is for businesses to list the Web or SOA-type services that they provide so that other companies searching for such services can more easily locate and arrange to use them.

Service Bus

The SB, more commonly referred to as the enterprise service bus (ESB), provides a transportation pathway between the data and the end-user application interface. Using an ESB does not necessarily mean SOA is being implemented, but ESB or some sort of SB use is almost always part of an SOA deployment. According to Hicks (n.d.), Oracle's idea of an ESB includes multiple

protocols that "separate integration concerns from applications and logic." What this means is that ESBs have now become commercialized, and can be licensed for use much like other UDDI-based services. So, companies searching for ESB solutions as part of an SOA effort now have multiple choices and do not necessarily have to re-create the wheel by building their own ESB.

Common Services

It seems apparent from many of the SOA definitions that many of the technologies included in an SOA definition, and by default SOA implementations, are established and conventional protocols. To better understand the services provided in many SOA definitions, a brief explanation of some of the more commonly used underlying technologies is provided. A particular service may or may not be explicitly Web based, but in the end it matters little since the services provided by the architecture should be transparently designed, implemented, and provided. The general consensus from most involved in Web services is that the services are meant to be modular. This means that no single document encompasses all of them, and furthermore, that the specifications are multiple and (more or less) dynamic. This results in a small number of core specifications. Those core services can be enhanced or supported by other services as "the circumstances and choice of technology dictate" ("Web Service," 2007).

XML allows users to define and specify the tags used to capture and exchange data, typically between distinct and usually incompatible systems from different companies or organizations. This means that XML is a good example of middleware; it also means that XML enables Web services. XML was one of the initial drivers that provided the ability to conduct e-business for many businesses in the Internet era. XML cannot really be considered a service, but as the language used to write many of the Web services or service stack protocols.

SOAP, like all protocols, consists of a set list of instructions detailing the action(s) to be taken in a given circumstance. SOAP is designed to call, access, and execute objects. The original SOAP was typically for communications between computers, and usually involved XML-based messages. SOAP and its underlying XML programming comprised one of the first Web service communication stacks. One of the original Web services that SOAP provided was called remote procedure call (RPC), which allowed a remote computer to call a procedure from another computer or network. More recently, SOAP has taken on a somewhat modified meaning so that the acronym now means service-oriented architecture protocol. In both cases, what SOAP does is to use existing communications protocols to provide its services. The more common early SOAP contracts included XML applications written for HTTP (hypertext transfer protocol), HTTPS (HTTP over secure socket layer), and SMTP (simple mail transfer protocol), among others. It should be apparent from these that many early SOAP implementations involved e-commerce or e-business applications, which means that the concern at the time when many applications were first developed was to move sales and other data collected in Web portals to back-end data stores.

CORBA is an OMG-developed standard that allows different software components that are usually written in different languages and installed on different computers to work together (Zhao & Siau, 2007). CORBA was developed in the early 1990s, and while not overtly an SOA at the time, it actually performs many of the functions in an SOA, using an IIOP- (Internet inter-orb protocol) based service stack.

EJB is a component typically situated on the server that "encapsulates the business logic of an application" ("EJB," 2007). EJB enables the creation of modular enterprise (and other) applications. The intent of EJB is to facilitate the creation of middleware that acts as a go-between

tying front-end applications to back-end applications or data sources.

SIP is a signaling protocol designed for use in telecommunications at the application layer. It has generally become one of the primary protocols used in VoIP (voice over Internet protocol), H.323, and other communications standards. SIP can be seen as a primary provider of Web services for Internet-based voice communications such as VoIP (Sulkin, 2007).

Contract (Services)

Components of a service contract typically include primary and secondary elements. The primary elements consist of the header, functional requirements, and nonfunctional requirements. Subelements for the header consist of the name, version, owner, RACI, and type. Under functional requirements are functional requirement descriptions, service operations, and invocation. Nonfunctional requirements include security constraints, QoS, transactional requirements (the service part of a larger transaction), service-level agreement, and process ("SOA," 2007). The contract generally includes metadata about itself, who owns it, and how it is brokered, bound, and executed.

Interface

At this level of service provision, the interface referred to is a segment of code that connects the service with the data and/or business logic (process). The interface describes how data will be moved into and out of the data source by the service, and must be designed to comply with the physical (data, data structures, etc.) and process (business logic) requirements of the existing and/or legacy system.

Implementation

The implementation specifies the contract and interface to be used for each service requested, and contains the direct pathway into the data and business logic.

Architecture

The service component of SOA has been discussed, though admittedly at a high level. However, the architecture component has not yet been addressed and it will be helpful to speak briefly about the architecture segment of SOA. Architecture in general refers to the art (or science) behind the design and building of structures. Alternatively, an architecture may refer to a method or style of a building or a computer system. So, if SOA is taken literally as a description of its function, it could be taken to mean a structured way of organizing or arranging the services in a business or organization.

SOA FRAMEWORK

It is apparent from the existing definitions and models that service-oriented architecture is commonly seen as an architecture or way of assembling, building, or composing the information technology infrastructure of a business or organization. As such, SOA is not a technology in itself; rather, it is a way of structuring or arranging other technologies to accomplish a number of other tasks. This naturally leads to the problem of a multiplicity of definitions of SOA since many relatively similar structural arrangements of services are possible. Many of the definitions also indicate that the arrangement and relationships between modules should be loosely coupled rather than tightly coupled. This allows for customization of services based on need, and on-demand rather than some predetermined structure, but the downside is that it also leads toward a plethora of definitions and approaches to SOA implementation.

Some of the common features that seem sensible to include in a formal definition of SOA would relate to a common framework, such as that specified by Krafzig et al. (2005) or one of the other standards bodies. In other words, a framework would include metadata describing the various important features of SOA, how those features can be arranged, and the libraries or location of services that allow adopting organizations to arrange bindings or contracts between themselves and the service provider, independent of whether the service provider is internal or external. We propose the framework depicted in Figure 1 as a starting point for visualizing SOA.

Several of the standards bodies have taken a stance in creating or calling for a metamodel, at least in some form. Among them are the Open Group, OASIS, OMG, W3C, and to a lesser extent industry-related bodies such as Javaworld.com, XML.com, IBM, and Oracle.

UDDI has become a very well-known structured repository for services and service components, which speaks to the universality of the library or centralized database of services. However, more standardization efforts will be necessary to enhance the interoperability of UDDI.

It also appears, especially with the industry definitions of SOA, that the contracts, bindings, interfaces, service buses, and other implementation-related portions of SOA are important elements to be considered when attempting to give an overall definition of SOA. This unfortunately could easily represent a stumbling block in garnering consensus on a definition of SOA since each of these companies has invested significant time, human, and other likely resources toward development of their specific pieces of the SOA pie. Each company has invested heavily and thus will likely be less willing to risk that investment and any potential return and customer lock-in in order to simply agree on standards. We observed a similar occurrence of this type of behavior in the recently ended format war in the high-definition DVD market. Similarly, if the standards bodies have political or industry leanings, agreement on

Figure 1. SOA framework

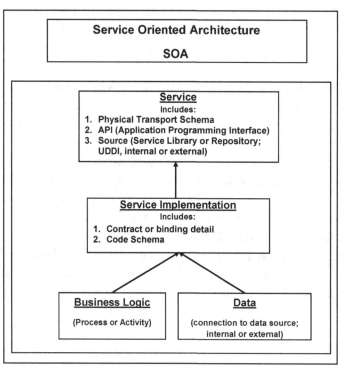

a common SOA definition and standards could be difficult to achieve.

Another more recent development comes from Shah and Kalin (2007). They proposed that organizations adopting SOA follow a specific path based on an analysis of business challenges, including SOA business drivers and IT barriers. This led them to speculate that a specific adoption model be used to guide the SOA implementation process. They indicated that an ad hoc SOA model is better where the benefits of new services are specific to each individual service, where the technologies may be inconsistently applied (different implementations for the same service in different projects), where services cannot be reused, and where the increases in technological complexity translate into decreased system response times. Shah and Kalin ended with a call for a strategy- or program-based SOA adoption model that is situational.

We propose that a common definition of SOA is possible and necessary, and call for negotiations among interested bodies with the aim of reaching a common definition of SOA. We realize that in practice it might prove difficult or even nearly impossible to expect such a consensus to be arrived at, but a common definition and structure of SOA would go a long way toward dealing with some of the confusion, misinformation, and hype regarding the entire subject. Difficult though it might be to expect this, a realization that SOAP, CORBA, RPC, and XML among many other technological tools have reached a point of relative agreement amongst users if not ubiquity, at least related to their underlying standards, should provide some evidence that agreements can be reached. Next, we will examine SOA from the research perspective.

POSSIBILITIES FOR RESEARCH

Research into SOA is extremely limited at this point in time. What studies exist can be classified into several distinct categories. The first includes exploratory or recommendation-type efforts that propose various means to approach SOA implementation. These investigations may or may not include proprietary industry software, but most of these research efforts propose the use of patterns or blueprints and a metamodel of SOA as a means to understanding the SOA perspective. Second, in this category are research proposals that examine company-specific technologies or tools (i.e., IBM proposing the use of Rational Software, including the Rational Unified Process) in relation to SOA design and implementation. Neither of the first two types of SOA research generally involve ideas on how to measure SOA in terms of success or failure, or even suggest metrics. Finally, the third type of research articles focus on empirical research.

SOA Development or Deployment Patterns and Blueprints, and the Meta-Approach

Stal (2006) took a roughly similar approach to what we are attempting to do in this article; he advocated using architectural patterns and blueprints (software engineering patterns) as a means to enable or foster efficient deployment of SOA. He supported loose coupling of services in a registry or library to the extent that he thought that removing the services' dependency on the registry's or provider's distinct location would benefit the deployment of SOA. Stal maintained that this would eliminate, or at least minimize, a layer in the SOA framework. He also proposed a more tightly defined and controlled integration of middleware using XML or similar tools. Basically, Stal suggested a metamodel and pattern approach to defining SOA, but did not suggest

what the research might accomplish or how the research into SOA would be framed. Kim and Lim (2007) also proposed a distinct means to implementing SOA, using in this instance, business process management, in addition to a variant of the SOA framework specifically dealing with the telecommunications industry. Similar to Stal, Kim and Lim did not propose empirical research into SOA, but rather focused on implementation and standards in a specific industry.

Shan and Hua (2006) proposed an SOA approach for the Internet banking industry. They also compiled a list of patterns that have been proven successful for other online service industries. However, the models they used and ended up with are very detailed regarding how SOA should be implemented for first online companies in general, and then Internet banking specifically. This again does not propose or frame specific research but rather suggests an implementation approach and a structure for SOA.

The ESB is explained in detail, but from a general perspective rather than a company-specific approach in Schmidt, Hutchison, Lambros, and Phippen's (2005) expository. The article is informative regarding ESB implementation and design patterns, but it is not research oriented.

Crawford, Bate, Cherbakov, Holley, and Tsocanos (2005) proposed a different way to structure SOA, what they called on-demand SOA. They essentially proposed an even looser coupling of services and their connecting elements than in other perspectives of SOA. They argued that this would allow much more flexibility to the adopting organizations and the end users.

Company-Specific and Commercial Tool-Based SOA Deployment

Brown, Delbaere, Eeles, Johnston, and Weaver (2005) presented an industry-oriented perspective on the SOA puzzle. They suggested an approach to service orientation using the proprietary IBM Rational platform. Their recommendations follow similar paths as some previous research, but are also filtered through the IBM Rational lens. The article is primarily illustrative in nature, suggesting how to best implement SOA using IBM Rational tools. In a similar vein, Ferguson and Stockton (2005) also detailed IBM's programming model and product architecture.

De Pauw, Lei, Pring, and Villard (2005) described the benefits of Web Services Navigator, a proprietary tool created to provide a better visualization of SOA and Web services in a loosely coupled architecture. The tool can help with design-pattern, business-logic, and business-process analysis, and thus help with SOA architecture design and implementation.

Jones (2005) suggested that SOA, service, and Web service standards were "on the way" and provided a list of existing tools, such as UML (Unified Modeling Language) and/or the rational unified process that could aid the SOA (or service) design process. However, he also advocated the push toward formal definitions of such SOA basics as services, to the end of providing a more coherent and cohesive structure that he thought would enhance the ability of developers and adopters to understand and deploy SOA.

Research-Based Perspectives on SOA

Chen, Zhou, and Zhang (2006) proposed an ontologically based perspective on SOA, Web services, and knowledge management. They attempted, with some success, to integrate two separate research streams into one. They presented a solution to show that semantic- and syntactic-based knowledge representations could both be depicted with a comprehensive ontology that also described Web service composition. While their framework represents a step toward automated (Web) service composition, more research is still needed.

Borkar, Carey, Mangtani, McKinney, Pate, and Thatte (2006) suggested a way of handling XML-based data in an SOA or service environment. Their idea involved the use of data both able to be queried and unable to be queried, and would necessarily also involve XML-formatted data. This represents empirical research into a part of SOA, namely, the underlying services, and is at least a step in the right direction, although it does not enter the realm of research into the efficacy or ROI of SOA.

Duke, Davies, and Richardson (2005) recommended and provided details on using the Semantic Web to organize an organization's approach to SOA and Web service orientation. They suggested that combining the Semantic Web and SOA into what they called Semantic SOA would provide benefits to adopting organizations. Then they further proposed an ontological model of the Semantic SOA, attempting essentially to create a meta-metamodel of SOA using their experience with the telecommunications industry as a case example. This is one of the few high-level articles that can also be seen as empirical research.

Zhang (2004) explored the connection between Web services and business process management, and described the modular nature of the service (and Web service) perspective. He detailed the software industry's approach to Web services and provided evidence that standards development would quickly mature, beginning in 2005. He maintained that once standards were agreed upon, a connection to business process management would be easier to sell to businesses. Zhang also developed a prototype e-procurement system that composed external services to operate.

Malloy, Kraft, Hallstrom, and Voas (2006) developed an extension to WSDL. They insisted that Web services' specifications were "typically informal and not well-defined," and proposed what they called an intermediate step between requiring more formal and rigorous service specifications and the informal nature of the existing service specifications. They accomplished this balance by extending WSDL to include support for application arguments that would help automate and expand the ability of services to operate in multiple environments. They provided an example of how their WSDL extension could allow a single service to function successfully in different applications using multiple zip code formats (five vs. nine digits, and hyphens vs. no hyphens).

Verheecke, Vanderperren, and Jonckers (2006) proposed and developed a middleware level that they called the Web services management layer (WSML). They saw the primary advantage of their approach in that it provided a reusable framework. They further believed that the use of their framework would enable "dynamic integration, selection, composition, and client-side management of Web Services in client applications" (p. 49). They were aware that their approach could cause some problems in a distributed system since implementation of it resulted in a centralized architecture.

Hutchinson, Henzel, and Thwaits (2006) described a case in which an SOA-based system was deployed for a library extension collaboration project. Much of the case details the SOA approach itself, and explains the experiences of the project developers and implementers. They noted that while the SOA architecture could be expected to reduce the operational maintenance costs overall, the way the system was specified and delivered in this particular case might require more work from IT to keep some services, such as flash players, up to date. While the authors did not specifically mention it in the article, perhaps a more loosely coupled architecture might alleviate some of those operational maintenance costs.

Li, Huang, Yen, and Cheng (2007) proposed a methodology to migrate the functionality of legacy systems to a Web services or SOA architecture. They used a case study to investigate the efficacy of their proposed methodology, finding that while it was possible to make such a migration from legacy systems to SOA (or Web services), the changes that it required from the organization were considerable, and some process reengineering would likely be necessary.

MEASURING SOA AND SOC SUCCESS

Another tricky issue in SOA and SOC implementation is the measurement or evaluation of success. Traditionally, software (or system) successes and failures have been estimated by the usual suspects: traditional measures such as ROI, net present value (NPV), breakeven, internal rate of return (IRR), or other similar financially based approaches. Similarly, software itself has usually been measured in terms of errors or productivity via numeric methodologies such as lines of code, COCOMO (constructive cost model), and similar estimation techniques. These approaches are all based firmly on the idea that if we can assign some number to a system, then we can compare them across projects, systems, or organizations. The problem is analogous to the question often asked regarding enterprise resource planning (ERP) systems: If all of the Fortune 100 companies implement the same piece of software, such as SAP, then what allows one organization to differentiate itself from another if they have standardized on SAP's best processes and best practices? One way to answer that question is to examine other measures of success such as competitive advantages (Siau, 2003), competitive necessity, flexibility, agility (Erickson, Lyytinen, & Siau, 2005), nimbleness, responsiveness, and other relevant intangibles. We would even propose that the best way to evaluate SOA or SOC implementation is not ROI. Intangible but critical factors such as competitive necessity, agility, on-demand abilities, and responsiveness should be the decisive factors.

Nah, Islam, and Tan (2007) proposed a framework and critical success factors for estimating the success of ERP implementations. They empirically assessed a variety of implementation success factors including top-management support, project team competence, and interdepartmental cooperation, among many others. While the study answered a number of important questions regarding ERP implementations, the issue of assessing intangibles in terms of success factors remains a problem, not only for ERP-type implementations but also for other system types as well, especially for SOA since the SOA approach can be seen as an alternative in many ways to ERP.

Langdon (2007) noted that while many economic-based studies indicate that IT projects add value at the macrolevel, little has been done to assess how value is added at the more micro or individual project level. Specifically, Langdon proposed and evaluated a research model that included (IS) integration and flexibility as capabilities that could lead to IT business value. Of course, flexibility and integration are only two components of a larger IT capabilities structure, but the study indicates that the first steps have been taken to study intangibles in the context of an IT systems development project.

Two intangibles in the IT success-factor context are the oft-cited agility or nimbleness of a company or organization. An entire genre of systems development has emerged based on the principle of agility. However, there is little empirical evidence supporting the value added from such development approaches (Erickson et al., 2005). Since a growing number of SOA installations are constructed as ad hoc, which is in a basic sense agile, we propose that in environments where agility and nimbleness are important, so in turn are SOA and SOC important.

CONCLUSION

From the literature, it appears that only a few efforts can be said to be empirical research. A majority of the research efforts involved created tools or language extensions that would increase the interoperability of services, while other research proposed standards modifications. Many of the remaining articles published proposed new tools or the use of existing proprietary tools, described an approach to SOA from specific perspectives, or proposed model or metamodel changes. A limited number of case studies detailing SOA, Web services, or service deployments or implementation efforts provide experience reports on how best to implement such systems.

As far as we can determine, virtually no research has been formally done regarding the benefits and drawbacks of SOA or Web services. Two problems with this are likely to revolve around the nebulous nature of SOA and Web services in terms of the widely varying definition and the emerging standards issue. An effort to identify SOA and Web services metrics would help to get research into this area started.

Another area of interest involving SOA and Web services adoption is the cultural and structural impacts on the organization or business. A number of articles note the importance of those elements, but little has been accomplished in terms of research specifically connecting SOA or Web services with cultural and structural changes in organizations.

A variety of standards bodies are working separately toward formal definitions including metamodels, and a number of SOA vendors, among them some of the very large and established software industry players, have emerged. While the effort toward standardization is direly needed and commendable, a more collaborative approach would, in our opinion, benefit the industry and implementing companies and organizations as well. The seeming result of the rather haphazard approach to SOA appears to indicate that an increasing number of implementing organizations are finding it difficult to assess the cost benefit of the entire services approach. Research efforts at this point appear to be in a similar state of disarray. Until a more coherent picture of SOA emerges, its image is likely to remain slightly out of focus, and research in the area is likely to remain somewhat unfocused as a result.

REFERENCES

Borkar, V., Carey, M., Mangtani, N., McKinney, D., Patel, R., & Thatte, S. (2006). XML data services. *International Journal of Web Services Research, 3*(1), 85-95.

Brown, A., Delbaere, M., Eeles, P., Johnston, S., & Weaver, R. (2005). Realizing service oriented solutions with the IBM Rational Software Development Platform. *IBM Systems Journal, 44*(4), 727-752.

Chen, Y., Zhou, L., & Zhang, D. (2006). Ontology-supported Web service composition: An approach to service-oriented knowledge management in corporate financial services. *Journal of Database Management, 17*(1), 67-84.

Crawford, C., Bate, G., Cherbakov, L., Holley, K., & Tsocanos, C. (2005). Toward an on demand service architecture. *IBM Systems Journal, 44*(1), 81-107.

De Pauw, Lei, M., Pring, E., & Villard, L. (2005). Web services navigator: Visualizing the execution of Web services. *IBM Systems Journal, 44*(4), 821-845.

Dorman, A. (2007). FrankenSOA. *Network Computing, 18*(12), 41-51.

Duke, A., Davies, J., & Richardson, M. (2005). Enabling a scalable service oriented architecture with Semantic Web services. *BT Technology Journal, 23*(3), 191-201.

EJB. (2007). *Wikipedia.* Retrieved October 12, 2007, from http://en.wikipedia.org/wiki/Ejb

Erickson, J., Lyytinen, K., & Siau, K. (2005). Agile modeling, agile software development, and extreme programming: The state of research. *Journal of Database Management, 16*(4), 80-89.

Ferguson, D., & Stockton, M. (2005). Service oriented architecture: Programming model and product architecture. *IBM Systems Journal, 44*(4), 753-780.

Havenstein, H. (2006). Measuring SOA performance is a complex art. *Computer World, 40*(2), 6.

Hicks, B. (n.d.). *Oracle Enterprise Service Bus: The foundation for service oriented architecture.* Retrieved October 18, 2007, from http://www.oracle.com/global/ap/openworld/ppt_download/middleware_oracle%20enterprise%20service%20bus%20foundation_250.pdf

Hutchinson, B., Henzel, J., & Thwaits, A. (2006). Using Web services to promote library-extension collaboration. *Library Hi Tech, 24*(1), 126-141.

Jones, S. (2005). Toward an acceptable definition of service. *IEEE Software, 22*(3), 87-93.

Kim, J., & Lim, K. (2007). An approach to service oriented architecture using Web service and BPM in the Telcom OSS domain. *Internet Research, 17*(1), 99-107.

Krafzig, D., Banke, K., & Slama, D. (2005). *SOA elements.* Prentice Hall. Retrieved October 2, 2007, from http://en.wikipedia.org/wiki/Image:SOA_Elements.png

Langdon, C. (2007). Designing information systems to create business value: A theoretical conceptualization of the role of flexibility and integration. *Journal of Database Management, 17*(3), 1-18.

Lee, J., Siau, K., & Hong, S. (2003). Enterprise integration with ERP and EAI. *Communications of the ACM, 46*(2), 54-60.

Li, S., Huang, S., Yen, D., & Chang, C. (2007). Migrating legacy information systems to Web services architecture. *Journal of Database Management, 18*(4), 1-25.

Malloy, B., Kraft, N., Hallstrom, J., & Voas, J. (2006). Improving the predictable assembly of service oriented architectures. *IEEE Software, 23*(2), 12-15.

Nah, F., Islam, Z., & Tan, M. (2007). Empirical assessment of factors influencing success of enterprise resource planning implementations. *Journal of Database Management, 18*(4), 26-50.

Object Management Group (OMG). (2007). Retrieved September 25, 2007, from http://colab.cim3. net/cgi-bin/wiki.pl?OMGSoaGlossary#nid34QI

Open Group. (2007). Retrieved September 25, 2007, from http://opengroup.org/projects/soa/doc. tpl?gdid=10632

Organization for the Advancement of Structured Information Standards (OASIS). (2006). Retrieved September 25, 2007, from http://www.oasis-open. org/committees/tc_home.php?wg_abbrev=soa-rm

Ricadela, A. (2006, September 4). The dark side of SOA. *Information Week*, pp. 54-58.

Schmidt, M., Hutchison, B., Lambros, P., & Phippen, R. (2005). Enterprise service bus: Making service oriented architecture real. *IBM Systems Journal, 44*(4), 781-797.

Shah, A., & Kalin, P. (2007, July 6). SOA adoption models: Ad-hoc versus program-based. *SOA Magazine*.

Shan, T., & Hua, W. (2006). Service oriented solution framework for Internet banking. *Internet Journal of Web Services Research, 3*(1), 29-48.

Siau, K. (2003). Interorganizational systems and competitive advantages: Lessons from history. *Journal of Computer Information Systems, 44*(1), 33-39.

Siau, K., & Tian, Y. (2004). Supply chains integration: Architecture and enabling technologies. *Journal of Computer Information Systems, 44*(3), 67-72.

SOA. (2007). *Wikipedia.* Retrieved September 25, 2007, from http://en.wikipedia.org/wiki/Service-oriented_architecture#SOA_definitions

Stal, M. (2006). Using architectural patterns and blueprints for service oriented architecture. *IEEE Software, 23*(2), 54-61.

Sulkin, A. (2007). SOA and enterprise voice communications. *Business Communications Review, 37*(8), 32-34.

Trembly, A. (2007). SOA: Savior or snake oil? *National Underwriter Life & Health, 111*(27), 50.

UNL-IBM System in Global Innovation Hub. (2007). *Making SOA relevant for business.* Retrieved October 9, 2007, from http://cba.unl.edu/outreach/ unl-ibm/documents/SOA_Relevant_Business.pdf

Verheecke, B., Vanderperren, W., & Jonckers, V. (2006). Unraveling crosscutting concerns in Web services middleware. *IEEE Software, 23*(1), 42-50.

Walker, L. (2007). IBM business transformation enabled by service-oriented architecture. *IBM Systems Journal, 46*(4), 651-667.

Web service. (2007). *Wikipedia.* Retrieved October 18, 2007, from http://en.wikipedia.org/wiki/ Web_service

World Wide Web Consortium (W3C). (2007). Retrieved September 25, 2007, from http://colab.cim3. net/cgi-bin/wiki.pl?WwwCSoaGlossary#nid34R0

XML.com. (2007). Retrieved September 25, 2007, from http://www.xml.com/pub/a/ws/2003/09/30/ soa.html

Zhang, D. (2004). Web services composition for process management in e-business. *Journal of Computer Information Systems, 45*(2), 83-91.

Zhao, L., & Siau, K. (2007). Information mediation using metamodels: An approach using XML and common warehouse metamodel. *Journal of Database Management, 18*(3), 69-82.

This work was previously published in the Journal of Database Management, Vol. 19, Issue 3, edited by K. Siau, pp. 42-54, copyright 2008 by IGI Publishing (an imprint of IGI Global).

Chapter 9
Approximate Query Answering with Knowledge Hierarchy

Wookey Lee
Inha University, Korea

Myung-Keun Shin
Telecom Business Division, SK C&C, Korea

Soon Young Huh
Korea Advanced Institute of Science and Technology, South Korea

Donghyun Park
Inha University, South Korea

Jumi Kim
Small Business Institute, Korea

ABSTRACT

Approximate Query Answering is important for incorporating knowledge abstraction and query relaxation in terms of the categorical and the numerical data. By exploiting the knowledge hierarchy, a novel method is addressed to quantify the semantic distances between the categorical information as well as the numerical data. Regarding that, an efficient query relaxation algorithm is devised to modify the approximate queries to ordinary queries based on the knowledge hierarchy. Then the ranking measures work very efficiently to cope with various combinations of complex queries with respect to the number of nodes in the hierarchy as well as the corresponding cost model.

INTRODUCTION

Database query processing has mostly focused on addressing exact answers in terms of Boolean model.

DOI: 10.4018/978-1-60566-904-5.ch009

There are a number of circumstances in which a user desires an approximate answer rather than the exact answer. At first, when a user does not always understand all about the data schema or the queries contain errors syntactically or semantically, then the query results may be null or be thrown up too much.

Then the user feels to amend or modify the query. Secondly, in data mining environment, when an initial query is answered and that can be considered as an anchor point from which the query can be relaxed to find more detailed information. Manual relaxation, however, for the unsatisfactory queries is usually a drudgery and time-consuming process, which strongly requires a knowledge-based schema for the database or datawarehouse as well as query relaxation mechanism.

The query relaxation process can be explained in more detail by the following example: Consider an illustrative recruiting scenario in which the query:

Q: *Skill == 'C++' ∧ Salary == $40,000 ∧ Age == 40*

Assume that no result record comes out with the conventional query answering systems. Then in our approach, the first step to relax the query condition is as follows:

Q_R: *Skill in ('Cobol' 'C++' 'Java') ∧ $35,000 ≤ Salary ≤ $45,000 ∧ 37 ≤ Age ≤ 43.*

And then, we sort the relaxed query results in terms of a ranking measure between the original query and the objects, which will prove very useful for the applicants as they obtain a richer result of information. Finally, we get the results sorted by ranking distance *D*, such as (1) < Martin, C++, $40000, 40, *D*: 0.00 >, (2) < Albert, *Java*, $43000, 40, *D*: 0.10 >, (3) < Harry, C++, $37000, 38, *D*: 0.21 >, and (4) < Neal, Cobol, $38000, 41, *D*: 0.39 >. In order to achieve this, a method of obtaining the approximate value and to measure the distance between the target value and the approximate value needs to be provided. For the numerical domain, such as Salary and Age, the difference between two values can be used as a semantic distance measure. For the categorical domain such as Skill, the approximate values can be calculated by using a predetermined item distance table (Motro, 1990) or by the abstract hierarchy (Chu et al., 1996; Chen, Zhou, & Zhang, 2006).

The approaches based on the semantic distance approach (Motro, 1990; Muslea, 2004; Lee *at al.*, 2007) uses the notion of semantic distance to represent the degree of similarity between data values. Since query answering systems employing the semantic distance approach provide quantitative measures between target values and neighborhood values as a query result, users can retrieve approximate values more effectively using the measures as references to compare with different approximate values. However, for categorical data, the semantic distance approach has two problems because it employs a two dimensional table to store distances among all pairs of data values. First, to find neighbor values of a target value, the system has to scan all the records related to the target value. Second, when a new value is added to a domain, it is required to consider distances between the value and all existing attribute values. This task contains a large amount of overhead to be done by a human operator, and moreover, human operators are liable to lose consistency in assigning distance data to a large number of values. In contrast, the approaches based on the abstraction hierarchy are suitable to dealing with categorical data. However, abstraction approaches could not properly handle other data types, such as the number, money, date and time, etc, and do not provide quantitative similarity measure among data values.

To overcome these problems, we propose a hierarchical quantified knowledge (HQK) that integrates abstraction approach and semantic distance approach. The HQK uses the hierarchy structure of abstraction approach and provides a quantitative measure between data values in the hierarchy. The abstraction hierarchy facilitates finding neighbor values for a target value quite easily. The distance information embedded in the HQK provides a more efficient method than the one based on a table. Maintenance of distance information due to the addition of a new value can be minimized since the change is localized in the hierarchy. This paper will demonstrate how to calculate the similarity distance between two data values and introduce the query relaxation algorithm with HQK.

The rest of the paper is organized as follows. Section 2 reviews prior related approaches. Section 3 proposes the HQK as a new knowledge representation framework. Section 3 explains details of the query relaxation algorithm and examples using the HQK. Section 4 presents the experiment result. The final section will summarize and introduce proposed concepts for future exploratory research.

RELATED WORKS

Several approaches for finding best matches instead of the exact match have been proposed, such as nearest neighbour searches (Chan, 1998; Beygelzimer, Kakade, & Langford, 2005), rank aggregation (Liu et al., 2007), top-K queries (Chakrabarti et al., 2003; Mouratidis, Bakiras, & Papadias, 2006; Lee *at al*., 2007), and preference searches (Klein & Konig-Ries, 2004). These approaches mostly deal with either numeric conditions or concepts such as importance or relevance. In addition, the conceptual database interface (Siau, Tan, & Chan, 1992; Lee & Lim, 2007) has been proposed to facilitate end users interacting with the database, where they have showed that the visualized conceptual level query could provide an effective and efficient assistance for end users than the complicated logical level query (Chan, Wei, & Siau, 1993; Siau, Chan, & Wei, 2004). The conceptual database interface, however, differs from our approach where we provide a structured query processing capability based on the query relaxation. Also, approximate query answering approaches (Babcock et al., 2003; Calado & Ribeiro-Neto,2003; Liu & Chu, 2007) have been proposed that have tried to provide relevant information with wider scope. Typical steps for approximate query answering consist of query analysis, query relaxation, and providing information relevant to the query. In order to facilitate query relaxation and to provide relevant information on the query, a knowledge representation framework is required. The knowledge representation framework is one of the most important factors in deciding the configuration and corresponding performance of the approximate query answering system.

Studies on knowledge representation have been extensively performed using semantic distance models or abstraction models (Shin et al., 2008). In the semantic distance approach, each and every pair of data values within the data set is assumed to have semantic distances (Motro, 1990), and thus this approach provides a straightforward method for query relaxation providing ranked results sorted by the semantic distance. FLEX (Motro, 1990) reaches a high tolerance to incorrect queries by iteratively interpreting the query at lower levels of correctness. FLEX is also cooperative in the sense that, for any empty result query, it provides either an explanation for the empty result or some assistance for turning the query into a nonempty result one. For categorical data, the distance between two data values is stored in a separate table. Since every pair of data is supposed to have a semantic distance, the table size usually becomes extremely large in an explosive fashion when a realistic application domain is considered.

In approximate query answering, the data abstraction is useful in associating data values with each other for query relaxation. Chu et al. (1996) introduced type abstraction hierarchy, which synthesize the database schema and tuples into an abstract form. Chu et al. used three type of operation, such as generalization, specialization, and association to relax a query. Shin *et al*. (2001) proposed the approximate query answering mechanism with the knowledge abstraction database. This paper shows that integrating the semantic distance notion to the abstraction hierarchy would overcome the weaknesses of the previous approaches and can provide a more

Figure 1. Hierarchical data abstraction with domain abstraction

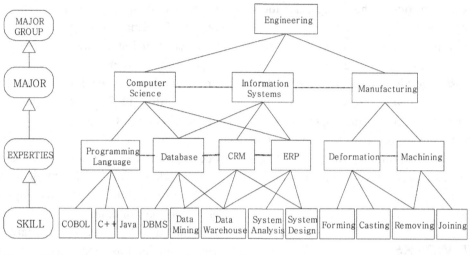

effective and extendable approximate query answering mechanism that can support a wider range of approximate queries.

HIERARCHICAL QUANTIFIED DATA ABSTRACTION

In this section we propose a hierarchical quantified data abstraction that combines abstraction hierarchy with a semantic distance notion.

Hierarchical Data Abstraction and Distance Metric

HQK is a knowledge representation framework that facilitates multilevel representation of data and meta-data for an underlying corporate database using data abstraction. Figure 1 shows an instance of the HQK that represents the abstraction information on Engineering. Values constituting the hierarchy may be parts of the underlying database or artificial values added to describe the semantic relationship among the existing data values. HQK consists of two types of abstraction hierarchies: *value abstraction*

hierarchy and *domain abstraction hierarchy*. In the value abstraction hierarchy, there are abstraction relationships of *specific node/abstract node.* One node in a level can be generalized into an abstract node placed in an upper level. Thus, the abstraction hierarchy is constructed on the basis of abstraction/specification relationships among abstract nodes and specific nodes in various abstraction levels. This abstraction relationship can be interpreted as an "IS-A" relationship. For instance, COBOL is a Programming Language while Programming Language is a (branch of) Computer Science. As such, higher levels provide a more generalized data representation than lower ones and the root node can be interpreted as the most abstract but representative name of the hierarchy. In Figure 1, the root node is Engineering which can act as a representative of the hierarchy.

The leaf nodes including COBOL, C++, etc., are given with the *level* value 1, and the level value increases by one each time they are generalized with an abstract node. A specific node may have multiple abstract nodes that are located in different levels, so that COBOL has Programming Language in level 2 and Computer Science in level 3 as its abstract node. The *n level abstract node* of a specific node is the abstract node that is located in *n* level higher than the specific node. Note that, the *level difference value n* between two arbitrary nodes is defined as the larger number of abstracted levels from the two nodes to their least common abstract node. The *n level neighbor nodes* are the nodes that share a common abstract node in level difference *n*. Figure 1 shows the explanation of the level difference and neighbour nodes. For example, COBOL and Database in Figure 1 have a level difference of 2, and System Analysis and System Design are an example of level 1 neighbor nodes.

Now we present the concept of the distance metric with which formal properties are derived. To develop the distance metric, first, we assume basic distance. The *basic distances* are specified on the two types of links, *vertical link* and *horizontal link*. The vertical link connects a specific node and its 1 level abstract node, and the horizontal link connects two different level 1 neighbor nodes. The basic distance is defined modifying the distance measure of Lee & Lim (2007). This measure shows how closely two nodes are related in the hierarchy. Let *z* represent the least common abstract node of *x* and *y*. Then, the basic distance between *x* and *y*, *bd*(*x, y*) is defined as

$$bd(x,y) = 1 - \frac{2 * N3}{N1 + N2 + 2 * N3}.$$

N1 is the number of nodes on the path from *x* to *z*. *N2* is the number of nodes on the path from *y* to *z*. *N3* is the number of nodes on the path from *z* to root. For example, to calculate the basic distance between Engineering and Computer Science in Frgure 1, we get *N1*=1, *N2*= 2, *N3*=1, respectively. So,

bd(Engineering, Computer Science) =

$$1 - \frac{2 \cdot 1}{1 + 2 + 2 \cdot 1} = 0.6$$

Note that the distance represents that the deeper the position of the two nodes, the smaller the basic distance is. Figure 2 shows an example of the HQK with the basic distance.

Herein, we define the distance between two arbitrary nodes that satisfies the requirement of the distance metric. It is possible to consider only the basic distances on the path for distance calculation; however, this approach cannot always guarantee property 2, implying that sometimes the calculated distance between the two nodes having the level difference 3 might be closer than those having the level difference 2. Therefore, the distances between two arbitrary nodes in the HQK are formulated using the level difference and the basic distances on the shortest path.

Definition 1. *The distance between two arbitrary nodes x and y in the HQK, D(x, y), is defined as*

$$D(x,y) = \text{level difference of } x \text{ and}$$

$$y - 1 + \frac{\underset{\substack{Z_0, Z_1, \ldots, Z_{r+1} \in N \\ Z_0 = x, Z_{r+1} = y}}{MIN} \left(\sum_{i=0}^{r} bd(Z_i, Z_{i+1}) \right)}{r + 1}$$

where $Z_0, Z_1, \ldots, Z_{r+1}$ is the path of *x* and *y* so that the distance can minimize the sum of the basic paths with the level distance.

Property 1. *For two different nodes x and y in the HQK, the distance of definition 1, D(x, y), is ranged according to the level difference n, as*

$$n - 1 < D(x,y) \leq n$$

where n is the level difference of x and y.

Property 2. *For arbitrary nodes x, y and z in the HQK, if the level difference of x and y is smaller than the level difference of x and z, then,*

$$D(x,y) < D(x,z)$$

The distance of Definition 1 satisfies the requirement of the distance metric. The distance

Figure 2. Hierarchical quantified data abstraction on Engineering

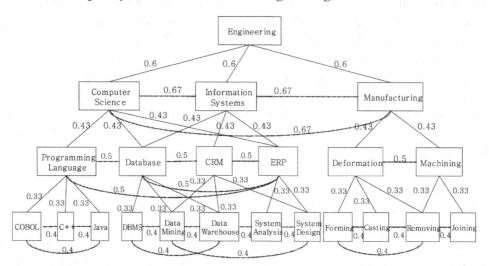

between two arbitrary nodes can be determined, and the distances are grouped with respect to the level difference (**Properties** 1 and 2).

Data Model and Operations

In this section we present the simplified data model and some operations to manage the HQK. Figure 3 shows two relations (DOMAIN_AB-STRACTION, VALUE_ABSTRACTION), which comprise a knowledge database which represents the HQK. Using these relations, we consider the following operations. With the operations, the details of approximate query answering processes and diverse query relaxation path will be explained later.

- **GetDomain**(*x*, *y*) produces the domain *D* of attribute *x* of relation *y*.
- **GetAbstractNode**(*n*, *D*, *l*) returns the *l* level abstract node of node *n* in domain *D* (for *l*=1, 2, 3,…). If *n* is the root, which has no parent, null is returned. This function refers to the VALUE_ABSTRACTION to find the abstract node.
- **GetSpecificNode**(*n*, *D*, *l*) returns the *l* level specific nodes of node *n* in domain

D. If *n* is the leaf, which has no child, null is returned. This function refers to the VALUE_ABSTRACTION to find the specific nodes.

QUERY RELAXATION

When the query results may be null or too much, and the user wants to relax the query with the database and its additional information. It can be done by relaxing the search conditions to include the additional information called the HQK. The HQK can be adopted in the process of query relaxation as the *approximate equal* and the *conceptual equal* in a formal way. In the HQK, an abstract node and its subordinate specific nodes have an IS_A relationship called *conceptual equal*. The *conceptual equal* implies two types of concepts as follows. At first, an abstract node semantically subsumes its subordinate specific nodes, and secondly, an abstract node is a high level representation for its subordinate specific nodes. On the other hand, neighbor nodes are *approximate equals* since they have the same abstract node that is *conceptual equal* to each neighbor nodes. The results of the *approximate equal* search may

Figure 3. Simplified data model to manage the HQK

DOMAIN_ABSTRACTION

domain	abstract_domain	HQK	level
MAJOR GROUP	NULL	Major & Skill	4
MAJOR	MAJOR GROUP	Major & Skill	3
EXPERTISE	MAJOR	Major & Skill	2
SKILL	EXPERTISE	Major & Skill	1

VALUE_ABSTRACTION

specific_node	domain	abstract_node	distance
Computer Science	MAJOR	Engineering	0.6
Programming Language	EXPERTISE	Computer Science	0.43
Database	EXPERTISE	Computer Science	0.43
COBOL	SKILL	Programming Language	0.33
C++	SKILL	Programming Language	0.33
Java	SKILL	Programming Language	0.33
...	...	...	...

not provide the exact answer queried by the user, but still include information that may be helpful for the user.

We use a *similar-to* operator symbolized as '=?' that represnts an approximate condition (Chu et al., 1996; Motro, 1990). The approximate condition is specified simply by using '=?' in the *where* clause of the SQL statement. To explicitly express level 2 or higher approximate searches, we extend the similar-to operator with '=#?' where # is a numeric value larger than 1 and indicates the level of approximate to search for. For example, in the HQK '=3?' makes the system search over 3 level approximates.

There can be one or more approximate conditions in a query. So, the distance between target conditions and the approximate answer is a combination of the individual distances between the corresponding conditions, and the individual distances may be given more weight than others, and the individual distances should be normalized. We define the distance of the approximate query as

$$D_{query} = \sum_{i=1}^{n} \frac{w_i}{r_i} \cdot D(tv_i, rv_i)$$

(1)

where w_i is the weight value for each condition, and r_i is the range value for each condition, and tv_i and rv_i are the target value and relaxed value of each condition, and D is a distance between the target value and the relaxed value, and n is the number of the approximate conditions in the query, and tv_i is classified two domains, such as HQK and numerical domain. w_i represents the importance of the target domain. The range value is a normalization factor used to scale distances, and dividing a distance by the range yields a measure of proximity that is independent of the particular domain and metric. According to the domain of the approximate condition, range value, r, and the distance, D, is defined as:

$$r_i = \begin{cases} \text{height of the HiQdA - 1} & \text{for } tv_i \in \text{HiQdA domain;} \\ \max(tv_i) - \min(tv_i) & \text{for } tv_i \in \text{Numerical domain.} \end{cases}$$

$$D(tv_i, rv_i) = \begin{cases} \text{distance of Definition 1} & \text{for } tv_i \in \text{HiQdA domain;} \\ |tv_i - rv_i| & \text{for } tv_i \in \text{Numerical domain.} \end{cases}$$

Query Relaxation Algorithm

Figure 4 represents the query relaxation algorithm for the HQK domain data. The input of the algorithm is an approximate query, Q, which includes one or more *similar-to* operators. The algorithm translates each approximate condition to ordinary

Figure 4. Query relaxation algorithm

```
Input:
    original approximate query Q
Output:
    relaxed query Q'
(1)    translate_query(){
(2)        condition type t;
(3)        int l;  // search level
(4)        Q' = Q;
(5)        for each approximate condition C_i in Q'{
(6)            if C_i is a selection condition{
(7)                (t, l) = analyze_selection(C_i);
(8)                if t == 'approximate query' {
(9)                    C_i' = generalize_condition(C_i, l);
(10)                   C_i" = specialize_condition(C_i', l);
(11)                   replace C_i with C_i" in Q';
(12)               }
(13)               if t == 'conceptual query' {
(14)                   C_i' = specialize_condition (C_i, l);
(15)                   replace C_i with C_i' in Q';
(16)               }
(17)           }
(18)           else { // Ci is a join condition
(19)               (t, l) = analyze_join(C_i);
(20)               C_i'= two attributes of C_i are appropriately
                           joined with ABSTRACTION;
(21)               replace C_i with C_i' in Q';
(22)           }
(23)       } // for C_i
(24)       return Q';
(25)   } // translate_query()
```

relaxed condition that does not include the *similar-to* operator. As a first step of the translation, we decide whether the condition is a selection query or a join query (line 6, 18). Next, we analyze the condition more deeply to find the condition type, t, and the search level, l (line 7, 19). The condition type indicates whether the condition is an approximate query or a conceptual query, and the search level indicates the number of the abstraction or the specification to relax the target value. For the approximate selection query, the target value is generalized and, then, specialized to gain the relaxed query (line 9, 10). For the conceptual selection query, the relaxed query is obtained by specifiying the target value (line 14).

The sub functions used in the algorithm are described in detail in the following.

```
Input: Condition C that consists of rela-
tion R, attribute A,
operator ?#= and target value v_t
Output:(i)condition type t, (ii) search
level l
(1)    analyze_selection(C) {
(2)        D_ta = GetDomain(R, A);
(3)        if v_t ∈ D_ta then {
(4)            t = 'approximate query';
(5)            if # is not null then l = #;
(6)            else l = 1;   // default search
level
(7)        }
(8)        else {
(9)            t = 'conceptual query';
(10)           D_tv = get domain of target value;
(11)           l   = level difference between
```

D_{ta} and D_{tv};

```
(12)    }
(13) } // analyze_selection()
```

Input: Condition C that consists of relation R1, attribute A1,

operator ?#=, relation R2 and attribute A2

Output: (i) condition_type t, (ii) search level l

```
(1)   analyze_join(C) {
(2)       D_a1 = GetDomain(R1, A1);
(3)       D_a2 = GetDomain(R2, A2);
(4)       l = level difference between D_a1
and D_a2;
(5)       if l == 0 then
(6)           t = 'approximate query';
(7)       else
(8)           t = 'conceptual query';
(9)   } // analyze_join()
```

Input: (i) Condition C that consists of relation R, attribute A, operator ?#= and target value v_t

        (ii) search level l

Output: generalized condition C'

```
(1)   generalize_condition(C, l) {
(2)       v_abstract = GetAbstractNode(v_t, l);
(3)       rewrite C' with v_abstract;
(4)       return C';
(5)   } // generalize_condition()
```

Input: (i) Condition C that consists of relation R, attribute A, operator ?#= and target value v_t

        (ii) search level l

Output: specialized condition C'

```
(1)   specialize_condition(C, l) {
(2)       v_specific = GetSpecificNode(v_t, l);
(3)       rewrite C' with v_specific;
(4)       return C';
(5)   } // specialize_condition()
```

Query Relaxation Example

In this section we explain an approximate selection and a conceptual join query as examples of query relaxation. For the explanation, let's define two relations EMPLY_SKILL(id, skill, level) and EXPRT_FOR_TASK (task, required_expertise). The underlined attributes indicate the primary key. The EMPLY_SKILL relation provides the skill of an employee, while the EXPRT_FOR_TASK relation prescribes the relationships between individual tasks and the expertise requirements for the task. At first, the approximate selection provides not only the exact match but also its approximate equal values. For example, consider the query 'find the five employees who have the requisite skills in both Java and DBMS,' which is written as

Q: *Skill1 == 'Java' $\wedge$ Skill2 == 'DBMS'*.

If there is no employee who can satisfy the query condition or there are an insufficient number of qualified candidates, then other employees with related skills need to be obtained by approximating the scope of the query. The query Q has tow selection conditions, and each condition is decided as approximate query with 1 level search (line 7 in Figure 5). Then the generalized query

Q_g: *Skill1* is-a '*Programming Language*' $\wedge$ *Skill2* is-a '*Database*'

is made by finding 1-level abstract node of Java and DBMS (line 9 in Figure 5). Finally, the relaxed query

Q_r: *Skill1* in ('*COBOL*', '*C++*', '*Java*') $\wedge$

Skill2 in ('*DBMS*', '*Data Mining*', '*Data Warehouse*')

is made by finding 1-level specific node of Programming Language and Database (line 10 in

Figure 5). As a result of the relaxed query, the system will return the employees who have the required skills in Programming Language and Database in addition to ones who have skills in Java and DBMS.

As a second example, the conceptual join is used when the two attributes in the join condition have different domains and thus are in different abstraction levels. In the explanatory two relations, note that the domain of the required_expertise attribute in the EXPRT_FOR_TASK relation is the EXPERTISE and is more general than that of the skill attribute in the EMPLY_SKILL relation. In such capacity, a user may want to find people whose skills belong to the expertise area required for performing a certain task, e.g., Software Design task. The query is written as

Q: *EXPRT_FOR_TASK.task* == '*Software Design*' ∧

EXPRT_FOR_TASK.requried_expertise =? *EMPLY_SKILL.skill.*

In second condition, both join attribute domains are different from each other but since one domain, EXPERTISE, is the abstract domain of the other, SKILL, the query is valid as a conceptual join query (line 19 in Figure 5). Subsequently, abstraction must be performed on the lower domain attribute, EMPLY_SKILL.skill. Since the ABSTRACTION relation provides pairs of specific value and abstract value, joining the two relations on the basis of common abstract nodes can be performed using the ABSTRACTION relation as an intermediary. A relaxed ordinary query can be written as

Q: *EXPRT_FOR_TASK.task* == '*Software Design*' ∧

EXPRT_FOR_TASK.requried_expertise == *VALUE_ABSTRACTION.abstract_node* ∧

EMPLY_SKILL.skill == *VALUE_ABSTRACTION.specific_node.*

EXPERIMENTS

In this section, we explain the number of pairs to be managed by semantic distance and HQK method, and the number of records to be retrieved for query relaxation. We also explain a cost model on semantic distance, abstraction, and HQK approach, and show experiment results with the cost model.

Let c, h, and l be the average number of children of each node (for c=2, 3, 4...), the height of the HQK, and the approximate search level respectively. Compared with the existing semantic distance approaches, the HQK considerably reduces the number of pairs to be managed by the classification of the similar data values using data abstraction. Then, the number of pairs in the HQK and the semantic distance approach can be calculated as follows.

- For the HQK,
  - the number of pairs = the number of l-level neighbour groups ×
  - (the number of pairs among 1-level neighbor nodes +
  - the number of abstraction relation)

$$= (1 + c + c^2 + \cdots + c^{h-2}) \times (_c C_2 + c)$$

$$= [(c^{h-1} - 1) / (c - 1)] \times [c(c - 1) / 2 + c]$$

$$= (c^h - c)(c + 1) / 2(c - 1)$$

- For the semantic distance approach,

the number of nodes in a hierarchy =

$$1 + c + c^2 + \cdots + c^{h-1} = (c^h - 1) / (c - 1), \text{ so}$$

Figure 5. Cost for a query relaxation and execution

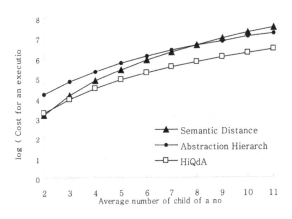

the number of pairs =

$$_{(c^h-1)/(c-1)}C_2 = (c^h - 1)(c^h - c) / 2(c-1)^2$$

Thus, the ratio of the semantic distance approach to the HQK is always greater than or equal to 1.

$$\frac{(c^h - 1)(c^h - c) / 2(c-1)^2}{(c^h - c)(c+1) / 2(c-1)} = \frac{(c^h - 1)}{(c^2 - 1)} \geq 1,$$

(for $c, h > 1$)

The ratio between two approaches increases enormously, as the height of hierarchy is gained or the average number of children of a node increases as shown in Table 1. For example, if the height of the hierarchy is 3 and each node has 4 children on average, then the semantic distance approach should maintain 4.2 times as many pairs in the HQK approach.

Table 2 shows the number of the records retrieved according to the query type, when the query is translated by the algorithm in Figure 5. For example, in the approximate selection query, we must retrieve the records of 1 in line (7), l in line (9), and $c + c^2 ... + c^l$ in line (10). In the semantic distance approach, however, in order to gain the approximate values, we must compare a target value with all the other values within the domain, so that we must retrieve the records of $c^{h-1} - 1$. For example, in c=4, h=4, and l=1, by transforming the approximate selection query, we must retrieve 9 records in the case of the HQK, and 63 records in the case of the semantic distance approach. Accordingly, the HQK is superior to the semantic distance approach in performing the approximate query relaxation.

Table 3 shows the simplified cost model for experiment. The cost model consists of three costs, such as the creation cost, the relaxation cost, and the execution cost. The creation cost (*CC*) is summarized to create an abstraction hierarchy or semantic distance matrix table that consists of numerical data and categorical data. For categorical data, we use the number of pairs to be managed as the creation cost. For numerical data, the semantic distance method needs the full scan cost, where the abstraction hierarchy method needs sorting costs to make the hierarchy. As for the relaxation cost (*RC*), we use the numbers of records to be retrieved for approximate selection queries. See Table 2.

In relaxing numerical data, the cost for the semantic distance method is 0 due to the corresponding range values, where the Abstraction Hierarchy method needs a cost to relax the hierarchy. The query execution cost (*EC*) can be measured by the

Table 1. The ratio of pairs to be assessed of semantic distance approach to the HQK

Height of hierarchy (h)	2	3	3	3	4	4	4
Average number of children (c)	3	3	4	5	3	4	5
Ratio $(c^h - 1)/(c^2 - 1)$	1	3.25	4.2	5.17	10	17	26

Table 2. The number of records to be retrieved for query relaxation

Approach	Selection/Join	Approximate Query	Conceptual Query
HQK	Selection Query	$1 + c + c^l$	$2 + c^l$
	Join Query	2	2
Semantic Distance	Selection Query	$c^{h-1} - 1$	N/A
	Join Query	N/A	N/A

Table 3. Simplified cost model for experiment

Data Type	Operation	Semantic Distance	Abstraction Hierarchy	HQK
Categorical data	Creation Cost	$CC_{cat}^{SD} = \dfrac{(c^h - c)(c+1)}{2(c-1)^2}$	$CC_{cat}^{AH} = \dfrac{(c^h - 1)(c^h - c)}{2(c-1)^2}$	$CC_{cat}^{HiQdA} = \dfrac{(c^h - 1)(c^h - c)}{2(c-1)^2}$
	Relaxation Cost	$RC_{cat}^{SD} = c^{h-1} - 1$	$RC_{cat}^{AH} =$ $1 + l + c + c^2 ... + c^l$	$RC_{cat}^{HiQdA} =$ $1 + l + c + c^2 ... + c^l$
	Execution Cost	$EC_{cat}^{SD} = c^l$	$EC_{cat}^{AH} = c^l$	$EC_{cat}^{HiQdA} = c^l$
Numerical data	Creation Cost	$CC_{num}^{SD} = c^{h-1}$	$CC_{num}^{AH} = c^{h-1} \log(c^{h-1})$	$CC_{num}^{HiQdA} = c^{h-1}$
	Relaxation Cost	$RC_{num}^{SD} = 0$	$RC_{num}^{AH} =$ $1 + l + c + c^2 ... + c^l$	$RC_{num}^{HiQdA} = 0$
	Execution Cost	$EC_{num}^{SD} = c^l$	$EC_{num}^{AH} = 2c^l$	$EC_{num}^{HiQdA} = c^l$

number of records to be retrieved. It is assumed that the abstraction hierarchy method and the HQK method are determined by the search levels; however the cost of the abstraction hierarchy method is twice that needed for retrieval by the HQK method due to the wide range of the records.

Figure 5 and 6 represent the total cost changes for the approximate query that includes the query relaxation cost and the execution cost. Given parameters as height h=4, search level l=2, one categorical data, and three numerical data, the x-axis represents the aver-

Figure 6. Cost for the creation, query relaxation, and execution

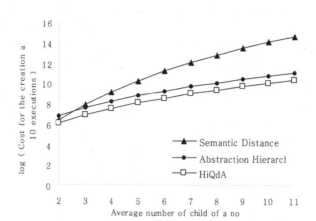

age number of child and y-axis represents log $(RC_{cat} + EC_{cat} + 3(RC_{num} + EC_{num}))$ for Figure 5, $\log(2(CC_{cat} + 10RC_{cat} + 10EC_{cat}) + 3(2(CC_{num} + 10RC_{num} + 10EC_{num}))$ for Figure 6, respectively.

Note that the semantic distance method costs "0" on the relaxation stage for the numerical domain, but the relaxation cost for the categorical domain increases exponentially. Thus, it is very much sensitive for the semantic distance method on the size of the categorical data. When the size of the categorical data is small, the corresponding total cost is negligible, however, the relaxation cost (RC_{cat}^{SD}) increases exponentially as the size of the categorical data does. Therefore, on condition that the size of the categorical data is big, in this experiment the average number of child node is more than 7, the total cost of the semantic distance method is the biggest among all the three methods regardless of other conditions.

The cost of the abstraction hierarchy method is increased and depends linearly on the search level for the categorical domain and numerical domain. When the data size is small, the execution cost (EC_{num}^{AH}) is twice and the relaxation cost (RC_{num}^{AH}) is higher than semantic distance method (RC_{num}^{SD}), so it is higher than the semantic distance method. The HQK method follows the advantage of the

abstraction hierarchy ($RC_{cat}^{HiQdA} = RC_{cat}^{AH}$) on the categorical data, and also follows the advantage of the semantic distance method ($RC_{num}^{HiQdA} = RC_{num}^{SH}$) on the numerical domain. Therefore the cost of the HQK method is not increased exponentially and less than those of the abstraction hierarchy method.

CONCLUSION

We have addressed the query relaxation algorithm with hierarchical quantified data abstraction (HQK) to relax the query condition of the categorical data domain. The HQK has an abstraction-based hierarchy that facilitates finding neighbor values for a target value quite easily. All that is needed is to identify an abstract node of the target value and retrieve all the specific nodes of the identified abstract nodes. The query relaxation algorithm has formulated this abstraction / specification features of the abstraction hierarchy according to the query type and the search level. We have defined the distance metric that calculates distances between two arbitrary nodes in the HQK, which enables to handle the quantitative similarity of categorical data. Also, we have introduced the cost model for creation of abstraction hierarchy, query relaxation and execution, and showed empirically that our approach is more efficient than other approaches.

For future research, a generic HQK derivation mechanism should be conceived in formal fashion. In addition, in order to support approximate query answering efficiently, nearest neighbor searches can be provided. However, since most researches on nearest neighbor searches are devised to consider numerical domains, there are difficulties in treating the categorical domain. Using features of the HQK, we plan to build a new index structure that deals with categorical data as well as numerical data. The range information on each attribute can be saved in the internal node of R-tree based data structure. The abstract node of the HQK can be used as the range information of specific nodes and this will lead us to develop a multi-dimensional index structure which can treat categorical data. Applying this structure, we will research a method to support the nearest neighbor queries efficiently. Also, in order to demonstrate the real advantages of this approach, it would be necessary to proceed into research to identify the need for user studies with human users.

REFERENCES

Babcock, B., Chaudhuri, S., & Das, G. (2003). Dynamic Sample Selection for Approximate Query Processing. In *Proceedings of the 2003 ACM SIGMOD International Conference on Management of Data, San Diego, California, USA* (pp. 539-550).

Beygelzimer, A., Kakade, S., & Langford, J. (2005). Cover trees for nearest neighbor. In *Proceedings of the 23rd international conference on Machine learning, Pittsburgh, Pennsylvania, USA* (pp. 97-104).

Calado, P. P., & Ribeiro-Neto, B. (2003). An Information Retrieval Approach for Approximate Queries. *IEEE Transactions on Knowledge and Data Engineering, 15*(1), 236–239. doi:10.1109/TKDE.2003.1161593

Chakrabarti, M., Ortega, M., Mehrotra, S., & Porkaew, K. (2003). Evaluating refined queries in top-k retrieval systems. *IEEE Transactions on Knowledge and Data Engineering, 15*(5), 256–270.

Chan, H., Wei, K., & Siau, K. (1993). User-Database Interface: The Effect of Abstraction Levels on Query Performance. *Management Information Systems Quarterly, 17*(4), 441–464. doi:10.2307/249587

Chan, T. M. (1998). Approximate Nearest Neighbor Queries Revisited. *Discrete & Computational Geometry, 20*(3), 359–374. doi:10.1007/PL00009390

Chen, Y., Zhou, L., & Zhang, D. (2006). Ontology-Supported Web Service Composition: An Approach to Service-Oriented Knowledge Management in Corporate Financial Services. *Journal of Database Management, 17*(1), 67–84.

Chu, W., Yang, H., Chiang, K., Minock, M., Chow, G., & Larson, C. (1996). CoBase: A scalable and extensible cooperative information system. *Journal of Intelligent Information Systems, 6*(2/3), 223–259. doi:10.1007/BF00122129

Klein, M., & Konig-Ries, B. (2004). Combining Query and Preference - an Approach to Fully Automatize Dynamic Service Binding. In *Proceedings of IEEE International Conference on Web Services* (pp. 788-791).

Lee, W., Kang, S., Lim, S., Shin, M., & Kim, Y. (2007). Adaptive Hierarchical Surrogate for Searching Web with Mobile Devices. *IEEE Transactions on Consumer Electronics, 53*(2), 796–803. doi:10.1109/TCE.2007.381762

Lee, W., & Lim, T. (2007). Architectural Measurements on the World Wide Web as a Graph. *Journal of Information Technology and Architecture*, *4*(2), 61–69.

Liu, S., & Chu, W. (2007). CoXML: A Cooperative XML Query Answering System. In *Proceedings of the 8th International Conference on Web-Age Information Management*, Huang Shan, China, (pp. 614-621).

Liu, Y., Liu, T., Qin, T., Ma, Z., & Li, H. (2007). Supervised rank aggregation. In *Proceedings of the 16th international conference on World Wide Web*, Banff, Alberta, Canada (pp. 481-490).

Motro, A. (1990). FLEX: A Tolerant and Cooperative User Interface to Databases. *IEEE Transactions on Knowledge and Data Engineering*, *2*(2), 231–246. doi:10.1109/69.54722

Mouratidis, K., Bakiras, S., & Papadias, D. (2006). Continuous monitoring of top-k queries over sliding windows. In *Proceedings of the 2006 ACM SIGMOD international conference on Management of data table of contents*, Chicago, IL, USA (pp. 635-646).

Muslea, I. (2004). Machine Learning for Online Query Relaxation. In *Proceedings of the tenth ACM SIGKDD international conference on Knowledge discovery and data mining*, Seattle, Washington, USA (pp. 246-255).

Shin, M., Huh, S., Park, D., & Lee, W. (2008). Relaxing Queries with Hierarchical Quantified Data Abstraction. *Journal of Database Management*, *19*(4), 76–90.

Siau, K., Chan, H., & Wei, K. (2004). Effects of Query Complexity and Learning on Novice User Query Performance with Conceptual and Logical Database Interfaces. *IEEE Transactions on Systems, Man, and Cybernetics. Part A, Systems and Humans*, *34*(2), 276–281. doi:10.1109/TSMCA.2003.820581

Chapter 10
Abstract DTD Graph from an XML Document:
A Reverse Engineering Approach

Joseph Fong
City University of Hong Kong, China

Herbert Shiu
City University of Hong Kong, China

ABSTRACT

Extensible Markup Language (XML) has become a standard for persistent storage and data interchange via the Internet due to its openness, self-descriptiveness and flexibility. This chapter proposes a systematic approach to reverse engineer arbitrary XML documents to their conceptual schema – Extended DTD Graphs — which is a DTD Graph with data semantics. The proposed approach not only determines the structure of the XML document, but also derives candidate data semantics from the XML element instances by treating each XML element instance as a record in a table of a relational database. One application of the determined data semantics is to verify the linkages among elements. Implicit and explicit referential linkages are among XML elements modeled by the parent-children structure and ID/IDREF(S) respectively. As a result, an arbitrary XML document can be reverse engineered into its conceptual schema in an Extended DTD Graph format.

INTRODUCTION

As Extensible Markup Language (XML) (Bray, 2004) has become the standard document format, the chance that users have to deal with XML documents with different structures is increasing. If the schema of the XML documents in Document Type Definition (DTD) (Bosak, 1998) is given or derived from the XML documents right away (Kay, 1999;

Moh, 2000), it is easier to study the contents of the XML documents. However, the formats of these schemas are hard to read, not to mention rather poor user-friendliness.

XML has been the common format for storing and transferring data between software applications and even business parties, as most software applications can generate or handle XML documents. For example, a common scenario is that XML documents are generated and based on the data stored in a relational database — and there have been

DOI: 10.4018/978-1-60566-904-5.ch010

various approaches for doing so(Thiran, 2004; Fernandez, 2001). The sizes of XML documents that are generated based on the data stored in databases can be very large. Most probably, these documents are stored in a persistent storage for backup purposes, as XML is the ideal format that can be processed by any software applications in the future.

In order to handle the above scenario, it is possible to treat XML element instances in an XML document as individual entities, and the relationships from the different XML element types can be determined by reverse engineering them for their conceptual models, such as Extended DTD Graphs with data semantics. As such, users can have a better understanding of the contents of the XML document and further operations with the XML document become possible, such as storing and querying (Florescu 1999; Deutsch, 1999; Kanne, 2000).

This chapter proposes several algorithms that analyze XML documents for their conceptual schema. Two main categories of XML documents exist — data-centric and narrative. As the contents of narrative XML documents, such as *DocBook* (Bob Stayton, 2008) documents, are mainly unstructured and their vocabulary is basically static, the necessity of handling them as structured contents and reverse engineering them into conceptual models is far less than that of handling data-centric ones. Therefore, this chapter will concentrate on data centric XML documents.

Referential Integrity in XML Documents

XML natively supports one referential integrity mechanism, which are ID/IDREF(S) types of attribute linkages. In every XML document, the value of an ID type attribute appears at most once and the value of the IDREF(S) attribute must refer to one ID type attribute value(s). An IDREF(S) type attribute can refer to any XML element in the same document, and each XML element can

define at most one ID type attribute. Due to the nature of ID/IDREF(S) type attributes in XML documents, relationships among different XML element types can be realized and it is possible to use them to implement data semantics.

This chapter will discuss the various data semantics and the possible ways to implement them. The algorithms presented in the chapter are based on the observations of the common XML document structures.

1. Using the nested structure of an XML document (the relationship between a parent element and its child element(s)), in which the child elements implicitly refer to their parent element.
2. For an IDREF or IDREFS type attribute, the defining element is referred to the element(s) with an ID type attribute by the referred value. Such linkages are similar to the foreign keys in a relational database. The two associated element types are considered to be linked by an explicit linkage.
3. As an IDREFS type attribute can refer to more than one element, there is a one-to-many cardinality from the referring element type and the referred element type(s).

The schema of an XML document can restrict the order of the XML elements — and the order of the elements may be significant — which depends on the intentions of the original XML document designer. For example, two XML documents with their corresponding DTD's are shown in Table 1 and Figure 1.

The two XML documents shown in Table 1 are storing the same data, which are the data of two couples. For the former one, its couple elements use the two IDREF type attributes to denote the corresponding husband and wife elements. However, the use of ID/IDREF cannot ensure a particular husband or wife element must be referred by one couple element only. For the latter XML document, the DTD restricts that the husband and

Table 1. Two equivalent XML documents that can represent the same data

DTD	XML Document
<!ELEMENT couples (husband*,wife*,couple*)> <!ELEMENT husband EMPTY> <!ELEMENT wife EMPTY> <!ATTLIST husband hid ID #REQUIRED name CDATA #REQUIRED> <!ATTLIST wife wid ID #REQUIRED name CDATA #REQUIRED> <!ATTLIST couple hid IDREF #REQUIRED wid IDREF #REQUIRED>	<?xml version="1.0"?> <couples> <husband hid="A123456" name="Peter"/> <husband hid="B234567" name="John"/> <wife wid="X123456" name="Amy"/> <wife wid="Y234567" name="Bonnie"/> <couple hid="A123456" wid="X123456"/> <couple hid="B234567" wid="Y234567"/> </couples>
<!ELEMENT couples (husband,wife)*> <!ELEMENT husband EMPTY> <!ELEMENT wife EMPTY> <!ATTLIST husband hid ID #REQUIRED name CDATA #REQUIRED> <!ATTLIST wife wid ID #REQUIRED name CDATA #REQUIRED>	<?xml version="1.0"?> <couples> <husband hid="A123456" name="Peter"/> <wife wid="X123456" name="Amy"/> <husband hid="B234567" name="John"/> <wife wid="Y234567" name="Bonnie"/> </couples>

wife elements must exist as a pair. Furthermore, the use of ID type attributes hid and wid ensures any husband and wife element instance must exist in the document at most once.

Extended DTD Graph

As XML element instances are treated as individual entities, the relationships from the element types are therefore related not only to the structure of the XML document but also to the linkages from the different types. As such, DTD cannot clearly indicate the relationships.

An Extended DTD Graph for XML is proposed to add data semantics into a DTD Graph so that the data semantics can be clearly identified, which is an excellent way of presenting the structure of an XML document. As such, in order to visualize the data semantics determined based on the XML document with its optional schema, it will provide the notations to be used for presenting the various data semantics. This chapter uses the authors' notations of the Extended DTD graph for presenting the structure and the data semantics from the elements, as follows:

Figure 1. The DTD tree of the two equivalent XML document for Table 1

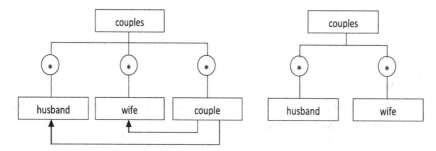

Figure 2. A sample Extended DTD Graph

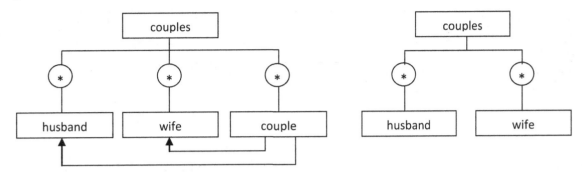

1. The vertexes as squares are drawn on the graph for elements, and vertexes as circles are drawn for occurrence operators (?, + and *) and selection operator (|).
2. Attributes and simple elements are omitted from the graph, as they specify a particular attribute of their defining and parent elements respectively.
3. Data semantics, other than one-to-one and one-to-many cardinality relations, are presented in the graph as arrows pointing from the referring element to the referred element with suitable descriptions as legends.

Based on the above criteria, it is possible to consider the ELEMENT declarations only for constructing the Extended DTD graph. Three types of ELEMENT declarations can be identified as follows:

1. An ELEMENT declaration defines sub-elements only.
2. An ELEMENT declaration involves sub-elements and #PCDATA as its contents.
3. An ELEMENT declaration that defines #PCDATA as its contents only.

The above three types correspond to the following three examples:

```
<!ELEMENT PARENT (CHILD1+, CHILD2*)>
<!ELEMENT MIXED_ELEMENT (#PCDATA | CHILD1
| CHILD2)*>
<!ELEMENT SIMPLE_ELEMENT (#PCDATA)>
```

For each ELEMENT declaration of the first type, the content model expression can be tokenized as individual elements and occurrence indicators and sequence separators (,), and represented as a tree structure with the element name as the root node. For example, the first example above can be visualized as the following tree diagram. In Figure 2, the sequence "," is implied in the diagram.

DTD's mostly contain more than one ELEMENT declaration but each element type can only appear once. Therefore, to construct the complete DTD graph for a DTD, the tree structures of all ELEMENT declarations in a DTD are constructed first and they are eventually merged by replacing each sub-element node in a tree by the tree structure of that element. Such merging is repeated until there is only one tree structure or all sub-elements have been replaced with their corresponding tree structures.

Cardinality / Participation

Element types are visualized as rectangles in the graph and a cardinality relationship is presented as an arrow pointing from the referring element type to the referred element type, with double-line and single line for total participation and partial participation respectively. The cardinality types,

Table 2 The arrows illustrating various cardinalities with participation types

Participation / Cardinality	Partial	Total
One-to-one	1/1-----------------------→	1/1 ═══════════════→
One-to-many	1/m----------------------→	1/m═════════════→
Many-to-one	m/1----------------------→	m/1═════════════→
Many-to-many	m/m------------------------------------→	m/m ═══════════════→

including one-to-one (1/1), one-to-many (1/m), many-to-one (m/1) and many-to-many (m/m), are shown as legends of the arrows. If the cardinality relationship is implemented as explicit ID/IDREF(S) linkages, the name of the ID type attribute of the referring element is appended to the legend, such as 1/m (parent_id). To identify explicit linkages from implicit linkages, cardinality relationships due to ID/IDREF(S) type attributes are shown as arrows with a curved line. Table 2 presents the eight possible combinations of arrows and legends.

N-ary Relationship

An *n-ary* relationship is implemented as a particular element type involved in more than two binary relationships. To represent such a relationship, a diamond-shaped vertex is used for such element types. Figure 3 presents a sample diagram with an *n-ary* relationship.

Aggregation

An aggregation denotes that the involved element types must exist as a unity. In Figure 3, an aggregation exists as the defining characteristic of mandatory participation between parent and child elements. As such, a rectangle is to be drawn enclosing all involved element types.

RELATED WORK

In order to have a complete picture of the reasons behind the algorithms for determining various data semantics, this chapter explains the existing approaches of constructing XML documents, especially those exported from relational databases.

The Determination of XML Schema

There is some existing work concerning the extraction of schema, such as DTD, from XML documents (Chidlovskii, 2001; Min, 2003). The outputs of these algorithms are the schemas that can validate the XML documents. However, the derived schemas provide no semantic interpretation other than the containment structures of the XML documents. The algorithms proposed in this chapter concern the determination of data semantics from the XML element instances rather

Figure 3. A sample diagram with an n-ary relationship

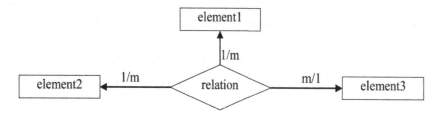

than simply XML schema among XML elements. Compared with the approach proposed by Goldman and Widom(Goldman, 1997) that directly manipulates semi-structured databases, such as an XML document, the algorithm proposed here provides the user with a clear picture of the data semantics from the XML element instances before further manipulating them.

The Determination of Data Semantics from XML Documents

One approach exists that can reverse engineer data semantics from XML documents(Fong, 2004), but the algorithm maps some predefined templates of document structures to data semantics, and the algorithm can only be implemented with DOM(W3C, 2003), which needs to read the entire XML document to the memory — and that is inappropriate for huge XML documents. The methodology presented in this chapter, however, determines basic candidate data semantics from arbitrary XML documents with SAX(Saxproject, 2004), which is applicable to XML documents of any size. Some of the determined data semantics may not be the intentions of the original writer and needs user supervision for verification.

The Implementation of Inheritance among XML Elements

Schema for Object-oriented XML (SOX)(W3C, 2005) introduced the idea of element and attribute inheritance, which enables an element to extend another element so that the derived element can have all attributes defined by the base element with its own new attributes.

Due to the limitations and low extensibility of DTD(Sahuguet, 2000), XML Schema Definition (XSD)(Sperberg, 2000) is becoming the popular replacement schema of DTD. Unlike DTD, XSD is an XML document itself and it can define more restrictive constraints and clear definitions of the XML documents to be validated. In other words,

the set of capabilities for defining the structures and data types of XSD are the superset of that of DTD. As such, there has been research and software for converting DTD to XSD(Mello, 2001; W3C, 2000).

There are other alternative schemas, such as RELAX NG (Relaxng, 2003) and Schematron (Schematron, 2008) and Lee and Chu(Lee, 2000) evaluated six common XML schemas, including DTD and XSD.

By constructing a graph by placing vertexes for elements — and the elements that are involved in a parent-child relation, which is defined by ELEMENT declaration in DTD, are connected with edges — it is possible to derive a graphical representation of the DTD that is commonly known as a DTD graph. Up to now, there is no formal standard for DTD graphs and various researchers are using their own conventions as in (Klettke, 2002; Shanmugasundaram, 2001; Lu, 2003; Böttcher, 2003), and the graph introduced in (Funderburk, 2002) is the first one that was denoted as a DTD graph.

There is a graphical representation of XSD(Fong, 2005) which derives an XML conceptual schema of an XML Tree Model from an XML schema of XSD. Its approach is different from this chapter's approach by deriving an Extended DTD Graph from an XML document.

As the conventions of most graphs for presenting the structure of an XML document are applicable to different schema languages, the graph is also known as Semantic graph(An, 2005). Some researchers proposed other graphical representations of XML schemas, such as the use of UML(Booch, 1999).

The Application of Extended DTD Graph

Data Graph is a DTD in graph. (Zhao, 2007) described that DTD can be a good common data model when the majority of data sources are XML sources for the interoperability between

Table 3. A comparison between the proposed and other existing approaches

	Proposed approach	Other approaches
Input	XML document with optional schema	XML document
Output	Conceptual schema with data semantics	Schema without data semantics
Completeness	All common data semantics can be determined	Schemas that can validate the XML document can be derived
User friendliness	Algorithms can be implemented with a user friendly GUI, such as the prototype.	Commercial products exist that provide a user friendly GUI.
Performance	Good	Not available as no mathematical proofs were provided.

relational databases and XML databases. Reserve engineering XML document into DTD graph is similar to data mining XML document into a data tree(Zhang, 2006). The former is a database schema while the later is an internal data in tree structure. (Trujillo, 2004) demonstrated that a DTD can be used to define the correct structure and content of an XML document representing main conceptual Multidemension model for data warehouses.

Compared with the approach proposed by Goldman and Widom(Goldman, 1997) that directly manipulates semi-structured databases such as an XML document, the algorithm proposed in this chapter enables the user to have a clear picture of the data semantics from the XML element instances before further manipulating them. Table 3 provides a comparison between the proposed algorithms and other existing approaches.

REVERSE ENGINEERING METHODOLOGY

There are basically two different definitions in a DTD, which are ELEMENT and ATTLIST. Each ATTLIST definition defines the attributes of a particular element, whereas ELEMENT defines its possible containments, and each ELEMENT definition can be represented in a tree structure with the element name as the root element with its child sub-elements as leaves, and there must

be another ELEMENT definition for each of its child elements.

It is not mandatory to define the ELEMENT declaration prior to all its child elements, and it is actually uncertain which element is the root element of the corresponding XML documents. The root element of the XML document is defined by the DOCTYPE declaration before the root element start tag.

Implementations of Various Data Semantics in XML

The following subsections provide all possible implementations of various data semantics, some of which are consistent with those proposed by other researchers (Lee, 2003; Lee, 2000).

Cardinalities

One-to-many cardinalities can be realized by both explicit and implicit referential linkages. By implicit referential linkages, a parent element can have child elements of the same type, such as,

```
<PURCHASE_ORDER>
  <PURCHASE_ORDER_LINE .../>
  <PURCHASE_ORDER_LINE .../>
</PURCHASE_ORDER>
```

The parent element PURCHASE_ORDER and the child elements PURCHASE_OR-

Figure 4. The DTD graph of the XML document shown in Listing 1

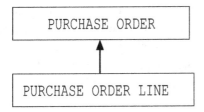

DER_LINE are implicitly in a one-to-many relationship. If the occurrences of child element PURCHASE_ORDER_LINE are at most one for all PURCHASE_ORDER elements, they are in a one-to-one relationship instead.

If the schema of the XML document is given, it can specify the ID/IDREF(S) type attributes. If an XML element defines an IDREF attribute and all such elements refer to the same element type, there is a one-to-many relationship between the referred and referring XML elements. For example, sample DTD and XML documents are shown in Listing 1 and Figure 4.

Listing 1. many-to-one cardinality implemented by an IDREF type attribute

```
<!ELEMENT PURCHASE_ORDER ...>
<!ELEMENT PURCHASE_ORDER_LINE ...>
<!ATTLIST PURCHASE_ORDER
    PO_ID ID #REQUIRED
    ...
>
<!ATTLIST PURCHASE_ORDER_LINE
    PO_ID IDREF #REQUIRED
    ...
>
<PURCHASE_ORDER PO_ID="PO001" ... />
...
<PURCHASE_ORDER_LINE
    PO_ID="PO001"
    ... />
<PURCHASE_ORDER_LINE
    PO_ID="PO001"
    ... />
```

For explicit referential linkages, to determine if the cardinality is one-to-one or one-to-many, it is necessary to scan the entire XML document. An XML element type may be involved in more than one one-to-many relationship. In other words, all elements of such XML element types define more than one linkage. For example, if an XML element type defines an IDREF(S) type attribute, all elements of such XML element type actually define two linkages, one implicit linkage by the nested structure and one explicit linkage by the IDREF(S) type attribute. If the two linkages are both one-to-many relationships, the two referred element types by such a referring element type can be considered to be in a many-to-many relationship. For example, the XML document in Listing 2 and Figure 5 illustrates a many-to-many relationship.

Listing 2. A many-to-many cardinality implemented by an element type with two IDREF type attributes

```
<!ELEMENT KEYWORD ...>
<!ELEMENT TOPIC ...>
<!ELEMENT MESSAGE ...>
<!ATTLIST KEYWORD
KEYWORD_ID ID #REQUIRED
    ...
>
<!ATTLIST TOPIC
TOPIC_ID ID #REQUIRED
    ...
>
<!ATTLIST MESSAGE
MSG_ID ID #REQUIRED
TOPIC_ID IDREF #REQUIRED
KEYWORD_ID IDREF #REQUIRED
    ...
>
<KEYWORD KEYWORD_ID="KW001" NAME="XML"/>
<KEYWORD KEYWORD_ID="KW002"
NAME="DATABASE"/>
...
<TOPIC TOPIC_ID="TP001" NAME="Reverse En-
```

Figure 5. The DTD Graph for the XML document shown in Listing 2

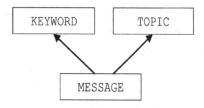

```
gineer an XML document"/>
<TOPIC TOPIC_ID="TP002" NAME="Exporting a
database as an XML document"/>

...

<MESSAGE MSG_ID="MG001"
TOPIC_ID="TP001"
KEYWORD_ID="KW001"
.../>
<MESSAGE MSG_ID="MG002"
TOPIC_ID="TP002"
KEYWORD_ID="KW002"
.../>
```

For an XML element type that defines two linkages and hence two one-to-many relationships, the two referred XML element types can be considered to be in a many-to-many relationship.

The linkages from the XML elements in an XML document are identified by the referring element name, linkage name and the referred element name. The algorithm shown in Algorithm 1 is used to determine the following table (Table 4) of the linkages.

Figure 6 illustrates the meanings of the four attributes.

There are eight XML elements in the document and there is only one implicit linkage from them. The values of the above four linkage attributes for such implicit linkage are shown in Table 5.

According to the combination of the values of the four attributes, it is possible to determine the cardinality data semantics for the involved elements. The rules are show in Table 6.

The algorithm is composed of two passes of parsing of the same XML document. The first pass assigns a synthetic element identity to each XML element in the document and determines all ID type attribute values and their corresponding element types. For the second pass, the XML document is traversed again and the linkages of each XML element are investigated and their attributes are stored. Finally, the stored linkage attributes are consolidated to give the four linkage attributes mentioned above and in Table 4.

The algorithm shown below can determine whether the XML document is valid, in particular whether a non-existing ID value is referred by an IDREF(S) type attribute. If the XML document is valid, three tables can be obtained — *ReferringInfo*, *ReferredInfo* and *ElementNameCount*. The key for the former two tables is the composite key (*RGE*, *RDE*, *L*), that is, the referring element name, the referred element name and the linkage name, whereas the key for the *ElementNameCount* is simply the element name. With three such tables,

Table 4. The attributes and their sources for determining data semantics

Attribute	Description	Value
MaxReferring	The maximum number of referred elements referred by a single referring element	Get from Referring Info with key *(RGE, RDE, L)*
MaxReferred	The maximum number of the referring elements that is referring to the same referred element with the same linkage type.	Get from Referred Info with key *(RGE, RDE, L)*
SumReferring	The number of referring elements that possess the linkage.	Get from ReferringInfo with key *(RGE, RDE, L)*
NumberElements	The number of referring elements in the document.	Get from ElementNameCount with key RGE

Figure 6. MaxReferring, MaxReferred, SumReferring & NumberElements example

```
<?xml version="1.0"?>
<message id="ID1" ... >
 <message id="ID2" ... >
  <message id="ID3" ... >
   <message id="ID4" ... >
   <message id="ID5" ... >
  </message>
  <message id="ID6" ... >
   <message id="ID7" ... >
   <message id="ID8" ... >
  </message>
 </message>
</message>
```

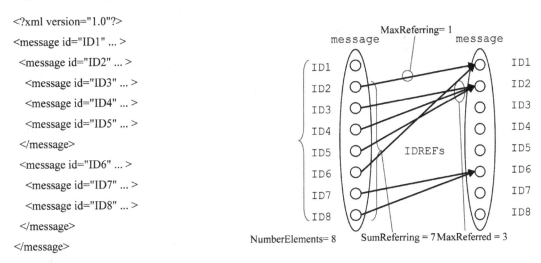

Table 5. Descriptions of variables in reverse engineering algorithms

Attribute Name	Value	Explanations
MaxReferring	1	All linkages are implicit and each child element has one implicit parent element only.
MaxReferred	3	The root message element with attribute id value ID1 is referred by two sub elements (with attribute id values ID2 and ID6). The message element with attribute id value ID2 is referred by three sub elements (with attribute id values ID3, ID4 and ID5). The message element with attribute id value ID6 is referred by two sub elements (with attribute id values ID7 and ID8). Therefore, the value of MND is 3.
SumReferring	7	Except the root message element with attribute id value ID1, all other message elements define such linkages. The value of NL is therefore 7.
NumberElements	8	There are eight message elements.

Table 6. Matrix for determining cardinality & participation based on the determined linkage attributes

		Participation	
		Total	Partial
Cardinality	One-to-one	MaxReferring= 1 MaxReferred = 1 SumReferring= NumberElements	MaxReferring = 1 MaxReferred= 1 SumReferring < NumberElements
	One-to-many	MaxReferring = 1 MaxReferred > 1 SumReferring = NumberElements	MaxReferring = 1 MaxReferred > 1 SumReferring < NumberElements
	Many-to-one	MaxReferring > 1 MaxReferred = 1 SumReferring = NumberElements	MaxReferring > 1 MaxReferred = 1 SumReferring < NumberElements
	Many-to-many	MaxReferring > 1 MaxReferred > 1 SumReferring = NumberElements	MaxReferring > 1 MaxReferred > 1 SumReferring < NumberElements

it is possible to derive the linkage attributes as shown in Table 4.

The complete algorithm is presented in Algorithm 1 along with a list of definitions for the variables to be used.

The above operation can be represented by the following SQL,

```
SELECT
    RGE, RDE, L,
    ReferringInfo.MaxReferring,
    ReferredInfo.MaxReferred,
    ReferringInfo.SumReferring,
    ElementNameCount.NumberElements
FROM
    ReferringInfo
    INNER JOIN ReferredInfo
        ON ReferringInfo.RGE = Referred-
Info.RGE
        AND ReferringInfo.RDE = Referred-
Info.RDE
        AND ReferringInfo.L =
ReferredInfo.L
```
```
    INNER JOIN ElementNameCount
        ON ReferringInfo.RGE =
ElementNameCount.E
```

Once the four attributes of a linkage are determined, the data semantics can be determined by using the matrix shown in Table 6. According to the determined one-to-one and one-to-many relationships, it is then possible to consolidate the related ones into many-to-many and *n-ary* relationships.

As mentioned above, if an XML element type defines two linkages that are determined to be many-to-one cardinalities, the two referred XML element types are considered to be in a many-to-many relationship. Similarly, if an XML element type defines more than two linkages that are determined to be many-to-one cardinalities, the referred XML element types are considered to be in an *n-ary* relationship. Therefore, based on the one-to-many cardinalities determined by the previous algorithm, the many-to-many and *n-ary* relationships can be determined, and the algorithm is shown in Algorithm 2.

Algorithm 1. The algorithm for determining linkage information by traversing the XML document

Variable name	Definition
EID	The current element ID. While processing the XML document sequentially, the EID determines the ID to be assigned to individual element encountered.
E	The current element to be handled.
A	An attribute of the current element to be handled.
AV	The attribute value of attribute *A*.
L	A linkage of the current element. It can be an implicit linkage with its parent element or an explicit linkage with an IDREF(S) type attribute. For a non-root element without IDREF(S) attribute, the element has only one implicit linkage to its parent element. Otherwise, the element can have more than one linkage, one implicit linkage and at least one explicit linkages.
L_{value}	The Element ID of the linkage *L* for the current element *E*. For example, if *L* is an implicit linkage, L_{value} is the element ID of the parent element of *E*. Otherwise, L_{value} is the attribute value of IDREF value and the value should be an ID type attribute of an element in the same document.
NG	The number of referring element of the same element name is referring to the same referred element with the same link.
RGE	The referring element of a link.
RDE	The referred element by a link.

continued on the following page

Algorithm 1. continued

Pass One:

Let *EID* = 1;

Repeat until all XML document elements are read

  Let *E* be the current element to be processed

  If ∃ record in $Table_{ElementNameCount}$ where *ElementName* = element name of *E*

    Get record (*ElementName, NumberElement*) from $Table_{ElementNameCount}$

    Increment *NumberElement* by 1;

    Update (*ElementName, NumberElement*) into $Table_{ElementNameCount}$;

  Else

    Add (*ElementName*, 1) into $Set_{ElementNameCount}$;

  End If

  Add (*EID, ElementName*) into $Set_{ElementIDName}$;

  If there exists ID type attribute *A* of element *E* with attribute value *AV*

    Add (*AV, ElementName*) into $Set_{ElementIDName}$;

  End If

  Increment *EID* by 1;

  Navigate to the next element *E* in the XML document

Pass Two:

Repeat until all XML document elements are read

  Let *RGE* is the current element to be handled

  For each linkage, *L*, of *RGE*

   For each linkage value, L_{value} of linkage *L* of *RGE*

    Get record (*EID,ElementName*) from $Table_{ElementIDName}$

     where primary key value is L_{value}

    If no such record exist in $Table_{ElementIDName}$

     XML document is invalid

    Else

     Let *RDE* = *ElementName* of the record obtained from $Table_{ElementIDName}$

    End If

    Get record (*RGE, RDE, L,* L_{value}*, ND*) from $Table_{RawReferredInfo}$ for primary key (*RGE, RDE, L,* L_{value});

    If record exists

     Increment *ND* of the record by 1; Update the record to $Table_{RawReferredInfo}$;

    Else

     Add record (*RGE, RDE, L,* L_{value}, 1) to the $Table_{RawReferredInfo}$;

    End If

---

continued on the following page

Algorithm 1. continued

For each referred element type, *RDE*

  Let *NG* = number of *RDE* referred by this linkage, *L;*

  Get record (*RGE, RDE, L,MaxReferring, SumReferring*) from the *Table$_{ReferringInfo}$* for primary key (*RGE, RDE, L*);

  If record exists

    If *NG > MaxReferring* from the record

      Update *MaxReferring* of the record to be *NG*

    End If

    Increment *SumReferring* of the record by 1;

    Update the record to the *Table$_{ReferringInfo}$;*

  Else

    Add record (*RGE, RDE, L, NG*, 1) to the *Table$_{ReferringInfo}$;*

  End If

  End For

 End For

End For

Navigator to the next element *RGE* in the XML document

Consolidate the records with same combination of (*RGE, RDE, L*) in table *RawReferredInfo*;

let *MaxReferred* = maximum of the *ND* values of all records;

Add record (*RGE, RDE, L, MaxReferred*) to the table *ReferredInfo;*

The many-to-one relationship to be considered should be those implemented by explicit linkages; that is, those defined by ID/IDREF(S) linkages. Otherwise, an element type exhibits implicit a one-to-many relationship due to nested structure and defines a many-to-one relationship that will be considered to be a many-to-many relationship, but the two referred elements are actually not related at all.

Participation

Participation concerns whether all instances of a particular element type are involved in a relationship with the corresponding element type.

For implicit referential linkage by a parent-child relation, such as the following DTD ELEMENT declaration,

```
<!ELEMENT PARENT (CHILD*)>
```
and there are no other ELEMENT declarations that define CHILD as their child elements, all CHILD element instances must appear as the child element of a PARENT element, and hence the participation can be considered to be total, as all instances of CHILD must be involved in the one-to-many cardinality relation with PARENT. If no schema is provided, and if all instances of an element type always appear as the child elements of the same parent element

Algorithm 2. The algorithm for determining many-to-many and n-ary relationships

---
Get referring XML element types from one-to-many cardinalities;
For each referring XML element $T_{referring}$ type
    Get referred XML element types, $S_{referred}$ referred by $T_{referring}$ via explicit linkages;
    If the size of the set $S_{referred}$ = 2
    XML element types in $S_{referred}$ = many-to-many relationship with $T_{referring}$;
  Else
    If size of $S_{referred}$ > 2
XML element types in $S_{referred}$ = n-ary relationship with $T_{referring}$;

---

type, the participation is also considered to be total.

For explicit referential linkage by ID/IDREF(S) attributes, if all instances of an element type use the same attribute with values referring instances of the same element type, the relationship is considered to be total participation. Otherwise, the relation is considered to be partial. The DTD of the XML document can only identify the ID/IDREF(S) type attributes but it cannot restrict the referring and referred element types. As such, actually parsing the XML document is required to determine the type of participation.

The DTD Graph of participation is same as the DTD Graph of cardinality except the double lines to show total participation as shown in table 2.

Aggregation

An aggregation means that the creation of a whole part of an element depends on the existences of its component sub elements. An aggregation is signified by the scenario that elements of different types are considered to be a single entity and all constituting elements must exist altogether. An XML document by itself does not provide any facility to enforce such a constraint. At best, the schema can hint at the correlations of the existence of the elements in the corresponding XML document.

For implicit referential linkage by an aggregation, such as the following DTD ELEMENT declaration,

```
<!ELEMENT AGGREGATION (COMPONENT_1, COMPO-
NENT_2, .... COMPONENT_N) +>
```

For example, the following ELEMENT declaration can restrict the existence of the elements, enrollment, student and course.

```
<!ELEMENT enrollment (student, course)+>
```

Besides, no student or course elements exist in the document that are not the sub-element of an enrollment element. For example, if there is another ELEMENT declaration in the same DTD, such as,

```
<!ELEMENT student_list (student*)>
```

student elements can exist in the document as the sub-elements of a student_list element. As such, the co-existence relationship of enrollment, student and course elements no longer holds.

Such a co-existence relationship specified in the schema can be extended to more than one nested level. For example, if the existence of a course element must be accompanied by a lecturer element and a tutor element, that is,

```
<!ELEMENT course (lecturer, tutor)+>
```

the elements, enrollment, student, course, lecturer and tutor, must exist as a whole. Then, all these elements are considered as an aggregation. From another perspective, an aggregation is actually composed of two one-to-one cardinality relations

Algorithm 3. The algorithm for determining aggregation

```
Let Set_temporary = empty;
For each ELEMENT declaration for element E_parent
  For each child element, element_child
    If element_child = mandatory and non-repeatable
    Add an aggregation relation (E_parent, E_child) to Set_temporary;

Let Set_aggregation and Set_root = empty;
For each relation R (E_parent, E_child) in Set_temporary
  If (∃ tree, T, in Set_aggregation) ∧ (E_parent is a node in T) ∧ (E_child is not a node in T)
  Add a path E_parent to E_child to T;
  Else
  (∃ tree, T, in Set_aggregation) ∧ (E_child is a node of T) ∧ (E_parent is not a node)
    If (E_child = root node) ∧ (E_child not in Set_root of T)
    Add the path E_parent to E_child to T;
    Else
      Add E_child to Set_root
  Remove the sub-tree starting with E_child from T;
  If ∃ sub-tree starting with E_child in multiple nodes
    Add sub-tree to Set_aggregation;
  Else
  ∃ tree T_i with a node for E_parent and T_j with E_child as root node;
    Merge trees T_i and T_j with a path from node for E_parent in T_i to root of T_j
  Else
  ¬∃ sub-tree in Set_aggregation with node for either E_parent and E_child;
    Add a new tree with a path E_parent to E_child to Set_aggregation;
```

(course – lecturer and course – tutor) which are both total participation.

An exceptional case is that if the sub-elements are actually the attribute of the parent element, such as in example one, it is inappropriate to consider that the involved elements are in an aggregation. As a result, user supervision is needed in the process.

Based on the DTD of the XML document, it is possible to determine the aggregation from the elements. As the requirements of an aggregation is the co-existence of the involved elements and the order of the sub-elements for a parent element is insignificant, the nested structure of the elements should first be simplified with the algorithm presented in Algorithm 3 where T is an aggregation tree.

The determination of aggregation is separated into two parts. The first part first discovers the pair of parent and child elements that must co-exist. Once the pairs are determined, the second part of the algorithm treats each pair as a path from parent element to the child element in a sub-tree, and these sub-trees are merged to form a bigger tree.

Eventually, the nodes in each tree must co-exist, and they are in aggregation. The second part is straightforward except there is a tricky point that if a child element is found to be a non-root node of a particular sub-tree, it implies that such an element can have more than one parent element, and the aggregation that includes such element must start with the parent element.

For example, for a list of ELEMENT declaration in the DTD,

```
<!ELEMENT A (B, C)>
<!ELEMENT B (D)>
<!ELEMENT C (D)>
<!ELEMENT D (E, F)>
```

The determined pairs of raw aggregation are (A, B), (A, C), (B, D), (C, D), (D, E) and (D, F). Merging the raw aggregation is shown in Figure 7.

Unary Relationship

Unary relation is a specify type of one-to-one or one-to-many relationship, in which the referring and referred elements are of the same element type. Therefore, unary relation can be realized by both implicit and explicit referential linkages, that is, nested structure of the same element type and IDREF(S) attribute that refers to elements of the same type. Listing 3 illustrates two XML documents contain elements of unary relationships by implicit and explicit referential linkages respectively.

In Listing 3, the ID attribute and PARENT_ID attribute are ID type and IDREF type attributes respectively for the latter XML document. For the DTD graph (Figure 8), the same set of arrows shown in Table 2 can be used for unary relationship as well. The difference is that arrow is starting from and end at the same element type.

For the former XML document above, more than one MESSAGE elements can associate with the parent MESSAGE element, and the parent MESSAGE element and the child MESSAGE elements are therefore in a one-to-many relationship. As they are of the same element type, they are in a unary relationship as well. Regarding the latter XML document, all MESSAGE elements appear in the XML document in the same level under the same parent element. The IDREF type attribute are implementing the one-to-many relationship and it is a unary relation because the referring and referred elements are all MESSAGE elements.

As a result, unary relationship is a specific relationship of one-to-one or one-to-many relationship; it is possible to identify unary relationships from usual one-to-one or one-to-many

Figure 8. DTD Graph for u-ary relationship

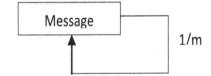

Figure 7. DTD Graph for Aggregation

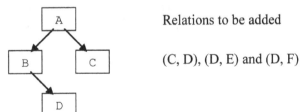

Relations to be added

(C, D), (D, E) and (D, F)

While adding the path (C, D) to the sub-tree, as D is not a root node, D should be removed from the sub-tree and it is considered to be an individual sub-tree with D as the single node.

Relations to be added

(D, E) and (D, F)

After the path (D, E) and (D, F) is added to the sub-tree with node D as the root node, two sub-trees are obtained,

As such, the elements A, B and C, and the elements D, E and F, are considered as being two individual aggregation.

Listing 3. Two possible formats for unary relationship

```
<MESSAGE ID="MSG01" ...>
 <MESSAGE ID="MSG02" ... />
 <MESSAGE ID="MSG03" ... />
 <MESSAGE ID="MSG04" ...>
   <MESSAGE ID="MSG05" .../>
   <MESSAGE ID="MSG06" .../>
 </MESSAGE>
</MESSAGE>
```

```
<MESSAGE ID="MSG01">
<MESSAGE ID="MSG02" PARENT_ID="MSG01">
<MESSAGE ID="MSG03" PARENT_ID="MSG01">
<MESSAGE ID="MSG04" PARENT_ID="MSG01">
<MESSAGE ID="MSG05" PARENT_ID="MSG04">
<MESSAGE ID="MSG06" PARENT_ID="MSG04">
```

relationships after they are derived from the XML document.

CASE STUDY AND PROTOTYPE

To illustrate the applicability and correctness of the algorithms mentioned in this chapter, a prototype was built that implements the algorithms proposed in this chapter. For actually drawing the DTD graph, the algorithm proposed by (Shiren, 2001) is used to define the layout of the vertexes on the graph. With such a prototype, a sample XML document with DTD file as shown in Listing 4 is provided to the prototype.

For this case study, both ID/IDREF type attributes are considered and the minimum number of common attributes is one. All elements with at least one attribute are sorted in ascending order of the lengths of their attribute lists. Therefore, the order of the elements to be processed is:

```
element1, element2, element3
```

According to the DTD of the XML document, only one ELEMENT declaration is used for constructing the Extended DTD Graph, as the contents of other element types are EMPTY.

```
<!ELEMENT test (element1*,element2*,elem
ent3*)>
```

Therefore, only those explicit one-to-many relationships are to be added to the graph, and the graph will become the one shown in Figure 9 and 10. The detailed derivation of the reverse engineering can be referred to (Shiu, 2006).

CONCLUSION

In order to make use of the XML document, software developers and end-users must have a thorough understanding of the contents in the XML document, especially those historical and huge XML documents. Sometimes the schemas of XML documents are missing and the XML documents cannot be opened to be inspected on the screen due to their huge size. Therefore, it is necessary to determine as much information as possible regarding the relationships from the elements in the document.

By reverse engineering the XML document with DTD, all explicit linkages can be determined and the resultant DTD Graph can be used to verify the correctness of ID/IDREF(S) linkages, as any incorrect IDREF(S) linkage will be indicated as an extra cardinality and shown in the Extended DTD graph. This chapter provides algorithms to help

Listing 4. test.xml and test.dtd

```
<?xml version="1.0"?>
<test>
 <element1 id="id1"/>
 <element1 id="id2"/>
 <element2 id="id3"/>
 <element2 id="id4"/>
 <element3 id="id5" idref1="id1" idref2="id3"/>
 <element3 id="id6" idref1="id2" idref2="id4"/>
 <element3 id="id7" idref1="id1" idref2="id4"/>
 <element3 id="id8" idref1="id2" idref2="id3"/>
</test>
```

```
<!ELEMENT test (element1*,element2*,element3*)>
<!ELEMENT element1 EMPTY>
<!ELEMENT element2 EMPTY>
<!ELEMENT element3 EMPTY>
<!ATTLIST element1
 id ID #REQUIRED>
<!ATTLIST element2
 id ID #REQUIRED>
<!ATTLIST element3
 id ID #REQUIRED
 idref1 IDREF #REQUIRED
 idref2 IDREF #REQUIRED>
```

Figure 9. The determined data semantics

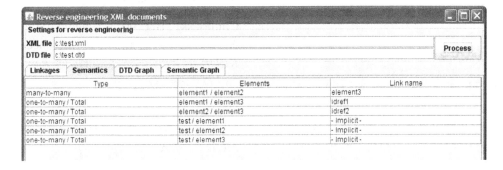

the users to understand the relationships from the elements by reverse engineering data semantics from the XML document, including:

1. Cardinality relationships
2. Participation relationships
3. *n-ary* relationships
4. Aggregations
5. Many-to-many relationships (a special case of cardinality relationships)
6. Unary relationships

In summary, to visualize the determined data semantics, a new Extended DTD Graph is proposed. XML documents natively support one-to-one, one-to-many and participation, data semantics. With a corresponding schema, such as DTD, the ID and IDREFS attributes of the elements can be identified, and many-to-many, *n-ary* and aggregations can also be determined.

Figure 10. Extended DTD Graph based on the DTD and the determined cardinality References

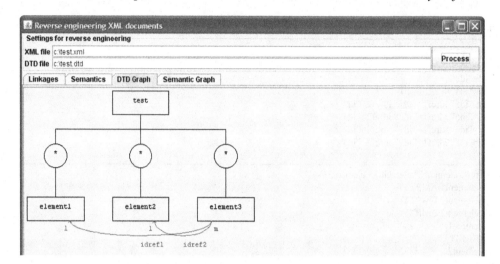

ACKNOWLEDGMENT

This book chapter is funded by Strategic Research Grant 7002325 of City University of Hong Kong

REFERENCES

An, Y., Borgida, A., & Mylopoulos, J. (2005). Constructing Complex Semantic Mappings Between XML Data and Ontologies. *International Semantic Web Conference ISWC 2005* (pp. 6-20).

Booch, G., Christerson, M., Fuchs, M., & Koistinen, J. (1999). *UML for XML schema mapping specification*. Retrieved from http://xml.coverpages.org/fuchs-uml_xmlschema33.pdf

Bosak, J., Bray, T., Connolly, D., Maler, E., Nicol, G., Sperberg-McQueen, C. M., et al. (1998). *Guide to the W3C XML Specification (XMLspec) DTD, Version 2.1*. Retrieved from http://www.w3.org/XML/1998/06/xmlspec-report-v21.htm

Böttcher, S., & Steinmetz, R. (2003). A DTD Graph Based XPath Query Subsumption Test. *Xsym, 2003*, 85–99.

Bray, T., Paoli, J., Sperberg-McQueen, C. M., Maler, E., & Yergeau, F. (2004). *Extensible Markup Language (XML) 1.0* (3rd ed.). Retrieved from http://www.w3.org/TR/2004/REC-xml-20040204

Chidlovskii, B. (2001). Schema Extraction from XML Data: A Grammatical Inference Approach. *KRDB '01 Workshop (Knowledge Representation and Databases)*

Deutsch, A., Fernandez, M., & Suciu, D. (1999). Storing Semi-structured Data with STORED. *SIGMOD Conference, Philadelphia, Pennsylvania*.

Fernandez, M., Morishima, A., & Suciu, D. (2001). Publishing Relational Data in XML: the SilkRoute Approach. *A Quarterly Bulletin of the Computer Society of the IEEE Technical Committee on Data Engineering, 24*(2), 12–19.

Florescu, D., & Kossmann, D. (1999). Storing and Querying XML Data Using an RDBMS. *A Quarterly Bulletin of the Computer Society of the IEEE Technical Committee on Data Engineering, 22*(3), 27–34.

Fong, J., & Cheung, S. K. (2005). Translating relational schema into XML schema definition with data semantic preservation and XSD graph . *Information and Software Technology, 47*(7), 437–462. doi:10.1016/j.infsof.2004.09.010

Fong, J., & Wong, H. K. (2004). XTOPO, An XML-based Technology for Information Highway on the Internet . *Journal of Database Management, 15*(3), 18–44.

Funderburk, J. E., Kiernan, G., Shanmugasundaram, J., Shekita, E., & Wei, C. (2002). XTABLES: Bridging relational technology and XML. *IBM Systems Journal, 41*(4).

Goldman, R., & Widom, J. (1997). DataGuides: Enabling Query Formulation and Optimization in Kanne, CC.,(2000). Guido Moerkotte. Efficient storage of xml data. In *Proc. of ICDE, California, USA* (p. 198).

Kay, M. (1999) DTDGenerator – A tool to generate XML DTDs. Retrieved from http://users.breathe.com/mhkay/saxon/dtdgen.html

Klettke, M., Schneider, L., & Heuer, A. (2002). Metrics for XML document collections. *Akmal Chaudri and Rainer Unland, XMLDM Workshop, Prague, Czech Republic* (pp.162-176).

Koike, Y. (2001). A Conversion Tool from DTD to XML Schema. Retrieved from http://www.w3.org/2000/04/schema_hack/

Lee, D. W., & Chu, W. W. (2000). Comparative Analysis of Six XML Schema Languages. *SIGMOD Record, 29*(3). doi:10.1145/362084.362140

Lee, D. W., & Chu, W. W. (2000). Constraints-Preserving Transformation from {XML} Document Type Definition to Relational Schema. *International Conference on Conceptual Modeling / the Entity Relationship Approach* (pp. 323-338).

Lee, D. W., Mani, M., & Chu, W. W. (2003). Schema Conversion Methods between XML and Relational Models. *Knowledge Transformation for the Semantic Web*.

Lu, S., Sun, Y., Atay, M., & Fotouhi, F. (2003). A New Inlining Algorithm for Mapping XML DTDs to Relational Schemas. In *Proc. Of the First International Workshop on XML Schema and Data Management, in conjunction with the 22nd ACM International Conference on Conceptual Modeling (ER2003)*.

Mello, R., & Heuser, C. (2001). A Rule-Based Conversion of a {DTD} to a Conceptual Schema (LNCS 2224).

Min, J. K., Ahn, J. Y., & Chung, C. W. (2003). Efficient extraction of schemas for XML documents . *Information Processing Letters, 85*(1). doi:10.1016/S0020-0190(02)00345-9

Moh. C., Lim, e., & Ng, W. (2000). DTD-Miner: A tool for mining DTD from XML documents. In *Proceedings of the Second International Workshop on Advanced Issues of E-Commerce*.

Relaxng (2003). RELAX NG. Retrieved from http://www.relaxng.org/

Sahuguet, A. (2000). Everything You Ever Wanted to Know About DTDs, But Were Afraid to Ask. *WebDB-2000*.

Shanmugasundaram, J., Shekita, E., Kiernan, J., Krishnamurthy, R., Viglas, E., Naughton, J., et al. (2008). *Shematron*. Retrieved from http://www.schematron.com

Shiren, Y., Xiujun, G., Zhongzhi, S., & Bing, W. (2001). Tree's Drawing Algorithm and Visualizing Method. In *CAD/Graphics'2001*.

Shiu, H. (2006). *Reverse Engineering Data Semantics from Arbitrary XML document*. Unpublished master's thesis, City University of Hong Kong, Hong Kong, China.

Sperberg-McQueen, C., & Thompson, H. (2000). *W3C XML schema*. Retrieved from http://www.w3.org/XML/Schema

Stayton, B. (2008). *DocBook*. Retrieved from http://www.docbook.org

Tatarinov, I. (2001). A general technique for querying XML documents using a relational database system. *SIGMOD Record*, *30*(3), 261–270.

Thiran, P. H., & Estiévenart, F. Hainaut. J.L., & Houben, G.J. (2004). Exporting Databases in XML - A Conceptual and Generic Approach. In *Proceedings of CAiSE Workshops (WISM'04)*.

Trujillo, J., & Luján-Mora, S. (2004). Applying UML and XML for Designing and Interchanging Information for Data Warehouses and OLAP Applications. *Journal of Database Management*, *15*(1), 41–72.

World Wide Web Consortium. (W3C). (1998). *Schema for object-oriented XML*. Retrieved from http://www.w3.org/TR/1998/NOTE-SOX-19980930

World Wide Web Consortium. (W3C). (2003). *Document object model DOM*. Retrieved from http://www.w3.org/DOM

World Wide Web Consortium. (W3C). (2004). *Simple API for XML, SAX*. Retrieved from http://www.saxproject.org

Zhang, J., Liu, H., Ling, T., Bruckner, R., & Tija, A. (2006). A framework for efficient association rule mining in XML data. *Journal of Database Management*, *17*(3), 19–40.

Zhao, L., & Siau, K. (2007). Information mediation using metamodels: An approach using XML and common warehouse metamodel. *Journal of Database Management*, *18*(3), 69–82.

Chapter 11

A Dynamic Model of Adoption and Improvement for Open Source Business Applications

Michael Brydon
Simon Fraser University, Canada

Aidan R. Vining
Simon Fraser University, Canada

ABSTRACT

This chapter develops a model of open source disruption in enterprise software markets. It addresses the question: Is free and open source software (FOSS) likely to disrupt markets for enterprise business applications? The conventional wisdom is that open source provision works best for low-level system-oriented technologies while large, complex enterprise business applications are best provided by commercial software vendors. The authors challenge the conventional wisdom by developing a two-stage model of open source disruption in business application markets that emphasizes a virtuous cycle of adoption and lead-user improvement of the software. The two stages are an initial incubation stage (the I-Stage) and a subsequent snowball stage (the S-Stage). Case studies of several FOSS projects demonstrate the model's ex post predictive value. The authors then apply the model to SugarCRM, an emerging open source CRM application, to make ex ante predictions regarding its potential to disrupt commercial CRM incumbents.

INTRODUCTION

Many commercial software firms face the possibility that free and open source software (FOSS) will disrupt their markets. A "disruptive innovation" is a new product, service, or business model that initially enters a market as a low-priced, lower-quality alternative to the products of market incumbents

but which, through a process of rapid improvement, eventually satisfies mainstream consumers and supplants some or all incumbents (Christensen, 1997; Markides, 2006). Prototypical examples of disruptive innovations include discount online brokerages (which won significant market share away from established full-service brokerages) and personal computers (which evolved into a viable substitute for larger, more expensive mini and mainframe computers). The disruptive effect of FOSS on com-

DOI: 10.4018/978-1-60566-904-5.ch011

mercial software markets has been variable so far. On the one hand, the Apache project has forced commercial vendors of web servers to either exit the market (IBM, Netscape), offer their products for free (Sun), or bundle their software at zero price with other offerings (Microsoft's IIS). On the other, FOSS entrants in the desktop operating system and office productivity software markets have had almost no impact on incumbents. Despite the economic significance of the software industry, there has been little formal analysis of the factors that lead to major disruption by FOSS in some markets but negligible disruption in others. This is especially true of enterprise applications—the complex software programs that support critical, cross-functional business processes, such as order management, financial reporting, inventory control, human resource planning, and forecasting.

What drives FOSS? Like all forms of open innovation, FOSS is characterized by recursive interdependence between user adoption and technological improvement (West & Gallagher, 2006). To this point, open source production has worked most effectively for software developed by hackers (software experts) for use by hackers. However, enterprise applications differ in important ways from well-known FOSS successes, such as Apache, the Perl programming language, and the Linux operating system. The intrinsic and culture-specific motivations that drive voluntary participation in FOSS projects by software experts are likely to be weaker or non-existent for business-oriented software (Fitzgerald, 2006). Accordingly, one might expect FOSS to have less disruptive impact on the market for enterprise applications. However, an alternative scenario is possible. Under certain conditions profit-maximizing firms have clear incentives to contribute to the development of open source enterprise software, such as enterprise resource planning (ERP), customer relationship management (CRM), and supply chain management (SCM) packages. The willingness of firms to pay programmers to write code and contribute it to a FOSS project as part of their employees'

regular duties reduces or eliminates dependence on conventional hacker-level incentives in predicting who will contribute to FOSS projects. Instead, the emphasis shifts to understanding the conditions that lead profit-maximizing firms to invest in projects from which they cannot fully appropriate the benefits of their investment.

We estimate the probable impact of FOSS in enterprise software markets by developing a dynamic model of FOSS adoption and improvement. The objective is to help predict whether open source entrants will disrupt commercial incumbents in a particular software market. The model draws on both the *disruptive technology* and the *adoption of technology* literatures because neither literature alone can fully account for the high variability in the level of disruption achieved by FOSS.

The disruptive technology literature emphasizes the role of technological improvement over time in fostering disruption. For example, Christensen (1997) illustrates the disruption dynamic by plotting the historical performance improvement demanded by the market against the performance improvements supplied by the technology, as shown in Figure 1. Improvements in performance over time are undoubtedly critical to disruption; however, little is said about the precise mechanisms by which the improvements —or "sustaining innovations"—are achieved. As Danneels (2004) points out, an *ex post* analysis of general trends is of little use when making *ex ante* predictions about the disruptive potential of a particular technology. The key to predicting whether a technology is potentially disruptive or "merely inferior" (Adner, 2002) is the identification of plausible mechanisms for rapid and significant improvement along dimensions of performance that matter to mainstream users.

Models from the adoption of technology literature, in contrast, tend to focus on specific attributes of the innovation or environment in order to predict the innovation's adoptability. The critical shortcoming of most adoption models for our purposes is that they are static. Disruption is

Figure 1. Changes in performance over time for incumbent and disruptive technologies (Christensen, 2006, p. 40)

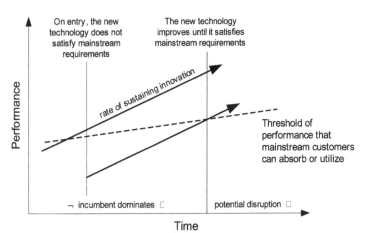

a fundamentally dynamic process where the attributes of both the innovation and the adopters of the innovation change over time. We attempt to capture these dynamics by modeling disruption as two distinct stages.

The paper proceeds as follows: Section 1 reviews the adoption literature and focuses on Fichman and Kemerer's (1993) distinction between organizational and community adoptability. Section 2 examines the open source model of production and the incentives for firm-level contribution to the production of a public good. In Section 3, we draw on the concepts of organizational and community adoptability to develop a two-stage model of FOSS adoption and disruption. We assess the *ex post* predictive power of the model in Section 4 by examining the development histories and subsequent disruptive impacts of several established FOSS projects. In Section 5, we apply the model to one type of enterprise software, CRM, to predict, *ex ante,* whether SugarCRM, a relatively new FOSS entrant, will disrupt the commercial CRM market. We summarize our conclusions and suggest some implications for theory and practice in Section 6.

INNOVATION AND TECHNOLOGY ADOPTION

A number of different adoption models in the literature seek to explain variability in the market success of new technologies (e.g., Ravichandran, 2005; Riemenschneider, Hardgrave, & Davis, 2002; Rai, Ravichandran, & Samaddar, 1998; Iacovou, Benbasat, & Dexter, 1995; Taylor & Todd, 1995). The theoretical foundations of these models are diverse (Fichman, 2000). Variously, they build on classic communication and diffusion mechanisms (e.g., Rogers, 1995), institutional theory (e.g., Tingling & Parent, 2002), organizational learning (e.g., Attewell, 1992) or on industrial economics (e.g., Katz and Shapiro, 1994). The purpose here is not to provide another general adoption model but rather to develop a middle-range theory that is applicable to the specific context of open source production and the markets for enterprise software (Fichman, 2000; Merton, 1967, p. 39).

The initial point of our analysis is Fichman and Kemerer's (1993) Adoption Grid, as reproduced in Figure 2. The grid integrates the "Diffusion of Innovations perspective" (Rogers, 1995) and the "Economics of Technology Standards perspec-

Figure 2. Adoption Grid (Fichman & Kemerer, 1993)

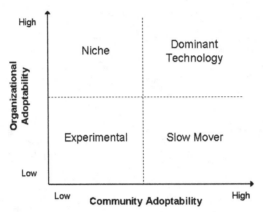

tive", each of which emphasizes a complementary set of adoption antecedents. The original Diffusion of Innovations perspective identified five attributes—relative advantage, compatibility, complexity, observability, and trialability—that affect the likelihood that a given population will adopt a new idea, product, or practice (hereafter, a "technology"). Although the subsequent literature has augmented and extended these attributes (e.g., Moore & Benbasat, 1991; Davis, 1989), the model retains its original focus on the technology and the technology's fit within the adopting population. Fichman and Kermerer (1993, p. 9) aggregate these attributes as *organizational adoptability*, arguing that "[…] organizations are more likely to be willing and able to adopt innovations that offer clear advantages, that do not drastically interfere with existing practices, and that are easier to understand. […]. Adopters look unfavorably on innovations that are difficult to put through a trial period or whose benefits are difficult to see or describe".

The Economics of Technology Standards perspective, in contrast, focuses on increasing returns to adoption. In considering this perspective, it is useful to make a distinction between direct increasing returns (network benefits or positive network externalities) and indirect increasing returns (Katz & Shapiro, 1994). The fax machine is a classic example of a technology that exhibits direct network benefits: the value a machine to a given user increases when the technology is adopted by others. However, indirect sources of increasing returns to adoption, such as learning-by-using and technology interrelatedness, are often more important in the enterprise software context. Learning-by-using is the process whereby the technology's price-performance ratio improves as users accumulate experience and expertise in using it (Attewell, 1992). Occasionally, the technology is reinvented during adoption and the resulting improvements feed back to the supplier and other adopters, further amplifying indirect benefits (Rogers, 1995). Technological interrelatedness considers a technology's ability to attract the provision of complementary technologies by third parties. In some cases, complementarity is straightforward: the adoption of Blu-Ray video players relies on the availability of movies in this format and televisions that can display higher resolutions. In other cases, complementarity may emerge in the form of propagating organizations, such as consultants, publishers, and standards organizations (Fichman, 2000). Fichman and Kemerer summarize a technology's *community adoptability* in terms of four attributes: prior technology drag, irreversibility of investments, sponsorship, and expectations. The presence of increasing returns to adoption mediate all four attributes to varying degrees.

The historical evidence shows that community adoptability can trump organizational adoptability in determining market outcomes when a technology exhibits strong increasing returns to adoption. Superior technology-related attributes (such as relative advantage) do not always ensure dominance, as the outcomes of the standards wars between Betamax and VHS and between DOS and Mac OS illustrate (Hill, 1997). However, relying on community adoptability as the basis for predicting market success is problematic because the presence of direct and indirect increasing returns can create a "logic of opposition" (Robey & Boudreau, 1999). Direct increasing returns, learning-by-using, and the existence of complements can all catalyze the rapid adoption of a new technology (e.g., the MP3 format for digital audio). Alternatively, increasing returns can be a potent source of prior technology drag (e.g., the QWERTY keyboard). A technology market that exhibits strong increasing returns to adoption often tips in favor of a single product or standard. Organizations that choose to bypass the established standard in order to adopt a new and "better" technology must forego the benefits of the standard's installed base (Shapiro & Varian, 1999; Farrell & Saloner, 1986). For example, firms that migrate to the desktop version of Linux from Microsoft Windows face high switching costs (independent of any quality differences between the two products) because of numerous incompatibilities with the large installed base of Windows.

Variations in organizational adoptability and community adoptability define the four quadrants of the Adoption Grid (Figure 2). Innovations in the *experimental* quadrant rate poorly in terms of both organizational and community adoptability and are unlikely to succeed in the market without further development. Innovations in the *niche*

quadrant rank highly in terms of organizational adoptability but poorly in terms of community adoptability. Niche innovations typically achieve quick adoption by a small base of dedicated users who value the product's attributes. However, either the absence of increasing returns to adoption or the presence of barriers to community adoptability (the logic of opposition) dampens adoption beyond the niche. Innovations in the *slow mover* quadrant provide community benefits but do not offer a compelling rationale (in terms of improved functionality or fit) for organizational adoption. These technologies are usually adopted only when replacement of the firm's existing generation of technology becomes necessary (Hovav, Patnayakuni, & Schuff, 2004). Finally, innovations in the *dominant technology* quadrant score well in terms of both organizational and community adoptability.

In some cases technologies become dominant by "disrupting" their markets. A technology is disruptive in the specific sense proposed by Christensen (1997) if it satisfies several conditions (Tellis, 2006, p. 34). The four conditions relevant for our purposes are:

- The technology initially underperforms the incumbent technologies along dimensions mainstream customers have historically valued.

- The disruptive technology has features that are valued by a relatively small group of customers. For example, the new technology is generally cheaper, simpler, smaller, or more convenient than the dominant technology.

- The new technology steadily improves in performance over time until it satisfies the requirements of the mainstream market (recall Figure 1). Disruption can only occur once the new technology satisfies the requirements threshold of mainstream customers.

Since the disruptive technology retains the features (cheaper, simpler, smaller, or more convenient) that led to its initial adoption, and since increases in performance provide diminishing returns for users once the requirements threshold of mainstream customers is attained, the disruptive entrant is able to displace the previously dominant technology in the mainstream market. Disruption is thus, at its core, a dynamic process in which a mechanism for technological improvement over time is central.

A REVIEW OF OPEN SOURCE PRODUCTION

There are two requirements for open source production. The first requirement is the form of licensing—often referred to as copyleft—which precludes the enforcement of exclusionary property rights for the good (Weber, 2004). Under a FOSS license, the program's source code can be downloaded, compiled, used, and modified by anyone. The second requirement is the availability of low-cost, ubiquitous networks and collaborative tools that enable software development and testing by large, geographically-dispersed groups. Open source software is thus "free" in two senses. First, the joint presence of non-excludability provided by FOSS licensing and the availability of low-cost telecommunications means that the software can be acquired at low cost. Second, unrestricted access to the software's source code means that users are able to adapt and improve the software.

Although low cost and the freedom to innovate make FOSS attractive to potential adopters, it is less clear why developers might choose to participate in the provision of such software. The central problem is that FOSS is a public good (Lerner & Tirole, 2002; Weber, 2004). Like all software, FOSS is non-rivalrous in consumption (consumption by one users does not preclude consumption by other users). But, in contrast to commercial software, FOSS licensing explicitly stipulates non-excludability (no one can be denied consumption or use of the good). Economic theory predicts that markets will undersupply pure public goods because individual contributors to the production of the good are not financially rewarded for their investment of time and other resources (Arrow, 1970; Weimer & Vining, 2005). The question facing any potential adopter of FOSS software—but especially firms seeking complex, mission-critical systems—is whether provision and continuous improvement of a public good will be reliably sustained over time.

Critics of what might be called the "naive pure public goods" characterization of FOSS point out that a blanket prediction of undersupply is an oversimplification of the incentive structures facing developers. Benkler (2002), for example, notes that Internet-based collaboration tools permit developers to make small, incremental contributions to open source projects at low, essentially negligible, personal opportunity cost. Others have emphasized the non-pecuniary and *delayed* or *indirect* pecuniary rewards that individuals receive from membership in the hacker culture (Roberts, Hann, & Slaughter, 2006; Weber, 2004; Himanen, Torvalds, & Castells, 2002; Lerner & Tirole, 2002). It is also important to recognize that the popular image of a lone hacker working voluntarily on a piece of shared code is no longer representative of the largest, most established FOSS projects. For example, although the initial releases of the Linux kernel was the result of massive personal investments by Linus Torvalds, further refinement is increasingly dominated by professional software developers as part of their contracts with their employers (Lyons, 2004; Morton, 2005). Not surprisingly, developers who are paid to contribute to an open source project are more likely to spend time doing so than volunteers (Hertel et al., 2003).

So what is the motivation for profit-maximizing firms to participate in FOSS? The economic incentives of for-profit firms are diverse. Some firms, such as IBM, Sun, and HP, expect to benefit by stimulating the adoption of a wide spectrum of FOSS products in order to sell complementary products and/or consulting services (Dahlander, 2007). Other firms, such as Redhat and MySQL AB have a similar interest, but have focused their attention on a single FOSS project. In some cases, dual licensing models are used in which the for-profit firm develops and sells an enhanced version of a commercial product built on a FOSS core. For example, MySQL AB maintains an FOSS version of the MySQL database system, but sells a commercial version of the database as well as technical support and training. Firms that maintain dual (FOSS and commercial) licenses have incentives to use revenues from their commercial products and services to cross-subsidize the development of the open software at the center of their technological system.

Of special interest in this research are "user firms" that choose to contribute to the development of FOSS. User-firms are organizations—such as banks, utilities, consumer goods firms, governments, and non-profits—that rely on software to support the production and delivery of their core products and services but whose core business model does not necessarily involve the production and sale of computer hardware, software, or services. There are many aspects of organizational adoptability that attract user-firms to FOSS. The most obvious is initial price—an entire stack of software applications can be assembled without paying licensing fees. User-firms may also adopt FOSS to avoid lock-in and excessive dependence on a particular commercial vendor (Hicks & Pachamanova, 2007). Finally, and most importantly from the perspective of this paper, user-firms adopt FOSS because it provides them with the flexibility to innovate and customize. There are several examples of firms exploiting this flexibility. Siemens' ICN division constructed its award-winning ShareNet knowledge management system by modifying an open source content management system from ArsDigita (MacCormack, 2002). Google has recently initiated the Android Open

Handset Alliance in an attempt to enable broader participation in the innovation process for mobile phones. According to Google, Android permits all players in the mobile phone industry—including users, content providers, handset manufacturers, and wireless service providers—to contribute to evolution of mobile phone functionality (Dano, 2008).

Product modification by "lead-users" can be a valuable source of innovation and product improvement (von Hippel, 1998). Such innovations typically have a high potential for market success for two reasons (Franke, von Hippel, & Schreier, 2006). First, lead-users have incentives to innovate because the expected payoffs from finding solutions to their problems are large. Second, as leads, they anticipate emerging market trends and the requirements of mainstream users. Lead-user development has traditionally functioned well in FOSS due to the capability of the lead-users and the ease with which software products can be modified. For example, computer specialists have contributed much of the source code for system-oriented software such as Linux utilities, Sendmail, and Perl. As information technology professionals, lead-users understand how the software could be modified to make their primary jobs easier (Weber, 2004). They also possess the specialized knowledge and skills required to implement solutions to their software problems. An "innovation toolkit" has been shown to be a critical enabler of lead-user development and such a toolkit is implicit in the norms and collaboration infrastructure provided by FOSS projects. Finally, FOSS licenses and the established culture of hacker community encourage users to contribute their solutions to the project, thereby ensuring a positive feedback loop between software adoption and its improvement.

The conditions that foster lead-user improvement of systems-oriented FOSS seem much less likely to occur, however, for business software. First, individual users of enterprise applications tend not to be software experts. They possess valuable local knowledge about the business processes that the software supports but lack the specialized knowledge and skills to navigate a version control system, to modify source code, or communicate with the software developer community. Thus, most users of enterprise business software lack the technical expertise required to access the innovation toolkit provided by the open source model. Second, firms normally discourage any valuable internal innovation from permeating the boundaries of the firm (Liebeskind, 1996). Consequently, we might expect any lead-user development that does occur to be kept within the firm rather than contributed to the FOSS community.

We argue, however, that user firms have both the means and the motivation to act as leads in the development of enterprise FOSS. A fundamental reason that firms exist is to enable the division of labor and foster specialization within the firm. Accordingly, firms can and do hire experienced FOSS developers to implement the functionality desired by non-technical users of enterprise business software. The question is thus not whether a firm *can* participate in the improvement of enterprise FOSS, but rather *why* a firm would be willing to forego the advantages of proprietary control over its enhancements. We hypothesize two reasons, both of which are unrelated to altruism or the open source culture of reciprocity. First, firms typically adopt packaged enterprise applications (whether commercial or open source) to implement important but *non-strategic* functionality (Hitt & Brynjolfsson, 1996). According to Beatty and Williams (2006), "The vast majority of firms that chose to undertake ERP projects based their decision on vendor promises that their organizations would realize significant cost savings in their core business." An analysis of performance following ERP implementation supports the view that such systems are better at providing internal gains in efficiency and productivity (e.g., decreases in the number of employees per unit of revenue) than in conferring sustainable competitive advantage based on differentiation (Poston &

Grabski, 2001). Firms will not view the enforcement of property rights for incremental enterprise software customization as a high priority if they recognize that such modifications are unlikely to confer sustainable competitive advantage. Instead, firms may be more concerned with the significant maintenance liability that arises whenever packaged software is customized (Beatty & Williams, 2006). Local modifications to packaged software may not be compatible with future releases. Thus, firms face a dilemma: they must either forego the new version's improvements or re-implement their customizations to make them compatible with the new release. A firm that customizes and enhances a FOSS application can eliminate its maintenance liability by contributing its changes to the project's main source tree. If accepted by the project's maintainers, the modifications will be included in subsequent releases of the software and receive institutionalized support (Ven & Mannaert, 2008). A survey of embedded Linux developers showed that a primary motivation for revealing source code was to increase the probability of "external development support" (Henkel, 2006). Thus, a firm may be willing to pass a potentially-valuable software innovation to the open source community (and thus competitors) in order to maximize compatibility with future releases of the software package and to benefit from continued maintenance and development by others.

A DYNAMIC MODEL OF OPEN SOURCE ADOPTION AND DISRUPTION

Open source software has the potential to satisfy the conditions discussed previously for disruption. Although most FOSS projects are initially less capable than their commercial counterparts, the lack of licensing fees makes FOSS attractive to cost-sensitive users. And although being a low-price alternative to an existing technology is typically insufficient to disrupt existing markets, lead-user contribution of source code provides FOSS business applications with a mechanism to improve over time. We propose here to model the process of FOSS disruption as two distinct stages: an initial *incubation* stage (I-Stage) and a subsequent *snowball* stage (S-Stage). During the I-Stage, the software is developed and refined until it achieves a threshold level of functionality and compatibility with existing practices. These improvements along the organizational adoptability dimension may permit the software to attract a critical mass of adopters. Rogers (1995) defines "critical mass" as the level of adoption that ensures that the innovation's further rate of adoption is self-sustaining. As we discuss below, the notion of critical mass in our model is more specific: it triggers the transition from the I-Stage to the S-Stage. The S-Stage is characterized by gradual, but cumulatively significant changes in both the adoption and improvement mechanisms. These changes are similar in scope to the distinct pre- and post-critical mass "diffusion regimes" identified by Cool, Dierickx, & Szulanski (1997). The change in adoption mechanism occurs as attributes of organizational adoptability (that is, properties of the technology itself) become relatively less important than attributes of community adoptability. For example, adoption beyond a niche typically requires what Moore (2002) calls

a "whole product solution"—the provision of complementary products (such as middleware for connections to existing systems) and services (such as consulting and education) from propagating organizations. The change in improvement mechanism typically occurs as the development process shifts from developers to lead-users and from a small, cohesive team to a large, heterogeneous community (Long & Siau, 2007).

The two stages of our model can be conceived as a specific trajectory through the quadrants of the Adoption Grid shown in Figure 3. First, the I-Stage results in development effort that moves the technology from the experimental quadrant to the niche quadrant. The key to this transition is a threshold increase along the organizational adoptability dimension. Second, in the absence of barriers such as prior technology drag, the S-Stage results in improvements that move the technology from the niche quadrant to the dominant technology quadrant. Increasing returns and determinants of community adoptability, rather than the intrinsic attributes of the technology, drive adoption during the S-Stage.

Why then is all FOSS not disruptive? Despite the advantages of low cost and flexibility, most FOSS projects fail to achieve adoption beyond the original development team and leave the experimental quadrant. Of the tens of thousands

Figure 3. A Dynamic Model of Adoption and Disruption

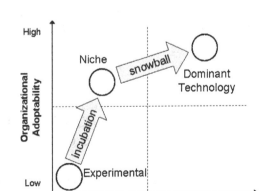

of software development projects hosted on SourceForge.net, a central repository for FOSS, only a small proportion are viable products with established niche markets (Hunt & Johnson, 2002). According to one analysis, "the typical [SourceForge.net] project has one developer, no discussion or bug reports, and is not downloaded by anyone" (Healy & Schussman, 2003, p. 16). The difficulty development projects encounter moving from the experimental to niche quadrants during I-Stage development should come as no surprise. Success in the I-Stage requires that "somebody" make significant investments to provide a pure public good of an uncertain value.

For the small proportion of FOSS projects that attract a critical mass of adoption, the internal mechanisms used to achieve success during the I-Stage are seldom transparent and can vary significantly from project to project. In many prominent FOSS projects, the threshold level of organizational adoptability was achieved through the efforts of a single individual or by a small group of hackers. As noted above, the incentives for such investments are often highly idiosyncratic. In other cases, the threshold level of organizational adoptability was achieved when the property rights holder granted the source code for an established product to the FOSS community. A more deliberate and increasingly common means of achieving a high level organizational adoptability for a new FOSS product is for a for-profit firm to develop a the product under an open source license with the expectation of selling complementary commercial products and services (Dahlander, 2005). Regardless of the internal mechanisms of the I-Stage, some FOSS projects rate sufficiently high along the organizational adoptability dimension to attract a critical mass and make the transition to the S-Stage.

We define the transition from the I-Stage to the S-Stage in terms of a critical mass of adopters (rather than a critical level of functionality or relative advantage) because of the importance of adoption in the improvement of FOSS. As

in the I-Stage, development during the S-Stage requires individuals to make investments in a pure public good. However, compared to the I-Stage, the scale of S-Stage investments is much lower, reciprocity is more easily observable, and value of the final outcome is much more certain. Although only a small proportion of adopters of the most successful FOSS projects actually contribute code, non-developers may contribute to the project in other important ways, such as clarifying requirements, submitting bug reports, or providing valuable knowledge to other users through discussion forums and mailing lists. Even users who do nothing other than download the software (and thus apparently free ride on the efforts of project participants) can contribute incrementally to the increasing returns associated with FOSS adoption because the decision by providers of complementary products to support a particular FOSS project often depends critically on the size of the installed base of users.

It is important to note that these indirect increasing returns to adoption in FOSS are independent of any direct network benefits associated with the technology itself. Thus, a project such as the Apache web server can achieve dominance due to learning-by-using during the S-Stage even though the software itself exhibits only weak network benefits.[1] Conversely, the presence of increasing returns in the incumbent market can prevent S-Stage improvement for a new technology. This can occur if the market has already tipped in favor of an incumbent or if several similar and competing technologies split the pool of early adopters with the result that no technology achieves critical mass.

EX POST PREDICTION: FOSS CASE STUDIES

We assess the predictive value of our model by examining the development and adoption histories of a number of well-known FOSS projects. The flow chart in Figure 3 summarizes the main determinants of adoption and disruption that our model posits in terms of four sequential questions: (1) Does the software have sufficient organizational adoptability to attract a niche of adopters? (2) Does a mechanism for S-Stage improvement exist that is subject to increasing returns to adoption? (3) Are there significant barriers to an S-Stage transition, such as prior technology drag? (4) Is there a competing product with similar advantages that divide community attention and resources?

The Apache Web Server

One of the earliest freely available web servers was developed by a group at the National Center for Supercomputer Applications (NCSA), a research lab sponsored by the US government. The market for web servers developed quickly at the start of the Internet boom in the early 1990s and several core members of the NCSA web server development team left NCSA to join Netscape, a commercial developer of web browser and server software. By October 1994, Netscape's Communications Server 1.0, was selling for $1,495 while its Commerce Server 1.0 was selling for $5,000.[2] The NCSA web server continued to be both popular and freely available; however, the loss of key personnel meant that the mechanism for collecting and applying updated excerpts of source code (or "patches") ceased to function effectively. In 1995, an independent web site developer named Brian Behlendorf and a small group of developers took over responsibility for managing patches and later that year they released "a patchy server". By 2005, Apache was running on roughly 70% of all web servers (Netcraft Inc., 2005).

The transition from the experimental to niche quadrant for the NCSA server occurred due to development subsidized by the US government. As both the NCSA and Netscape web servers had similar functionality (and development teams), the NCSA server's relative advantage in organizational adoptability was initially due to its low cost and its ability to run on multiple server platforms. In contrast, Apache's S-Stage transition to market dominance can be attributed to improvements in its community adoptability. First, the emergence of standard protocols for content (HTML), transfer between web servers and browsers (HTTP) and eventually security (SSL) eliminated the risk of a single firm controlling both sides of a of a two-sided network (Parker & Van Alstyne, 2005). Open standards meant that all web servers were essentially compatible with all web browsers, thus eliminating an important sources of prior technology drag. Second, Apache's architecture was designed to be highly modular. The flexibility provided by modularity was essential during the period when the concept of a "web server" was being continuously redefined. Complementary modules were developed, such as mod_ssl, which permitted the Apache web server to draw on the encryption and authentication services of the OpenSSL package to provide secure transactions. In their survey of adoption of security-related modules by Apache users, Franke and von Hippel (2005) found that lead-user development played an important role in the provision of modules. Although only 37% of users in the sample reported having sufficient programming skills within their server maintenance groups to modify Apache source code (that is, to exploit the innovation toolkit), and although less than 20% of the respondents reported making actual improvements to the code, 64% of users were able and willing to install modular enhancements to the web server developed by lead-users. A third element in Apache's increase in community adoptability during the S-Stage was the emergence of a well-regarded governance mechanism for the web server project. The Apache community (formalized in 1999 as the Apache Foundation) facilitated inputs by lead-users through effective patch management and emerged as a credible sponsor of the project. The Apache Foundation has since become the sponsoring organization for a large number of FOSS projects, many of which have no direct relationship to web servers. Similarly, the O'Reilly Group, a publisher of technical books, contributed to the expectation that Apache would become dominant by promoting books describing the use of the Apache web server in concert with the Linux operating system, MySQL database and the Perl/Phython/PHP scripting languages. Combined with the Linux operating system, these tools comprise the "LAMP stack" of complementary FOSS applications.

Eclipse

Eclipse is an open source development framework used for writing software in Java and other standardized programming languages. The product was originally developed commercially by Object Technology International (OTI) but was acquired by IBM in 1996 as a replacement for VisualAge, IBM's own commercial development environment. IBM subsequently invested an estimated $40 million in further refinements to Eclipse. However, rather than releasing it as a commercial product, IBM granted the source code to the Eclipse Foundation in 2001 (McMillan, 2002) and has since remained a major supporter of the Eclipse project (Babcock, 2005). By late 2005, Eclipse had acquired a market share in the integrated development environment (IDE) market of 20-30% and continues to grow, primarily at the expense of incumbent commercial products such as Borland's JBuilder and BEA's WebLogic Workshop (Krill, 2005).

Eclipse's I-Stage development resulted from the commercial development efforts of OTI and IBM. At the time that Eclipse was converted to a FOSS project, it already compared favorably along the organizational adoptability dimension to enterprise-level tools from incumbent commercial vendors. Eclipse's S-Stage improvement has been rapid, due largely to the sponsorship of IBM, the relative absence of prior technology drag (due to support for standardized computer languages), the modularity of Eclipse, and the accessibility of the

innovation toolkit to the professional programmers that constitute the Eclipse user base. In addition, the reaction of commercial incumbents to the entry of Eclipse both increased its community adoptability and reduced barriers to adoption. Rather than compete with a high-performing FOSS product, incumbents such as Borland and BEA have ceded the basic IDE market to Eclipse and have repositioned their commercial products as complements to the Eclipse core. The membership of these former competitors in the Eclipse Foundation has increased expectations that the Eclipse platform will become a dominant standard.

MySQL Relational Database

MySQL is a FOSS relational database management system (RDBMS) controlled by MySQL AB, a for-profit firm that retains copyright to most of the program's source code. Owing to MySQL's dual license, the program is available under both the GNU General Public License (GPL) and a commercial software license. Unlike the GPL, the commercial license enables firms to sell software that builds on or extends the MySQL code. MySQL's I-Stage development depended primarily on the development effort of the founding members of MySQL AB. Once in the niche quadrant, however, MySQL competed with other multiplatform FOSS RDBMSs, notably PostgreSQL and Interbase (now Firebird). In terms of organizational adoptability, both PostgreSQL and Interbase initially had significant technical advantages over MySQL, including support for atomic transactions and stored procedures. However, such features mattered less to developers of dynamic web sites than stability, speed, and simplicity—particular strengths for MySQL. MySQL's edge over PostgreSQL in terms of these attributes led to MySQL's inclusion in the LAMP stack, an important factor in attracting complementary products such as middleware and education materials.

The impact of prior technology drag on the community adoptability of MySQL has been relatively small, despite the presence of well-established incumbents such as Oracle, IBM, and Microsoft in the client/server database market. One explanation for this is "new market disruption" (Christensen, 1997). Dynamic website development was a relatively new activity that was not particularly well served by the commercial incumbents. Many of the small firms and experimental web design units within larger firms had neither the resources nor the functional imperative to acquire enterprise-level client/server databases and thus favored the simpler, low-cost alternatives offered by the open source community. In addition, the standardized use of SQL by all RDBMSs and existing middleware standards such as ODBC, JDBC, and Perl DBI minimized prior technology drag. According to the MySQL AB website, the program is now the world's most popular database.

Much of MySQL's improvement along the organizational adoptability dimension resulted from the continued development efforts of MySQL AB (based, ostensibly, on feedback from lead-users). However, as MySQL became more widely adopted, it also attracted and incorporated complementary technologies from other FOSS projects. For example, InnoDB is a separate FOSS project that provides a more sophisticated alternative to MySQL's MyISAM storage engine. Integration with InnoDB permitted MySQL to close the gap with PostgreSQL and Interbase by offering many of the advanced RDBMS features absent from MySQL's original storage engine.

Despite its improvements, however, a clear demarcation remains between the enterprise-level RDBMS segment dominated by Oracle and IBM and the middle and low-end segments now dominated by MySQL. The heterogeneity in consumer requirements responsible for market segmentation generally becomes less important as performance of products in all segments exceed customer requirements (Adner, 2002). However, the S-Stage improvement that would permit MySQL to challenge enterprise-level incumbents

has likely been adversely affected by competition from other FOSS databases. SAP AG released its SAP DB database under an open source license 2000. Shortly thereafter, Computer Associates transferred its Ingres database (a commercial predecessor of PostgreSQL) to the open source community. The coexistence of these mature, enterprise-level FOSS databases created competition for database specialists within the open source community and has made it difficult of any of the products to achieve the critical mass required for S-Stage improvement. At one point, MySQL entered into an agreement with SAP to rebrand SAP DB as MaxDB and "combine the performance and stability of MySQL and the enterprise-level functionality of [SAP DB]."[1] However, this agreement was terminated in 2007 and SAP DB as reverted to a closed-source license under SAP's control.

OpenOffice

The OpenOffice suite of desktop productivity tools (a word processor, spreadsheet, and presentation design program) is meant to compete with Microsoft's dominant Office suite. The original product, known as StarOffice, was created by StarDivision, a commercial firm, but was purchased by Sun Microsystems in 1999. Sun released the source code for the product to the OpenOffice project in 2000, but continues to develop a commercial version of StarOffice that includes a number of proprietary enhancements to the OpenOffice core. The I-Stage development of OpenOffice thus resembles the early development of Eclipse: a fledgling but viable product was purchased by a large software vendor and released as a fully functional FOSS project. The organizational adoptability of the niche product rested on two advantages over Microsoft Office: the ability to run on multiple platforms and the absence of a licensing fee. Despite its promising start, however, OpenOffice remains in the niche quadrant for three reasons. First, Microsoft Office imposes significant prior technology drag. Although OpenOffice is *almost* fully compatible with Microsoft Office, the lack of full compatibility imposes costs on those who choose not to participate in the dominant Microsoft Office network. Microsoft, as the incumbent technology standard, has strong incentives to prevent OpenOffice from achieving complete compatibility with Microsoft Office's proprietary file formats (Hill, 1997). Second, OpenOffice suffers from a relative disadvantage in the number and quality of complementary products such as learning materials, templates, and add-ins. Third, and more controversially, the widespread piracy of Microsoft Office, particularly in the developing world, has partially neutralized OpenOffice's cost advantage. Indeed, Microsoft's reluctance to impose stricter piracy controls on its Office suite amounts to a versioning strategy to combat the emergence of disruptive alternatives (Farrell & Saloner, 1986).

Of the relatively small number of adopters of OpenOffice who have overcome the prior technology drag imposed by the dominant commercial incumbent, many are non-programmers and are therefore unable to enhance OpenOffice's source code (Brown, 2005). Although we argued above that firm-level contributions eliminate the need for users to also be developers, the components of the OpenOffice suite are primarily intended for individual use within the firm, not firm-level use. Firms may be willing to underwrite improvements to an enterprise database or web server at the core of their enterprises. To this point, however, they have been less willing to pay to fix stability problems or interface annoyances in a PowerPoint clone. The barriers to adoption imposed by Microsoft Office combined with the lack of strong mechanisms for firm- or individual-level user development prevent OpenOffice from achieving the S-Stage improvement required for transition to the dominant technology quadrant. Barring an exogenous and significant increase in community adoptability—for example, widespread legislation

mandating the use of non-proprietary file formats by government agencies—OpenOffice will remain in the niche quadrant and fail to achieve dominant status.

Summary of the *Ex Post* Case Studies

Table 1 summarizes each of the FOSS examples in terms of the mechanisms used for I-Stage development and S-Stage improvement. Both Apache and MySQL have already achieved disruption in their markets (or market segment in the case of MySQL). Eclipse is almost certain to achieve dominance, given the supportive response from commercial incumbents and the potential for significant learning-by-using effects in a market in which *all* users are software developers. OpenOffice, in contrast, illustrates the failure of a major FOSS project to ignite the virtuous cycle of S-Stage adoption and improvement despite offering a base level of functionality that is comparable to commercial competitors.

The I-Stage investment required to move a technology or product from the experimental quadrant to the niche quadrant is significant. Grants to the FOSS community of commercial products with established niches have become increasingly common, especially for products that have failed to achieve the dominant position in tippy markets. For example, both SAP DB and Ingres were mature, enterprise-level products competing in a market segment dominated by Oracle and IBM prior to being converted to FOSS. Such grants are seen by some as a way for commercial software firms to abandon underperforming products without alienating the product's installed base. In the cases of Eclipse and StarOffice, the contributors' motivations may have been more strategic, prompted by direct competition with Microsoft.

Once in the niche quadrant, the forces of community adoption appear to be more important than the overall organizational adoptability of the technology. S-Stage improvement leads

Table 1. Summary of FOSS cases

FOSS project	Mechanism for I-Stage development	Key attributes of organizational adoptability (niche quadrant)	Mechanism for S-Stage improvement	Key attributes of community adoptability (dominant technology quadrant)
Apache web server	Grant of web server code from NCSA	Low cost, modular structure, multiplatform	Lead-user development by web administrators	Adherence to emerging W3 standards, sponsorship by the Apache Foundation, increased expectations due to central role in the LAMP stack
Eclipse integrated development framework	Grant of code by IBM; subsequent investments by IBM in the FOSS project	Low cost, enterprise-level functionality	Commitment to development by major commercial tool vendors; lead-user development	Adherence to standards, multiplatform, development of modules for multiple languages, sponsorship of IBM
MySQL relational database	Development effort by founders of MySQL AB	Low cost, speed, simplicity	Lead-user requests for features, development by MySQL AB	Integration into LAMP stack, formal sponsorship of MySQL AB, informal sponsorship through O'Reilly LAMP books
Open Office personal productivity software	Grant of source code by Sun Microsystems	Low cost, basic functionality, basic compatibility with Microsoft Office file formats	Development by Sun (StarOffice)	Slow adoption due to prior technology drag (network benefits, complementary assets), some incompatibility with MS Office formats

to increasing adoption and increasing adoption feeds further S-Stage improvement. For Apache, Eclipse, and, to a lesser extent, MySQL, lead-user development continues to be the dominant improvement mechanism because many users of such products have strong technical skills. Apache and MySQL benefit from firm-level contributions, since they occupy critical roles in a firm's technology infrastructure. On the other hand, all three of the disruptive FOSS projects have benefited from open industry standards, which reduced or eliminated prior technology drag.

Community adoptability becomes more difficult to assess when multiple FOSS projects compete against one another. The probability that multiple FOSS projects achieve niche status within the same market segment increases as commercial products are converted to FOSS projects. For example, the conversion of Interbase to an FOSS project in 2000 by Borland created competition within the mid-tier FOSS database segment for both users and developers. Much the same problem exists in the high-end segment due

to the conversion of SAP DB and Ingres to FOSS licenses. As the economics of technology standards literature predicts, and the confusion around SAP DB/MaxDB vividly illustrates, predicting the dominant technology in the face of competing standards is extremely difficult.

EX ANTE PREDICTION: CRM AND THE THREAT OF FOSS DISRUPTION

CRM software enables firms to develop, document, and improve relationships with their customers. At its most basic level, CRM software provides the data and interfaces necessary for sales force automation. More generally, however, CRM "requires a cross-functional integration of processes, people, operations, and marketing capabilities that is enabled through information, technology, and applications" (Payne & Frow, 2005, p. 168). CRM is thus similar to ERP and SCM systems in terms of its scope, organizational impact and technological requirements. All three types of enterprise software involve significant organization-wide commitments to shared processes and infrastructure. Moreover, all three provide support for important, but ultimately non-strategic, business processes. We therefore believe that our model and analysis extend beyond CRM and apply to enterprise software generally.

Commercial CRM software firms can be divided into three major strategic groups. The first group consists of the three leading CRM vendors: SAP, Oracle, and Siebel (now owned by Oracle). These firms target large organizations with complex, high-performance CRM implementations. The second group consists of a larger number of smaller vendors that target small-to-medium size businesses (SMB) and includes Microsoft, Pivotal, Onyx, and SalesLogix (Close, 2003). The third strategic group consists of software-as-a-service (SaaS) CRM vendors, such as Salesforce.com. Application service providers rent access to SaaS-enabled CRM software over the Internet for a subscription fee. Salesforce.com actively targets the SMB segment with particular emphasis on non-users (i.e., SMBs that have yet to adopt any CRM product).

The CRM industry's separation into strategic groups is consistent with segmentation theories in information goods' markets. Suppliers of information goods incur high initial development costs in order to produce the first copy of the product. Once produced, however, the marginal cost of producing an additional copy is effectively zero and suppliers of information goods face no physical limitations on production capacity. Consequently, the competitive equilibrium price of an undifferentiated information good available from multiple suppliers approximates the good's zero marginal cost (Shapiro & Varian, 1999). Suppliers in information markets therefore risk a catastrophic price collapse if their products become commoditized. Such collapses have occurred in several markets, including web browsers, encyclopaedias, and online stock quotes. In general, there are three generic strategies for avoiding

ruinous price-based competition in markets for information goods: differentiation, domination, and lock-in (Shapiro & Varian, 1999). Suppliers seek to avoid commoditization by differentiating their offerings based on some combination of their own capabilities and the heterogeneous requirements of customers. Accordingly, Oracle, and SAP compete on the advanced features, scalability, and reliability of their CRM software. Since many SMBs are unwilling to pay for these attributes, an opportunity exists for lower cost, lower functionality mid-tier CRM vendors (Band et al., 2005). Domination, in contrast, requires cost leadership through supply-side economies of scale in fixed-cost activities such as administration, distribution and marketing. For this reason, competition *within* a segment often leads to consolidation. Finally, first movers may be able to retain a degree of pricing power by erecting high switching costs that lock-in customers. Lock-in is common in enterprise software markets because of the high switching costs that flow from differences in underlying data models and formats, and the existence of indirect increasing returns to adoption. Moreover, the magnitude of the ongoing revenue streams generated from upgrades, customization, and integration provide explicit disincentives for vendors to reduce switching costs. A study of packaged enterprise software by Forrester estimated that the annual cost for such maintenance activities is 2.75 times the initial license fee (Gormley et al,, 1998).

Commercial CRM software vendors have attempted each of the three generic strategies for avoiding price-based competition: they have differentiated themselves into high- and mid-range segments, moved towards domination of a segment by consolidation, and erected high switching costs through proprietary data models and product-specific training. The result is a relatively stable two-tiered CRM market. However, the stability of this market structure is threatened by three potential sources of disruption. The first is prototypical, low-end disruption from contact management products, such as Maximizer and Act. Although such tools are superficially similar to CRM software (they contain customer data, for example), contact management products are intended for single users or workgroups and do not provide the enterprise-wide integration of true CRM tools. The second and third potential sources of disruption are business model disruptions rather than product disruptions. Business model disruption alters the way in which an existing product is offered to customers rather than defining a new product (Markides, 2006). The SaaS model for CRM pioneered by Salesforce.com constitutes a business model disruption because it permits customers to use CRM without installing and maintaining CRM software. Software providers service all their clients from a single central resource over the Internet. The lower up-front cost of SaaS to consumers leads to increased adoption, which in turn leads to greater economies of scale for the software provider. This virtuous cycle of adoption may ultimately permit Salesforce.com to achieve market dominance. The third candidate for disrupting the CRM market is emerging FOSS enterprise applications, such as Hipergate, Vtiger, Compiere, CentricCRM, and SugarCRM. Of these FOSS entrants, SugarCRM is currently the clear frontrunner.

According to our dynamic model, both low-end disruption (by Act and Maximizer) and business model disruption by a single firm (e.g., Salesforce.com) are unlikely. The I-Stage development required to upgrade existing contact management packages to full CRM functionality requires a significant investment by either the software's developer or by others. However, both the mid- and high-end segments of the CRM market are already contested by firms with mature products and installed customer bases. There is little incentive for Act or Maximizer to make large investments in order to enter these highly competitive segments. The community adoptability of Salesforce.com, in contrast, is bounded by the ease with which competitors can match both its SaaS delivery

mechanism and its pricing model. The presence of high switching costs means that the structure of the commercial CRM market will change more as a result of consolidation than disruption by other vendors of closed-source software.

Disruption by a FOSS CRM program, such as SugarCRM, is more likely. SugarCRM is a dual-licensed application built on top of the Apache-MySQL-PHP stack. The application is entirely web-based, allowing it to be offered in SaaS mode, much like Salesforce.com. Sugar-CRM's functionality, simplicity, and low cost have allowed it to establish a position in the niche quadrant. According to SugarCRM's website, the product has been downloaded more than 5.2 million times.[3]

Professional software developers backed by venture financing undertook the I-Stage development of SugarCRM. The founders of SugarCRM Inc., all former employees of a commercial CRM vendor, secured more than $26M in three rounds of financing in the eighteen months following the company's incorporation in 2004. Given its establishment as a niche product, the question is whether SugarCRM possess a plausible mechanism for S-Stage improvement? Following our *ex post* analyses from the previous section, we decompose this question into two parts: (1) whether commercial and open source competitors in the CRM market impose significant barriers to community adoptability, and (2) whether the SugarCRM community has the capacity to improve the product to a point to where it is functionally comparable to the offerings from mid-tier incumbents.

Barriers to Community Adoptability

The lack of direct network benefits in the CRM market means that the primary source of prior technology drag is switching costs. The use of proprietary data models and user interfaces for CRM software mean that changing to a different CRM product involves significant data migration and retraining. Consequently, SugarCRM will appeal to non-users—firms that have been to this point unable to justify the cost of commercial CRM products. However, some firms that have already adopted CRM may perceive that they are excessively dependent on their current CRM vendor and may seek to avoid long-term vendor hold-up (an extreme form of lock-in) by switching to a FOSS CRM provider.

Extreme vendor dependence also arises in the enterprise software market due to the irreversibility of investments. Enterprise applications typically exhibit increasing returns to adoption *within* the firm. Specifically, many of the benefits of enterprise systems accrue from sharing data across multiple business processes and functional areas. The benefits of integration are difficult to assess during a localized pilot or trial and thus implementation of an application such as CRM requires a significant, organizational-wide commitment in training and process redesign. The risk of making such large-scale investments and then being stranded with a non-viable technology may lead some firms to favor well-established CRM vendors, such as Oracle and SAP. However, FOSS licensing and access to source code also reduce vendor dependence. The risk of being stranded with an orphaned FOSS technology depends more on the viability of an entire community of adopters than on the viability of a single firm. The relatively large amount of venture financing accumulated by SugarCRM Inc. has established it as a credible sponsor of the SugarCRM community and has reinforced expectations that the community of adopters will continue to grow.

Mechanisms for S-Stage Improvement

In our view, FOSS CRM has a plausible mechanism for S-Stage improvement. New adopters of CRM and firms seeking to decrease their vendor dependence will help FOSS CRM achieve a critical mass. As discussed previously, these users have incentives to improve the product and contribute their improvements back to the main project. The SugarForge.org website provides a forum for SugarCRM developers to share their enhancements with others. To cite one of many examples on SugarForge, a developer working for a call center recently posted the source code for a small program that integrates SugarCRM with the Asterisk telephony application. Such incremental enhancements by lead-users can help FOSS CRM make the transition from the niche quadrant to the dominant quadrant and disrupt the commercial CRM market.

Whether SugarCRM *in particular* will disrupt the commercial CRM market is more difficult to answer for two reasons. First, heterogeneous requirements across different vertical markets (e.g., financial services and consumer products) may lead to a large number of vertical-specific customizations. In these circumstances, the community may decide to fork the code into different projects for different vertical markets rather than attempt to manage the complexity of a single large code base. The resulting fragmentation of the developer base threatens the S-Stage development of a FOSS project. This risk is illustrated by the emergence of CiviCRM, a FOSS CRM intended specifically for non-profit and non-governmental organizations. Second, the economic opportunities facing incumbent commercial CRM vendors are at least as favorable as those facing SugarCRM Inc. Any incumbent commercial vendor could convert its application to a FOSS license and rely on revenue from complementary products and services to replace lost license revenue. At this point, major CRM incumbent firms have the benefit of larger installed bases and networks of complements.

Summary: Predicting Disruption by FOSS

As the flow chart in Figure 4 shows, SugarCRM satisfies the conditions in our model for successful disruption. However, the flow chart also suggests

Figure 4. A flow chart to predict disruption by FOSS

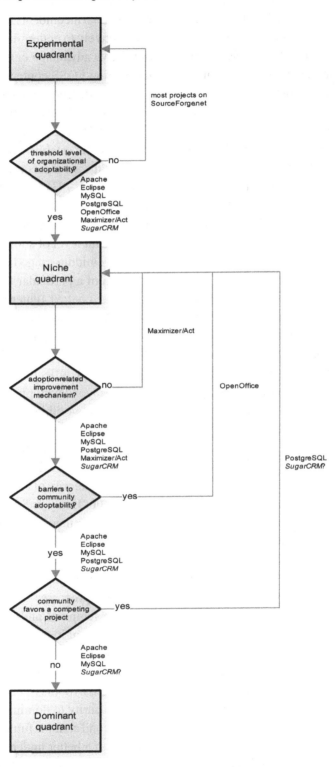

possible defensive responses by commercial incumbents to the emergence of niche FOSS competitors. Commercial software vendors may be able to erect barriers to community adoptability by maximizing prior technology drag or by attempting to control the ecology of complementors that support the new entrant. A possible example of the latter response is Oracle's acquisition of InnoDB. Commercial vendors may also release (or threaten to release) a competing FOSS or "community" version of their products. For example, Sun's release of its Unix-based operating system, OpenSolaris, may have been an attempt to further fragment the open source community that develops and maintains Linux. Oracle's scaled-down Express Edition provides price-sensitive users of client/ server database with a free alternative to FOSS products such as MySQL. The requirement to achieve a critical mass of adoption before S-Stage improvement can become self-sustaining means that such tactics by commercial incumbents can be effective in slowing or preventing disruption by FOSS entrants.

IMPLICATIONS FOR THEORY AND PRACTICE

In this paper, we present a dynamic model of adoption and disruption that can help managers better understand the process of disruption by free and open source software. We illustrate the application of the model by analyzing the history of four well-known FOSS projects and applying the model to the case of SugarCRM, a FOSS CRM project. We predict that the FOSS model of production will disrupt the existing commercial CRM market; however, we cannot make theory-based predictions about whether a particular FOSS CRM project, such as SugarCRM, will be disruptive. SugarCRM currently rates highest among FOSS CRM products along the dimension of community adoptability. However, a measure of Christensen's influence on practice is that firms are now more

aware of the effects of disruptive innovations. Commercial incumbents facing disruption may act preemptively to undermine SugarCRM's sources of relative advantage or to displace it entirely as the leading FOSS contender.

The model contributes to the developing theory of disruptive innovation (Christensen, 2006; Danneels, 2004) by explaining the disruption process in terms of an established model of adoption. We build on the synthesis provided by Fichman and Kermerer's (1993) Adoption Grid to identify two temporally distinct stages that must occur before a FOSS project can move from an experimental to dominant level of adoption. Our model can be seen as a middle-range theory that describes the adoption of a particular technology (FOSS) in a particular context (enterprise applications such as CRM, ERP, and SCM).

Our work suggests several avenues for future theoretical and empirical research. First, our hypothesized inflection point between I-Stage and S-Stage development challenges the notion of a monolithic FOSS production method. Several researchers have noted inconsistencies in cross-sectional studies of practices as they are embodied in a few FOSS successes versus those in the vast majority of FOSS projects (Niederman, et al., 2006; Healy & Schussman, 2003). We believe that our theoretical understanding of many aspects of the FOSS phenomenon not addressed in this paper—including governance structures, software development techniques, and innovation-generating processes—will have to become more dynamic, temporal, and consequently contingent. Moreover, longitudinal studies of FOSS showing dramatic shifts in, for example, project governance and internal project dynamics, are required to support our hypothesis of a two-stage progression from obscurity to dominance.

A second area for future research is the development of a better understanding of the expanding role of user-firms in FOSS development. For example, much of the economic rationale for firm-level lead-user development rests on the assumption that a user-firm can work within the FOSS community to have the firm's modifications and enhancements incorporated into a particular project. However, it is not clear how conflicting objectives between multiple firms within a FOSS project might be resolved or whether firms have incentives to behave strategically within the project. In this way, the dynamics of firm-level participation in FOSS resemble those of firm-level participation in standard-setting bodies (Foray, 1994).

Finally, the policy implications of our two-stage model have not been addressed. As our analysis of existing FOSS projects show, some valuable software applications become public goods by accident. Substantial sunk investments are made during the I-Stage with the expectation that the resulting software will be a commercially-viable private good. The public policy implications of subsidizing I-Stage development in order to exploit S-Stage expansion and refinement have not been explored, but are worthy of further research.

ACKNOWLEDGMENT

The authors acknowledge the Social Sciences and Humanities Research Council of Canada (SSHRC) Initiatives for the New Economy (INE) program for financial support.

REFERENCES

Adner, R. (2002). When are technologies disruptive? A demand-based view of the emergence of competition. *Strategic Management Journal, 23*(8), 667–688. doi:10.1002/smj.246

Arrow, K. (1970). *Social choice and individual values* (2nd ed.). New Haven, CT: Yale University Press.

Attewell, P. (1992). Technology diffusion and organizational learning: the case of business computing. *Organization Science, 3*(1), 1–19. doi:10.1287/orsc.3.1.1

Babcock, C. (2005). Eclipse on the rise. [Electronic version]. *InformationWeek*. Retrieved January 29, 2006.

Band, W., Kinikin, E., Ragsdale, J., & Harrington, J. (2005). *Enterprise CRM suites, Q2, 2005: Evaluation of top enterprise CRM software vendors across 177 criteria*. Cambridge, MA: Forrester Research Inc.

Beatty, R., & Williams, C. (2006). ERP II: Best practices for successfully implementing an ERP upgrade. *Communications of the ACM, 49*(3), 105–109. doi:10.1145/1118178.1118184

Benkler, Y. (2002). Coase's penguin, or, Linux and the nature of the firm. *The Yale Law Journal, 112*(3), 1–42. doi:10.2307/1562247

Brown, A. (2005). If this suite's a success, why is it so buggy? [Electronic version]. *The Guardian*, Retrieved March 15, 2006.

Christensen, C. M. (1997). *The innovator's dilemma: When new technologies cause great firms to fail*. Boston, MA: Harvard Business School Press.

Christensen, C. M. (2000). After the gold rush. *Innosight*. Retrieved January 30, 2006.

Christensen, C. M. (2006). The ongoing process of building a theory of disruption. *Journal of Product Innovation Management, 23*(1), 39–55. doi:10.1111/j.1540-5885.2005.00180.x

Close, W. (2003). *CRM suites for North American MSBs markets: 1H03 magic quadrant*. Stamford, CT: Gartner Inc. Markets.

Cool, K. O., Dierickx, I., & Szulanski, G. (1997). Diffusion of innovative within organizations: Electronic switching in the Bell system, 1971-1982. *Organization Science, 8*(5), 543–560. doi:10.1287/orsc.8.5.543

Dahlander, L. (2005). Appropriation and appropriability in open source software. *International Journal of Innovation Management, 9*(3), 259–285. doi:10.1142/S1363919605001265

Dahlander, L. (2007). Penguin in a new suit: A tale of how de novo entrants emerged to harness free and open source software communities. *Industrial and Corporate Change, 16*(5), 913–943. doi:10.1093/icc/dtm026

Danneels, E. (2004). Disruptive technology reconsidered: A critique and research agenda. *Journal of Product Innovation Management, 21*(4), 246–258. doi:10.1111/j.0737-6782.2004.00076.x

Dano, M. (2008). Android founder makes the case for Google's mobile strategy. *RCR Wireless News, 27*(34), 1–8.

Davis, F. (1989). Perceived usefulness, perceived ease of use, and user acceptance of information technology. *MIS Quarterly, 13*(3), 318–339. doi:10.2307/249008

Farrell, J., & Saloner, G. (1986). Installed base and compatibility: Innovation, product preannouncements, and predation. *The American Economic Review, 76*(5), 940–955.

Fichman, R. G. (2000). The diffusion and assimilation of information technology innovations. In R. Zmud (Ed.), *Framing the domains of IT management: Projecting the future through the past.* Cincinnati, OH: Pinnaflex Publishing.

Fichman, R. G., & Kemerer, C. F. (1993). Adoption of software engineering process innovations: The case of object orientation. *Sloan Management Review, 34*(2), 7–22.

Fitzgerald, B. (2006). The Transformation of Open Source Software. *MIS Quarterly, 30*(3), 587–598.

Foray, D. (1994). Users, standards and the economics of coalitions and committees. *Information Economics and Policy, 6*(3-4), 269–293. doi:10.1016/0167-6245(94)90005-1

Franke, N., & von Hippel, E. (2003). Satisfying heterogeneous user needs via innovation toolkits: The case of Apache security software. *Research Policy, 32*(7), 1199–1216. doi:10.1016/S0048-7333(03)00049-0

Franke, N., von Hippel, E., & Schreier, M. (2006). Finding commercially attractive user innovations: A test of lead user theory. *Journal of Product Innovation Management, 23*(4), 301–315. doi:10.1111/j.1540-5885.2006.00203.x

Gormley, J., W. Bluestein, J. Gatoff & H. Chun (1998). The runaway costs of packaged applications. *The Forrester Report, 3*(5). Cambridge, MA: Forrester Research, Inc.

Healy, K., & Schussman, A. (2003). *The ecology of open source software development.* Open Source, MIT. Working paper. http://opensource.mit.edu/papers/healyschussman.pdf. Last accessed January 8, 2007.

Henkel, J. (2006). Selective revealing in open innovation processes: The case of embedded Linux. *Research Policy, 35*(7), 953–969. doi:10.1016/j.respol.2006.04.010

Hertel, G., Niedner, S., & Herrmann, S. (2003). Motivation of software developers in open source projects: an Internet-based survey of contributors to the Linux kernel. *Research Policy, 32,* 1159–1177. doi:10.1016/S0048-7333(03)00047-7

Hicks, C., & Pachamanova, D. (2007). Back-propagation of user innovations: The open source compatibility edge. *Business Horizons, 50*(4), 315–324. doi:10.1016/j.bushor.2007.01.006

Hill, C. W. L. (1997). Establishing a standard: Competitive strategy and technological standards in winner-take-all industries. *The Academy of Management Executive, 11*(2), 7–25.

Himanen, P., Torvalds, L., & Castells, M. (2002). *The Hacker Ethic.* New York: Random House.

Hitt, L., & Brynjolfsson, E. (1996). Productivity, profit, and consumer welfare: Three different measures of information technology's value. *MIS Quarterly, 20*(20), 144–162.

Hovav, A., Patnayakuni, R., & Schuff, D. (2004). A model of internet standards adoption: The case of IPv6. *Information Systems Journal, 14*(3), 265–294. doi:10.1111/j.1365-2575.2004.00170.x

Hunt, F., & Johnson, P. (2002). On the Pareto distribution of SourceForge projects. In *Proceedings of the Open Source Software Development Workshop,* Newcastle, UK (pp. 122-129).

Iacovou, C. L., Benbasat, I., & Dexter, A. S. (1995). Electronic data interchange and small organizations: Adoption and impact of technology. *MIS Quarterly, 19*(4), 465–485. doi:10.2307/249629

Katz, M. L., & Shapiro, C. (1994). Systems competition and network effects. *The Journal of Economic Perspectives, 8*(2), 93–115.

Krill, P. (2005). Borland upgrading IDE while preparing for eclipse future. [Electronic version]. *InfoWorld.* Retrieved January 30, 2006.

Lerner, J., & Tirole, J. (2002). Some simple economics of open source. *The Journal of Industrial Economics, 50*(2), 197–234.

Liebeskind, J. P. (1996). Knowledge, strategy, and the theory of the firm. *Strategic Management Journal, 17,* 93–107.

Long, Y., & Siau, K. (2007). Social network structures in open source software development teams. *Journal of Database Management, 18,* 25–40.

Lyons, D. (2004). Peace, love and paychecks. [Electronic version]. *Forbes.* Retrieved January 30, 2006.

MacCormack, A. (2002) *Siemens ShareNet: Building a knowledge network.* Harvard Business School Publishing, Case 603036, Cambridge, MA.

Markides, C. (2006). Disruptive innovation: In need of better theory. *Journal of Product Innovation Management, 23*(1), 19–25. doi:10.1111/j.1540-5885.2005.00177.x

McMillan, R. (2002). Will Big Blue eclipse the Java tools market? [Electronic version]. *JavaWorld.* Retrieved January 27, 2006.

Moore, G. A. (2002). *Crossing the chasm: Marketing and selling high-tech products to mainstream customers* (revised edition). New York: HarperBusiness Essentials.

Moore, G. C., & Benbasat, I. (1991). Development of an instrument to measure the perceptions of adopting an information technology innovation. *Information Systems Research, 2*(3), 192–222. doi:10.1287/isre.2.3.192

Morton, A. (2005). *Lead Maintainer, Linux Production Kernel.* IT Conversations: SDForum Distinguished Speaker Series. Retrieved January 31, 2006.

Netcraft Inc. (2005). *October 2005 web server survey.* Retrieved December 5, 2006 from http://news.netcraft.com/archives/2005/10/04/october_2005_web_server_survey.html.

Niederman, F., Davis, A., Greiner, M., Wynn, D., & York, P. (2006). A research agenda for studying open source I: A multi-level framework. *Communications of the AIS, 18*(7), 2–38.

Parker, G. G., & Van Alstyne, M. W. (2005). Two-sided network effects: A theory of information product design. *Management Science, 51*(10), 1494–1504. doi:10.1287/mnsc.1050.0400

Payne, A., & Frow, P. (2005). A strategic framework for customer relationship management. *Journal of Marketing, 69*(4), 167–176. doi:10.1509/jmkg.2005.69.4.167

Poston, R., & Grabski, S. (2001). Financial impacts of enterprise resource planning implementations. *International Journal of Accounting Information Systems, 2*(4), 271–294. doi:10.1016/S1467-0895(01)00024-0

Rai, A., Ravichandran, T., & Samaddar, S. (1998). How to anticipate the Internet's global diffusion. *Communications of the ACM, 41*(10), 97–106. doi:10.1145/286238.286253

Ravichandran, T. (2005). Organizational assimilation of complex technologies: An empirical study of component-based software development. *IEEE Transactions on Engineering Management, 52*(2), 249–268. doi:10.1109/TEM.2005.844925

Riemenschneider, C. K., Hardgrave, B. C., & Davis, F. D. (2002). Explaining software developer acceptance of methodologies: A comparison of five theoretical models. *IEEE Transactions on Software Engineering, 28*(12), 1135–1145. doi:10.1109/TSE.2002.1158287

Robey, D., & Boudreau, M. (1999). Accounting for the contradictory organizational consequences of information technology: Theoretical directions and methodological implications. *Information Systems Research, 10*(2), 167–185. doi:10.1287/isre.10.2.167

Rogers, E. M. (1995). *Diffusion of innovations* (4th ed.). New York, NY: The Free Press.

Shapiro, C., & Varian, H. R. (1999). *Information rules: A strategic guide to the network economy.* Cambridge, MA: Harvard Business School Press.

Taylor, S., & Todd, P. A. (1995). Understanding information technology usage: A test of competing models. *Information Systems Research, 6*(2), 144–176. doi:10.1287/isre.6.2.144

Tellis, G. J. (2006). Disruptive technology or visionary leadership? *Journal of Product Innovation Management, 23*(1), 34–38. doi:10.1111/j.1540-5885.2005.00179.x

Tingling, P., & Parent, M. (2002). Mimetic isomorphism and technology evaluation: Does imitation transcend judgment? *Journal of the Association for Information Systems, 3*(5), 113–143.

Ven, K., & Mannaert, H. (2008). Challenges and strategies in the use of open source software by independent software vendors. *Information and Software Technology, 50*(9), 991–1002. doi:10.1016/j.infsof.2007.09.001

von Hippel, E. (1998). Economics of product development by users: The impact of 'sticky' local information. *Management Science, 44*(5), 629–644. doi:10.1287/mnsc.44.5.629

von Hippel, E. (2005). *Democratizing innovation.* Cambridge, MA: MIT Press.

Weber, S. (2004). *The success of open source.* Cambridge, MA: Harvard University Press.

Weimer, D., & Vining, A. (2005). *Policy Analysis: Concepts and Practice.* Upper Saddle River, NJ: Pearson Prentice-Hall.

West, J., & Gallagher, S. (2006). Challenges of open innovation: the paradox of firm investment in open-source software. *R & D Management, 36*(3), 319–331. doi:10.1111/j.1467-9310.2006.00436.x

ENDNOTES

[1]   All leading web servers rely on the same standard protocols including HTML, HTTP

and SSL. The strong network benefits thus occur at the protocol level, rather than the level of the application software that implements the protocols.

2   Netscape's company name at the time was Mosaic Communications. They changed it shortly after. An order form is shown at http://www.dotnetat.net/mozilla/mcom.10.1994/MCOM/ordering_docs/index.html.

3   From http://www.sugarforge.org/: 1.5 million downloads as of 22 March, 2006; 5.2 million downloads as of 23 December, 2008.

Chapter 12
Aiding the Development of Active Applications:
A Decoupled Rule Management Solution

Florian Daniel
University of Trento, Italy

Giuseppe Pozzi
Politecnico di Milano, Italy

ABSTRACT

Active applications are characterized by the need for expressing, evaluating, and maintaining a set of rules that implement the application's active behavior. Typically, rules follow the Event-Condition-Action (ECA) paradigm, yet oftentimes their actual implementation is buried in the application code, as their enactment requires a tight integration with the concepts and modules of the application. This chapter proposes a rule management system that allows developers to easily expand its rule processing logic with such concepts and modules and, hence, to decouple the management of their active rules from the application code. This system derives from an exception manager that has previously been developed in the context of an industry-scale workflow management system and effectively allows developers to separate active and non-active design concerns.

INTRODUCTION

Until the emergence of the first operating systems and high-level programming languages allowed developers to disregard hardware peculiarities, computers had to be programmed directly in machine code Then, only in the eighties, Database Management Systems (DBMSs) provided efficient, external data management solutions, and in the nineties Workflow Management Systems (WfMSs)

extended this idea and extracted entire processes from still rather monolithic software systems. We believe that in similar way also active (also known as reactive) behaviors, which are present in many modern applications (see for instance Section 2), can be more efficiently managed by proper active software supports, such as active rules and rule engines (Section 3).

The basic observation underlying this idea is that, when abstracting from the particular application and domain, most of the active behaviors in software systems adhere to the rather regular and

DOI: 10.4018/978-1-60566-904-5.ch012

stable ECA (Event-Condition-Action) paradigm. ECA rules have first been introduced in the context of active DBMSs, where operations on data may raise events, conditions check the status of the database, and actions perform operations on data. Our previous experience in the field of WfMSs (Casati, Ceri, Paraboschi, and Pozzi, 1999; Combi and Pozzi, 2004) allowed us to successfully apply high-level ECA rules to WfMSs for the specification and handling of expected exceptions that may occur during process execution. By leveraging this experience, in this paper, we propose an ECA paradigm accompanied by a suitable rule language, where events represent data, temporal, application or external events, conditions check the state of data or of the application, and actions may act on data, applications, or external resources. Active rules may thus not only refer to the data layer, but as well to the whole application, comprising data and application-specific characteristics. Elevating active rules from the data layer to the application layer allows designers to express a broader range of active behaviors and, more importantly, to address them at a suitable level of abstraction (Section 4). This could turn out beneficial for example in requirements engineering approaches, such as the ones described by Loucopoulos and Kadir (2008) or by Amghar, Meziane, and Flory (2002), as well as in re-engineering approaches like the one described in Huang, Hung, Yen, Li, and Wu (2006).

For the execution and management of ECA rules, we further propose an open ECA server (OES), which runs in a mode that is completely detached from the execution of the actual application, so as to alleviate the application from the burden of event management. OES is highly customizable, which allows developers to easily add application- or domain-specific features to the rule engine (Section 5 describes the customization process, Section 6 illustrates a use case of the system). Instead of implementing the OES system from the scratch, we shall show how we unbundled and reconfigured the necessary com-

ponents from a previously developed exception manager for a WfMS (Casati et al., 1999) (Section 7) – unbundling is the activity of breaking up monolithic software systems into smaller units (Gatziu and Koschel, 1998). We thus move from the ECA server we developed within the EC project WIDE to manage exceptions in the context of Sema's FORO commercial WfMS, where the exception manager (FAR) was tightly bundled into FORO.

RATIONALE AND BACKGROUND

Active mechanisms or behaviors have been extensively studied in the field of active DBMSs as a flexible and efficient solution for complex data management problems. Many of the results achieved for relational or object-oriented active databases have recently been extended to tightly related research areas such as XML repositories and ontology storage systems. To the best of our knowledge, only few works (Dittrich, Fritschi, Gatziu, Geppert, and Vaduva, 2003; Chakravarthy and Liao, 2001; Cugola, Di Nitto, and Fuggetta, 2001) try to elevate the applicability of active rules from the data level to the application level and to eliminate the tedious mapping from active behavior requirements to data-centric active rules (Section 8 discusses related works in more detail). Besides DBMSs, there are several application areas, which could significantly benefit from an active rule support that also takes into account their application- or domain-specific peculiarities. Among these application areas, we mention here:

- WfMSs or in general business process management systems allow one to define the system-assisted execution of office/ business processes that may involve several actors, documents, and work items. Active mechanisms could be exploited for an efficient enactment of the single tasks or work items, and the management of time constraints during process execution (Combi and Pozzi, 2003; Combi and Pozzi, 2004).

- Web services and (Web) applications, which use Web services as data sources or incorporate their business logic (Li, Huang, Yen, and Chang, 2007), may rely on an asynchronous communication paradigm where an autonomous management of incoming and outgoing events (i.e., messages) is crucial. Suitable active rules could ease the integration of Web services with already existing (Web) applications. Active rules could further serve for the coordination of service compositions, similar to the coordination of actors and work items in a WfMS (Charfi and Mezini, 2004; Daniel, Matera, and Pozzi, 2006).

- Exception handling is gaining more and more attention as a cross-cutting aspect in both WfMSs and service compositions. The adoption of active rules for the specification of exception handlers to react to application events has already proved its viability in the context of WfMSs (Casati et al., 1999; Combi, Daniel, and Pozzi, 2006). Their adoption for handling exception also in service compositions would thus represent a natural evolution.

- Time-critical systems or production and control systems, as well as the emerging approaches to self-healing software systems (Mok, Konana, Liu, Lee, and Woo, 2004; Minsky, 2003), intrinsically contain features or functionalities that are asynchronous with respect to the normal execution of the system (e.g., alerting the user of the occurrence of a production error). Their execution may indeed be required at any arbitrary time during system execution, and may thus not be predictable. Active rules are able to capture this peculiarity at an appropriate level of abstraction.

- Adaptive applications or context-aware, ubiquitous, mobile, and multi-channel applications incorporate active or reactive behaviors as functional system requirements (Wyse, 2006). The event-condition-action paradigm of active rules thus perfectly integrates with the logic of adaptivity, proper of such classes of software systems. The use of a dedicated rule engine for the execution of rules representing adaptivity requirements fosters the separation of concerns and the possibility of evolution of the overall system (Daniel, Matera, and Pozzi, 2006; Daniel, Matera, and Pozzi, 2008: Beer et al., 2003: Bonino da Silva Santos, L. O., van Wijnen, R. P., & Vink, P., 2007).

SUPPORTING ACTIVE BEHAVIORS IN APPLICATIONS

The above mentioned application areas show a wide range of potential applications of active mechanisms and rule engines. Current approaches, however, mainly operate on the data level and do not provide an adequate abstraction to also address application logic when specifying events, conditions, and actions. As a consequence, developing applications with active behaviors requires developers to address – each time anew – some typical problems:

- the definition of a set of events that trigger active behaviors and the development of suitable event management logic (the *event manager*);
- the implementation of generic and application-specific action *executors*, which enable the enactment of the actual active behaviors;
- possibly, the design of appropriate *rule metadata*, required to control rule execution and prioritization;

Figure 1. Without decoupled support for the management of active rules, each application internally needs to cater for suitable rule management functions and rule metadata

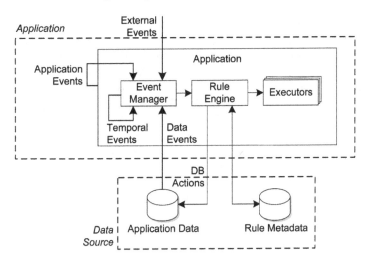

- the specification of a suitable *rule specification formalism*; and
- the development of an according rule interpretation and execution logic (the *rule engine*).

Figure 1 arranges the previous design concerns into a possible architecture for active applications. Of course, in most cases, the described modules and features might not be as easily identifiable, because the respective functions are buried in the application code or because they are just not thought of as independent application features. Nevertheless, conceptually we can imagine the internal architecture be structured like in Figure 1.

Typically, we classify events as *application events*, *data events*, *temporal events*, or *external events*. Application events originate from the inside of the application; data events originate from the application's data source; temporal events originate from the system clock; and external events originate from the outside of the application. All possible events in active applications can be re-conducted to these four classes of events (Eder and Liebhart, 1995).

Given the previous considerations, developing active application may represent a cumbersome undertaking. We however believe that developers can largely be assisted in the development of such applications by introducing a dedicated, detached rule execution environment that extracts the previously described active components from applications and acts as intermediate layer between the application's data and its application logic. This further fosters the separation of concerns between application logic and (independent) active behaviors and the reuse and maintainability of active rules.

The idea is graphically shown in Figure 2. Applications provide for the necessary *application events* (now *external events* with respect to the rule engine) and the set of action *executors* that enact the respective active behaviors; each application may have its own set of executors. The *customizable rule engine* allows the applications to delegate the capturing of data events, temporal events, and external events as well as the management of the set of rules that characterize the single applications. The rule engine includes the necessary logic for maintaining suitable *rule metadata* for multiple applica-

Figure 2. The introduction of a decoupled rule engine may largely assist the development of active applications

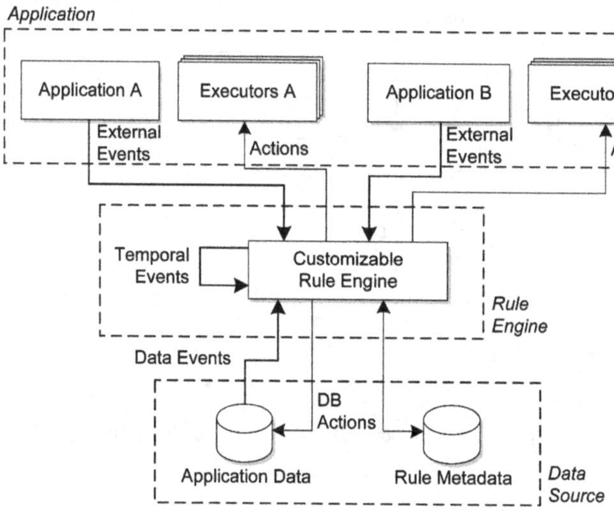

tions. The described architecture requires thus to address the following research topics:

- the specification of a customizable *rule specification language*;
- the development of a proper *runtime framework* for rule evaluation;
- the provisioning of easy *extension/customization mechanisms* for the tailoring of the generic rule engine to application-specific requirements.

In the following, we propose the OES system, a rule execution environment that provides an implementation of the idea expressed in Figure 2. OES is based on the so-called OpenChimera language for rule specification and provides for advanced customization support.

THE OES SYSTEM

The OES system consists of two main logical components that complement each other: the OpenChimera rule language for the definition of active behaviors and the OES rule engine

for the execution of OpenChimera rules. Both rule language and rule engine are extensible and easily customizable, in order to be able to manage application-specific events, conditions, and actions.

The OpenChimera Language

The OpenChimera language is derived from the Chimera-Exception language (Casati et al., 1999), a language for the specification of expected exceptions in WfMSs. Chimera-Exception is based, in turn, on the Chimera language (Ceri and Fraternali, 1997) for active DBMSs. OpenChimera builds on an object-oriented formalism, where classes are typed and represent records of typed attributes that can be accessed by means of a simple dot-notation. Rules adhere to the following structure:

```
define trigger <TriggerName>
  events      <Event> [(,<Event>)+]
  condition [<Cond> [(,<Cond>)+]|none]
  actions     <Action> [(,<Action>+)]
  [order <PriorityValue>]
end
```

A trigger <TriggerName> has one or more disjunctive triggering events (<Event>), a condition with one or more conjunctive conditional statements (<Cond>), and one or more actions (<Action>) to be performed in case the condition of the triggered rule holds. Rules may have an associated priority (<PriorityValue>) in the range from 0 (lowest) to 1000 (highest). Priorities enable the designer to define a rule execution order.

Events

Events in OES can be specified according to the following taxonomy:

- *Data events* enable the monitoring of operations that change the content of data stored in the underlying (active) DBMS. Similarly to rules in active databases, monitored events are insert, delete, and update. Data events are detected at the database level by defining suitable rules (or triggers) for the adopted active DBMS.
- *External events* must be first registered by applications in order to be handled properly. External events are recognized by means of the raise primitive, which – when an external event occurs – provides the name of the triggering event and suitable parameters (if needed).
- *Temporal events* are related to the occurrence of a given timestamp and are based on the internal clock of the system. In order to cope with a worldwide environment, all the temporal references of these events are converted to the GMT time zone. Temporal events are categorized as instant, periodic and interval events:
- *Instant events* are expressed as constants preceded by an @-sign (e.g. @timestamp "December 15th, 2008, 18:00:00");
- *Periodic events* are defined using the during keyword, separating the start of the

event from the respective time interval (e.g. 1/days during weeks denotes the periodic time defined by the first day of each week). The full notation and additional details can be found in (Casati et al., 1999);
- *Interval events* are expressed as elapsed duration since instant, where instant is any type of event used as anchor event (e.g. elapsed (interval 1 day) since modify (amount)).

Conditions

Conditions bind elements and perform tests on data. Since the adopted mechanism for rule execution is detached, i.e. the triggering event and the rule execution take place in two separate transactions, at rule execution time the context of the triggering event is reconstructed for condition evaluation. For instance, if we consider a data event triggered by the modification of a tuple, the occurred predicate of the OpenChimera language is used to select only the tuples that have really been modified and on which the trigger can, possibly, execute the specified action.

Actions

Standard actions that can be performed include changes to the database and notifications via e-mail messages. Other application-specific actions can be defined by means of external executors. Several executors may be available, each one typically dedicated to one specific action. As we shall show in Section 5, the customization of the actions that are available for rule definition represent the real value of the OES system.

The OES Rule Engine

The internal architecture of the OES system, detailed in Figure 3, is composed of: Rule Compiler, Event Manager, Scheduler, Interpreter, DB access API, and Dispatcher. The main features

Figure 3. The architecture of the autonomous ECA server OES

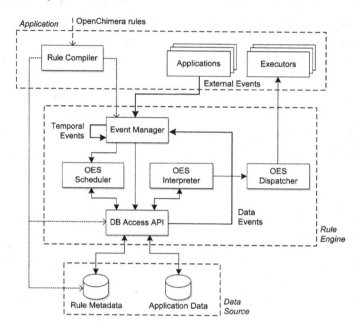

of the constituent modules are described in the following.

- *OES Rule Compiler*: The Compiler accepts rules at rule creation time and translates them into an intermediate execution language, proper configurations of the Event Manager, and suitable rule metadata that are accessed at rule evaluation time. The Compiler is invoked by specifying (i) the name of the file containing the source code of the rule and (ii) the name of a file containing a Data Dictionary for the specific application domain, which is basically a standard text file describing the data types used for type checking at compile time.

Besides rule compilation, the Compiler is also in charge of rule management: commands inside a source file provided in input to the compiler allow the developer to add new rules (define trigger), to remove existing rules (remove trigger), or to modify existing rules (modify trigger), thus enabling an incremental rule definition and a flexible rule management.

- *OES Event Manager*: The Event Manager is sensitive to external and temporal events. For the correct interpretation of interval events, the module registers those events that are used as anchor events and raises the actual event only once the respective interval has elapsed. Instant and periodical events are managed by means of a proper WakeUpRequest service. Finally, the Event Manager may invoke the OES Scheduler directly if a real-time event is raised.

- *OES Scheduler*: The Scheduler periodically determines the rule instances which have been triggered by monitoring the rule metadata and schedules triggered rules for execution according to the rules' priorities. The Scheduler is automatically invoked in a periodical fashion, but it can also be invoked directly by the Event Manager: this forces an immediate scheduling of the respective rule, still respecting possible priority constraints.

- *OES Interpreter*: The Interpreter is called by the OES Scheduler to execute a specific rule in the intermediate language. The

Interpreter evaluates the rule's condition and computes respective parameters. If a condition holds, actions are performed via the DB access API or via the OES Dispatcher.

- *OES Dispatcher*: The Dispatcher provides a uniform interface for the execution of actions by external executors and hides their implementation details to OES. External executors play a key role in the customization of the system.
- *OES DB Access API*: The DB Access API provides a uniform access to different DBMSs. At installation time, OES is configured with the driver for the specific DBMS adopted. Specific drivers are needed, since OES also exploits some DBMS-specific functionalities for the efficient execution of database triggers.

CUSTOMIZING THE OES SYSTEM

As described in the previous section, OES comes with a default set of generic events and actions; domain-specific events and actions can be specified in form of external events and suitable external executors. Hence, if the default set of events and actions suffices the needs of the developer, he/she can immediately define rules without performing any additional customization. If, instead, domain-or application-specific events and actions are required, he/she needs to customize the OES system.

Customizing Events

New events are specified as *external events*, which are supported by the OES system through a proper raising mechanism. External events must be registered in the OES system, in order to enable their use in the definition of OpenChimera triggers. If notified of the occurrence of an external event,

OES inserts a respective tuple into the rule metadata. The metadata is periodically checked by the OES Scheduler and enables condition evaluation and action execution.

When customizing events, the customizer has to implement the external program(s) that might raise the event(s). Communications between external program(s) and OES are enabled through a CORBA message passing mechanism. We observe that if the adopted DBMS has no active behavior, no data event can be defined; temporal and external events, instead, can be normally defined, detected, and managed as they do not require any specific active behavior from the DBMS.

Customizing Conditions

The syntax of OpenChimera conditions can be extended with new data types, abstracting tables in the underlying database. The definition of new types occurs by means of a so-called *Data Dictionary*, which is a standard text file containing a name and a set of attributes for each new data type. At rule compilation time, the OES Compiler, besides rule definitions themselves, requires the Data Dictionary to evaluate the proper use of data types for the variables included in the trigger definition. The definition of the Data Dictionary is the only situation where the Compiler has to read data that are specific to the application domain.

OES adopts a detached trigger execution model, where the triggering part of a rule is detected in one transaction, and the condition and action parts of the trigger are executed in another transaction. The definition of suitable data types in the Data Dictionary allows OES to reconstruct at condition evaluation time the status of the transaction in which the rule was triggered.

Customizing Actions

Adding a new action to the syntax of the OpenChimera language requires adding suitable descriptions and action executors to a so-called *Action Dictionary*. At rule compilation time, if the OES Compiler encounters an action that is not included in the set of predefined actions, it checks whether the specified action is included in a specific view in the database (the view Action-Dictionary can be seen in Figure 6) by searching the specified action in the ActionName attribute of the table Action. If the action is described in the view and its signature (as specified by the Action_Tag table) complies with the parameters of the rule to be compiled, the action is valid. If the OES Compiler fails in finding a matching tuple in the Action Dictionary, a suitable error message is generated. At rule execution time, the OES Interpreter processes the rule and the OES Dispatcher invokes the specified executor, as defined by the Action Dictionary, launching it as a child process.

Executors in OES can be characterized according to three orthogonal aspects: the location of the executor, dynamic vs. static parameters, and XML support:

- *Location*. Executors can be either *local* applications, running on the same system where OES is running, or *remote* services accessible via the Internet. We observe that services, even if running on the same system as OES, are always considered remote services.

- *Parameters*. Executors typically require input data. Parameters can be *dynamically* computed by the OES Interpreter at run time, or they can be *statically* defined. If dynamic parameters are required, the Interpreter performs a query over the application data, computes the actual parameters, and writes them into an XML file. Static parameters can be directly taken from the definition of the action and added to the XML file.

- *XML support*. Some executors are able to parse XML files, others do not. If an executor parses XML, it is up to the executor to extract the parameters correctly. If an executor does not parse XML, an intermediate parser is used to extract the parameters from the XML file and to invoke the executor, suitably passing the required parameters.

According to the above criteria, executors are divided into the following categories:

a) *Commands*. Local applications with static parameters that are not capable of parsing XML. The Dispatcher of OES constructs the command line and invokes the local system service according to the parameters stored in the Executor table of Figure 6. Such an executor is identified by the attribute CommandType="CMD", e.g. this may happen for a periodical backup service performed via the tar command of a Unix system.

b) *Executors capable of reading XML files*. Dynamic parameters are computed by the OES Interpreter and stored in an XML file. The executor, in turn, can be a local application or a client connecting to a remote service. Executors reading XML files are classified as follows:

   b1) *Local applications*. The Dispatcher of OES invokes the local application and passes it the name of the XML file with the parameters.

   b2) *Client connecting to an XML-enabled remote service*. The Dispatcher of OES starts a client application that connects to the remote service and sends the XML file via the HTTP POST method. The executor, in turn, may reply with another XML file, e.g. containing the results or the return code of the service.

c) *Executors not capable of reading XML files*. Dynamic parameters are computed by the OES Interpreter and stored in an XML file.

The invocation of the executors is performed via specific, intermediate parsers, which extract the necessary parameters from the XML file and invoke the executors by suitably passing the required dynamic parameters. Analogously to XML-enabled executors, not XML-enabled executors are classified as follows:

c1) *Local applications.* The parser invokes the local application passing it the dynamic parameters in the appropriate format.

c2) *Client connecting to a remote service which is not XML-enabled.* The parser sets up a client-server connection with the remote service and passes it the dynamic parameters in the appropriate format, possibly receiving results back.

It can be observed that executors not capable of reading XML files are internally treated like executors capable of reading XML files by leveraging an intermediate layer of suitable parsers, one parser for each specific executor. Figure 4 summarizes the taxonomy of executors.

CASE STUDY – THE AUCTION WEB SITE

In order to show how to customize OES in practice, we consider an auction web-site, where a seller can monitor the auction prices at which the market accepts to sell goods.

The potential seller of a given good would like to be notified via an e-mail message if the auction price of the same good sold by other sellers exceeds predefined limits, in order to understand whether the prices paid by the buyers of that good meet his/her expectations or not. If yes, the seller posts the offer to the auction web site; if not, he/she keeps the good. Auction prices are checked every 30 minutes during working days. Figure 5 shows an excerpt of the data structure underlying the auction software, to be used for the integration with OES: the good table represents the current status of the auctions, the notification table represents the notifications set up by the sellers, and the customer table identifies the sellers.

As we shall show in the following, supporting the required e-mail feature requires the OES system to be extended with two new actions: one (updateAuctionPrice) for the periodic update of the auction prices, and one (sendEMail) to send the e-mail notification message.

Customizing OpenChimera and the Rule Engine

The event for the periodic update of the stock price in the underlying database is a *periodic temporal event*, while the event triggering the sending of the e-mail notification is a *data event*. As both events are default OpenChimera events, no customization of OpenChimera events needs to be performed.

The definition of suitable conditions over the database tables described in Figure 5, requires

Figure 4. Taxonomy of executors

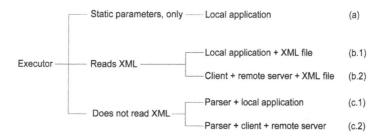

the definition of according data types in the Data Dictionary. More precisely, the three data types good, notification, and customer, referring to the respective tables in the database, must be included into the Data Dictionary, in order to be able to bind variables to them and formulate proper data queries.

The two new actions (updateAuctionPrice and sendEMail) can be made available to the OpenChimera environment by means of two new tuples in the Action table of the OES system. In table Action_Tag of Figure 6, the three tuples with attribute ActionName set to sendEMail or upda-

teAuctionPrice, respectively, serve this purpose and conclude the customization of the OpenChimera syntax. For the customization of the rule engine, we need to implement and to register the two actions sendEMail and updateAuctionPrice as external executors.

As for the sendEMail action, the transmission of the e-mail message to the specified e-mail address is performed free of charge by the Web site. Our executor for the new defined sendEmail action thus connects to a suitable Web server and requests the transmission of the messages. We assume that the executor myMailer serves this

Figure 5. The goods, customer, and notification tables as defined by the management software

good

name	value	timeStamp
myPhone	89.99	09:14 GMT 28-Nov-2008
myTennisBat	182.49	09:25 GMT 28-Nov-2008

notification

customerId	goodName	price	active
19153	myPhone	99.99	yes
19161	myPhone	84.99	yes
19153	myTennisBat	197.50	no

customer

Id	eMailAddress
19153	seller@auction
19161	peter@auction

Figure 6. Action-Dictionary view: Action, Executor, and Action_Tag tables. By joining them on the ExecutorId and on the ActionName attributes, we obtain the Action-Dictionary view. The Action_Tag table is used to check the signature of executors at rule compilation time. The names of system tables and of related attributes are capitalized

Action

ActionName	Priority	CommandType	CommandRequest	ExecutorId
sendSMS	10	XML	/usr/local/bin/myBrowser	22
sendEMail	5	XML	/usr/bin/myMailer	25
Backup	1	CMD	/usr/local/bin/tar	30
updateAuctionPrice	20	XML	/usr/local/bin/myUpdateAuction	6

Executor

ExecutorId	Location	Par1	Par2	Par3
22	http://freesms.jumpy.it			
6	http://luxuryauction.com			
30	localhost	-xvf	/usr/home/agents	/dev/rmt8
25	http://mymailer.mail			

Action_Tag

ActionName	Tag	Pos
sendSMS	CellNumber	1
sendSMS	CellMessage	2
sendEMail	ESubject	1
sendEMail	EAddressee	2
sendEMail	EText	3
updateAuctionPrice	GoodName	1

purpose. The definition of the new action requires thus the insertion of a new tuple into the Action table and the definition of proper attributes (see Figure 6):

- ActionName defines the name of the action;
- Priority defines the default priority for the action (i.e. 10), which can be overwritten by means of the order statement in the rule definition;
- CommandType defines whether the action corresponds to an executor not capable of reading XML files and with static parameters ("CMD"), or an XML-enabled executor ("XML");
- CommandRequest defines the actual invocation command to be launched by the Dispatcher;
- ExecutorId is the unique identifier of the executor.

We consider now the action named sendEMail with executor id 25: CommandType is "XML", indicating that the executor is XML-enabled. CommandRequest is the name of the executor that receives the XML file via the command line, connects to the remote server, and forwards the XML file. The first tuple of the Action table thus binds the sendEMail action to a proper executor.

To complete the definition of the action, we have to specify how static parameters can be passed to the executor. Static parameters are defined by tuples in the Executor table (see Figure 6):

- ExecutorId is the unique identifier of the executor;
- Location defines the location where the executor can find the remote service, if needed. In fact, if the executor requires a remote service, the executor runs as a client, connects to a valid URL defined by Location, and sends out the XML file created by the

Interpreter. If Location is set to localhost, no remote service is needed;
- Par1, Par2, Par3 define the static parameters that may be used by local commands which are not capable of reading XML files. We recall that this kind of executors is labeled "CMD" in the attribute CommandType of the Action table.

As can be seen in Figure 6, the sendEMail action requires dynamic parameters that will be computed at runtime and stored in an XML file. Specified parameters are translated into suitable tags in the XML file and sorted according to the order in which they appear in the source code of the rule. Dynamic parameters are specified in the Action_Tag table:

- ActionName defines the name of the action;
- Tag is the name of the tag inside the XML file (tag names must match the Data Dictionary);
- Pos defines the order of the parameters to be used in the OpenChimera language.

Thus, if the action is sendEMail, the three corresponding tuples of Action_Tag define that the XML file to be sent to the executor must be constructed as follows: the first dynamic parameter is the subject of the e-mail message, the second dynamic parameter is the e-mail address of the seller, and the third dynamic parameter is the text of the e-mail message.

The specification of the executor for the updateAuctionPrice action is analogous to the one of the sendEMail executor. The information we need to store represents the auction price at a given time instant. To access this information, we again use an executor that uses the Web to accomplish its task by searching the Web for the auction price and storing it into the application's data source.

To make the action updateAuctionPrice available, we deploy a suitable executor, namely myUpdateAuction, available in the directory /usr/local/bin. Again, its inclusion into OES requires inserting a suitable tuple in the ActionDictionary view of Figure 6. The name of the action is updateAuctionPrice, its priority is 20, its type is "XML", the executor is myUpdateAuction, and the id is 6. Dynamic parameters for the executor are defined by the Action_Tag table: for the current action, the only dynamic parameter needed is the name of the stock. The executor myUpdateAuction thus receives in input an XML file containing the name of the stock and connects to the remote server. The invoked remote service replies with another XML file, from which myUpdateAuction reads the auction price and its timestamp as defined by the remote server, and stores these data in the database.

Specifying the Active Rules

Now we can specify the actual rules to define the required active behavior. For presentation purposes, we assume that all customers are interested in the "myPhone" good, only.

The myUpdateAuction executor accesses the DBMS and stores the good name, the current auction price and its timestamp in the good table. According to the customized syntax of the OpenChimera language, we can now define the periodicalAuctionUpdate rule as follows.

```
define trigger periodicalAuctionUpdate
  events      30/minutes during days
  condition   good(G), G.name="myPhone"
  actions     updateAuctionPrice(G.name)
end
```

The event part of the rule states that the rule must be invoked every 30 minutes. The condition part considers all the instances G of the good type (i.e., all the tuples inside the table named good) and selects only the tuples where G.name

equals "myPhone". The action part invokes the executor myUpdateAuction, corresponding to the updateAuctionPrice action. The OES Interpreter computes the required dynamic parameter by assigning the value "myPhone" to the tag GoodName inside the XML file passed to the myUpdateAuction executor. The periodicalAuctionUpdate rule thus periodically stores the price of the chosen stock in the database.

A second rule is needed to compare the stored price with the minimum price the seller is interested in. The respective data are stored in the database and can be accessed by the following rule priceOfGoodReached, in order to trigger possible e-mail notifications:

```
define trigger priceOfGoodReached
  events      modify(good.value)
  condition   good(G), notification(N),
customer(C),
              G.name=N.goodName,
N.customerId=C.Id,
              occurred(modify(good.
value),G),
              G.value>N.price,
N.active="yes"
  action      sendEMail("Monitored good
has reached minimum price",
              C.eMailAddress,
              "Good " + G.name + " reached
your specified
              minimum price. Its current
price is "
              + G.value + " euros."),
N.active="no"
end
```

The event part of the rule states that the rule must be invoked each time the attribute value of a tuple inside the good table is changed (data event). The condition part has a twofold goal. First, it aims at binding the instances of goods (G), of notification (N) and of customer (C). The binding states that the good must be related to a request of notification by an interested customer: this is performed by a join operation. Second, the conditions part verifies that tuples selected from the good table are only those for which there has been a change of the value attribute since the last execution of the rule (occurred(modify(good.value),G)), that the new price exceeds the specified threshold (G.value>N.Max)), and that the notification service is active (N.active="yes"). The action part is executed after all the conditions are true. The action invokes the executor sendEMail whose parameters are the subject of the email message, the e-mail address of the seller, and the body of the e-mail message including the auction price of the good. In order to prevent a continuous sending of the same message, a second action disables the notification service (N.active="no") for the sent message. Users can easily enable the service again through their stock management software.

IMPLEMENTATION

The OES system described in this paper is derived from the exception manager FAR (FORO Active Rules), developed within the EC project WIDE and aimed at managing expected exceptions in the workflow management system FORO (Casati et al., 1999). In the following, we shortly outline the architecture of the FAR system and show how OES has been unbundled from FAR. Then, we discuss termination, confluence, and security in OES.

The FAR System

Exception handling in WfMSs typically involves a wide scenario of events and actions. In the case of the FAR system, the rule engine is able to manage the following four categories of events (Casati et al., 1999): data events, temporal events, workflow events (e.g. the start or the end of a task or of a case), and external events. Concerning the actions that can be enacted through FAR, the rule engine supports the following actions: data manipula-

tion actions, workflow actions (e.g. the start or completion of a task or a process instance, the assignment of a task or case to a specific agent), and notification actions.

Figure 7 graphically summarizes the FORO/FAR architecture. Exceptions are specified by means of the active rule language Chimera-Exception (Casati et al., 1999), from which we derived the OpenChimera language adopted in OES. Besides data events (originating from an active Oracle database shared with the FORO system), temporal events and external events, FAR is directly notified of workflow events coming from the FORO workflow engine. On the action side, database actions are directly supported by the FAR system, while notifications and workflow actions are performed via the FORO workflow engine.

Unbundling the Rule Engine

The implementation of the OES system leveraged as much as possible the already existing implementation of the FAR system. Instead of developing a new rule engine from scratch, we decided to unbundle (Gatziu, Koschel, von Bultzingsloewen, and Fritschi, 1998; Silberschatz and Zdonik, 1997) the necessary functionalities and modules from the FORO/FAR system. When unbundling the rule engine from FORO/FAR, we had to re-consider all the interactions of the tightly-coupled, bundled modules. In particular, we had to consider how events are notified to the rule engine and how the rule engine enacts actions.

An extension of FAR's built-in support for both external events and external executors provided efficient means to enable users of OES (i.e., developers of active applications) to define application-specific events and actions. The unbundled OES system thus inherits the support for data events, temporal events, and external events from the FAR system, while workflow events are not supported any longer, due to the unbundling of the rule engine from the WfMS. Analogously,

Figure 7. FAR architecture and dependencies with FORO. FAR is bundled into FORO

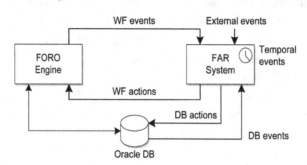

we were able to reuse FAR solutions to support the execution of database actions and the flexible definition of external executors for customizable actions; again, workflow-specific actions were discarded. The introduction of intermediate parsers allows OES to select appropriate executors according to the specifications received from the rule engine.

In order to be capable of detecting events and of performing actions, the unbundled OES system must implement suitable communication channels among the modules composing the system. For example, OES must be able to start transactions over a given DBMS and to invoke external applications, possibly passing some parameters. For the communication between internal modules, OES leverages CORBA and shared tables in the underlying database. While a shared database works fine for internal modules, the adoption of a specific DBMS (i.e., Oracle) may cause interoperability difficulties with external modules, such as external executors for customized actions. Therefore, the communication with external executors added to the OES system is based on XML as common format for accessing and sharing information. Data is passed in form of XML documents, containing possible static and/or dynamic parameter values or responses from the external executors.

Remarks

Termination

An active system guarantees *termination* if its rules are not allowed to trigger each other indefinitely. If we define a rule $r1$ that reacts to the event $e1$ by executing the action $a1$, which in turn triggers the event $e1$, the active system enters an endless loop if the condition of $r1$ always holds (*self-triggering*). We may also define a rule $r1$ that reacts to the event $e1$ by executing the action $a1$, which in turn triggers the event $e2$ of a rule $r2$ whose action $a2$ triggers again $e1$. Should the conditions of $r1$ and $r2$ always hold, the active system enters an endless loop (*cross-triggering*). Similarly, an active system may encounter a situation of *cascaded triggering*, if the endless cycle involves more than two rules.

Potential situations of non-termination can be avoided by *static* and *dynamic* checks. Compile time (static) detection is performed at rule compilation time by the OES Compiler: for each potential loop, it issues a proper warning message. The static check is performed by a suitable termination analysis machine, properly adapted to OES from (Casati et al., 1999). The resolution of possible loops is up to the developer.

Run time (dynamic) detection of loops is more complex in OES than in FAR, as involved actions can be external to OES itself. A self-triggering situation may occur when an action $a1$ invokes the server $s1$, which in turn invokes a server $s2$ that is external and unknown to OES, and $s2$ invokes another server $s3$, whose actions trigger the event $e1$ of $r1$. This self-triggering situation is very hard to detect, as it comes from subsequent server invocations outside OES. A simple yet effective *avoidance mechanism* is limiting the maximum cascading level for rules: rules are simply not allowed to trigger other rules indefinitely. OES (like most active DBMSs) adopts this solution and uses an upper limit for cascaded activations that can be easily configured. With respect to generic DBMSs, OES however does not limit this technique to data events only.

Confluence

In a system featuring active behaviors, *confluence* means that the final effect of the processing of multiple concurrently triggered rules is independent of the ordering by which rules are triggered and executed. The problem of confluence arises in many situations, like SQL triggers and stored procedures in most conventional database applications. Typically, those situations generate non-confluent behaviors, because actions are performed over sets of tuples, which by definition come with no ordering criteria.

The same consideration applies to OES: each rule is intrinsically non-confluent, because it associates a set-oriented, declarative condition with a tuple-oriented imperative action, and there is no language construct to impose a rule-internal order on the bindings that are selected by the condition evaluation part. If in OES we assume to trigger a rule t_1, its condition part may for instance return a set of n unordered data tuples to which the rule's actions are to be applied; at this point, we cannot say for sure in which order the actions are enacted, as this typically depends on the underlying active DBMS.

If, instead, we assume to trigger two (or more) rules t_1, t_2, the usage of priorities (i.e., the order token of OpenChimera) enables the designer to

define an ordering among the rules t_1, t_2, where the highest priority rule is processed first. This option enables the designer to state a partial order among the triggered rules t_1, t_2, but not an order that is internal to each rule.

Security

Security in OES relates to three different aspects: rule definition, event generation, and action execution. At *rule definition* time, the customizer logs into OES and uses the OES Compiler. As triggers and rule metadata are stored inside the DBMS, the security level provided by OES is the one provided by the DBMS.

At *event generation* time, security issues concern data events, temporal events, and external events. Data events require to access the DBMS and to insert, delete, or update data: again, the security level provided by OES is the one provided by the underlying DBMS. Temporal events are triggered by the internal clock of OES: their security level is the one provided by the operating system on which OES is running. External events are triggered by external applications: the security level of the entire system is the one implemented by the external application, which has however to be registered into OES by the customizer prior to being able to trigger any event.

At *action execution* time, security issues concern database actions and external actions. Database actions are preformed locally by OES itself, which connects to the local DBMS and performs all the actions defined by the involved rule over locally stored data: the security level provided by OES is the same as the one provided by the DBMS. External actions, instead, require OES to reach executors external to OES itself. The same criteria as those for external applications apply.

RELATED WORK

We consider now some relevant research areas where event management plays a key role.

Active Database Management Systems

The scenario of event management in active DBMSs is the most relevant one.

Samos (Dittrich et al., 2003) is a very complex active OODBMS, which provides several active functionalities, including event management similar to the one of OES. Samos runs coupled to the Object-Store passive OODBMS, only. OES, which is not an active DBMS but a pure event manager, can be mapped onto any active DBMS accepting the SQL language, and it provides suitable interfaces for most common DBMSs. Samos provides a very powerful event definition language, including relationships in event capturing (before..., after...), event composition (sequence..., conjunction...), and an execution model which accepts both attached and detached exception management. On the contrary, OES provides a very simple model featuring a numeric prioritization of rules and the only detached mode of execution.

Sentinel (Chakravarthy, 1997) was started as an OODBMS with event based rules capable of defining composite events by an extended set of operators. Later on, the authors (Chakravarthy and Liao, 2001) extended the system to include asynchronous events for a distributed cooperative environment, obtaining a server which is not connected to any particular DBMS, but runs as a message broker. With respect to Sentinel, OES adopts a more simplified event definition mechanism and language. OES can detect database modification events at the very database level, without requiring services from external event detectors, as required by Chakravarthy and Liao, 2001. According to OES, the event detection takes place only locally, even if in a distributed database environment, and

the consequent action – if needed – may require communication with other sites of the distributed environment. Thus, in OES distributed events cannot be defined directly but need to be mapped as sets of local events and of local actions. Local actions may also include communications among the sites of the distributed environment.

EvE (Geppert, Tombros, and Dittrich, 1998) is an event engine implementing event-driven execution of distributed workflows. Similarly to OES, EvE adopts a registration, detection, and management mechanism, and it runs on a distributed, multi-server architecture. The main differences of OES, with respect to EvE, are that: a) OES does not use rules to schedule tasks according to a process model for the managed business process defined inside the WfMS; b) OES does not select executors (brokers in EvE's terminology) at runtime, choosing from a pool of resources since only one executor is defined for every action; c) OES does not require a WfMS environment as a core unit. In fact, OES can be run as a completely autonomous ECA server and the definition of events is not related to any WfMS. OES is extremely free, autonomous, can reference heterogeneous executors and allows one to define almost any type of event.

Framboise (Fritschi, Gatziu, and Dittrich, 1998) is a framework for the construction of active DBMSs inheriting the rule language of Samos. Framboise represents a database middleware, extending (Dittrich et al., 2003) to provide individual and customizable active services for any arbitrary passive DBMS. With respect to Framboise, OES aims at providing active services exploiting ECA rules over an existing active DBMS, capable of accepting standard SQL statements and the definition of triggers. While the language of OES is much simpler than Framboise's, OES does not necessarily require a DBMS, thus limiting itself to manage temporal and external events. On the other hand, if the application domain requires a DBMS, data events can be managed by OES provided that the DBMS supports active behaviors. OES can be more conveniently mapped on most commercial active DBMS, without requiring to recompile the kernel of the active DBMS itself neither requiring to modify existing applications.

Workflow Management Systems

Some WfMSs - e.g., Mentor (Wodtke, Weißenfels, Weikum, Kotz Dittrich, and Muth, 1997), Meteor (Krishnakumar and Sheth, 1995) - allow one to define a task to be executed whenever a specified exception is detected and the related event is raised. Pitfalls for this solution are that there is a wide separation between the normal evolution flow and the exception management flow, and that an exception can only start as a new activity. Additionally, the detection of the event must be formally performed whenever a task is terminated and before the next one is started: the detection cannot be performed while a task is running. In other systems - e.g., ObjectFlow (Hsu and Kleissner, 1996) - a human agent is formally dedicated to the detection of asynchronous exceptions: after the event occurs, task execution is aborted and suitably defined execution paths are executed.

The use of OES coupled to a WfMS to manage asynchronous events overcomes some of these limitations. In fact, the detection of an event can take place even during the execution of a task, and not only after the completion of the task and before the successor is activated. Furthermore, the management of the exception can be completely automated, and may not require any human intervention to identify compensation paths.

Active Middleware Systems

Middleware technology aims at providing low- to medium-level services, which can be exploited by higher-level applications. In this area, Siena (Carzaniga, Rosenblum, and Wolf, 2001) is a wide area notification service, and it is mainly focused on scalability issues. With respect to OES, Siena can capture a reduced number of events, e.g. temporal events are not considered.

Amit (Adi and Etzion, 2004) is a "situation manager" which extends the concept of composite events. An event is a significant instantaneous atomic occurrence identified by the system; a situation requires the system to react to an event. The middleware aims at reducing the gap between events and situations. Amit comes with a situation definition language enabling one to capture events (immediate, delayed, deferred) and to detect situations. Applications are then notified when required situations occur.

López de Ipiña and Katsiri (2001) developed a CORBA-based event-condition-action (ECA) rule matching service, featuring a composite event matching engine. The provided rule specification language is translated to an intermediate language (CLIPS), while the architecture of the system has few similarities with the one proposed by OES. However, the expressiveness, the ease of coding, the customizability of external executors, and the variety of considerable events of the OpenChimera language are much richer.

CONCLUSION AND FUTURE WORK

In this paper, we described the autonomous, open ECA server OES and its active rule language, OpenChimera. OpenChimera supports the definition and the management of generic active rules following the Event-Condition-Action (ECA) paradigm, while the OES rule engine, derived from the FAR exception handler (Casati et al., 1999) of the FORO WfMS, supports the execution of OpenChimera rules.

OES comes with a standard set of events and actions. Events cover data manipulation events, temporal events, and events raised by external applications; the standard set of actions includes data manipulation actions. It is possible to customize the OES system to application- or domain-specific needs by adding new events and actions. OES can be coupled and customized with relatively little effort with any existing system that requires event and rule management solutions. The extended system allows designers to easily define application-specific active rules and to insulate active application requirements from the core application logic.

OES therefore fosters separation of concerns in the application development process (i.e., active and non-active requirements) and provides a robust solution to a cross-cutting implementation issue: active rule management. The nature of the OES rule engine minimizes the efforts required to integrate OES into other applications and further supports a flexible management of rules even after application deployment, i.e., during runtime. At design time, the built-in support for the detection of infinite loops represents a valuable tool to developers who typically have to deal with a multitude of rules and interdependencies.

ACKNOWLEDGMENT

We are grateful to Catia Garatti and Marco Riva for the implementation of the OES system, starting from FAR, and we thank prof. Stefano Ceri of Politecnico di Milano, Italy, prof. Stefano Paraboschi of the University of Bergamo, Italy, and prof. Fabio Casati of the University of Trento, Italy, for fruitful discussions and suggestions.

REFERENCES

Adi, A., & Etzion, O. (2004). Amit - the situation manager. *The VLDB Journal*, *13*(2), 177–203. doi:10.1007/s00778-003-0108-y

Amghar, Y., Meziane, M., & Flory, A. (2002). Using business rules within a design process of active databases. In S. Becker (Ed.), *Data Warehousing and Web Engineering* (pp. 161-184), Hershey, PA: IRM Press.

Beer, W., Volker, C., Ferscha, A., & Mehrmann, L. (2003) Modeling context-aware behavior by interpreted ECA rules. In H. Kosch, L. Böszörményi, & H. Hellwagner (Eds.), *Euro-Par 2003* (LNCS 2790, pp. 1064-1073).

Bonino da Silva Santos, L. O., van Wijnen, R. P., & Vink, P. (2007). A service-oriented middleware for context-aware applications. *MPAC*, (pp. 37-42). New York: ACM Press.

Carzaniga, A., Rosenblum, D. S., & Wolf, A. L. (2001). Design and evaluation of a wide-Area event notification service. *ACM Transactions on Computer Systems*, *19*(3), 332–383. doi:10.1145/380749.380767

Casati, F., Ceri, S., Paraboschi, S., & Pozzi, G. (1999). Specification and implementation of exceptions in workflow management systems. *ACM Transactions on Database Systems*, *24*(3), 405–451. doi:10.1145/328939.328996

Ceri, S., & Fraternali, P. (1997). *Designing database applications with objects and rules: the IDEA methodology*. Reading, MA: Addison-Wesley.

Ceri, S., Fraternali, P., Bongio, A., Brambilla, M., Comai, S., & Matera, M. (2002). *Designing Data-Intensive Web Applications*. San Francisco, CA: Morgan Kauffmann.

Chakravarthy, S. (1997). Sentinel: An object-oriented DBMS with event-based rules. In J. Peckham (Ed.), *SIGMOD Conference* (pp. 572-575). New York: ACM Press.

Chakravarthy, S., & Liao, H. (2001). Asynchronous monitoring of events for distributed cooperative environments. In H. Lu, & S. Spaccapietra (Eds.), *Proceedings of CODAS'01* (pp. 25-32). Beijing: IEEE Computer Society.

Charfi, A., & Mezini, M. (2004). Hybrid Web service composition: business processes meet business rules. In M. Aiello, M. Aoyama, F. Curbera, & M. P. Papazoglou (Eds.), *Proceedings of ICSOC'04* (pp. 30-38). New York: ACM Press.

Combi, C., Daniel, F., & Pozzi, G. (2006). A portable approach to exception handling in workflow management systems. In R. Meersman & Z. Tari (Eds.), *OTM Conferences (1)*, LNCS 4275 (pp. 201-218). Montpellier, France: Springer Verlag.

Combi, C., & Pozzi, G. (2003). Temporal conceptual modelling of workflows. In I. Song, S. W. Liddle, T. Wang Ling, & P. Scheuermann (Eds.), *Proceedings of ER'03* (LNCS 2813, pp. 59-76).

Combi, C., & Pozzi, G. (2004). Architectures for a temporal workflow management system. In H. Haddad, A. Omicini, R. L. Wainwright, & L. M. Liebrock (Eds.), *Proceedings of SAC'04* (pp. 659-666). New York: ACM Press.

Cugola, G., Di Nitto, E., & Fuggetta, A. (2001). The JEDI event-based infrastructure and its application to the development of the OPSS wfMS. *IEEE Transactions on Software Engineering*, *27*(9), 827–850. doi:10.1109/32.950318

Daniel, F., Matera, & Pozzi, G. (2008). Managing runtime adaptivity through active rules: the Bellerofonte framework. *Journal of Web Engineering*, *7*(3), 179–199.

Daniel, F., Matera, M., & Pozzi, G. (2006). Combining conceptual modeling and active rules for the design of adaptive web applications. In N. Koch & L. Olsina (Eds.), *ICWE'06 Workshop Proceedings* (article no.10). New York: ACM Press.

Dittrich, K. R., Fritschi, H., Gatziu, S., Geppert, A., & Vaduva, A. (2003). Samos in hindsight: experiences in building an active object-oriented DBMS. *Information Systems Journal*, *28*(5), 369–392. doi:10.1016/S0306-4379(02)00022-4

Eder, J., & Liebhart, W. (1995). The workflow activity model WAMO. In S. Laufmann, S. Spaccapietra, & T. Yokoi (Eds.), *Proceedings of CoopIS'95* (pp. 87-98). Vienna, Austria.

Fritschi, H., Gatziu, S., & Dittrich, K. R. (1998). Framboise - an Approach to framework-based active database management system construction. In G. Gardarin, J. C. French, N. Pissinou, K. Makki, & L. Bouganim (Eds.), *Proceedings of CIKM '98* (pp. 364-370). New York: ACM Press.

Gatziu, S., Koschel, A., von Bultzingsloewen, G., & Fritschi, H. (1998). Unbundling active functionality. *SIGMOD Record*, *27*(1), 35–40. doi:10.1145/273244.273255

Geppert, A., Tombros, D., & Dittrich, K. R. (1998). Defining the semantics of reactive components in event-driven workflow execution with event histories. *Information Systems Journal*, *23*(3-4), 235–252. doi:10.1016/S0306-4379(98)00011-8

Hsu, M., & Kleissner, C. (1996). Objectflow: towards a process management infrastructure. *Distributed and Parallel Databases*, *4*(2), 169–194. doi:10.1007/BF00204906

Huang, S., Hung, S., Yen, D., Li, S., & Wu, C. (2006). Enterprise application system reengineering: a business component approach . *Journal of Database Management*, *17*(3), 66–91.

Krishnakumar, N., & Sheth, A. P. (1995). Managing heterogeneous multi-system tasks to support enterprise-wide operations. *Distributed and Parallel Databases*, *3*(2), 155–186. doi:10.1007/BF01277644

Li, S. H., Huang, S. M., Yen, D. C., & Chang, C. C. (2007). Migrating legacy information systems to web services architecture. *Journal of Database Management, 18*(4), 1–25.

López de Ipiña, D., & Katsiri, E. (2001). An ECA rule-matching service for simpler development of reactive applications, *Middleware 2001*. IEEE Distributed Systems Online, *2*(7).

Loucopoulos, P., & Kadir, W. M. N. W. (2008). BROOD: Business rules-driven object oriented design. *Journal of Database Management Systems, 19*(1), 41–73.

Minsky, N. H. (2003). On conditions for self-healing in distributed software systems. [Los Alamitos, CA: IEEE Computer Society.]. *Proceedings of AMS, 03*, 86–92.

Mok, A. K., Konana, P., Liu, G., Lee, C., & Woo, H. (2004). Specifying timing constraints and composite events: an application in the design of electronic brokerages. *IEEE Transactions on Software Engineering, 30*(12), 841–858. doi:10.1109/TSE.2004.105

Chapter 13
Dimensions of UML Diagram Use:
Practitioner Survey and Research Agenda

Brian Dobing
University of Lethbridge, Canada

Jeffrey Parsons
Memorial University of Newfoundland, Canada

ABSTRACT

The Unified Modeling Language (UML) is an industry standard for object-oriented software engineering. However, there is little empirical evidence on how the UML is used. This chapter reports results of a survey of UML practitioners. The authors found differences in several dimensions of UML diagram usage on software development projects, including frequency, the purposes for which they were used, and the roles of clients/users in their creation and approval. System developers are often ignoring the "Use Case-driven" prescription that permeates much of the UML literature, making limited or no use of either Use Case Diagrams or textual Use Case descriptions. Implications and areas requiring further investigation are discussed.

INTRODUCTION

The Unified Modeling Language (UML) emerged in the mid-1990s through the combination of previously competing Object-Oriented Analysis and Design (OOAD) approaches (Rumbaugh, Blaha, Premerlani, Eddy, and Lorensen, 1991; Jacobson, Christerson, Jonsson, and Overgaard, 1992; Booch, 1994), along with other contributions to modeling complex systems (e.g., Harel, 1987). Control over its formal evolution was placed in the hands of the

DOI: 10.4018/978-1-60566-904-5.ch013

Object Management Group (www.omg.org), which oversaw a major revision to Version 2 in 2006 (Selic, 2006) and recently released the UML 2.2 (Object Management Group, 2009). The UML became widely accepted as the standard for OOAD soon after its introduction (Kobryn, 1999) and remains so today (Evermann and Wand, 2006). A large number of practitioner articles and dozens of textbooks have been devoted to articulating various aspects of the language, including guidelines for using it. More recently, a substantial body of research on the UML has emerged, including ontological analysis of its modeling constructs (Evermann and Wand,

2001a, 2001b) and a more recent empirical assessment (Evermann and Wand, 2006), analysis of the language's complexity (Siau and Cao, 2001, 2002; Erickson and Siau, 2007), related learning difficulties (Siau and Loo, 2006) and means to address them (Batra and Satzinger, 2006), and experiments that evaluate various aspects of the effectiveness of UML models (Burton-Jones and Weber, 2003, Burton-Jones and Meso, 2006). Batra (2008, p.i) also lists a number of recent UML research areas.

The UML was not developed based on any theoretical principles regarding the constructs required for an effective and usable modeling language for analysis and design; instead, it arose from (sometimes conflicting) "best practices" in parts of the software engineering community (Booch, 1999; Booch, Rumbaugh, and Jacobson, 1999). This resulted in a language containing many modeling constructs, which has thus been criticized on the grounds that it is excessively complex (Dori, 2002; Kobryn, 2002; DeJong, 2006). However, more recently research has suggested the "practical complexity" is not as great (Siau, Erickson and Lee, 2005; Erikson and Siau, 2007). At the same time, the UML has also been criticized for lacking the flexibility to handle certain modeling requirements in specific domains (Duddy, 2002) . As a consequence, the UML has evolved to allow for the definition of "profiles" that have enabled Domain Specific Languages (Cook, 2000; DeJong, 2006).

While the UML is intended to be "largely process-independent," some of the key originators recommend a Use Case-driven process (e.g., Booch et al., 1999, p.33). A majority of UML books since then have endorsed this view, and most contain at least some further prescriptions for applying the language in modeling (Stevens and Pooley, 2000; Schneider and Winters, 2001; Larman, 2005). As would be expected with a best practices approach, their prescriptions sometimes differ. While some accept the original view that only Use Case Narratives (or, more simply, Use

Cases) be used to verify requirements with users (Jacobson, Ericsson, and Jacobson, 1994), others explicitly or implicitly indicate that other UML diagrams can be used for this purpose, e.g., Activity Diagrams "can be safely shared with customers, even those unfamiliar with software engineering" (Schneider and Winters, 2001, p.67).

There are also differences in guidelines for using the language, and Use Case Narratives in particular (Dobing and Parsons, 2000). This is not surprising since the official UML documentation (currently 2.2) has never provided guidance on Narrative format, stating only that "use cases are typically specified in various idiosyncratic formats such as natural language, tables, trees, etc." (Object Management Group, 2009, p.592). However, there is no shortage of information on Use Cases. As of November 2009, Amazon.com lists nine books with "Use Case" in the title (related to system modeling), but none with "Class Diagram" (although there are many UML books covering both). Finally, when the Use Case-driven approach is used, concerns have been raised about the potential communication disconnect (Dobing and Parsons, 2000) that can occur when Use Cases are the primary communication tool among analysts and the clients/users on the project team while Class Diagrams play that role among analysts and programmers. While Use Case Narratives have been found to be the most comprehensible artifact for managers, users and domain experts, and even more so when used with Use Case Diagrams (Gemino and Parker, 2008), they are the least comprehensible for designers and programmers (Arlow and Neustadt, 2004) when they require knowledge of the organizational context that programmers do not have. Conversely, Class Diagrams are highly comprehensible by programmers, but not clients/users (Arlow and Neustadt, 2004).

In view of these issues, it would not be surprising to find a variety of practices followed by UML practitioners. We believe understanding current practice can make an important contribution to both theoretical and applied research on UML. From a theoretical perspective, understanding how the language is used can support or challenge theoretical analyses of UML capabilities and deficiencies (Evermann and Wand, 2001a, 2001b). From a practical perspective, usage patterns can inform best practices.

However, to our knowledge, only two previous surveys addressed the extent to which UML diagrams are used in practice (Zeichick, 2002; Grossman, Aronson, and McCarthy, 2005) and neither examined why analysts choose to use some diagrams and ignore others. (We are defining "UML diagram" to include Use Case Narratives, even though they are generally used to describe Use Cases in text form.) Moreover, there have been few field studies of any type on the UML; Erikson (2008, p.iv) summarizes those that have been done. This is particularly surprising in view of the explosion of academic interest in UML. Our research seeks to address this issue by surveying UML use in practice.

Our objective was to study three key dimensions of UML diagram usage: how often each diagram was being used, the reasons why analysts chose to use or avoid them (emphasizing their role in facilitating team communication), and the roles of clients/users in their creation and approval. Such an understanding can also support the development of theory to explain observed usage patterns. From a practical point of view, understanding how the language is used can help support its evolution. For example, if certain parts of the language are not widely used or seen as useful, further research is needed to understand why this is so, and may lead to evolution or elimination of those parts.

RESEARCH METHODOLOGY

The research began with participation in a local UML user group, along with mostly informal interviews of about a dozen UML practitioners (none belonging to that user group and most in different cities) and some of their clients. Their approaches to using UML all differed to some degree from each other, some substantially. Some of the differences can be attributed to situational factors. For example, one project began with the database, and the associated Class Diagram, already in place. In other projects, analysts took a Use Case-driven approach and relied on someone else to do the Class Diagram later. Some clients wrote most of the Use Cases themselves, while others reviewed them.

The level of Use Case modeling varied, even in systems of roughly the same size, from a small number (less than 20) of relatively short Use Cases to much larger sets of detailed Use Cases and Scenarios (usually defined as paths through a Use Case illustrating its application to particular instances) that attempted to capture very complex rules and regulations. The use of other UML diagrams depended on the analyst's knowledge of how to use them, client requests (e.g., one client insisted on at least one Activity Diagram for every Use Case), system domain, and other factors. Some learned the UML by starting with only a few of the diagram types while others took a more ambitious approach and attempted to use them all.

To get a broader picture of UML usage, a web survey was developed based on the preliminary interviews and a literature review. The survey contained 38 questions, many with multiple parts (e.g., a list of possible reasons for not using a particular UML diagram). Both the survey and this paper use UML 1.5 terminology, such as "Collaboration Diagrams" rather than the newer "Communication Diagrams." The original survey was first reviewed by colleagues and then pretested with two people involved in the interviews and one who had not been. Minor wording changes were made to several questions as a result. The pretest data were retained because the changes made were consistent with what these subjects had in mind.

Table 1. Respondent Experience in Years and Projects

	Mean	Median	Max	Std Dev	N
Yrs Experience IT	15.1	14.0	45	9.2	96
Yrs Experience OO Prog	8.4	7.5	25	5.1	95
Yrs Experience OOAD	7.4	6.0	25	4.7	95
Yrs Experience UML	4.7	5.0	10	2.4	101
Yrs Experience OO DB	2.5	0.5	20	4.1	84
All IT Projects	27.0	15.0	200	32.6	93
No. of UML Projects	6.2	4.0	51	7.0	168
Other OO Projects	4.0	2.0	50	7.6	127

The survey was intended for the population of analysts familiar with object-oriented techniques and UML in particular. To obtain a sample of such analysts, the OMG was contacted and they agreed to support the project. Their members were informed by email of the survey and the OMG endorsement. A link to the survey was also provided from the main OMG web page. OMG members were encouraged to share the link with others using the UML in their organizations. Subsequently, an invitation to participate in the survey was posted to the comp.object Usenet newsgroup. No participation incentive was offered. Some limitations of this approach are discussed later. However, other researchers in this area (e.g., Johnson and Hardgrave, 1999; Grossman et al., 2005) have used similar methods due to the difficulty of finding more representative samples.

RESULTS

Almost 2700 hits on the survey site were recorded during the survey period from March 21, 2003 to March 31, 2004. About half (1369) provided no response to any item. After eliminating these responses along with test data, minimal responses, meaningless or invalid responses, and inappropriate respondents (primarily students), there were 284 usable responses. While these criteria are difficult to define precisely, invalid responses were easily identified in practice based on either meaningless numerical entries (e.g., 1 for all entries including budget, number of classes, etc.) or comments that showed the response was not serious. Any response that had meaningful comments was included, no matter how incomplete. The 284 analyzed responses either contained data on UML diagram usage (182) or reasons why the UML was not being used (102). Of the 182 analysts using UML diagrams, most (171) responded that they were using the UML while 11 indicated they were using some UML diagrams in conjunction with other modeling approaches.

Demographic Data

The survey gathered some data on respondent experience in IT, but did not ask about age, gender or nationality. Respondents have a wide range of experience in the IT field, reporting up to 45 years and 200 projects (Table 1). Their UML experience is understandably less. In all cases, the minimum value reported was zero except for Years of Experience in IT (2 years) and All IT Projects (3). While respondents report more project experience with UML than other object-oriented approaches, it represents less than a quarter of their projects and about a third of their years of experience. The figures reported for Years of Experience with OOAD include both UML and non-UML experience.

Table 2. "Typical" Project Sizes

	Budget (US 000$)	Person Years	Lines Of Code	Use Cases	Classes
Mean	5 342	57.5	478 910	88	1311
Median	1 000	6.5	50 000	35	150
Maximum	75 000	3 000	5 000 000	800	25 000
Std Dev	12 000	297	1 050 000	137	4 215
N	71	118	64	75	95

The survey also asked in what type of industry the respondent was primarily employed, either as a direct employee or as a consultant. Respondents could select only one industry. Of the respondents using the UML who provided their industry type, 47% were in software development, 13% in financial services, and 8% each in education, aerospace and defense, and health care and pharmaceuticals. About 44% also indicated they were associated with their industry through a consulting firm.

The survey asked respondents, "How large are the typical object oriented and/or UML projects you have worked on?" Table 2 shows the results, with budgets in U.S. dollars (with euros and Canadian dollars taken at par). The Use Cases and Classes measures reflect both the size of the project and the extent to which these diagrams were used and exclude responses where they were not used at all. The inclusion of a few very large reported project sizes skewed the means, so the medians are also reported.

Overall UML Diagram Usage

Table 3 shows the relative usage of UML analysis diagrams, with our results compared to others (Zeichick, 2002; Grossman et al., 2005). To keep our survey to a reasonable length, we only asked about Use Case Narratives and UML diagrams covering system structure and behavior that are used to document system functionality. This excluded the Object Diagram, which is closely related to the Class Diagram, and the Component and Deployment Diagrams, used in application architecture modeling. Respondents were asked, "What proportion of the object-oriented/UML projects that you have been involved with have used the following UML components?" The five-point Usage scale was: None, <1/3, 1/3 – 2/3, > 2/3 and All. The question asked about diagrams used in projects rather than personally by the respondent because the initial interviews found that team members often specialized in one or a few diagrams (e.g., focusing on Use Case Narratives or the Class Diagram).

Although the UML is often presented as being used with a Use Case-driven approach in the UML literature, and in particular by the Unified Process (Jacobson et al., 1999), only 44% of respondents report that Use Case Narratives are used in two-thirds or more of their projects. Over a third of the respondents say their projects never use them, or use them less than a third of the time (15% and 22%, respectively). Class Diagrams were the most frequently used, with 73% of respondents using them in two-thirds or more of their projects. Use Case Narratives were ranked fourth, behind Sequence Diagrams and Use Case Diagrams. Only 3% of respondents report that their projects never use Class Diagrams, while Collaboration Diagrams have the highest non-usage rate of 25%. The number of respondents to this question varied from 152 (Statechart) to 172 (Class Diagram).

Our results are reasonably consistent with other studies (Table 3), except for a much lower

Table 3. UML Diagram Usage

UML Diagram	Usage[1]	Never Used (%)	>2/3 usage (%)	>1/3 usage (%)	G[2] (%)	Z[3] (%)
Class	4.19**	3	73	87	93	75
Use Case Diagram	3.56**	7	51	72	NA	89
Sequence	3.51	8	50	75	89	75
Use Case Narrative	3.25	15	44	63	93	NA
Activity	2.87**	22	32	55	60	52
Statechart	2.82*	19	29	53	63	52
Collab'tion	2.54**	25	22	42	50	37

[1] Usage is measured on a scale from 1 (Never Used) to 5 (Used on All Projects)

[2] From Grossman et al. (2005)

[3] From Zeichick (2002)

*,** Significantly different from Use Case Narrative mean,

** $p<=0.01$, * $p<0.05$ (t-test)

Use Case Narrative usage in our study compared to Grossman et al. (2005) and a possibly related lower use of Use Case Diagrams than in Zeichick (2002). In all three studies, Collaboration Diagrams were found to be the least frequently used. The differences may be attributable to question wording; for example, Grossman et al. (2005) simply asked if the diagram was being used rather than in what percentage of projects. The usage data in all three studies are based on respondents rather than projects. Due to the low correlations (maximum of 0.2) between UML experience and diagram usage, weighting usage by the respondent's number of UML projects increases the averages only slightly.

Most projects made only partial use of the seven UML diagram types studied (Table 4). Of the 135 respondents who reported project usage levels for all seven UML diagrams studied, 51% reported that five or more of them were used in at least a third of their projects while 21% reported five or more used in at least two-thirds of their projects.

Usage rates of the different UML diagram types were all positively correlated with each other, from an r^2 of 0.64 between Use Case Narratives

Table 4. Number of UML Diagram Types Used

UML Diagram Types Used	>1/3 Projects (%)	>2/3 Projects (%)
0	6	13
1	4	14
2	8	13
3	10	23
4	21	16
5	16	10
6	19	3
7	16	8

and Use Case Diagrams to 0.16 between Use Case Narratives and Statechart Diagrams. Thus, there is apparently no general tendency for projects to use certain diagrams at the expense of others (which would result in a negative correlation). For example, given that Sequence Diagrams and Collaboration Diagrams are "semantically close" so that "only minor visual information may be lost" when transforming one to the other (Selonen, Koskimies, and Sakkinen, 2003, p.45), one might expect to find that projects use either the Collaboration Diagram or the Sequence Diagram but not both. However, among our respondents, usage of the two was correlated at 0.38 (p < 0.01). There were 24 respondents (out of 153) who reported that all their projects use Collaboration Diagrams and 19 of the 24 reported always using Sequence Diagrams as well.

In contrast, of the 50 always using Sequence Diagrams in their projects, 18 used Collaboration Diagrams less than one-third of the time (and 11 of these never used them). While 87 respondents reported a higher usage level for Sequence than for Collaboration Diagrams, only 12 reported the opposite. Analysts clearly prefer using Sequence Diagrams but many apparently value depicting the same information in different ways for different purposes. Their isomorphic nature also means that Sequence and Collaboration Diagrams share underlying data, so the incremental cost of producing both (after committing to either one) is low with some UML tools.

UML Diagram Usage Patterns

The survey collected demographic data about respondents, their organizations, use of tools, and types of systems being built. Not all respondents completed these sections so the sample sizes for this analysis are somewhat smaller. Differences that are not reported were statistically insignificant.

Organization Size

There are a number of significant positive relationships between organization size measures and the use of UML diagrams. Comparing organizations above to those at or below $10 million in annual revenue, the former are significantly more likely to use Use Case Narratives (p=0.001), Use Case Diagrams (p=0.02) and Sequence Diagrams (p=0.02) and they use an average 4.75 diagram types compared to 3.65 for smaller organizations (p=0.01). Comparing usage by organizations with 50 or more IT employees to those with fewer, the former are more likely to use Sequence Diagrams (p=0.01) and Activity Diagrams (p=0.03). However, those with more employees use only slightly more Use Case Narratives and total number of diagram types. Both points used to divide the samples were chosen to create roughly equal subsamples so they are somewhat arbitrary. Moreover, the two size measures are not independent (r=0.72).

Project Size

Larger projects might be expected to make wider use of UML diagram types, but this is generally not the case. A similar analysis using the five project size measures (Table 2) found that respondents reporting larger than average budgets reported more use of Use Case Narratives and more diagram types used over a third of the time (p<0.05). Larger projects based on person-years also reported greater use of Use Case Narratives (p<0.05). However, no other comparisons were significant.

UML Tools

The availability of UML tools is also related to the use of UML diagram types. Those with tools are significantly more likely to use Class Diagrams (p=0.02) and Sequence Diagrams (p<0.001) with usage levels higher for all remaining diagram types as well (none significant). Respondents from larger organizations might be expected to have better access to tools and they do, but only slightly so this does not explain why larger organizations are using more diagram types. Correlations between the organization size measures (annual revenue and number of employees) and spending on tools are also low (0.25 and 0.29, respectively, neither significant) even though tool cost is typically partly dependent on the number of installations.

Organizational UML Usage

Overall usage of the UML in an organization could affect practices within individual projects. For example, analysts (and presumably organizations) could begin learning the UML by focusing on a subset of diagrams (Ambler, 2002, pp.46-47). The survey data do not permit any direct testing to determine whether individual analysts are taking this approach. However, respondents from organizations using the UML in 40% or fewer of their projects use an average of 2.4 diagram types two-thirds of the time or more. Those from organizations using the UML in over 40% of projects average a significantly greater (p = 0.02) 3.3 diagram types and are also making significantly (p = 0.03) more use of Sequence Diagrams (3.84 usage level compared to the 3.51 average in Table 3 and 3.23 level for those using the UML 40% of the time or less). Usage levels of all the remaining diagram types are very similar to those reported in Table 3 for both groups.

Respondent Experience

There are generally weak relationships between respondent experience and their projects' UML diagram usage. Experience measures (Table 1) were correlated with use of each UML diagram type (Table 3). The strongest relationships involved Statechart Diagrams and years of experience in OOAD (0.45, p<0.01) and years of experience with the UML (0.35, p<0.01). Class Diagram usage also correlated significantly (p<0.01) with these two

experience measures at 0.36 and 0.40 respectively, and with years of object-oriented programming (0.31). No other correlations between experience measures and diagram type usage exceeded 0.30 (and thus they explained less than 10% of the observed variance).

Industry

The survey provided 15 possible industrial classifications, with all but one receiving 12 or fewer responses (insufficient to be useful in analysis). The 46 respondents working in the software development industry, who do not always have identifiable clients in the same sense as those working in other organizations, had somewhat (but not significantly) lower use of Use Case Narratives, Sequence Diagrams and Activity Diagrams.

In our initial informal interviews, consultants were always described (by themselves and by others) as enthusiastic proponents of Use Case Narratives and the Use Case-driven philosophy. While we expected similar results from the survey, instead consultants reported lower Use Case Narrative usage than non-consultants (but not significantly, p=0.07). However, consultants were significantly more likely (p=0.04) to use Collaboration Diagrams.

System Type

Respondents were asked to indicate the application area(s) in which their systems were being built. The seven choices (with the number of responses in parentheses) were e-commerce (90), administrative (71), embedded (36), manufacturing (28), customer relationship management (26), data mining (21) and mobile commerce (17). There were also 58 who provided "other" categories, although many used this option to further describe one of the existing categories. Building software tools (6) was the most common selection not listed in the survey.

Use Case Narratives were used most by those developing customer relationship management

Table 5. UML Diagram Usage by Project Type

UML Diagram	New System	Replacement System	Enhancement of System
Class	4.19	4.82	4.38
Use Case Diag	3.62	3.90	3.56
Sequence	3.55	3.95	3.43
Use Case Narr	3.08	3.82	3.23
Activity	2.99	2.95	2.69
Statechart	2.87	2.75	2.63
Collaboration	2.59	2.95	2.45

(3.57) and e-commerce systems (3.48), and least by those developing embedded systems (2.64). (The numbers shown use the same five-point scale as in Table 3.) T-test significance levels were 0.01 and 0.001, respectively, after excluding respondents who selected both the system types being compared. However, embedded system projects had the highest reported usage of Sequence Diagrams (3.56), while customer relationship management had the least (2.14) (p<0.005). Activity Diagrams were used most in developing manufacturing systems (3.12) and least in embedded (2.58), but this difference was not significant.

Respondents were also asked to identify the proportion of their object oriented/UML projects that were new systems, complete replacements of existing systems, or enhancements to existing systems. Most entered percentages that totaled 100, but others entered the number of each type and these were converted to percentages. There were 154 usable responses, averaging 56% new, 20% replacement and 24% enhancements. Table 5 computed the usage of each UML diagram (computed as in Table 3) for those who reported at least 50% of their projects were of that type; there were 96 responses for new systems, 23 for replacement projects and 34 for enhancement projects. (Some responses were split 50/50 between two types and were counted twice while others were split more evenly among all three types and were not counted at all.) Most notable is the greater use of

Class Diagrams and Use Case Narratives when developing replacement systems.

Information Provided by UML Diagrams

There are a number of reasons for using multiple diagram types to describe system functionality, beginning with the possibility that different diagrams convey different information. To investigate this, the survey asked which diagrams provide new information beyond that contained in Use Case Narratives. The Use Case Narratives were chosen as the benchmark because a Use Case-driven approach had been endorsed by much of the early UML literature. Both the interviews and a literature review (Dobing and Parsons, 2000) showed that Use Case Narratives varied widely in level of detail, so simply knowing that Use Case Narratives are being employed does not answer the question of how much information they contain. In contrast, the level of redundancy across other pairs of diagrams is largely determinable from their syntax. The question used a five-point scale from "No New Info" to "All New Info," with "Some New Info" as the midpoint (3). This item was only seen by those whose projects had used both Use Case Narratives and the other diagram in question so there were fewer respondents, from 89 (Collaboration Diagram) to 125 (Class Diagram).

Table 6. New Information (Not in Use Case Narratives) from UML Diagrams

UML Diagram	New Information[1]	Some – All New Information (%)
Class	3.51	86
Use Case	2.42**	48
Sequence	3.37	78
Activity	2.89**	63
Statechart	3.38*	79
Collaboration	2.98**	67

[1] New information is measured on a scale from 1 (No New Information) to 5 (All New Information)

*,** Significantly different from Class Diagram mean, ** $p <= 0.01$, * $p < 0.05$ (t-test)

Table 6 shows that the diagram of highest value for conveying new information not already contained in the Use Case Narratives was the Class Diagram, with a score of 3.51 on the five-point scale, and 86% of respondents believe it offers at least some new information (at least 3 on the 5-point scale). The Use Case Diagram was least useful in providing additional information, which is not surprising given its role is to depict the Use Cases and their relationships to actors and to each other.

Stronger relationships were expected between the belief that a UML diagram provides additional information beyond the Use Case Narrative and the usage level of that diagram. For Activity Diagrams, the correlation was 0.42 ($p < 0.01$). However, other correlations of this type were all weak (i.e., none exceeded 0.30, so none explained more than 10% of the variance).

There was also a strong correlation (0.77) between the beliefs that Collaboration and Sequence Diagrams provide new information beyond Use Case Narratives, the highest correlation found among all pairs of diagrams. This could be attributed to the isomorphic relationship between Collaboration and Sequence Diagrams (i.e., that they convey similar information but in different ways).

Role of UML Diagrams

Table 7 examines reasons for including each UML diagram in a project, with the focus on communication within the project team. Each respondent who reported using a particular diagram at least a third of the time was asked about four possible purposes. As expected, Use Case Narratives had the highest score for "Verifying and validating requirements with client representatives on the project team" at 4.00 (on a 5-point scale). The use of other diagrams for this purpose was higher than expected, based on interview responses and our review of the UML literature. These high levels of client involvement show that use of the more technical diagrams of the UML is not limited to the technical members of the development team. The survey also included a single item that asked, "How successful has the UML been in facilitating communication with clients?" The items used a five-point scale from Not to Very Successful. The mean was 3.28 with 25% choosing the lowest two levels.

Of those respondents who reported using a particular diagram at least a third of the time, Table 8 shows the percentage who rated them from "Moderately Useful" to "Essential" for four different purposes. The results show higher than expected levels of usefulness for all UML diagrams in "Verifying and validating requirements

Table 7. Roles for UML Diagrams

UML Diagram	Client Validation[1]	Implement[2]	Document[3]	Clarify[4]
Use Case Narrative	4.00	3.62[†]	3.15[††]	3.52[††]
Activity	3.50**	3.43[††]	3.35[††]	3.50[††]
Use Case Diagram	3.36**	3.06[††]	2.90[††]	3.17[††]
Sequence	2.91**	3.71[†]	3.76[††]	4.14[†]
Class	2.90**	4.06	4.18[††]	4.35[††]
Statechart	2.63**	3.51[††]	3.35[††]	3.74[††]
Collab'tion	2.62**	3.25[††]	2.96[††]	3.40[††]

[1] Verifying and validating requirements with client representatives on the project team

[2] Specifying system requirements for programmers

[3] Documenting for future maintenance and other enhancements

[4] Clarifying understanding of application among technical members of the project team

** Significantly different from Use Case Narrative mean,

** $p <= 0.01$ (t-tests)

[†],[††] Significantly different from Class Diagram mean,

[††] $p <= 0.01$, [†] $p < 0.05$ (t-tests)

with users." Only Statecharts, at 49%, were under the 50% level.

The other three purposes listed are more related to communication within the project team, among analysts, programmers and maintenance staff. For these three purposes, the Class Diagram was considered most useful with the Use Case Diagram least useful (but all diagram types were rated as at least "moderately useful" by over 60% of respondents). As noted earlier, the Use Case Diagram provides an overview of the project while programming tends to focus on implementing particular functionality. In Table 8, the usefulness levels reported for Sequence Diagrams are all

Table 8. Percent of Respondents Who Believe Each UML Diagram is at Least Moderately Useful

UML Diagram	Client Validation[1]	Implement[2]	Document[3]	Clarify[4]
Use Case Narrative	87	79	68	74
Activity	77	81	73	80
Use Case Diagram	74	62	61	66
Sequence	62	84	85	92
Class	57	89	92	93
Statechart	49	79	71	82
Collab'tion	51	70	62	74

[1] Verifying and validating requirements with client representatives on the project team

[2] Specifying system requirements for programmers

[3] Documenting for future maintenance and other enhancements

[4] Clarifying understanding of application among technical members of the project team

Table 9. Reasons for not using Some UML Diagrams (% responses)

UML Diagram	Not well understood by analysts	Not useful for most projects	Insufficient value to justify cost	Information captured redundant	Not useful with clients	Not useful with programmers
Class	50	13	13	25	25	25
Sequence	32	23	36	14	23	23
Use Case Narrative	29	26	37	29	11	26
Use Case Diagram	32	32	42	19	29	42
Statechart	35	42	28	12	28	33
Activity	48	23	35	35	14	25
Collab'tion	27	32	24	49	29	24

significantly higher (p<0.01) on the three project team communication measures than those for the isomorphic Collaboration Diagram.

These reported levels of client involvement with the full range of UML diagrams exceed those generally recommended in the literature and, in particular, seem inconsistent with the dominant Use Case-driven philosophy. Concerns have been raised about a potential disconnect that could result from relying on Use Case Narratives when working with clients and Class Diagrams when working with technical team members (Dobing and Parsons, 2000). The survey results confirm that Use Case Narratives are indeed the primary diagram for communication with clients and Class Diagrams for communication within the technical members of the team. However, all diagrams received at least "moderately useful" ratings from over 50% of respondents across all forms of communication (Table 8), except using Statechart Diagrams for communication with clients which was 49%. In particular, Use Case Narratives are widely used among the technical members of project teams. This suggests that the disconnect problem may well have been addressed in practice, if not in the UML literature.

Those who reported that their projects used a particular diagram less than a third of the time (including not at all) were asked why they were

not using it more often. There were fewer respondents for these questions, ranging from only 8 for Class Diagrams to 59 for Collaboration Diagrams. Table 9 shows the percentage of respondents who selected each possible reason. Respondents were encouraged to select all reasons that applied so row totals exceed 100%. A lack of understanding by analysts was the primary factor among the few not using Class Diagrams (50%). Similar concerns were expressed by 48% of respondents about Activity Diagrams. Leading concerns for the remaining diagrams were over how useful they are (Statechart), their value (Sequence and Use Case Diagrams and Narratives) and the degree of redundancy (Collaboration, presumably with respect to Sequence Diagrams).

Client Participation

Client participation has long been considered crucial to successful system development. The survey asked about the client's role in relation to each of the UML diagram types being studied. Respondents were able to select more than one (e.g., they could report that clients helped to develop Use Case Narratives, reviewed some or all of them upon completion and had formal approval authority). The results are summarized in Table 10. For example, 76% of respondents who

Table 10. Client Participation

UML Diagram	Develop (%)	Review (%)	Approve (%)	N
Use Case Narr	76	63	54	78
Use Case Diag	57	69	46	77
Activity	47	60	19	57
Sequence	37	52	16	87
Class	33	53	20	103
Collaboration	38	48	13	48
Statechart	28	36	20	61

used Use Case Narratives reported that clients were involved in their development. When UML diagram types are ranked on the level of client participation, the order is very similar (with only Class and Collaboration Diagrams transposed) to "comprehensibility" rankings for managers, users and domain experts (Arlow and Neustadt, 2004, p.91).

The results show that clients were most likely to be involved in developing, reviewing and approving Use Case Narratives and the Use Case Diagram. Of the remaining diagrams, Activity Diagrams are probably the easiest for clients to understand and almost half the analysts report some involvement by clients in their development, consistent with the quote from Schneider and Winters (2001) in the Introduction. While clients were less likely to be involved in developing the Class Diagram, just over half were involved in reviewing this widely used diagram. The wide range of client involvement practices in our interviews and survey results is not unexpected given that most organizations have relatively limited experience with the UML.

Not surprisingly, clients were least likely to be involved in developing or reviewing Statechart Diagrams. The fact that about one quarter to a third were involved in these tasks may reflect the technical sophistication of some clients in the survey sample, since the composition of OMG membership includes many large companies in the computer industry.

Respondents were also asked about possible difficulties that had occurred which "could be attributed to the UML." They could check any or all of the five categories listed. User interface concerns were checked most frequently (36%), followed by roles and responsibilities of particular users (21%), security (18%), data requirements (18%), and system capabilities and functionality (13%).

Respondents Not Using the UML

Some limited analysis was also done based on the 102 responses from those not using the UML. Software development was also the largest organization type for this group (31%) with education second (25%). These respondents were less experienced than the UML practitioners (averaging 8.1 years IT experience and 16.3 IT projects vs. 15.1 years and 27.0 projects for UML practitioners). The sample selection method suggests this group is probably more knowledgeable about the UML (and more interested in it) than the average non-practitioner. The primary reasons given by those not using the UML or any object-oriented approach were a lack of people familiar with the UML (51%) and a lack of suitable projects (16%). Of those whose organizations were using an object-oriented approach but not the UML, 55% cited a lack of people familiar with the UML while 23% said they had no suitable projects, 17% said it was too complex, 17% said it was not yet standardized or accepted and 15% indicated their tools were not compatible with the UML. Respondents could select more than one answer so the percentage total exceeds 100%.

DISCUSSION AND RECOMMENDATIONS

This appears to have been the first survey investigating both how often, and more importantly, why UML diagrams are used (or not used) in systems analysis. We found variations on all three of the major dimensions studied, including frequency of use for each diagram type, the purposes for which they were being used, and the role of clients/users in their creation and approval. While the UML is "unified" in that it brought together elements from disparate modeling notations, considerable variations remain in its use. These variations are somewhat inconsistent with the notion of the UML as a "unified" language in the sense of implying coordinated and cohesive use of diagram types within a development project. Moreover, we found that use of only a subset of UML diagrams on a project is widespread. The data also show a variety of reasons why certain UML diagrams are not used.

While surveys can address which UML diagrams are used, they cannot easily determine if they are being used appropriately. As one respondent put it, "Used, vs. used appropriately, is probably a telling difference. Many places are using the components but in a relatively brain-dead manner." Of course, this type of comment can be made about most technologies, particularly when, as with the UML, they are relatively new and complex.

The findings of this research can be useful in a number of ways. First, information on UML use can provide valuable input in the evolution of the standard. For example, on the issue of complexity, the language could be simplified by eliminating Collaboration Diagrams. Based on our findings, Collaboration Diagrams are used less often,

deemed to be less useful, and appear to offer little additional value in relation to Sequence Diagrams. Statechart Diagrams are also used less often than most and seem to be less useful most of the time, but are rated highly for providing new information in some situations (e.g., real-time systems) and have low redundancy. Admittedly, both these diagrams also have some strong supporters. As one interview subject said about Statecharts, "When they are useful, they are very useful."

Second, some projects do not follow a Use Case-driven approach with over a third of the respondents saying they use them less than a third of the time. At the same time, there is limited empirical evidence to support the proposition that Use Case Narratives are a more effective way to communicate with clients than are the other UML diagrams. Some respondents were particularly critical of Use Cases, referring to them as "close to useless," "imprecise," and "just unformatted text notes," noting that the "ambiguity of Use Cases in particular is problematic" and they "tend to become remarkably complex and highly error prone." (These comments come from four different respondents.) Research is needed to determine an appropriate level of granularity and level of detail for Use Case Narratives.

Third, more attention may be needed on the issue of how clients/users can be better prepared to participate in development and review of artifacts beyond Use Case Narratives. As one respondent put it, "The only problem is communicating with people not familiar with the UML." We found that the use of diagrams other than Use Case Narratives among clients/users was higher than expected based on the extant prescriptive literature on 'how to use' the language. The UML practitioner literature generally seems to assume that UML diagrams, except for Use Case Diagrams and Narratives, are too complex or technical to be understood by clients. However, our results show that clients frequently approve, review, and even help develop all of the UML diagrams. But those respondents who chose to comment on this issue generally took the opposite view, saying that the UML is "too geeky and techie for non-technical people," their "eyes glaze over" and there is "little involvement of key business people." The views of clients and intended users of systems on the usability and usefulness of UML have received little attention from researchers (including this study). Nor has much consideration been given to how to prepare clients for this level of involvement.

Fourth, research is needed to understand which UML diagrams can best facilitate communication between clients and analysts, particularly as the use of the UML to support Agile Modeling grows (Ambler, 2002). In addition, work might be needed to modify these diagrams (e.g., by simplifying or otherwise changing the syntax and grammar of the diagram type) to enable them to support communication and verification more effectively.

Research on Activity Diagrams might be particularly interesting. Following Use Cases, the respondents expressed the sharpest disagreement on their usefulness, with the critics saying they are "very time-consuming to produce," have "unclear semantics and an unclear connection to the rest of the UML Diagrams," do not represent "the concept of a 'business process,'" and are redundant "if Use Cases are well written and well modeled" (from four different respondents). Some also noted that Activity Diagrams are not well covered in the UML literature and not well supported by UML tools. A search using ABI/ Inform Global (November 2009) found only three research articles with "Activity Diagram" in the title so this could an unmined opportunity for researchers.

Another related question is how to best use UML diagrams with Agile methods. There have been several books on this subject, beginning with Ambler (2002), but few journal research articles have been published.Fifth, as noted earlier, 36% of respondents agreed that they had experienced "difficulties … [with user interfaces] that could be attributed to the UML." User interfaces have become much more complex over the past decade

with the use of both visual programming and web environments, complicating development using any methodology or notation. Based on accompanying comments, respondents would welcome better ways to integrate user interface design with UML modeling. One approach is to distinguish between "System" and "Essential" Use Case Narratives (Constantine and Lockwood, 1999), where Essential Use Cases are independent of technology (and user interfaces) while System Use Cases include these details. Currently, the UML has no standards for Use Case Narratives (OMG, 2005) or System Use Cases in particular, which might explain why many respondents experienced user interface issues that they attributed to the UML. Another approach is to use prototyping or other screen design tools in conjunction with the UML. One respondent noted that, "It is easier for clients to understand the functionality of software through user interface sketches" while another said that clients had difficulty validating Use Case Narratives "without any draft of the [user interface]." The principle that system analysis should be technology independent long precedes the development of the UML and is widely accepted among leading writers in the field but, as several respondents pointed out, some difficulties can arise when applying this principle in practice. Another respondent noted difficulties in creating a vocal interface, pointing out that not all interfaces are purely visual. There are some very interesting research opportunities in this area.

Respondents provided fewer comments on other difficulties with the UML. Concerns about security are to be expected but no suggested solutions were mentioned. One difficulty with database design is that many respondents were using a Relational, rather than Object-Oriented, DBMS. Difficulties identifying the "roles and responsibilities of particular users" suggest that there may be problems mapping the UML "actor" to specific individuals or job descriptions. There are some strong parallels with this issue and user interfaces; at least some clients prefer to work with more concrete designs that clearly show who does what rather than with more abstract approaches that take a higher level view. More research is needed on how clients can more effectively validate designs.

Sixth, some respondents discussed additional modeling constructs they used to supplement the UML. While this might seem to make a complex modeling language even more so, some of these constructs could be used to replace UML diagrams. Entity-relationship diagrams remain popular (but 15 of the 17 who discussed using them also use the Class Diagram). Data Flow and Process Flow Diagrams are still being used as well. Six respondents reported using tools for user interface design to address some of the issues mentioned above.

Finally, there have been numerous attempts to evaluate UML from a theoretical standpoint including assigning ontological semantics to UML constructs (Evermann and Wand, 2001a; Opdahl and Henderson-Sellers, 2001) and assessing the complexity of the UML (Siau and Cao, 2001, 2002; Siau, Erickson, and Lee, 2005; Erickson and Siau, 2007). In cases such as these, theoretical conclusions can be substantiated or refuted by empirical data on usage. To illustrate, some UML constructs appear to have no ontological counterpart and such constructs may not be suitable for conceptual modeling (Evermann and Wand, 2001a). We then might expect that diagrams that have more such constructs would be less useful and less used in conceptual modeling. In terms of this study, this would correspond to less use of such diagrams/constructs for verifying and validating requirements with users. Our study did not examine use at the level of constructs within diagrams, but future empirical studies might do an analysis at that level of detail (perhaps for a single diagram type).

SURVEY RESPONDENT CHARACTERISTICS: PROFILE AND LIMITATIONS

Given the lack of any defined population of UML practitioners from which to obtain a random sample, we chose to survey primarily OMG members and those who use its web site. This may have produced biased responses. However, given that the goals of this research were to examine how UML practitioners (the target population) were using the language, rather than the extent to which it is being used in software development in general, the participation of the OMG seemed appropriate. While respondents may not be representative of all UML practitioners, they can be considered leading edge adopters. Their UML experience was naturally low when this survey was conducted, with medians of five years and four projects. As such, respondents might not be typical of the eventual set of UML practitioners (which could become the majority of system developers if object-oriented system development and the UML become more widely accepted). Based on other research in technology adoption, albeit in different areas (e.g., Brown and Venkatesh, 2003), early adopters might approach the UML quite differently from those who come later.

In addition, there are some obvious limitations with using a convenience sample. The number of people who received or read the invitation to participate is unknown because of the possibility of it being forwarded. Visitors to the OMG site need not be members, so the results should not be considered as a survey of OMG's membership even prior to inviting readers of the comp.object Usenet newsgroup. It is also likely that some people found the survey through search engines, since the survey was, for some time, the top result of a Google search on "UML survey." Despite the lack of control over respondents, reviewing the comments and contact information suggests that the group as a whole does belong to the target population and are reasonably diverse on a range of demographic measures. Moreover, whether they worked for OMG member companies or found the survey by other means, the respondents clearly were very interested in the UML. Whether respondents are representative of the target population of all analysts who use the UML is unknown.

A majority of respondents opted to remain anonymous so they could have submitted two or more responses, but there was no reason for them to do so and there are no obvious patterns of duplicate responses. It is also conceivable that results could be skewed by heavy participation by a single organization. However, responses came from a wide variety of organization types and sizes and there were no bursts of unusual activity levels. Among those who did provide an email address, no company domain had more than one response except for email providers (15 from Yahoo! accounts, five from Hotmail, etc.). So there is no evidence to suggest the results were manipulated by any individual or group.

The survey took a Use Case-driven approach, consistent with a majority of the books written on the UML up to the time of this survey. However, only 44% of respondents reported using Use Case Narratives in at least two-thirds of their UML/object-oriented projects. Measuring the value of the information provided by different UML diagrams by comparing them to Use Case Narratives therefore seems insufficient and new measures are needed.

The measures used for project size were also problematic. Low numbers of Classes and Use Case Narratives used in some "typical" projects probably reflect limited usage of those diagram types rather than the real size of the project, and many projects are not using them at all. Some unrealistically low budgets (which were coded as missing data) were perhaps intended to be in thousands of dollars while others appear to exclude salaries. On the other hand, some larger budgets might have included training and tool acquisition costs that do not reflect project size. Lines of code is commonly used as a measure of project size, and

was used here because of its simplicity. However, respondents may or may not have included shared code, comments, etc. and programming style can also affect code size. Low correlations among these size measures also suggest a lack of reliability. Budget and number of classes correlated at 0.65 while person-years and lines of code correlated at 0.44 (both with $p<0.01$). But the next largest correlation is only 0.25.

Measures of user/client involvement have a long history in the IS literature. This survey measures only the perspective of IT professionals rather than the clients themselves. In the earlier interviews, there were several cases of strong disagreement between the clients and analysts on their roles and even on appropriate use of some UML diagram types. There can also be differences in what 'client' means across different organizations and situations. Are clients those sponsoring the system or does this term also include the intended direct users? Some external consultants might view the IT Department that hires them as the client, while those developing commercial software may have certain types of clients in mind but have limited interaction with them.

CONCLUSION

The UML has rapidly become the de facto standard for object-oriented systems development. However, this survey suggests there is no standard approach to using the UML within a group of arguably leading edge practitioners. There is considerable variation in use of diagrams across projects and in the role clients/users play in the development of UML models. Clearly, in view of the popular interest in the UML, further research is needed to better understand UML use in order to gain insight on how it can be effectively used to support systems development. The results of this survey suggest several aspects of UML adoption and use that need to be studied.

ACKNOWLEDGMENT

The authors would like to thank the Object Management Group, and Richard Soley in particular, for their support of our research. Thanks also to Dinesh Batra and other anonymous reviewers for their helpful suggestions and comments. Funding for this research was provided by the Natural Sciences and Engineering Research Council of Canada.

Some of the results in this chapter appeared earlier in the Communications of the ACM - "How the UML is Used," May 2006.

REFERENCES

Ambler, S. (2002). *Agile Modeling: Effective Practices for Extreme Programming and Unified Process*. New York: John Wiley.

Arlow, J., & Neustadt, I. (2004). *Enterprise Patterns and MDA: Building Better Software with Archetype Patterns and UML*. Boston: Addison-Wesley.

Batra, D. (2008). Unified Modeling Language (UML) Topics: The Past, the Problems, and the Prospects. *Journal of Database Management, 19*(1), i–vii.

Batra, D., & Satzinger, J. (2006). Contemporary Approaches and Techniques for the Systems Analyst. *Journal of Information Systems Education, 17*(3), 257–265.

Booch, G. (1994). *Object-Oriented Analysis and Design with Applications* (2nd ed.). Redwood City, CA: Benjamin/Cummings.

Booch, G. (1999). UML in Action. *Communications of the ACM, 42*(10), 26–28. doi:10.1145/317665.317672

Booch, G., Rumbaugh, J., & Jacobson, I. (1999). *The Unified Modeling Language User Guide*. Reading, MA: Addison Wesley.

Brown, S., & Venkatesh, V. (2003). Bringing Non-Adopters Along: The Challenge Facing the PC Industry. *Communications of the ACM, 46*(4), 76–80. doi:10.1145/641205.641208

Burton-Jones, A., & Meso, P. (2006). Conceptualizing Systems for Understanding: An Empirical Test of Decomposition Principles in Object-Oriented Analysis. *Information Systems Research, 17*(1), 101–114. doi:10.1287/isre.1050.0079

Burton-Jones, A., & Weber, R. (2003). Properties do not have properties: Investigating a questionable conceptual modeling practice. In *Proceedings of the 2nd Annual Symposium on Research in Systems Analysis and Design,* St. John's, Canada.

Constantine, L. L., & Lockwood, L. A. D. (1999). *Software for Use*. Reading, MA: Addison-Wesley.

Cook, S. (2000). The UML Family: Profiles, Prefaces, and Packages. In *Proceedings of UML 2000 - The Unified Modeling Language. Advancing the Standard* (LNCS 1939, pp. 255-264).

DeJong, J. (2006, June 15). Of Different Minds About Modeling. *SD Times*. Retrieved from http://www.sdtimes.com/article/special-20060615-02.html.

Dobing, B., & Parsons, J. (2000). Understanding the Role of Use Cases in UML: A Review and Research Agenda. *Journal of Database Management, 11*(4), 28–36.

Dori, D. (2002). Why Significant UML Change is Unlikely. *Communications of the ACM, 45*(11), 82–85. doi:10.1145/581571.581599

Duddy, K. (2002). UML2 Must Enable A Family of Languages. *Communications of the ACM, 45*(11), 73–75. doi:10.1145/581571.581596

Erickson, J. (2008). A Decade and More of UML: An Overview of UML Semantic and Structural Issues and UML Field Use. *Journal of Database Management, 19*(3), i–vii.

Erickson, J., & Siau, K. (2007). Theoretical and Practical Complexity of Modeling Methods. *Communications of the ACM, 50*(8), 46–51. doi:10.1145/1278201.1278205

Evermann, J., & Wand, Y. (2001a). Towards ontologically based semantics for UML constructs. *Proceedings of the 20th International Conference on Conceptual Modeling*, Yokohama, Japan (pp. 354-367).

Evermann, J., & Wand, Y. (2001b). An Ontological Examination of Object Interaction in Conceptual Modeling. In *Proceedings of the 11th Workshop on Information Technologies and Systems*, New Orleans, Louisiana (pp. 91-96).

Evermann, J., & Wand, Y. (2006). Ontological Modeling Rules For UML: An Empirical Assessment. *Journal of Computer Information Systems, 46*(5), 14–29.

Gemino, A., & Parker, D. (2009). Use Case Diagrams in Support of Use Case Modeling: Deriving Understanding from the Picture. *Journal of Database Management, 20*(1), 1–24.

Grossman, M., Aronson, J., & McCarthy, R. (2005). Does UML make the grade? Insights from the software development community. *Information and Software Technology, 47*(6), 383–397. doi:10.1016/j.infsof.2004.09.005

Harel, D. (1987). Statecharts: A visual formalism for complex systems. *Science of Computer Programming, 8*(3), 231–274. doi:10.1016/0167-6423(87)90035-9

Jacobson, I., Booch, G., & Rumbaugh, J. (1999). *The Unified Software Development Process.* Reading, MA: Addison-Wesley.

Jacobson, I., Christerson, M., Jonsson, P., & Overgaard, G. (1992). *Object-Oriented Software Engineering: A Use Case Driven Approach.* Reading, MA: Addison-Wesley.

Jacobson, I., Ericsson, M., & Jacobson, A. (1994). *The Object Advantage: Business Process Reengineering with Object Technology*. Reading, MA: Addison-Wesley.

Johnson, R., & Hardgrave, B. (1999). Object-oriented methods: current practices and attitudes. *Journal of Systems and Software, 48*(1), 5–12. doi:10.1016/S0164-1212(99)00041-2

Kobryn, C. (1999). UML 2001: A Standardization Odyssey. *Communications of the ACM, 42*(10), 29–37. doi:10.1145/317665.317673

Kobryn, C. (2002). Will UML 2.0 Be Agile or Awkward? *Communications of the ACM, 45*(1), 107–110. doi:10.1145/502269.502306

Larman, C. (2005). *Applying UML and Patterns: An Introduction to Object-Oriented Analysis and Design and Iterative Development* (3rd ed.). Upper Saddle River, NJ: Prentice Hall.

Moore, A. (2001). Extending UML to Enable the Definition and Design of Real-Time Embedded Systems. *Crosstalk: The Journal of Defense Software Engineering, 14*(6), 4–9.

Object Management Group. (2009). *OMG Unified Modeling Language: Superstructure*, Version 2.2. Retrieved November 4, 2009 from http://www.omg.org/spec/UML/2.2/Superstructure/PDF/

Odell, J., Van Dyke, P., & Bauer, B. (2000). Extending UML for Agents. In *Proceedings of the Agent-Oriented Information Systems Workshop at the 17th National conference on Artificial Intelligence*, Austin, Texas (pp. 3-17).

Opdahl, A. L., & Henderson-Sellers, B. (2001). Grounding the OML metamodel in ontology. *Journal of Systems and Software, 57*, 119–143. doi:10.1016/S0164-1212(00)00123-0

Rumbaugh, J., Blaha, M., Premerlani, W., Eddy, F., & Lorensen, W. (1991). *Object-Oriented Modeling and Design*. Englewood Cliffs, NJ: Prentice Hall.

Schneider, G., & Winters, J. (2001). *Applying Use Cases: A Practical Guide* (2nd ed.). Boston: Addison-Wesley.

Selic, B. (2006). UML 2: A model driven development tool. *IBM Systems Journal, 45*(3), 607–620.

Selonen, P., Koskimies, K., & Sakkinen, M. (2003). Transformations between UML diagrams. *Journal of Database Management, 14*(3), 37–55.

Siau, K., & Cao, Q. (2001). Unified Modeling Language (UML) - a complexity analysis. *Journal of Database Management, 12*(1), 26–34.

Siau, K., & Cao, Q. (2002). How Complex Is the Unified Modeling Language? *Advanced Topics in Database Research, 1*, 294–306.

Siau, K., Erickson, J., & Lee, L. Y. (2005). Theoretical vs. Practical Complexity: The Case of UML. *Journal of Database Management, 16*(3), 40–57.

Siau, K., & Loo, P. Identifying Difficulties in Learning UML. *Information Systems Management, 23*(3), 43–51. doi:10.1201/1078.1058053 0/46108.23.3.20060601/93706.5

Stevens, P., & Pooley, R. (2000). *Using UML: Software Engineering with Object and Components*. Reading, MA: Addison-Wesley.

Zeichick, A. (2002, July 15). Modeling Usage Low; Developers Confused About UML 2.0, MDA. *SD Times*. Retrieved from http://www.sdtimes.com/article/story-20020715-03.html

Chapter 14
A 360-Degree Perspective of Education in 3-D Virtual Worlds

Brenda Eschenbrenner
University of Nebraska-Lincoln, USA

Fiona Fui-Hoon Nah
University of Nebraska-Lincoln, USA

Keng Siau
University of Nebraska-Lincoln, USA

ABSTRACT

Three-dimensional virtual world environments are providing new opportunities to develop engaging, immersive experiences in education. These virtual worlds are unique in that they allow individuals to interact with others through their avatars and with objects in the environment, and can create experiences that are not necessarily possible in the real world. Hence, virtual worlds are presenting opportunities for students to engage in both constructivist and collaborative learning. To assess the impact of the use of virtual worlds on education, a literature review is conducted to identify current applications, benefits being realized, as well as issues faced. Based on the review, educational opportunities in virtual worlds and gaps in meeting pedagogical objectives are discussed. Practical and research implications are also addressed. Virtual worlds are proving to provide unique educational experiences, with its potential only at the cusp of being explored.

INTRODUCTION

Advanced technological media have the potential to enhance online learning and education. As courses move to on-line formats, challenges emerge in meeting some of the common and core objectives in learning and education, which include engagement, interactivity, collaboration, and experimentation.

DOI: 10.4018/978-1-60566-904-5.ch014

Many instructors have looked to a range of technologies such as wikis and blogs (Guru & Siau, 2008) to discussion forums on Blackboard to better achieve these objectives but there are limitations faced.

One particular technology that presents new opportunities to achieving these objectives is three-dimensional (3-D) virtual world technology which provides a common space for individuals to interact and creates a learning environment that can better suit their needs. One may establish replications of reality in this virtual space for individuals to explore or interact with. Stoerger (2008) suggests that one of the key elements of a virtual world is the visual creativity that it affords, while Gaimster (2008) identifies the rich immersive experiences as highlights of virtual worlds. Johnson and Levine (2008) suggest that a distinctive characteristic of virtual worlds is that users can determine the course of events to be experienced because of their ability to interact with peers (through their avatars) and objects in the environment. Whatever the purpose, the nature of virtual reality is such that students have the potential to become engaged in a simulated activity and collaborate in a dispersed setting that more closely replicates the advantages of being face-to-face.

In addition, changes in educational paradigms are creating a need for new technologies to support new learning environments. Dickey (2005a) cites that creating *interactive* learning environments is a current trend being supported by the increasing paradigm shift towards constructivism. The paradigm advocates that knowledge is *constructed* and learners need to be more engaged in the learning process. Therefore, environments that are conducive to learners being able to manipulate and explore are more conducive to constructivist activities and learning. Coffman and Klinger (2007) suggest that being immersed in an environment that supports creativity and discovery provides a better means for students to transfer their knowledge to real-world applications. Also, Barab et al. (2000) cite that many learning environments are becoming more collaborative in nature. Therefore, technology incorporated into a curriculum should engage students in the learning process, allow students to experiment and explore so as to construct their own knowledge, and provide an adequate platform for rich communication and cooperation to take place. Johnson and Levine (2008) have noted that virtual world environments provide platforms for rich expressions as well as social interactions.

3-D virtual world environments may prove to enhance existing technologies' capabilities to better achieve these goals. The environments offer abilities to communicate and collaborate with others in a shared virtual space that is created by the users and foster potential for educational and cooperative activities. Typically, the virtual environments are created by the users. These capabilities afford new opportunities for creativity to abound and for idea generation and experimentation to flourish. Users can learn through their own discovery processes, as well as learn through their interactions and collaborative efforts with others.

Accounts of educational applications of virtual worlds provide insights into various opportunities that exist and are being realized, along with issues that have been encountered. This article addresses these applications and opportunities by focusing on 3-D virtual world environments in educational contexts. Specifically, this article reviews the literature that addresses current applications, benefits, and issues of virtual worlds in education, then summarizes opportunities and gaps of these virtual worlds for consideration in education, and highlights implications for both practice and research.

3-D VIRTUAL WORLDS IN EDUCATION

Educational institutions continually explore new opportunities to bring the classroom online as technology continues to grow in sophistication and capabilities (Erickson & Siau, 2003). Some pursue this endeavor to create greater opportunities to reach students through distance education programs. However, some have extended this concept of using Internet-based technologies to teach by creating more sophisticated virtual realities or virtual worlds to expand on the interaction that takes place among students as well as with their instructors. Bryson (1996) has defined virtual reality as "the use of computers and human-computer interfaces to create the effect of a three-dimensional world containing interactive objects with a strong sense of three-dimensional presence" (p. 62). He notes three important attributes of virtual reality environments: computer-generated, three-dimensional, and interactive. Also, he emphasizes that virtual reality environments entail creating an effect of interacting with things and are characterized by the interface. Other features and characterizations of 3-D virtual worlds include the illusion of 3-D space that allows real-time interaction/interactive capabilities, avatars that are digital representations of users, chat tools facilitating communication, first person viewpoints, navigation freedom, and abilities of participants to share space as well as time and to design their own spaces (Dickey, 2005a, 2005b; Mikropoulos, 2001; Ondrejka, 2008)

3-D virtual worlds extend the functionality of other technologies by generating more dynamic environments in that individuals can participate or view objects, simulations, or others in a 3-D space. Mennecke, McNeill, Ganis, and Roche (2008) suggest that the popularity of these 3-D virtual environments has been increasing because of "stunning visuals, animations, role playing opportunities, and social communities" as well as "the interaction that users experience" (p. 373). Engagement is being enhanced by the nature of a shared environment.

For instance, Dickey (2005b) found from her case studies of educational institutions (one using the Active World environment for an undergraduate business computing course and the other an object modeling course) that these 3-D virtual worlds afford various opportunities for students and instructors. In the business computing course, students utilized the virtual world to complete and submit assignments, review their grades, locate web-linked resources, collaborate with other students, and communicate by way of a chat tool. In the object modeling course, the instructor used

chat tools to promote discussion, and presented examples of 3-D objects.

The opportunities realized included promoting collaborative and cooperative learning (Siau, 2003), self-defining the learning context, creating interactive experiences with materials or models that may not be replicable in a traditional classroom (Siau et al., 2006), and providing engaging, constructivist activities. Students indicated that they felt a sense of presence in the environment, while instructors indicated that a significant drop in attrition rates occurred (Dickey, 2005b). Instructors also noted that the environment advocated constructivist approaches in that it provided collaboration opportunities, real-time communication, as well as a visual learning environment. The researcher noted that the sense of anonymity promoted more daring interactions among students/avatars.

Virtual worlds have also been designed to create simulations of real world phenomena to provide an environment for experiential learning and training. An example is the simulation of a toddler's initial cognitive experience when joining a daycare to improve caregiver's awareness of these experiences (Passig, Klein, & Noyman, 2001). In a research study that focused on validating virtual environments as a means to study child pedestrian behaviors, Schwebel, Gaines, and Severson (2008) demonstrated that virtual environments can replicate the real-world environment such that behaviors are consistent in both.

Also, Mantovani, Castelnuovo, Gaggioli, and Riva (2003) cite specific health care related learning applications that include creating simulations for emergency training, mental health training (e.g., experience hallucinations of schizophrenia patients), brain and body interactivity training, and telesurgical training (focused on teaching certain skill sets). The authors suggest that learning environment and individual factors such as the material to be learned, characteristics of learners, as well as the learning and interactive experience can influence the process of learning and resulting outcomes.

Various 3-D virtual world environments utilized in educational contexts exist today to support these endeavors. For example, Active Worlds Educational Universe, launched in 1999, is a browser-based virtual environment that consists of user-created 3-D worlds inhabited by avatars (Dickey, 2005a; Peterson, 2006). Avatars are digital personas used to represent a person's identity in a virtual world environment (Conway, 2007). An avatar is typically a caricature, a full body, or can be just a head shot. In Active Worlds, avatars can be customized if the user is registered, otherwise users are restricted to standardized avatars that can walk, run, slide, and fly throughout the virtual world (Dickey, 2005a; Peterson, 2006). Users can interact within the environment or access Web pages. Sensors or triggers can be placed throughout the world such that when an avatar encounters one, pre-specified actions will occur (e.g., transporting to a new location).

Similarly, Adobe Atmosphere (established in 2001) is a 3-D virtual world environment that allows avatars to navigate and interact with one another (Dickey, 2005a). Worlds are created by users and can be linked together. Another example of virtual world environments that is increasing in popularity is Second Life. Second Life was launched in 2003 by Linden Lab (Joly, 2007). Individuals are able to create avatars, also called residents of Second Life, that can be navigated to explore the environment, socialize with other avatars, participate in activities, and produce and trade items and services. Avatars don't necessarily have to be human, they can range from animal forms to a "giant bowl of Jell-O" (Graves, 2008 p. 49).

Nearly 12 million unique avatar accounts exist in early 2008 in Second Life (Mennecke et al., 2008). Also, Second Life provides textual, visual, and auditory communication channels (Junglas, Johnson, Steel, Abraham, & Loughlin, 2007). Ondrejka (2008) and Goral (2008) clarify that

Second Life is not a game, but has a plethora of opportunities being pursued by various educational and research communities. Schultze, Hiltz, Nardi, Rennecker, and Stucky (2008) indicate that over 100 universities have conducted classes or sessions in Second Life. Also, Second Life has created a new avenue for business opportunities. The Linden Dollar currency can be exchanged for U.S. dollars and objects can be set to "copy" or as "for sale" to facilitate economic exchange (Jennings & Collins, 2007).

Second Life is unique in that the environment is created by its users. Linden Lab offers the foundational and communication tools for residents to build their own unique worlds and experiences. Educational institutions can purchase islands in Second Life for around US$700 per region (Second Life, 2008).

According to the Second Life website (www.secondlife.com), Second Life functionality that supports educational endeavors includes (Second Life, 2008):

- Conducting distance education courses
- Simulations and interactive content
- Training seminars
- Collaborative work efforts
- Studies in new media
- Security through private island purchases
- Skill practice or opportunities to experiment with new ideas

Hence, various applications of 3-D virtual world environments in an educational context are possible and are discussed below.

Current Applications

Educational applications of 3-D virtual world environments continue to grow and are capitalizing on the unique capabilities that these virtual environments can offer. These capabilities provide avenues for novel expressions to emerge, a new means to "participate" in classes, as well as new ways to reach wider audiences. Rich forms of communications provide new venues for class or group discussions.

For example, capabilities associated with Second Life include (Jennings & Collins, 2007):

- Accenting site with logos, maps, welcome signs, and various forms of greetings
- Offering promotional materials to visitors (e.g., free t-shirts for avatar)
- Sidewalks, pathways/footpaths, bridges, and elevators for avatar to navigate within site
- Links to other Internet websites and teleports to other Second Life locations
- Communication tools – text or audio
- Space for classrooms, auditoriums (includes podium, video screen, chalkboard, and seating for avatars), libraries, theater, offices (includes chairs and desk), research labs, sandbox (for building), role-playing, student projects, assignment distribution and submission, apartments/housing, art galleries, visitor centers, resource centers, meetings for campus organizations, and socializing (e.g., bars, restaurants, dance clubs, beaches, gardens, game rooms, coffee shops)
- Creating sense of openness (e.g., buildings with mesh ceilings and no walls, bubbles floating in the air, pane glass windows looking at ocean/patios/vegetation)
- Replication of real-world environment and building connections with real-world (e.g., animal life, natural vegetation, historic buildings, campus layout)
- Social accommodations (e.g., offering beverages, listening to radio, vending machines)
- Simulations of events, games, etc.

In regards to the structure that shapes these virtual worlds in educational applications, Jennings and Collins (2007) have noted that some institutions are choosing to develop a "reflective virtual campus environment" or developing a replication of its physical campus and orchestrating connections to the real-world, while others are developing an "operative virtual campus environment" or creating a virtual location that is unique from its physical campus and performing activities virtually (p. 184). Hence, the applications for higher education are various and they are provided in Table 1. These applications are categorized into three categories or types based on their purpose: (i) replicating reality and existing activities, (ii) developing novel spaces and conducting activities unique to the virtual world environment, (iii) those focusing on accomplishing both of the above.

Some instructors have chosen to hold classes fully through Second Life, while others are utilizing a hybrid method (Jennings & Collins, 2007). Richter, Anderson-Inman, and Frisbee (2007) identify five different types of learner engagement that are possible in Second Life: demonstrative, experiential, diagnostic, role play, and constructivist. For example, Schultze et al. (2008) suggest that students could participate in role-playing scenarios such as discussing an ethical dilemma and debating over the various perspectives that arise. All students could ask questions and vote. Therefore, applications and opportunities of Second Life in education continue to emerge, and with these developments certain benefits and issues have been identified.

Benefits

A variety of potential beneficial outcomes experienced when utilizing 3-D virtual worlds in an educational context have been cited. Benefits that were identified based on our review include conducting educational activities in a risk-free environment, enhancements in collaboration and communication, engaging learners, and being

Table 1. Examples of educational applications in 3-D virtual environments for higher education

Organization	Application	Source
1. Replicating Reality – Utilizing Alternative Space for Existing Activities		
Appalachian State University and Clemson University	3-D virtual world created to improve online learning for master's degree students.	"ASU Partners", 2008
Ball State University – Middletown Island	Intellagirl conducts freshman English-composition class.	Foster, 2007b
Bard College	Students practice using a 3D replica of an optical telescope before using the real device.	Johnson & Levine, 2008
Duke University's Fuqua School of Business	Partnering with ProtonMedia to create 3-D spaces for education or "telepresence portal."	"Bringing Virtual Worlds," 2008
INSEAD - France and Singapore	School/library is open-air building with auditorium seating 36. Clickable computer screens provide access to other web pages and library offers hot tea. Research lab provides notecards to describe research and request consent. Public space/beach provides clickable kiosks to obtain more information about INSEAD, space for reflecting and conversing, bar with drinks available, and listening to radio.	Jennings & Collins, 2007
Northwestern University	Students design productions and develop appropriate stage configuration in virtual theater.	Johnson & Levine, 2008
Princeton University	Created island that includes lecture hall, art museum, and performance location.	Graves, 2008
2. Developing Novel Space – Conducting Activities Unique to Virtual World		
Immersive Education project - Boston College, Harvard University, Amherst College, Columbia University, Massachusetts Institute of Technology, Sweden's Royal Institute of Technology, Japan's University of Aizu, the Israeli Association of Grid Technologies, National Aeronautics and Space Administration (NASA), Sun Microsystems, the City of Boston, and the New Media Consortium	Created tours inside Egyptian tomb, created interactive lessons (Croquet and Project Wonderland), developed park and replica of Boston's subway system to tour city's neighborhoods, developed Restaurant Game to help waiters/waitresses acquire skills/training through simulations of restaurant experiences.	Foster, 2007a
Indiana University	Created a Virtual Solar System project for astronomy undergraduate course.	Barab et al., 2000
Lehigh Carbon Community College and adjunct at De-Sales University (professor at both)	Professor created Literature Alive – provides guided tours of famous literary locations (e.g., Dante's Inferno).	Foster, 2007b
Vassar College – Vassar Island	Re-creation of Sistine Chapel – visitors can fly to ceiling or view tapestries designed for the walls.	Foster, 2007b
3. Replicating Reality and Developing Novel Space		
Boise State University	EDTech island utilized for teaching educational games and providing students testing area (building own objects), includes information center, and condominium.	Goral, 2008
Bowling Green State, Ohio	Use virtual campus for teaching, research, office hours (space pods situated into mountain sides), exhibiting art and music, and presentations by guest speakers. In process of creating a writing center ran by graduate students.	Goral, 2008

continued on the following page

Table 1. continued

Organization	Application	Source
Bradley University	Students have conducted analyses of avatar fans of musicians that conduct performances in Second Life as well as other topics such as online hackers.	Foster, 2007b
Georgia Institute of Technology	Augmented Reality lab created software to associate actual physical spaces with virtual – creating ability to combine video feeds from the real world with Second Life avatars.	Goral, 2008
Johnson & Wales University	Created a Virtual Morocco in conjunction with Ministry of Tourism of Morocco. Includes monuments and opportunities to learn about Moroccan culture. Students created and developed plans and prototypes, and worked with individuals from other countries on project. Virtual BLAST (Balloon-borne Large-Aperture Sub-millimeter Telescope) brought attention to scientific ballooning projects by flying over the Second Life main grid and stopping to visit various educational and scientific locations. Entrepreneurship students create business plans and develop prototypes in Second Life	Mason, 2007
Massachusetts Institute of Technology	75% of island dedicated to student projects, remainder replicates physical campus (including outdoor theater area). Avatars can address a crowd with a megaphone and determine average viewpoint by avatars moving to right or left of line on platform. Sponsored contest for students to design dormitories.	Foster, 2007b
Montclair State University	Use mountain sides for displaying syllabus and spheres for deadlines, Literature Alive spots include Willow Springs and encountering evil in Young Goodman Brown, and provide sun bathing area as well as covered deck near lake.	Foster, 2007b
New Media Consortium	Created New Media Consortium campus for educational experiences	Johnson & Levine, 2008
Ohio University or Ohio University Without Boundaries	Entry way provides historical information and historic replicas of campus (along with Standards and Privacy Statement). Locations include Welcome Center (video display of learning initiatives), Art and Music Center, Classroom and Meeting Center (with seating capacity of 25), Learning Center (displaying e-learning activities), Student Center (coffee shop, stage which includes microphone, pool tables, kiosk publicizing real-world entertainment activities, student video lounge, vending machines, and reading space), Featured Games (simulation of fast food restaurant – avatar selects food to learn nutritional value), Stocker Center and Sandbox (building objects by permission). Collaborated with The Princeton Review for SAT preparation.	Jennings & Collins, 2007; Goral, 2008
Simon Fraser University	Professor produced films for posting on YouTube and created cartoons for first-year calculus students.	Conway, 2007

able to utilize an alternative space for conducting courses and associated tasks, explained as follows:

(i) Conducting Activities in a Risk-free Environment

As noted previously, a variety of activities and tasks can be conducted in 3-D virtual worlds, and many of these can be carried out with less apprehension by the learner. For instance, some have cited the benefits of Second Life that include providing a platform in which students can conduct role-playing, experiment with new ideas, enhance their skill sets, and create simulations in essentially a risk-free way and in a safe environment (Graves, 2008; Johnson & Levine, 2008; Wood, Solomon, & Allan, 2008). Dickey (2005a) cites previous research demonstrating benefits of virtual environments including being able to experiment without concern for "real-world repercussions" and being able to "learn by doing." Ondrejka

(2008) cites that some students have cited a greater level of comfort in asking questions, and are able to develop a sense of shared learning. Goral (2008) cites exploring new domains of interest and innovation as possibilities in Second Life. Students who are interested in on-line courses may be more attuned to those taught via avatars because it could provide opportunities to introduce more creativity into the classroom (Conway, 2007).

(ii) Collaboration and Communication

Benefits of using 3-D virtual worlds in education include enhanced collaboration and communication capabilities. In research conducted in virtual world environments, the creation of an avatar increased the individual user's sense of telepresence or copresence, which has been suggested to improve communication, as well as social and educational experiences in virtual environments (Peterson, 2006; Wood, Solomon, & Allan, 2008). Active Worlds allows non-verbal communication cues and emotional states to be displayed by one's avatar in real-time, which extends the capabilities of technologies that are only text-based. According to Bronack, Reidl, and Tashner (2006) who utilize the AET Zone, a 3-D virtual world created with an Active Worlds Inc. universe server and developed for Appalachian State University, the benefits of education in virtual worlds include "a sense of presence, immediacy, movement, artifacts, and communications unavailable within traditional Internet-based learning environments" (p. 220). Bronack, Reidl, and Tashner (2006) also noted that they are able to have interactions with their students in "more fluid and natural ways" (p. 230), are allowing students to select their own paths of learning, resources, and activities, and are "encouraging cross-class collaboration" (p. 230). Their students have indicated that they have found the interactions with other students to be stimulating and the experience to be enriching. Dickey (2005a, 2005b) has also cited that the chat tools and communication capabilities in environments such as Active Worlds provide a platform for collaborative and cooperative learning, which is highly valued in the socio-constructivist paradigm.

Some have noted the ability to interact with individuals who are physically located throughout the world (Graves, 2008). Having the ability to create an avatar that is not only human in form but can be modeled to be almost identical to oneself can help to enhance on-line communication (Foster, 2007a). Goral (2008) cites the benefits of collaborating and interacting with others who are geographically dispersed, engaging with others in discussions of similar interests, and engaging in rich forms of communication. Johnson and Levine (2008) identify the benefits of learning a foreign language and about remote locations by interacting with natives from these remote locations. Chang Liu, director of Virtual Immersive Technologies and Arts for Learning Lab that is associated with Ohio University Without Boundaries, argues that Second Life is "a very rich form of communication and the main task of education is communication" (Goral, 2008 p. 62). Also, Second Life has been cited as providing a culturally diverse experience and providing livelier communication in distance education courses (Foster, 2007b). Research conducted by Jarmon, Traphagan, and Mayrath (2008) indicates that team projects and the associated virtual social relationships can enhance the learning experience. Gaimster (2008) has also suggested that having positive social interactions can influence academic achievement.

(iii) Engagement

Increased engagement has also been associated with the use of 3-D virtual world environments in education and is important for learning success according to the constructivist methodology (Coffman & Klinger, 2007). In research conducted by Mikropoulos (2001), brain activity was measured for tasks performed in real as well as virtual reality environments. Research findings demonstrated subjects were more attentive, responsive, and utilized less mental effort in the virtual world, demonstrating that knowledge transfer is possible (such that knowledge gained in one world can be transferred to the other world).

Mason (2007) cites students being more engaged in learning tasks and spending more time thinking and discussing the subject material, while Richter, Anderson-Inman, and Frisbee (2007) cite perceptions of immersion into another world and engaging in learning in the first person (which is more interactive and experiential). Second Life experiences can be created such that information is available when the learner needs and wants it (Ondrejka, 2008). Dickey (2005b) has also cited that allowing learners to interact with information in the first person facilitates constructivist-based learning activities, and that the user-extensible options in Active Worlds provide greater opportunity for learner engagement. Also, Dickey (2005a) has cited that previous research indicates that being able to interact with virtual objects may assist in developing a stronger conceptual understanding, depending on the content.

Using virtual worlds increases enthusiasm for learning and introduces some to an experience (in virtual worlds) that they may have never realized (Foster, 2007b).

(iv) Alternative Space for Instruction and Tasks

Some educational professionals see opportunities to conduct courses or related activities in places other than the classroom including visiting simulations of places that no longer exist in real life (Graves, 2008). One associate dean has even cited that these virtual campuses could be a back-up to the physical location in cases of natural disasters such as Katrina (Graves, 2008). Others, who are situated in more risky locations, find Second Life a safer venue to have undergraduates conduct field research projects (Foster, 2007b) or activities that

may be too dangerous or expensive in real-life (Johnson & Levine, 2008).

Conway (2007) suggests that teaching through an academic avatar that follows the traditional classroom instructional methods in a virtual environment can provide the instructor opportunities to spend more time on spontaneous and productive interactions through group work or class discussions in the real-world classroom by freeing up precious time. Experiential learning programs can be designed such that relevant skills can be practiced and acquired (Mason, 2007). Dickey (2005a) has cited the ability to personalize one's learning space.

(iv) Visualization for Difficult Content

Some subject-matter is more difficult to learn through material that is presented in a static format. For example, Barab et al. (2000) indicated that concepts such as "lines of nodes" and the variety of scales and sizes are typically disregarded in introductory astronomy courses because of the difficulty in understanding these concepts which are dynamic and 3-D in nature. Hence, their use of a 3-D virtual environment allowed students to more easily grasp these concepts.

Hence, virtual worlds present their own unique set of opportunities, but with that, their own unique issues.

Issues

Applications of virtual environments in an educational context pose unique issues. These issues include identifying value-added educational applications; being able to read people's natural physical cues; technological issues; costs; behavioral, health and safety issues; and user adoption. Issues cited for virtual world environments in education are discussed as follows:

(i) Appropriate Value-Added Educational Applications

Identifying appropriate value-added educational content and activities in which 3-D virtual worlds can be effectively utilized has been cited as an issue. Mantovani, Castelnuovo, Gaggioli, and Riva (2003) indicate two challenges to utilizing virtual worlds in education: 1) determining situations in which virtual world learning presents value beyond what traditional education can provide, and 2) determining how to effectively utilize and adapt these worlds to support learning. Although 3-D virtual worlds may be utilized to conduct educational games, some indicate that promoting games in learning environments is degrading to education (Foster, 2007a). Furthermore, existing virtual worlds may not be designed for optimal teaching (e.g., integrating quizzes) (Schultze et al., 2008). Johnson and Levine (2008) suggest that some faculty, especially those who are novices to virtual worlds, attempt to "retrofit" existing teaching practices and strategies to the new virtual environment.

(ii)   Inability to read "natural" physical cues

There has been discontent with not being able to read natural body language. Although an avatar can present certain facial expressions, one professor indicates that these forced expressions are meaningless and doesn't provide sound evidence of a student's attentiveness or boredom (Graves, 2008). Dickey (2005a) also notes that the *traditional* classroom setting provides a broader range of non-verbal communication. Similarly, Wood, Solomon, and Allan (2008) suggest that it is more challenging to gauge student comprehensions without natural body language.

(iii)   Technological Issues

Technological issues that may arise include proprietary applications with limited adaptability to other contexts as well as system usability (Mantovani, Castelnuovo, Gaggioli, & Riva, 2003). Bryson (1996) cites virtual reality issues

that include the re-invention of interfaces that accommodate the three-dimensional versus traditional two-dimensional designs and requiring exceptionally high system performance such that the virtual-reality effect can be experienced. In previous applications of Second Life in education, Schultze et al. (2008) reported that some learners did not have enough hardware power or bandwidth to properly utilize Second Life and most of the discussions were focused on the features of Second Life and not the to-be-learned topic. Dickey (2005a) indicates that in some virtual environments, such as Active Worlds and Adobe Atmosphere, only text communication is available. Also, in Active Worlds, objects can not easily be built or moved while in Adobe Atmosphere because the object-building process is time intensive and requires some basic skills before one can become proficient.

(iv)   Costs

Concerns have also been generated over costs (Dickey, 2005a; Mantovani, Castelnuovo, Gaggioli, & Riva, 2003). Schultze et al. (2008) note that a common concern for *any* implementation of technology in education is costs. Costs may include not only the purchase of one's own island, but also the cost associated with building and maintaining the island. Costs to consider include initial set-up expenses as well as recurring licensing and/ or rental fees ("What Does It Cost", 2008). For instance, if one wanted a private and customized island that could accommodate 50 individuals, it could cost anywhere from $10,000 to $20,000. If a fully customized and completely private virtual world that was able to accommodate thousands of individuals was desired, the cost could reach one million dollars. However, if one wanted to rent public space from existing campuses, the costs could include rentals of $200-300 each day, management fees of $20-30 for each participant, and customization costs of $1,000-2,000 for each simulation. Although the latter option provides easier affordability, it also presents new issues of utilizing public spaces which poses other potential issues, such as safety issues, addressed as follows.

(v)   Behavioral, Health, and Safety Issues

Other issues that may arise include health and safety issues (e.g., simulator sickness, ocular problems, addictive behaviors) (Gaimster, 2008; Mantovani, Castelnuovo, Gaggioli, & Riva, 2003; Wood, Solomon, & Allan, 2008). Also, activities may become more playful than educational, and monitoring behavior can present challenges (Graves, 2008). For example, Ohio University's Second Life campus experienced a virtual shooting and Woodbury University students were engaging in "disruptive and hostile behavior" (Graves, 2008 p. 50). Bugeja (2008) cites that the two most common violations in Second Life are assault and harassment. He indicates that issues may arise when the company's terms of service agreements may conflict with academic due process in cases such as violence, or students are required to agree to these service terms in order to participate in this virtual world. Questions to be considered, as posed by the author, include: Has the professor included warnings if he/she required an exercise to be performed in a virtual world? Is your institution aware of harassment issues in virtual worlds or has issued guidelines on its use?

(vi)   User Adoption

Lack of experience with using virtual worlds can raise issues for teachers (Dickey, 2005a; Gaimster, 2008; Mantovani, Castelnuovo, Gaggioli, & Riva, 2003; Wood, Solomon, & Allan, 2008) as well as students (Dickey, 2005a). For instance, concerns include acquiring the skills to function in a virtual world, such as being able to teleport and master basic communication (Graves, 2008), and becoming acquainted with the virtual social space (Jarmon, Traphagan, & Mayrath, 2008). As

noted by Dickey (2005a), in virtual environments, such as Active Worlds, in which text-only communication is available, those individuals who do not have adequate typing or written language skills may suffer. Virtual worlds have been noted as not scaling well when too many avatars are participating simultaneously (Mennecke et al., 2008). Another issue is trust (Gaimster, 2008; Siau & Shen, 2003, Siau et al., 2004). Are the teachers and students going to trust the technology, the environments, and the people that they meet in the environments?

In experiences with conducting a single session class in Second Life, Schultze et al. (2008) indicated that learners (ranging in age from 25 to 50) encountered many problems in navigation, as well as experienced disorientation and confusion. However, a four-week set of sessions with learners who had significant online gaming experience and were averaging 20 years of age indicated that Second Life was simple, but the graphics appeared outdated. In addition, Baber et al. (2000) found that learners spent a significant amount of time learning the software for their 3-D virtual world learning environment, resulting in a delay of exploring the to-be-learned subject matter. They, however, felt that this could have been avoided if they would have used a scaffolding approach in accomplishing technical skills and subject-matter concepts.

EDUCATIONAL OPPORTUNITIES IN 3-D VIRTUAL WORLDS

Based on the review above, we present Figure 1 which summarizes aspects of 3-D virtual worlds and their implications for educational opportunities. The use of virtual worlds in an educational context generates certain issues as well as affords various capabilities. When considering educational opportunities, certain factors can be considered to address the issues that are inherent. For example, it is important to assure that individu-

Figure 1. Virtual world implications in education

VIRTUAL WORLD FACTORS, CAPABILITES, and EXPERIENCES in EDUCATIONAL OPPORTUNITIES

ISSUES
- Meeting technology requirements
- Utilizing virtual world functions and navigating around
- Integrating effectively (e.g., supporting learning and not distracting)
- Identifying domain-specific value and value-added activities
- Focus on task and not technology
- Designing for optimal learning and teaching
- Health and safety (e.g., inappropriate behavior)

CAPABILITIES
- Simulations (some not possible in real life)/role-playing
- Visualizations
- Experimentation (more risk free)/exploration
- Collaboration (greater diversity)
- Communication channel variety (e.g., text, audio, visual)
- Alternative spaces for socializing/education/research/entertainment/business
- Ability to replicate reality or create new world/objects
- Ability to move and navigate (one's avatar and other objects)
- Information available on demand
- More natural interactions (e.g., communicating with other avatars)
- Ability to conduct some normal class functions (e.g., retrieving assignments, posting syllabi)
- Opportunities to practice, train, gain assistance (e.g., tutoring), and acquire skills at lower costs and risks
- Avenue for promotion and marketing tools
- Provide easy access or connections points to other resources

FACTORS
- Sufficient technology resources
- Appropriate orientation and training in a virtual world
- Effective strategies for integration (focus on subject material and not technology) – allow time for being accustomed to a virtual world
- Assessment criteria for determining derived value
- Participating in learning community - leveraging other tools, acquiring feedback, and sharing experiences
- Discipline in usage – appropriate policies and codes of conduct
- Safety measures – e.g., restricted island usage

Educational Opportunities

EXPERIENCES
- Sense of presence, immediacy, openness, and community
- Rich and real-time communication
- Interactivity
- Creative expression/avenue for creativity
- Motivation/engagement/immersion – greater time spent on subject
- Adaptability (e.g., to learners needs)
- Innovation
- Greater comfort with taking risks and asking questions

als engaging in 3-D virtual world environments have the appropriate technological requirements, training, orientation, and time to become accustomed to the virtual world so the technology is not distracting to their learning. Also, utilizing assessment criteria for determining the value that can be derived from the use of 3-D virtual world environments in education can help determine "when" and "where" they can be applied. Participating in a learning community in which tools and experiences can be shared to address concerns can help to identify "how" educational value can be derived, such as joining the Second Life education (SLED) listserv to communicate with other educators or browse the Second Life

Education Wiki. Appropriate safety measures and disciplinary policies should also be considered to address health and safety concerns.

The 3-D virtual world environments provide many capabilities, including simulations and visualizations that cannot feasibly take place in reality but can be incorporated in the design of educational opportunities. These capabilities also generate various experiences that can be leveraged as well. For example, the ability to experiment and explore in 3-D virtual world environments can generate educational opportunities that foster innovation. The ability to move one's avatar, communicate through various channels, and conduct more natural interactions can foster rich and real-

Table 2. Fink's (2003) Taxonomy of significant learning – application to 3-D virtual world environments

Category	Description	3-D Virtual Environment Affordances
Foundational Knowledge	Being able to understand and remember – the basic knowledge that is foundational to other learning	Provides ability to acquire information when needed and understand concepts (some too difficult to learn through traditional instruction but possible through 3-D visualizations)
Application	Engaging in other actions or thinking (e.g., critical, creative), acquiring certain skills, and managing complex projects – basis for other learning to be useful	Environment provides creative expression opportunities, ability to practice, and encourages critical thinking and risk-taking
Integration	Identifying and comprehending connections between different ideas, people, or realms – creation of intellectual power	Collaboration and cooperative activities allow connections between people; environment allows viewing creations from multiple perspectives; creating simulations allow opportunities to understand entire dynamic relationships
Human Dimension	Understanding important aspects of one's self or others, includes understanding personal and social implications – derivation of human significance of subject matter	Interactions with others can provide insights into social and personal factors
Caring	Changes in feelings, interests, or values in which the student cares about subject – acquisition of energy needed for learning	Engaging and becoming immersed in a subject can generate increased sense of caring
Learning How to Learn	Learn how to learn: becoming a more successful student, engaging in inquiry, or self-directing learning – support more effective and continuous learning	No immediate application identified; may depend on learning tasks

time communication which can enhance educational activities focused on collaboration. Also, providing opportunities to practice or participate in simulations can generate greater engagement and interactivity.

Hence, educational opportunities in 3-D virtual world environments can be derived through the virtual world's existing capabilities and associated experiences. These opportunities can be enhanced by consideration of various factors that address the associated issues that accompany 3-D virtual world experiences. To appropriately address the potential of 3-D virtual world environments in meeting pedagogical objectives, we compare the capabilities of these environments to a taxonomy of learning objectives to identify the possibilities as well as the gaps that remain, described as follows.

GAPS IN 3-D VIRTUAL WORLD ENVIRONMENT CAPABILITIES IN EDUCATION

The 3-D virtual world environments have demonstrated potential usage in an educational context, but gaps may remain. To assess the potential as well as the gaps, we compare these capabilities to Fink's (2003) taxonomy of significant learning. Fink identified a need to broaden Bloom's taxonomy of educational objectives considering "individuals and organizations involved in higher education are expressing a need for important kinds of learning that do not emerge easily from the Bloom taxonomy" (Fink, 2003 p. 29). Therefore, Fink created a new taxonomy that focuses on learning in terms of change. The taxonomy and its relation to 3-D virtual world environments are listed in Table 2.

As noted in Table 2, all but one of Fink's categories of significant learning can potentially be addressed in some regards in 3-D virtual world environments. Learners are able to acquire a foundational knowledge as well as learn its application. Through collaborative, interactive, and cooperative activities, learners can integrate knowledge and understand its social and individual implications. Also, learners can become more engaged and immersed in an activity, and they can develop a deeper sense of caring for the topic. However, no indications of educational applications in such environments indicate that students become more capable, self-directed learners or have developed strategies (e.g., metacognitive strategies) that imply that they have learned how to learn. Therefore, many educational opportunities exist and much potential for meeting various pedagogical objectives are possible in 3-D virtual world environments. Gaps may remain in the ability for students to "learn how to learn."

IMPLICATIONS

Practical Implications

Various opportunities have arisen and continue to evolve in applying 3-D virtual worlds in the field of education. Examples for business-related courses include:

- Strategic Management: create competition in which each team manages an existing business or designs a new business that markets a particular product or service. The activities can include conducting research and development, making manufacturing production decisions, establishing prices, and developing advertising campaigns.
- Operations Management: create simulations of supply chains
- Management Information Systems: create virtual simulation of data and information flowing through an enterprise resource planning system, or a simulation of e-commerce(electronic commerce)/u-commerce (ubiquitous commerce) transactions
- Management/Leadership: role playing as a manager training/evaluating/managing employees, facilitate virtual presentations from guest speakers who are geographically dispersed
- International Management: meeting individuals from across cultures and collaborating with students from other universities on projects
- Marketing: role playing sales presentations or advertising strategies, experiment with brand management, create a service enterprise to provide marketing/advertising services to businesses (or other organizations) joining 3-D virtual world environments, and experimenting with and studying consumer behavior and product development (Park et al., 2008; Wood, et al. 2008)
- Finance: create simulations of actively trading stocks
- Economics: study the entire ecosystem within a 3-D virtual world environment that is emerging

The examples given above are a few of the many educational opportunities that exist for business-related courses. Many others exist outside the domain of business as well. Hence, the potential for applications of virtual worlds in any field of education is just starting to be realized and will continue to develop.

Therefore, it will be important for instructors to consider all the capabilities and derived experiences that are associated with 3-D virtual worlds (see Figure 1), and consider the pedagogical objectives they want to achieve (see Table 2). These capabilities can be leveraged in various manners to provide new or enhanced educational opportunities. For pedagogical objectives that are focused on innovation, exploration, and risk-taking, an instructor can capitalize on virtual worlds' abilities to provide platforms for prompting these experiences. If practice or training of certain skills is necessary, simulations can be created in virtual worlds to promote such activities. Also, if collaboration is desired, an educator can take advantage of the rich communication media available in 3-D virtual worlds, such as the audio, visual, and textual features of Second Life.

However, instructors will also want to take into account various factors that address issues inherent in a 3-D virtual world environment. Assessing the value that can be derived as well as incorporating appropriate disciplinary measures will be essential for an optimal education experience to be achieved. John Lester (SL: Pathfinder Linden) of Linden Lab suggests the following strategies for success in utilizing Second Life in education (Lester, 2006):

1. Explore and learn about Second Life as much as possible
2. Converse with other educators currently utilizing Second Life
3. Develop concise, measurable goals
4. Write a paper about your Second Life experiences and utilize other venues to share your knowledge
5. Be open to the potential of Second Life and the variations in activities possible
6. Think creatively about new uses for instruction and avoid applying old models of thinking
7. Capitalize on feedback from students' experiences

Specific projects are being undertaken to enhance and capitalize on the educational opportunities within 3-D virtual worlds. For example, the SaLamander Project's goal is to "survey, collect, and describe 3D objects, materials, resources, and environments in Second Life created specifically for use in teaching and learning or with the potential to be useful in such activities" (Richter,

Anderson-Inman, & Frisbee, 2007, p. 21). Hence, educators will benefit from accessing these developing resources as well as communicating with the existing community of educators in 3-D virtual world environments.

Research Implications

Based on the literature review conducted, researchers will need to be aware of issues that have arisen as well as the experiences and capabilities that are possible in 3-D virtual world environments. For example, 3-D virtual environments require advanced technology resources, appropriate training and orientation before users can be expected to perform specific tasks, and adequate time for users to become familiar with the environment. Also, safety measures may be needed, such as acquiring one's own island so usage is restricted, so that behaviors can be properly monitored.

The capabilities and opportunities that exist in virtual environments provide much potential for insightful research experiments. Research that may not have been practical or feasible in real life can be created through simulations in environments. With abilities to collaborate and a variety of communication channels, researchers can study social behaviors in various contexts. Also, the experiences of creative expression and innovation that are possible in virtual worlds can be studied at an individual level with a variety of tasks.

Various educational institutions are citing plans for future research in 3-D virtual world environments. For example, Louisiana has implemented a statewide initiative to explore the value of virtual world environments for higher education, which includes the purchase and development of five islands in Second Life (Graves, 2008). The Immersive Education project is developing virtual-reality software for Second Life spaces that incorporates Web cameras, Internet-based telephony, three-dimensional graphics that are interactive, as well as other digital media (Foster, 2007a). The ultimate goal is to develop interactive activities that can capture a student's attention similar to gaming environments enticements. Some of the environments being developed have publicly available code (i.e., open source) (see Long & Siau, 2007; Crowston & Scozzi, 2008) allowing others to customize as needed. Other endeavors include developing best practices and open standards. Using Second Life as a laboratory, business professors are exploring it as developmental ground for entrepreneurs (Foster, 2007b).

Mennecke et al. (2008) highlight three broad themes to provide perspective on future research: psychological, sociological, and technical. The psychological theme encompasses the individual personality, dispositions, and traits that influence a user's experience. Sociological theme recognizes the dynamic interactions of agents (i.e., avatars) and the influence of these on group outcomes and individual experiences. Finally, the technical theme addresses the progression of interweaving existing technologies with virtual worlds and improving functionality. Therefore, future research can expand on Figure 1 to study the influence of specific psychological, social, and technical factors, along with the capabilities and experiences that are possible in 3-D virtual worlds on educational experiences (see Figure 2).

Schultze et al. (2008) suggest that pedagogical techniques need to be explored that promote effective collaboration as well as constructivist learning in 3-D virtual world environments. Junglas, Johnson, Steel, Abraham, and Loughlin (2007) argue that social psychological theories that have been previously applied to understand learning styles in the real world need to be readdressed in the virtual world. Junglas and Steel (2007) indicate that future research can more closely examine variations in the capabilities that 3-D virtual worlds can provide, including visualization, simulation, and social presence. Hence, future research can explore additional applications of 3-D virtual world environments in education.

One method of doing so is to conduct a focus group study or Delphi study of individuals currently utilizing 3-D virtual worlds for teaching and research. Focus sessions can identify criteria for evaluating value-added activities as well as strategies for effectively integrating 3-D virtual worlds into a curriculum. Factors that are associated with adoption of 3-D virtual worlds into educational activities by educators can be explored as well. Also, experiments of various constructivist activities and their effect on learning outcomes can be conducted. The learning experience may vary among individuals; hence, additional research can focus on individual learner profiles that are more likely to capitalize on the learning experience in 3-D virtual worlds.

Figure 2. Virtual worlds in education

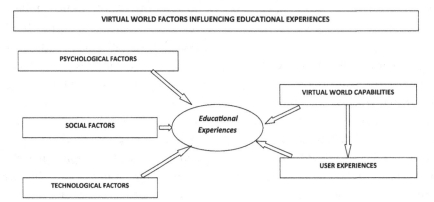

CONCLUSION

In summary, virtual reality environments present new opportunities for education. The unique opportunities of creating an interactive environment occupied by avatars with advanced communication abilities have opened up new avenues for a variety of educational experiences. This article specifically reviews aspects of 3-D virtual world environments to assess current applications, benefits that are being realized, and issues that have emerged. In the context of educational opportunities, factors, capabilities, and derived experiences in 3-D virtual world environments are identified. The capabilities range from creating simulations and role-playing to collaboration. The derived experiences include a sense of presence as well as promoting innovation to name a few. However, factors to be taken into account for educational opportunities include proper training and orientation, appropriate strategies for integration (Langdon, 2006), and criteria for determining value-added activities. Hence, this review provides various practical implications for those interested in exploring educational opportunities in 3-D virtual world environments, as well as provides suggestions for future research. As educational applications of 3-D virtual worlds are beginning to evolve, their true potential and influence on education is yet to be fully explored and discovered.

REFERENCES

ASU partners with Clemson to create virtual world technology. (2008). *Techniques: Connecting Education & Careers, 83*(2), 60.

Barab, S. A., Hay, K. E., Squire, K., Barnett, M., Schmidt, R., & Karrigan, K. (2000). Virtual solar system project: Learning through a technology-rich, inquiry-based, participatory learning environment. *Journal of Science Education and Technology, 9*(1), 7–25. doi:10.1023/A:1009416822783

Bringing virtual worlds to business school. (2008). *BizEd, 7*(1), 34.

Bronack, S., Riedl, R., & Tashner, J. (2006). Learning in the zone: A social constructivist framework for distance education in a 3-dimensional virtual world. *Interactive Learning Environments, 14*(3), 219–232. doi:10.1080/10494820600909157

Bryson, S. (1996). Virtual reality in scientific visualization. *Communications of the ACM, 39*(5), 62–71. doi:10.1145/229459.229467

Bugeja, M. J. (2008). Second thoughts about Second Life. *Education Digest, 73*(5), 18–22.

Coffman, T., & Klinger, M. B. (2007). Utilizing virtual worlds in education: The implications for practice. *International Journal of Social Sciences, 2*(1), 29–33.

Conway, C. (2007). Professor Avatar. *Inside Higher Ed*. Retrieved April 24, 2008, from http://www.insidehighered.com/views/2007/10/16/conway.

Crowston, K., & Scozzi, B. (2008). Bug fixing practices within free/libre open source software development teams. *Journal of Database Management, 19*(2), 1–30.

Davis, S., Siau, K., & Dhenuvakonda, K. (2003). A fit-gap analysis of e-business curricula vs. industry need. *Communications of the ACM, 46*(12), 167–177. doi:10.1145/953460.953497

Dickey, M. D. (2005a). Brave new (interactive) worlds: A review of the design affordances and constraints of two 3D virtual worlds as interactive learning environments. *Interactive Learning Environments, 13*(1-2), 121–137. doi:10.1080/10494820500173714

Dickey, M. D. (2005b). Three-dimensional virtual worlds and distance learning: Two case studies of Active Worlds as a medium for distance education. *British Journal of Educational Technology, 36*(3), 439–451. doi:10.1111/j.1467-8535.2005.00477.x

Erickson, J., & Siau, K. (2003). e-ducation. *Communications of the ACM, 46*(9), 134–140. doi:10.1145/903893.903928

Finke, L. D. (2003). *Creating Significant Learning Experiences*. San Francisco, CA: Jossey-Bass, John Wiley & Sons Inc.

Foster, A. (2007a). 'Immersive *education*' submerges students in online worlds made for learning. *The Chronicle of Higher Education, 54*(17), A22.

Foster, A. (2007b). Professor avatar. *The Chronicle of Higher Education, 54*(4), A24–A26.

Gaimster, J. (2008). Reflections on interactions in virtual worlds and their implication for learning art and design. *Art, Design, & . Communication in Higher Education, 6*(3), 187–199. doi:10.1386/adch.6.3.187_1

Goral, T. (2008). Sizing up Second Life. *University Business, 11*(3), 60–64.

Graves, L. (2008). A Second Life for higher ed. *U.S. News & World Report, 144*(2), 49–50.

Guru, A., & Siau, K. (2008). Developing the IBM I Virtual Community – iSociety. *Journal of Database Management, 19*(4), i–xiii.

Jarmon, L., Traphagan, T., & Mayrath, M. (2008). Understanding project-based learning in Second Life with pedagogy, training, and assessment trio. *Educational Media International, 45*(3), 157–176. doi:10.1080/09523980802283889

Jennings, N., & Collins, C. (2007). Virtual or virtually U. *International Journal of Social Sciences, 2*(3), 180-186. Retrieved April 7, 2008, from http://www.waset.org/ijss/v2/v2-3-28.pdf

Johnson, L. F., & Levine, A. H. (2008). Virtual worlds: Inherently immersive, highly social learning spaces. *Theory into Practice, 47*(2), 161–170. doi:10.1080/00405840801992397

Joly, K. (2007). A Second Life for higher education? *University Business*. Retrieved April 17, 2008 from http://www.universitybusiness.com/viewarticle.aspx?articleid=797.

Junglas, I. A., Johnson, N. A., Steel, D. J., Abraham, D. C., & Loughlin, P. M. (2007). Identify formation, learning styles and trust in virtual worlds. *The Data Base for Advances in Information Systems, 38*(4), 90–96.

Junglas, I. A., & Steel, D. J. (2007). The virtual sandbox. *The Data Base for Advances in Information Systems, 38*(4), 26–28.

Langdon, C. S. (2006). Designing information systems capabilities to create business value: A theoretical conceptualization of the role of flexibility and integration. *Journal of Database Management, 17*(3), 1–18.

Lester, J. (2006). Pathfinder Linden's guide to getting started in Second Life. In D. Livingstone and J. Kemp (Eds.) *Proceedings of the Second Life Education Workshop at the Second Life Community Convention, San Francisco* (pp. v.-vii.). United Kingdom: University of Paisle. Retrieved May 28, 2008, from http://www.simteach.com/SLCC06/slcc2006-proceedings.pdf

Long, Y., & Siau, K. (2007). Social network structures in open source software development teams. *Journal of Database Management, 18*(2), 25–40.

Mantovani, F., Castelnuovo, G., Gaggioli, A., & Riva, G. (2003). Virtual reality training for health-care professionals. *CyberPscyhology & Behavior, 6*(4), 389–395. doi:10.1089/109493103322278772

Mason, H. (2007). Experiential education in Second Life. In *Proceedings of the Second Life Education Workshop 2007* (pp. 14-18). Retrieved May 28, 2008 from http://www.simteach.com/slccedu07proceedings.pdf.

Mennecke, B., McNeill, D., Ganis, M., & Roche, E. M. (2008). Second Life and other virtual worlds: A roadmap for research. *Communications of the Association for Information Systems*, *22*, 371–388.

Mikropoulos, T. A. (2001). Brain activity on navigation in virtual environments. *Journal of Educational Computing Research*, *24*(1), 1–12. doi:10.2190/D1W3-Y15D-4UDW-L6C9

Ondrejka, C. (2008). Education unleashed: Participatory culture, education, and innovation in *Second Life*. In K. Salen (Ed.), *The Ecology of Games: Connecting Youth, Games, and Learning, The John D. and Catherine T. MacArthur Foundation Series on Digital Media and Learning* (pp. 229-252). Cambridge, MA: The MIT Press.

Park, S., Nah, F., DeWester, D., Eschenbrenner, B., & Jeon, S. (2008). Virtual world affordances: Enhancing brand value. *Journal of Virtual Worlds Research*, *1*(2), 1–18.

Passig, D., Klein, P., & Noyman, T. (2001). Awareness of toddler's initial cognitive experiences with virtual reality. *Journal of Computer Assisted Learning*, *17*, 332–344. doi:10.1046/j.0266-4909.2001.00190.x

Peterson, M. (2006). Learner interaction management in an avatar and chat-based virtual world. *Computer Assisted Language Learning*, *19*(1), 79–103. doi:10.1080/09588220600804087

Richter, J., Anderson-Inman, L., & Frisbee, M. (2007). Critical engagement of teachers in Second Life: Progress in the SaLamander project. In *Proceedings of the Second Life Education Workshop 2007* (pp. 19-26). Retrieved May 28, 2008 from http://www.simteach.com/slccedu07proceedings.pdf.

Schultze, U., Hiltz, S. R., Nardi, B., Rennecker, J., & Stucky, S. (2008). Using synthetic worlds for work and learning. *Communications of the Association for Information Systems*, *22*, 351–370.

Schwebel, D., Gaines, J., & Severson, J. (2008). Validation of virtual reality as a tool to understand and prevent child pedestrian injury. *Accident; Analysis and Prevention*, *40*(4), 1394–1400. doi:10.1016/j.aap.2008.03.005

Second Life. (2008). Retrieved on April 23, 2008 from www.secondlife.com.

Siau, K. (2003). Evaluating the usability of a group support system using co-discovery. *Journal of Computer Information Systems*, *44*(2), 17–28.

Siau, K., Nah, F., Eschenbrenner, B., & Guru, A. (2007). An augmented approach to support collaborative distance learning of unified modeling language. *Americas Conference on Information Systems (AMCIS 2007)*, Colorado, USA.

Siau, K., & Shen, Z. (2003). Building customer trust in mobile commerce. *Communications of the ACM*, *46*(4), 91–94. doi:10.1145/641205.641211

Siau, K., Sheng, H., & Nah, F. (2006). Use of a classroom response system to enhance classroom interactivity. *IEEE Transactions on Education*, *49*(3), 398–403. doi:10.1109/TE.2006.879802

Siau, K., Sheng, H., Nah, F., & Davis, S. (2004). A qualitative investigation on consumer trust in mobile commerce. *International Journal of Electronic Business*, *2*(3), 283–300. doi:10.1504/IJEB.2004.005143

Stoerger, S. (2008). Virtual worlds, virtual literacy: An educational exploration. *Knowledge Quest*, *36*(3), 50–56.

What does it cost to use a virtual world learning environment? (2008). *Training & Development*, *62*(11), 88.

Wood, N., Solomon, M. R., & Allan, D. (2008). Welcome to the matrix: E-learning gets a Second Life. *Marketing Education Review*, *18*(2), 47–53.

Chapter 15
Using Graphics to Improve Understanding of Conceptual Models

Kamal Masri
Simon Fraser University, Canada

Drew Parker
Simon Fraser University, Canada

Andrew Gemino
Simon Fraser University, Canada

ABSTRACT

Making Entity-Relationship diagrams easier to understand for novices has been a topic of previous research. This study provides experimental evidence that suggests using small representative graphics (iconic graphics) to replace standard entity boxes in an ER diagram can have a positive effect on domain understanding for novice users. Cognitive Load Theory and the Cognitive Theory of Multimedia Learning are used to hypothesize that iconic graphics reduce extraneous cognitive load of model viewers leading to more complete mental models and consequently improved understanding. Domain understanding was measured using comprehension and transfer (problem solving) tasks. Results confirm the main hypothesis. In addition, iconic graphics were found to be less effective in improving domain understanding with English as second language (ESL) participants. ESL results are shown to be consistent with predictions based on the Cognitive Load Theory. The importance of this work for systems analysts and designers comes from two considerations. First, the use of iconic graphics seems to reduce the extraneous cognitive load associated with these complex systems. Secondly, the reduction in extraneous load enables users to apply more germane load which relates directly with levels of domain understanding. Thus iconic graphics may provide a simple tool that facilitates better understanding of ER diagrams and the data structure for proposed information systems.

DOI: 10.4018/978-1-60566-904-5.ch015

INTRODUCTION

The entity relationship (ER) diagram (Chen, 1976), remains an important element in information systems documentation and development (Batra, 2005). As information systems become more sophisticated, information systems professionals recognize that an understanding of the conceptual structure of a system becomes increasingly important in implementation decisions (Moody, 1996). The conceptual data model often holds the key to understanding what a system is able to accomplish and, perhaps more importantly, unable to accomplish. For this reason, developing useful ER diagrams able to communicate these capabilities is of growing importance. While much research attention has been focused on how to develop consistent and complete ER diagrams, less research has been directed on how to make ER diagrams more understandable, particularly to users who have little or no experience with the diagramming methods (Topi & Ramesh, 2002). One of the main roles of ER diagramming is to support communication between developers and users (who are often novices modelers) (Kung & Solvberg, 1986). Therefore, we believe it is important to research techniques for improving understanding of ER diagrams for novice users.

This chapter addresses research opportunities identified by Wand & Weber's (2002) framework. Specifically, we rely on cognitive theory to investigate the effects of using small pictorial representations, what we call iconic images, embedded in ER diagrams on model viewer's understanding. Although our findings are specific to ER diagrams, these findings suggest the potential for further research into the use of multimedia elements in other conceptual modeling techniques leading to new applications of existing systems development methodologies.

The following section of this chapter provides a brief overview of conceptual modeling and comparative research in the field. Next, descriptions of the Cognitive Load Theory (Sweller, 1988;

Sweller & Chandler, 1994) and the Cognitive Theory of Multimedia Learning (Mayer, 2001) are presented. This is followed by an overview of the experimental procedures including hypotheses generation, method, and results. The chapter closes with a discussion of the results along with research implications and conclusions.

COMPARATIVE RESEARCH IN CONCEPTUAL MODELING

Conceptual modeling provides the means to organize requirements for a system to form a meaningful whole (Andrade, et al., 2004). ER diagramming is an example of conceptual modeling that focuses on data structure. Approaches to IS development often include conceptual modeling tools to communicate and validate requirements. Curtis, Krasner and Iscoe (1988) found that problems of fluctuating and conflicting requirements in software design projects can be associated with communication breakdown. They identified a need for increased communication in requirements development. The breakdown in communications can happen across many levels.

Figure 1 offers a generic model of interactions between parties involved during systems development projects. The three parties are: 1) Stakeholders of the to-be system (e.g. end-users, managers), 2) Systems Analysts (intermediaries), and 3) Developer/Designers of the to-be system. Stakeholders often have the best understanding of the business process and the needs of the new system. Systems analysts are typically responsible for determining *what* should be built (requirements) via direct communication with stakeholders, while developers/designers are responsible for *how* the system will be put together to meet business objectives. Communication between systems analysts and stakeholders involves a two stage iterative process: *requirements gathering* and *requirements validation*. Stage 1, requirements gathering, is a process that analysts use to understand the busi-

Figure 1. Interaction among the various players during system development

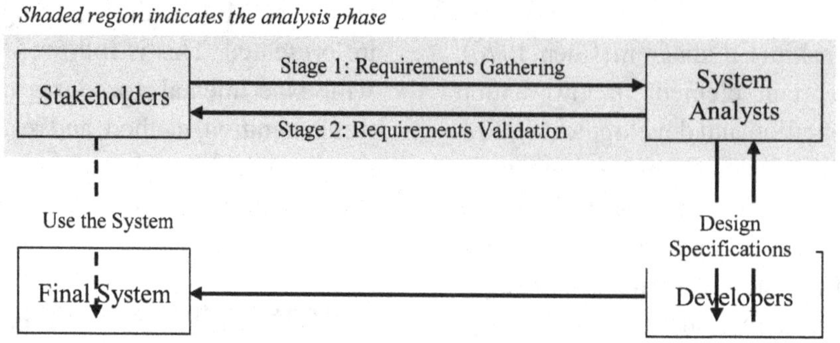

Shaded region indicates the analysis phase

ness and technical requirements of the system; whereas, stage 2, requirements validation, is the process stakeholders use to approve requirements as conceptualized and documented by the analysts. In practice, stages 1 and 2 occur in an iterative process of discovery and learning. Developing a common understanding of the system documentation, which often includes conceptual models, as presented to stakeholders is often important to the overall success of a development project.

Research in requirements gathering and validation has focused on the importance of conceptual modeling (Topi & Ramesh, 2002; Wand & Weber, 2002) which occurs early in the analysis phase of information systems projects. The large number of techniques available to analysts suggests that comparison of conceptual modeling techniques is of particular importance. Comparative research can be separated into three major categories (Gemino & Wand, 2004; Rockwell & Bajaj, 2005): 1) product comparisons (modeling effectiveness), 2) process comparisons (modeling efficiency), and 3) understanding-level comparisons (readability efficiency).

Product comparison research focuses on comparing modeling effectiveness of competing techniques from model designers' perspective. Some research consider modeling dimensions such as syntactic, semantic, communicability and usability (Y.-G. Kim & March, 1995; Yadav, Bravoco, Chatfield, & Rajkumar, 1988), while others

consider abilities of analysts to learn competing techniques (Jarvenpaa & Machesky, 1989; Wang, 1996) or abilities of end-users to produce the models using competing techniques (Batra, Hoffer, & Bostrom, 1990; Batra & Wishart, 2004).

Process comparisons focus on *how* conceptual models are created or analyzed and place less attention on the ensuing products generated from the process. For example, Vessey & Conger (1994) compared three different techniques by documenting the cognitive processes novice systems analysts use to produce models by closely monitoring participants as they created these models. Kim, Hahn & Hahn (2000) studied the cognitive processes involved in understanding multiple diagrams representing different elements of the same system. They tested the hypothesis that visual cues and contextual information relating diagrams to each other enable viewers to better identify problems embedded within the diagrams. Their results supported the hypothesis suggesting that visual cues increased the probability of model viewers identifying errors with the model but did not attempt to measure user understanding.

The third category of research investigates effectiveness of modeling techniques from a problem solving (understanding) perspective which is often overlooked by the first two categories. Understanding-level comparisons focus on the final outcome of the conceptual modeling process; that is, whether or not the person viewing the system understands the domain being represented. This category has attracted more attention recently.

Understanding-level research often relies on cognitive theory or ontological models to predict and explain documented effects. Agarwal, De, & Sinha (1999) used the theory of cognitive fit (Vessey, 1991) to compare the comprehensibility of object-oriented and process oriented models. Bodart, Patel, Sim, & Weber (2001) generated propositions using the theory of semantic networks (Collins & Quillian, 1969) to conclude that optional properties in ER diagrams impede deep-level understanding of users. The cognitive theory of multimedia learning (Mayer, 2001) provided theoretical background to investigate additions of animation and narration in requirements validation (Gemino, 2004), and to reach similar conclusions as Bodart et al. (2001) regarding the impact of optional properties in ER diagrams (Gemino & Wand, 2005). Finally, Wand & Weber's (1990) representation model based on the theory of ontology was used to investigate how model decomposition impacts analysts' understanding of a domain (Burton-Jones & Meso, 2006) and the effect number of concepts presented has on the readability of the model (Bajaj, 2004). Following the lead of these studies, we rely on the cognitive theory of multimedia learning (Mayer, 2001) and the cognitive load theory (Sweller, 1988; Sweller & Chandler, 1994) to investigate the effects of embedding iconic images in ER diagrams.

This chapter details an experiment designed to test the level of understanding developed by model viewers reading ER diagrams with and without iconic graphics. Cognitive load theory and the cognitive theory of multimedia learning are used to hypothesize that embedding iconic graphics will increase the sophistication of mental models developed by viewers leading to higher scores on transfer tasks. The transfer task involves participants answering a set of problem solving questions as a measure of the level of domain understanding attained by the viewer (Mayer, 1989,

1996, 2001). Consequently, improved understanding as measured by the transfer task may lead to improved requirements validation (Figure 1). It is important to note that the research is designed to measure domain understanding only. It does not address task efficiency.

Research exists to support the use of icons in the field of Human-Computer Interaction which can be used to support the structure of our research. For example, adding pictorial icons to text warning messages in industrial training manuals improved comprehension and recall of the warning messages (Young & Wogalter, 1990). Combining icons with text labels was found to be more effective in facilitating learning of application programs than using labels or icons alone (Wiedenbeck, 1999). Pictorial icons were found to enhance learning in a computer-based training exercise (Kunnath, Cornell, Kysilka, & Witta, 2007). Finally, contextualizing the problem domain increased performance of interpreting icons (Siau, 2005).

The use of iconic images in system analysis was suggested by Moody (1996) who introduced the idea of a graphical entity relational model to simplify the ER model for non-technical users. The graphical entity relational model had multiple levels of abstractions that included context data models using entities to represent subject areas, subject area data models consisting of detailed ER models, and foreign entities used to relate the different subject areas. Images were only included in the context data model and their effectiveness on user understanding was not directly measured. Our research is differentiated from Moody (1996) by directly measuring the effects of embedding iconic images into detailed ER diagrams on user understanding while grounding the research in cognitive theory.

THEORETICAL BACKGROUND

Davis (1982) provided three reasons to explain problems encountered in requirements gathering and validation: 1) the constraints on humans as information processors and problem solvers, 2) the variety and complexity of information requirements, and 3) the complex patterns of interaction among users and analysts in defining requirements. It is not surprising that complex conceptual models will result from complex systems requirements. In addition, requirements validation can be considered a learning process (Gemino & Wand, 2003) where stakeholders use information presented in the model, coupled with prior knowledge of the problem domain (Khatri, Vessey, Ramesh, Clay, & Park, 2006), to build understanding. Theories of how humans develop understanding from presented information are therefore important in improving our understanding of the conceptual modeling process.

Cognitive Load Theory

We have focused on two related cognitive theories to develop our hypotheses. Cognitive Load Theory (CLT) defines the cognitive constraints associated with humans (Sweller, 1988; Sweller & Chandler, 1994). The Cognitive Theory of Multimedia Learning (CTML) provides principles to improve messages and promote learning (Mayer, 2001). The main assumptions of the cognitive load theory are limited working memory and its interaction with a practically unlimited long term memory (Sweller & Chandler, 1994). Working memory has the capacity to process approximately seven items of information at any given time (Miller, 1956). However, schema acquisition allows the individual items used by working memory to vary in complexity without using additional working memory space (Sweller & Chandler, 1994).

For example, a "dog" can be considered a single element occupying one of the seven locations in working memory for an individual familiar with

dogs; or, a dog can be decomposed into its various descriptive elements (paws, eyes, ears, tail, etc) with each element occupying one of the working memory locations for an individual not familiar with dogs. Schema acquisition relies on prior experiences and knowledge that enables individuals to construct bigger chunks of information to use as single elements in working memory. This supports the evidence that long term memory provides the basis of intellectual performance and differentiates the problem solving skills (i.e., speed and accuracy) between novices and experts. The CLT suggests properly designed learning mechanisms will enable learners to use material stored in long term memory to reduce the burden (cognitive load) on working memory. The CLT proposes three sources of cognitive load: intrinsic, extraneous, and germane. It argues that using learning mechanisms structured to reduce either of the intrinsic or extraneous sources of cognitive load allows an increase of germane cognitive load causing improved learning and understanding.

Intrinsic Cognitive Load

Intrinsic Cognitive Load is strongly related to the interactivity of elements in the task being learned. Sweller and Chandler (1994) argue the more elements that need to be simultaneously assimilated in a particular task will increase the intrinsic cognitive load on working memory thus reducing an individual's overall ability to process information. The definition of an element is subjective and dependent on the learner's prior knowledge. For example, when viewing the same ER diagram, an element might be a property of an entity to a novice viewer whereas a more experienced viewer might view an entity with all its corresponding properties as an element.

Intrinsic cognitive load is determined by the interactivity of elements in an instructional message. Conceptual models present elements of the system (e.g., entities and attributes) and their associated interactivity (e.g., relationships) to describe the problem domain. Intrinsic cognitive load is expected to be high with more complex models. Element interactivity and its associated cognitive load can be influenced by model design by omitting some interacting elements (Paas, Renkl, & Sweller, 2003; Sweller & Chandler, 1994). For example, the choice of using optional or mandatory properties in ER diagrams can influence element interactivity.

Extraneous Cognitive Load

The intrinsic nature of the task involves schema acquisition and knowledge construction by combining new information with prior knowledge. The process of manipulating elements of the message to construct knowledge (such as locating and mentally arranging elements of a conceptual model) involves extraneous cognitive activity. This manipulation is not relevant to schema acquisition and knowledge construction. The CLT argues that reducing this irrelevant cognitive activity by carefully presenting the information will facilitate learning (Sweller & Chandler, 1994). We propose that embedding iconic images into conceptual models helps to reduce extraneous cognitive load by supporting the process of efficiently manipulating model elements in preparation for knowledge construction.

Germane Cognitive Load

Intrinsic and extraneous cognitive loads are additive and consume working memory capacity. Remaining capacity is used for knowledge construction (developing understanding) (Paas, Tuovinen, Tabbers, & Van Gerven, 2003). Germane cognitive load enhances learning by allowing remaining working memory capacity to be devoted to schema acquisition and knowledge construction (Paas, Renkl, et al., 2003). In other words, germane cognitive load is the effort imposed by the learner to understand the material presented. The amount of effort used for understanding is dependent on the amount of available cognitive resources and the willingness or capabilities of the learner to exert the additional load (Seufert, Jänen, & Brünken, 2007).

Balancing intrinsic and extraneous cognitive activity is therefore essential to maximizing the efficiency of working memory. Challenging tasks like reading ER diagrams, with high intrinsic cognitive loads, are susceptible to extraneous cognitive overload. In these situations, extraneous cognitive load will reduce cognitive resources available for knowledge construction, significantly impeding the learning process. Reducing extraneous cognitive load therefore becomes essential to promote learning and understanding. A primary goal in requirements validation should be to minimize the effects of extraneous cognitive load on complex modeling tasks for model users.

COGNITIVE THEORY OF MULTIMEDIA LEARNING

The Cognitive Theory of Multimedia Learning (CTML) was developed by Mayer using a variety of empirical research (Mayer, 1989, 1996, 2001). The theory's main objective is to use multimedia presentations to reduce extraneous cognitive load.

The CTML is founded on three major assumptions: 1) Dual Channels, 2) Limited Capacity, and 3) Active Processing. The dual channel assumption is based on the dual coding theory (Paivio, 1986, 1991). Individuals are assumed to have two separate processing channels for interpreting visual and auditory information. The two channels complement each other since receiving simultaneous information through each channel improves overall recall compared to receiving information through only one channel (Paivio, 1986). The theory of working memory (Baddeley, 1992) along with assumptions from the cognitive load theory (Sweller, 1988) provide the framework for the limited capacity assumption. Baddeley's theory

Figure 2. The Cognitive Theory of Multimedia Learning (Mayer, 2001, p. 44)

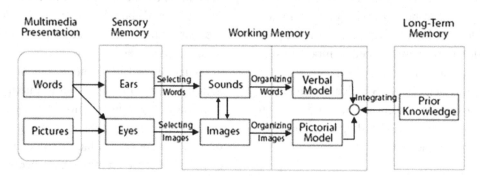

states that individuals have limits to the amount of information processed by each channel and held in working memory. Finally, the active processing assumption is based on generative theory (Wittrock, 1990) that suggests people are active processors of information rather than passive processors. Active processing implies individuals pay attention, organize incoming information, and integrate the information with knowledge stored in long term memory (prior knowledge). The implication for multimedia message design is that information presented must have a coherent structure. The messages should provide the receiver guidance for building structure.

Multimedia presentation, as defined by Mayer (1989) is "the presentation of material using both words and pictures" (Mayer, 2001, p. 2). Unlike the popular definition of "multimedia," Mayer's definition is not associated to the media (such as computers) used to deliver the message nor to the presentation mode (such as animation); instead, he associates it to the sensory mode. According to the sensory modality description, a textbook with pictures would be considered multimedia as readers will visually process pictures and convert words into sounds for verbal processing (auditory processing). Adding iconic images or pictures to static conceptual models would produce multimedia diagrams that fit the description defined by Mayer (1989). An overview of the CTML is shown in Figure 2.

The CTML suggests three cognitive processes are employed by learners to make sense of a message. First, incoming information is selected into one of two available channels where verbal information is processed through the auditory channel and visual information is processed through the pictorial channel. Second, the information is organized in working memory to form verbal and pictorial based models. These models are created by building connections among pieces of information received through either channel. The third process involves integration of the two models to create a single integrated representation of the information to be assimilated with prior knowledge from long term memory. This implies the level of understanding of the message will depend on the learner's prior knowledge.

The foundations of the CTML enabled Mayer (2001) to suggest seven design principles to assist designers to create effective multimedia presentations. The principles with a description of each are presented in Table 1.

HYPOTHESES

Having developed our theoretical background, we are now able to consider the research hypotheses. Standard methods for presenting entities in ER diagrams use an entity name surrounded by a simple box as shown in Appendices 1a and 2a.

Table 1. The Seven Principles of the Cognitive Theory of Multimedia Learning

Design Principal	Description
Multimedia Principle	Recipients learn better from words and pictures than from words alone.
Spatial Contiguity Principle	Recipients learn better when corresponding words and pictures are presented near rather than far from each other on a page or screen.
Temporal Contiguity Principle	Recipients learn better when corresponding words and pictures are presented simultaneously rather than successively.
Coherence Principle	Recipients learn better when extraneous material is excluded rather than included in the presentation.
Modality Principle	Recipients learn better from animation and narration than from animation and on-screen text (spoken text rather than printed text).
Redundancy Principle	Recipients learn better from animation and narration than from animation, narration, and text.
Individual Differences Principle	Design effects are stronger for low-knowledge learners than for high-knowledge learners, and for high-spatial learners rather than for low-spatial learners.

The use of iconic graphics, as a substitute for the standard entity in an ERD is illustrated by Appendices 1b and 2b. We argue below that incorporating a relevant graphical icon with an entity name instead of a standard box with an entity name can increase the domain understanding developed by model viewers.

Hypotheses for this experiment are based on the multimedia principle from the CTML (Table 1). The multimedia principle suggests that incorporating graphical images in messages will improve learner understanding. Words and pictures are qualitatively different as words describe information in an abstract manner while pictures present information in an intuitive manner (Mayer, 2001). The iconic graphic provides more content and reduces the extraneous cognitive load associated with the ER diagram. Lowering the extraneous load allows more cognitive capacity to be used for knowledge construction to increase the sophistication of the cognitive model developed by the model viewer. Model viewers who are provided with iconic graphics should therefore perform better on tasks related to domain understanding than model viewers provided with standard boxes to describe entities.

The level of understanding is assessed using three variables. Multiple variables are necessary as three learning outcomes are associated with any learning process: 1) no learning, 2) retention (remembering), and 3) understanding (Mayer, 2001). No learning is self evident. Retention is the ability to reproduce presented information. Understanding is the ability to apply constructed knowledge for use in new situations. Mayer (2001) suggests using recognition and recall tasks to measure retention, and transfer tests to measure understanding.

The goal of this study is to identify the impact of embedded iconic images on understanding, but it is important to test the impact of iconic images on retention as well as understanding to be consistent with research grounded in the CTML. The research hypotheses are:

H1: Participants using conceptual models with embedded iconic graphics will show higher levels of retention (higher scores on recognition and recall) than participants using standard ER diagrams.

H2: Participants using conceptual models with embedded iconic graphics will develop higher levels of understanding (higher transfer scores) than participants using standard ER diagrams.

H1 is necessary to establish a framework for interpreting the results of the primary hypothesis

H2. Care must be taken when evaluating modeling techniques to carefully control for informational equivalence (Siau, 2004). Siau (2004) introduced the notion of informational and computational equivalence (Larkin & Simon, 1987) as mechanisms for evaluating effectiveness of modeling techniques. Comparison of different techniques is more valid if these techniques are informationally equivalent as significance detected will not be attributed to the different information provided by the technique. Informational equivalence is defined as "two representations are informationally equivalent if all the information in the one is also inferable from the other, and vice versa" (Larkin & Simon, 1987, p. 67).

Hypothesis H2 suggests that higher transfer scores result from incorporating iconic graphics into the ERD. But different transfer scores might also result from having different information. Retention is defined as the ability to reproduce presented information. Therefore, retention provides a baseline for informational equivalency. If the information provided by both treatments is not equivalent, i.e. has significantly different retention scores, then differences in transfer score may be related to differences in retention instead of a lowered extraneous load. Since representations in both treatments groups are identical except for the icons, we expect differences in understanding (H2) to be attributed to the use of embedded iconic images. Significant differences in H1 may indicate that the treatment condition is not informationally equivalent to the control group leading to concerns whether different information in the treatment is the cause of measured significant differences in H2.

METHOD

Participants

A total of 206 valid responses from 211 participants were collected. Undergraduates were paid $10 to participate in the experiment. Previous research has established differences between novice and expert modelers (Batra & Davis, 1992; Lee & Truex, 2000; Shanks, 1997). Gemino & Wand (2004) note participants with high domain or modeling technique knowledge may have difficulty in overcoming developed expertise leading to biases. Students with similar expected levels of modeling and domain experience were therefore considered an appropriate population. Table 2 lists a breakdown of key pretest variables by treatment group.

Instruments

Two business cases, "Voyager Bus Company" (Voyager) and "Far East Repair" (Far East), were used. These two cases adapted from previous studies (Batra, et al., 1990; Bodart, et al., 2001; Gemino & Wand, 2005) were used to control for case effect bias. Four experimental groups were created: two treatment groups (one for each case), and two control groups. Participants received a one page text description of the case, an ER diagram with or without the treatment condition, and a training page that explained the grammar used. The ER diagrams for both cases are presented in Appendices 1a through 2b.. The training document is displayed as Appendix 3. The graphics used for the treatment conditions were obtained from cli-part.com (all images embedded in the ER diagrams are © 2006 JupiterImages Corporation).

Procedures

The procedure used for the study is based on Mayer (2001) and follows examples of previous research (Bodart, et al., 2001; Burton-Jones & Meso, 2006; Gemino, 2004; Gemino & Wand, 2005; Khatri, et al., 2006). A computer laboratory, equipped with 27 workstations and customized software, was used to collect the data. Sessions varied in size from 11 to 26 participants lasting approximately one hour. Experimental material was distributed

Table 2. Summary of important pretest variables

	Case: Far East			Case: Voyager	
	Graphic	Standard		Graphic	Standard
N	52	51		51	52
Age (mean)	20.2	20.3		20.7	20.7
Gender (% Male)	67.3%	52.9%		54.9%	50.0%
ESL (%)	50.0%	58.8%		62.7%	65.4%
ERD Courses (mean)	0.92	0.90		1.20	1.27
Used ERD (Total)	4	2		2	3
Case Knowledge[1] (mean)	1.77	1.43		1.76	1.83
PDK[2] (mean)	0.36	-0.36		0.07	-0.07

[1] Mean of question 5 listed in Table 3 where 1 indicates no knowledge on a seven point self reporting scale

[2] standardized means of questions 5 to 10 listed in Table 3

randomly. Participants seated next to each other did not receive the same case or treatment condition. Participants were monitored and asked to work independently.

Sessions began with a brief training period to review the one page explanation of the grammar (Appendix 3). The training was followed by a pretest to capture demographics, prior experiences, prior domain knowledge, and prior knowledge of ER diagrams (Table 3).

The three experimental tasks were administered immediately after the pretest. The recognition task was first. Participants had 15 minutes to review

the material and answer 12 "Yes/No/Unknown" questions listed in Table 4. The recognition score was defined as the number of correct answers. The participants were told all case materials would be taken away at the conclusion of the first task. This way, participants completed the final two tasks using only their mental models. Participants could not revisit any completed task.

The recall task followed. Participants were asked the following question: "Using what you have learned about this company, please write down an explanation of how the company operates." Six minutes were allotted to complete the

Table 3. Information collected during the pretest for each case

Voyager Case	Far Eastern Case
1. Number of System Analysis course taken	1. Number of System Analysis course taken
2. Level of ERD knowledge (1 to 7)	2. Level of ERD knowledge (1 to 7)
3. Used ERD in a business setting (Yes/No)	3. Used ERD in a business setting (Yes/No)
4. English as first language (Yes/No)	4. English as first language (Yes/No)
5. Level of knowledge of a bus tour company (1 to 7)	5. Level of knowledge of a machine repair facility (1 to 7)
6. Taken a bus tour (Yes/No)	6. Worked as a mechanic (Yes/No)
7. Worked as a bus driver (Yes/No)	7. Worked in a warehouse (Yes/No)
8. Made reservations for a bus trip (Yes/No)	8. Replaced a part of an engine (Yes/No)
9. Traveled by bus to a special event (Yes/No)	9. Had your engine overhauled (Yes/No)
10. Organized a set of short bus trips (Yes/No)	10. Helped to organize a repair shop (Yes/No)

Table 4. Recognition Questions used for the Far Eastern Repair Facility case

1. Do all repairs require parts?
2. Can a repair be worked on by more than one mechanic?
3. Are all repairs assigned to at least one mechanic
4. Are there parts stored in the warehouse that are not used for repairs?
5. Does Far Eastern collect different information for different machine types?
6. Does Far Eastern differentiate their local customers in any way?
7. Can a mechanic who does not have a special skill be assigned to more than one repair?
8. Do all the mechanics related to the same repair, pool their hours to create a single entry for hours worked?
9. Can a piece of equipment undergo more than one repair?
10. Can more than one part be listed in a single repair detail?
11. Is the cylinder volume recorded for all pumps that are repaired?
12. Can a part be supplied by more than one manufacturer?

recall exercise. The recall score was defined as the total number of distinct and correct idea units listed. One rater scored the recall responses using scoring procedures from previous research (Mayer & Moreno, 1998). The treatment condition was hidden from the rater to eliminate rater bias.

The final task was the transfer task composed of four questions each describing a specific problem. Examples are provided in Table 5. Participants were asked to record as many solutions as they could think of for each question. Two minutes were allotted per question. The total number of responses as well as the number of acceptable responses for all four questions was determined by a single rater. A template of possible acceptable answers was prepared. Examples of acceptable answers for the first question (Table 5) included:

parts not available, mechanics with required skill not available, and machine already repaired but customer not yet contacted.

The open-ended nature of these questions allowed participants to provide answers based either on information attained from the case material or from other experiences. One example of a solution to question 1 (Table 5) that would be outside the case information was "Far Eastern burned down." The structure of the transfer task may have encouraged participants to record solutions regardless whether these solutions were based on knowledge from the case or otherwise. We worked to isolate this effect from transfer scores. We chose to compute the ratio of acceptable answers provided by each participant to the total number of solutions noted. Analysis of this

Table 5. Problem solving questions used for the Far Eastern Repair Facility case

1. A customer of Far Eastern has called to complain that the machine they sent for repair has not been repaired yet. What possible reasons can you provide for what might have gone wrong?
2. Far Eastern is experiencing a very large increase in the number of machines that they should repair. What problems might Far Eastern experience because of this increase in repairs?
3. Customers of Far Eastern are not happy when the actual repair price is higher than the estimated repair price. The sales person says that it is not his fault because the estimation is so difficult. Provide as many possibilities as you can think of that make the accurate estimation of the total repair price difficult.
4. Far Eastern is considering investing in a machine that can be used to repair large turbine engines. How would the current data structure be affected by the purchase of the new machine? Try to think of as many affects as possible.

Table 6. Means and Standard Deviations of the dependent variables (by case and treatment condition)

Dependent Variable	Case: Far East		Cse: Voyager	
	Graphic n=52	Standard n=51	Gaphic n=51	Standard n=52
Recognition	7.08 (1.79)	7.04 (1.84)	708 (1.41)	7.27 (1.68)
Recall	6.92 (3.31)	6.20 (3.18)	882 (4.83)	9.52 (5.85)
Transfer (Acceptable)	10.00 (4.39)	7.90 (4.09)	1.73 (4.53)	9.37 (4.08)
Transfer (All Responses)	14.87 (5.59)	13.92 (4.86)	1.12 (5.11)	15.81 (5.31)
Transfer Ratio: *Acceptable/All Responses*	0.67 (0.22)	0.55 (0.19)	0.70 (0.22)	0.59 (0.18)

ratio provides a more accurate analysis of the differences between treatment groups.

RESULTS

Table 6 lists means and standard deviations for the three dependent variables (recognition, recall, and transfer) as well as total number of responses and ratio of acceptable to total for the transfer task (*Transfer Ratio*).

Multivariate Analysis of covariance (MAN-COVA) was used to test for statistical significance. MANCOVA was chosen because of multiple dependent variables and the need to control for covariates. MANCOVA assumptions were investigated prior to analysis. Histograms and P-P plots were constructed and used to verify the normality assumption. The homogeneity of variances assumptions was verified using the Box's statistic.

Two covariates were used in the model: previous domain knowledge (PDK), as defined in Table 2, and English as a second language (ESL). Both covariates were found to be significant for some of transfer ratios and recall scores although the level of significance varied between cases. Table 7 provides complete results of the MANCOVA analysis.

Covariates

Previous research (Shaft & Vessey, 1995, 1998) has indicated important differences between application experts and novices. Differences are also expected through considerations of the cognitive load theory (Sweller & Chandler, 1994), the cognitive theory of multimedia learning (Mayer, 2001), and findings of Khatri et al. (2006). The CLT suggests that high PDK will lower the intrinsic cognitive load. The individual differences principle outlined by the CTML again suggests that design effects will have a lower impact for those with high PDK. Khatri et al. (2006) suggests the level of previous domain knowledge has an effect on the level of understanding achieved. Results in Table 7 suggest that PDK may have some effect on understanding as significance was detected in the Far East case. The impact was not observed in the Voyager case. The lack of significance may have to do with the instrument used to measure PDK.

The results from ESL imply the precise semantics associated with ER modeling may be more difficult for individuals with less familiarity with the language. The ESL covariate shows a strong relationship with recall and transfer ratios. ESL significance reported by Table 7 indicates a possible effect of the experimental condition between ESL and non-ESL groups. Simple Analysis of

Table 7. MANCOVA results for the treatment condition and covariates (ESL and PDK)

	Case: Far East						Case: Voyager					
	Treatment:		Covariates:				Treatment:		Covariates:			
			EL		PDK				EL		PDK	
	F	ig.	F	sig.	F	Sig.	F	ig.	F	ig.	F	ig.
Recog.	0.04	0.84	1.72	0.19	1.05	0.31	0.35	0.56	0.37	0.54	1.08	0.30
Recall	1.65	0.20	5.87	0.02	2.78	0.10	0.48	0.49	6.08	0.02	1.02	0.31
Transfer Ratio	11.16	0.00	4.41	0.04	6.10	0.02	8.73	0.00	4.30	0.04	1.17	0.28

Variance (ANOVA) was used to investigate the degree and direction of any difference. Table 8 displays ANOVA results for the ESL group and Table 9 displays analysis results for the non-ESL group. Results indicate the treatment condition had a higher positive impact on the non-ESL group for transfer ratios.

The effects of ESL need to be interpreted cautiously. An alternative explanation for at least a portion of the results may be related to possible task bias. The yes/no type of answer in the recognition task requires less language skills than responding in point form or complete sentences which is the format for the recall and transfer tasks. The potential task bias might explain why recognition results differ less than recall and transfer results across Table 8 and Table 9. It may not be clear, for ESL participants, whether comprehension and understanding was measured as opposed to

written language skill. Therefore, a portion of the ESL findings may be the result of task bias. The results for non-ESL participants would more likely reflect the true effect of iconic graphics.

Treatment Effects

Having established the significance of the covariates, we turn our attention to the treatment variable. The results provide support for hypothesis H2 only (Table 7). H2, the hypothesis that embedded graphics will improve understanding, is confirmed for both cases. Both cases showed significant transfer ratio score differences between treatment and non-treatment conditions after accounting for covariate influence ($F=11.16$ and $F=8.73$ for Far East and Voyager respectively).

The results in Table 7 show no evidence of significant differences across treatment groups for

Table 8. ANOVA analysis for participants with English as a second language (ESL)

	Case: Far East						Case: Voyager					
	Graphic		Standard				Graphic		Standard			
	N26		N=30		ANOVA		N=32		N=34		ANOVA	
	Man	sd.	Mean	sd.	F	Sig.	Mean	sd.	Mean	sd.	F	Sig.
Recog.	6.65	1.98	7.00	1.80	0.47	0.50	6.97	1.51	7.24	1.79	0.42	0.52
Recall	5.92	3.14	5.77	3.29	0.03	0.86	7.38	4.17	9.03	5.67	1.81	0.18
Transfer:												
Acept.	7.77	3.76	6.37	3.39	2.16	0.15	8.66	3.71	8.65	3.95	0.00	0.99
All	12.08	4.03	12.00	4.28	0.01	0.95	13.31	4.41	15.06	5.27	2.12	0.15
Ratio	0.63	0.26	0.51	0.18	4.24	0.04	0.65	0.25	0.58	0.18	1.90	0.17

Table 9. ANOVA analysis for participants with English as native language (non-ESL)

	Case: Far East						Case: Voyager					
	Graphic		Standard				Graphic		Standard			
	N26		N=21		ANOVA		N=19		N=18		ANOVA	
	Man	sd.	Mean	sd.	F	Sig.	Mean	sd.	Mean	sd.	F	Sig.
Recog.	7.50	1.50	7.10	1.95	0.65	0.43	7.26	1.24	7.33	1.50	0.02	0.88
Recall	7.92	3.22	6.81	2.98	1.48	0.23	11.26	4.99	10.44	6.23	0.20	0.66
Transfer:												
Acept.	12.23	3.85	10.10	4.07	3.39	0.07	14.21	3.57	10.72	4.10	7.65	0.01
All	17.65	5.61	16.67	4.37	0.44	0.51	18.16	4.83	17.22	5.25	0.32	0.58
Ratio	0.71	0.19	0.61	0.18	3.69	0.06	0.79	0.09	0.61	0.17	15.28	0.00

recognition or recall. Lack of significant differences between the treatment groups for recognition and recall across the two cases may imply that treatment and control groups received informationally equivalent experimental material.

In summary, the results of the MANCOVA support hypothesis H2 that suggests the use of iconic graphics generates a significant increase in the level of understanding when compared with participants viewing standard ER models. In addition, two covariates were shown to be significantly related to levels of understanding: PDK and ESL. The effect of the treatment condition was strongest for participants with English as their native language.

DISCUSSION AND RESEARCH IMPLICATIONS

This study presented experimental findings on the use of embedded graphics in ER diagrams. The motivations for the study were based on an objective to improve overall effectiveness of ER diagramming for model viewers. Standard ER diagrams were adapted to include entities represented as iconic images and text titles. ER diagrams were chosen for their continued popularity in systems analysis and the ease of representing entities with embedded graphics. An experiment was conducted with two

cases used in previous research (Batra, et al., 1990; Bodart, et al., 2001). The cognitive load theory and the cognitive theory of multimedia learning provided the theoretical foundation to generate hypotheses predicting the impact of embedded graphics on retention and understanding.

Results provide support for our primary hypotheses generated from the CTML and CLT. Iconic graphics did not have any significant impact on retention as measured by recognition and recall tasks; however, in both cases, iconic graphics did support significantly higher levels of understanding as measured by the transfer task. These results suggest iconic graphics can positively impact the level of understanding gained by persons viewing ER diagrams. These results should encourage further research into the use of graphics and other multimedia enhancements in standard ER diagrams.

In addition to the effect of iconic graphics, the study also indicated that previous domain knowledge (PDK) and English as a second language (ESL) are two important variables to consider in any measurement of understanding. PDK was investigated as an element in explaining higher levels of understanding based on assumptions from the CLT (Sweller & Chandler, 1994), CTML (Mayer, 2001), and findings from Khatri et al (2006) that previous domain knowledge may play an important role in IS analysis and design.

PDK findings did not provide robust results. We believe this may in large part be due to the measurement instrument for PDK. Pretest results for the Far East case indicated a low self reported prior case knowledge of 1.7 (1 is no knowledge). Only 9 (of 33) participants who reported a score greater than one also answered positively to two or more of the PDK related pretest questions (Questions 6 to 10 in Table 3). We believe this may have caused a statistical anomaly leading to a significant result. PDK is likely an important factor that impacts understanding, but this experiment may not have a robust enough data set to provide valid inferences.

ESL was introduced to isolate possible effects due to language processing. Our results indicate that embedding graphics in ER diagrams provided a larger effect on understanding for non-ESL participants. As noted earlier, comparison of the ESL and non-ESL group is preliminary and may be affected by task bias. The initial ESL result may seem counterintuitive because use of representative images would typically be expected to allow users to relate textual description to graphical elements perhaps surpassing the limitations of written language. However, working with a foreign language can lead to additional sources of intrinsic cognitive load. Since the effects of cognitive load are cumulative, the CLT would suggest that an increase in intrinsic cognitive load necessarily results in a decreased ability of the user to exert germane cognitive load used for knowledge construction and understanding. ESL users would be subject to higher overall intrinsic and extraneous cognitive loads compared to those working in their native language. Therefore, any positive effect of using graphics on reducing extraneous cognitive load for ESL users would not necessarily compensate for the increase in intrinsic load required to process language (See Figure 3).

This result should not be surprising as ER diagrams often pose a significant challenge for users even when presented in their native language. The results perhaps suggest that increased precision of semantics in ER diagrams requires a high familiarity with the language. As 'offshoring' and multilingual communication requirements become more the norm, this finding could prove more important in considering methods to support effective communication.

An alternative explanation may provide some additional insight into the ESL results. The comprehension task required only yes/no type answers whereas retention and transfer tasks required written answers. It is possible the written tasks may have been more difficult for ESL participants to complete which introduces a task bias accounting for some of the measured variance.

It is clear that more work needs to be done to fully uncover the impact of presentation on model

Figure 3. Cognitive Loads on working memory of ESL vs. non-ESL groups

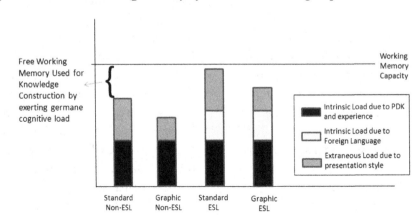

viewer understanding. We expect model viewer characteristics such as language, domain experience, and modeling experience to be important considerations in multilingual contexts.

CONCLUSION, LIMITATIONS, AND FUTURE RESEARCH

This study provides evidence that iconic graphics embedded in ER diagrams can have a positive effect on domain understanding for viewers with relatively low levels of familiarity with ER diagrams. The importance of this work for practicing Systems Analysts and designers comes from two key elements of their job. First, modern IS projects are complex. The ability to understand large and complex projects requires tools that break these projects into meaningful, manageable components. The use of iconic graphics seems to reduce the extraneous cognitive load associated with these complex systems and deserves further attention. Secondly, the reduction in extraneous cognitive load seems to enable novice users to apply more germane cognitive load which relates directly with levels of domain understanding. ER diagrams are used as communication tools among systems experts, and among project stakeholders. A supporting tool, like iconic graphics, that more efficiently and effectively presents the modeled system has the potential to facilitate better understanding of the current and proposed information system. While the alteration in the diagram may seem small, the effect on understanding can be significant as shown in this chapter.

A limitation of these findings is using students as participants to review the two cases. While using student subjects does not represent experienced system analysts, students are a good sample for the general population of system users to which these conceptual models are often addressed (Gemino and Wand, 2004). Some effect differences were also found across cases which may suggest the potential for additional work in indentifying when

case differences impact measures of recognition, recall and transfer.

Another limitation is the size and complexity of the ER diagrams selected for the cases. Although the ER diagrams used in this study are smaller than the average model used in practice, it was an important consideration to control the effects of other variables not considered in this study. For example, the CTML's spatial and temporal contiguity principles suggest that splitting a diagram onto multiple sheets of paper (or computer screens) will not be as effective as having the diagram presented in one location. Previous research (J. Kim, et al., 2000) has considered this issue and future research could more carefully consider the effects in combination with graphical representations. There is also a need for more thorough discussion and development of cases that can be used for this type of experimental research. It is difficult to establish external validity but use of widely accepted cases would improve the impact of results from similar experiments.

One important consideration is the choice of icons to be used. It seems natural to expect the use of icons to be more effective as graphics would more closely represent the domain experience of the viewer. We, therefore, suggest that embedding icons using actual domain relevant images captured with digital cameras to enhance entities would more likely provide a better opportunity to promote understanding of conceptual models. Further research into the effect of icons with differing levels of domain relevance can address this issue.

Another interesting consideration is the impact of using icons on task efficiency. It is possible that icons could have an impact on understanding or recall efficiency. The research was designed to control for time used during each experimental task which limited the ability to measure task efficiency in conjunction with performance levels. Further research without a time restriction may be able to uncover the impact on task efficiency.

Results from this experiment suggest improvements can be made in presenting information in a way that is more effective than standard text based diagrams. This study focused on a single CTML principle. Further improvements are likely when more of the principles are considered. For example, including graphical elements combined with narration and user interactivity (such as computer aided navigation of the conceptual model) may lead to better understanding than standard techniques. We therefore suggest that further efforts should be made in developing conceptual models with a lower cognitive burden for systems analysis and design. Developing these methods will lead to improved communication of system requirements and, consequently, increased rates of success in information systems development projects.

The issues raised by results involving ESL in this study suggest new directions for future research. Possibility of interaction between writing skills and measurement of understanding suggests that researchers should measure ESL (or language) when studying conceptual models' impact on understanding.

Further research will be required to extend the findings to other diagramming techniques. Class diagrams under the UML represent a strong candidate for embedding graphics to improve understanding. Class diagrams consist of class objects associated with attributes and operations. The potentially large number of attributes and operational elements per class requires an inexperienced user to spend valuable cognitive resources to manipulate these elements in preparation for knowledge construction. This can lead to an increase in extraneous cognitive load. It is predicted by the CLT and the CTML that a reduction of this load with help from multimedia elements will improve the process of knowledge construction and overall understanding.

REFERENCES

Agarwal, R., De, P., & Sinha, A. P. (1999). Comprehending object and process models: An empirical study. *IEEE Transactions on Software Engineering*, *25*(4), 541–556. doi:10.1109/32.799953

Andrade, J., Ares, J., Garcia, R., Pazos, J., Rodriguez, S., & Silva, A. (2004). A methodological framework for generic conceptualisation: problem-sensitivity in software engineering. *Information and Software Technology*, *46*(10), 635–649. doi:10.1016/j.infsof.2003.11.003

Baddeley, A. (1992). Working Memory. *Science*, *255*(5044), 556–559. doi:10.1126/science.1736359

Bajaj, A. (2004). The effect of the number of concepts on the readability of schemas: an empirical study with data models. *Requirements Engineering*, *9*(4), 261–270. doi:10.1007/s00766-004-0202-8

Batra, D. (2005). Conceptual Data Modeling Patterns: Representation and Validation. *Journal of Database Management*, *16*(2), 84–106.

Batra, D., & Davis, J. G. (1992). Conceptual data modelling in database design: similarities and differences between expert and novice designers. *International Journal of Man-Machine Studies*, *37*(1), 83–101. doi:10.1016/0020-7373(92)90092-Y

Batra, D., Hoffer, J. A., & Bostrom, R. P. (1990). Comparing Representations with Relational and EER Models. *Communications of the ACM*, *33*(2), 126–139. doi:10.1145/75577.75579

Batra, D., & Wishart, N. A. (2004). Comparing a rule-based approach with a pattern-based approach at different levels of complexity of conceptual data modelling tasks. *International Journal of Human-Computer Studies*, *61*(4), 397–419. doi:10.1016/j.ijhcs.2003.12.019

Bodart, F., Patel, A., Sim, M., & Weber, R. (2001). Should optional properties be used in conceptual modelling? A theory and three empirical tests. *Information Systems Research, 12*(4), 384–405. doi:10.1287/isre.12.4.384.9702

Burton-Jones, A., & Meso, P. (2006). Conceptualizing Systems for Understanding: An Empirical Test of Decomposition Principles in Object-Oriented Analysis. *Information Systems Research, 17*(1), 38–60. doi:10.1287/isre.1050.0079

Chen, P. P.-S. (1976). The Entity-Relationship Model-Toward a Unified View of Data. *ACM Transactions on Database Systems, 1*(1), 9–36. doi:10.1145/320434.320440

Collins, A. M., & Quillian, M. R. (1969). Retreival Times from Semantic Memory. *Journal of Verbal Learning and Verbal Behavior, 8*, 240–247. doi:10.1016/S0022-5371(69)80069-1

Curtis, B., Krasner, H., & Iscoe, N. (1988). A Field Study of the Software Design Process for Large Systems. *Communications of the ACM, 31*(11), 1268–1287. doi:10.1145/50087.50089

Davis, G. B. (1982). Strategies for information requirements determination. *IBM Systems Journal, 21*(1), 4–30.

Gemino, A. (2004). Empirical comparisons of animation and narration in requirements validation. *Requirements Engineering, 9*(3), 153–168. doi:10.1007/s00766-003-0182-0

Gemino, A., & Wand, Y. (2003). Evaluating modeling techniques based on models of learning. *Communications of the ACM, 46*(10), 79–84. doi:10.1145/944217.944243

Gemino, A., & Wand, Y. (2004). A framework for empirical evaluation of conceptual modeling techniques. *Requirements Engineering, 9*(4), 248–260. doi:10.1007/s00766-004-0204-6

Gemino, A., & Wand, Y. (2005). Complexity and clarity in conceptual modeling: Comparison of mandatory and optional properties. *Data & Knowledge Engineering, 55*(3), 301–326. doi:10.1016/j.datak.2004.12.009

Jarvenpaa, S. L., & Machesky, J. J. (1989). Data analysis and learning: an experimental study of data modeling tools. *International Journal of Man-Machine Studies, 31*(4), 367–391. doi:10.1016/0020-7373(89)90001-1

Khatri, V., Vessey, I., Ramesh, V., Clay, P., & Park, S.-J. (2006). Understanding Conceptual Schemas: Exploring the Role of Application and IS Domain Knowledge. *Information Systems Research, 17*(1), 81–99. doi:10.1287/isre.1060.0081

Kim, J., Hahn, J., & Hahn, H. (2000). How Do We Understand a System with (So) Many Diagrams? Cognitive Integration Processes in Diagrammatic Reasoning. *Information Systems Research, 11*(3), 284–303. doi:10.1287/isre.11.3.284.12206

Kim, Y.-G., & March, S. T. (1995)... *Comparing Data Modeling Formalisms, 38*(6), 103–115.

Kung, C. H., & Solvberg, A. (1986). *Activity modelling and behaviour modelling.* Paper presented at the Proceedings of the IFIP WG 8.1 working conference on comparative review of information systems design methodologies: improving the practice, North-Holland, Amsterdam.

Kunnath, M. L. A., Cornell, R. A., Kysilka, M. K., & Witta, L. (2007). An experimental research study on the effect of pictorial icons on a user-learner's performance. *Computers in Human Behavior, 23*(3), 1454–1480. doi:10.1016/j.chb.2005.05.005

Larkin, J. H., & Simon, H. A. (1987). Why a Diagram is (Sometimes) Worth Ten Thousand Words. *Cognitive Science, 11*(1), 65–100. doi:10.1016/S0364-0213(87)80026-5

Lee, J., & Truex, D. P. (2000). Exploring the impact of formal training in ISD methods on the cognitive structure of novice information systems developers. *Information Systems Journal, 10*(4), 347–367. doi:10.1046/j.1365-2575.2000.00086.x

Mayer, R. E. (1989). Models for Understanding. *Review of Educational Research, 59*(1), 43–64.

Mayer, R. E. (1996). Learning strategies for making sense out of expository text: The SOI model for guiding three cognitive processes in knowledge construction. *Educational Psychology Review, 8*(4), 357–371. doi:10.1007/BF01463939

Mayer, R. E. (2001). *Multimedia Learning*. New York: Cambridge University Press.

Mayer, R. E., & Moreno, R. (1998). A Split-Attention Effect in Multimedia Learning: Evidence for Dual Processing Systems in Working Memory. *Journal of Educational Psychology, 90*(4), 312–320. doi:10.1037/0022-0663.90.2.312

Miller, G. A. (1956). The magical number seven, plus or minus two: some limits on our capacity for processing information. *Psychological Review*, 81–97. doi:10.1037/h0043158

Moody, D. (1996). Graphical Entity Relationship models: Towards a more user understandable representation of data. *Conceptual Modeling ER '96* (LNCS 1157, pp. 227-244). Berlin / Heidelberg: Springer.

Paas, F., Renkl, A., & Sweller, J. (2003). Cognitive load theory and instructional design: Recent developments. *Educational Psychologist, 38*(1), 1–4. doi:10.1207/S15326985EP3801_1

Paas, F., Tuovinen, J. E., Tabbers, H., & Van Gerven, P. W. M. (2003). Cognitive Load Measurement as a Means to Advance Cognitive Load Theory. *Educational Psychologist, 38*(1), 63–71. doi:10.1207/S15326985EP3801_8

Paivio, A. (1986). *Mental Representations: A Dual Coding Approach*. Oxford, UK: Oxford University Press.

Paivio, A. (1991). Dual coding theory: Retrospect and current status. *Canadian Journal of Psychology, 45*(3), 255–287. doi:10.1037/h0084295

Rockwell, S., & Bajaj, A. (2005). COGEVAL: Applying Cognitive Theories to Evaluate Conceptual Models. In K. Siau (Ed.), *Advanced Topics in Database Research* (Vol. 4). Hershey, PA: Idea Group Publishing.

Seufert, T., Jänen, I., & Brünken, R. (2007). The impact of intrinsic cognitive load on the effectiveness of graphical help for coherence formation. *Computers in Human Behavior, 23*(3), 1055–1071. doi:10.1016/j.chb.2006.10.002

Shaft, T. M., & Vessey, I. (1995). The Relevance of Application Domain Knowledge: The Case of Computer Program Comprehension. *Information Systems Research, 6*(3), 286–299. doi:10.1287/isre.6.3.286

Shaft, T. M., & Vessey, I. (1998). The Relevance of Application Domain Knowledge: Characterizing the Computer Program Comprehension Process. *Journal of Management Information Systems, 15*(1), 51–78.

Shanks, G. (1997). Conceptual Data Modelling: An Empirical Study of Expert and Novice Data Modellers. *Australian Journal of Information Systems, 4*(2), 63–73.

Siau, K. (2004). Informational and computational equivalence in comparing information modeling methods. *Journal of Database Management, 15*(1), 73–86.

Siau, K. (2005). Human-computer interaction: The effect of application domain knowledge on icon visualization. *Journal of Computer Information Systems, 45*(3), 53–62.

Sweller, J. (1988). Cognitive load during problem solving: Effects on learning. *Cognitive Science*, *12*(2), 257–285.

Sweller, J., & Chandler, P. (1994). Why Some Material Is Difficult to Learn. *Cognition and Instruction*, *12*(3), 185–223.

Topi, H., & Ramesh, V. (2002). Human Factors Research on Data Modeling: A Review of Prior Research, An Extended Framework and Future Research Directions. *Journal of Database Management*, *13*(2), 3–19.

Vessey, I. (1991). Cognitive Fit: A Theory-Based Analysis of the Graphs Versus Tables Literature. *Decision Sciences*, *22*(2), 219–240. doi:10.1111/j.1540-5915.1991.tb00344.x

Vessey, I., & Conger, S. (1994). Requirements Specification: Learning Object, Process, and Data Methodologies. Association for Computing Machinery. *Communications of the ACM*, *37*(5), 102–113. doi:10.1145/175290.175305

Wand, Y., & Weber, R. (1990). An Ontological Model of an Information System. *IEEE Transactions on Software Engineering*, *16*(11), 1282–1292. doi:10.1109/32.60316

Wand, Y., & Weber, R. (2002). Information Systems and Conceptual Modeling - A Research Agenda. *Information Systems Research*, *13*(4), 363–376. doi:10.1287/isre.13.4.363.69

Wang, S. (1996). Two MIS analysis methods: An experimental comparison. *Journal of Education for Business*, *71*(3), 136–141.

Wiedenbeck, S. (1999). The use of icons and labels in an end user application program: an empirical study of learning and retention. *Behaviour & Information Technology*, *18*(2), 68–82. doi:10.1080/014492999119129

Wittrock, M. C. (1990). Generative processes of comprehension. *Educational Psychologist*, *24*(4), 345–376. doi:10.1207/s15326985ep2404_2

Yadav, S. B., Bravoco, R. R., Chatfield, A. T., & Rajkumar, T. M. (1988). Comparison Of Analysis Techniques For Information Requirement Determination. *Communications of the ACM*, *31*(9), 1090–1097. doi:10.1145/48529.48533

Young, S. L., & Wogalter, M. S. (1990). Comprehension and Memory of Instruction Manual Warnings: Conspicuous Print and Pictorial Icons Human Factors. *The Journal of the Human Factors and Ergonomics Society*, *32*(6), 637–649.

APPENDICES

Appendix 1a: The Far East Repair standard ERD used during the experiment (Figure 4)

Figure 4.

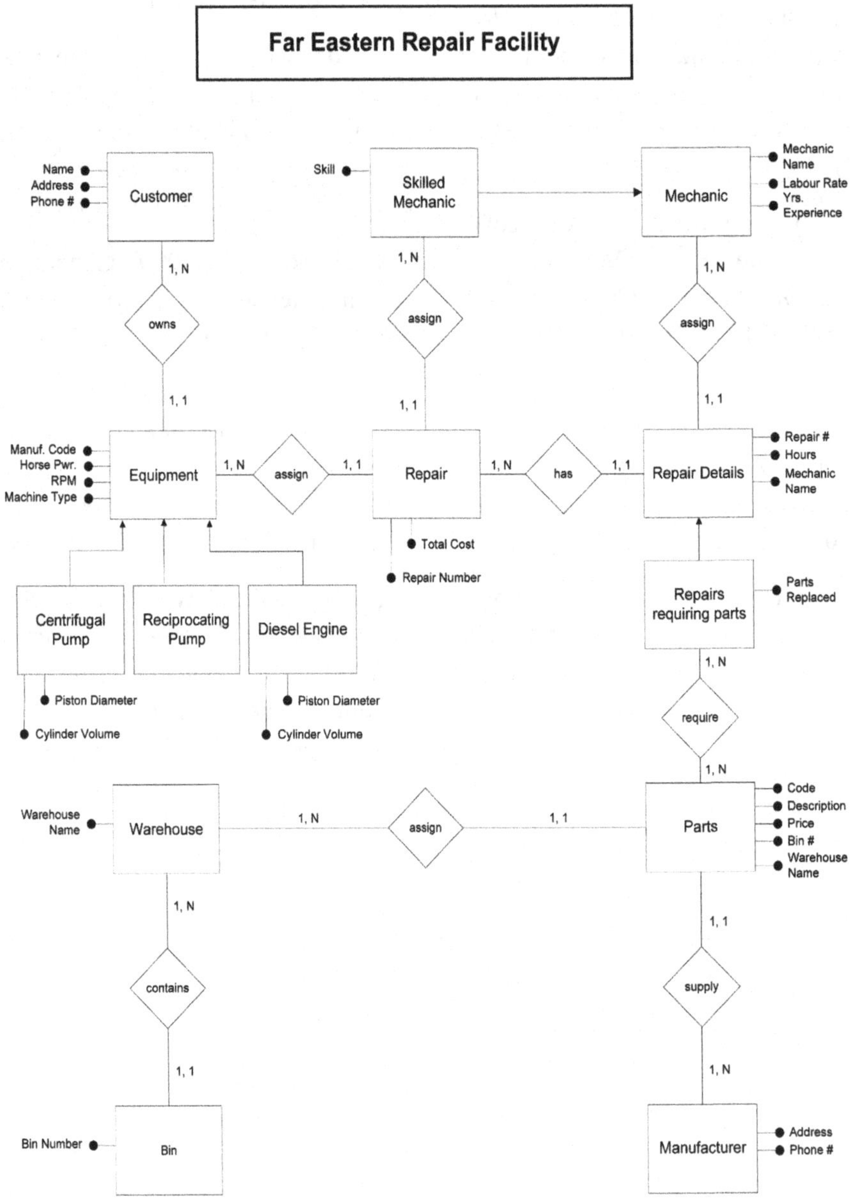

Appendix 1b: The Far East Repair treatment condition ERD (Figure 5)

Figure 5.

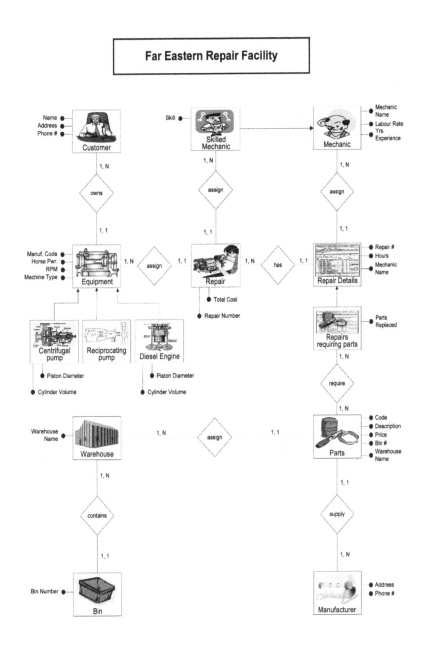

Appendix 2a: The Voyager standard ERD (Figure 6)

Figure 6.

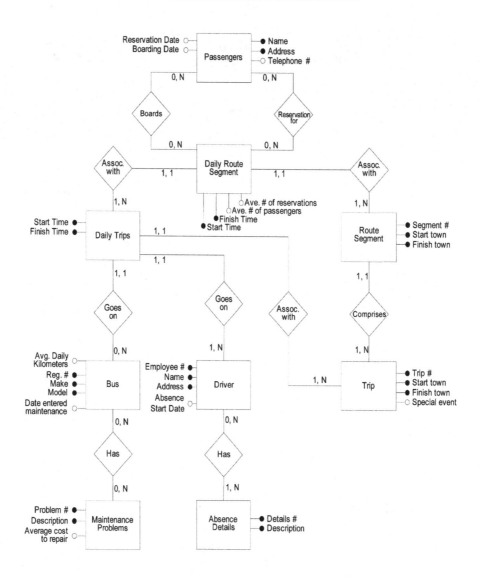

Appendix 2b: The Voyager treatment condition ERD (Figure 7)

Figure 7.

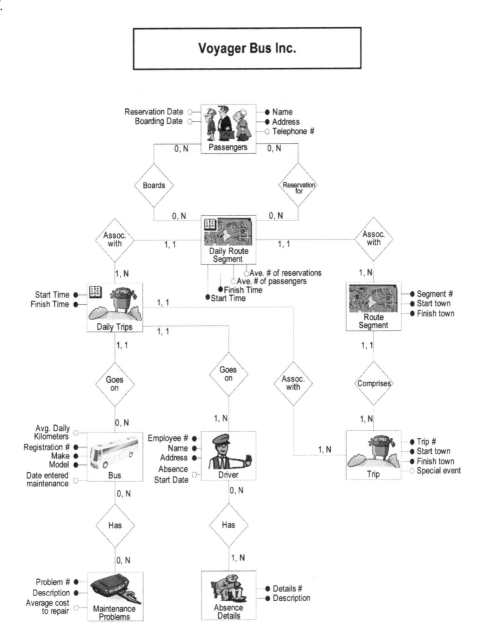

Appendix 3: Training documentation (Explanation of Grammar used by the ERDs) (Figure 8)

Figure 8.

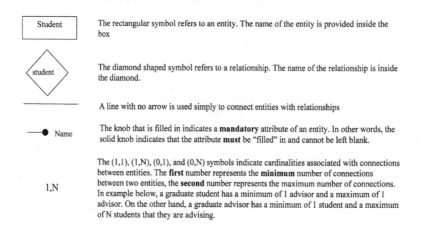

Student	The rectangular symbol refers to an entity. The name of the entity is provided inside the box
student	The diamond shaped symbol refers to a relationship. The name of the relationship is inside the diamond.
	A line with no arrow is used simply to connect entities with relationships
Name	The knob that is filled in indicates a **mandatory** attribute of an entity. In other words, the solid knob indicates that the attribute **must** be "filled" in and cannot be left blank.
1,N	The (1,1), (1,N), (0,1), and (0,N) symbols indicate cardinalities associated with connections between entities. The **first** number represents the **minimum** number of connections between two entities, the **second** number represents the maximum number of connections. In example below, a graduate student has a minimum of 1 advisor and a maximum of 1 advisor. On the other hand, a graduate advisor has a minimum of 1 student and a maximum of N students that they are advising.

Example:
In this example, all Faculty members have a name and office number and some, but not necessarily all of the faculty are graduate advisors. Graduate advisors can have more than one graduate student as an advisee. All students have a name and student number and there are two types of students. A graduate student must have one and only one graduate advisor. Undergrads do not have a graduate advisor.

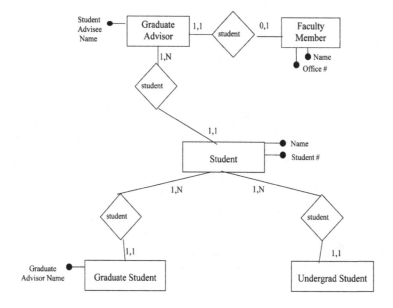

Chapter 16

Beyond Open Source:
The Business of 'Whole' Software Solutions

Joseph Feller
University College Cork, Ireland

Patrick Finnegan
University of New South Wales, Australia

Jeremy Hayes
University College Cork, Ireland

ABSTRACT

Researchers have argued that competitive necessities will require open source software companies to participate in cooperative business networks in order to offer the complete product / service (whole product) demanded by customers. It is envisaged that these business networks will enhance the business models of participant firms by supplementing their value adding activities and increasing responsiveness to customers. However, while such propositions have intuitive appeal, there is a paucity of empirical research on such networks. This study examines Zea Partners, a network of small open source companies cooperating to deliver the 'whole product' in the area of Content Management Systems (CMS). It investigates how network participation augments the business models of the participant companies, and identifies the agility challenges faced by the business network. The chapter concludes that reconciling the coordination needs of OSS networks with the operational practices of participant firms is of crucial importance if such networks are to achieve adaptive efficiency to deliver whole products in a 'bazaar-friendly' manner.

INTRODUCTION

Researchers (Agerfalk et al., 2006; Feller et al. 2006a; Fitzgerald, 2006) have recently argued that Open Source Software firms should adopt a 'whole product' approach (cf. Moore, 1999) by forming a network / ecosystem of partners with complementary

capabilities "to offer a professional product and service in an agile, bazaar-friendly manner" (Fitzgerald, 2006, p.294). This 'whole product' approach is consistent with the challenges of 'productizing OSS' discussed by Woods and Guliani (2005) as well as developments in the production and use of other complex product/service offerings as discussed by Davidow and Malone (1992). This approach is regarded as appropriate when there is a need for firms

DOI: 10.4018/978-1-60566-904-5.ch016

to quickly deliver a variety of customised products, and when the nature of the product development process means that individual organisations do not have sufficient competencies to deal with all parts of product design (Davidow and Malone, 1992; Huang, 2001). In such circumstances, market forces require organisations with similar goals to align themselves in IT-mediated partner networks in order to meet customer requirements (Stafford 2002).

Moore (1999) popularised the concept of the 'whole product' as the cornerstone of market-driven, rather than product-driven, businesses. However, the concept resonates with the dynamics of the open source software phenomenon, which, due to the licensing structure, emphasises services and meta-services surrounding the artefact. Indeed, Woods and Guliani (2005) describe as the challenge of 'productizing' open source software as the need to offer support, implementation, modification and related services. Thus, networks of co-operating small open source software organizations may represent what Clemons and Row (1992) term a "move-to-the middle" where networks of organisations interact in order to deliver value (in the form of the whole product) to the end consumer.

This paper examines Zea Partners, a business network of firms developing Content Management Systems and selling related services, all based around the Zope application server. It investigates how participation in the network augments the business models of participant firms in order to adopt a 'whole product' approach, and identifies the challenges faced by the network in trying to ensure the business agility necessary to offer the 'whole product'. The paper begins by discussing the theoretical foundation for the study. Next, the research objective and research methods are discussed. The case environment is then outlined and the findings presented. The paper illustrates that participation in the network allows firms to share business model components within a centrally managed network, and to engage in agile

competitive practices by making network-level changes in response to changes in the external environment. The need to address adaptability and alignment issues in addition to business agility is highlighted, however. Consequently, the paper concludes that reconciling the coordination needs of OSS networks with the operational practices of participant firms is a critical issue if such networks are to achieve adaptive efficiency to deliver whole products in a bazaar-friendly manner.

THEORETICAL FOUNDATION

OSS has been investigated from a variety of disciplinary and theoretical perspectives. The two dominant research themes, however, have been (1) OSS software engineering tools and techniques and (2) the socio-cultural analysis of OSS communities. The open source model of software development has been popularised as a realistic option for commercial organisations in recent years (Agerfalk and Fitzgerald, 2008; Watson et al. 2008). Commercial organisations, however, are under-represented in OSS research, not just in terms of quantity, but more importantly in terms of depth of research. In particular, there is a need for greater research on commercial aspects (Agerfalk and Fitzgerald, 2008) and business model issues surrounding OSS (Feller *et al.* 2006b). In this section, we draw on the wider literature on business models and business networks to develop the theoretical grounding for our study. In particular, we examine how extant research on business models and networks can improve our understanding of the issues facing firms seeking to form the type of agile business ecosystems envisaged by Fitzgerald (2006).

In keeping with the increasing commercialisation of OSS, researchers such as Watson et al. (2008), Krishnamurthy (2005), Weber (2004), Spiller and Wichmann (2002), Raymond (2001) and Hecker (2000) have documented a series of OSS business models. However, much of this work concentrates on the source of the revenue stream and neglects other aspects of the business models. This is not surprising, as the terms 'business model' and 'revenue model' are frequently, and incorrectly, used interchangeably. Looking outside the OSS literature, it is evident from the work of Timmers (1999), Mahadevan (2000), and Osterwalder and Pigneur (2002) that business models must examine value-adding activities in the context of a supply chain or business network. Osterwalder and Pigneur (2002) propose a comprehensive approach, and detail an ontology that focuses on four aspects of the organisation: product innovation, infrastructure management, customer relationship and financials. Mahadevan (2000) defines a business model as a blend of three streams: value, revenue, and logistics. The value stream is concerned with the value proposition for buyers, sellers and market makers. The revenue stream identifies how the organisations will earn revenue, and the logistics stream involves detailing how supply chain issues will affect the organisations involved. Timmers (1999) argued that architectures for business models can be identified through the deconstruction and reconstruction of a value chain. Value chain elements are identified, as are the possible ways that information can be integrated both within the value chain and between the respective value chains of interacting parties. Furthermore, Evans and Wurster (2000) argue that as more advanced information standards are introduced, levels of collaboration between organizations can be achieved that were previously only possible within a vertically integrated hierarchical intra-organisational structure. Recently, there has been a focus on the business model aspects of 'open innovation' (Chesbrough 2003, 2006; West et al. 2006) where firms supplement, or even supplant, internal research and development efforts by leveraging a variety of sources for knowledge inflows including suppliers, partners, customers, competitors, academic researchers, etc. Thus, many economic entities have recognised the importance of the composition of the supply chain

(or business network) to the overall performance of the firm (Christiaanse 2005).

The benefits of cooperative business relationships have been advocated for decades (Kaufman, 1966; Van de Ven, 1976; Cash and Konsynski, 1985; Henderson, 1990; Finnegan et al., 2003). These relationships have been described as Business webs (Tapscott et al, 2000), partnerships (Henderson, 1990), networks (Nelson, 1988; Joynt, 1991; Finnegan et al, 2003), strategic alliances (Joynt, 1991; Bronder and Pritzl, 1992; Lei and Slocum, 1992), virtual organisations (Davidow and Malone, 1992; Goldman et al., 1995), joint ventures (Kanter, 1989; Oliver, 1990; Campell et al., 1991) service consortia, and stakeholder or value-chain partnerships (Kanter, 1989), promotional and obligation networks (Campell et al., 1991), agency federations, trade associations, social service joint programs, corporate-financial interlocks and agency-sponsor linkages (Oliver, 1990).

The reasons for such business cooperation include; resource procurement and allocation (Galaskiewicz, 1985; Clemons and Row, 1992; Alter and Hage, 1993), political advantages (Galaskiewicz, 1985), risk sharing and acquiring expertise (Alter and Hage, 1993), stability (Oliver, 1990), legitimacy (Galaskiewicz, 1985; Oliver, 1990), efficiency (Oliver, 1990; Clemons and Row, 1992), and innovating (Ticoll *et al.,* 1998). Participants in business networks believe that collaboration will result in adaptive efficiency; the ability to change rapidly while providing customised services or products at a low cost (Alter and Hage, 1993). Thus, the ability to quickly assess new business opportunities, to identify suitable trading partners, and to effectively coordinate delivery of products and services across the business network is important (Sadeh et al. 2003). Following this logic, agility is seen as an important characteristic of business networks.

Agility is a business-wide capability that includes organisational structures, information systems, logistics processes, and mindsets

(Christopher 2000). The term agility has created significant interest in the business world (Lo 1998) and is recognised as a prerequisite for success in dynamic or turbulent environments (Christopher 2000; Camarinha-Matos et al. 2003). Fingar (2000) believes that "the ability to change is now more important than the ability to create… Change becomes a first class design goal and requires business and technology architectures whose components can be added, modified, replaced and configured" (p.66). Sharifi and Zhang (1999) argue that the concept of agility has two main attributes: responding to change promptly and appropriately, and capitalising on the opportunities that are created by change. In a business network, agility is highly dependent not only on the skills of the individual firms, but also on the flexibility of the supporting infrastructure (Camarinha-Matos et al. 2003). Infrastructure flexibility has been identified as an important characteristic of the agile organisation (Christopher 2000), and is dependent on both internal and external factors (Thomke and Reinertsen, 1998). External factors include changes in the needs of the end customer, while internal factors include changes in the development process. Thomke and Reinertsen (1998) argue that design flexibility can be brought about by (1) following a development strategy that can endure a higher probability of design changes, (2) having the ability to produce late changes to the product design in order to better integrate it with the technology and the needs of the customer, and (3) preventing late changes to the product design by making design commitments at a very late stage in the development process.

To conclude, agile business networks designed to meet customer demands for customised products are reasonably well understood outside the OSS domain. Within the OSS field, recent work by Woods and Guliani (2005), Feller et al. (2008), Fitzgerald (2006), (Agerfalk and Fitzgerald, 2008) and Watson et al. (2008) has drawn attention to the importance of networks to OSS business models. However, small OSS firms have emerged from various OSS communities and, thus, cannot be considered to be the same as the type of firms that have been the subject of research on business networks to-date. Therefore, there is a need for further research on the development of agile bazaar-friendly business ecosystems to deliver whole products in the OSS domain.

RESEARCH OBJECTIVE AND METHOD

The objective of this study is to explore the emerging phenomenon of a business network of OSS firms cooperating to deliver the 'whole product'. Two research questions were formulated to support this objective:

RQ1: How does an OSS network affect the business models of participant organisations?

RQ2: What challenges are faced in ensuring that the network is agile?

Case studies are regarded as the most commonly used qualitative research method in IS, and are especially useful for studying organisational aspects of IS (Benbasat et al, 1987). Cases are most appropriate when the objective involves studying contemporary events, without the need to control variables or subject behaviour (Yin, 1994). The single case study method is considered to be a potentially rich and valuable source of data, while suited to exploring relationships between variables in their given context (Yin, 1994; Benbasat et al., 1987). We thus adopted a "soft positivist" epistemology as discussed by Kirsch (2004) and our method follows in the tradition of Eisenhardt (1989) and Madill et al. (2000); it is designed to reveal pre-existing, relatively stable and objectively extant phenomena and the relationships among them in a manner that is not limited to examining only pre-identified constructs.

The subject of the case study (Zea Partners) was chosen as it represented an interesting case in the area of open source business practice in that it is one of a small number of such networks aiming to deliver the 'whole product' in an OSS environment. The researchers first conducted a thorough archival search to determine the existence of public domain material on the network and participant companies. As a result of this preliminary analysis, the researchers prepared a case study protocol (cf. Yin, 1994). Based on this protocol, 16 interviews took place with key personnel from participant firms over a 17-month period from November 2004 to April 2006. In Addition, the researchers had 5 separate interviews with the network founder (elite interviewing, cf. Marshall and Rossman, 1989), and also participated in 4 intensive workshops with network members during this time, which facilitated member checking. The choice of interviewees was based on a number of factors. These were:

1. Willingness to co-operate. In order to obtain useful material, it was necessary for a potential interviewee to be interested in the study, and willing to co-operate.
2. History of network involvement. Interviewees had to have been involved in ongoing network planning and / or project activity over a period of time. A consequence of this selection criterion was that the views of recent members were not studied.
3. Seniority. In order to get contextual material on business strategy and experience with network activities, it was necessary to speak with senior staff within each partner firm. A consequence of this selection criterion was that the views of junior staff were not studied.

Interviews, conducted using an interview guide (cf. Patton, 1980), were generally of one to two-hour duration with follow-up telephone interviews used to clarify and refine issues that emerged during transcription. Interviews were complemented by comprehensive reviews of documents and presentations at the workshops. The content analysis was conducted using Osterwalder and Pigneur's (2002) business model framework as well as Aitken et al.'s (2002) and Lee's (2004) agility frameworks. This is in line with Lee and Baskerville (2003) who, in addressing the issue of generalization, describe the process of generalizing from theory to empirical description (whereby the research seeks to apply findings confirmed in one setting to another one).

CASE ENVIRONMENT

Zea Partners was founded in 2003 as the Zope Europe Association (ZEA), and changed its name to Zea Partners in 2006. Headquartered in Belgium, Zea Partners operates as an international network of businesses that build software and deliver services around the application server technology called Zope; widely used for developing content management systems, intranets, portals, and related applications. Zea Partners consists of 19 firms; 3 managing partners and 16 associate partners located in the Netherlands, Italy, Norway, Belgium, Germany, the United Kingdom, Lithuania, the USA, Spain, France, and South Africa. The management team seeks project contracts on behalf of network members and performs network management activities such as marketing and project management. They also develop the network's business strategy in conjunction with the managing partners.

The partner companies are typically small (10 people or less). These companies have recognized that their size limits the contract (deal) sizes for which they could effectively compete, as well as their geographic range. One of the benefits of the network is, thus, that a number of companies can pool their resources to compete for larger contracts on a global scale. More importantly, in the context of competing on the basis of a whole product, the network allows partners to offer a full range of value chain activities, rather than concentrating exclusively on their own specialities (e.g. development, consultancy, training, etc.). The network is currently working on ensuring that all partners can conduct marketing under the one brand.

According to the network's Founder, the goal is *"to say that we have the whole product. We are going to group together all the people who need a whole product made but can't invest the resources to do it, and then take that whole product and make it offerable by anyone in the network. It has so many benefits on profitability it's just amazing. It's really the only way to impact profitability."* He sees this as being the value proposition of the Network, and acknowledges that, through partnering, the network can compete for larger deal sizes without competing directly with the large international consulting companies. In comparing the Zea Partners network with such consulting companies, he notes the increased flexibility offered to customers. In particular, he argues that: *"instead of having a cathedral[1] model of Accenture, or something like that, we want to have multiple players in multiple countries. We can move things around as new trends emerge, new specialities emerge, stuff like that."* He also highlights the importance of the fact *"that the people in the network are the people that created Silva, the creators of Plone, the creators of Workflow, the creators of Multilingual, the creators of each one of these things. And we want to explain to customers that it's in their interests to have a relationship that rewards these people. It's in their interests, first, because the guy who wrote it can get the job done at a pretty effective rate."*

However, due to the early stage of development at which the network finds itself, co-ordination amongst partners is still on a person-to-person basis. There is an acknowledged need amongst members to evolve the organisation of the network towards the use of quotas, geographical regions etc. To date, coordination has meant observing trademark and domain rules, as well as some network terms and conditions to ensure that products/services delivered by partners meet the expecta-

tions of the customer. Finally, he acknowledges that it is critical to build trust amongst partners so that invoices are paid on time and other responsibilities are met.

FINDINGS

The Osterwalder and Pigneur business model ontology was used as a lens to investigate how the presence of the Zea Partners network affects the business models of the member firms. The results are summarised in Table 1, classified as per the pillars of the Osterwalder and Pigneur (2002) framework, and are discussed below.

Zea Partners enhances the value that member firms can offer to a specific *target customer segment* (*Value Proposition*) by allowing smaller organisations to group together to deliver the whole product as part of a consortium. The fact that the network spans many geographic territories with multiple languages and specialised local knowledge means that a consortium made up of small organisations can compete with the larger consultancy firms. This co-operation increases the range of projects in which members can become involved. Zea Partners covers 12 different countries which, from a geographical spread makes it comparable with a large company. In terms of targeting customers, the Zea Partners brand is purposefully designed to be a mark that distinguishes participants in the network as being leaders in the market. Thus, organisations must already have a good reputation before they can join the network. The Zea Partners network also enhances the business model of participants by adding to the range of *capabilities* that underpin their value propositions. Many of the Zea Partners members are small start-ups that consist of two to four people with mostly specialised technical expertise. A major benefit of Zea Partners membership has, thus, been the ability to access Zea Partners' expertise in areas such as project management, customer relationship management, requirements

Table 1. Effects of Zea Partners network on participants' business models

Business Model Pillar		Effect of Zea Partners on member's business models
Product Innovation	Target Customer Segment	Enhances reputation and branding of participants by providing a single 'market leader' brand.
	Value Proposition	Extends geographic coverage, supports the ability to offer specialised expertise, products and services in many languages and leveraging local knowledge.
	Capabilities	Enhances existing capabilities by providing a broader range of business capabilities, especially project management and customer Relationship Management.
Customer Relationship	Information Strategy	ZEA aims to provide lead referrals and to contribute to the sharing of experiences and knowledge.
	Feel & Serve	Facilitates profile building through common branding.
	Trust & Loyalty	Leverages access to expertise of software originators to build customer trust.
Infrastructure Management	Resources	Lowers friction when building teams, through information sharing, common methodology, tracking results, reporting bugs, etc.
	Activity Configuration	Enables members to act as a "value shop" configuration. Network reduces the information asymmetry between client and consultant resulting in customers 'joining' the community.
	Partner Network	ZEA network means that members do not have to outsource to partners outside the network.
Financials	Revenue Model	Increases deal size for members by creating "whole product" consortia.
	Cost Structure	Enables cost-sharing amongst members.
	Profit/Loss	Increases revenue and lowers expenses through sharing among members, leading to bigger profits.

management, tendering and sales to complement technical expertise. According to the founder of one of the participant companies (Infrae), the development of *capabilities* within Zea Partners is vital to delivering a professional service. In relation to the production of documentation, he noted that *"over time we gradually removed all dependencies on the community, because it was completely unpredictable"*.

With regard to *information strategy*, Zea Partners' stated aim is to *"learn together, share experiences and refer leads to each other"*. However, as yet, resource problems have limited Zea Partners' ability to meet their ideal in terms of *information strategy*. Nevertheless, Zea Partners are proving very successful in enhancing the manner in which a participant firm reaches its customers (*Feel and Serve*). The market for Zope and Plone is characterised by customers approaching firms

in the network with whom they want to do business. A key value added by Zea Partners is that the profile-building activities of the network results in 'leads' for member firms. In some countries where the demand for Plone services exceeds supply, Zea Partners can partner with member firms in that country by co-signing the deal but leaving the local participant with ownership of the customer. Furthermore, a key aspect of customer relationships amongst open source firms is that *trust and loyalty* can be enhanced by providing access to the originator of the software. Thus, Zea Partners aims to assemble project teams that contain relevant software originators from participant firms.

The OSS network model necessitates the inter-organisational management of business infrastructure. A key challenge has been integrating different participants in a seamless manner to deliver the 'whole product' to customers. Zea Partners aims to lower friction in inter-organisational teams by establishing a common approach through the use of *resources* e.g. standing contracts, having customer references on file, having a common methodology; a common way of thinking about a problem, assigning work, tracking results and reporting bugs. This is summed up by the Zea Partners Founder as being the *"big difference between a rabble and an army. You can take a thousand people that speak different languages, that never worked together and they can get defeated by 50 people that are well trained"*. This approach is also evident in the Zea Partners approach to the *configuration of activities* and processes at the level of individual firms and at network level. The Zea Partners network allows members to act as a 'value shop' (cf. Stabell and Fjelstad, 1998) or service provider and carry out the phases of this configuration (problem-finding and acquisition, problem-solving, choice, execution, control and evaluation) as if they were one integrated organisation. One of the areas where Zea Partners differs from the "value shop" concept (as per Stabell and Fjeldstad, 1998) is that in the traditional "value shop" model the information asymmetry between the client and the service provider (in this case a consultancy firm) is one of the main value drivers and results in high prices. This is not seen as desirable by Zea Partners. Instead the network endeavours to reduce this asymmetry so that the customer, instead of being a recipient of content management, becomes a participant in the OSS community: *"there are certain people that need support contracts. There has not been a need for it in any of the projects we have been involved in. I'm a big believer in teaching the people to know enough about the solution to mostly fix it themselves"* (Chief Architect, Plone Solutions). Finally, in relation to infrastructure management, the *partner network* aspect of the business model is a service that Zea Partners completely operates on behalf of its members. Thus they do

not need to outsource activities to non-member organisations.

Enhancing the *financial aspects* of the business models of participants is a key objective of the Zea Partners network. Zea Partners aims to increase the 'deal size' that members can tender for leading to increased profit margin. A key aspect of the Zea Partners' approach is, thus, the sharing of resources and common expenses. Thus participants can focus on key value adding activities of their business models, while sharing the resources, costs and risks of secondary value activities. An interesting revenue model arising in relation to OSS companies providing consulting services is an effort to move away from a 'bill-by-the hour' model to fixed price. This move is occurring as the constant innovation with OSS results in the need for much less customisation, and thus, shorter development times. However, fixed price billing creates challenges for network-based project management as time overruns cut into the profit margins of the participant providing the service.

The discussion of Table 1 above refers to the effects of the Zea Partners network on the business models of the network participants, and not the business model(s) of Zea Partners itself. However, the various effects, taken as whole, result in the Zea Partners network operating as an entity in its own right, and engaging in agile competitive practices. Aitken *et al.,* (2002) present a framework for understanding agility in the context of internal activities such as marketing, production, design, organisation, management and people. This framework is utilised in the present study as a tool for describing the agile characteristics of Zea Partners, as summarised in Table 2 and discussed below.

The members of Zea Partners are already independently able to utilise recognition of the Zope and Plone brands as a marketing tool, but this is only relevant to client firms already aware of Zope/Plone. The unified brand image of Zea

Table 2. Agile Characteristics of Zea Partners

Activity Area	Key Characteristics
Marketing	Network provides and maintains unified Zope and Zea Partners brand.
Production	Network provides harmonised and integrated collection of diverse production processes and capabilities to deliver the whole product.
Design	Network provides harmonised and integrated collection of diverse design processes and capabilities to deliver the whole product.
Organisation	Network serves as competency rallying mechanism to deliver multi-lingual, whole product services across a wide geographic area.
Management	Network distributes responsibility and revenue through simple, decentralised and transparent network governance structures.
People	Network provides customers with access to original software authors and/or experts with unique competencies.

Partners promotes agile marketing in several ways, such as simplifying brand management (one brand versus many) and allowing the network to devote resources to unified brand building, reducing the burden on individual members (e.g., in order to increase brand awareness of Zea Partners and its member organisations, the founder is active in giving interviews, attending conferences etc.). The long-term goal of Zea Partners is to build up sufficient resources so that the network can project a professional image on behalf of the member organisations that simply would not possess the resources to do this individually.

The most important characteristic of Zea Partners vis-à-vis production is its ability to leverage the large amount of diverse skills possessed by the member organisations. According to the Chief Architect of Plone Solutions, *"the thing that will make the network strong is that there is no single point of failure; you can swap out components or companies. If one company does not have the domain knowledge we normally have another company…It's very agile and very flexible"*. Thus, the network allows delivery of the 'whole product', which would not be possible for the smaller members to do as a stand-alone provider. Likewise, many design issues associated with delivering the whole product are addressed through leveraging common experience with a common set of tools, working practices, communication norms and culture that serve to harmonise and integrate the practices of individual firms.

In terms of organisational activity, while the network facilitates matching member competency with customer need, Zea Partners does not currently use explicit coordination processes to schedule work. Previous attempts to do so have had negative results – for example, an incident in which a member firm was advised not to accept new work for a certain time period based on a client's intention, only to find that the client organisation was unable to sign the contracts in the agreed time frame, thus trapping the member firm into a period of non-productivity. However, by not having explicit scheduling mechanisms in place, Zea Partners believes that it is more agile than traditional consulting firms as the network is able to allocate resources more dynamically and effectively and thus to smooth out the peaks and valleys that are a characteristic of technology consulting and development work.

From a management perspective, the goal of Zea Partners is to ensure that network management and governance does not impede realising the potential benefits associated with the fact that open source software is by nature highly decentralised. The founder of Zea Partners believes that this fact results in *"a higher velocity of innovation,"* and that firms in the open source space are thus better equipped to adapt to the very specific needs of clients. For example, while a larger proprietary software development firm may decide not to support a particular language because the market is not big enough to sustain it, open source firms can leverage the work of individual developers and smaller groups who wish to support that language. Having a decentralised governance / management structure and a decentralised approach to consulting, means that if a need is encountered for an unanticipated skill set, it is less of a problem to meet the need than it would be in the traditional consulting model. Finally, in relation to people, Zea Partners leverages the availability of access to the original author(s) and/or core maintainer(s) of the software products to respond to customer demand in an agile fashion.

Zea Partners is made up of a number of autonomous organisations, each having different philosophies, operating in different countries and meeting the needs of a diverse group of clients; meaning that it can draw from a wider variety of experiences. The Chief Architect of Plone noted that there are consequential social and management challenges; *"you will, of course, get the complexity that comes from coordinating different companies with different working styles, and the whole chemistry thing where not all people have worked with the other people all the time."* The business agility challenges that are faced by the network were analysed using the work of Lee (2004) as a lens. He expands on the concept of internal agility by also considering the adaptability of a supply chain as well as the alignment of players within that supply chain. Lee's work is used to frame the content analysis of agility-related challenges facing Zea Partners, and is summarised in Table 3. The categorisation of challenges according to this classification reveals that the challenges extend beyond agility to matters of adaptability and alignment. Consequently, while Zea Partners has been able to engage in agile competitive practices, the challenges that management have articulated indicate the need to move beyond short-term agile practices to consider structural and technological changes in OSS markets, and creating performance incentives.

CONCLUSION

This paper has responded to the need to expand our understanding of economic and business aspects of the OSS phenomenon (cf. Feller *et al.* 2006b) by exploring the business model and agility aspects of participation by open source companies in a business network designed to deliver the 'whole product' (cf. Fitzgerald, 2006). This participation is seen by those studied as a business imperative in order for small OSS firms to compete for large 'deal sizes' with traditional integrated companies. In a study of 13 companies, Morgan and Finnegan (2007) found that support from the open source community was less important to them than support from a trusted third party. Network participation is, thus, an important factor when competing for contracts with larger firms, and the ability of the small firms to access experts from other firms in the network can facilitate building trust and loyalty aspect of the customer relationship.

The study also indicates that participation in the network allows small firms to, in effect, outsource some elements of their business model to the network. This is particularly evident in the division of responsibility for customer-facing activities between participants and the central network. It is this division of responsibility that results in the network being able to engage in agile competitive practices as network-level changes can be made rapidly in response to changes in the external environment. Thus, the challenges that the network faces in ensuring that the multitude of reciprocal interdependencies necessary for the delivery of a whole product do not adversely affect the agility of the network. Nevertheless, it is clear that agile practices are only the first step for the network in competing in the software and consulting sector. It is evident that further work is necessary to address adaptability and alignment issues.

Table 3. Key Challenges for Zea Partners

AGILITY	
Objectives: To respond to short-term changes in demand or supply quickly and to handle external disruptions smoothly.	**Key Challenges:** • Co-ordinate information flow amongst network participants to 'smooth out peaks and valleys' associated with traditional work. • Foster collaborative relationships with partners based on the need for particular competencies. • Develop network level competencies (e.g. project management) to complement the core activities of participants.
ADAPTABILITY	
Objectives: To adjust the network's design to meet structural shifts in markets; to modify supply network to strategies, products, and technologies.	**Key Challenges:** • Leverage partner expertise in different geographical regions to understand market for the total product. • Plan for the introduction of new members into the network to meet requirements for particular competencies. Also, ensure an adequate evaluation of potential members. • Create an understanding of the needs of different types of customers (typically niche markets that traditional competitors don't serve). • To effectively manage the expertise of network partners to ensure that the competencies of the network evolve in response to changes in the product technologies that originate outside the network.
ALIGNMENT	
Objectives: To create incentives for better performance.	**Key Challenges:** • To exchange information and knowledge freely amongst network partners. • Manage partner responsibilities in delivering the whole product in a manner that allows partners to focus on their core competencies. • Effectively provide non-core competencies in a manner that participants can confidently delegate important business model components to the network. • Equitably share risks, costs, and gains of initiatives. • Enable customers to understand the business value of engaging with and contributing to the OSS community.

The need for agility, adaptability and alignment is a problem in all business networks. However, Zea Partners is not typical of other business networks, which rely on formal coordination mechanisms and legal agreements. Rather we observe that the relatively informal characteristics, found in the Zea Partners network, reflects the informal structures characteristic of the online communities of OSS developers from which the firms emerged. Reconciling these two approaches to the coordination issue is a critical issue for future research if OSS networks are to achieve adaptive efficiency (cf. Alter and Hage, 1993) and to deliver whole products in a 'bazaar-friendly' manner (Fitzgerald, 2006).

Overall, our study contributes to the understanding of the commercialisation of open source software. Previous studies of commercial firms have been dominated by studies of single firms, whether OSS start-ups such as RedHat and JBoss (e.g. Krishnamurthy, 2005; Watson et al, 2005) or very large multi-nationals like Apple, IBM and Sun (e.g. West, 2003). Our study examines the perspective of small/micro firms engaged in a cooperative business network in a manner that takes a more complete consideration of the business model concept than has been done to date in the OSS domain. Nevertheless, the methodology utilised for the study was exploratory, and thus the findings need further investigation. This study should be duplicated as part of the process of validating its findings in a context that is not just exploratory. In particular, further research is needed to replicate the study by assessing the results in a wider variety of networks.

ACKNOWLEDGMENT

The present work was funded by the European Commission (via IST Project 004337) and by the Irish Research Council for the Humanities and Social Sciences (via the *O3C Business Models* project).

REFERENCES

Agerfalk, P., Finnegan, P., Hayes, J., Lundell, B., & Ostling, M. (2006). 12 (not so) easy pieces: Grand challenges for Open Source Software. *Panel Presentation at the 14th European Conference on Information Systems, Gotenburg, Sweden, June.*

Ågerfalk, P., & Fitzgerald, B. (2008). Outsourcing to an Unknown Workforce: Exploring Opensourcing as a Global Sourcing Strategy. *MIS Quarterly, 32*(2), 385–409.

Alter, C., & Hage, J. (1993). *Organisations working together.* London: Sage Publications.

Benbasat, I., Goldstein, D. K., & Mead, M. (1987). The case research strategy in studies of Information Systems. *MIS Quarterly, 11*(3), 369–386. doi:10.2307/248684

Bronder, C., & Pritzl, R. (1992). Developing strategic alliances: A conceptual framework for successful co-operation. *European Management Journal, 10*(4), 412–421. doi:10.1016/0263-2373(92)90005-O

Camarinha-Matos, L. M., Afsarmanesh, H., & Rabelo, R. J. (2003). Infrastructure developments for agile virtual enterprises. *International Journal of Computer Integrated Manufacturing, 16*(4-5), 235–254. doi:10.1080/0951192031000089156

Campell, J. L., Hollingsworth, J. R., & Lindberg, L. N. (Eds.). (1991). *The governance of the American economy.* New York: Cambridge University Press.

Cash, J. I., & Konsynski, B. R. (1985). IS redraws competitive boundaries. *Harvard Business Review, 63*(2), 131–142.

Chesbrough, H. (2005). Open Innovation: A New Paradigm for Understanding Industrial Innovation. In H. Chesbrough, W. Vanhaverbeke, & J. West (eds.), *Open Innovation: Researching a New Paradigm* (pp. 1-14). Oxford, UK: Oxford University Press.\

Chesbrough, H. (2006). *Open Business Models: How to Thrive in the New Innovation Landscape.* Boston: Harvard Business School Press.

Christiaanse, E. (2005). Performance benefits through integration hubs. *Communications of the ACM, 48*(4), 95–100. doi:10.1145/1053291.1053294

Christopher, M. (2000). The agile supply chain – competing in volatile markets. *Industrial Marketing Management, 29*(1), 37–44. doi:10.1016/S0019-8501(99)00110-8

Clemons, E. K., & Row, M. C. (1992). Information technology and industrial cooperation: The role of changing transaction costs. *Journal of Management Information Systems, 9*(2), 9–28.

Davidow, W. H., & Malone, M. S. (1992). *The virtual corporation.* New York: HarperCollins.

Eisenhardt, K. M. (1989). Building theories from case study research. *Academy of Management Review, 14*(4), 532–550. doi:10.2307/258557

Evans, P., & Wurster, T. S. (2000). *Blown to bits: How the new economics of information transforms strategy.* Boston, MA: Harvard Business School Press.

Feller, J., Finnegan, P., Fitzgerald, B., & Hayes, J. (2008). From Peer Production to Productization: A Study of Socially Enabled Business Exchanges in Open Source Service Networks. *Information Systems Research, 19*(4), 475–493. doi:10.1287/isre.1080.0207

Feller, J., Finnegan, P., Hayes, J., & Lundell, B. (2006a, June 8-10). Business models for Open Source Software: Towards a mature understanding of the concept and its implications for practice. *Panel Presentation at the IFIP 2.13 Conference on Open Source Software, Genoa Italy 8th-10th June.*

Feller, J., Finnegan, P., Kelly, D., & MacNamara, M. (2006b, July 12-15). Developing Open Source Software: A Community-based Analysis of Research. In *Proceedings of the IFIP 8.2 Working Conference on Social Exclusion--Societal and Organisational Implications for Information Systems, Limerick, Ireland.*

Fingar, P. (2000). Component-based frameworks for e-commerce. *Communications of the ACM, 43*(10), 61–66. doi:10.1145/352183.352204

Finnegan, P., Galliers, R. D., & Powell, P. (2003). Applying Triple Loop Learning to planning electronic trading systems. *Information Technology & People, 16*(4), 461–483. doi:10.1108/09593840310509662

Fitzgerald, B. (2006). The transformation of Open Source Software. *MIS Quarterly, 30*(3), 587–598.

Galaskiewicz, J. (1985). Interorganisational relations. *Annual Review of Sociology, 11*, 281–304. doi:10.1146/annurev.so.11.080185.001433

Goldman, S. L., Nagel, R. N., & Preiss, K. (1995). *Agile competitors and virtual organisations: Strategies for enriching the customer*. New York: Van Nostrand Reinhold.

Hecker, F. (2000). Setting up shop: The business of Open-Source Software [Working paper]. Retrieved from http://www.hecker.org/writings/setting-up-shop

Henderson, J. C. (1990). Plugging into strategic partnerships: The critical IS connection. *Sloan Management Review, 30*(3), 7–18.

Huang, C. (2001). Using Intelligent Agents to Manage Fuzzy Business Processes. *IEEE Transactions on Systems, Man, and Cybernetics. Part A, Systems and Humans, 31*(6), 508–523. doi:10.1109/3468.983409

Joynt, P. (1991). International dimensions of managing technology. *Journal of General Management, 16*(3), 73–84.

Kanter, R. M. (1989). The future of bureaucracy and hierarchy in organisational theory: A report from the field. In P. Bourdieu & J. Coleman (Eds.), *Social Theory for a Changing Society*. Boulder: Westview.

Kaufman, F. (1966). Data systems that cross company boundaries. *Harvard Business Review, 44*(1), 141–155.

Kirsch, L. J. (2004). Deploying common systems globally: The dynamics of control. *Information Systems Research, 15*(4), 375–395. doi:10.1287/isre.1040.0036

Krishnamurthy, S. (2005). An analysis of open source business models. In J. Feller, B. Fitzgerald, S. Hissam, & K. Lakhani (Eds.), *Perspectives on free and open source software*. Cambridge, MA: MIT Press.

Lee, A. S., & Baskerville, R. L. (2003). Generalizing generalizability in Information Systems research. *Information Systems Research, 14*(3), 221–243. doi:10.1287/isre.14.3.221.16560

Lee, H. (2004). The Triple-A Supply Chain. *Harvard Business Review, 82*(10), 102–112.

Lei, D., & Slocum, J. W. (1992). Global strategy, competence-building and strategic alliances. *California Management Review, 35*(1), 81–97.

Lo, W. K. (1998). Agility, job satisfaction and organizational excellence: Their factors and relationships. *Third Proceedings of ISO 9000 and Total Quality Management* (pp. 330–336).

Madill, A., Jordan, A., & Shirley, C. (2000). Objectivity and reliability in qualitative analysis: Realist, contextualist and radical constructionist epistemologies. *The British Journal of Psychology, 91*(1), 1–20. doi:10.1348/000712600161646

Mahadevan, B. (2000). Business models for Internet-based e-commerce: An anatomy. *California Management Review, 42*(4), 55–69.

Marshall, C., & Rossman, B. G. (1989). *Designing Qualitative Research,* Thousand Oaks, CA: Sage Publications.

Moore, G. (1999). *Crossing the Chasm.* New York: Harper-Perennial.

Morgan, L., & Finnegan, P. (2007). Benefits and Drawbacks of Open Source Software: An Exploratory Study of Secondary Software Firms. In J. Feller, B. Fitzgerald, W. Scaachi, & A. Sillitti (Eds.), *IFIP International Federation for Information Processing, Volume 234, Open Source Development, Adoption and Innovation* (pp. 307-312). Boston, MA: Springer.

Nelson, R. E. (1988). Social network analysis as intervention tool. *Group and Organisation Studies, 13*(1), 139–158.

Oliver, C. (1990). Determinants of interorganisational relationships: Integration and future directions. *Academy of Management Review, 15*(2), 241–265. doi:10.2307/258156

Osterwalder, A., Ben Lagha, S., & Pigneur, Y. (2002, July 3–7). An ontology for developing e-business models. In *Proceedings of IFIP DSIAge 2002,* Cork, Ireland.

Osterwalder, A., & Pigneur, Y. (2002, June 17–19). An e-business model ontology for modelling ebusiness. In *Proceedings of the 15th Bled eCommerce Conference,* Bled, Slovenia.

Patton, M. Q. (1980). *Qualitative evaluation and research methods.* Newbury Park, CA: Sage Publications.

Raymond, E. S. (2001). *The Cathedral and the Bazaar* (2nd Ed.). Sebastopol, CA: O'Reilly.

Sadeh, N. M., Hildum, D. W., & Kjenstad, D. (2003). Agent-based e-supply chain decision support. *Journal of Organizational Computing and Electronic Commerce, 13*(3-4), 225–241. doi:10.1207/S15327744JOCE133&4_05

Sharifi, H., & Zhang, Z. (1999). A methodology for achieving agility in manufacturing organisations: An introduction. *International Journal of Production Economics, 62*(1-2), 7–22. doi:10.1016/S0925-5273(98)00217-5

Spiller, D., & Wichmann, T. (2002). *Basics of Open Source Software markets and business models. FLOSS Final Report - Part 3.* Berlin: Berlecon Research.

Stabell, C. B., & Fjeldstad, O. D. (1998). Configuring value for competitive advantage: On chains, shops, and networks. *Strategic Management Journal, 19*(5), 413–437. doi:10.1002/(SICI)1097-0266(199805)19:5<413::AID-SMJ946>3.0.CO;2-C

Stafford, T. (2002). Trust, transactions, and relational exchange: Virtual integration and agile supply chain management. In *Proceedings of the 8th Americas Conference on Information Systems (AMCIS 02).*

Tapscott, D., Ticoll, D., & Lowy, A. (2000). *Digital capital: Harnessing the power of business webs.* Cambridge, MA: Harvard Business School Press.

Thomke, E., & Reinertsen, D. G. (1998). Agile product development: Managing development flexibility in uncertain environments. *California Management Review, 41*(1), 8–30.

Ticoll, D., Lowy, A., & Kalakota, R. (1998). Joined at the bit: The emergence of the e-business community. In Tapscott, D. (Ed.) *Blueprint to the digital economy: Creating wealth in the era of e-business*, New York: McGraw-Hill.

Timmers, P. (1999). *Electronic Commerce: Strategies and models for business-to-business trading*, Chichester: Wiley.

Van de Ven, A. H. (1976). On the nature, formation and maintenance of relations among organisations. *Academy of Management Review*, *1*(4), 24–36. doi:10.2307/257722

Watson, R. T., Boudreau, M., York, P. T., Greiner, M. E., & Wynn, D. (2008). The Business of Open Source. *Communications of the ACM*, *51*(4), 41–46. doi:10.1145/1330311.1330321

Watson, R. T., Wynn, D., & Boudreau, M. (2005). Jboss: The evolution of Professional Open Source Software. *MIS Quarterly Executive*, *4*(3), 329–341.

Weber, S. (2004). *The success of open source*, Cambridge, MA: Harvard University Press.

West, J. (2003). How open is open enough? Melding proprietary and open source platform strategies. *Research Policy*, *32*(7), 1259–1285. doi:10.1016/S0048-7333(03)00052-0

West, J., Vanhaverbeke, W., & Chesbrough, H. (2006). Open Innovation: A Research Agenda. In H. Chesbrough, W. Vanhaverbeke, & J. West (eds.), *Open Innovation: Researching a New Paradigm* (pp. 285-307). Oxford, UK: Oxford University Press.

Woods, D., & Guliani, G. (2005). *Open source for the enterprise*. Sebastopol, CA: O'Reilly Media.

Yin, R. K. (1994). *Case study research, design and methods*. Newbury Park: Sage Publications.

ENDNOTE

[1] Raymond (2001) first articulated the much cited contrast between the hierarchical cathedral model characterising proprietary software and the distributed model of the open source bazaar.

Chapter 17
The Application–Based Domain Modeling Approach:
Principles and Evaluation

Iris Reinhartz-Berger
University of Haifa, Israel

Arnon Sturm
Ben-Gurion University of the Negev, Israel

ABSTRACT

Domain analysis provides guidelines and validation aids for specifying families of applications and capturing their terminology. Thus, domain analysis can be considered as an important type of reuse, validation, and knowledge representation. Metamodeling techniques, feature-oriented approaches, and architectural-based methods are used for analyzing domains and creating application artifacts in these domains. These works mainly focus on representing the domain knowledge and creating applications. However, they provide insufficient guidelines (if any) for creating complete application artifacts that satisfy the application requirements on one hand and the domain rules and constraints on the other hand. This chapter claims that domain artifacts may assist in creating complete and valid application artifacts and presents a general approach, called Application-based DOmain Modeling (ADOM), for this purpose. ADOM enables specifying domains and applications similarly, (re)using domain knowledge in applications, and validating applications against the relevant domain models and artifacts. The authors demonstrate the approach, which is supported by a CASE tool, on the standard modeling language, UML, and report experimental results which advocate that the availability of domain models may help achieve more complete application models without reducing the comprehension of these models.

INTRODUCTION

Domain Engineering enables identifying, modeling, constructing, cataloging, and disseminating the commonalities and differences of applications in a domain (Prieto-Diaz, 1990; Champeaux, 1993; Nakatani et al. 1999; Czarnecki & Eisenecker, 2000). A *domain* in this context is an area of knowledge which uses common concepts that are accepted by practitioners in that area. Similarly, software product line engineering provides aids for specifying sets of software-intensive systems that share common,

DOI: 10.4018/978-1-60566-904-5.ch017

managed sets of features satisfying the specific needs of particular market segments or missions (Pohl et al., 2005; SEI-CMU, 2008). In this discipline, the term 'software product line' replaces 'domain'. Domain engineering and software product line methods receive special attention from communities which deal with reuse, validation, and knowledge representation (Meekel et al., 1997; Addy, 1998; SEI-CMU, 2008). Important reasons for this tendency might be the increasing variability of information and software systems, the need to acquire expertise in different, evolving domains, and the requirements to develop "similar" artifacts taking into consideration business drivers, such as time-to-market, cost, productivity, and quality.

A core activity in domain engineering and software product line engineering is domain analysis, which identifies a domain and captures its ontology (Valerio et al., 1997). It should specify the basic elements of the domain, organize an understanding of the relationships among these elements, and represent this understanding in a useful way (Czarnecki & Eisenecker, 2000). Departing from "regular" reuse techniques, domain analysis methods are expected to provide some kind of support to specification of variability within the domain and not just to the commonality. Several methods and architectures have been developed to support domain analysis through modeling. However, these mainly focus on the specification and representation of the domain knowledge and lack in guiding and validating the reuse of domain knowledge in particular application models.

In this chapter, we present the Application-based DOmain Modeling (ADOM) approach which provides aids for capturing and representing domain knowledge, creating application artifacts from them, and validating these artifacts according to the domain knowledge. ADOM's framework consists of three layers: language, domain, and application. The language layer includes metamodels of modeling languages (or methods), such as UML. In the domain layer, the domain elements, structure, and behavior are modeled using a modeling language that is defined in the language layer. Finally, in the application layer, the designated applications are modeled using the knowledge and constraints presented in the domain layer and the modeling constructs specified in the language layer.

ADOM supports different inter-layer activities, and in particular domain layer artifacts may be used for creation and validation of application layer artifacts, while applications may be generalized into domain artifacts in a process of knowledge elicitation. Furthermore, ADOM can be used with different modeling languages for performing various modeling tasks (e.g., business modeling, requirements analysis, and design). However, when adopting ADOM to a specific modeling language, this language is used in both application and domain layers, easing the inter-layer activities. Here we use the standard modeling language, UML, for demonstrating ADOM's principles and capabilities in both application and domain layers. This dialect of ADOM is called ADOM-UML.

The rest of the chapter is organized as follows. The next section reviews related work in the area of domain analysis. Following, ADOM-UML is presented, describing the domain layer and its provided guidelines, the application layer, and the validation mechanism between these layers. This section also includes an overview of the CASE tool used for ADOM-UML. Next, experimental results regarding the usefulness of ADOM-UML in terms of application model correctness and completeness are reported. Finally, conclusions and future research plans are outlined.

LITERATURE REVIEW

Domain analysis deals with identifying stakeholders and their objectives in a domain, defining selection criteria, identifying boundary conditions, examples, and counter examples, characterizing main common features and variants of the domain, determining relations to other domains, dividing the domain into sub-domains, acquiring domain information from experts, legacy systems, literature, and prototyping, describing domain terminology, and building overall domain models.

Three main groups of domain analysis methods are architectural-based, feature-oriented, and metamodeling. Architectural-based methods (e.g., Neighbors, 1989; Meekel et al., 1997) define the domain knowledge in components, libraries, or architectures, which may be reused in an application as they are, but can be also modified to support the particular requirements at hand. They usually do not provide the designer with guidelines to support a specific application design; rather they allow selecting the relevant elements required by the designated application, while adaptation and assembly of these elements are usually out of the method scope. Furthermore, these methods do not support validation of specific applications according to the domain constraints and rules.

Feature-oriented methods (e.g., Gomaa & Kerschberg, 1995; Kang et al., 1990; Kang et al., 1998; Gomaa, 2004) suggest that a system specification will be derived by tailoring the domain model according to the features desired in a specific system. That is, a specific system uses the reusable architecture and instantiates a subset of features from the domain model. Deursen & Klint (2002) suggest a formal textual notation for feature diagrams, which can be used as a basis for tool development and as mediation between the options provided by software applications and the user requirements. They further show how feature diagrams can be directly mapped to UML class diagrams and consequently be generated to Java code. These methods usually guide the application designer of how to select the required features, while validation is supported by checking whether the feature constraints defined in the domain model hold in the specific application. The main limitation of these methods is that they only partially support adding application-specific

features, through closed variation points, affecting the completeness of the created application models.

Metamodeling techniques (e.g., Schleicher & Westfechtel, 2001; Gomaa and Eonsuk-Shin, 2002; Nordstrom et al., 1999) enable definition of domains as metamodels that serve both for capturing domain knowledge and validating particular applications in the domain. Following these techniques the domain and application models are described in two abstraction levels and support only closed variability, i.e., choosing from predefined sets of variants determined at the domain level. The UML-based language for specifying domain-specific patterns (France, 2004; Kim & Shen, 2008), which can be considered as a metamodeling approach, modifies UML metamodel in order to express the domain variability in terms of element multiplicity. When specifying a particular application, stereotypes are used for connecting the application elements to the relevant domain (pattern) elements. Kim (2007) suggests a conformance mechanism which validates application models against the relevant domain models. However, this mechanism does not include special treatments for application-specific additions. For example, if a direct association in the structural domain model (termed Static Pattern Specification, SPS) is replaced by indirect associations through an additional application-specific class in the class diagram, the conformance mechanism will result with the conclusion that the class diagram does not conform to the SPS, limiting the possible variants of a SPS.

To summarize, the main lack of current domain analysis methods is their partial support for inter-layer activities, namely guiding the creation of complete and valid applications from domain models and validating application models against the relevant domain rules and constraints. The Application-based DOmain Modeling (ADOM) aims at filling this lack.

Table 1. Defined multiplicity indicators (stereotypes) in ADOM-UML

Abbreviated notation	Full notation	Meaning
<<optional many>>	<<multiplicity min = 0 max = *>>	The element may appear any number (including 0) of times in any application model of that domain
<<optional single>>	<<multiplicity min = 0 max = 1>>	The element should appear at most once in any application model of that domain
<<mandatory many>>	<<multiplicity min = 1 max = *>>	The element must appear at least once in any application model of that domain
<<mandatory single>>	<<multiplicity min = 1 max = 1>>	The element must appear exactly once in any application model of that domain
	<<multiplicity min = n max = m>>	The element must appear between n to m times in any application model of that domain

THE APPLICATION-BASED DOMAIN MODELING (ADOM) APPROACH

The Application-based DOmain Modeling (ADOM) approach is based on a three layered framework, which is embedded within the classical framework for metamodeling presented in OMG-MOF (2003). The application layer, which is the lowest layer, consists of models of particular applications, including their structure (scheme) and behavior. The language layer, which is uppermost layer, includes metamodels of modeling languages. Finally, the intermediate domain layer consists of specifications of various domains, such as web applications, multi agent systems, and process control systems. The application and domain layers are included within the model layer (M1) of the classical framework for metamodeling, while the language layer consolidates with the metamodel layer (M2) of this framework. As noted, in ADOM-UML the language used in both application and domain layers is UML.

A domain model in ADOM-UML captures generic knowledge (know-how), in terms of common elements and the allowed variability among them. In particular, the UML stereotypes mechanism is used in the domain layer in order to denote multiplicity-related variability. Each element in the domain layer is associated with a multiplicity indicator (stereotype), which specifies a range for the number of variants of the specific

domain element that may or should be included in an application model in that domain. This is done using two tagged values with this stereotype: min and max. The most commonly used multiplicity indicators are mandatory many, mandatory single, optional many, and optional single, whose meanings are summarized in Table 1. Note that other multiplicity indicators can be specified using the general <<multiplicity>> stereotype with its associated min and max tagged values.

An application model can be constructed on the basis of the knowledge captured in the domain model. In this case, we refer to the application model as an *instantiation* of the domain model. Instantiation can be mainly achieved by configuration or specialization operations, performed at design time (when the application model is created). *Configuration* is the selection of a subset of existing elements from a domain model for the purpose of specifying a lawful specific application model. *Specialization*, on the other hand, is the result of concretization of a domain model element into a specific application model element. The generic (domain) elements can be specialized through operations of refinement, sub-typing, and contextual adoption, so that one generic element may be specialized into more than one element (variant) in the specific application model (Soffer et al., 2007). The relations between a generic element and its instantiations are maintained by UML stereotypes. In addition, some generic elements

Figure 1. The PCS domain model in ADOM-UML: A use case diagram

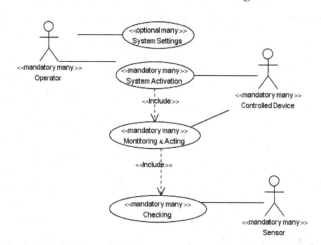

may be omitted and some new specific elements may be inserted to the specific (application) model. Nevertheless, the domain knowledge embedded in the generic model must be maintained in the specific one.

The Domain Layer in ADOM-UML

As noted, models within the domain layer capture the commonality and variability within the domain. This is done by attaching a multiplicity indicator to each element specifying the minimal and maximal number of instantiations of that element in a specific application model. As an example, consider a domain of process control systems (PCS). Applications in this domain monitor and control the values of certain variables through a set of components that work together to achieve a common objective or purpose (Duffy, 2004). Application areas within this domain include engineering and industrial control systems, control systems in the human body, and financial derivation-tracking products.

During the functional requirements analysis of applications in this domain, operators, controlled devices, and sensors are identified as mandatory actors. However, a particular application in the domain may have more than one type of operators, controlled devices, and sensors. Similarly, System

Activation, Monitoring & Acting, and Checking are recognized as mandatory use cases that may be instantiated more than once in a particular application in the domain, while System Settings is an optional use case. Figure 1 depicts these elements, as well as the relationships between them, in a use case diagram.

The domain class diagram, presented in Figure 2, defines the terminology in the domain. According to this model, all applications in the domain should define their sensors, controlled elements and values, and controlled devices. In particular, each application in the PCS domain should have exactly one controller, which exhibits at least one operation for monitoring and acting. A PCS application should also have at least one controlled element, each of which exhibits at least one attribute specifying its identity, zero or more enumerated attributes specifying its statuses, at least one Boolean operation checking certain conditions, and at least one operation for monitoring and activating the controlled element at hand. A controller may be connected to zero or more types of controlled elements, while a controlled element must be connected to at least one type of controller.

The behavior of applications in this domain is manifested in two ways: the sequence diagram depicted in Figure 3 specifies a typical scenario

Figure 2. The PCS domain model in ADOM-UML: a class diagram

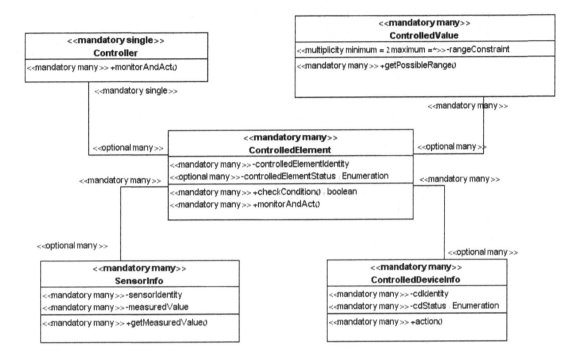

of monitoring the controlled values and activating the controlled devices accordingly[1], while the state diagram in Figure 4 describes the changes in the status of a controlled device over the time. In a typical monitoring and acting scenario, for example, a controller object may appear or not. If it appears, it may activate the monitoring and acting operation of its controlled elements, which in turn sample their controlled values and sensors and activate the relevant controlled devices, if required. A controlled device has a single state presenting that it is off, while several states may represent its activation ("on").

Domain Models Guidance in ADOM-UML

As explained and demonstrated previously, domain models capture the domain knowledge and specify a variety of rules and constraints that should be enforced on all applications in the domain. A special and important type of rules that does not depend on the used modeling language and its semantics is multiplicity-related variability. Domain models enable specifying mandatory and optional elements: mandatory elements must be instantiated in any application in the domain, while optional ones most likely appear in applications in the domain, but may not appear in particular applications in that domain. ADOM also distinguishes between domain elements that may be instantiated several times in the same application in the domain ("many") and domain elements that may be instantiated at most once in a particular application ("single"). Furthermore, ADOM defines three types of elements: relational, dependent, and first order. A relational element explicitly connects other elements (e.g., associations and messages), while a dependent element relies on other elements such that the omission of these elements from the model implies the omission of the dependent element (e.g., attributes and operations). First order elements are elements which are not dependent neither relational. The

Figure 3. The PCS domain model in ADOM-UML: a sequence diagram of monitoring & acting

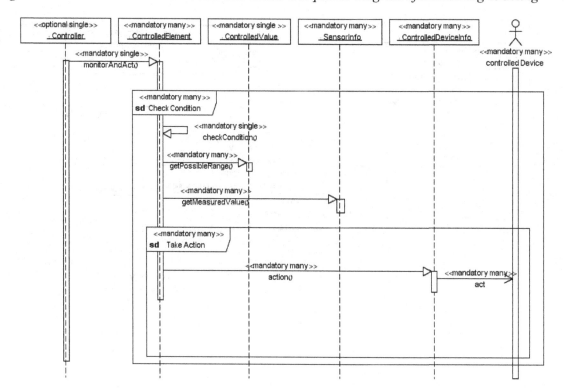

meanings of the multiplicity indicators are slightly different for the three defined elements types. The multiplicity indicator of a first order element specifies the range of times this domain element can be instantiated in any application model of that domain, while a multiplicity indicator of a relational element specifies the range of times this domain element can be instantiated in any application model of that domain **giving that its connected elements have been instantiated**. Finally, a multiplicity indicator of a dependent element specifies the range of times this domain

element can be instantiated in any application model of that domain **giving that its dependees have been instantiated**.

Examples of rules that can be specified for the process control systems (PCS) domain, guiding the creation of application models in this domain, are given below.

Rule 1 (from the use case diagram): An application in the PCS domain interacts with three types of actors, **Operator**, **Sensor**, and **Controlled Device**, each of which must be

Figure 4. The PCS domain model in ADOM-UML: a state diagram of a controlled device

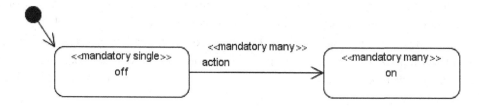

instantiated at least once in any application in this domain.

Rule 2 (from the use case diagram): Each application in the domain has at least one use case in the following categories: **System Activation**, **Monitoring & Acting**, and **Checking**.

Rule 3 (from the class diagram): Each application in the domain has exactly one class classified as **Controller** and at least one class in each of the following categories: **SensorInfo**, **ControlledDeviceInfo**, **ControlledElement**, and **Controlled Value**. Furthermore, the domain model provides additional knowledge on the structure of each concept, including its attributes, operations, and relations to other concepts. Each **ControlledElement** class, for example, has at least one attribute classified as **controlledElementIdentity**, at least one operation classified as **monitorAndAct,** and at least one

operation classified as **checkCondition** (each of which returns a Boolean value). In addition, **ControlledElement** may have enumerated attributes classified as **controlledElementStatus**.

Rule 4 (from the sequence diagram): Each application in the domain deals with monitoring and acting in the following way. The **Controller** activates a **monitorAndAct** operation on the **ControlledElements**. This operation acts in two stages: in the first stage the condition is checked, while in the second stage the action takes place. The activation part of the sequence is embedded within the condition checking part and each one of them can appear several times.

Rule 5 (from the state diagram): Each **ControlledDevice** has exactly one "**off**" state and at least one "**on**" state. The transition between "**off**" and "**on**" states is done by an **action**, while no additional

Figure 5. The HCC application model in ADOM-UML: a use case diagram

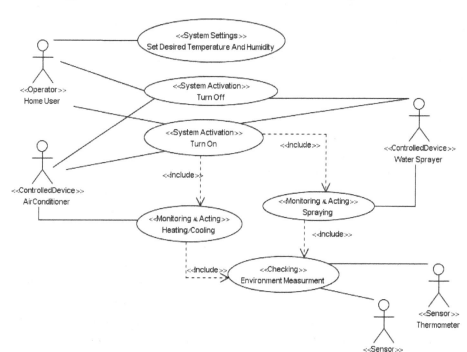

information is provided in the domain level about the transitions between "**on**" and "**off**" states.

The Application Layer in ADOM-UML

An application model, specified in the application layer of ADOM, aims at satisfying the (particular) requirements at hand, while not violating the domain constraints. For this purpose, elements in an application model can be classified according to domain elements specified in the domain layer. In ADOM-UML this is done using the stereotypes mechanism. Each element, be it relational, dependent, or first order, can be stereotyped by a domain counterpart of the same meta-class. Differently from profiles, in which stereotypes are specified as classes and associated to meta-classes from the language (metamodel) layer, stereotypes in ADOM-UML are directly specified using the relevant meta-classes. For example, stereotypes that can be used for actors, use cases, classes, attributes, operations, associations, messages, and states will be respectively specified in the domain layer as actors, use cases, classes, attributes, operations, associations, messages, and states. The purpose of this decision is to ease the task of creating application specifications from domain models, since the same modeling constructs are applied in both application and domain layers. However, as is explained and demonstrated next, relational and dependent elements can use stereotypes from their relevant context (i.e., their connected elements and dependees, respectively). An application element is required to preserve the constraints of its stereotypes in the relevant domain model.

Returning to the PCS example, the variety of applications in this domain is quite large. Applications in the domain defer in the number of the controlled elements, the numbers and types of controlled values and sensors, whether the system is configurable, how the system monitors controlled values and acts, etc. In this section, two applications in the domain are specified: a Home Climate Control (HCC) application and a Water Level Control (WLC) system. The HCC application ensures that the temperature in the rooms of a house remains in the closed range [TL, TH] and the humidity in these rooms remains in the closed range [HL, HH]. Each room has its own limit values (TL, TH, HH, and HL) which are configurable. The actual levels of temperature and humidity are measured by thermometers and humidity gauges, respectively. An air conditioner and a water sprayer are installed in each room, enabling changing the temperature and humidity at will. The ADOM-UML model of the HCC application appears in Figures 5, 6, 7, 8, and 9. Note that these diagrams include application-specific elements that are not stereotyped according to the domain, e.g., the size attribute of Room and the service company attribute of Air Conditioner. Furthermore, relationships (associations) are not always stereotyped even if they originate from the domain model (e.g., when the domain relationship name is not explicitly specified). Thus, the association of an application relationship to its domain counterpart is done through its stereotype (if exists) and context, i.e. the elements which it connects. Pay attention that the objects and procedure calls in the sequence diagram are not explicitly stereotyped, since their stereotypes can be concluded from the class diagram. As explained latter, application-specific elements can be added as long as they do not violate the domain constraints.

The purpose of the WLC application is to monitor and control the water levels in tanks, ensuring that the actual water level is always in the closed range [Lowest Limit, Highest Limit]. The values of the lowest and highest limits are configurable. The actual level is measured by a boundary stick. The tanks are also coupled to emptying faucets that drain water from the tank and to filling faucets that inject water into the tank. The ADOM-UML

Figure 6. The HCC application model in ADOM-UML: a class diagram

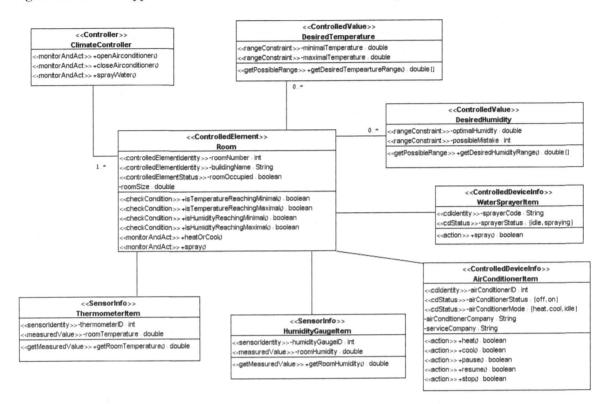

model of the WLC application is presented in Figures 10, 11, 12, and 13.

Although different, both applications use the knowledge captured in the PCS domain model and preserve its constraints. In particular, they both maintain the five rules exemplified before. Note that these rules may not explicitly appear in the requirement specification of a particular application, as they may be common property of the domain.

Validating Application Models against Domain Models in ADOM-UML

To check the validity of application models in a domain, an automatic validation procedure is taken. This procedure refers to the adherence of the application model to the domain model. It does not refer to the verification of the specific application requirements in the application model. In other words, the validation capability of ADOM checks the fulfillment of the domain constraints and rules in the application model. The inputs of this procedure are an application model and a domain model. The application model could be developed using the domain model or without it. In the latter case, preprocessing is required, in which the application elements are classified according to the domain elements.

The validation in ADOM is performed in three phases: element reduction, element unification, and model matching.

Element Reduction

In this step, application-specific elements are omitted from the application model. These elements are recognized using the classification (stereotypes) mechanism and the context within which

Figure 7. The HCC application model in ADOM-UML: a sequence diagram of heating/cooling

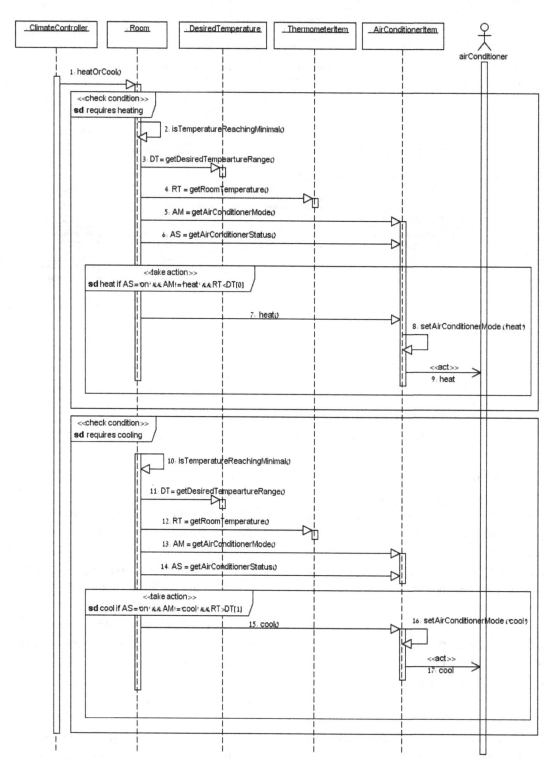

Figure 8. The HCC application model in ADOM-UML: a state diagram of a water sprayer

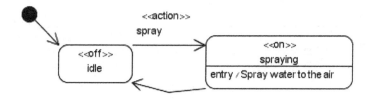

Figure 9. The HCC application model in ADOM-UML: a state diagram of an air-conditioner

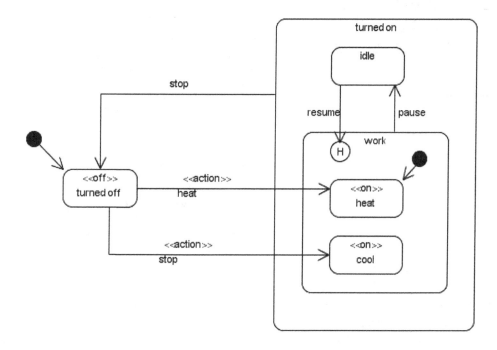

Figure 10. The WLC application model in ADOM-UML: a use case diagram

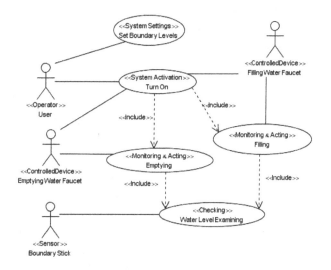

Figure 11. The WLC application model in ADOM-UML: a class diagram

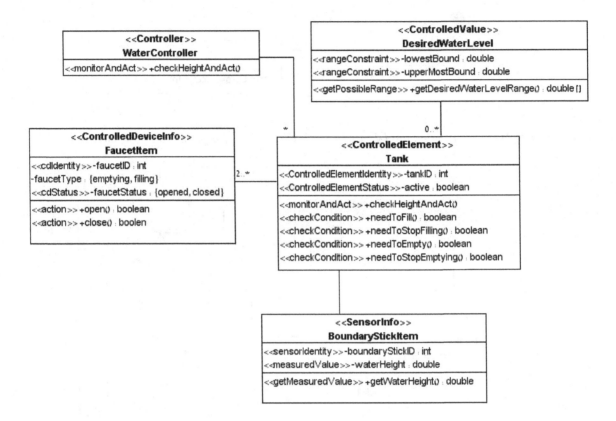

particular elements participate (for relational and dependent elements). As a consequence, compensating operations may be required for percolating the omission to the remaining model. If, for example, the application model includes three classes, A, B, and C, which are connected with two bi-directional associations A-B and B-C, and B is determined as application-specific, then the omission of B from the model will require adding a bi-directional association between A and C in order to specify that in the original (application) model there were navigational paths from A to C and vice versa. The resultant model, after making these changes to the application model, is termed a *reduced model*.

Element Unification

In this step, elements that have the same classification (stereotype) in the reduced model are unified, leaving only one element for each category. Stereotypes, called actual multiplicity, are associated to these elements in order to denote the number of elements that are classified the same in the reduced model. Similarly to the multiplicity indicators in domain models, actual multiplicity stereotypes have two values, minimum and maximum, which respectively specify the minimal and maximal application elements that are classified as the corresponding domain element in the particular application. Finally, the resultant model, termed the *verifiable model*, can be matched to the domain model. The verifiable model of the HCC application appears in Figure 14, whereas the verifiable model of the WLC application appears

Figure 12. The WLC application model in ADOM-UML: a sequence diagram of filling/stop filling

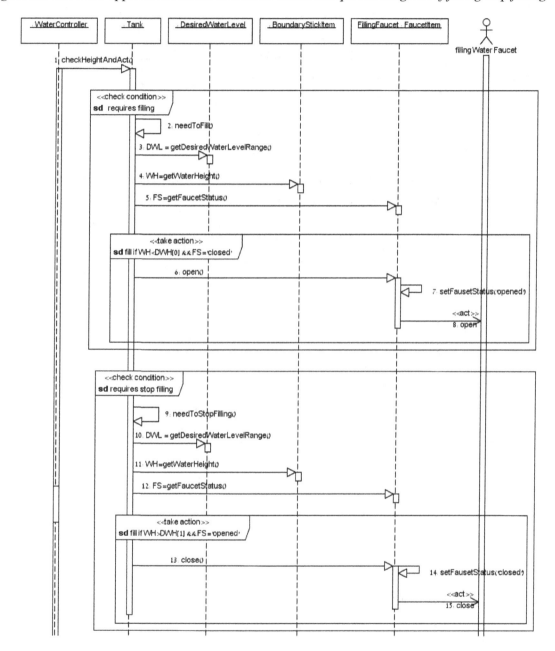

in Figure 15. For clarity purposes, we reduced the notation <<ActualMultiplicity min=m max=n> to <m..n> in these figures.

Note that for first order elements the minimal and maximal tagged values of the actual multiplicity are equal. However, these tagged values may be different for dependent and relational elements.

The actual multiplicity of dependent elements is calculated over all the dependees of the same type, whereas the actual multiplicity of relational elements is calculated over all their connected elements. The actual multiplicity of the action operation of Controlled Device Info in the HCC verifiable model, for example, is 1..5, since both

Figure 13. The WLC application model in ADOM-UML: a state diagram of a faucet

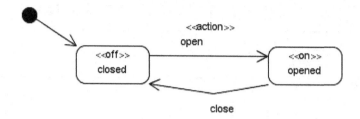

Figure 14. The verifiable model of the HCC application: (a) the use case diagram, (b) the class diagram, (c) the state diagram, and (d) the sequence diagram

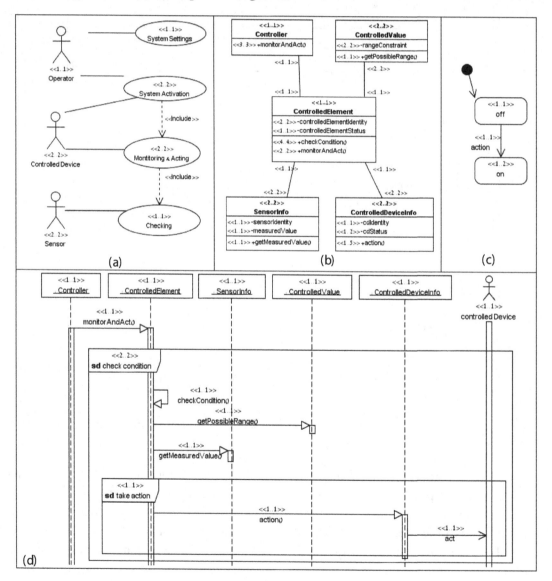

Figure 15. The verifiable model of the WLC application: (a) the use case diagram, (b) the class diagram, (c) the state diagram, and (d) the sequence diagram

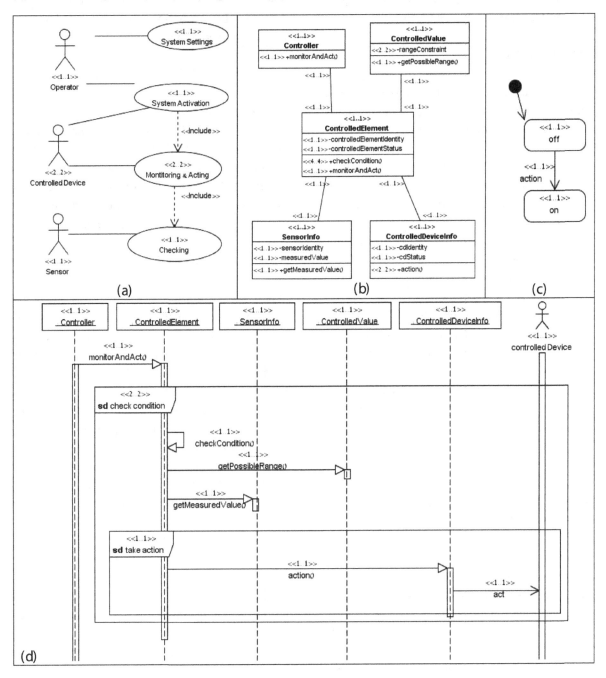

Air-conditioner and Water Sprayer are classified as controlled devices in the HCC application and the Air-conditioner has 5 action operations (heat, cool, pause, resume, stop), while the Water Sprayer has only one (spray). Thus, action appears between 1 to 5 times in a controlled device element. The actual multiplicity of all the messages in the sequence diagrams in both applications is

1..1, since each message appears exactly once in its owning frame (although each sequence diagram contains two frames of each type).

Model Matching

This step matches the verifiable model with the domain model, where matching models satisfy the following conditions:

1. All the classified elements in the verifiable model are termed as elements of the same meta-classes from the domain model. All the non-classified elements in the verifiable model have counterparts of the same meta-classes in the domain model. These counterparts have no names in the domain model (e.g., associations).
2. For each element in the verifiable model, the values of the actual multiplicity are within the boundaries of the multiplicity indicator of the relevant element in the domain model.
3. Each element in the domain model that does not appear in the verifiable model is optional (i.e., has minimal multiplicity in the domain model of 0).

Supporting ADOM-UML with a CASE Tool

Creating domain and application models in ADOM is not a trivial task. Thus, we developed a tool which supports guiding and validating the creation of valid application models in ADOM-UML. This tool plugs into an existing UML tool, called TOPCASED (2008). TOPCASED promotes model-driven engineering and formal methods as key technologies. It uses the eclipse modeling framework (Eclipse Foundation, 2008) for manipulating the modeling tool and models. We mainly chose this CASE tool since it is open source and enabled us adding the following ADOM-related functionality: domain model

creation, application model guiding, and application model validation[2]. At its current stage, this ADOM-related functionality is supported only in UML class and activity diagrams.

Domain Model Creation

The creation of domain models is supported by defining an ADOM-UML profile that includes the different multiplicity stereotypes with their associated tagged values. These stereotypes are assigned to the top level Element class in the UML metamodel, allowing specification the commonality and variability of all domain elements.

Application Model Guiding

When creating a new modeling project, the modeler requests the tool to semi-automatically create an application model from the selected domain model. A profile based on the selected domain model is created, including the different domain model elements, each of which attached to the relevant element types. Domain elements that are described by classes, for examples, are translated to stereotypes which are attached to the Class meta-class. The modeler can use this profile when developing the application model. The tool adds to the current application model one instantiation for each mandatory first order domain element. For each such instantiated element, all its mandatory dependent elements are instantiated (once each). After creating the initial application model, the modeler can continue developing the application model by adding, removing, and updating various model elements, as well as assigning the proper domain classifiers (stereotypes) to them.

Application Model Validation

At any moment in the application development process, the modeler can choose to activate this option, which executes the three-step algorithm specified in the previous section, and results with a report of errors that refer to violation of domain model constraints. Figure 16 is a screenshot from the tool, showing an error report resulted when validating an erroneous HCC application model against the PCS domain model. "-1" represents infinity in this report.

EXPERIMENTING WITH ADOM-UML

In this section we report about our experience regarding the usefulness of the ADOM approach in general and ADOM-UML in particular for creating correct and complete application models. According to Major and McGregor (1999), *correctness* is measured as how accurately the model represents the information specified within the requirements. For defining the correctness of a model, a source that is assumed to be (nearly) infallible is identified. This source, termed a "test oracle", is usually a human expert whose

personal knowledge is judged to be sufficiently reliable to be used as a reference. The accuracy of the model representation is measured relatively to the results expected by the oracle. *Completeness*, on the other hand, deals with the necessity and usefulness of the model to represent the real life application, as well as the lack of required elements within the model (Major & McGregor, 1999). In other words, completeness is judged as to whether the information being modeled is described in sufficient details for the established goals. This judgment is based on the model's ability to represent the required situations, as well as on the knowledge of experts.

In order to check whether domain analysis with ADOM-UML may contribute to development of more complete and correct applications, we conducted an experiment, whose hypotheses, settings, and results are detailed next.

Figure 16. An error report resulted when validation an erroneous HCC application model against the PCS domain model

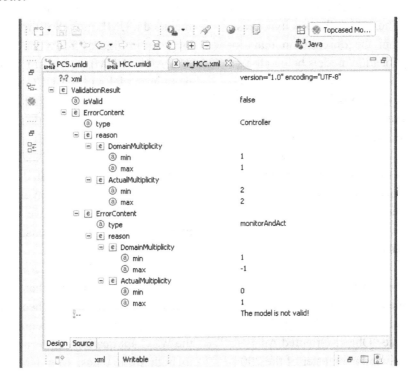

Experiment Hypotheses

In the experiment we aimed at checking the following three hypotheses.

Hypothesis #1: **Application models are more completely developed when a domain model is available.** This hypothesis is derived from the observation that domain models may include relevant elements and constraints that do not explicitly appear in the requirements of each application in the domain. Furthermore, "best practices" can be incorporated into the domain models as optional elements (i.e., elements whose minimal multiplicity is 0), helping the designer not to miss information.

Hypothesis #2: **Application models are more correctly developed when a domain model is available.** Here, again, wrong interpretation of requirements may be avoided by the domain artifacts and knowledge.

Hypothesis #3: **The comprehension of application models remains unchanged when the relevant domain model and elements are added.** The reason for this hypothesis originates from the observation that domain and application models belong to two different abstraction levels. When answering concrete questions about the applications, the more abstract domain elements might generalize the needed information, blurring the sought answer. However, the existence of these domain elements may help answer questions which relate to generalized application information.

Experiment Settings

The subjects of the experiment were third year students in a four-year engineering B.Sc. program at Ben-Gurion University of the Negev, Israel, who took the course "Object-Oriented Analysis and Design" at the winter semester of the 2004-

5 academic year. All of them were students of the Information Systems Engineering program and had no previous knowledge or experience in system modeling and specification. During the course, the students studied mainly UML and its applicability to software analysis and design, while the last lecture was devoted to ADOM.

The experiment took place during the final three-hour examination of the course. The examination contained two tasks, one of which was related to the reported experiment. In this task the students were asked to respond to nine true/false comprehension questions about the HCC application and to build a model of a WLC application. The students were told that both applications belong to the same PCS domain. The comprehension questions are listed along with their expected answers in the appendix, which also includes the modeling question that refers to the WLC application. An acceptable model to this application is given in Figures 10-13.

The students were divided arbitrarily into two groups of 34 and 36 students. Each group got a different test form type, ADOM-UML and "regular" UML, respectively. The "regular" UML test form included a UML model of the HCC application, as given in Figures 5-9 without the stereotypes. The ADOM-UML test form included the PCS domain model and the HCC application model as given in Figures 1-4 and 5-9, respectively. The students were provided with alternating form types according to their seating positions, so this arbitrary division into the two experimental groups closely approximated random division. Executing a t-test on the average grades of the students in their studies, we indeed found that no significant difference exists between the two groups ($t = 0.32$, $p \sim 0.75$).

In order to validate the correctness and completeness of the models that participate in the experiment, as well as to check that the comprehension questions can be accurately answered and the WLC application can be accurately modeled in both form types, four UML design experts examined them carefully. Only after reaching an agreement on all the aforementioned issues, the experiment was conducted.

We also addressed ethical concerns that may rise using the author's students as participants (Singer & Vinson, 2002). In particular, the students were notified at the beginning of the semester about the exam being used as an experiment; the students had the opportunity of getting a grade in the course without participating in the experiment (by taking term B of the exam); the grades of the two test forms were normalized; and confidentiality was kept throughout the entire data grading and analysis processes, so no identification of the subjects can be done.

Experiment Results

The comprehension and modeling questions were checked according to a pre-defined detailed grading policy, which included potential errors along with the number of points that should be reduced for each error. Each comprehension question could score a maximum of 2 points (18 points in total), while the modeling question could score as much as 32 points. Incomplete answers, or incorrect answers, scored less according to the detailed grading policy.

Table 2 summarizes the average scores of the comprehension, modeling, and overall grades. A t-test, which was used to analyze these results, showed that although the average comprehension score of the ADOM-UML group was higher than that of the "regular" UML group, it was not found as statistically significant (p<0.094). This

outcome can be considered as in-line with our third hypothesis, as we claimed that domain models sometimes help find generalized answers (i.e., answers that are relevant to several applications in the domain or to several instantiations of the same domain element) and sometimes blur the sought answers (for questions that are individual to the specific application). Since the questions in the experiment belong to both categories, no significant differences were found.

However, the statistical analysis shows that the availability of the domain model was very important for modeling a new application in the domain. This is especially true, since the students that participated in the experiment were non-experts (in the domain, the modeling language, and the development task).

In order to carry out an in-depth analysis of the domain model influence on both correctness and completeness of application models, we further checked the average amount of points reduced due to incompleteness and incorrectness, whereas incompleteness referred to missing elements and correctness was measured in terms of redundancy, incorrect facts, and inconsistency among the diagrams. Note that some of the points were reduced due to miscellaneous defects (Shull et al., 2000) and, thus, they are omitted from the calculations regarding correctness and completeness.

Table 3 presents the average amount of points reduced due to incompleteness and incorrectness. As claimed in hypothesis #1, the results clearly show that ADOM-UML helped gain a more complete model. We believe that the main reason for this outcome is using the ADOM-UML domain

Table 2. Results of the comprehension, modeling, and overall grades

	Average score		t	p-value
	ADOM-UML	**Regular UML**		
Comprehension	**76.31%**	68.98%	1.698	<0.094
Modeling	**89.11%**	77.73%	3.605	**<0.001**
Overall	**84.50%**	74.58%	3.214	**<0.002**

model as guidelines for building the application model, rather than starting from scratch or from a similar application. These guidelines were applied properly as the students had another application from the same domain (the HCC model) that applied the same guidelines.

Regarding correctness, Table 3 shows that the students had fewer errors when using ADOM-UML. However, this was not found as statistically significant (p<0.062). The main differences between the two groups were that students who used the "regular" UML test forms had significantly less errors related to the class diagram, while students who used the ADOM-UML test forms had significantly less errors related to messages in the sequence diagram and to states and their transitions in the state diagram. We believe that the reason for the statistical insignificance of these results was the similarity between the two applications: the given HCC model and the requested WLC model. Our belief relies on the observation that the students who got "regular" UML test forms consider the HCC model as a reference for modeling the WLC system. This could be done since the particular applications are very similar. However, in the general case, only the domain model can serve as a template to guide the developer in the development of new domain-specific applications.

SUMMARY AND FUTURE WORK

In this chapter we presented and exemplified the principles of the Application-based DOmain Modeling (ADOM) approach, which enables specifying both domain and application models with similar software engineering techniques and languages. Furthermore, the approach provides means for using domain models for guiding and validating application models in certain domains: when developing a particular application in the domain, the domain model is used as a reference for guiding the modeler to create complete and valid application models and the application model can be validated against the relevant domain model in order to detect completeness and correctness errors. An ADOM-UML tool was developed in order to support these activities.

We empirically evaluated our approach on undergraduate students, i.e., inexperienced users who need additional tools and techniques in order to develop qualitative application models. The results presented in this chapter suggest that the availability of the domain model help develop better application models, mainly with respect to their completeness, without affecting their comprehension. When developing totally new applications inexperienced designers tend to create erroneous models, but even experienced ones cannot anticipate the implication of a change on an overall model (Sunye et al, 2001). Indeed, Lange et al. (2006) showed that model defects often remain undetected, even if practitioners check the model attentively. These results may advocate and justify the costs and efforts required in developing complete and correct domain models for mature, stable, economically viable domains, as these domain models can be used for guiding the development of high quality applications in these domains.

The separation in ADOM between the model (the application and domain layers) and meta-model (the language layer) levels enables adopting

Table 3. The average percentages of points reduced due to completeness and correctness errors

p-value	t	Regular UML	ADOM-UML	Inspected aspect
<0.002	-3.324	10.84%	**5.59%**	Completeness
<0.062	-1.904	7.66&	**5.34%**	Correctness

ADOM and its associated activities to different modeling languages and tasks. We have already adopted ADOM for business process modeling with UML activity diagrams (Reinhartz-Berger et al., 2005) and EPC (Soffer et al., 2007), for requirement and design modeling with Object-Process Methodology (Sturm et al., 2006), and for web site development with Tersus (Tersus, 2006).

In the future, we plan to continuously evaluate the effectiveness of using ADOM (by novice and experienced users) to support the construction of consistent, correct, and complete application models in various modeling languages. In addition, we work on developing a formal and accurate process for instantiating and utilizing domain models, which we believe will help improve the accuracy, correctness, and completeness of the resultant application models. Finally, continuous improvements and enhancements for the CASE tool are planned.

REFERENCES

Addy, E.A. (1998). A framework for performing verification and validation in reuse-based software engineering, *5*(1), 279-292.

Czarnecki, K., & Eisenecker, U. W. (2000). *Generative Programming - Methods, Tools, and Applications*. Addison-Wesley.

de Champeaux, D., Lea, D., & Faure, P. (1993). *Object-Oriented System Development*. Addison Wesley.

Deursen, van A. & Klint, P. (2002). Domain-Specific Language Design Requires Feature Descriptions, Journal of Computing and Information Technology, *10*(1), 1-17.

Duffy, D. J. (2004). *Domain Architectures: Models and Architectures for UML Applications*. New York: John Wiley & Sons.

Eclipse Foundation. (2008). *Eclipse modeling frameworks*. Retrieved from http://www.eclipse.org/modeling/emf/

France, R. B., Kim, D.-K., Ghosh, S., & Song, E. (2004). A UML-Based Pattern Specification Technique . *IEEE Transactions on Software Engineering*, *30*(3), 193–206. doi:10.1109/TSE.2004.1271174

Gomaa, H. (2004). *Designing Software Product Lines with UML: From Use Cases to Pattern-based Software Architectures*. The Addison-Wesley Object Technology Series.

Gomaa, H., & Eonsuk-Shin, M. (2002). Multiple-View Meta-Modeling of Software Product Lines. In *Proceedings of the Eighth IEEE International Conference on Engineering of Complex Computer Systems*.

Gomaa, H., & Kerschberg, L. (1995). Domain Modeling for Software Reuse and Evolution. In *Proceedings of Computer Assisted Software Engineering Workshop* (CASE 95).

Kang, K., Cohen, S., Hess, J., Novak, W. & Peterson, A. (1990). Feature-Oriented Domain Analysis (FODA) Feasibility Study, CMU/SEI-90-TR-021 ADA235785.

Kang, K. C., Kim, S., Lee, J., Kim, K., Shin, E., & Huh, M. (1998). FORM: A feature-oriented reuse method with domain-specific reference architectures. *Annals of Software Engineering*, *5*(1), 143–168. doi:10.1023/A:1018980625587

Kim, D. K. (2007). The Role-Based Metamodeling Language for Specifying Design Patterns. In T. Taibi (Ed.), *Design Pattern Formalization Techniques* (pp. 183-205). Hershey, PA: IGI Global.

Kim. D. K., & Shen, W. (2008). Evaluating Pattern Conformance of UML Models: A Divide-and-Conquer Approach and Case Studies. *Software Quality Journal*.

Lange, C. F. J., Chaudron, M. R. V., & Muskens, J. (2006). In Practice: UML Software Architecture and Design Description. *IEEE Software, 23*(2), 40–46. doi:10.1109/MS.2006.50

Major, M., & McGregor, J. (1999). *Using Guided Inspection to Validate UML Models.* Paper presented at the 24th Annual IEEE/NASA Software Engineering Workshop.

Meekel, J., Horton, T. B., France, R. B., Mellone, C., & Dalvi, S. (1997). From domain models to architecture frameworks. In *Proceedings of the 1997 symposium on Software reusability* (pp. 75-80).

Nakatani, L. H., Ardis, M. A., Olsen, R. G., & Pontrelli, P. M. (1999). Jargons for domain engineering, In *Proceedings of the 2nd Conference on Domain-Specific Languages* (pp. 15-24).

Neighbors, J. (1989). Draco: A Method for Engineering Reusable Software Systems. In T. Biggerstaff & A. Perlis (Eds.), *Software Reusability. Volume I: Concepts and Models* (pp. 295-319). Reading, MA: ACM Press, Frontier Series, Addison-Wesley.

Nordstrom, G., Sztipanovits, J., Karsai, G., & Ledeczi, A. (1999). Metamodeling - Rapid Design and Evolution of Domain-Specific Modeling Environments. In *Proceedings of the IEEE Sixth Symposium on Engineering Computer-Based Systems (ECBS)* (pp. 68-74).

OMG-MOF (2003). Meta-Object Facility (MOF™), version 1.4.

OMG-UML (2003). The Unified Modeling Language (UML™), version 1.5.

OMG-UML (2006). UML 2.0 Superstructure, 2006.

Pohl, K., Gunter, B., & van der Linden, F. (2005). *Software Product Line Engineering – Foundations, Principles, and Techniques.* Springer.

Prieto-Diaz, R. (1990). Domain analysis: an introduction. *ACM SIGSOFT Software Engineering Notes, 15*(2), 47–54. doi:10.1145/382296.382703

Reinhartz-Berger, I., Soffer, P., & Sturm, A. (2005). A Domain Engineering Approach to Specifying and Applying Reference Models. In *Proceedings of Enterprise Modeling Information Systems Architecture (EMISA'05)* (pp. 50-63).

Schleicher, A., & Westfechtel, B. (2001). Beyond Stereotyping: Metamodeling Approaches for the UML, In *Proceedings of the 34th Annual Hawaii International Conference on System Sciences* (pp.1243-1252).

SEI-CMU. (2008). *A Framework for Software Product Line Practice, Version 5.0.* Retrieved from http://www.sei.cmu.edu/productlines/framework.html

Shull, F., Rus, I., & Basili, V. (2000). How Perspective-Based Reading Can Improve Requirements Inspections. *IEEE Computer, 33*(7), 73–79.

Singer, J., & Vinson, N. G. (2002). Ethical Issues in Empirical Studies of Software Engineering. *IEEE Transactions on Software Engineering, 28*(12), 1171–1180. doi:10.1109/TSE.2002.1158289

Soffer, P., Reinhartz-Berger, I., & Sturm, A. (2007). *Facilitating Reuse by Specialization of Reference Models for Business Process Design.* Accepted to the 8th Workshop on Business Process Modeling, Development, and Support (BPMDS'07), in conjunction with CAiSE'07.

Sturm, A., Dori, D., & Shehory, O. (2006). Domain Modeling with Object-Process Methodology, In *Proceedings of the Eighth International Conference on Enterprise Information Systems, ICEIS (3)* (pp. 144-151).

Sunye, G., Pollet, D., Le Taraon, Y., & Jezkel, J.-M. (2001). Refactoring UML models. In *Proceedings of UML 2001* (LNCS 2185, pp. 134-148).

Tersus (2006). Retrieved from http://www.tersus.com

TOPCASED. (2008). Retrieved from http://topcased.gforge.enseeiht.fr/

Valerio, A., Giancarlo, S., & Massimo, F. (1997). Domain analysis and framework-based software development. *ACM SIGAPP Applied Computing Review*, *5*(2), 4–15. doi:10.1145/297075.297081

ENDNOTES

[1] In order to be comprehensible to both UML 1.x (OMG-UML, 2003) and UML 2.x (OMG-UML, 2006) users, we use here elements that exist in both versions. The only exception is frame combined fragments, which are used in UML 2.x sequence diagrams for referring to sequences of messages. We could replace these combined fragments with notes in UML 1.x.

[2] This ADOM-UML CASE Tool can be freely downloaded from http://mis.hevra.haifa.ac.il/~iris/ADOM-UMLtool.zip.

APPENDIX. THE EXPERIMENT QUESTIONNAIRE

Part 1: The HCC comprehension questions and expected answers

For each statement, state weather it is true or false and shortly explain why.

1. There are two types of devices that are controlled by the system.
    True – air-conditioners and water sprayers.
2. The system checks its sensor data, the thermometer and the humidity gauge, only through the Heating/Cooling use case.
    False – also from spraying.
3. The only possibility for the home user to activate the system is by turning it on, in addition to setting the desired temperature and humidity.
    False – also turning off.
4. According to the model, it can certainly be determined that a room is uniquely identified by its room number.
    False – there is no evidence for it in the model.
5. There are three controlled values that are controlled by the system.
    False – only temperature and humidity.
6. There can be a situation in which the water sprayer is working and the air-conditioner is not.
    True – there is no contradiction to any specification.
7. In each situation when the air-conditioner is on and the room temperature is lower than the lowest bound of the desired temperature, the heating operation of the air-conditioner is activated.
    False – only if the air-conditioner did not heat before.
8. In case that the air-conditioner is on, it cools or heats.
    False – it can be idle.
9. There are at least two sensors in each room.
    True – one thermometer and one humidity gauge.

Part 2: The WLS modeling question (abbreviated summary)

The Water Level Control (WLC) application, similarly to the HCC system, belongs to a domain of Process Control Systems (PCS). Its purpose is to monitor and control the water levels in tanks in order to ensure that the actual water level is always in the closed range [Lowest Limit, Highest Limit]. The values of the lowest and highest limits are defined per water tank and are configurable. In each tank, a boundary stick which measures the actual height of the water in the tank is installed. The tank is also coupled to filling and emptying faucets which respectively inject and drain water when the water height in the tank reaches its lowest or highest desirable limits.

You are requested to provide the following four diagrams for the WLC application: (1) the system use case diagram, (2) the system class diagram, (3) a sequence diagram of tank filling, and (4) a state diagram of a water faucet

Chapter 18
The Use of Ontology for Data Mining with Incomplete Data

Hai Wang
Saint Mary's University, Canada

Shouhong Wang
University of Massachusetts Dartmouth, USA

ABSTRACT

Ontology has recently received considerable attention. Based on a domain analysis of knowledge representations in data mining, this chapter presents a structure of ontology for data mining as well as the unique resources for data mining with incomplete data. This chapter demonstrates the effectiveness of ontology for data mining with incomplete data through an experiment.

INTRODUCTION

Knowledge management has become one of the important topics in the database management field (Zhang and Zhao 2006). There have been two important research themes in knowledge management: data mining (Cunningham *et al.* 2006; Fayyad *et al.* 1996) and ontology (Green and Rosemann 2004; Kim 2002). Data mining is the process of trawling through data to find interesting patterns (Hand 1998). As such a process reveals previously unknown relationships among the data, data mining has become a widely used knowledge discovery technique (Brachman *et al.* 1996). On the other hand, ontology is a science that studies explicit

DOI: 10.4018/978-1-60566-904-5.ch018

formal specifications of the resources and relations among them in the domain (Gruber 1993). An ontology is a specification of a conceptualization (Gruber 1995), and intended for knowledge sharing among applications (Welty 2003). In the past few years, the two themes have become well-recognized substrate for research into knowledge management (Nilakanta *et al.* 2006; Li and Zhong 2006). Yet, potential benefits of joining the two themes have not been explored.

Intuitively, the use of ontology for data mining can be beneficial for knowledge management in the following aspects.

1. To share common understanding of the context of data mining among data miners. For example, given a set of marketing survey

Figure 1. Primitive Ontology

data, the data miners would like to know the scope of the database, the definitions of the data items, the meta-data (e.g., proportion of missing values) of the database, and the *a priori* knowledge of data mining on the database (e.g., applicable theories of market segments).

2. To use the ontology as a tool to accumulate and extend human knowledge. Following the above example, the data miners can use the ontology as a vehicle to record data mining activities and data mining results for marketing planning. The ontology is updated based on the available data mining techniques and data mining results.

3. To make specifications of the data mining resources (e.g., data and data mining tools) and their relations explicit so that computers can automate data mining process. Following the above example, if many marketing survey databases share the same ontology, then an intelligent software agent can extract and aggregate data mining results on these databases at a collective level.

Clearly, applications of ontology to data mining can be promising for effective knowledge management. However, little research on this issue has been reported in the literature. In this paper, we first discuss the key knowledge elements of data mining, and propose a generic structure of ontology for the domain. We then place the emphasis on ontology development for novel data mining with incomplete data. Through a project of ontology-based data mining system, we demonstrate the effectiveness of ontology in data mining.

ONTOLOGY FOR DATA MINING

Ontology

According to Resource Description Framework (RDF) (W3C 2007), a primitive ontology consists of a pair of resource objects and a relational linkage between them. It is formalized as shown in Figure 1. A large ontology for an entire domain is a composition of a set of primitive ontology.

Resources in ontology are knowledge representations, including data, procedures, rules, ideas that guide actions and decisions (Beckman 1999; Alter 1996); Tobin 1996; van der Spek and Spijkervet 1997). In this study, an ontology is a network of all these resources that shows the paths of data mining actions for the data miner to achieve a certain goal.

Categories of Resources of Data Mining

An ontology for the domain is usually large. To make a large ontology manageable to the developer and user, the entire ontology must be partitioned into parts. The partition is done through categorizing resources and identifying their relations pertinent to the domain. Taxonomy of formalized generic resource categories can help people to better understand and share the ontology. Based on the available limited literature on ontology associated with data mining (e.g., (Bernstein *et al.* 2005; Kim 2002; Li and Zhong 2006; Welty 2003), and their references) we propose generic resource categories for the domain of data mining as follows.

Task

Data mining is a task to discover unsuspected patterns of the data for decision making. A task is formally described as a hierarchical structure of its sub-tasks. For instance, the task of marketing data mining with incomplete data can be to identify new segments of consumers. It can have two sub-tasks: (1) to reveal new consumer segments based on complete data; and (2) to verify the new consumer segments using a data set with missing values.

Data

Data is the key resource in data mining. Definitions of the data items and metadata of the database are all the attributes of the data resource. In data mining with incomplete data, the data resource includes data with complete values and data with missing values.

Procedure

One of the major objectives of data mining is to support the data miner to conduct data mining processes through the execution of structured procedures. Each structural procedure is usually formalized by defining the sequence (e.g., when) and instructions (e.g., how). An algorithm is a primitive procedure, and a complex procedure is a set of algorithms. The formal descriptions of procedures represent explicit expertise of data mining. The combination of the structured procedures can be the data miner's selection.

Hypothesis

Hypothetical concepts are powerful appliances to symbolize *a priori* knowledge representations for data mining. In fact, the ultimate objective of data mining is to verify hypotheses which have been kept in the data miner's mind. For instance, common conjectures of the correlations of data

variables are often used for data mining (e.g., consumers who purchase product A are also purchase product B). Profound data mining requires sophisticated hypotheses in order to accomplish a significant task.

Instrument

An elementary model that can be used for the data miner for operations, deriving conclusions, or testing hypotheses, is called an instrument. An instrument could a statistical tool, an artificial intelligence model (e.g., neural networks), or a nondefinitional model (e.g., reasoning logic, simulation, inference engine, search engine).

Reference

A free-format document other than the resources discussed above is called a reference. A reference may not be applied for data mining directly, but could be useful for knowledge sharing. For instance, the history of data mining on the database is a useful document for the data miner to learn what data mining results have been obtained.

Relations between Resources

The relations between the resources could be diversified. Yet, there are generic semantics that commonly exist among these resources and can be used for general purposes of knowledge management for data mining. The general relations between resources in the business data mining domain are articulated in Table 1.

Construction of an Ontology

An ontology for data mining is a synthesis of the above six categories of resources based on the contingency of knowledge sharing among data miners. The first step of the development of an ontology is to identify the independent resources in each of categories (task, data, procedure, hypothesis,

Table 1. The relations between resources

	Task	Data	Procedure	Hypothesis	Instrument	Reference
Task	Has_a	Associates	Uses	Associates	Uses	Explained
Data		Is_a	Applied	Associates	Applied	Described
Procedure			Has_a	Applies	Applies	Described
Hypothesis				Is_a	Applied	Explained
Instrument					Is_a	Explained
Reference						Has_a

instrument, and reference). The second step of the development is to synthesize these resources by creating a semantic network and specifying the relations between them. The third step of the development of an ontology is to maintain the ontology through adding or deleting resources on the ontology and modifying the relations between them. The updated ontology reflects the current structure of knowledge for data mining.

AN ILLUSTRATIVE EXAMPLE OF THE USE OF ONTOLOGY FOR DATA MINING

In this section, we illustrate the development of ontology for data mining using a simple example. This example is based on a well known supermarket data mining story that consumers who purchase beer are more likely to purchase diaper at the same time. This story sounds interesting because such a purchase pattern is unsuspected and might stimulate a business decision for the supermarket. The ontology behind the data mining example is fairly simple. The task of this data mining process is to find an unusual customers' purchase pattern. The data used in this example are customers' purchase records, including the merchandise items purchased by the customer each time. The procedure for this task includes data retrieval and evaluation of the correlation of any two merchandise items purchased by the same customers each time. The hypothesis in this case

can be "customer who purchase product A is more likely to purchase product B, given that A and B are not known to be related to each other." The instrument used for this data mining case can be a simple SQL query with COUNT function. The above description can be briefly formalized into an ontology, as depicted in Figure 2.

The ontology in Figure 2 can be further formalized using a computer language such as Web ontology language (OWL 2007). Several advantages of the use of ontology can be perceived from this example.

1. Knowledge of this data mining process is described explicitly, and can be easily shared by people.
2. The ontology can be re-used for similar data mining tasks. For instance, a music store can also use the ontology with few changes for its data mining.
3. More importantly, the formalized ontology can be used by computer software to automate the data mining process. In this case, computer can detect similar unusual purchase patterns for all products.

UNIQUE RESOURCES IN DATA MINING WITH INCOMPLETE DATA

In this section we focus on the sub-domain of data mining with incomplete data. Data mining with incomplete data is an important area, since data

Figure 2. The Ontology of the Illustrative Data Mining Example

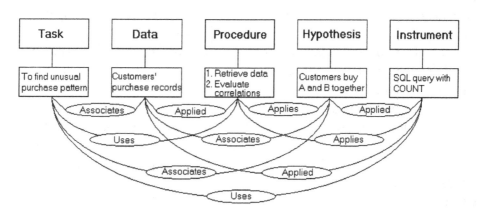

mining commonly deals with survey data (Brin *et al.* 2003; Zhang *et al.* 2006) and surveys and questionnaires are often only partially completed by respondents. The possible reasons for incomplete data could be numerous, including negligence, deliberate avoidance for privacy, ambiguity of the survey question, and aversion (Brown and Kros 2003). The extent of damage of missing data is unknown when it is virtually impossible to return the survey or questionnaires to the data source for completion, but is one of the most important parts of knowledge for data mining to discover. In fact, missing data is an important debatable issue in the knowledge engineering field (Tseng *et al.* 2003).

There have been three traditional approaches to handling missing data in data mining. One of the convenient solutions to incomplete data is to eliminate from the data set those records that have missing values (Little and Rubin, 2002). This, however, ignores potentially useful information in those records. In cases where the proportion of missing data is large, the data mining conclusions drawn from the screened data set are more likely misleading. Another simple approach of dealing with missing data is to use generic "unknown" for all missing data items. However, this approach does not provide much information that might be useful for interpretation of missing data. The

third solution to dealing with missing data is to estimate the missing value in the data item through imputation methods (Dempster and Rubin 1983). In the case of time series data, interpolation based on two adjacent data points that are observed is possible. In general cases, one may use some expected value in the data item based on statistical measures (Dempster *et al.* 1977). However, data in data mining are commonly of the types of ranking, category, multiple choices, and binary. Imputation is generally inadequate for data mining. More importantly, a meaningful treatment of missing data shall always be independent of the problem being investigated (Batista and Monard, 2003).

The above mentioned three traditional statistical approaches to missing values are commonly used in standard data mining tools (e.g., SPSS and SAS), but not particularly helpful for data mining as data mining ought to discover valuable knowledge about the patterns of the missing data as well as the potential impacts of the missing data on the mining results. For instance, a data miner often wishes to know how reliable a data mining result is, if only the complete data entries are used; when and why certain types of values are often missing; what variables are correlated in terms of having missing values at the same time; what reason for incomplete data is likely, etc. These valuable pieces of knowledge can be discovered only after the missing part of the data set is fully explored (Wang and Wang 2004).

Next, we consider two special resources of ontology for data mining with incomplete data: hypotheses for conceptual construction and instruments for enhanced mining, to allow the data miner to deal with incomplete data in a non-traditional way.

Hypotheses for Conceptual Construction

Conceptual construction on incomplete data reveals the patterns of the missing data as well as the potential impacts of these missing data on the mining results. It is a knowledge development process that consists of two phases. In the first phase, complete data are used for data mining to discover preliminary knowledge. In the second phase, incomplete data are included to verify and extend the preliminary knowledge through new concept construction. To construct new concepts on incomplete data, the data miner needs to develop hypotheses as a base for the construction and test the hypotheses. For example, suppose a data miner is investigating the profile of the consumers who are interested in a particular product. Using the complete data, the data miner has found that the variable income is an important factor of the consumers' purchasing behavior. To understand more about the impact of missing values in income, the data miner must develop new knowledge through mining the incomplete data.

Five typical types of hypotheses in data mining with incomplete data are described as follows.

1. *Reliability* - A hypothesis of reliability hypothesizes the scope of the missing data in terms of the preliminary knowledge based only on complete data. To test a hypothesis of reliability, the data miner can define index S_M/S_C where S_M is the number of data

samples with missing values, and S_C is the number of data samples with complete values. Generally, the higher S_M/S_C is, the lower the reliability of the observation of the clusters would be. Index $V_M(i)/V_C(i)$, where $V_M(i)$ is the number of missing values in variable i and $V_C(i)$ is the number of samples used for the data mining process in variable i, would more pertinent for a test when i is an important factor. Normally, the higher $V_M(i)/V_C(i)$ is, the lower the reliability of the factor would be.

2. *Complementing* - A hypothesis of complementing hypothesizes what variables are more likely to have missing values at the same time; that is, the inclusive correlation of missing values related to the problem being investigated. The data miner can define index $V_M(i,j)/V_M(i)$ where $V_M(i,j)$ is the number of missing values in both variables i and j, and $V_M(i)$ is the number of missing values in variable i. This concept discloses the inclusive correlation of two variables in terms of missing values. The higher the value $V_M(i,j)/V_M(i)$ is, the stronger the inclusive correlation of missing values would be.

3. *Clashing* - A hypothesis of clashing hypothesizes what variables are unlikely to have missing values at the same time; that is, the exclusive correlation of missing values related to the problem being investigated. Index $V_M(i,j)/V_M(i)$ can also be used to measure clashing. The lower the value $V_M(i,j)/V_M(i)$ is, the stronger the exclusive correlation of missing values would be.

4. *Hiding* - A hypothesis of hiding hypothesizes how likely an observation with a certain range of values in one variable is to have a missing value in another variable. The data miner can define index $V_M(i)|x(j) \in (a,b)$ where $V_M(i)$ is the number of missing values in variable i, $x(j)$ is the occurrence of variable j (e.g., education years), and (a,b)

is the range of x(j). This index is to disclose the hiding relationships between variables *i* and *j*.

5. *Conditional effects* – A hypothesis of conditional effects hypothesizes the potential changes to the understanding of the problem caused by the missing values. To develop the concept of conditional effects, the data miner assumes different possible values for the missing values, and then observe the possible changes of the nature of the problem. For instance, the data miner can define index $\Delta P|\forall z(i)$=k where ΔP is the change of the data mining result perceived by the data miner, $\forall z(i)$ represents all missing values of variable *i*, and k is the possible value variable *i* might have for the survey. Typically, k=\{*max, min, p*\} where *max* is the maximal value of the scale, *min* is the minimal value of the scale, and *p* is the random variable with the same distribution function of the values in the complete data. By setting different possible values of k for the missing values, the data miner is able to observe the change of the data mining result.

The above five typical types of hypotheses for conceptual construction are general. Clearly, specifics of hypotheses for a particular data mining task always depend on the data miner's *a priori* knowledge.

Instruments for Enhanced Data Mining

The second special type of resource for data mining with incomplete data is instruments for enhanced data mining. Enhanced data mining is carried out through two phases. In the first phase, observations with missing data are transformed into fuzzy observations. Since missing values make the observation fuzzy, according to fuzzy set theory (Zadeh, 1978), an observation with missing values can be transformed into fuzzy patterns that are equivalent to the observation. For instance, suppose there is an observation $A=\mathbf{X}(x_1, x_2, \ldots x_c \ldots x_m)$ where x_c is the variable with missing value, and $x_c \in \{ r_1, r_2 \ldots r_p \}$ where r_j (j=1, 2, ... p) is the possible occurrence of x_c. Let $\mu_j = P_j(x_c = r_j)$, the fuzzy membership (or possibility) that x_c belongs to r_j (j=1, 2, ...p), and $\sum_j \mu_j = 1$. Then, $\mu_j [\mathbf{X} |(x_c = r_j)]$ (j=1, 2, ... p) are fuzzy patterns that are the equivalence to the observation *A*.

In the second phase of enhanced data mining, an instrument is applied to the entire data set. The instruments used for enhanced data mining are variations of traditional data mining tools, such as discriminant analysis (Hand 1981), self-organizing maps (SOM) (Kohonen, 1989; Deboeck and Kohonen, 1998), and neural networks (Wang, 2000; Wang 2002). They are different from the original ones in that they are capable of retaining information of fuzzy membership for each fuzzy pattern. For instance, using a SOM-based enhanced data mining model (Wang 2003), the data miner is allowed to compare SOM based on complete data and fuzzy SOM based on all incomplete data to perceive covert patterns of the data set. The data miner is allowed to conduct what-if trials by including different portions of the incomplete data to disclose more accurate facts. A data mining model of Hopfield neural networks (Hopfield and Tank 1986) utilizes information of fuzzy patterns of incomplete data to make the data mining results more accurate than that based only on complete data. More importantly, the model produces rich information about the uncertainty of the data mining results (Wang 2005).

A PROJECT OF ONTOLOGY FOR DATA MINING WITH INCOMPLETE DATA

An ontology provides a guide for the data miner as well as computer software to utilize the data mining resources at different levels of the tasks. The knowledge structure represented by the ontology facilitates task-related problem solving. Technically, an ontology provides a network of information repository and tools that are capable of supporting the data miner to transform unstructured data mining activities to structured processes.

To learn more about ontology in data mining, a project was conducted to investigate the effectiveness of ontology for novel data mining with incomplete data. We developed an ontology with a small scale using the proposed resource structure for ontology development and the domain knowledge discussed in the previous section. We then developed a software system, called MidOn (Mining Incomplete Data through the Ontology), that can support data mining processes in accordance with the ontology knowledge structure. We finally tested the MidOn system. The following subsections describe the project and our experiences.

The Ontology for the Project

The resources of the ontology developed for the project are briefly summarized below.

1. *Task* – The general task of this project is data mining on a survey data set with incomplete data through classification. It will discover the following specific knowledge.
   a. Critical factors for the classification problem.
   b. Implications of the missing values in these critical factors.
   c. Impact of the missing values on the accuracy of prediction of the classification problem.
2. *Data* – A survey data set that can lead to classification (e.g., favour/not-favour in a marketing survey of consumers' opinions on a product).
3. *Procedure* – The procedure for this data mining task includes the following major steps.

   a. Choose variables of the survey, and retrieve observations with complete data (S_1) and observations with incomplete data (S_2) in accordance with the specified format.
   b. Apply the instrument linear discriminant analysis (LDA) to the data set S_1, and obtain the correct-classification rate.
   c. For Task-a, find the minimal number of important variables, called critical factors, that contribute a significant portion of the correct-classification rate, through an iteration of executions of LDA on S_1.
   d. For Task-b, test hypothesis-a through hypothesis-d using statistical Data Analysis Tools.
   e. For Task-c, test hypotheses-e using the instrument LDA.
4. *Hypothesis* – Five hypotheses for data mining with incomplete data are used for the project.
   a. Reliability - As the survey contains missing values, the preliminary knowledge based only on complete data is not generally valid.
   b. Complementing – Two variables are more likely to have missing values at the same time.
   c. Clashing - Two variables are unlikely to have missing values at the same time.
   d. Hiding – Observations with a certain range of values in one variable is to have a missing value in another variable.
   e. Conditional effects – The preliminary knowledge based only on complete data might be no longer true when the missing value of a variable takes a certain possible value.
5. *Instrument* – The instrument used for the project include Data Analysis Tools built in Microsoft Excel and linear discriminant

analysis (LDA). These simple data mining instruments are easy to learn and use for our experiments.

6. *Reference* – The references include explanations of the data mining task, data format, procedures, hypotheses and examples, and the two instruments.

MidOn: Mining Incomplete Data Based on the Ontology

The computing environment of MidOn is Microsoft Excel. This makes it easy to integrate the data base, basic statistical data analysis tools, the program of procedures, and the user-computer interface into a single computing environment. Using Microsoft Excel, the data base is held by the spreadsheet, the program of procedures is implemented by macros (Visual Basic for Applications), and the user-computer interface is supported by the build-in graphics utilities. Technical details of the system architecture are depicted in Figure 3.

MidOn includes three major modules, as described below.

1. The largest module of MidOn is the execution functions for the procedures of the ontology. The user can call these functions through the menus.

2. The second module of MidOn is the navigation functions that reflect the relations between the resources of the ontology (Table 1). MidOn provides the graphical user interface for navigation.

3. The third module of MidOn is general operational functions for the data mining process, such as data selection.

An Experiment

In this section we present an experiment to demonstrate the use of MidOn for data mining with incomplete survey data. This experiment is not intended to establish any statistically significant results; rather, it is merely to show that the ontology-based data mining system can be useful for knowledge development through discovering unsuspected patterns of incomplete data. The data miner in this experiment was a group of three MBA students who were taking individual study

Figure 3. The Architecture of MidOn

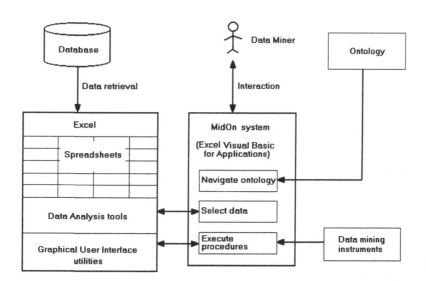

of data mining from one of the authors. They had no experience of data mining before the individual study. The use of MidOn to analyze a set of data was an assignment for them to receive practical experiences of data mining. They worked in group on this assignment for the credit of the individual study. The reference resources of the ontology provided them sufficient information of MidOn for their assignment.

The data assigned in this study came from a student opinion of teachers survey (see Appendix) at a Canadian university. In this case, twenty one questions describe the characteristics of a teacher's performance. Each question is rated on a five-point scale for students to answer. A high mark for a question indicates a positive answer to the question. The twenty questions related to the evaluation of effectiveness of teaching for a class session represent the twenty variables (v1 through v20). The last one question was associated to the classification of teachers. Data of 4235 survey samples were given to the data mining group. Among them, 1857 (44%) observations were incomplete. Among the complete data set, 86% (2045) were class-1 (effective as above the mean) and 14% were class-2 (ineffective as below the mean). Among the incomplete data, observations of class-2 (ineffective) were 48% (891).

The assignment for the group of the three MBA as the data miner was to follow the semantics of MidOn to develop knowledge on this data set.

Interestingly, after less than four hours of learning and doing, they went through the data mining procedures and developed new knowledge. To our judgment, their knowledge on the data set was correct although it can certainly be further expanded. Their data mining results for each of procedures are summarized below.

1. The correct-classification rate for the complete data set was 75.3%. The very relevant variables (critical factors) were v1, v14, v15, v16, v18, and v20 that lead to 64.5% correct-classification rate.

2. The rate of incomplete observations for the entire survey was as high as 44%; however, the average missing data rate in the critical factors (v1, v14, v15, v16, v18, and v20) was 9.8%, indicating that the critical factors were less ignored by students. Among the six critical factors, the rate of missing values in v20 was the highest at 12.4%, indicating that the dependability of ineffective teaching on this variable (i.e., the usefulness of the textbook and teaching material) might not be as reliable as other critical factors.

3. The rate of missing values in v15 was 7.8%; however, 69.2% of the missing values came from the observations with v18=[1,3]. This indicated that students who were not satisfied with feedback often disregarded whether they received grade promptly.

4. The values of v15 and v16 were often missing together. Among all observations with incomplete data, 36.6% observations had missing values in the both variables. This indicated that students who omitted the opinion on prompt grading often disregarded whether helpful comments were provided.

5. Among the six critical factors, v1 and v14 were unlikely to have missing values together. Among all observations with incomplete data, only 4.1% observations had missing values in the both variables. This indicated that students who expressed the opinion on the clarity and understandability of the instructor were also concerned with the measures of tests and assignments.

6. Among the six critical factors, v20 had the highest rate of missing values (12.4%). Twenty five (25) observations with missing values in v20 only were found in the incomplete data set. After setting 1 though 5 for the missing values of v20 of these observations and adding them to the complete data set, LDA was applied for the trials. The range of the trial correct-classification rates was 64.3%-64.7%, compared with the

preliminary result 64.5%. This indicated that missing values in v20 seemed to have moderate impact on the preliminary result.

DISCUSSION

The MidOn system is a prototype of ontology-based knowledge discovery system for data mining with incomplete data. MidOn contains general knowledge of data mining in the ontology, including predefined tasks, data organization, data mining procedures, domain-based hypotheses, and data mining instruments. The novice data miner is allowed to interact with MidOn to generate knowledge through the development and testing hypotheses. MidOn is not designed to replace the data miner for so called "knowledge discovery automation"; rather, it transmits *a priori* data mining knowledge to the data miner for relevant and accurate data mining. While the system makes no claim to best possible data mining, the experiment does show that ontology contributes data mining with incomplete data in this case.

CONCLUSION

This paper discusses the crucial combination ontology and data mining for knowledge management. The competence of a data mining depends not only on the amount of information discovered, but also on *a priori* knowledge as the base for the data mining. To provide a tool of data mining for knowledge management, this paper proposes a framework of ontology for data mining based primarily on the domain analysis of the resources involved in data mining. This framework shifts the data mining activities from *ad hoc* styles to knowledge management through ontology.

For knowledge sharing, an ontology of the data mining domain can have six typical categories resources: task, data, procedure, hypothesis, instrument, and reference. The relationships of the resources can be generalized. The use of ontology would allow the data miner to fully utilize *a priori* knowledge of data mining to develop his/her own knowledge based on a specific data set. We have developed MidOn, a prototype of ontology-based data mining tool, for mining incomplete data in a non-traditional way. Our experiences with MidOn demonstrate the effectiveness of ontology in data mining for knowledge discovery.

This study raises new tasks for parties involved in data mining and knowledge management. For enterprises, knowledge sharing through ontology is crucial for the success of data mining for the enterprise. For software developers, new semantic techniques and tools for knowledge management in data mining are imperative. Isolated data mining tools are no longer adequate for knowledge management. New knowledge management techniques need to be fully integrated into the data mining environment. For data miners, new skills are required in the knowledge management era. They must better understand the ontology of data mining, and possess the ability of transforming their own knowledge into ontology for data mining.

ACKNOWLEDGMENT

The first author is supported in part by the Natural Sciences and Engineering Research Council of Canada (NSERC Grant No. 312423). This article is an enhanced version of the following article: Wang, H., and Wang, S. (2008). Ontology for Data Mining and Its Application to Mining Incomplete Data, Journal of Database Management, 19(4), 20-29.

REFERENCES

W3C. (2008). World Wide Web Consortium. Retrieved December 20, 2008 from http://www.w3.org/

Alter, S. (1996). *Information Systems: A Management Perspective*, New York: Benjamin/Cummings Publishing.

Batista, G., & Monard, M. (2003). An analysis of four missing data treatment methods for supervised learning. *Applied Artificial Intelligence, 17*(5/6), 519–533. doi:10.1080/713827181

Beckman, T. J. (1999). The current state of knowledge management. In J. Liebowitz (Ed.), *Knowledge Management Handbook* (pp. 1.1-1.22), Boca Raton, FL: CRC Press.

Bernstein, A., Provost, F., & Hill, S. (2005). Toward intelligent assistance for a data mining process: An ontology-based approach for cost-sensitive classification. *IEEE Transactions on Knowledge and Data Engineering, 17*(4), 503–518. doi:10.1109/TKDE.2005.67

Brachman, R. J., Khabaza, T., Kloesgen, W., Piatetsky-Shapiro, G., & Simoudis, E. (1996). Mining business databases. *Communications of the ACM, 39*(11), 42–48. doi:10.1145/240455.240468

Brin, S., Rastogi, R., & Shim, K. (2003). Mining optimized gain rules for numeric attributes. *IEEE Transactions on Knowledge and Data Engineering, 15*(2), 324–338. doi:10.1109/TKDE.2003.1185837

Brown, M. L., & Kros, J. F. (2003). Data mining and the impact of missing data. *Industrial Management & Data Systems, 103*(8), 611–621. doi:10.1108/02635570310497657

Cunningham, C., Song, I. Y., & Chen, P. P. (2006). Data warehouse design to support customer relationship management analysis. *Journal of Database Management, 17*(2), 62–88.

Deboeck, G., & Kohonen, T. (1998). *Visual Explorations in Finance with Self-Organizing Maps*, London, UK: Springer-Verlag.

Dempster, A., & Rubin, D. (1983). Incomplete data in sample surveys. In W. G. Madow, I. Olkin, & D. Rubin (Eds.), *Sample Surveys Vol. II: Theory and Annotated Bibliography* (pp. 3-10), New York: Academic Press.

Dempster, A. P., Laird, N. M., & Rubin, D. B. (1977). Maximum likelihood from incomplete data via the EM algorithm. *Journal of the Royal Statistical Society. Series B. Methodological, 39*(1), 1–38.

Fayyad, U., Piatetsky-Shapiro, G., & Smyth, P. (1996). The KDD process for extracting useful knowledge from volumes of data. *Communications of the ACM, 39*(11), 7–34.

Green, P., & Rosemann, M. (2004). Applying ontologies to business and systems modeling techniques and perspectives: Lessons learned. *Journal of Database Management, 15*(2), 105–117.

Gruber, T. (1993). A translation approach to portable ontology specifications. *Knowledge Acquisition, 5*(2), 199–220. doi:10.1006/knac.1993.1008

Gruber, T. (1995). Toward principles for the design of ontologies used for knowledge sharing. *International Journal of Human-Computer Studies, 43*(5/6), 907–928. doi:10.1006/ijhc.1995.1081

Hand, D. J. (1981). *Discrimination and Classification*. New York: Wiley.

Hand, D. J. (1998). Data mining: Statistics and more? *The American Statistician, 52*(2), 112–118. doi:10.2307/2685468

Hopfield, J. J., & Tank, D. W. (1986). Computing with neural circuits. *The Sciences, 233*, 625–633.

Kim, H. (2002). Predicting how ontologies for the semantic Web will evolve. *Communications of the ACM, 45*(2), 48–54. doi:10.1145/503124.503148

Kohonen, T. (1989). *Self-Organization and Associative Memory* (3rd ed.). New York: Springer-Verlag.

Li, Y., & Zhong, N. (2006). Mining ontology for automatically acquiring Web user information needs . *IEEE Transactions on Knowledge and Data Engineering, 18*(4), 554–568. doi:10.1109/TKDE.2006.1599392

Little, R. J. A., & Rubin, D. B. (2002). *Statistical Analysis with Missing Data* (2nd ed.). New York: John Wiley and Sons.

Nilakanta, S., Miller, L. L., & Zhu, D. (2006). Organizational memory management: Technological and research issues. *Journal of Database Management, 17*(1), 85–94.

OWL. (2008). Web Ontology Language (OWL). Retrieved December 20, 2008 from http://www.w3.org/TR/owl-features/

Tobin, D. (1996). *Transformational Learning: Renewing Your Company through Knowledge and Skills*. New York: John Wiley & Sons.

Tseng, S., Wang, K., & Lee, C. (2003). A preprocessing method to deal with missing values by integrating clustering and regression techniques. *Applied Artificial Intelligence, 17*(5/6), 535–544. doi:10.1080/713827170

van der Spek, R., & Spijkervet, A. (1997). Knowledge management: dealing intelligently with knowledge. In Liebowitz & Wilcox (Eds.), *Knowledge Management and Its Integrative Elements*. Boca Raton, FL: CRC Press.

Wang, S. (2000). Neural networks. In M. Zeleny (Ed.), *IEBM Handbook of IT in Business* (pp. 382-391). London: International Thomson Business Press.

Wang, S. (2002). Nonlinear pattern hypothesis generation for data mining. *Data & Knowledge Engineering, 40*(3), 273–283. doi:10.1016/S0169-023X(01)00059-3

Wang, S. (2003). Application of self-organizing maps for data mining with incomplete data Sets. *Neural Computing & Applications, 12*(1), 42–48. doi:10.1007/s00521-003-0372-1

Wang, S. (2005). Classification with incomplete survey data: A Hopfield neural network approach. *Computers & Operations Research, 32*(10), 2583–2594. doi:10.1016/j.cor.2004.03.018

Wang, S., & Wang, H. (2004). Conceptual construction on incomplete survey data. *Data & Knowledge Engineering, 49*(3), 311–323. doi:10.1016/j.datak.2003.10.007

Welty, C. (2003). Ontology research . *AI Magazine, 24*(3), 11–12.

Zadeh, L. A. (1978). Fuzzy sets as a basis for a theory of possibility. *Fuzzy Sets and Systems, 1*, 3–28. doi:10.1016/0165-0114(78)90029-5

Zhang, D., & Zhao, J. L. (2006). Knowledge management in organizations. *Journal of Database Management, 17*(1), 1–7.

Zhang, S., Qin, Z., Ling, C., & Sheng, S. (2005). Missing is useful: Missing values in cost-sensitivity decision trees. *IEEE Transactions on Knowledge and Data Engineering, 17*(12), 1689–1693. doi:10.1109/TKDE.2005.188

APPENDIX

The Questionnaire of Student Opinion of Teachers Survey

Q1(v1): The instructor explains difficult concepts clearly and understandably.

Q2(v2): Class sessions appear to be carefully planned.

Q3(v3): The instructor conveys strong interest and enthusiasm.

Q4(v4): Students are encouraged to express their views and participate in class.

Q5(v5): The instructor shows a genuine concern for student progress.

Q6(v6): The instructor stimulates students to think for themselves.

Q7(v7): Effective use is made of examples and illustrations.

Q8(v8): The instructor speaks in a way which can be clearly understood.

Q9(v9): The instructor makes it clear how each topic fits into the course.

Q10(v10): This course was a positive learning experience.

Q11(v11): Classes are held regularly to an agreed schedule.

Q12(v12): The various parts of the course are effectively co-ordinated.

Q13(v13): Course requirements are communicated clearly and explicitly.

Q14(v14): Tests and assignments are reasonable measures of student learning.

Q15(v15): Where appropriate, student work is graded promptly.

Q16(v16): Where appropriate, helpful comments are provided when student work is graded.

Q17(v17): There is close agreement between stated course objectives and what is taught.

Q18(v18): Test and assignments provide adequate feedback on student progress.

Q19(v19): The instructor is willing to schedule consultation time with the students.

Q20(v20): The text book(s) and course material are useful.

Q21: In comparison to other instructors, this instructor is an effective teacher.

Compilation of References

Abrahamson, E. (1991). Managerial fads and fashions: The diffusion and refection of innovations. *Academy of Management Review, 16*(3), 586–612.

Addy, E. A. (1998). A framework for performing verification and validation in reuse-based software engineering, *5*(1), 279-292.

Adi, A., & Etzion, O. (2004). Amit - the situation manager. *The VLDB Journal, 13*(2), 177–203. doi:10.1007/s00778-003-0108-y

Adner, R. (2002). When are technologies disruptive? A demand-based view of the emergence of competition. *Strategic Management Journal, 23*(8), 667–688. doi:10.1002/smj.246

Agarwal, R., De, P., & Sinha, A. P. (1999). Comprehending object and process models: An empirical study. *IEEE Transactions on Software Engineering, 25*(4), 541–556. doi:10.1109/32.799953

Ågerfalk, P., & Fitzgerald, B. (2008). Outsourcing to an Unknown Workforce: Exploring Opensourcing as a Global Sourcing Strategy. *MIS Quarterly, 32*(2), 385–409.

Agerfalk, P., Finnegan, P., Hayes, J., Lundell, B., & Ostling, M. (2006). 12 (not so) easy pieces: Grand challenges for Open Source Software. *Panel Presentation at the 14th European Conference on Information Systems, Gotenburg, Sweden, June.*

Agrawal, R., & Kiernan, J. (2002). Watermarking relational databases. *Proceedings of VLDB* (pp. 155-166).

Ahuja, M. K., Carley, K., & Galletta, D. F. (1997). *Individual performance in distributed design groups: An empirical study.* Paper presented at the SIGCPR Conference, San Francisco.

Alho, K., & Sulonen, R. (1998). *Supporting virtual software projects on the Web.* Paper presented at the Workshop on Coordinating Distributed Software Development Projects, 7th International Workshop on Enabling Technologies: Infrastructure for Collaborative Enterprises (WETICE '98).

Alter, C., & Hage, J. (1993). *Organisations working together.* London: Sage Publications.

Alter, S. (1996). *Information Systems: A Management Perspective*, New York: Benjamin/Cummings Publishing.

Alves-Foss, J., Conte de Leon, D., & Oman, P. (2002). *Experiments in the use of xml to enhance traceability between object-oriented design specifications and source code.* Paper presented at the 35th Annual Hawaii International Conference on System Sciences.

Ambler, S. (2002). *Agile Modeling: Effective Practices for Extreme Programming and Unified Process.* New York: John Wiley.

Amghar, Y., Meziane, M., & Flory, A. (2002). Using business rules within a design process of active databases. In S. Becker (Ed.), *Data Warehousing and Web Engineering* (pp. 161-184), Hershey, PA: IRM Press.

An, Y., Borgida, A., & Mylopoulos, J. (2005). Constructing Complex Semantic Mappings Between XML Data and Ontologies. *International Semantic Web Conference ISWC 2005* (pp. 6-20).

Andrade, J., Ares, J., Garcia, R., Pazos, J., Rodriguez, S., & Silva, A. (2004). A methodological framework for generic conceptualisation: problem-sensitivity in software engineering. *Information and Software Technology, 46*(10), 635–649. doi:10.1016/j.infsof.2003.11.003

Andrade, L., & Fiadeiro, J. (2000, October 15-19). *Evolution by contract*. Paper presented at the ACM Conference on Object-Oriented Programming, Systems, Languages, and Applications 2000, Workshop on Best-practice in Business Rules Design and Implementation, Minneapolis, Minnesota USA.

Andrade, L., Fiadeiro, J., Gouveia, J., & Koutsoukos, G. (2002). Separating computation, coordination and configuration. *Journal of Software Maintenance and Evolution: Research and Practice, 14*(5), 353-359.

Anthes, G. H. (2000, June 26). Software Development goes Global. *Computerworld Magazine.*

Arlow, J., & Neustadt, I. (2004). *Enterprise Patterns and MDA: Building Better Software with Archetype Patterns and UML*. Boston: Addison-Wesley.

Arrow, K. (1970). *Social choice and individual values* (2nd ed.). New Haven, CT: Yale University Press.

Astley, M., & Agha, G. A. (1998, 20-21 April). *Modular construction and composition of distributed software architectures*. Paper presented at the Int. Symposium on Software Engineering, for Parallel and Distributed Systems, Kyoto, Japan.

ASU partners with Clemson to create virtual world technology. (2008). *Techniques: Connecting Education & Careers, 83*(2), 60.

Atkins, D., Ball, T., Graves, T., & Mockus, A. (1999). Using version control data to evaluate the impact of software tools. *Proceedings of the 21st International Conference on Software Engineering* (pp. 324–333). Los Angeles: ACM Press.

Atkinson, C., & Kühne, T. (2003, September-October). Model-driven development: A metamodeling foundation. *IEEE Software, 20*(5), 36-41. Retrieved June 5, 2006, from http://doi.ieeecomputersociety.org/10.1109/MS.2003.1231149

Atkinson, C., & Kühne, T. (2005, October). Concepts for comparing modeling tool architectures. In L. Briand & C. Williams (Eds.), *Model Driven Engineering Languages and Systems: Eighth International Conference, MoDELS 2005* (pp. 398-413). Springer. Retrieved June 23, 2006, from http://dx.doi.org/10.1007/11557432 30

Attewell, P. (1992). Technology diffusion and organizational learning: the case of business computing. *Organization Science, 3*(1), 1–19. doi:10.1287/orsc.3.1.1

August, J. H. (1991). *Joint application design: The group session approach to system design*. Englewood Cliffs, NJ: Yourdon Press.

Babcock, B., Chaudhuri, S., & Das, G. (2003). Dynamic Sample Selection for Approximate Query Processing. In *Proceedings of the 2003 ACM SIGMOD International Conference on Management of Data, San Diego, California, USA* (pp. 539-550).

Babcock, C. (2005). Eclipse on the rise. [Electronic version]. *InformationWeek*. Retrieved January 29, 2006.

Baddeley, A. (1992). Working Memory. *Science, 255*(5044), 556–559. doi:10.1126/science.1736359

Bajaj, A. (2004). The effect of the number of concepts on the readability of schemas: an empirical study with data models. *Requirements Engineering, 9*(4), 261–270. doi:10.1007/s00766-004-0202-8

Baker, F.T. (1972). Chief programmer team management of production programming. *IBM Systems Journal, 11*(1), 56–73.

Band, W., Kinikin, E., Ragsdale, J., & Harrington, J. (2005). *Enterprise CRM suites, Q2, 2005: Evaluation of top enterprise CRM software vendors across 177 criteria*. Cambridge, MA: Forrester Research Inc.

Bandow, D. (1997). Geographically distributed work groups and IT: A case study of working relationships and IS professionals. In *Proceedings of the SIGCPR Conference* (pp. 87–92).

Barab, S. A., Hay, K. E., Squire, K., Barnett, M., Schmidt, R., & Karrigan, K. (2000). Virtual solar system project: Learning through a technology-rich, inquiry-based, participatory learning environment. *Journal of Science Education and Technology, 9*(1), 7–25. doi:10.1023/A:1009416822783

Basili, V.R., Briand, L.C., & Melo, W.L. (1996). A validation of object-oriented design metrics as quality indicators. *IEEE Transactions on Software Engineering, 22*(10), 751–761.

Baskerville, R., & Pries-Heje, J. (2001, July 27-29). *Racing the e-bomb: How the internet is redefining information systems development methodology.* Proceedings of the IFIP TC8/WG8.2 Working Conference on Realigning Research and Practice in Information Systems Development: The Social and Organizational Perspectice (pp. 49-68). Boise, Idaho.

Basset, T. (2004). Coordination and social structures in an open source project: Videolan. In S. Koch (Ed.), *Open source software development* (pp. 125-151). Hershey, PA: Idea Group.

Batista, G., & Monard, M. (2003). An analysis of four missing data treatment methods for supervised learning. *Applied Artificial Intelligence, 17*(5/6), 519–533. doi:10.1080/713827181

Batra, D. (2005). Conceptual Data Modeling Patterns: Representation and Validation. *Journal of Database Management, 16*(2), 84–106.

Batra, D. (2008). Unified Modeling Language (UML) Topics: The Past, the Problems, and the Prospects. *Journal of Database Management, 19*(1), i–vii.

Batra, D., & Davis, J. G. (1992). Conceptual data modelling in database design: similarities and differences between expert and novice designers. *International Journal of Man-Machine Studies, 37*(1), 83–101. doi:10.1016/0020-7373(92)90092-Y

Batra, D., & Satzinger, J. (2006). Contemporary Approaches and Techniques for the Systems Analyst. *Journal of Information Systems Education, 17*(3), 257–265.

Batra, D., & Wishart, N. A. (2004). Comparing a rule-based approach with a pattern-based approach at different levels of complexity of conceptual data modelling tasks.

International Journal of Human-Computer Studies, 61(4), 397–419. doi:10.1016/j.ijhcs.2003.12.019

Batra, D., Hoffer, J. A., & Bostrom, R. P. (1990). Comparing Representations with Relational and EER Models. *Communications of the ACM, 33*(2), 126–139. doi:10.1145/75577.75579

Beatty, R., & Williams, C. (2006). ERP II: Best practices for successfully implementing an ERP upgrade. *Communications of the ACM, 49*(3), 105–109. doi:10.1145/1118178.1118184

Beckman, T. J. (1999). The current state of knowledge management. In J. Liebowitz (Ed.), *Knowledge Management Handbook* (pp. 1.1-1.22), Boca Raton, FL: CRC Press.

Beer, W., Volker, C., Ferscha, A., & Mehrmann, L. (2003) Modeling context-aware behavior by interpreted ECA rules. In H. Kosch, L. Böszörményi, & H. Hellwagner (Eds.), *Euro-Par 2003* (LNCS 2790, pp. 1064-1073).

Bélanger, F. (1998). Telecommuters and Work Groups: A Communication Network Analysis. In *Proceedings of the International Conference on Information Systems (ICIS)* (pp. 365–369). Helsinki, Finland.

Benbasat, I., Goldstein, D. K., & Mead, M. (1987). The case research strategy in studies of Information Systems. *MIS Quarterly, 11*(3), 369–386. doi:10.2307/248684

Benkler, Y. (2002). Coase's penguin, or, Linux and the nature of the firm. *The Yale Law Journal, 112*(3), 1–42. doi:10.2307/1562247

Bergquist, M., & Ljungberg, J. (2001). The power of gifts: Organizing social relationships in open source communities. *Information Systems Journal, 11*(4), 305–315.

Bernstein, A., Provost, F., & Hill, S. (2005). Toward intelligent assistance for a data mining process: An ontology-based approach for cost-sensitive classification. *IEEE Transactions on Knowledge and Data Engineering, 17*(4), 503–518. doi:10.1109/TKDE.2005.67

Bertino, E., Ooi, B. C., Yang, Y., & Deng, R. (2005). Privacy and ownership preserving of outsourced medical data. *Proceedings of IEEE International Conference on Data Engineering* (pp. 521-532).

Bessen, J. (2002). *Open Source Software: Free Provision of Complex Public Goods*: Research on Innovation.

Beygelzimer, A., Kakade, S., & Langford, J. (2005). Cover trees for nearest neighbor. In *Proceedings of the 23rd international conference on Machine learning, Pittsburgh, Pennsylvania, USA* (pp. 97-104).

Bezroukov, N. (1999a). A second look at the Cathedral and the Bazaar. *First Monday, 4*(12).

Bezroukov, N. (1999b). Open source software development as a special type of academic research (critique of vulgar raymondism). *First Monday, 4*(10).

Bichler, M., Segev, A., & Zhao, J. L. (1998). Component-based e-commerce: Assesment of current practices and future directions. *SIGMOD Record, 27*(4), 7-14.

Bodart, F., Patel, A., Sim, M., & Weber, R. (2001). Should optional properties be used in conceptual modelling? A theory and three empirical tests. *Information Systems Research, 12*(4), 384–405. doi:10.1287/isre.12.4.384.9702

Bollinger, T., Nelson, R., Self, K.M., & Turnbull, S.J. (1999). Open-source methods: Peering through the clutter. *IEEE Software, 16*(4), 8–11.

Boneh, D., & Shaw, J. (1995). Collusion secure fingerprinting for digital data (extended abstract). *Crypto,* 452-465.

Boneh, D., & Shaw, J. (1998). Collusion secure fingerprinting for digital data. *IEEE Transactions on Information Theory, 44*(5), 1897-1905.

Bonino da Silva Santos, L. O., van Wijnen, R. P., & Vink, P. (2007). A service-oriented middleware for context-aware applications. *MPAC,* (pp. 37-42). New York: ACM Press.

Booch, G. (1994). *Object-Oriented Analysis and Design with Applications* (2nd ed.). Redwood City, CA: Benjamin/Cummings.

Booch, G. (1999). UML in Action. *Communications of the ACM, 42*(10), 26–28. doi:10.1145/317665.317672

Booch, G., Brown, A., Iyengar, S., Rumbaugh, J., & Selic, B. (2004, May). An MDA manifesto. *Business Process Trends/MDA Journal.* Retrieved June 15, 2006, from http://www.bptrends.com/publicationfiles/05-04COLIBMManifesto-Frankel-3.pdf

Booch, G., Christerson, M., Fuchs, M., & Koistinen, J. (1999). *UML for XML schema mapping specification.* Retrieved from http://xml.coverpages.org/fuchs-uml_xmlschema33.pdf

Booch, G., Rumbaugh, J., & Jacobson, I. (1999). *The Unified Modeling Language User Guide.* Reading, MA: Addison Wesley.

Borkar, V., Carey, M., Mangtani, N., McKinney, D., Patel, R., & Thatte, S. (2006). XML data services. *International Journal of Web Services Research, 3*(1), 85-95.

Bosak, J., Bray, T., Connolly, D., Maler, E., Nicol, G., Sperberg-McQueen, C. M., et al. (1998). *Guide to the W3C XML Specification (XMLspec) DTD, Version 2.1.* Retrieved from http://www.w3.org/XML/1998/06/xmlspec-report-v21.htm

Böttcher, S., & Steinmetz, R. (2003). A DTD Graph Based XPath Query Subsumption Test. *Xsym, 2003,* 85–99.

Boulding, K. E. (1956). General systems theory—The skeleton of a science. *Management Science, 2*(April), 197–208.

Brachman, R. J., Khabaza, T., Kloesgen, W., Piatetsky-Shapiro, G., & Simoudis, E. (1996). Mining business databases. *Communications of the ACM, 39*(11), 42–48. doi:10.1145/240455.240468

Bray, T., Paoli, J., Sperberg-McQueen, C. M., Maler, E., & Yergeau, F. (2004). *Extensible Markup Language (XML) 1.0* (3rd ed.). Retrieved from http://www.w3.org/TR/2004/REC-xml-20040204

Briand, L., Wüst, J., Ikonomovski, S., & Lounis, H. (1998). *A comprehensive investigation of quality factors in object-oriented designs: An industrial case study.* Technical Report ISERN-98-29, International Software Engineering Network.

Briand, L.C., Wüst, J., Daly, J.W., & Porter, D.V. (2000). Exploring the relationship between design measures and software quality in object-oriented systems. *Journal of Systems and Software, 51*(3), 245–273.

Brin, S., Rastogi, R., & Shim, K. (2003). Mining optimized gain rules for numeric attributes. *IEEE Transactions on Knowledge and Data Engineering, 15*(2), 324–338. doi:10.1109/TKDE.2003.1185837

Bringing virtual worlds to business school. (2008). *BizEd, 7*(1), 34.

Britton, L. C., Wright, M., & Ball, D. F. (2000). The use of co-ordination theory to improve service quality in executive search. *Service Industries Journal, 20*(4), 85–102.

Bronack, S., Riedl, R., & Tashner, J. (2006). Learning in the zone: A social constructivist framework for distance education in a 3-dimensional virtual world. *Interactive Learning Environments, 14*(3), 219–232. doi:10.1080/10494820600909157

Bronder, C., & Pritzl, R. (1992). Developing strategic alliances: A conceptual framework for successful co-operation. *European Management Journal, 10*(4), 412–421. doi:10.1016/0263-2373(92)90005-O

Brooks, F. P., Jr. (1975). *The Mythical Man-month: Essays on Software Engineering*. Reading, MA: Addison-Wesley.

Brooks, F.P. Jr. (1995). *The mythical man-month: Essays on Software engineering* (anniv. ed.). Reading, MA: Addison-Wesley.

Brown, A. (2005). If this suite's a success, why is it so buggy? [Electronic version]. *The Guardian,* Retrieved March 15, 2006.

Brown, A., Delbaere, M., Eeles, P., Johnston, S., & Weaver, R. (2005). Realizing service oriented solutions with the IBM Rational Software Development Platform. *IBM Systems Journal, 44*(4), 727-752.

Brown, M. L., & Kros, J. F. (2003). Data mining and the impact of missing data. *Industrial Management & Data Systems, 103*(8), 611–621. doi:10.1108/02635570310497657

Brown, S., & Venkatesh, V. (2003). Bringing Non-Adopters Along: The Challenge Facing the PC In-

dustry. *Communications of the ACM, 46*(4), 76–80. doi:10.1145/641205.641208

Bryson, S. (1996). Virtual reality in scientific visualization. *Communications of the ACM, 39*(5), 62–71. doi:10.1145/229459.229467

Bugeja, M. J. (2008). Second thoughts about Second Life. *Education Digest, 73*(5), 18–22.

Burton-Jones, A., & Meso, P. (2006). Conceptualizing Systems for Understanding: An Empirical Test of Decomposition Principles in Object-Oriented Analysis. *Information Systems Research, 17*(1), 101–114. doi:10.1287/isre.1050.0079

Burton-Jones, A., & Weber, R. (2003). Properties do not have properties: Investigating a questionable conceptual modeling practice. In *Proceedings of the 2nd Annual Symposium on Research in Systems Analysis and Design,* St. John's, Canada.

Butler, B., Sproull, L., Kiesler, S., & Kraut, R. (2002). Community effort in online groups: Who does the work and why? In S. Weisband & L. Atwater (Eds.), *Leadership at a Distance*. Mahwah, NJ: Lawrence Erlbaum.

Butler, B.S., & Gray, P.H. (2006). Reliability, mindfulness, and information systems. *MIS Quarterly, 30*(2), 211–224.

Calado, P. P., & Ribeiro-Neto, B. (2003). An Information Retrieval Approach for Approximate Queries. *IEEE Transactions on Knowledge and Data Engineering, 15*(1), 236–239. doi:10.1109/TKDE.2003.1161593

Camarinha-Matos, L. M., Afsarmanesh, H., & Rabelo, R. J. (2003). Infrastructure developments for agile virtual enterprises. *International Journal of Computer Integrated Manufacturing, 16*(4-5), 235–254. doi:10.1080/0951192031000089156

Campell, J. L., Hollingsworth, J. R., & Lindberg, L. N. (Eds.). (1991). *The governance of the American economy.* New York: Cambridge University Press.

Carmel, E. (1999). *Global Software Teams.* Upper Saddle River, NJ: Prentice-Hall.

Carmel, E., & Agarwal, R. (2001). Tactical approaches for alleviating distance in global software development. *IEEE Software*(March/April), 22–29.

Carzaniga, A., Rosenblum, D. S., & Wolf, A. L. (2001). Design and evaluation of a wide-Area event notification service. *ACM Transactions on Computer Systems, 19*(3), 332–383. doi:10.1145/380749.380767

Casati, F., Ceri, S., Paraboschi, S., & Pozzi, G. (1999). Specification and implementation of exceptions in workflow management systems. *ACM Transactions on Database Systems, 24*(3), 405–451. doi:10.1145/328939.328996

Cash, J. I., & Konsynski, B. R. (1985). IS redraws competitive boundaries. *Harvard Business Review, 63*(2), 131–142.

Ceri, S., & Fraternali, P. (1997). *Designing database applications with objects and rules: the IDEA methodology.* Reading, MA: Addison-Wesley.

Ceri, S., Fraternali, P., Bongio, A., Brambilla, M., Comai, S., & Matera, M. (2002). *Designing Data-Intensive Web Applications.* San Francisco, CA: Morgan Kauffmann.

Chakrabarti, M., Ortega, M., Mehrotra, S., & Porkaew, K. (2003). Evaluating refined queries in top-k retrieval systems. *IEEE Transactions on Knowledge and Data Engineering, 15*(5), 256–270.

Chakravarthy, S. (1997). Sentinel: An object-oriented DBMS with event-based rules. In J. Peckham (Ed.), *SIGMOD Conference* (pp. 572-575). New York: ACM Press.

Chakravarthy, S., & Liao, H. (2001). Asynchronous monitoring of events for distributed cooperative environments. In H. Lu, & S. Spaccapietra (Eds.), *Proceedings of CODAS'01* (pp. 25-32). Beijing: IEEE Computer Society.

Chan, H., Wei, K., & Siau, K. (1993). User-Database Interface: The Effect of Abstraction Levels on Query Performance. *Management Information Systems Quarterly, 17*(4), 441–464. doi:10.2307/249587

Chan, T. M. (1998). Approximate Nearest Neighbor Queries Revisited. *Discrete & Computational Geometry, 20*(3), 359–374. doi:10.1007/PL00009390

Charfi, A., & Mezini, M. (2004). Hybrid Web service composition: business processes meet business rules. In M. Aiello, M. Aoyama, F. Curbera, & M. P. Papazoglou (Eds.), *Proceedings of ICSOC '04* (pp. 30-38). New York: ACM Press.

Checkland, P. B., & Scholes, J. (1990). *Soft system methodology in action.* Chichester: John Wiley and Sons.

Chen, P. P.-S. (1976). The Entity-Relationship Model-Toward a Unified View of Data. *ACM Transactions on Database Systems, 1*(1), 9–36. doi:10.1145/320434.320440

Chen, Y., Zhou, L., & Zhang, D. (2006). Ontology-supported Web service composition: An approach to service-oriented knowledge management in corporate financial services. *Journal of Database Management, 17*(1), 67-84.

Chesbrough, H. (2005). Open Innovation: A New Paradigm for Understanding Industrial Innovation. In H. Chesbrough, W. Vanhaverbeke, & J. West (eds.), *Open Innovation: Researching a New Paradigm* (pp. 1-14). Oxford, UK: Oxford University Press.\

Chesbrough, H. (2006). *Open Business Models: How to Thrive in the New Innovation Landscape.* Boston: Harvard Business School Press.

Chidamber, S., & Kemerer, C.F. (1994). A metrics suite for object oriented design. *IEEE Transactions on Software Engineering, 20*(6), 476–493.

Chidamber, S.R., & Kemerer, C.F. (1991). Towards a metric suite for object oriented design. *Proceedings of the 6th ACM Conference of Object Oriented Programming, Systems, Languages and Applications* (pp. 197–211). Phoenix, AZ: ACM Press.

Chidamber, S.R., Darcy, D.P., & Kemerer, C.F. (1998). Managerial use of metrics for object-oriented software: An exploratory analysis. *IEEE Transactions on Software Engineering, 24*(8), 629–639.

Chidlovskii, B. (2001). Schema Extraction from XML Data: A Grammatical Inference Approach. *KRDB'01 Workshop (Knowledge Representation and Databases)*

Christensen, C. M. (1997). *The innovator's dilemma: When new technologies cause great firms to fail.* Boston, MA: Harvard Business School Press.

Christensen, C. M. (2000). After the gold rush. *Innosight.* Retrieved January 30, 2006.

Christensen, C. M. (2006). The ongoing process of building a theory of disruption. *Journal of Product Innovation Management, 23*(1), 39–55. doi:10.1111/j.1540-5885.2005.00180.x

Christiaanse, E. (2005). Performance benefits through integration hubs. *Communications of the ACM, 48*(4), 95–100. doi:10.1145/1053291.1053294

Christopher, M. (2000). The agile supply chain – competing in volatile markets. *Industrial Marketing Management, 29*(1), 37–44. doi:10.1016/S0019-8501(99)00110-8

Chu, W., Yang, H., Chiang, K., Minock, M., Chow, G., & Larson, C. (1996). CoBase: A scalable and extensible cooperative information system. *Journal of Intelligent Information Systems, 6*(2/3), 223–259. doi:10.1007/BF00122129

Ciborra, C. (2000). Drifting: From control to drift. In K. Braa, C. Sorensen & B. Dahlbom (Eds.), *Planet internet.* Lund: Studentlitteratur.

Clemons, E. K., & Row, M. C. (1992). Information technology and industrial cooperation: The role of changing transaction costs. *Journal of Management Information Systems, 9*(2), 9–28.

Close, W. (2003). *CRM suites for North American MSBs markets: 1H03 magic quadrant.* Stamford, CT: Gartner Inc. Markets.

Coffman, T., & Klinger, M. B. (2007). Utilizing virtual worlds in education: The implications for practice. *International Journal of Social Sciences, 2*(1), 29–33.

Cohen, M.D., March, J.G., & Olsen, J.P. (1972). A garbage can model of organizational choice. *Administrative Science Quarterly, 17*(1), 1–25.

Coleman, E.G., & Hill, B. (2004). The social production of ethics in debian and free software communities: Anthropological lessons for vocational ethics. In S. Koch (Ed.), *Open source software development* (pp. 273–295). Hershey, PA: Idea Group.

Collins, A. M., & Quillian, M. R. (1969). Retreival Times from Semantic Memory. *Journal of Verbal Learning and Verbal Behavior, 8*, 240–247. doi:10.1016/S0022-5371(69)80069-1

Combi, C., & Pozzi, G. (2003). Temporal conceptual modelling of workflows. In I. Song, S. W. Liddle, T. Wang Ling, & P. Scheuermann (Eds.), *Proceedings of ER'03* (LNCS 2813, pp. 59-76).

Combi, C., & Pozzi, G. (2004). Architectures for a temporal workflow management system. In H. Haddad, A. Omicini, R. L. Wainwright, & L. M. Liebrock (Eds.), *Proceedings of SAC'04* (pp. 659-666). New York: ACM Press.

Combi, C., Daniel, F., & Pozzi, G. (2006). A portable approach to exception handling in workflow management systems. In R. Meersman & Z. Tari (Eds.), *OTM Conferences (1)*, LNCS 4275 (pp. 201-218). Montpellier, France: Springer Verlag.

Conallen, J. (1999). Modeling web application architectures with UML. *Communications of the ACM, 42*(10), 63-70.

Constantine, L. L., & Lockwood, L. A. D. (1999). *Software for Use.* Reading, MA: Addison-Wesley.

Conte, S.D., Dunsmore, H., & Shen, V. (1986). *Software engineering metrics and models.* Menlo Park, CA: Benjamin/Cummings.

Conway, C. (2007). Professor Avatar. *Inside Higher Ed.* Retrieved April 24, 2008, from http://www.insidehighered.com/views/2007/10/16/conway.

Conway, M. E. (1968). How do committees invent. *Datamation, 14*(4), 28–31.

Cook, J.E., Votta, L.G., & Wolf, A.L. (1998). Cost-effective analysis of in-place software processes. *IEEE Transactions on Software Engineering, 24*(8), 650–663.

Cook, S. (2000). The UML Family: Profiles, Prefaces, and Packages. In *Proceedings of UML 2000 - The Unified Modeling Language. Advancing the Standard* (LNCS 1939, pp. 255-264).

Cool, K. O., Dierickx, I., & Szulanski, G. (1997). Diffusion of innovative within organizations: Electronic switching in the Bell system, 1971-1982. *Organization Science, 8*(5), 543–560. doi:10.1287/orsc.8.5.543

Cox, A. (1998). Cathedrals, Bazaars and the Town Council. Retrieved 22 March, 2004, from http://slashdot.org/features/98/10/13/1423253.shtml

Cox, I. J., Miller, M. L., & Bloom, J. A. (2001). *Digital watermarking: Principles and practice.* Morgan Kaufmann.

Crawford, C., Bate, G., Cherbakov, L., Holley, K., & Tsocanos, C. (2005). Toward an on demand service architecture. *IBM Systems Journal, 44*(1), 81-107.

Crowston K., Scozzi B., (2003). Open Source Software projects as virtual organizations: competency rallying for software development. *IEE Proceedings Software, 149*(1), 3-17.

Crowston, K. (1997). A coordination theory approach to organizational process design. *Organization Science, 8*(2), 157–175.

Crowston, K., & Howison, J. (2006). Hierarchy and centralization in free and open source software team communications. *Knowledge, Technology & Policy, 18*(4), 65–85.

Crowston, K., & Kammerer, E. (1998). Coordination and collective mind in software requirements development. *IBM Systems Journal, 37*(2), 227–245.

Crowston, K., & Osborn, C. S. (2003). A coordination theory approach to process description and redesign. In T. W. Malone, K. Crowston & G. Herman (Eds.), *Organizing Business Knowledge: The MIT Process Handbook.* Cambridge, MA: MIT Press.

Crowston, K., & Scozzi, B. (2002). Open source software projects as virtual organizations: Competency rallying for software development. *IEE Proceedings—Software Engineering, 149*(1), 3–17.

Crowston, K., & Scozzi, B. (2008). Bug fixing practices within free/libre open source software development teams. *Journal of Database Management, 19*(2), 1–30.

Crowston, K., Howison, J., & Annabi, H. (2006). Information systems success in Free and Open Source Software development: Theory and measures. *Software Process—Improvement and Practice, 11*(2), 123–148.

Crowston, K., Wei, K., Li, Q., & Howison, J. (2006). *Core and periphery in Free/Libre and Open Source software team communications.* Paper presented at the Hawai'i International Conference on System System (HICSS-39), Kaua'i, Hawai'i.

Crowston, K., Wei, K., Li, Q., Eseryel, U. Y., & Howison, J. (2005). *Coordination of Free/Libre Open Source Software development.* Paper presented at the International Conference on Information Systems (ICIS 2005), Las Vegas, NV, USA.

Cubranic, D. (1999). *Open-source software development.* Paper presented at the 2nd Workshop on Software Engineering over the Internet, Los Angeles.

Cugola, G., Di Nitto, E., & Fuggetta, A. (2001). The JEDI event-based infrastructure and its application to the development of the OPSS wfMS. *IEEE Transactions on Software Engineering, 27*(9), 827–850. doi:10.1109/32.950318

Cunningham, C., Song, I. Y., & Chen, P. P. (2006). Data warehouse design to support customer relationship management analysis. *Journal of Database Management, 17*(2), 62–88.

Curtis, B., Krasner, H., & Iscoe, N. (1988). A field study of the software design process for large systems. *Communications of the ACM, 31*(11), 1268–1287.

Curtis, B., Krasner, H., & Iscoe, N. (1988). A Field Study of the Software Design Process for Large Systems. *Communications of the ACM, 31*(11), 1268–1287. doi:10.1145/50087.50089

Curtis, B., Walz, D., & Elam, J. J. (1990). Studying the process of software design teams. In *Proceedings of the 5th International Software Process Workshop On*

Experience With Software Process Models (pp. 52–53). Kennebunkport, Maine, United States.

Cusumano, M.A. (2004). Reflections on free and open software. *Communications of the ACM, 47*(10), 25–27.

Cutosksy, M. R., Tenenbaum, J. M., & Glicksman, J. (1996). Madefast: Collaborative engineering over the Internet. *Communications of the ACM, 39*(9), 78–87.

Czarnecki, K., & Eisenecker, U. W. (2000). *Generative Programming - Methods, Tools, and Applications.* Addison-Wesley.

D'Souza, D. F., & Wills, A. C. (1998). *Objects, components, and frameworks with UML: The catalysis approach*: Addison-Wesley.

Dahlander, L. (2005). Appropriation and appropriability in open source software. *International Journal of Innovation Management, 9*(3), 259–285. doi:10.1142/S1363919605001265

Dahlander, L. (2007). Penguin in a new suit: A tale of how de novo entrants emerged to harness free and open source software communities. *Industrial and Corporate Change, 16*(5), 913–943. doi:10.1093/icc/dtm026

Daniel, F., Matera, & Pozzi, G. (2008). Managing runtime adaptivity through active rules: the Bellerofonte framework. *Journal of Web Engineering, 7*(3), 179–199.

Daniel, F., Matera, M., & Pozzi, G. (2006). Combining conceptual modeling and active rules for the design of adaptive web applications. In N. Koch & L. Olsina (Eds.), *ICWE'06 Workshop Proceedings* (article no.10). New York: ACM Press.

Danneels, E. (2004). Disruptive technology reconsidered: A critique and research agenda. *Journal of Product Innovation Management, 21*(4), 246–258. doi:10.1111/j.0737-6782.2004.00076.x

Dano, M. (2008). Android founder makes the case for Google's mobile strategy. *RCR Wireless News, 27*(34), 1–8.

Dashofy, E. M., Van der Hoek, A., & Taylor, R. N. (2005). A comprehensive approach for the development of modular software architecture description languages. *ACM Transactions on Software Engineering and Methodology, 14*(2), 199-245.

Davidow, W. H., & Malone, M. S. (1992). *The virtual corporation.* New York: HarperCollins.

Davis, F. (1989). Perceived usefulness, perceived ease of use, and user acceptance of information technology. *MIS Quarterly, 13*(3), 318–339. doi:10.2307/249008

Davis, G. B. (1982). Strategies for information requirements determination. *IBM Systems Journal, 21*(1), 4–30.

Davis, S., Siau, K., & Dhenuvakonda, K. (2003). A fit-gap analysis of e-business curricula vs. industry need. *Communications of the ACM, 46*(12), 167–177. doi:10.1145/953460.953497

de Champeaux, D., Lea, D., & Faure, P. (1993). *Object-Oriented System Development.* Addison Wesley.

De Pauw, Lei, M., Pring, E., & Villard, L. (2005). Web services navigator: Visualizing the execution of Web services. *IBM Systems Journal, 44*(4), 821-845.

de Souza, P. S. (1993). *Asynchronous Organizations for Multi-Algorithm Problems.* Unpublished Doctoral Thesis, Carnegie-Mellon University.

Deboeck, G., & Kohonen, T. (1998). *Visual Explorations in Finance with Self-Organizing Maps,* London, UK: Springer-Verlag.

Dedrick, J., & West, J. (2003). Why firms adopt open source platforms: A grounded theory of innovation and standards adoption. In J.L. King & K. Lyytinen (Eds.), *Proceedings of the Workshop on Standard Making: A Critical Research Frontier for Information Systems* (pp. 236–257), Seattle, WA.

DeJong, J. (2006, June 15). Of Different Minds About Modeling. *SD Times.* Retrieved from http://www.sdtimes.com/article/special-20060615-02.html.

Deligiannis, I., Shepperd, M., Roumeliotis, M., & Stamelos, I. (2003). An empirical investigation of an object-oriented design heuristic for maintainability. *Journal of Systems and Software, 65*(2), 127–139.

Demetriou, N., Koch, S., & Neumann, G. (2006). The development of the OpenACS community. In M. Lytras & A. Naeve (Eds.), *Open source for knowledge and learning management: Strategies beyond tools* (pp. 298–318). Hershey, PA: Idea Group.

Dempsey, B.J., Weiss, D., Jones, P., & Greenberg, J. (2002). Who is an open source software developer? *Communications of the ACM, 45*(2), 67–72.

Dempster, A. P., Laird, N. M., & Rubin, D. B. (1977). Maximum likelihood from incomplete data via the EM algorithm. *Journal of the Royal Statistical Society. Series B. Methodological, 39*(1), 1–38.

Dempster, A., & Rubin, D. (1983). Incomplete data in sample surveys. In W. G. Madow, I. Olkin, & D. Rubin (Eds.), *Sample Surveys Vol. II: Theory and Annotated Bibliography* (pp. 3-10), New York: Academic Press.

Denzin, N. K. (1978). *The research act: A theoretical introduction to sociological methods*: McGraw-Hill.

DeSanctis, G., & Jackson, B. M. (1994). Coordination of information technology management: Team-based structures and computer-based communication systems. *Journal of Management Information Systems, 10*(4), 85.

Deursen, van A. & Klint, P. (2002). Domain-Specific Language Design Requires Feature Descriptions, Journal of Computing and Information Technology, *10*(1), 1-17.

Deutsch, A., Fernandez, M., & Suciu, D. (1999). Storing Semi-structured Data with STORED. *SIGMOD Conference, Philadelphia, Pennsylvania.*

Di Bona, C., Ockman, S., & Stone, M. (Eds.). (1999). *Open Sources: Voices from the Open Source Revolution.* Sebastopol, CA: O'Reilly & Associates.

Dickey, M. D. (2005). Brave new (interactive) worlds: A review of the design affordances and constraints of two 3D virtual worlds as interactive learning environments. *Interactive Learning Environments, 13*(1-2), 121–137. doi:10.1080/10494820500173714

Dickey, M. D. (2005). Three-dimensional virtual worlds and distance learning: Two case studies of Active Worlds as a medium for distance education. *British Journal of Educational Technology, 36*(3), 439–451. doi:10.1111/j.1467-8535.2005.00477.x

Dinh-Tong, T.T., & Bieman, J.M. (2005). The FreeBSD project: A replication case study of open source development. *IEEE Transactions on Software Engineering, 31*(6), 481–494.

Dittrich, K. R., Fritschi, H., Gatziu, S., Geppert, A., & Vaduva, A. (2003). Samos in hindsight: experiences in building an active object-oriented DBMS. *Information Systems Journal, 28*(5), 369–392. doi:10.1016/S0306-4379(02)00022-4

Dobing, B., & Parsons, J. (2000). Understanding the Role of Use Cases in UML: A Review and Research Agenda. *Journal of Database Management, 11*(4), 28–36.

Dori, D. (2001). Object-process methodology applied to modeling credit card transactions. *Journal of Database Management, 12*(1), 4.

Dori, D. (2002). Why Significant UML Change is Unlikely. *Communications of the ACM, 45*(11), 82–85. doi:10.1145/581571.581599

Dorman, A. (2007). FrankenSOA. *Network Computing, 18*(12), 41-51.

Drucker, P. (1988). The coming of the new organization. *Harvard Business Review,* 3-15.

Dubé, L., & Paré, G. (2003). Rigor in information systems positivist case research: Current practices, trends, and recommendations. *MIS Quarterly, 27*(4), 597–635.

Duddy, K. (2002). UML2 Must Enable A Family of Languages. *Communications of the ACM, 45*(11), 73–75. doi:10.1145/581571.581596

Duffy, D. J. (2004). *Domain Architectures: Models and Architectures for UML Applications.* New York: John Wiley & Sons.

Duke, A., Davies, J., & Richardson, M. (2005). Enabling a scalable service oriented architecture with Semantic Web services. *BT Technology Journal, 23*(3), 191-201.

Dutoit, A.H., & Bruegge, B. (1998). Communication metrics for software development. *IEEE Transactions on Software Engineering, 24*(8), 615–628.

Eclipse Foundation. (2008). *Eclipse modeling frameworks.* Retrieved from http://www.eclipse.org/modeling/emf/

Eder, J., & Liebhart, W. (1995). The workflow activity model WAMO. In S. Laufmann, S. Spaccapietra, & T. Yokoi (Eds.), *Proceedings of CoopIS'95* (pp. 87-98). Vienna, Austria.

Egyed, A., & Medvidovic, N. (1999, Oct). *Extending Architectural Representation in UML with View Integration.* Proceedings of the 2nd International Conference on the Unified Modelling Language (UML), (pp. 2-16). Fort Collins, CO.

Eisenhardt, K. M. (1989). Building theories from case study research. *Academy of Management Review, 14*(4), 532–550. doi:10.2307/258557

EJB. (2007). *Wikipedia.* Retrieved October 12, 2007, from http://en.wikipedia.org/wiki/Ejb

Elliott, M.S., & Scacchi, W. (2004). Free software development: Cooperation and conflict in a virtual organizational culture. In S. Koch (Ed.), *Open source software development* (pp. 152–172). Hershey, PA: Idea Group.

Erickson, J. (2008). A Decade and More of UML: An Overview of UML Semantic and Structural Issues and UML Field Use. *Journal of Database Management, 19*(3), i–vii.

Erickson, J., & Siau, K. (2003). e-ducation. *Communications of the ACM, 46*(9), 134–140. doi:10.1145/903893.903928

Erickson, J., & Siau, K. (2007). Theoretical and Practical Complexity of Modeling Methods. *Communications of the ACM, 50*(8), 46–51. doi:10.1145/1278201.1278205

Erickson, J., Lyytinen, K., & Siau, K. (2005). Agile modeling, agile software development, and extreme programming: The state of research. *Journal of Database Management, 16*(4), 80-89.

Eriksson, H.-E., & Penker, M. (2000). *Business modelling with uml:* OMG Group, Wiley Computer Publishing, John Wiley & Sons, Inc.

Erlikh, L. (2000). Leveraging legacy system dollars for e-business. *IEEE IT Professional, 2*(3), 17 - 23.

Evans, H., & Dickman, P. (1999, October). *Zones, contracts and absorbing change: An approach to software evolution.* Paper presented at the Conference on Object-Oriented Programming, Systems, Languages and Applications (OOPSLA '99), Denver, Colorado, USA.

Evans, P., & Wurster, T. S. (2000). *Blown to bits: How the new economics of information transforms strategy.* Boston, MA: Harvard Business School Press.

Evermann, J., & Wand, Y. (2001). Towards ontologically based semantics for UML constructs. *Proceedings of the 20th International Conference on Conceptual Modeling,* Yokohama, Japan (pp. 354-367).

Evermann, J., & Wand, Y. (2001). An Ontological Examination of Object Interaction in Conceptual Modeling. In *Proceedings of the 11th Workshop on Information Technologies and Systems,* New Orleans, Louisiana (pp. 91-96).

Evermann, J., & Wand, Y. (2006). Ontological Modeling Rules For UML: An Empirical Assessment. *Journal of Computer Information Systems, 46*(5), 14–29.

Faraj, S., & Sproull, L. (2000). Coordinating Expertise in Software Development Teams. *Management Science, 46*(12), 1554–1568.

Farrell, J., & Saloner, G. (1986). Installed base and compatibility: Innovation, product preannouncements, and predation. *The American Economic Review, 76*(5), 940–955.

Fayad, M.E., & Schmidt, D.C. (1997). Object-oriented application frameworks. *Communications of the ACM, 40*(10), 32–39.

Fayyad, U., Piatetsky-Shapiro, G., & Smyth, P. (1996). The KDD process for extracting useful knowledge from volumes of data. *Communications of the ACM, 39*(11), 7–34.

Feller, J., Finnegan, P., Fitzgerald, B., & Hayes, J. (2008). From Peer Production to Productization: A Study of Socially Enabled Business Exchanges in Open Source Service Networks. *Information Systems Research*, *19*(4), 475–493. doi:10.1287/isre.1080.0207

Feller, J., Finnegan, P., Hayes, J., & Lundell, B. (2006, June 8-10). Business models for Open Source Software: Towards a mature understanding of the concept and its implications for practice. *Panel Presentation at the IFIP 2.13 Conference on Open Source Software, Genoa Italy 8th-10th June.*

Feller, J., Finnegan, P., Kelly, D., & MacNamara, M. (2006, July 12-15). Developing Open Source Software: A Community-based Analysis of Research. In *Proceedings of the IFIP 8.2 Working Conference on Social Exclusion--Societal and Organisational Implications for Information Systems, Limerick, Ireland.*

Feller, J., Fitzgerald, B., Hissam, S.A., & Lakhani, K.R. (Eds.). (2005). *Perspectives on free and open source software.* Cambridge, MA: MIT Press.

Fenton, N.E. (1991). *Software metrics□a rigorous approach.* London: Chapman & Hall.

Ferguson, D., & Stockton, M. (2005). Service oriented architecture: Programming model and product architecture. *IBM Systems Journal, 44*(4), 753-780.

Fernandez, M., Morishima, A., & Suciu, D. (2001). Publishing Relational Data in XML:the SilkRoute Approach. *A Quarterly Bulletin of the Computer Society of the IEEE Technical Committee on Data Engineering, 24*(2), 12–19.

Fernández, W. D., Lehmann, H., & Underwood, A. (2002, June 6-8). *Rigour and relevance in studies of IS innovation: A grounded theory methodology approach.* Proceedings of the European Conference on Information Systems (ECIS) 2002, (pp. 110-119).Gdansk, Poland.

Fichman, R. G. (2000). The diffusion and assimilation of information technology innovations. In R. Zmud (Ed.), *Framing the domains of IT management: Projecting the future through the past.* Cincinnati, OH: Pinnaflex Publishing.

Fichman, R. G., & Kemerer, C. F. (1993). Adoption of software engineering process innovations: The case of object orientation. *Sloan Management Review, 34*(2), 7–22.

Fingar, P. (2000). Component-based frameworks for e-commerce. *Communications of the ACM, 43*(10), 61–66. doi:10.1145/352183.352204

Finholt, T., Sproull, L., & Kiesler, S. (1990). Communication and Performance in Ad Hoc Task Groups. In J. Galegher, R. F. Kraut & C. Egido (Eds.), *Intellectual Teamwork.* Hillsdale, NJ: Lawrence Erlbaum and Associates.

Finke, L. D. (2003). *Creating Significant Learning Experiences.* San Francisco, CA: Jossey-Bass, John Wiley & Sons Inc.

Finnegan, P., Galliers, R. D., & Powell, P. (2003). Applying Triple Loop Learning to planning electronic trading systems. *Information Technology & People, 16*(4), 461–483. doi:10.1108/09593840310509662

Fiol, C.M., & Connor, O.J. (2003). Waking up! Mindfulness in the face of bandwagons. *Academy of Management Review, 28*(1), 54–70.

Fioravanti, F., & Nesi, P. (2001). Estimation and prediction metrics for adaptive maintenance effort of object-oriented systems. *IEEE Transactions on Software Engineering, 27*(12), 1062–1084.

Fischer, M., Pinzger, M., & Gall, H. (2003). Populating a release history database from version control and bug tracking systems. *Proceedings of the 19th IEEE International Conference on Software Maintenance* (pp. 23–32), Amsterdam, The Netherlands.

Fitzgerald, B. (2006). The transformation of Open Source Software. *MIS Quarterly, 30*(3), 587–598.

Florescu, D., & Kossmann, D. (1999). Storing and Querying XML Data Using an RDBMS. *A Quarterly Bulletin of the Computer Society of the IEEE Technical Committee on Data Engineering, 22*(3), 27–34.

Fogel, K. (1999). *Open source development with CVS.* Scottsdale: CoriolisOpen Press.

Fong, C. K. (2007, June). *Successful implementation of model driven architecture: A case study of how Borland Together MDA technologies were successfully implemented in a large commercial bank.* Retrieved November 23, 2007, from http://www.borland.com/resources/en/pdf/products/together/together-successful-implementation-mda.pdf

Fong, J., & Cheung, S. K. (2005). Translating relational schema into XML schema definition with data semantic preservation and XSD graph. *Information and Software Technology, 47*(7), 437–462. doi:10.1016/j.infsof.2004.09.010

Fong, J., & Wong, H. K. (2004). XTOPO, An XML-based Technology for Information Highway on the Internet. *Journal of Database Management, 15*(3), 18–44.

Foray, D. (1994). Users, standards and the economics of coalitions and committees. *Information Economics and Policy, 6*(3-4), 269–293. doi:10.1016/0167-6245(94)90005-1

Foster, A. (2007). 'Immersive *education*' submerges students in online worlds made for learning. *The Chronicle of Higher Education, 54*(17), A22.

Foster, A. (2007). Professor avatar. *The Chronicle of Higher Education, 54*(4), A24–A26.

Fowler, M. (1999). *Refactoring: Improving the design of existing code.* Boston: Addison-Wesley.

France, R. B., Ghosh, S., Dinh-Trong, T., & Solberg, A. (2006, February). Model-driven development using UML 2.0: Promises and pitfalls. *Computer, 39*(2), 59-66. Retrieved June 5, 2006, from http://doi.ieeecomputersociety.org/10.1109/MC.2006.65

France, R. B., Kim, D.-K., Ghosh, S., & Song, E. (2004). A UML-Based Pattern Specification Technique. *IEEE Transactions on Software Engineering, 30*(3), 193–206. doi:10.1109/TSE.2004.1271174

Franck, E., & Jungwirth, C. (2002). *Reconciling investors and donators: The governance structure of open source* (Working Paper No. No. 8): Lehrstuhl für Unternehmensführung und -politik, Universität Zürich.

Franke, N., & von Hippel, E. (2003). Satisfying heterogeneous user needs via innovation toolkits: The case of Apache security software. *Research Policy, 32*(7), 1199–1216. doi:10.1016/S0048-7333(03)00049-0

Franke, N., von Hippel, E., & Schreier, M. (2006). Finding commercially attractive user innovations: A test of lead user theory. *Journal of Product Innovation Management, 23*(4), 301–315. doi:10.1111/j.1540-5885.2006.00203.x

Fritschi, H., Gatziu, S., & Dittrich, K. R. (1998). Framboise - an Approach to framework-based active database management system construction. In G. Gardarin, J. C. French, N. Pissinou, K. Makki, & L. Bouganim (Eds.), *Proceedings of CIKM '98* (pp. 364-370). New York: ACM Press.

Funderburk, J. E., Kiernan, G., Shanmugasundaram, J., Shekita, E., & Wei, C. (2002). XTABLES: Bridging relational technology and XML. *IBM Systems Journal, 41*(4).

Gacek, C., & Arief, B. (2004). The many meanings of Open Source. *IEEE Software, 21*(1), 34–40.

Gaimster, J. (2008). Reflections on interactions in virtual worlds and their implication for learning art and design. *Art, Design, &. Communication in Higher Education, 6*(3), 187–199. doi:10.1386/adch.6.3.187_1

Galaskiewicz, J. (1985). Interorganisational relations. *Annual Review of Sociology, 11*, 281–304. doi:10.1146/annurev.so.11.080185.001433

Galbraith, J. R. (1973). *Designing Complex Organizations.* Reading, MA: Addison-Wesley.

Gallivan, M.J. (2001). Striking a balance between trust and control in a virtual organization: A content analysis of open source software case studies. *Information Systems Journal, 11*(4), 277–304.

Garlan, D., & Kompanek, A. J. (2000). *Reconciling the needs of architectural description with object-modeling notations.* Proceedings of the Third International Conference on the Unified Modeling Language - UML 2000, (pp. 498-512). York, UK.

Gatziu, S., Koschel, A., von Bultzingsloewen, G., & Fritschi, H. (1998). Unbundling active functionality. *SIGMOD Record, 27*(1), 35–40. doi:10.1145/273244.273255

Gemino, A. (2004). Empirical comparisons of animation and narration in requirements validation. *Requirements Engineering, 9*(3), 153–168. doi:10.1007/s00766-003-0182-0

Gemino, A., & Parker, D. (2009). Use Case Diagrams in Support of Use Case Modeling: Deriving Understanding from the Picture. *Journal of Database Management, 20*(1), 1–24.

Gemino, A., & Wand, Y. (2003). Evaluating modeling techniques based on models of learning. *Communications of the ACM, 46*(10), 79–84. doi:10.1145/944217.944243

Gemino, A., & Wand, Y. (2004). A framework for empirical evaluation of conceptual modeling techniques. *Requirements Engineering, 9*(4), 248–260. doi:10.1007/s00766-004-0204-6

Gemino, A., & Wand, Y. (2005). Complexity and clarity in conceptual modeling: Comparison of mandatory and optional properties. *Data & Knowledge Engineering, 55*(3), 301–326. doi:10.1016/j.datak.2004.12.009

Geppert, A., Tombros, D., & Dittrich, K. R. (1998). Defining the semantics of reactive components in event-driven workflow execution with event histories. *Information Systems Journal, 23*(3-4), 235–252. doi:10.1016/S0306-4379(98)00011-8

German, D. (2006). A study of contributors of PostgreSQL. *Proceedings of the International Workshop on Mining Software Repositories* (MSR'06), Shanghai.

Geuss, R. (1994). Ideology. In T. Eagleton (Ed.), *Ideology* (pp. 260–278). Essex, UK: Longman Group.

Ghosh, R.A., & Prakash, V.V. (2000). The Orbiten free software survey. *First Monday, 5*(7).

Glaser, B. (1978). *Theoretical sensitivity: Advances in the methodology of grounded theory*. Mill Valley: Sociology Press.

Glaser, B., & Strauss, A. L. (1967). *The discovery of grounded theory: Strategies for qualitative research*. Chigago: Aldine.

Goldman, R., & Widom, J. (1997). DataGuides: Enabling Query Formulation and Optimization in Kanne, CC.,(2000). Guido Moerkotte. Efficient storage of xml data. In *Proc. of ICDE, California, USA* (p. 198).

Goldman, S. L., Nagel, R. N., & Preiss, K. (1995). *Agile competitors and virtual organisations: Strategies for enriching the customer*. New York: Van Nostrand Reinhold.

Goldstein, H. (1999). *Multilevel statistical models*. London: Arnold.

Gomaa, H. (2004). *Designing Software Product Lines with UML: From Use Cases to Pattern-based Software Architectures*. The Addison-Wesley Object Technology Series.

Gomaa, H., & Eonsuk-Shin, M. (2002). Multiple-View Meta-Modeling of Software Product Lines. In *Proceedings of the Eighth IEEE International Conference on Engineering of Complex Computer Systems*.

Gomaa, H., & Kerschberg, L. (1995). Domain Modeling for Software Reuse and Evolution. In *Proceedings of Computer Assisted Software Engineering Workshop* (CASE 95).

Goral, T. (2008). Sizing up Second Life. *University Business, 11*(3), 60–64.

Gormley, J., W. Bluestein, J. Gatoff & H. Chun (1998). The runaway costs of packaged applications. *The Forrester Report, 3*(5). Cambridge, MA: Forrester Research, Inc.

Gottesdiener, E. (1997). Business rules show power, promise. *Application Development Trends, 4*(3, March 1997).

Grabowski, M., & Roberts, K. H. (1999). Risk mitigation in virtual organizations. *Organization Science, 10*(6), 704–721.

Graves, L. (2008). A Second Life for higher ed. *U.S. News & World Report, 144*(2), 49–50.

Gray, B., & Gorelick, J. (2004, March 1). Database piracy plague. *The Washington Times*. Retrieved from http://www.washingtontimes.com

Green, P., & Rosemann, M. (2004). Applying ontologies to business and systems modeling techniques and perspectives: Lessons learned. *Journal of Database Management, 15*(2), 105–117.

Greunz, M., & Stanoevska-Slabeva, K. (2002). *Modeling business media platforms*. 35th Annual Hawaii International Conference on System Sciences, Maui, HI.

Grinter, R. E. (1999). Systems architecture: Product designing and social engineering. *ACM SIGSOFT Software Engineering Notes, 24*(2), 11-18.

Grinter, R. E., Herbsleb, J. D., & Perry, D. E. (1999). The Geography of Coordination: Dealing with Distance in R&D Work. In *Proceedings of the GROUP '99 Conference* (pp. 306–315). Phoenix, Arizona, US.

Gross-Amblard, D. (2003). Query-preserving watermarking of relational databases and XML documents. *Proceedings of ACM Symposium on Principles of Database Systems (PODS)* (pp. 191-201).

Grossman, M., Aronson, J., & McCarthy, R. (2005). Does UML make the grade? Insights from the software development community. *Information and Software Technology, 47*(6), 383–397. doi:10.1016/j.infsof.2004.09.005

Grubb, P., & Takang, A. A. (2003). *Software maintenance: Concepts and practice*. Singapore: World Scientific Publishing.

Gruber, T. (1993). A translation approach to portable ontology specifications. *Knowledge Acquisition, 5*(2), 199–220. doi:10.1006/knac.1993.1008

Gruber, T. (1995). Toward principles for the design of ontologies used for knowledge sharing. *International Journal of Human-Computer Studies, 43*(5/6), 907–928. doi:10.1006/ijhc.1995.1081

Guo, H., Li, Y., & Jajodia, S. (2007). Chaining watermarks for detecting malicious modifications to streaming data. *Information Sciences, 177*(1), 281-298.

Guo, H., Li, Y., Liu, A., & Jajodia, S. (2006). A fragile watermarking scheme for detecting malicious modifications of relational databases. *Information Sciences, 176*(10), 1350-1378.

Guo, J., Li, Y., Deng, R. H., & Chen, K. (2006). Rights protection for data cubes. *Proceedings of Information Security Conference (ISC)* (pp. 359-372).

Guru, A., & Siau, K. (2008). Developing the IBM I Virtual Community – iSociety. *Journal of Database Management, 19*(4), i–xiii.

Hahsler, M., & Koch, S. (2005). Discussion of a large-scale open source data collection methodology. *Proceedings of the Hawaii International Conference on System Sciences (HICSS-38)*, Big Island, HI.

Halle, B. V. (1994). Back to business rule basics. *Database Programming and Design*(October 1994), 15-18.

Hallen, J., Hammarqvist, A., Juhlin, F., & Chrigstrom, A. (1999). Linux in the workplace. *IEEE Software, 16*(1), 52–57.

Hamilton, M.B. (1987). The elements of the concept of ideology. *Political Studies, 35*(1), 18–38.

Hand, D. J. (1981). *Discrimination and Classification*. New York: Wiley.

Hand, D. J. (1998). Data mining: Statistics and more? *The American Statistician, 52*(2), 112–118. doi:10.2307/2685468

Hann, I.-H., Roberts, J., Slaughter, S., & Fielding, R. (2002). Economic incentives for participating in open source software projects. In *Proceedings of the Twenty-Third International Conference on Information Systems* (pp. 365–372).

Hansen, M., Köhntopp, K., & Pfitzmann, A. (2002). The open source approach—opportunities and limitations with respect to security and privacy. *Computers & Security, 21*(5), 461–471.

Hansen, M.T., & Haas, M.R. (2001). Competing for attention in knowledge markets: Electronic document dissemination in a management consulting company. *Administrative Science Quarterly, 46*(1), 1–28.

Hanseth, O., Monteiro, E., & Hatling, M. (1996). Developing information infrastructure: The tension between standardization and flexibility. *Science, Technology & Human Values, 21*(4), 407-426.

Harel, D. (1987). Statecharts: A visual formalism for complex systems. *Science of Computer Programming, 8*(3), 231–274. doi:10.1016/0167-6423(87)90035-9

Harrison, D.A., Mykytyn, P.P. Jr., & Riemenschneider, C.K. (1997). Executive decisions about adoption of information technology in small business: Theory and empirical tests. *Information Systems Research, 8*(2), 171–195.

Havenstein, H. (2006). Measuring SOA performance is a complex art. *Computer World, 40*(2), 6.

Hay, D., & Healy, K. A. (1997). *Business rules: What are they really?* GUIDE (The IBM User Group). Retrieved from http://www.BusinessRulesGroup.org/):.

Hay, D., & Healy, K. A. (2000). *Defining business rules ~ what are they really?* (No. Rev 1.3): the Business Rules Group.

Healy, K., & Schussman, A. (2003). *The ecology of open source software development.* Open Source, MIT. Working paper. http://opensource.mit.edu/papers/healyschussman.pdf. Last accessed January 8, 2007.

Hecker, F. (2000). Setting up shop: The business of Open-Source Software [Working paper]. Retrieved from http://www.hecker.org/writings/setting-up-shop

Henderson, J. C. (1990). Plugging into strategic partnerships: The critical IS connection. *Sloan Management Review, 30*(3), 7–18.

Henderson-Seller, B. (1996). *Object-oriented metrics: Measures of complexity.* Upper Saddle River, NJ: Prentice Hall.

Henderson-Sellers, B. (2005, February). UML the good, the bad or the ugly? Perspectives from a panel of experts. *Software and Systems Modeling, 4*(1), 4-13. Retrieved June 5, 2006, from http://dx.doi.org/10.1007/s10270-004-0076-8

Henkel, J. (2006). Selective revealing in open innovation processes: The case of embedded Linux. *Research Policy, 35*(7), 953–969. doi:10.1016/j.respol.2006.04.010

Herbsleb, J. D., & Grinter, R. E. (1999). Architectures, coordination, and distance: Conway's law and beyond. *IEEE Software*(September/October), 63–70.

Herbsleb, J. D., & Grinter, R. E. (1999). *Splitting the organization and integrating the code: Conway's law revisited.* Paper presented at the Proceedings of the International Conference on Software Engineering (ICSE '99), Los Angeles, CA.

Herbsleb, J. D., Mockus, A., Finholt, T. A., & Grinter, R. E. (2001). *An empirical study of global software development: Distance and speed.* Paper presented at the Proceedings of the International Conference on Software Engineering (ICSE 2001), Toronto, Canada.

Herbst, H. (1996). *Business rule oriented conceptual modelling.* Verlag: Physica .

Herbst, H. (1996). Business rules in system analysis: A meta-model and repository system. *Information Systems, 21*(2), 147-166.

Hertel, G., Niedner, S., & Herrmann, S. (2003). Motivation of software developers in open source projects: an Internet-based survey of contributors to the Linux kernel. *Research Policy, 32*, 1159–1177. doi:10.1016/S0048-7333(03)00047-7

Hicks, B. (n.d.). *Oracle Enterprise Service Bus: The foundation for service oriented architecture.* Retrieved October 18, 2007, from http://www.oracle.com/global/ap/openworld/ppt_download/middleware_oracle%20enterprise%20service%20bus%20foundation_250.pdf

Hicks, C., & Pachamanova, D. (2007). Back-propagation of user innovations: The open source compatibility edge. *Business Horizons, 50*(4), 315–324. doi:10.1016/j.bushor.2007.01.006

Hill, C. W. L. (1997). Establishing a standard: Competitive strategy and technological standards in winner-take-all industries. *The Academy of Management Executive, 11*(2), 7–25.

Himanen, P., Torvalds, L., & Castells, M. (2002). *The Hacker Ethic*. New York: Random House.

Hirschheim, R., & Klein, H. K. (1989). Four paradigms of information systems development. *Communications of the ACM, 32*(10), 1199-1216.

Hitt, L., & Brynjolfsson, E. (1996). Productivity, profit, and consumer welfare: Three different measures of information technology's value. *MIS Quarterly, 20*(20), 144–162.

Hofmeister, C., Nord, R., & Soni, D. (1999). *Applied software architecture*. Reading, MA: Addison-Wesley.

Hofmeister, C., Nord, R., & Soni, D. (1999). *Describing software architecture with UML.* Proceedings of the First Working IFIP Conference on Software Architecture (WICSA1), (pp. 145-160). San Antonio, TX.

Hopfield, J. J., & Tank, D. W. (1986). Computing with neural circuits. *The Sciences, 233*, 625–633.

Hovav, A., Patnayakuni, R., & Schuff, D. (2004). A model of internet standards adoption: The case of IPv6. *Information Systems Journal, 14*(3), 265–294. doi:10.1111/j.1365-2575.2004.00170.x

Hsu, M., & Kleissner, C. (1996). Objectflow: towards a process management infrastructure. *Distributed and Parallel Databases, 4*(2), 169–194. doi:10.1007/BF00204906

Huang, C. (2001). Using Intelligent Agents to Manage Fuzzy Business Processes. *IEEE Transactions on Systems, Man, and Cybernetics. Part A, Systems and Humans, 31*(6), 508–523. doi:10.1109/3468.983409

Huang, S., Hung, S., Yen, D., Li, S., & Wu, C. (2006). Enterprise application system reengineering: a business component approach. *Journal of Database Management, 17*(3), 66–91.

Humphrey, W. (1995). *A discipline for software engineering*. Reading, MA: Addison-Wesley.

Humphrey, W. S. (2000). *Introduction to Team Software Process*: Addison-Wesley.

Hunt, F., & Johnson, P. (2002). On the pareto distribution of sourceforge projects. *Proceedings of the Open Source Software Development Workshop* (pp. 122–129), Newcastle, UK.

Hutchinson, B., Henzel, J., & Thwaits, A. (2006). Using Web services to promote library-extension collaboration. *Library Hi Tech, 24*(1), 126-141.

Iacovou, C. L., Benbasat, I., & Dexter, A. S. (1995). Electronic data interchange and small organizations: Adoption and impact of technology. *MIS Quarterly, 19*(4), 465–485. doi:10.2307/249629

Iannacci, F. (2005). Coordination processes in OSS development: The Linux case study. Retrieved 21 September, 2006, from http://opensource.mit.edu/papers/iannacci3.pdf

IBM (Cartographer). (2003). *Ibm websphere application server enterprise*

Jacobson, I., Booch, G., & Rumbaugh, J. (1999). *The unified software development process*. New York: Addison-Wesley.

Jacobson, I., Christerson, M., Jonsson, P., & Overgaard, G. (1992). *Object-Oriented Software Engineering: A Use Case Driven Approach*. Reading, MA: Addison-Wesley.

Jacobson, I., Ericsson, M., & Jacobson, A. (1994). *The Object Advantage: Business Process Reengineering with Object Technology*. Reading, MA: Addison-Wesley.

Jarmon, L., Traphagan, T., & Mayrath, M. (2008). Understanding project-based learning in Second Life with pedagogy, training, and assessment trio. *Educational Media International, 45*(3), 157–176. doi:10.1080/09523980802283889

Jarvenpaa, S. L., & Leidner, D. E. (1999). Communication and trust in global virtual teams. *Organization Science, 10*(6), 791–815.

Jarvenpaa, S. L., & Machesky, J. J. (1989). Data analysis and learning: an experimental study of data modeling tools. *International Journal of Man-Machine Studies, 31*(4), 367–391. doi:10.1016/0020-7373(89)90001-1

Jennings, N., & Collins, C. (2007). Virtual or virtually U. *International Journal of Social Sciences, 2*(3), 180-186. Retrieved April 7, 2008, from http://www.waset.org/ijss/v2/v2-3-28.pdf

Jensen, C., & Scacchi, W. (2005). Collaboration, Leadership, Control, and Conflict Negotiation in the Netbeans.org Open Source Software Development Community. In *Proceedings of the Hawai'i International Conference on System Science (HICSS 2005)*. Big Island, Hawai'i.

Johnson, L. F., & Levine, A. H. (2008). Virtual worlds: Inherently immersive, highly social learning spaces. *Theory into Practice, 47*(2), 161–170. doi:10.1080/00405840801992397

Johnson, N. F., Duric, Z., & Jajodia, S. (2000). *Information hiding: Steganography and watermarking. Attacks and countermeasures*. Kluwer.

Johnson, R. (1997). Frameworks=(components+patterns). *Communications of the ACM, 40*(10), 39–42.

Johnson, R., & Hardgrave, B. (1999). Object-oriented methods: current practices and attitudes. *Journal of Systems and Software, 48*(1), 5–12. doi:10.1016/S0164-1212(99)00041-2

Joly, K. (2007). A Second Life for higher education? *University Business*. Retrieved April 17, 2008 from http://www.universitybusiness.com/viewarticle.aspx?articleid=797.

Jones, C. (1986). *Programming productivity*. New York: McGraw-Hill.

Jones, M. (1998). *Information Systems and the Double Mangle: Steering a Course Between the Scylla of Embedded Structure and the Charybdis of Strong Symmetry*. IFIP WG8.2/8.6 Joint Working Conference, Helsinki, Finland.

Jones, S. (2005). Toward an acceptable definition of service. *IEEE Software, 22*(3), 87-93.

Joynt, P. (1991). International dimensions of managing technology. *Journal of General Management, 16*(3), 73–84.

Junglas, I. A., & Steel, D. J. (2007). The virtual sandbox. *The Data Base for Advances in Information Systems, 38*(4), 26–28.

Junglas, I. A., Johnson, N. A., Steel, D. J., Abraham, D. C., & Loughlin, P. M. (2007). Identify formation, learning styles and trust in virtual worlds. *The Data Base for Advances in Information Systems, 38*(4), 90–96.

Kalakota, R., & Robinson, M. (2001). *e-Business 2.0: Roadmap for Success*: Addison-Wesley.

Kang, K. C., Kim, S., Lee, J., Kim, K., Shin, E., & Huh, M. (1998). FORM: A feature-oriented reuse method with domain-specific reference architectures. *Annals of Software Engineering, 5*(1), 143–168. doi:10.1023/A:1018980625587

Kang, K., Cohen, S., Hess, J., Novak, W. & Peterson, A. (1990). Feature-Oriented Domain Analysis (FODA) Feasibility Study, CMU/SEI-90-TR-021 ADA235785.

Kanter, R. M. (1989). The future of bureaucracy and hierarchy in organisational theory: A report from the field. In P. Bourdieu & J. Coleman (Eds.), *Social Theory for a Changing Society*. Boulder: Westview.

Kaplan, B. (1991). Models of change and information systems research. In H.-E. Nissen, H. K. Klein & R. Hirschheim (Eds.), *Information Systems Research: Contemporary Approaches and Emergent Traditions* (pp. 593–611). Amsterdam: Elsevier Science Publishers.

Katz, M. L., & Shapiro, C. (1994). Systems competition and network effects. *The Journal of Economic Perspectives, 8*(2), 93–115.

Katzenbeisser, S., & Petitcolas, F. A. (2000). *Information hiding techniques for steganography and digital watermarking*. Artech House.

Kaufman, F. (1966). Data systems that cross company boundaries. *Harvard Business Review, 44*(1), 141–155.

Kay, M. (1999) DTD Generator – A tool to generate XML DTDs. Retrieved from http://users.breathe.com/mhkay/saxon/dtdgen.html

Kazman, R., Klein, M., & Clements, P. (2000). *ATAM: Method for Architecture Evaluation* (Technical report No. CMU/SEI-2000-TR-004): Software Engineering Institute.

Kelly, S., & Tolvanen, J.-P. (2008). *Domain-specific modeling.* Hoboken, NJ: John Wiley & Sons.

Kemerer, C.F., & Slaughter, S. (1999). An empirical approach to studying software evolution. *IEEE Transactions on Software Engineering, 25*(4), 493–509.

Khatri, V., Vessey, I., Ramesh, V., Clay, P., & Park, S.-J. (2006). Understanding Conceptual Schemas: Exploring the Role of Application and IS Domain Knowledge. *Information Systems Research, 17*(1), 81–99. doi:10.1287/isre.1060.0081

Kim, D. K. (2007). The Role-Based Metamodeling Language for Specifying Design Patterns. In T. Taibi (Ed.), *Design Pattern Formalization Techniques* (pp. 183-205). Hershey, PA: IGI Global.

Kim. D. K., & Shen, W. (2008). Evaluating Pattern Conformance of UML Models: A Divide-and-Conquer Approach and Case Studies. *Software Quality Journal.*

Kim, H. (2002). Predicting how ontologies for the semantic Web will evolve. *Communications of the ACM, 45*(2), 48–54. doi:10.1145/503124.503148

Kim, H. M., Sengupta, A., Fox, M. S., & Dalkilic, M. (2007). A measurement ontology generalizable for emerging domain applications on the Semantic Web. *Journal of Database Management, 18*(1), 20-42.

Kim, J., & Lim, K. (2007). An approach to service oriented architecture using Web service and BPM in the Telcom OSS domain. *Internet Research, 17*(1), 99-107.

Kim, J., Hahn, J., & Hahn, H. (2000). How Do We Understand a System with (So) Many Diagrams? Cognitive Integration Processes in Diagrammatic Reasoning. *Information Systems Research, 11*(3), 284–303. doi:10.1287/isre.11.3.284.12206

Kim, Y.-G., & Everest, G. C. (1994). Building an IS architecture: Collective wisdom from the field. *Information & Management, 26*(1), 1-11.

Kim, Y.-G., & March, S. T. (1995). *Comparing Data Modeling Formalisms, 38*(6), 103–115.

Kirsch, L. J. (2004). Deploying common systems globally: The dynamics of control. *Information Systems Research, 15*(4), 375–395. doi:10.1287/isre.1040.0036

Klein, K.J., Tosi, H., & Cannella, A.A. Jr. (1999). Multilevel theory building: Benefits, barriers, and new development. *Academy of Management Review, 24*(2), 243–248.

Klein, M., & Konig-Ries, B. (2004). Combining Query and Preference - an Approach to Fully Automatize Dynamic Service Binding. In *Proceedings of IEEE International Conference on Web Services* (pp. 788-791).

Kleppe, A., Warmer, J., & Bast, W. (2003). *MDA explained: The model driven architecture. Practice and promise.* Reading, MA: Addison-Wesley.

Klettke, M., Schneider, L., & Heuer, A. (2002). Metrics for XML document collections. *Akmal Chaudri and Rainer Unland, XMLDM Workshop, Prague, Czech Republic* (pp.162-176).

Kobryn, C. (1999). UML 2001: A Standardization Odyssey. *Communications of the ACM, 42*(10), 29–37. doi:10.1145/317665.317673

Kobryn, C. (2002). Will UML 2.0 Be Agile or Awkward? *Communications of the ACM, 45*(1), 107–110. doi:10.1145/502269.502306

Koch, S. (2004). Profiling an open source project ecology and its programmers. *Electronic Markets, 14*(2), 77–88.

Koch, S. (2004). Agile principles and open source software development: A theoretical and empirical discussion. *Extreme Programming and Agile Processes in Software Engineering: Proceedings of the 5th International Conference XP 2004* (pp. 85–93). Berlin: Springer-Verlag (LNCS 3092).

Koch, S., & Schneider, G. (2002). Effort, cooperation and coordination in an open source software project: GNOME. *Information Systems Journal, 12*(1), 27–42.

Kogut, B., & Metiu, A. (2001). Open-source software development and distributed innovation. *Oxford Review of Economic Policy, 17*(2), 248–264.

Kohonen, T. (1989). *Self-Organization and Associative Memory* (3rd ed.). New York: Springer-Verlag.

Koike, Y. (2001). A Conversion Tool from DTD to XML Schema. Retrieved from http://www.w3.org/2000/04/schema_hack/

Koontz, C. (2000). Develop a solid e-commerce architecture. *e-Business Advisor*(January).

Koru, A.G., & Tian, J. (2004). Defect handling in medium and large open source projects. *IEEE Software, 21*(4), 54–61.

Koru, A.G., & Tian, J. (2005). Comparing high-change modules and modules with the highest measurement values in two large-scale open-source products. *IEEE Transactions on Software Engineering, 31*(8), 625–642.

Kovari, P., Diaz, D. C., Fernandes, F. C. H., Hassan, D., Kawamura, K., Leigh, D., et al. (2003). *Websphere application server enterprise v5 and programming model extensions: Websphere handbook series* (First Edition ed.): International Business Machines Corporation.

Krafzig, D., Banke, K., & Slama, D. (2005). *SOA elements.* Prentice Hall. Retrieved October 2, 2007, from http://en.wikipedia.org/wiki/Image:SOA_Elements.png

Krammer, M. I. (1997). Business rules: Automating business policies and practicies. *Distributed Computing Monitor*(May 1997).

Kraut, R. E., & Streeter, L. A. (1995). Coordination in software development. *Communications of the ACM, 38*(3), 69–81.

Kraut, R. E., Steinfield, C., Chan, A. P., Butler, B., & Hoag, A. (1999). Coordination and virtualization: The role of electronic networks and personal relationships. *Organization Science, 10*(6), 722–740.

Kreft, I., & de Leeuw, J. (2002). *Introducing multilevel modeling.* London: Sage.

Krill, P. (2005). Borland upgrading IDE while preparing for eclipse future. [Electronic version]. *InfoWorld.* Retrieved January 30, 2006.

Krishnakumar, N., & Sheth, A. P. (1995). Managing heterogeneous multi-system tasks to support enterprise-wide operations. *Distributed and Parallel Databases, 3*(2), 155–186. doi:10.1007/BF01277644

Krishnamurthy, S. (2002). Cave or Community? An Empirical Examination of 100 Mature Open Source Projects. *First Monday, 7*(6).

Krishnamurthy, S. (2005). An analysis of open source business models. In J. Feller, B. Fitzgerald, S. Hissam, & K. Lakhani (Eds.), *Perspectives on free and open source software.* Cambridge, MA: MIT Press.

Kung, C. H., & Solvberg, A. (1986). *Activity modelling and behaviour modelling.* Paper presented at the Proceedings of the IFIP WG 8.1 working conference on comparative review of information systems design methodologies: improving the practice, North-Holland, Amsterdam.

Kunnath, M. L. A., Cornell, R. A., Kysilka, M. K., & Witta, L. (2007). An experimental research study on the effect of pictorial icons on a user-learner's performance. *Computers in Human Behavior, 23*(3), 1454–1480. doi:10.1016/j.chb.2005.05.005

Kuntzmann, A., & Kruchten, P. (2003). The rational unified process—an enabler for higher process maturity. Retrieved April 19, 2007 from http://www-128.ibm.com/developerworks/rational/library/content/03July/0000/0579/Rational_CMM_WhitePaper.pdf.

Langdon, C. S. (2006). Designing information systems capabilities to create business value: A theoretical conceptualization of the role of flexibility and integration. *Journal of Database Management, 17*(3), 1–18.

Lange, C. F. J., Chaudron, M. R. V., & Muskens, J. (2006). In Practice: UML Software Architecture and Design Description. *IEEE Software, 23*(2), 40–46. doi:10.1109/MS.2006.50

Larkin, J. H., & Simon, H. A. (1987). Why a Diagram is (Sometimes) Worth Ten Thousand Words. *Cognitive Sci-*

ence, 11(1), 65–100. doi:10.1016/S0364-0213(87)80026-5

Larman, C. (2005). *Applying UML and Patterns: An Introduction to Object-Oriented Analysis and Design and Iterative Development* (3rd ed.). Upper Saddle River, NJ: Prentice Hall.

Lawrence, P., & Lorsch, J. (1967). *Organization and Environment*. Boston, MA: Division of Research, Harvard Business School.

Ledeczi, A., Maroti, M., Bakay, A., Karsai, G., Garrett, J., Thomason, C., et al. (2001, 17 May). *The generic modeling environment*. Paper presented at the Workshop on Intelligent Signal Processing, Budapest, Hungary.

Lee, A. S., & Baskerville, R. L. (2003). Generalizing generalizability in Information Systems research. *Information Systems Research, 14*(3), 221–243. doi:10.1287/isre.14.3.221.16560

Lee, D. W., & Chu, W. W. (2000). Comparative Analysis of Six XML Schema Languages. *SIGMOD Record, 29*(3). doi:10.1145/362084.362140

Lee, D. W., & Chu, W. W. (2000). Constraints-Preserving Transformation from {XML} Document Type Definition to Relational Schema. *International Conference on Conceptual Modeling / the Entity Relationship Approach* (pp. 323-338).

Lee, D. W., Mani, M., & Chu, W. W. (2003). Schema Conversion Methods between XML and Relational Models. *Knowledge Transformation for the Semantic Web.*

Lee, H. (2004). The Triple-A Supply Chain. *Harvard Business Review, 82*(10), 102–112.

Lee, J., & Truex, D. P. (2000). Exploring the impact of formal training in ISD methods on the cognitive structure of novice information systems developers. *Information Systems Journal, 10*(4), 347–367. doi:10.1046/j.1365-2575.2000.00086.x

Lee, J., Siau, K., & Hong, S. (2003). Enterprise integration with ERP and EAI. *Communications of the ACM, 46*(2), 54-60.

Lee, W., & Lim, T. (2007). Architectural Measurements on the World Wide Web as a Graph. *Journal of Information Technology and Architecture, 4*(2), 61–69.

Lee, W., Kang, S., Lim, S., Shin, M., & Kim, Y. (2007). Adaptive Hierarchical Surrogate for Searching Web with Mobile Devices. *IEEE Transactions on Consumer Electronics, 53*(2), 796–803. doi:10.1109/TCE.2007.381762

Lehman, M. M., & Belady, L. A. (1985). *Program evolution: Processes of software change*. London: Academic Press, Inc.

Lei, D., & Slocum, J. W. (1992). Global strategy, competence-building and strategic alliances. *California Management Review, 35*(1), 81–97.

Leibovitch, E. (1999). The business case for Linux. *IEEE Software, 16*(1), 40–44.

Leist, S., & Zellner, G. (2006, April 23-27). *Evaluation of current architecture frameworks*. SAC'06, (pp. 1546-1553). Dijon, France.

Lerner, J., & Tirole, J. (2001). The open source movement: Key research questions. *European Economic Review, 45*, 819–826.

Lerner, J., & Tirole, J. (2002). Some simple economics of open source. *The Journal of Industrial Economics, 50*(2), 197–234.

Lester, J. (2006). Pathfinder Linden's guide to getting started in Second Life. In D. Livingstone and J. Kemp (Eds.) *Proceedings of the Second Life Education Workshop at the Second Life Community Convention, San Francisco* (pp. v.-vii.). United Kingdom: University of Paisle. Retrieved May 28, 2008, from http://www.simteach.com/SLCC06/slcc2006-proceedings.pdf

Li, S. H., Huang, S. M., Yen, D. C., & Chang, C. C. (2007). Migrating legacy information systems to Web services architecture. *Journal of Database Management, 18*(4), 1–25.

Li, Y., & Deng, R. (2006). Publicly verifiable ownership protection for relational databases. *Proceedings of ACM Symposium on Information, Computer and Communication Security (ASIACCS)* (pp. 78-89).

Li, Y., & Zhong, N. (2006). Mining ontology for automatically acquiring Web user information needs. *IEEE Transactions on Knowledge and Data Engineering, 18*(4), 554–568. doi:10.1109/TKDE.2006.1599392

Li, Y., Guo, H., & Jajodia, S. (2004). Tamper detection and localization for categorical data using fragile watermarks. *Proceedings of ACM Digital Rights Management Workshop (DRM)* (pp. 73-82).

Li, Y., Swarup, V., & Jajodia, S. (2003). Constructing a virtual primary key for fingerprinting relational data. *Proceedings of ACM Digital Rights Management Workshop (DRM)* (pp. 133-141).

Li, Y., Swarup, V., & Jajodia, S. (2003). A robust watermarking scheme for relational data. *Proceedings of 13th Workshop on Information Technology and Systems (WITS)* (pp. 195-200).

Li, Y., Swarup, V., & Jajodia, S. (2004). Defending against additive attacks with maximal errors in watermarking relational data. *Proceedings of 18th Annual IFIP WG11.3 Working Conference on Data and Applications Security (DBSEC)* (pp. 81-94).

Li, Y., Swarup, V., & Jajodia, S. (2005). Fingerprinting relational databases: Schemes and specialties. *IEEE Transactions on Dependable and Secure Computing, 2*, 34-45.

Liebeskind, J. P. (1996). Knowledge, strategy, and the theory of the firm. *Strategic Management Journal, 17*, 93–107.

Little, R. J. A., & Rubin, D. B. (2002). *Statistical Analysis with Missing Data* (2nd ed.). New York: John Wiley and Sons.

Liu, S., & Chu, W. (2007). CoXML: A Cooperative XML Query Answering System. In *Proceedings of the 8th International Conference on Web-Age Information Management*, Huang Shan, China, (pp. 614-621).

Liu, Y., Liu, T., Qin, T., Ma, Z., & Li, H. (2007). Supervised rank aggregation. In *Proceedings of the 16th international conference on World Wide Web*, Banff, Alberta, Canada (pp. 481-490).

Ljungberg, J. (2000). Open source movements as a model for organizing. *European Journal of Information Systems, 9*(4), 208–216.

Lo, W. K. (1998). Agility, job satisfaction and organizational excellence: Their factors and relationships. *Third Proceedings of ISO 9000 and Total Quality Management* (pp. 330–336).

Locke, K. (2001). *Grounded theory in management research*: SAGE Publications.

Long, Y., & Siau, K. (2007). Social network structures in open source software development teams. *Journal of Database Management, 18*(2), 25–40.

López de Ipiña, D., & Katsiri, E. (2001). An ECA rule-matching service for simpler development of reactive applications, *Middleware 2001*. IEEE Distributed Systems Online, *2*(7).

Lorenz, M., & Kidd, J. (1995). *Object oriented metrics.* Upper Saddle River, NJ: Prentice Hall.

Loucopoulos, P., & Kadir, W. M. N. W. (2008). BROOD: Business rules-driven object oriented design. *Journal of Database Management Systems, 19*(1), 41–73.

Loucopoulos, P., & Layzell, P. J. (1986, 1987). *Rubric: A rule based approach for the development of information systems.* Paper presented at the 1st European workshop on fault diagnosis, reliability and related knowledge based approaches, Rhodes.

Lu, S., Sun, Y., Atay, M., & Fotouhi, F. (2003). A new inlining algorithm for mapping xml dtds to relational schemas. In *Proc. Of the First International Workshop on XML Schema and Data Management, in conjunction with the 22nd ACM International Conference on Conceptual Modeling (ER2003)*.

Lundell, B., Lings, B., & Lindqvist, E. (2006). Perceptions and uptake of open source in Swedish organizations. In E. Damiani, B. Fitzgerald, W. Scacchi, M. Scotto, & G. Succi (Eds.), *IFIP international federation for information processing: Volume 203, open source systems* (pp. 155–163). Boston: Springer.

Lyons, D. (2004). Peace, love and paychecks. [Electronic version]. *Forbes.* Retrieved January 30, 2006.

Lyytinen, K. (1987). A taxonomic perspective of information dystems fevelopment: Theoretical constructs and recommendations. In R. J. Boland, Jr. & R. A. Hirschheim (Eds.), *Critical issues in information systems research* (pp. 3-41): John Wiley & Sons.

Lyytinen, K., Rose, G., & Welke, R. (1998). The brave new world of development in the internetwork computing architecture (InterNCA): Or how distributed computing platforms will change systems development. *Information Systems Journal, 8*(3), 241-253.

Lyytinen, K., Smolander, K., & Tahvanainen, V.-P. (1989). *Modelling CASE environments in systems development.* Proceedings of CASE'89 the First Nordic Conference on Advanced Systems Engineering, Stockholm.

MacCormack, A. (2002) *Siemens ShareNet: Building a knowledge network.* Harvard Business School Publishing, Case 603036, Cambridge, MA.

MacCormack, A., Rusnak, J., & Baldwin, C.Y. (2006). Exploring the structure of complex software designs: An empirical study of open source and proprietary code. *Management Science, 52*(7), 1015–1030.

Madanmohan, T. R., & Navelkar, S. (2002). *Roles and Knowledge Management in Online Technology Communities: An Ethnography Study* (Working paper No. 192): IIMB.

Madill, A., Jordan, A., & Shirley, C. (2000). Objectivity and reliability in qualitative analysis: Realist, contextualist and radical constructionist epistemologies. *The British Journal of Psychology, 91*(1), 1–20. doi:10.1348/000712600161646

Mahadevan, B. (2000). Business models for Internet-based e-commerce: An anatomy. *California Management Review, 42*(4), 55–69.

Major, M., & McGregor, J. (1999). *Using Guided Inspection to Validate UML Models.* Paper presented at the 24th Annual IEEE/NASA Software Engineering Workshop.

Malloy, B., Kraft, N., Hallstrom, J., & Voas, J. (2006). Improving the predictable assembly of service oriented architectures. *IEEE Software, 23*(2), 12-15.

Malone, T. W., & Crowston, K. (1994). The interdisciplinary study of coordination. *Computing Surveys, 26*(1), 87–119.

Mantovani, F., Castelnuovo, G., Gaggioli, A., & Riva, G. (2003). Virtual reality training for health-care professionals. *CyberPscyhology & Behavior, 6*(4), 389–395. doi:10.1089/109493103322278772

Markides, C. (2006). Disruptive innovation: In need of better theory. *Journal of Product Innovation Management, 23*(1), 19–25. doi:10.1111/j.1540-5885.2005.00177.x

Markus, M. L., & Robey, D. (1988). Information technology and organizational change: Causal structure in theory and research. *Management Science, 34*(5), 583–598.

Markus, M. L., Manville, B., & Agres, E. C. (2000). What makes a virtual organization work? *Sloan Management Review, 42*(1), 13–26.

Marshall, C., & Rossman, B. G. (1989). *Designing Qualitative Research*, Thousand Oaks, CA: Sage Publications.

Martin, J. (1989). *Information engineering*: Prentice-Hall.

Martin, P. Y., & Turner, B. A. (1986). Grounded theory and organizational research. *The Journal of Applied Behavioral Science, 22*(2), 141-157.

Mason, H. (2007). Experiential education in Second Life. In *Proceedings of the Second Life Education Workshop 2007* (pp. 14-18). Retrieved May 28, 2008 from http://www.simteach.com/slccedu07proceedings.pdf.

Massey, A. P., Hung, Y.-T. C., Montoya-Weiss, M., & Ramesh, V. (2001). When culture and style aren't about clothes: Perceptions of task-technology "fit" in global virtual teams. In *Proceedings of GROUP '01.* Boulder, CO, USA.

Mayer, R. E. (1989). Models for Understanding. *Review of Educational Research, 59*(1), 43–64.

Mayer, R. E. (1996). Learning strategies for making sense out of expository text: The SOI model for guiding three cognitive processes in knowledge construction. *Educational Psychology Review, 8*(4), 357–371. doi:10.1007/BF01463939

Mayer, R. E. (2001). *Multimedia Learning*. New York: Cambridge University Press.

Mayer, R. E., & Moreno, R. (1998). A Split-Attention Effect in Multimedia Learning: Evidence for Dual Processing Systems in Working Memory. *Journal of Educational Psychology, 90*(4), 312–320. doi:10.1037/0022-0663.90.2.312

McCabe, T. (1976). A complexity measure. *IEEE Transactions on Software Engineering, 2*(4), 308–320.

McCann, J. E., & Ferry, D. L. (1979). An approach for assessing and managing inter-unit interdependence. *Academy of Management Review, 4*(1), 113–119.

McConnell, S. (1999). Open-source methodology: Ready for prime time? *IEEE Software, 16*(4), 6–8.

McMenamin, S. M., & Palmer, J. F. (1984). *Essential systems analysis*. Englewood Cliffs, NJ: Yourdon Press.

McMillan, R. (2002). Will Big Blue eclipse the Java tools market? [Electronic version]. *JavaWorld*. Retrieved January 27, 2006.

Medvidovic, N., & Taylor, R. N. (2000). A classification and comparison framework for software architecture description languages. *IEEE Transactions on Software Engineering, 26*(1), 70-93.

Medvidovic, N., Egyed, A., & Rosenblum, D. S. (1999). *Round-trip software engineering using UML: From architecture to design and back*. Proceedings of the 2nd Workshop on Object-Oriented Reengineering (WOOR), Toulouse, France, Sept. 1999, 1-8.

Meekel, J., Horton, T. B., France, R. B., Mellone, C., & Dalvi, S. (1997). From domain models to architecture frameworks. In *Proceedings of the 1997 symposium on Software reusability* (pp. 75-80).

Mello, R., & Heuser, C. (2001). A Rule-Based Conversion of a {DTD} to a Conceptual Schema (LNCS 2224).

Mennecke, B., McNeill, D., Ganis, M., & Roche, E. M. (2008). Second Life and other virtual worlds: A roadmap for research. *Communications of the Association for Information Systems, 22*, 371–388.

Mens, K., Wuyts, R., Bontridder, D., & Grijseels, A. (1998). *Tools and environments for business rules*. Paper presented at the ECOOP'98, Brussels, Belgium.

Merisalo-Rantanen, H., Tuunanen, T., & Rossi, M. (2005). Is extreme programming just old wine in new bottles: A comparison of two cases. *Journal of Database Management, 16*(4), 41–61.

MetaCase. (n.d.). *MetaCase: Domain-specific modeling with MetaEdit+*. Retrieved June 5, 2006, from http://www.metacase.com

Metamodel.com: Community site for meta-modeling and semantic modeling. (n.d.). Retrieved June 5, 2006, from http://www.metamodel.com

Metiu, A., & Kogut, B. (2001). *Distributed Knowledge and the Global Organization of Software Development* (Working paper). Philadelphia, PA: The Wharton School, University of Pennsylvania.

Mikropoulos, T. A. (2001). Brain activity on navigation in virtual environments. *Journal of Educational Computing Research, 24*(1), 1–12. doi:10.2190/D1W3-Y15D-4UDW-L6C9

Miles, M. B., & Huberman, A. M. (1994). *Qualitative data analysis: An expanded sourcebook* (2nd ed.). Thousand Oaks, CA: Sage.

Miller, G. A. (1956). The magical number seven, plus or minus two: some limits on our capacity for processing information. *Psychological Review*, 81–97. doi:10.1037/h0043158

Mills, H. D. (1971). *Chief programmer teams: Principles and procedures*. Report FSC 71-5108, IBM Federal Systems Division, USA.

Min, J. K., Ahn, J. Y., & Chung, C. W. (2003). Efficient extraction of schemas for XML documents. *Information Processing Letters, 85*(1). doi:10.1016/S0020-0190(02)00345-9

Minsky, N. H. (2003). On conditions for self-healing in distributed software systems. [Los Alamitos, CA: IEEE Computer Society.]. *Proceedings of AMS, 03*, 86–92.

Mintzberg, H. (1979). *The Structuring of Organizations*. Englewood Cliffs, NJ: Prentice-Hall.

Mockus, A., Fielding, R. T., & Herbsleb, J. D. (2002). Two case studies Of Open Source Software development: Apache And Mozilla. *ACM Transactions on Software Engineering and Methodology, 11*(3), 309–346.

Moh. C., Lim, e., & Ng, W. (2000). DTD-Miner: A tool for mining DTD from XML documents. In *Proceedings of the Second International Workshop on Advanced Issues of E-Commerce*.

Mohr, L. B. (1971). Organizational technology and organizational structure. *16*, 444–459.

Mohr, L. B. (1982). *Explaining Organizational Behavior: The Limits and Possibilities of Theory and Research*. San Francisco: Jossey-Bass.

Mok, A. K., Konana, P., Liu, G., Lee, C., & Woo, H. (2004). Specifying timing constraints and composite events: an application in the design of electronic brokerages. *IEEE Transactions on Software Engineering, 30*(12), 841–858. doi:10.1109/TSE.2004.105

Monroe, R. T., Kompanek, A., Melton, R., & Garlan, D. (1997). Architectural styles, design patterns, and objects. *IEEE Software, 14*(1), 43-52.

Moody, D. (1996). Graphical Entity Relationship models: Towards a more user understandable representation of data. *Conceptual Modeling ER '96* (LNCS 1157, pp. 227-244). Berlin / Heidelberg: Springer.

Moon, J. Y., & Sproull, L. (2000). Essence of distributed work: The case of Linux kernel. *First Monday, 5*(11).

Moore, A. (2001). Extending UML to Enable the Definition and Design of Real-Time Embedded Systems.

Crosstalk: The Journal of Defense Software Engineering, 14(6), 4–9.

Moore, G. (1999). *Crossing the Chasm*. New York: Harper-Perennial.

Moore, G. A. (2002). *Crossing the chasm: Marketing and selling high-tech products to mainstream customers* (revised edition). New York: HarperBusiness Essentials.

Moore, G. C., & Benbasat, I. (1991). Development of an instrument to measure the perceptions of adopting an information technology innovation. *Information Systems Research, 2*(3), 192–222. doi:10.1287/isre.2.3.192

Morgan, L., & Finnegan, P. (2007). Benefits and Drawbacks of Open Source Software: An Exploratory Study of Secondary Software Firms. In J. Feller, B. Fitzgerald, W. Scaachi, & A. Sillitti (Eds.), *IFIP International Federation for Information Processing, Volume 234, Open Source Development, Adoption and Innovation* (pp. 307-312). Boston, MA: Springer.

Moriaty, T. (1993). The next paradigm. *Database Programming and Design*.

Morisio, M., Romano, D., & Stamelos, I. (2002). Quality, productivity and learning in framework-based development: An exploratory case study. *IEEE Transactions on Software Engineering, 28*(8), 340–357.

Morton, A. (2005). *Lead Maintainer, Linux Production Kernel*. IT Conversations: SDForum Distinguished Speaker Series. Retrieved January 31, 2006.

Motro, A. (1990). FLEX: A Tolerant and Cooperative User Interface to Databases. *IEEE Transactions on Knowledge and Data Engineering, 2*(2), 231–246. doi:10.1109/69.54722

Mouratidis, K., Bakiras, S., & Papadias, D. (2006). Continuous monitoring of top-k queries over sliding windows. In *Proceedings of the 2006 ACM SIGMOD international conference on Management of data table of contents*, Chicago, IL, USA (pp. 635-646).

Murdoch, D. J., & Chow, E. D. (1996). A graphical display of large correlation matrices. *The American Statistician, 50*(2), 178–180.

Muslea, I. (2004). Machine Learning for Online Query Relaxation. In *Proceedings of the tenth ACM SIGKDD international conference on Knowledge discovery and data mining*, Seattle, Washington, USA (pp. 246-255).

Nah, F., Islam, Z., & Tan, M. (2007). Empirical assessment of factors influencing success of enterprise resource planning implementations. *Journal of Database Management, 18*(4), 26-50.

Nakatani, L. H., Ardis, M. A., Olsen, R. G., & Pontrelli, P. M. (1999). Jargons for domain engineering, In *Proceedings of the 2nd Conference on Domain-Specific Languages* (pp. 15-24).

Neighbors, J. (1989). Draco: A Method for Engineering Reusable Software Systems. In T. Biggerstaff & A. Perlis (Eds.), *Software Reusability. Volume I: Concepts and Models* (pp. 295-319). Reading, MA: ACM Press, Frontier Series, Addison-Wesley.

Nejmeh, B. A. (1994). Internet: A strategic tool for the software enterprise. *Communications of the ACM, 37*(11), 23–27.

Nelson, R. E. (1988). Social network analysis as intervention tool. *Group and Organisation Studies, 13*(1), 139–158.

Netcraft Inc. (2005). *October 2005 web server survey.* Retrieved December 5, 2006 from http://news.netcraft.com/archives/2005/10/04/october_2005_web_server_survey.html.

Neumann, C. (2002). *Jsp- und Servlet-basierte frameworks für Web-applikationen.* Master's Thesis, Universität Karlsruhe, Germany.

Ng, W., & Lau, H. L. (2005). Effective approaches for watermarking XML data. *International Conference on Database Systems for Advanced Applications* (pp. 68-80).

Niederman, F., Davis, A., Greiner, M., Wynn, D., & York, P. (2006). A research agenda for studying open source I: A multi-level framework. *Communications of the AIS, 18*(7), 2–38.

Nilakanta, S., Miller, L. L., & Zhu, D. (2006). Organizational memory management: Technological and research issues. *Journal of Database Management, 17*(1), 85–94.

Nobrega, L., Nunes, N. J., & Coelho, H. (2006, June). The meta sketch editor: A reflexive modeling editor. In G. Calvary, C. Pribeanu, G. Santucci, & J. Vanderdonckt (Eds.), *Computer-Aided Design of User Interfaces V: Proceedings of the Sixth International Conference on Computer-Aided Design of User Interfaces (CADUI 2006)* (pp. 199-212). Berlin, Germany: Springer-Verlag.

Nordstrom, G., Sztipanovits, J., Karsai, G., & Ledeczi, A. (1999). Metamodeling - Rapid Design and Evolution of Domain-Specific Modeling Environments. In *Proceedings of the IEEE Sixth Symposium on Engineering Computer-Based Systems (ECBS)* (pp. 68-74).

O'Leary, M., Orlikowski, W. J., & Yates, J. (2002). Distributed work over the centuries: Trust and control in the Hudson's Bay Company, 1670–1826. In P. Hinds & S. Kiesler (Eds.), *Distributed Work* (pp. 27–54). Cambridge, MA: MIT Press.

Object Management Group (OMG). (2007). Retrieved September 25, 2007, from http://colab.cim3.net/cgi-bin/wiki.pl?OMGSoaGlossary#nid34QI

Object Management Group. (1999). *UML Profile for Enterprise Distributed Object Computing: Request for Proposals (ad/99-03-10)*: OMG.

Object Management Group. (2005). *Unified modeling language: Superstructure version 2.0* (No. formal/05-07-04).

Object Management Group. (2006). *OMG SysML Specification (ptc/06-05-04).*

Object Management Group. (2009). *OMG Unified Modeling Language: Superstructure*, Version 2.2. Retrieved November 4, 2009 from http://www.omg.org/spec/UML/2.2/Superstructure/PDF/

Odell, J., Van Dyke, P., & Bauer, B. (2000). Extending UML for Agents. In *Proceedings of the Agent-Oriented Information Systems Workshop at the 17th National conference on Artificial Intelligence*, Austin, Texas (pp. 3-17).

Oliver, C. (1990). Determinants of interorganisational relationships: Integration and future directions. *Academy of Management Review, 15*(2), 241–265. doi:10.2307/258156

OMG (Cartographer). (2001). *Omg unified modeling language specification*

OMG (Cartographer). (2002). *Software process engineering metamodel specification*

OMG-MOF (2003). Meta-Object Facility (MOF™), version 1.4.

OMG-UML (2003). The Unified Modeling Language (UML™), version 1.5.

OMG-UML (2006). UML 2.0 Superstructure, 2006.

Ondrejka, C. (2008). Education unleashed: Participatory culture, education, and innovation in *Second Life*. In K. Salen (Ed.), *The Ecology of Games: Connecting Youth, Games, and Learning, The John D. and Catherine T. MacArthur Foundation Series on Digital Media and Learning* (pp. 229-252). Cambridge, MA: The MIT Press.

Opdahl, A. L., & Henderson-Sellers, B. (2001). Grounding the OML metamodel in ontology. *Journal of Systems and Software, 57*, 119–143. doi:10.1016/S0164-1212(00)00123-0

Open Group. (2007). Retrieved September 25, 2007, from http://opengroup.org/projects/soa/doc.tpl?gdid=10632

Oreizy, P., Medvidovic, N., & Taylor, R. N. (1998, April 19-25). *Architecture-based runtime software evolution.* Paper presented at the International Conference on Software Engineering 1998 (ICSE'98), Kyoto, Japan.

Organization for the Advancement of Structured Information Standards (OASIS). (2006). Retrieved September 25, 2007, from http://www.oasis-open.org/committees/tc_home.php?wg_abbrev=soa-rm

Orlikowski, W. J. (2002). Knowing in practice: Enacting a collective capability in distributed organizing. *Organization Science, 13*(3), 249–273.

Osterwalder, A., & Pigneur, Y. (2002, June 17–19). An e-business model ontology for modelling ebusiness. In *Proceedings of the 15th Bled eCommerce Conference,* Bled, Slovenia.

Osterwalder, A., Ben Lagha, S., & Pigneur, Y. (2002, July 3–7). An ontology for developing e-business models. In *Proceedings of IFIP DSIAge 2002,* Cork, Ireland.

OWL. (2008). Web Ontology Language (OWL). Retrieved December 20, 2008 from http://www.w3.org/TR/owl-features/

Paas, F., Renkl, A., & Sweller, J. (2003). Cognitive load theory and instructional design: Recent developments. *Educational Psychologist, 38*(1), 1–4. doi:10.1207/S15326985EP3801_1

Paas, F., Tuovinen, J. E., Tabbers, H., & Van Gerven, P. W. M. (2003). Cognitive Load Measurement as a Means to Advance Cognitive Load Theory. *Educational Psychologist, 38*(1), 63–71. doi:10.1207/S15326985EP3801_8

Päivärinta, T., Halttunen, V., & Tyrväinen, P. (2001). A genre-based method for information system planning. In M. Rossi & K. Siau (Eds.), *Information modeling in the new millennium* (pp. 70-93). Hershey, PA: Idea Group.

Paivio, A. (1986). *Mental Representations: A Dual Coding Approach.* Oxford, UK: Oxford University Press.

Paivio, A. (1991). Dual coding theory: Retrospect and current status. *Canadian Journal of Psychology, 45*(3), 255–287. doi:10.1037/h0084295

Park, P. (1992). *Software size measurement: A framework for counting source statements.* Technical Report CMU/SEI-92-TR-20, Software Engineering Institute, Carnegie Mellon University, USA.

Park, S., Nah, F., DeWester, D., Eschenbrenner, B., & Jeon, S. (2008). Virtual world affordances: Enhancing brand value. *Journal of Virtual Worlds Research, 1*(2), 1–18.

Parker, G. G., & Van Alstyne, M. W. (2005). Two-sided network effects: A theory of information product design. *Management Science, 51*(10), 1494–1504. doi:10.1287/mnsc.1050.0400

Parnas, D. L. (1972). On the criteria to be used in decomposing systems into modules. *Communications of the ACM, 15*(2), 1053–1058.

Passig, D., Klein, P., & Noyman, T. (2001). Awareness of toddler's initial cognitive experiences with virtual reality. *Journal of Computer Assisted Learning, 17*, 332–344. doi:10.1046/j.0266-4909.2001.00190.x

Patton, M. Q. (1980). *Qualitative evaluation and research methods*. Newbury Park, CA: Sage Publications.

Payne, A., & Frow, P. (2005). A strategic framework for customer relationship management. *Journal of Marketing, 69*(4), 167–176. doi:10.1509/jmkg.2005.69.4.167

Payne, C. (2002). On the security of open source software. *Information Systems Journal, 12*(1), 61–78.

Pears, R., & Houliston, B. (2007). Optimization of multidimensional aggregates in data warehouses. *Journal of Database Management, 18*(1), 69-93.

Perens, B. (1999). The open source definition. In C. DiBona, S. Ockman, & M. Stone (Eds.), *Open sources: Voices from the open source revolution* (pp. 171–188). Cambridge, MA: O'Reilly & Associates.

Peterson, M. (2006). Learner interaction management in an avatar and chat-based virtual world. *Computer Assisted Language Learning, 19*(1), 79–103. doi:10.1080/09588220600804087

Pfaff, B. (1998). Society and open source: Why open source software is better for society than proprietary closed source software. from http://www.msu.edu/user/pfaffben/writings/anp/oss-is-better.html

Pfeffer, J. (1978). *Organizational Design*. Arlington Heights, IL: Harlan Davidson.

Pfeffer, J., & Salancik, G. R. (1978). *The External Control of Organizations: A Resource Dependency Perspective*. New York: Harper & Row.

Phillips, L.W. (1981). Assessing measurement error in key informant reports: A methodological note on organizational analysis in marketing. *Journal of Marketing Research, 18*(4), 395–415.

Pohl, K., Gunter, B., & van der Linden, F. (2005). *Software Product Line Engineering – Foundations, Principles, and Techniques*. Springer.

Pons, A. P., & Aljifri, H. (2003). Data protection using watermarking in e-business. *Journal of Database Management, 14*(4), 1-13.

Poston, R., & Grabski, S. (2001). Financial impacts of enterprise resource planning implementations. *International Journal of Accounting Information Systems, 2*(4), 271–294. doi:10.1016/S1467-0895(01)00024-0

Prasad, G. C. (n.d.). A hard look at Linux's claimed strengths…. from http://www.osopinion.com/Opinions/GaneshCPrasad/GaneshCPrasad2-2.html

Prieto-Diaz, R. (1990). Domain analysis: an introduction. *ACM SIGSOFT Software Engineering Notes, 15*(2), 47–54. doi:10.1145/382296.382703

Prieto-Diaz, R. (1993). Status report: Software reusability. *IEEE Software, 10*(3), 61–66.

Rai, A., Ravichandran, T., & Samaddar, S. (1998). How to anticipate the Internet's global diffusion. *Communications of the ACM, 41*(10), 97–106. doi:10.1145/286238.286253

Rational Software Corporation. (2001). Rational Unified Process [Online documentation, Version 2001A.04.00].

Ravichandran, T. (2005). Organizational assimilation of complex technologies: An empirical study of component-based software development. *IEEE Transactions on Engineering Management, 52*(2), 249–268. doi:10.1109/TEM.2005.844925

Raymond, E. S. (1998). The cathedral and the bazaar. *First Monday, 3*(3).

Raymond, E. S. (2001). *The Cathedral and the Bazaar* (2nd Ed.). Sebastopol, CA: O'Reilly.

Raymond, E.S. (1999). *The cathedral and the bazaar: Musings on Linux and open source by an accidental revolutionary.* Sebastopol, CA: O'Reilly & Associates.

Reid, R., & Dhillon, G. (2003). Integrating digital signatures with relational databases: Issues and organizational implications. *Journal of Database Management, 14*(2), 42-51.

Reinhartz-Berger, I., Soffer, P., & Sturm, A. (2005). A Domain Engineering Approach to Specifying and Applying Reference Models. In *Proceedings of Enterprise Modeling Information Systems Architecture (EMISA'05)* (pp. 50-63).

Relaxng (2003). RELAX NG. Retrieved from http://www.relaxng.org/

Ricadela, A. (2006, September 4). The dark side of SOA. *Information Week*, pp. 54-58.

Richter, J., Anderson-Inman, L., & Frisbee, M. (2007). Critical engagement of teachers in Second Life: Progress in the SaLamander project. In *Proceedings of the Second Life Education Workshop 2007* (pp. 19-26). Retrieved May 28, 2008 from http://www.simteach.com/slccedu-07proceedings.pdf.

Riehle, D., Tilman, M., & Johnson, R. (2000). *Dynamic object model* (No. WUCS-00-29): Dept. of Computer Science, Washington University.

Riemenschneider, C. K., Hardgrave, B. C., & Davis, F. D. (2002). Explaining software developer acceptance of methodologies: A comparison of five theoretical models. *IEEE Transactions on Software Engineering, 28*(12), 1135–1145. doi:10.1109/TSE.2002.1158287

Riemenschneider, C.K., Harrison, D.A. & Mykytyn, P.P. Jr. (2003). Understanding IT adoption decisions in small business: Integrating current theories. *Information & Management, 40*(4), 269–285.

Robey, D., & Boudreau, M. (1999). Accounting for the contradictory organizational consequences of information technology: Theoretical directions and methodological implications. *Information Systems Research, 10*(2), 167–185. doi:10.1287/isre.10.2.167

Robey, D., Khoo, H. M., & Powers, C. (2000). Situated-learning in cross-functional virtual teams. *IEEE Transactions on Professional Communication*(Feb/Mar), 51–66.

Robinson, K., & Berrisford, G. (1994). *Object-oriented ssadm*. Englewood Cliffs, NJ: Prentice Hall.

Robles-Martinez, G., Gonzalez-Barahona, J.M., Centeno-Gonzalez, J., Matellan-Olivera, V., & Rodero-Merino, L. (2003). Studying the evolution of libre software projects using publicly available data. *Proceedings of the 3rd Workshop on Open Source Software Engineering 25th International Conference on Software Engineering* (pp. 111–115), Portland, OR.

Robson, C. (2002). *Real world research, (2ⁿᵈ ed.)*. Blackwell Publishing.

Rockwell, S., & Bajaj, A. (2005). COGEVAL: Applying Cognitive Theories to Evaluate Conceptual Models. In K. Siau (Ed.), *Advanced Topics in Database Research* (Vol. 4). Hershey, PA: Idea Group Publishing.

Rogers, E. M. (1995). *Diffusion of innovations* (4ᵗʰ ed.). New York, NY: The Free Press.

Rosca, D., Greenspan, S., & Wild, C. (2002). Enterprise modeling and decision-support for automating the business rules lifecycle. *Automated Software Engineering, 9*(4), 361 - 404.

Rosca, D., Greenspan, S., Feblowitz, M., & Wild, C. (1997, January 1997). *A decision support methodology in support of the business rules lifecycle*. Paper presented at the International Symposium on Requirements Engineering (ISRE'97), Annapolis, MD.

Rosca, D., Greenspan, S., Wild, C., Reubenstein, H., Maly, K., & Feblowitz, M. (1995, November 1995). *Application of a decision support mechanism to the business rules lifecycle*. Paper presented at the 10th Knowledge-Based Software Engineering Conference (KBSE95), Boston, MA.

Ross, J. W., Weill, P., & Robertson, D. C. (2006). *Enterprise architecture as strategy: Creating a foundation for business execution*: Harvard Business School Press.

Ross, R. G. (1997). *The business rule book: Classifying, defining and modelling rules*: Data Base Newsletter.

Ross, R. G., & Lam, G. S. W. (1999). *Ruletrack: The brs meta-model for rule management*: Business Rule Solutions, Inc.

Ross, R. G., & Lam, G. S. W. (2003). *The brs proteus™ methodology* (Fourth ed.): Business Rule Solutions.

Rossi, G., & Schwabe, D. (2000). Object-oriented web applications modeling. In M. Rossi & K. Siau (Eds.), *Information modelling in the next millennium*. Hershey: IDEA Group Publishing.

Rouvellou, I., Degenaro, I., Rasmus, K., Ehnebuske, D., & McKee, B. (1999, November 1-5). *Externalizing business rules from enterprise applications: An experience report*. Paper presented at the Conference on Object-Oriented Programming, Systems, Languages, and Applications, Denver, Colorado.

Rouvellou, I., Degenaro, L., Rasmus, K., Ehnebuske, D., & McKee, B. (2000, June). *Extending business objects with business rules*. Paper presented at the 33rd International Conference on Technology of Object-Oriented Languages and Systems (TOOLS Europe 2000), Mont Saint-Michel/ St-Malo, France.

Rumbaugh, J., Blaha, M., Premerlani, W., Eddy, F., & Lorensen, W. (1991). *Object-Oriented Modeling and Design*. Englewood Cliffs, NJ: Prentice Hall.

Rumpe, B., Schoenmakers, M., Radermacher, A., & Schürr, A. (1999). *UML + ROOM as a Standard ADL*. Fifth IEEE International Conference on Engineering of Complex Computer Systems, (pp. 43-53).

S"oderstrom, E., Andersso, B., Johannesson, P., Perjons, E., & Wangler, B. (2002, May). Towards a framework for comparing process modelling languages. In *CAiSE '02: Proceedings of the 14ᵗʰ International Conference on Advanced Information Systems Engineering* (pp. 600-611). London: Springer-Verlag. Retrieved June 21, 2006, from http://portal.acm.org/citation.cfm?coll=GUIDE&dl=GUIDE&id=680389#

Saaren-Seppälä, K. (1988). *Wall chart technique: The use of wall charts for effective planning*. Helsinki: Kari Saaren-Seppälä Ky.

Sabherwal, R., & Robey, D. (1995). Reconciling variance and process strategies for studying information system development. *Information Systems Research, 6*(4), 303–327.

Sadeh, N. M., Hildum, D. W., & Kjenstad, D. (2003). Agent-based e-supply chain decision support. *Journal of Organizational Computing and Electronic Commerce, 13*(3-4), 225–241. doi:10.1207/S15327744JOCE133&4_05

Safavi-Naini, R., & Wang, Y. (2001). Collusion secure q-ary fingerprinting for perceptual content. *Digital Rights Management Workshop* (pp. 57-75).

Sahuguet, A. (2000). Everything You Ever Wanted to Know About DTDs, But Were Afraid to Ask. *Web-DB-2000*.

Samoladas, I., Stamelos, I., Angelis, L., & Oikonomou, A. (2004). Open source software development should strive for even greater code maintainability. *Communications of the ACM, 47*(10), 83–87.

Sandusky, R. J., Gasser, L., & Ripoche, G. (2004). *Bug Report Networks: Varieties, Strategies, and Impacts in an OSS Development Community*. Paper presented at the Proceedings of the ICSE Workshop on Mining Software Repositories, Edinburgh, Scotland, UK.

Sauer, C., Southon, G., & Dampney, C. N. G. (1997). *Fit, failure, and the house of horrors: Toward a configurational theory of IS project failure*. Proceedings of the eighteenth international conference on Information systems, (pp. 349-366). Atlanta, Georgia.

Sawyer, S., & Guinan, P. J. (1998). Software development: Processes and performance. *IBM Systems Journal, 37*(4), 552–568.

Scacchi, W. (1991). The software infrastructure for a distributed software factory. *Software Engineering Journal, 6*(5), 355–369.

Scacchi, W. (2002). Understanding the requirements for developing Open Source Software systems. *IEE Proceedings Software, 149*(1), 24–39.

Scacchi, W. (2005). Socio-technical interaction networks in Free/Open Source Software development processes. In S. T. Acuña & N. Juristo (Eds.), *Software Process Modeling* (pp. 1–27). New York: Springer.

Schleicher, A., & Westfechtel, B. (2001). Beyond Stereotyping: Metamodeling Approaches for the UML, In

Proceedings of the 34th Annual Hawaii International Conference on System Sciences (pp.1243-1252).

Schmidt, D. C. (2006, February). Guest editor's introduction: Model-driven engineering. *Computer, 39*(2), 25-31. Retrieved June 5, 2006, from http://doi.ieeecomputersociety.org/10.1109/MC.2006.58

Schmidt, M., Hutchison, B., Lambros, P., & Phippen, R. (2005). Enterprise service bus: Making service oriented architecture real. *IBM Systems Journal, 44*(4), 781-797.

Schneider, G., & Winters, J. (2001). *Applying Use Cases: A Practical Guide* (2nd ed.). Boston: Addison-Wesley.

Schneider, J. (1999). *Components, scripts, and glue : A conceptual framework for software composition.* Bern:University of Bern.

Schultze, U., Hiltz, S. R., Nardi, B., Rennecker, J., & Stucky, S. (2008). Using synthetic worlds for work and learning. *Communications of the Association for Information Systems, 22*, 351–370.

Schwebel, D., Gaines, J., & Severson, J. (2008). Validation of virtual reality as a tool to understand and prevent child pedestrian injury. *Accident; Analysis and Prevention, 40*(4), 1394–1400. doi:10.1016/j.aap.2008.03.005

Second Life. (2008). Retrieved on April 23, 2008 from www.secondlife.com.

SEI-CMU. (2008). *A Framework for Software Product Line Practice, Version 5.0.* Retrieved from http://www.sei.cmu.edu/productlines/framework.html

Selic, B. (2006). UML 2: A model driven development tool. *IBM Systems Journal, 45*(3), 607–620.

Selonen, P., Koskimies, K., & Sakkinen, M. (2003). Transformations between UML diagrams. *Journal of Database Management , 14*(3), 37-55.

Seufert, T., Jänen, I., & Brünken, R. (2007). The impact of intrinsic cognitive load on the effectiveness of graphical help for coherence formation. *Computers in Human Behavior, 23*(3), 1055–1071. doi:10.1016/j.chb.2006.10.002

Shaft, T. M., & Vessey, I. (1995). The Relevance of Application Domain Knowledge: The Case of Computer Program Comprehension. *Information Systems Research, 6*(3), 286–299. doi:10.1287/isre.6.3.286

Shah, A., & Kalin, P. (2007, July 6). SOA adoption models: Ad-hoc versus program-based. *SOA Magazine.*

Shan, T., & Hua, W. (2006). Service oriented solution framework for Internet banking. *Internet Journal of Web Services Research, 3*(1), 29-48.

Shanks, G. (1997). Conceptual Data Modelling: An Empirical Study of Expert and Novice Data Modellers. *Australian Journal of Information Systems, 4*(2), 63–73.

Shanmugasundaram, J., Shekita, E., Kiernan, J., Krishnamurthy, R., Viglas, E., Naughton, J., et al. (2008). *Shematron.* Retrieved from http://www.schematron.com

Shapiro, C., & Varian, H. R. (1999). *Information rules: A strategic guide to the network economy.* Cambridge, MA: Harvard Business School Press.

Sharifi, H., & Zhang, Z. (1999). A methodology for achieving agility in manufacturing organisations: An introduction. *International Journal of Production Economics, 62*(1-2), 7–22. doi:10.1016/S0925-5273(98)00217-5

Shaw, M., & Garlan, D. (1996). *Software architecture: Perspectives on an emerging discipline*: Prentice Hall.

Shin, M., Huh, S., Park, D., & Lee, W. (2008). Relaxing Queries with Hierarchical Quantified Data Abstraction. *Journal of Database Management, 19*(4), 76–90.

Shiren, Y., Xiujun, G., Zhongzhi, S., & Bing, W. (2001). Tree's Drawing Algorithm and Visualizing Method. In *CAD/Graphics'2001.*

Shiu, H. (2006). *Reverse Engineering Data Semantics from Arbitrary XML document.* Unpublished master's thesis, City University of Hong Kong, Hong Kong, China.

Shull, F., Rus, I., & Basili, V. (2000). How Perspective-Based Reading Can Improve Requirements Inspections. *IEEE Computer, 33*(7), 73–79.

Siau, K., & Cao, Q. (2001). Unified modeling language: A complexity analysis. *Journal of Database Management, 12*(1), 26-34.

Siau, K., & Cao, Q. (2002). How Complex Is the Unified Modeling Language? *Advanced Topics in Database Research, 1*, 294–306.

Siau, K. (2003). Evaluating the usability of a group support system using co-discovery. *Journal of Computer Information Systems, 44*(2), 17–28.

Siau, K. (2003). Interorganizational systems and competitive advantages: Lessons from history. *Journal of Computer Information Systems, 44*(1), 33-39.

Siau, K., & Shen, Z. (2003). Building customer trust in mobile commerce. *Communications of the ACM, 46*(4), 91–94. doi:10.1145/641205.641211

Siau, K. (2004). Informational and computational equivalence in comparing information modeling methods. *Journal of Database Management, 15*(1), 73–86.

Siau, K. (2005). Human-computer interaction: The effect of application domain knowledge on icon visualization. *Journal of Computer Information Systems, 45*(3), 53–62.

Siau, K., & Loo, P.Identifying Difficulties in Learning UML. *Information Systems Management, 23*(3), 43–51. doi:10.1201/1078.10580530/46108.23.3.20060601/93706.5

Siau, K., & Tian, Y. (2004). Supply chains integration: Architecture and enabling technologies. *Journal of Computer Information Systems, 44*(3), 67-72.

Siau, K., Chan, H., & Wei, K. (2004). Effects of Query Complexity and Learning on Novice User Query Performance with Conceptual and Logical Database Interfaces. *IEEE Transactions on Systems, Man, and Cybernetics. Part A, Systems and Humans, 34*(2), 276–281. doi:10.1109/TSMCA.2003.820581

Siau, K., Erickson, J., & Lee, L. Y. (2005). Theoretical vs. practical complexity: The case of UML. *Journal of Database Management, 16*(3), 40-57.

Siau, K., Erickson, J., & Lee, L. Y. (2005). Theoretical vs. Practical Complexity: The Case of UML. *Journal of Database Management, 16*(3), 40–57.

Siau, K., Nah, F., Eschenbrenner, B., & Guru, A. (2007). An augmented approach to support collaborative distance learning of unified modeling language. *Americas Conference on Information Systems (AMCIS 2007)*, Colorado, USA.

Siau, K., Sheng, H., & Nah, F. (2006). Use of a classroom response system to enhance classroom interactivity. *IEEE Transactions on Education, 49*(3), 398–403. doi:10.1109/TE.2006.879802

Siau, K., Sheng, H., Nah, F., & Davis, S. (2004). A qualitative investigation on consumer trust in mobile commerce. *International Journal of Electronic Business, 2*(3), 283–300. doi:10.1504/IJEB.2004.005143

Silva, A., & Videira, C. (2005). *UML, metodologias e ferramentas CASE* (Vol. 2, 2nd ed.). Portugal: Centro Atlântico.

Singer, J., & Vinson, N. G. (2002). Ethical Issues in Empirical Studies of Software Engineering. *IEEE Transactions on Software Engineering, 28*(12), 1171–1180. doi:10.1109/TSE.2002.1158289

Sion, R. (2004). Proving ownership over categorical data. *Proceedings of IEEE International Conference on Data Engineering (ICDE)* (pp. 584-596).

Sion, R., Atallah, M., & Prabhakar, S. (2003). Rights protection for relational data. *Proceedings of ACM SIGMOD International Conference on Management of Data* (pp. 98-108).

Smolander, K. (2003, January 6-9,). *The birth of an e-business system architecture: Conflicts, compromises, and gaps in methods.* Hawaii International Conference on System Sciences (HICSS'36), Hilton Waikoloa Village, Big Island, Hawaii.

Smolander, K., & Päivärinta, T. (2002, May 27 - 31). *Describing and communicating software architecture in practice: Observations on stakeholders and rationale.* Proceedings of CAiSE'02 - The Fourteenth International Conference on Advanced Information Systems Engineering, (pp. 117-133).Toronto, Canada.

Smolander, K., & Päivärinta, T. (2002, Aug 25-30). *Practical rationale for describing software architecture: Beyond programming-in-the-large.* Software Architecture:

System Design, Development and Maintenance - IFIP 17th World Computer Congress - TC2 Stream / 3rd Working IEEE/IFIP Conference on Software Architecture (WICSA3), (pp. 113-126). Montréal, Québec, Canada.

Smolander, K., Hoikka, K., Isokallio, J., Kataikko, M., & Mäkelä, T. (2002, April, 8-11). *What is included in software architecture? A case study in three software organizations.* Proceedings of 9th annual IEEE International Conference and Workshop on the Engineering of Computer-Based Systems (pp. 131-138). (ECBS) 2002, Lund, Sweden.

Smolander, K., Rossi, M., & Purao, S. (2002, December 18). *Software architecture: Metaphors across contexts.* AIS Theory Development Workshop, Barcelona.

Smolander, K., Rossi, M., & Purao, S. (2005, May 26-28). *Going beyond the blueprint: Unraveling the complex reality of software architectures.* 13th European Conference on Information Systems: Information Systems in a Rapidly Changing Economy, Regensburg, Germany.

Snijders, T.A.B., & Bosker, R.J. (2003). *Multilevel analysis: An introduction to basic and advanced multilevel modeling.* London: Sage.

SOA. (2007). *Wikipedia.* Retrieved September 25, 2007, from http://en.wikipedia.org/wiki/Service-oriented_architecture#SOA_definitions

Soffer, P., Reinhartz-Berger, I., & Sturm, A. (2007). *Facilitating Reuse by Specialization of Reference Models for Business Process Design.* Accepted to the 8th Workshop on Business Process Modeling, Development, and Support (BPMDS'07), in conjunction with CAiSE'07.

Sowa, J. F., & Zachman, J. A. (1992). Extending and formalizing the framework for information systems architecture. *IBM Systems Journal, 31*(3), 590-616.

SparxSystems. (n.d.). *Enterprise architect: UML design tools and UML CASE tools for software development.* Retrieved June 5, 2006, from http://www.sparxsystems.com/ products/ea.html

Sperberg-McQueen, C., & Thompson, H. (2000). *W3C XML schema.* Retrieved from http://www.w3.org/XML/Schema

Spiller, D., & Wichmann, T. (2002). *Basics of Open Source Software markets and business models. FLOSS Final Report - Part 3.* Berlin: Berlecon Research.

Stabell, C. B., & Fjeldstad, O. D. (1998). Configuring value for competitive advantage: On chains, shops, and networks. *Strategic Management Journal, 19*(5), 413–437. doi:10.1002/(SICI)1097-0266(199805)19:5<413::AID-SMJ946>3.0.CO;2-C

Stafford, T. (2002). Trust, transactions, and relational exchange: Virtual integration and agile supply chain management. In *Proceedings of the 8th Americas Conference on Information Systems (AMCIS 02).*

Stal, M. (2006). Using architectural patterns and blueprints for service oriented architecture. *IEEE Software, 23*(2), 54-61.

Stallman, R.M. (2002). *Free software, free society: Selected essays of Richard M. Stallman.* Boston: GNU Press.

Stamelos, I., Angelis, L., Oikonomou, A., & Bleris, G.L. (2002). Code quality analysis in open source software development. *Information Systems Journal, 12*(1), 43–60.

Star, S. L., & Griesemer, J. R. (1989). Institutional cology, "translations" and boundary objects: Amateurs and professionals in berkeley's museum of vertebrate zoology, 1907-39. *Social Studies of Science, 19*, 387-420.

Stayton, B. (2008). *DocBook.* Retrieved from http://www.docbook.org

Sternberg, R.J. (2000). Images of mindfulness. *Journal of Social Issues, 56*(1), 11–26.

Stevens, P., & Pooley, R. (2000). *Using UML: Software Engineering with Object and Components.* Reading, MA: Addison-Wesley.

Stewart, K. J., & Ammeter, T. (2002). An exploratory study of factors influencing the level of vitality and popularity of open source projects. In *Proceedings of the Twenty-Third International Conference on Information Systems* (pp. 853–857).

Stewart, K.J., & Gosain, S. (2006). The impact of ideology on effectiveness in open source software development teams. *MIS Quarterly, 30*(2), 291–314.

Stoerger, S. (2008). Virtual worlds, virtual literacy: An educational exploration. *Knowledge Quest, 36*(3), 50–56.

Strauss, A. L., & Corbin, J. (1990). *Basics of qualitative research: Grounded theory procedures and applications.* Newbury Park, CA: Sage Publications.

Sturm, A., Dori, D., & Shehory, O. (2006). Domain Modeling with Object-Process Methodology, In *Proceedings of the Eighth International Conference on Enterprise Information Systems, ICEIS (3)* (pp. 144-151).

Subramanian, G., & Corbin, W. (2001). An empirical study of certain object-oriented software metrics. *Journal of Systems and Software, 59*(1), 57–63.

Subramanyam, R., & Krishnan, M.S. (2003). Empirical analysis of ck metrics for object-oriented design complexity: Implications for software defects. *IEEE Transactions on Software Engineering, 29*(4), 297–309.

Sulkin, A. (2007). SOA and enterprise voice communications. *Business Communications Review, 37*(8), 32-34.

Sunye, G., Pollet, D., Le Taraon, Y., & Jezkel, J.-M. (2001). Refactoring UML models. In *Proceedings of UML 2001* (LNCS 2185, pp. 134-148).

Swanson, E.B., & Ramiller, N.C. (2004). Innovating mindfully with information technology. *MIS Quarterly, 28*(4), 553–583.

Sweller, J. (1988). Cognitive load during problem solving: Effects on learning. *Cognitive Science, 12*(2), 257–285.

Sweller, J., & Chandler, P. (1994). Why Some Material Is Difficult to Learn. *Cognition and Instruction, 12*(3), 185–223.

Tapscott, D., Ticoll, D., & Lowy, A. (2000). *Digital capital: Harnessing the power of business webs.* Cambridge, MA: Harvard Business School Press.

Tatarinov, I. (2001). A general technique for querying XML documents using a relational database system. *SIGMOD Record, 30*(3), 261–270.

Taylor, M. J., McWilliam, J., Forsyth, H., & Wade, S. (2002). Methodologies and website development: A survey of practice. *Information and Software Technology, 44*(6), 381-391.

Taylor, P. (1998, December 2). New IT mantra attracts a host of devotees. *Financial Times, Survey—Indian Information Technology,* p. 1.

Taylor, S., & Todd, P. A. (1995). Understanding information technology usage: A test of competing models. *Information Systems Research, 6*(2), 144–176. doi:10.1287/isre.6.2.144

Tellis, G. J. (2006). Disruptive technology or visionary leadership? *Journal of Product Innovation Management, 23*(1), 34–38. doi:10.1111/j.1540-5885.2005.00179.x

Tersus (2006). Retrieved from http://www.tersus.com

Thiran, P. H., & Estiévenart, F. Hainaut. J.L., & Houben, G.J. (2004). Exporting Databases in XML - A Conceptual and Generic Approach. In *Proceedings of CAiSE Workshops (WISM'04).*

Thomas, D. (2004, May-June). MDA: Revenge of the modelers or UML utopia? *IEEE Software, 21*(3), 15-17. Retrieved June 5, 2006, from http://doi.ieeecomputersociety.org/10.1109/MS.2004.1293067

Thomke, E., & Reinertsen, D. G. (1998). Agile product development: Managing development flexibility in uncertain environments. *California Management Review, 41*(1), 8–30.

Thompson, J. D. (1967). *Organizations in Action: Social Science Bases of Administrative Theory.* New York: McGraw-Hill.

Thuraisingham, B. (2005). Privacy-preserving data mining: Development and directions. *Journal of Database Management, 16*(1), 75–87.

Ticoll, D., Lowy, A., & Kalakota, R. (1998). Joined at the bit: The emergence of the e-business community. In Tapscott, D. (Ed.) *Blueprint to the digital economy: Creating wealth in the era of e-business,* New York: McGraw-Hill.

Timmers, P. (1999). *Electronic Commerce: Strategies and models for business-to-business trading*, Chichester: Wiley.

Tingling, P., & Parent, M. (2002). Mimetic isomorphism and technology evaluation: Does imitation transcend judgment? *Journal of the Association for Information Systems, 3*(5), 113–143.

Tobin, D. (1996). *Transformational Learning: Renewing Your Company through Knowledge and Skills.* New York: John Wiley & Sons.

Tolvanen, J.-P., & Rossi, M. (2003, October). MetaEdit+: Defining and using domain-specific modeling languages and code generators. In *OOPSLA '03: Companion of the 18th Annual ACM SIGPLAN Conference on Object-Oriented Programming, Systems, Languages, and Applications* (pp. 92-93). New York: ACM Press. Retrieved June 5, 2006, from http://doi.acm.org/10.1145/949344.949365

TOPCASED. (2008). Retrieved from http://topcased.gforge.enseeiht.fr/

Topi, H., & Ramesh, V. (2002). Human Factors Research on Data Modeling: A Review of Prior Research, An Extended Framework and Future Research Directions. *Journal of Database Management, 13*(2), 3–19.

Torvalds, L. (1999). The Linux edge. *Communications of the ACM, 42*(4), 38–39.

Trembly, A. (2007). SOA: Savior or snake oil? *National Underwriter Life & Health, 111*(27), 50.

Trujillo, J., & Luján-Mora, S. (2004). Applying UML and XML for Designing and Interchanging Information for Data Warehouses and OLAP Applications. *Journal of Database Management, 15*(1), 41–72.

Tseng, S., Wang, K., & Lee, C. (2003). A pre-processing method to deal with missing values by integrating clustering and regression techniques. *Applied Artificial Intelligence, 17*(5/6), 535–544. doi:10.1080/713827170

Turk, D., France. R., & Rumpe, B. (2005). Assumptions underlying agile software-development processes. *Journal of Database Management, 16*(4), 62–87.

Tushman, M.L., & Scanlan, T.J. (1981). Characteristics and external orientations of boundary spanning individuals. *Academy of Management Journal, 24*(1), 83–98.

UNL-IBM System in Global Innovation Hub. (2007). *Making SOA relevant for business.* Retrieved October 9, 2007, from http://cba.unl.edu/outreach/unl-ibm/documents/SOA_Relevant_Business.pdf

Vaas, L. (2003, September 24). Putting a stop to database piracy. *eWeek: Enterprise News and Reviews.* Retrieved from http://www.eweek.com/print_article/0,3084,a=107965,00.asp

Valerio, A., Giancarlo, S., & Massimo, F. (1997). Domain analysis and framework-based software development. *ACM SIGAPP Applied Computing Review, 5*(2), 4–15. doi:10.1145/297075.297081

Valloppillil, V. (1998). Halloween I: Open Source Software. from http://www.opensource.org/halloween/halloween1.html

Valloppillil, V., & Cohen, J. (1998). Halloween II: Linux OS Competitive Analysis. from http://www.opensource.org/halloween/halloween2.html

van Assche, F., Layzell, P. J., Loucopoulos, P., & Speltinex, G. (1988). *Rubric: A rule-based representation of information system constructs.* Paper presented at the ESPRIT Conference, Brussels, Belgium.

Van de Ven, A. H. (1976). On the nature, formation and maintenance of relations among organisations. *Academy of Management Review, 1*(4), 24–36. doi:10.2307/257722

van der Spek, R., & Spijkervet, A. (1997). Knowledge management: dealing intelligently with knowledge. In Liebowitz & Wilcox (Eds.), *Knowledge Management and Its Integrative Elements.* Boca Raton, FL: CRC Press.

Ven, K., & Mannaert, H. (2008). Challenges and strategies in the use of open source software by independent software vendors. *Information and Software Technology, 50*(9), 991–1002. doi:10.1016/j.infsof.2007.09.001

Verheecke, B., Vanderperren, W., & Jonckers, V. (2006). Unraveling crosscutting concerns in Web services middleware. *IEEE Software, 23*(1), 42-50.

Vessey, I. (1991). Cognitive Fit: A Theory-Based Analysis of the Graphs Versus Tables Literature. *Decision Sciences, 22*(2), 219–240. doi:10.1111/j.1540-5915.1991.tb00344.x

Vessey, I., & Conger, S. (1994). Requirements Specification: Learning Object, Process, and Data Methodologies. Association for Computing Machinery. *Communications of the ACM, 37*(5), 102–113. doi:10.1145/175290.175305

Victor, B., & Blackburn, R. S. (1987). Interdependence: An alternative conceptualization. *Academy of Management Review, 12*(3), 486–498.

Visual Studio 2005: Domain-specific language tools. (n.d.). Retrieved June 5, 2006, from http://msdn.microsoft.com/vstudio/dsltools

Vixie, P. (1999). Software engineering. In C. DiBona, S. Ockman, & M. Stone (Eds.), *Open sources: Voices from the open source revolution* (pp. 91–100). Cambridge, MA: O'Reilly & Associates.

von Hippel, E. (1998). Economics of product development by users: The impact of 'sticky' local information. *Management Science, 44*(5), 629–644. doi:10.1287/mnsc.44.5.629

von Hippel, E. (2005). *Democratizing innovation.* Cambridge, MA: MIT Press.

VU (Cartographer). (2003). *Gme 3 user's manual*

W3C. (2008). World Wide Web Consortium. Retrieved December 20, 2008 from http://www.w3.org/

Walker, L. (2007). IBM business transformation enabled by service-oriented architecture. *IBM Systems Journal, 46*(4), 651-667.

Walz, D. B., Elam, J. J., & Curtis, B. (1993). Inside a software design team: knowledge acquisition, sharing, and integration. *Communications of the ACM, 36*(10), 63–77.

Wan Kadir, W. M. N., & Loucopoulos, P. (2003, 23-26 June). *Relating evolving business rules to software design.* Paper presented at the International Conference on Software Engineering Research and Practice (SERP), Las Vegas, Nevada, USA.

Wan Kadir, W. M. N., & Loucopoulos, P. (2004). Relating evolving business rules to software design. *Journal of Systems Architecture, 50*(7), 367-382.

Wand, Y., & Weber, R. (1990). An Ontological Model of an Information System. *IEEE Transactions on Software Engineering, 16*(11), 1282–1292. doi:10.1109/32.60316

Wand, Y., & Weber, R. (2002). Information Systems and Conceptual Modeling - A Research Agenda. *Information Systems Research, 13*(4), 363–376. doi:10.1287/isre.13.4.363.69

Wang, S. (1996). Two MIS analysis methods: An experimental comparison. *Journal of Education for Business, 71*(3), 136–141.

Wang, S. (2000). Neural networks. In M. Zeleny (Ed.), *IEBM Handbook of IT in Business* (pp. 382-391). London: International Thomson Business Press.

Wang, S. (2002). Nonlinear pattern hypothesis generation for data mining. *Data & Knowledge Engineering, 40*(3), 273–283. doi:10.1016/S0169-023X(01)00059-3

Wang, S. (2003). Application of self-organizing maps for data mining with incomplete data Sets. *Neural Computing & Applications, 12*(1), 42–48. doi:10.1007/s00521-003-0372-1

Wang, S. (2005). Classification with incomplete survey data: A Hopfield neural network approach. *Computers & Operations Research, 32*(10), 2583–2594. doi:10.1016/j.cor.2004.03.018

Wang, S., & Wang, H. (2004). Conceptual construction on incomplete survey data. *Data & Knowledge Engineering, 49*(3), 311–323. doi:10.1016/j.datak.2003.10.007

Watermarking relational data: Framework, algorithms and analysis. *The VLDB Journal, 12*(2), 157-169.

Watson, R. T., Boudreau, M., York, P. T., Greiner, M. E., & Wynn, D. (2008). The Business of Open Source. *Communications of the ACM, 51*(4), 41–46. doi:10.1145/1330311.1330321

Watson, R. T., Wynn, D., & Boudreau, M. (2005). Jboss: The evolution of Professional Open Source Software. *MIS Quarterly Executive, 4*(3), 329–341.

Watson-Manheim, M. B., Chudoba, K. M., & Crowston, K. (2002). Discontinuities and continuities: A new way to understand virtual work. *Information, Technology and People, 15*(3), 191–209.

Wayner, P. (2000). *Free For All*. New York: HarperCollins.

Web service. (2007). *Wikipedia*. Retrieved October 18, 2007, from http://en.wikipedia.org/wiki/Web_service

Webb, E., & Weick, K. E. (1979). Unobtrusive measures in organizational theory: A reminder. *Administrative Science Quarterly, 24*(4), 650–659.

Weber, S. (2004). *The success of open source*, Cambridge, MA: Harvard University Press.

Weick, K.E., Sutcliffe, K.M., & Obstfeld, D. (1999). Organizing for high reliability: Processes of collective mindfulness. In R.I. Sutton & B.M. Staw (Eds.), *Research in organizational behavior* (vol. 21, pp. 81–123). Greenwich, CT: JAI Press.

Weimer, D., & Vining, A. (2005). *Policy Analysis: Concepts and Practice*. Upper Saddle River, NJ: Pearson Prentice-Hall.

Weisband, S. (2002). Maintaining awareness in distributed team collaboration: Implications for leadership and performance. In P. Hinds & S. Kiesler (Eds.), *Distributed Work* (pp. 311–333). Cambridge, MA: MIT Press.

Welty, C. (2003). Ontology research. *AI Magazine, 24*(3), 11–12.

West, J. (2003). How open is open enough? Melding proprietary and open source platform strategies. *Research Policy, 32*(7), 1259–1285. doi:10.1016/S0048-7333(03)00052-0

West, J., & Dedrick, J. (2005). The effect of computerization movements upon organizational adoption of open source. *Proceedings of the Social Informatics Workshop: Extending the Contributions of Professor Rob Kling to the Analysis of Computerization Movements,* Irvine, CA.

West, J., & Gallagher, S. (2006). Challenges of open innovation: the paradox of firm investment in open-source software. *R & D Management, 36*(3), 319–331. doi:10.1111/j.1467-9310.2006.00436.x

West, J., Vanhaverbeke, W., & Chesbrough, H. (2006). Open Innovation: A Research Agenda. In H. Chesbrough, W. Vanhaverbeke, & J. West (eds.), *Open Innovation: Researching a New Paradigm* (pp. 285-307). Oxford, UK: Oxford University Press.

What does it cost to use a virtual world learning environment? (2008). *Training & Development, 62*(11), 88.

Wiedenbeck, S. (1999). The use of icons and labels in an end user application program: an empirical study of learning and retention. *Behaviour & Information Technology, 18*(2), 68–82. doi:10.1080/014492999119129

Witten, B., Landwehr, C., & Caloyannides, M. (2001). Does open source improve system security? *IEEE Software, 18*(5), 57–61.

Wittrock, M. C. (1990). Generative processes of comprehension. *Educational Psychologist, 24*(4), 345–376. doi:10.1207/s15326985ep2404_2

Wodtke, D., Weißenfels, J., Weikum, G., Kotz Dittrich, A., & Muth, P. (1997). The Mentor workbench for enterprise-wide workflow management. In J. Peckham (Ed.), *Proceedings of SIGMOD'97* (pp. 576-579). New York: ACM Press.

Woo, J. H., Lee, B. S., Lee, M. J., Loh, W. K., & Whang, K. Y. (2007). Temporal aggregation using a multidimensional index. *Journal of Database Management, 18*(2), 62-79.

Wood, N., Solomon, M. R., & Allan, D. (2008). Welcome to the matrix: E-learning gets a Second Life. *Marketing Education Review, 18*(2), 47–53.

Wood-Harper, T. (1985). Research methods in information systems: Using action research. In E. Mumford, R. A. Hirschheim, G. Fitzgerald & T. Wood-Harper (Eds.), *Research methods in information systems*. New York: North-Holland Publishers.

Woods, D., & Guliani, G. (2005). *Open source for the enterprise.* Sebastopol, CA: O'Reilly Media.

World Wide Web Consortium (W3C). (2007). Retrieved September 25, 2007, from http://colab.cim3.net/cgi-bin/wiki.pl?WwwCSoaGlossary#nid34R0

World Wide Web Consortium. (W3C). (1998). *Schema for object-oriented XML.* Retrieved from http://www.w3.org/TR/1998/NOTE-SOX-19980930

World Wide Web Consortium. (W3C). (2003). *Document object model DOM.* Retrieved from http://www.w3.org/DOM

World Wide Web Consortium. (W3C). (2004). *Simple API for XML, SAX.* Retrieved from http://www.saxproject.org

Wyse, J. E. (2006). Location-aware query resolution for location-based mobile commerce: performance evaluation and optimization. *Journal of Database Management, 17*(3), 41–65.

XML.com. (2007). Retrieved September 25, 2007, from http://www.xml.com/pub/a/ws/2003/09/30/soa.html

Yadav, S. B., Bravoco, R. R., Chatfield, A. T., & Rajkumar, T. M. (1988). Comparison Of Analysis Techniques For Information Requirement Determination. *Communications of the ACM, 31*(9), 1090–1097. doi:10.1145/48529.48533

Yin, R. K. (1994). *Case study research, design and methods.* Newbury Park: Sage Publications.

Yin, R.K. (2003). *Case study research: Design and methods* (3rd ed.). Newbury Park, CA: Sage.

Yoder, J. W., Balaguer, F., & Johnson, R. (2001, October 14-18). *Adaptive object models for implementing business rules.* Paper presented at the Third Workshop on Best-Practices for Business Rules Design and Implementation, Conference on Object-Oriented Programming, Systems, Languages, and Applications (OOPSLA 2001), Tampa Bay, Florida, USA.

Young, S. L., & Wogalter, M. S. (1990). Comprehension and Memory of Instruction Manual Warnings: Conspicuous Print and Pictorial Icons Human Factors. *The Journal of the Human Factors and Ergonomics Society, 32*(6), 637–649.

Zadeh, L. A. (1978). Fuzzy sets as a basis for a theory of possibility. *Fuzzy Sets and Systems, 1,* 3–28. doi:10.1016/0165-0114(78)90029-5

Zaniolo, C., Ceri, S., Faloutsos, C., Snodgrass, R., Subrahmanian, V. S., & Zicari, R. (1997). *Advanced database systems*: Morgan Kaufmann.

Zeichick, A. (2002, July 15). Modeling Usage Low; Developers Confused About UML 2.0, MDA. *SD Times.* Retrieved from http://www.sdtimes.com/article/story-20020715-03.html

Zhang, D. (2004). Web services composition for process management in e-business. *Journal of Computer Information Systems, 45*(2), 83-91.

Zhang, D., & Zhao, J. L. (2006). Knowledge management in organizations. *Journal of Database Management, 17*(1), 1–7.

Zhang, J., Liu, H., Ling, T., Bruckner, R., & Tija, A. (2006). A framework for efficient association rule mining in XML data. *Journal of Database Management, 17*(3), 19–40.

Zhang, S., Qin, Z., Ling, C., & Sheng, S. (2005). Missing is useful: Missing values in cost-sensitivity decision trees. *IEEE Transactions on Knowledge and Data Engineering, 17*(12), 1689–1693. doi:10.1109/TKDE.2005.188

Zhao, L., & Siau, K. (2007). Information mediation using metamodels: An approach using XML and common warehouse metamodel. *Journal of Database Management, 18*(3), 69-82.

Zhou, X., Pang, H. H., & Tan, K. L. (2007). Query-based watermarking for XML data. *Proceedings of ACM Symposium on Information, Computer and Communication Security (ASIACCS)* (pp. 253-264).

Zhu, J., Tian, Z., Li, T., Sun, W., Ye, S., Ding, W., et al. (2004). Model-driven business process integration and management: A case study with the Bank SinoPac regional service platform. *IBM Journal of Research and*

Development, 48(5/6), 649-669. Retrieved November 23, 2007, from http://www.research.ibm.com/journal/rd/485/zhu.pdf

Zuboff, S. (1988). *In the Age of the Smart Machine*. New York: Basic Books.

About the Contributors

Keng Siau is the E. J. Faulkner Chair Professor of Management Information Systems (MIS) and Full Professor of Management at the University of Nebraska, Lincoln (UNL). He is the Director of the UNL-IBM Global Innovation Hub, Editor-in-Chief of the Journal of Database Management, North America Regional Editor of the Requirements Engineering journal, and Co-Editor-in-Chief of the Advances in Database Research series. He received his Ph.D. degree from the University of British Columbia (UBC). His master and bachelor degrees are in Computer and Information Sciences from the National University of Singapore. Professor Siau has over 200 academic publications. He has published more than 100 refereed journal articles, and these articles have appeared in journals such as Management Information Systems Quarterly, Journal of the Association for Information Systems, Communications of the ACM, IEEE Computer, Information Systems Journal, Journal of Strategic Information Systems, Information Systems, ACM SIGMIS's Database, IEEE Transactions on Systems, Man, and Cybernetics, IEEE Transactions on Professional Communication, IEEE Transactions on Information Technology in Biomedicine, IEICE Transactions on Information and Systems, Data and Knowledge Engineering, Journal of Information Technology, International Journal of Human-Computer Studies, and others. He served as the Organizing and Program Chairs of the International Conference on Evaluation of Modeling Methods in Systems Analysis and Design (EMMSAD) (1996 – 2005). He also served on the organizing committees of AMCIS 2005, ER 2006, AMCIS 2007, EuroSIGSAND 2007, EuroSIGSAND 2008, and ICMB 2009. He received the International Federation for Information Processing (IFIP) Outstanding Service Award in 2006, and the IBM Faculty Award in 2006 and 2008.

John Erickson is an assistant professor in the College of Business Administration at the University of Nebraska at Omaha. His research interests include UML, software complexity and Systems Analysis and design issues. He has published in journals such as the CACM, JDM, and in conferences such as AMICIS, ICIS WITS, EMMSAD, and CAiSE. He has also co-authored several book chapters.

* * *

Michael Brydon is an Associate Professor in the Faculty of Business Administration at Simon Fraser University in Vancouver, Canada. He received his Ph.D. in Management Information Systems from the University of British Columbia and M.Eng. and B.Eng. degrees in Engineering Management from the Royal Military College of Canada. His research interests lie at the intersection of decision theory, economics, and computer science and include computational economies, decision-theoretic valuation of real options, and markets for public goods such as knowledge and open source software. Recent articles have appeared in Decision Support Systems, Information & Management and Information and Technology Management.

Kevin Crowston joined the School of Information Studies at Syracuse University in 1996. He received his PhD in information technologies from the Sloan School of Management, Massachusetts Institute of Technology (MIT) in 1991. Before moving to Syracuse he was a founding member of the Collaboratory for Research on Electronic Work at the University of Michigan and of the Centre for Coordination Science at MIT. His current research focuses on new ways of organizing made possible by the extensive use of information technology.

Florian Daniel is a postdoctoral researcher at the University of Trento. He holds a Ph.D. in Information Technology (2007) and a M.Sc. in Computer Engineering (2003) from Politecnico di Milano, Italy. His main research interests include Web engineering, mashups, service and UI composition, conceptual modeling in Web engineering, active/context-aware Web applications and business intelligence applications. Contact him at daniel@disi.unitn.it

Brian Dobing is an Associate Professor of Information Systems in the Faculty of Management at the University of Lethbridge. His research interests include system development using the Unified Modeling Language, influence of culture on web site design, and visual programming languages. His research has been published journals such as Communications of the ACM, Journal of Database Management, Journal of Internet Research, and the Journal of Computer Information Systems. He is a member of the Editorial Board for the Journal of Database Management and Journal of Information Systems Education.

Brenda Eschenbrenner is currently pursuing her PhD in Management Information Systems, with concentrations in accounting, information technology, and human cognition, at the University of Nebraska—Lincoln. Her research interests include virtual world environments, human acceptance and use of current and emerging technologies, factors contributing to information system proficiency, and technology applications in education and training. She has over 10 years of work experience including management positions with a former Fortune 500 company and involvement with system implementation efforts.

Joseph Feller, Ph.D., is a senior lecturer in Business Information Systems at University College Cork, Ireland. His research focuses on open source software and other forms of collaborative production. He has published four books and his work has appeared in leading international journals and conferences including Information Systems Research, Information Systems Journal, Journal of Strategic Information Systems, Journal of Database Management, the International Conference on Information Systems, the European Conference on Information Systems, and working conferences of IFIP. He has also published widely in practitioner-oriented publications and is a frequent contributor to the Cutter Consortium. He was program chair for the IEEE/ACM workshop series on open source software engineering (2001–2005) and the Third International Conference on Open Source Systems (IFIP 2.13) and has edited several journal special issues on the subject of open source.

Patrick Finnegan received his PhD from the University of Warwick, England, and is currently an Associate Professor in Information Systems in the Australian School of Business at the University of

New South Wales, Australia, as well as a Senior Editor of the Information Systems Journal. He previously held an Associate Professorship in Management Information Systems at University College Cork, Ireland, and was President of the Irish Association for Information Systems. His research on Inter-Organizational Systems and Electronic Business has been published in leading international journals and conferences, including Information Systems Research, Information Technology and People, The Information Systems Journal, The International Journal of Electronic Commerce, DATABASE, Electronic Markets, ICIS and ECIS.

Joseph Fong received his PhD degree in computing at University of Sunderland in 1993, and is an associate professor at computer science department of City University of Hong Kong. He is a fellow member of the Hong Kong Computer Society and the honorary founder chairman of Hong Kong Web Society. He has published above 100 publications including US and Hong Kong patents, SCI journals, conference proceedings, and text books. His research interests are in database reengineering and interoperability, XML and hybrid Learning, and has been organizing many international eLearning conferences.

Andrew Gemino is an associate professor of management information systems in the faculty of business administration at Simon Fraser University. His primary research interests are in the evaluation of conceptual modeling techniques and information technology project management. His papers have been published in the Journal of Management Information Systems, Communications of the ACM, Requirements Engineering Journal, Journal of Asynchronous Learning Networks and Data and Knowledge Engineering. He is funded through grants from the National Sciences and Research Council (NSERC) and the Social Sciences and Humanities Research Council (SSHRC). Andrew is currently President of the AIS Special Interest Group on Systems Analysis and Design (SIGSAND).

Huiping Guo is an assistant professor in the Department of Computer Science at California State University, Los Angeles. She received her PhD degree in computer science from University of Ottawa in 2003 and did postdoctoral research for two years at George Mason University. Her research interests focus on multimedia communications, digital rights management and information security.

Jeremy Hayes is a Lecturer in Business Information Systems at University College Cork. His research interests are in the area of electronic business models, inter-organisational systems, open source software, and business agility. He has published his research findings at international conferences and journals including the European Journal of Operational Research, Information Systems Research, Journal of Database Management, the European Conference on Information Systems (ECIS) and IFIP working conferences.

Wan Mohd Nasir Wan Kadir received his B.Sc. from Universiti Teknologi Malaysia in 1994, and his MSc and PhD degrees from UMIST, Manchester in 1996 and 2005 respectively. He is an academic member of staff at the Software Engineering Department, Faculty of Computer Science and Information Systems, Universiti Teknologi Malaysia, and currently, he is the Head of the Department. He is also a member of pro-tem committee of Malaysian Software Engineering Interest Group (MySEIG). His research interests include architecture-based software evolution, requirements traceability, component reusability, business rules, object- oriented design and CASE tools.

Jumi Kim received the Ph.D. in the Department of Industrial and Manufacturing Systems Engineering at Iowa State University. She got her B.S. in Industrial Engineering from the Kangnung National University of Korea, and a M.S. in Industrial Engineering from the Seoul National University of Korea. She is now a senior researcher in Korea Small Business Institute. Her research interests are in simulation optimization, web based information systems, and data mining.

Stefan Koch is associate professor of information business at the Vienna University of Economics and Business Administration, Austria. He received an MBA in management information systems from Vienna University and Vienna Technical University, and a PhD from Vienna University of Economics and Business Administration. Currently he is involved in the undergraduate and graduate teaching program, especially in software project management and ERP packages. His research interests include cost estimation for software projects, the open source development model, software process improvement, the evaluation of benefits from information systems, and ERP systems. He edited a book, Free/Open Source Software Development, for an international publisher in 2004 and acted as guest editor for Upgrade for a special issue on libre software. He has published more than 10 papers in peer-reviewed journals, and over 30 in international conference proceedings and book collections.

Wookey Lee received the B.S., M.S., and Ph.D. in Industrial Engineering from Seoul National University, Korea. Currently, he is a Professor in the department of Industrial Engineering, Inha University, Incheon, Korea. He finished the MSE in Carnegie-Mellon University, PA, USA and he has been a visiting scholar at CS, UBC, Canada. He got the best paper award in KORMS. He is now Editor-in-chief in the Journal of Information Technology and Architecture. His research interests include Web Structuring, mobile and multimedia DB, Data Warehousing, and EA.

Yingjiu Li is currently an assistant professor in the School of Information Systems at Singapore Management University. He received his PhD degree in Information Technology from George Mason University in 2003. His research interests include application security, privacy protection, and data rights management.

Pericles Loucopoulos is professor of information systems in the Business School, Loughborough University, United Kingdom and adjunct professor at the University of Manchester. He is the co-editor-in-chief of the Journal of Requirements Engineering, associate editor for Information Systems and serves on the editorial boards of the Information Systems Journal, the Journal of Computer Research, Business Process Management Journal, International Journal of Computer Science & Applications, the International Journal of Computing and ICT research, among others. He is a fellow of the British Computer Society and has served as general chair and programme chair of six international conferences and has been a member of over 150 Programme Committees of international conferences. He has published over 150 papers in academic journals and conference proceedings on the engineering of information, and the tools, methods and processes used to design, develop and deploy information systems in order to meet organisational goals. He has written or edited 10 books related to requirements and information systems engineering.

Kamal Masri is a lecturer in management information systems in the Faculty of Business Administration at Simon Fraser University. He spent over 12 years involved in all aspects of developing specialized information systems for a variety of industries including: health care, transportation, education, and sports and entertainment. His main research interest is the effective use of conceptual models and effective systems development.

Fiona Fui-Hoon Nah is an Associate Professor of Management Information Systems (MIS) at the University of Nebraska-Lincoln. Her research interests include human-computer interaction, 3-D virtual worlds, computer-supported collaborative work, knowledge-based and decision support systems, enterprise resource planning, and mobile and ubiquitous commerce. She has published her research in journals such as Journal of the Association for Information Systems, Communications of the Association for Information Systems, Communications of the ACM, IEEE Transactions on Education, International Journal of Human-Computer Studies. She is an Associate Editor of Journal of the Association for Information Systems and Journal of Electronic Commerce Research. She also serves on the Editorial Board of more than ten other MIS journals. She is a co-Founder and Past Chair of the Association for Information Systems Special Interest Group on Human-Computer Interaction, and is a featured volunteer for the Association for Information Systems (June 2008). She received her Ph.D. in MIS from the University of British Columbia, and her M.S. and B.S. (Honors) in Computer and Information Sciences from the National University of Singapore. She was previously on the faculty of School of Computing, National University of Singapore, and the Krannert School of Management, Purdue University.

Christian Neumann holds a PhD from the Department of Information Business at the Vienna University of Economics and Business Administration, Austria. He received his masters degree in engineering and management from the University of Karlsruhe, Germany. His research interests include quality of open source projects, usability of frameworks, cost estimation, and software investment analysis. He is now working for an international management consulting company.

Drew Parker is an Associate Professor of Information Systems in the Faculty of Business Administration at Simon Fraser University. He is interested in online team performance, adoption of information technology and internet-related business applications. Papers have appeared in journals including the Journal of Management Information Systems, Journal of Asynchronous Learning Networks, Journal of Educational Media International, European Journal of Operational Research, INFOR, and Journal of the Operational Research Society.

Jeffrey Parsons is Professor of Information Systems in the Faculty of Business Administration at Memorial University of Newfoundland. His research interests include systems analysis and design using UML, database management, and the semantic web. His research has been published in journals such as Management Science, Communications of the ACM, ACM Transactions on Database Systems, Journal of Management Information Systems, and IEEE Transactions on Software Engineering. He serves as a senior editor for the Journal of the Association for Information Systems and is on the editorial board of the Journal of Database Management, and is Program Co-chair of the 2008 Americas Conference on Information Systems (AMCIS).

Giuseppe Pozzi is associate professor of Computer Engineering at the Politecnico di Milano, Italy, where he teaches the classes of Database Systems and of Workgroup and Workflow Systems. He received a M.Sc in E.E. in 1986 and a Ph.D. in 1992 from Politecnico di Milano, respectively. His main research interests include temporal and active database systems, workflow management systems, temporal information in workflow systems. Contact him at giuseppe.pozzi@polimi.it

Iris Reinhartz-Berger received her B.Sc. degree in Applied Mathematics and Computer Science from the Technion, Israel Institute of Technology in 1994. She obtained a M.Sc. degree in 1999 and a PhD in 2003 in Information Management Engineering from the Technion, Israel Institute of Technology. She is currently a faculty member at the Department of Management Information Systems, Haifa University, Israel. Her research interests include conceptual modeling, modeling languages and techniques for analysis and design, domain analysis, development processes, and methodologies. Her work has been published in journals and international conferences.

Matti Rossi is a professor of information systems at Helsinki School of Economics. He has worked as research fellow at Erasmus University Rotterdam and as a visiting assistant professor at Georgia State University, Atlanta. He received his PhD degree in business administration from the University of Jyväskylä in 1998. He is currently the European and African representative in the Association of Information Systems. He has been the principal investigator in several major research projects funded by the technological development center of Finland and Academy of Finland. His research papers have appeared in journals such as CACM, Journal of AIS, Information and Management, and Information Systems, and over thirty of them have appeared in conferences such as ICIS, HICSS and CAiSE.

João Saraiva is currently a PhD student (in the area of computer science and engineering) at Instituto Superior Técnico (IST/UTL) since 2007. He is also a researcher at INESC-ID, as a member of the Information Systems Group (GSI) since 2004, where he participates in ProjectIT (PhD focus), WebComfort, and EscolaNaNet projects. His professional and research interests are in modeling and metamodeling, modeldriven engineering, domain-specific modeling, CMS and ECM systems, and CASE and CSCW tools.

Barbara Scozzi is an assistant professor at the Politecnico of Bari, Italy. She received her PhD in management engineering from the University of Rome Tor Vergata/Polytechnic of Bari in 2001. Since 1997 she has been involved in many research projects at the Politecnico di Bari. Her main research interests are coordination, knowledge management and innovation in business organizations.

Myung-Keun Shin received the BS and MS in computer science and the PhD in information & communication from Korea Advanced Institute of Science and Technology, Korea. He is currently a researcher in the Telecom Business Division, SK C&C, Korea. His research interests are knowledge management system, database transaction processing, and information retrieval, etc.

Herbert Shiu was the project manager of a funded research project under the Department of computer Science at City University of Hong Kong. He graduated with a B.Sc. in Computer Science from the University of Hong Kong in 1992, a MSc, and MPhil in Computer Science from City University of Hong Kong in1998 and 2006 respectively. He is now a PhD student at City University of Hong Kong. His current research interests are in database, XML and object-oriented software design and development.

Alberto Rodrigues da Silva is professor of information systems at the Department of Computer Science and Engineering at Technical University of Lisbon (IST/UTL) Portugal. He is also a senior researcher at INESC-ID and director at the SIQuant Company. His professional and research interests are in modeling and metamodeling, model-driven engineering, requirement engineering, enterprise knowledge-based platforms, and CSCW and CASE Tools.

Kari Smolander is a professor of software engineering in the Department of Information Technology, Lappeenranta University of Technology, Finland. He has a PhD (2003) in computer science from Lappeenranta University of Technology and a Licentiate (1993) and Master (1988) degree from University of Jyväskylä, Finland. In addition to his long teaching experience, he has worked several years in industry and in 1990's he was the main architect in the development of MetaEdit CASE tool. He has published more than 50 refereed research papers in international journals and conferences. His current research interests include architectural aspects of systems development and organizational view of software development.

Arnon Sturm is a faculty member within the department of Information Systems Engineering at Ben-Gurion University. He obtained a M.Sc. degree in 1999 and a PhD in 2004 in Information Management Engineering from the Technion, Israel Institute of Technology. His research concentrates on software engineering and in particular domain engineering and software development methods. Prior to his studies, Arnon has gained extensive experience in developing software systems in the industry. He also served as a member of a software engineering team that addressed problems of software development.

Kris Ven graduated from the Faculty of Applied Economics of the University of Antwerp, Belgium, in 2002. He is currently working in the Department of Management Information Systems at the University of Antwerp. He is preparing a PhD on the organizational adoption of open source software. Related research interests include the link between innovation in organizations and open source software, and the adoption of open source software by public administrations. He has authored and presented several papers at international conferences on open source software and information systems.

Jan Verelst received his PhD in Management Information Systems from the Faculty of Applied Economics of the University of Antwerp, Belgium, in 1999. He is working in the Department of Management Information Systems at the University of Antwerp, where he teaches courses on analysis and design of information systems. He is also an executive professor at the Management School of the University of Antwerp. His research interests include conceptual modeling of information systems, evolvability and maintainability of information systems, empirical software engineering, and open source software.

Aidan R. Vining is the CNABS Professor of Business & Government Relations in the Segal Graduate School of Business, Simon Fraser University in Vancouver, Canada. He obtained his Ph.D. at the University of California, Berkeley. He also has an MBA from the University of California, Riverside and an LLB from King's College, London University. His research interests focus on both public policy and business strategy, especially strategy and organizational incentives. Recent articles have appeared in the Journal of Policy Analysis and Management, the Journal of Management Studies, Industrial and Corporate Change, American Behavioral Scientist, Journal of Public Affairs, and Public Administration

Review. He is a co-author of Policy Analysis; Concepts and Practice (4th. Edition, Pearson Prentice-Hall, 2005) and Cost-Benefit Analysis: Concepts and Practice (3rd. Edition, Pearson Prentice-Hall, 2006.)

Hai Wang is an Assistant Professor of Computing and Information Systems at Saint Mary's University. He received his PhD from University of Toronto. His research interests are in areas of database, data mining, knowledge management, and performance modeling. His papers have been published in VLDB, Performance Evaluation, ACM SIGMETRICS Performance Evaluation Review, Knowledge and Information Systems, Journal of the Operational Research Society, Managerial and Decision Economics, International Journal of Mobile Communications, Data and Knowledge Engineering, and others.

Shouhong Wang is a Professor of Management Information Systems at University of Massachusetts Dartmouth. He received his PhD from McMaster University. His research interests include data mining, knowledge management, and business intelligence. He has published over 90 papers in academic journals, including Information Resources Management Journal, Journal of Organizational and End User Computing, Journal of Management Information Systems, Information & Management, International Journal of Information Management, Information Systems Management, Management Science, Decision Sciences, Journal of The Operational Research Society, and others.

Shuhong Wang is currently a Research Fellow in the Faculty of Informatics at University of Wollongong. He received his PhD degree in Mathematics from Peking University in 2005. His research interests include cryptography and its application in information security.

Index